VICTORIS
CARPATIO
VENETI
OPVS

5—

the guinness book of records 1492

The World Five Hundred Years Ago

EDITOR: *Deborah Manley*

EDITORIAL CONSULTANT: *Dr. Geoffrey Scammell*

Facts On File
New York • Oxford

CONTRIBUTORS

DR EWAN ANDERSON: University of Durham
DR FELIPE FERNÁNDEZ-ARMESTO: Oxford Comparative Colonial History Project
PROFESSOR DAVID BIRMINGHAM: University of Kent at Canterbury
Ms BLUNDEN
DR DON BROTHWELL: Institute of Archaeology, University College London
CLIVE CARPENTER
DR PETER CATTERMOLE
DR CHRISTOPHER CULLEN: School of Oriental and African Studies, University of London
DR BASIL DAVIDSON: Centre of West African Studies, University of Birmingham
ALAN DAWSON
DR WILLIAM DOLBY: University of Edinburgh
PROFESSOR MARK ELVIN: Australian National University, Canberra
DR IAN FRIEL
JEAN GIMPEL: Historian of technology and the cycles of civilization
PROFESSOR DENYS HAY: Professor Emeritus, University of Edinburgh
DR JOHN HEMMING: Director of The Royal Geographical Society
DR DONALD HILL
GEOFFREY HINDLEY: Secretary for the Society of the History of Medieval Technology and Science
DR COLIN IMBER: University of Manchester
DR MURRAY LAST: University College London
DR MARTIN LOWRY: University of Warwick
PROFESOR MANUEL LUCENA SALMORAL: Universidad de Alcalá y Henares, Madrid
PROFESSOR KAN-WEN MA: The Wellcome Institute for the History of Medicine
PROFESSOR MICHAEL MALLETT: University of Warwick
PROFESSOR DEREK MASSARELLA: Chuo University, Tokyo
NORRIS McWHIRTER, CBE: Founding Editor of The Guinness Book of Records
PROFESSOR W R MEAD: Emeritus Professor of Geography, University College London
DR PATRICK MOORE, CBE
DR RANJIT NAIR and colleagues of National Institute of Science, Technology and Development Studies, New Delhi
PETER NEWBY
DR MALYN NEWITT: University of Exeter
RICHARD NEWNHAM
DR PAULA NUTTALL
JOANNE O'BRIEN: ICOREC
DR MARK OVERTON: University of Newcastle upon Tyne
MARTIN PALMER: ICOREC
PROFESSOR YURI PINYAGIN: Perm State University, Russia
PROFESSOR MICHAEL PEARSON: University of New South Wales, Australia
DR ROY PORTER: The Wellcome Institute for the History of Medicine
CAROLINE PRENTICE: The Wellcome Institute for the History of Medicine
PROFESSOR DAVID B QUINN: Emeritus Professor, University of Liverpool
PROFESSOR A RAHMAN: Former Director, National Institute of Science, Technology and Development Studies, New Delhi
DR PETER ROWAN
YASMIN SHARIFF: ARIBA
BRIAN SPENCER: The Museum of London
REAY TANNAHILL: Author of 'Food in History'
DAVE TERRY: Member of the British Society of Sports History
DR DELLA THOMPSON: Oxford University Press
DR TIM UNWIN: Royal Holloway and Bedford New College, University of London
DAVID WILEMAN
BRIAN WILLIAMS
PROFESSOR LEA E WILLIAMS: Brown University, Rhode Island
DR SYLVIA WRIGHT: Education Department, Royal Academy of Arts
IGOR ZAITSEV: Editor of the Russian Edition of The Guinness Book of Records

Picture Agencies and Sources: Ancient Art & Architecture Library, Archiv für Kunst und Geschichte, Bibliotheque Nationale (Paris), Bodleian Library, Bridgeman Art Library Ltd, British Library, British Museum, Central Library (Zürich), Cleveland Museum of Art, E T Archive, Mary Evans, Explorer, Giraudon, Robert Harding Picture Library, Image Select International, Images Colour Library, INCAFO, Mary Rose Trust, National Portrait Gallery, Pictor International, Anne Ronan Collection, Scala, Science Museum, Science Photo Library, Spectrum Colour Library, Syndication International, Dave Terry, Roger Viollet, Zefa.

Special thanks for their assistance with illustrations for this edition are extended to: Gary Fisk; Jurgen Raible; Catherine Cheval; Brigitte Baumbusch; Simon Conti.

Design: Kathy Aldridge. **Cover design:** Barry Lowenoff. **Maps and diagrams:** Rob Burns and Peter Harper. **Picture editor:** Alexander Goldberg.

Facts On File, Inc. 460 Park Avenue South New York NY 10016

Library of Congress Cataloging-in-Publication Data
The Guinness book of records 1492: the world five hundred years ago/
editors, Deborah Manley and Geoffrey Scammell
p. cm.
Includes bibliographical references and index.
ISBN 0-8160-2772-2
1. Curiosities and wonders. 2. World records. 3. Civilization.
I. Manley, Deborah. II. Scammell, Geoffrey Vaughan.
AG243.G863 1992
031.02--dc20 91-58588
CIP

Facts On File books are available at special discounts when purchased in bulk quantities for businesses, associations, institutions or sales promotions. Please call our Special Sales Department in New York at 212/683-2244 (dial 800/322-8755 except in NY, AK or HI).

Printed and bound in Spain by Printer Industria Gráfica, S.A., Barcelona the guinness book of records 1492

Contents

As this book appears, the world is looking back to 1492 in what is probably the most widely spread and most sharply focused retrospect ever made. Some look back in anger, to what is seen as the start of an era of imperialist brutality and ecological degradation. Others behold with satisfaction the supposed beginnings of an age of freedom and progress. No one today can look back at 1492 with indifference.

Native Americans are offended by the suggestion that Columbus accomplished anything new. Claims to have preceded him are advanced on behalf of every imaginable rival. The significance of his Atlantic crossing has been belittled and denied. Yet the traditional resonances of 1492 – which are the justification of this book – remain intact. The opening of reliable routes, both ways across the Atlantic, had a permanent, transforming effect on the world. No other single event contributed so much towards making our unified world of today different from those of antiquity and the middle ages, which were composed of discrete patches, like a decayed mosaic.

Columbus can be commemorated not – in deference to the Americans and the Vikings – as the discoverer of America, but as the discoverer of these routes. Strictly speaking, it was only in 1493 that he completed the job. On the first crossing, his outward course was tentative: it was rarely followed by later shipping. His second voyage, in 1493, established the ideal route out, south-west from the Canaries to the Lesser Antilles. The way back, north from the West Indies to catch the westerly winds, was only slightly modified after his time. Taken together, the voyages of 1492–3 forged an enduring link, not just between Europe and America, but right across the civilized and densely populated 'middle belt' of the world. A single network of communications now stretched from China across the caravan-roads of Asia and the shipping-lanes of the Indian Ocean to the Mediterranean and almost to the threshold of the civilizations of Mesoamerica. What had formerly been a planet of sundered or barely-communicating cultures was bound to become 'one world', the whole breadth of which could be crossed by cultural contagion, human migration and commercial exchange.

This remarkable impact was registered with modest means, by a man of little education and humble origins. Just as some snobs suppose that the works of Shakespeare could never have been written by a simple actor from a Stratford grammar school, so it has seemed incredible, in similar circles, that a poor weaver's son from Genoa could have made the discoveries of Columbus. He is often said to have concealed some secret identity or to have got his ideas from someone else. Yet what we know about his provenance and the formation of his plans makes a credible story, of the kind of truth which excels fiction.

He was born at an uncertain date around the middle of the 15th century, probably in 1451 or early in 1452, in or near Genoa. From his natural course of life in his father's business, he could have bettered himself by any of three means of social advancement common in his day. He might have joined the Church, like his younger brother: in later life, Columbus affected a sense of religious vocation and had a fancy for a friar's habit. He might have gone to war: indeed, he later claimed to have started on a warrior's life and liked to present himself as 'a commander of knights and conquests'. In the event, he chose the third possible option and went to sea.

Christopher Columbus, born Genoa, Italy 1451, died Valladolid, Spain 20 May 1506, seafarer. A 16th century portrait by an unknown artist.

Social values at the time were strongly influenced by the code of chivalry, and seaborne deeds of derring-do commanded, in popular literature, enormous prestige. The sea was the 'chief office' of a famous Castilian knight. Young men's heads were turned by the stories Cervantes later lampooned, in which romantic deeds overseas were rewarded with the lordship of exotic islands.

Like many 15th-century heroes 'on the make', Columbus sought to give his life this sort of storybook trajectory. He was always trying to escape, from the world of restricted social opportunity in which he was born, into an aristocratic fantasy.

Woodcut illustration of Columbus' record of his journey of discovery, with an imaginative interpretation of the Caribbean islands.

Mutineers on his first Atlantic crossing knew what he was after: he was risking all their necks, they grumbled, just 'to make himself a great lord'. Columbus registered a big advance late in the 1470s when, working as an agent for Genoese merchants in Lisbon, he married a daughter of a deceased governor of Porto Santo near Madeira. Her family belonged to the nobility – albeit the most peripheral in the kingdom. She came, moreover, from an Atlantic colonial frontier world with which Columbus was becoming deeply familiar.

In a series of mainly commercial voyages between 1477 and 1485 he traversed virtually the whole of the Atlantic as it was known in his day, from Iceland and the British Isles, through the Portuguese and Spanish island colonies, to a newly-opened gold-trading factory on the southern edge of the charted ocean, near the mouth of the River Volta in West Africa. He began to plan an Atlantic journey of exploration of his own, such as had offered – and occasionaly delivered – fame and status to a number of earlier navigators. His plans are commonly represented as having sprung fully armed, to be pursued with single-minded conviction: 'as if kept in a chamber' – said an influential early source – 'locked with his own key'. In reality, they seem to have developed gradually and to have wavered between different objectives. At different times, Columbus proposed a voyage in search of undiscovered islands, an ocean crossing to the far extremity of the known world and a quest for a new or 'Antipodean' continent, such as America ultimately proved to be. None of these notions was original and all had existing supporters and doubters. While seeking sponsorship during the 1480s, Columbus was also engaged in a process of belated self-education. This enabled him to commend his plans with increasing confidence and with an ever more elaborate show of scholarship. Whether academic study had a formative influence on his intentions is uncertain: in surviving sources, he produced no systematic geography of an academic nature until late in the 1490s.

In a legend of his own making, Columbus represented himself as dedicated to a long and lonely search for patronage in the face of academic derision and courtly disdain. Yet at the royal court of Castile, where he was lobbying perhaps from 1485 and certainly in 1486, his suit seems rather to have prospered by degrees. By tireless self-recommendation, he built up critical masses of support: among Franciscan friars who had access to the monarchs; among household servants of the heir to the throne, some of whom went on to the household of the king and queen; among the seafaring community of Palos, near the mouth of the Río Tinto, where most of the equipment and men that were to take him across the ocean would be supplied; among rich fellow-Genoese and Florentines in Seville who were prepared to subscribe financial backing for his venture; and among an overlapping group of financial servants or agents of the crown who came together in the 1480s to fund Castile's first great Atlantic project, the conquest of the Canary Islands.

A tinted woodcut from the 1493 record of the Columbus voyage shows the people of the New World timorously approaching the strangers.

By early in 1492 the Columbus lobby had built up enough momentum, and could raise sufficient funds, for the monarchs to sanction his enterprise. With his impecunious royal patrons he seems finally to have set Asia as his objective, presumably because of the Orient's reputation for rich trade goods and precious metals. When he sailed from Palos on 3 August 1492, Columbus carried a 'Chaldean interpreter' and letters for the ruler of China.

Enough survives of Columbus' detailed record for us to sense the excitement of a journey into the unknown: the phoney landfalls, the struggle to maintain a course due west, the murmurs of mutineers, the daily search of the horizon, the nightly scanning of the skies, the nervous conjectures about how far they had gone and how far they had to go. On 7 October, just over a month since the last sight of land, Columbus' nerve cracked: he gave in to pressure from subordinates and altered course to the south-west. On 12 October – at an unidentifiable spot, almost certainly in the Bahamas – the continuous history of encounter between the Old World and the New began. Columbus spent three months in explorations which gave him an extensive knowledge of the northern coasts of Cuba and Hispaniola. He sailed in the growing conviction that he was approaching a rich civilization. Shortly before he left for home in January 1493, he found gold samples in promising quantities: if he could make it back through the storms of the North Atlantic, he was sure of a welcome in Spain.

When he returned to parade plumed Indians and exotic parrots through the streets of Barcelona, many observers assumed that he had indeed reached the environs of the Orient. But there were advocates of other solutions: it was said that Columbus must merely have found more islands like the Canaries or stumbled on an Antipodean world. The discoverer himself was committed to the Asian thesis. On performance of his promises depended the security of all the rewards the monarchs gave him: the titles of Don and Admiral and Governor and Viceroy, the prospect of vast wealth, the expectation of founding a great dynasty, the place in the acceptance world which he had craved.

Columbus had already achieved enough to satisfy any rational ambition. Yet his implacability doomed him to misery. He went on defending an 'Asian' label for his discoveries in defiance of the evidence and, at times, of his own avowed perceptions. He insisted on ruling his islands in person, with ignominious results – for his ability to manage men, strong on shipboard, deserted him on dry land. To vindicate a half-ruined reputation he made a last Atlantic journey in 1502, discovering a long stretch of the coast of Central America but losing his fleet and wrecking his health. The bitterness of his late career was allayed by the consolations of religion. He was comforted by a celestial 'voice' with which he conversed. He claimed literally to have located the Earthly Paradise. He compiled Biblical texts which, he said, were prophecies of his own discoveries and evidence of the imminence of the Last Days.

He grew rich on the proceeds of placer-gold from Hispaniola but complained unremittingly of poverty. He was hailed as a 'new apostle' but presented himself as a Jeremiah or a Job. In April 1506, practically on his deathbed, he wrote a last, pathetic letter, promising to give 'greater service than ever . . .'.

Columbus on his own could not 'put a girdle round the earth': he did more, perhaps than any other individual to unstraiten the laces. The discovery of 1492–3, though uniquely effective and uniquely significant, belongs in the contexts of slowly unfolding processes of exploration, economic change and technical advance which have brought into mutual contact all the peoples who inhabit our planet. Therefore, *The Guinness Book of Records 1492* sets the records broken by Columbus alongside other quantifiable achievements, worldwide, over a period of about one hundred years from *c.* 1450. The picture which emerges is of a dynamic world in which a number of expanding cultures were reaching out from their traditional spheres, and in which the scale and range of Columbus' achievement seems thoroughly characteristic.

FELIPE FERNANDEZ-ARMESTO

This world and beyond

STRUCTURE AND DIMENSIONS
NATURAL PHENOMENA • WEATHER
GEOGRAPHERS AND MAPS • GEOLOGY
THE UNIVERSE • ASTROLOGY • THE ANIMAL KINGDOM • THE PLANT KINGDOM

Structure and dimensions

During this period the most important sources of geographical information were found in ancient Greek writings. Although Aristotle (384–322 BC) had shown the world was round, his views were largely lost to the early medieval Catholic world in the West, or at least only partially known through Arab sources. Cosmas wrote his *Christian Topography* in Alexandria in Egypt in late antiquity to prove from scripture that the Earth is not a globe but flat and square. So the re-assertion of what had been known to antiquity was a long and slow process of Western re-discovery. It started from the 12th century onwards and by 1492 was widely accepted.

World dimensions

First scientific proof that the Earth is spherical ■ This was given by the Greek philosopher Pythagoras (born 472 BC). Among his proofs may be cited the fact that the bright star Canopus can be seen from Alexandria in Egypt, but not from Athens in Greece – which could not be the case if the Earth were flat. Also, Pythagoras pointed out that the shadow of the Earth cast upon the Moon during a lunar eclipse is curved, indicating that the Earth's surface must also be curved. This knowledge led to the deduction that it would be possible to reach East Asia by sailing to the west from Europe.

However, Cosmas Indicopleustes, writing in Alexandria, Egypt, in late antiquity, suggested that the Earth was indeed flat. He explained away noon shadows by suggesting that the Sun was smaller and nearer Earth. The idea of the spherical Earth was in widespread circulation by the 13–14th centuries.

First measurement of the size of the Earth ■ Eratosthenes of Cyrene (*c.* 275–195 BC) was librarian in Alexandria, Egypt. He noted that at the town of Syene (Aswan) at noon in midsummer the Sun was directly overhead, but 7.5° from the vertical at Alexandria. He measured the distance between Syene and Alexandria, and calculated from this that the Earth's circumference must be 252 000 stades. We are not sure of the length of the stades used, but it may be the Earth's circumference according to Eratosthenes works out at 24 600 miles *39 360 km* and the diameter as 7850 miles *12 560 km* – values rather larger than those adopted by Columbus in his voyage in 1492.

Most celebrated geography ■ The most widely consulted geography of the world at this period was the *Geography* of Claudius Ptolemy of Alexandria, Egypt (*c.* 100–170 AD). It was in eight books and gave latitudes and longitudes of about 8000 locations. Through translations into Arabic it was well known to Muslim geographers, and it was published in Latin translations in Europe *c.* 1406, and became the major text on geography. The first printed edition was made in Bologna, Italy, in 1477. Ptolemy's *Geography* contained a serious miscalculation whereby the circumference of the Earth was underestimated. This resulted in a major underestimate of the distance which would have to be covered in sailing westwards from Europe in order to reach East Asia.

First Arab versions of Ptolemy ■ Ptolemy's *Geography* was translated into Arabic by Thabit ibn Kurra, a leading scholar of the ninth century AD, and another translation was made by Ibn Khurdadbih, also of the ninth century AD. In about the middle of the 10th century Al-Khwārizmi produced a reworking of Ptolemy's *Geography* in which Islamic geographical data were interpolated.

First Western editions of Ptolemy ■ The translation into Latin by Jacobus Angelus was first published at Vicenza, Italy, in 1475 and contained no maps. Later editions contained new commentaries and annotations by leading geographers and were accompanied by important maps which showed the increase in geographical knowledge at this period. An influential edition was published at Ulm, Germany, in 1482, including five new maps, one of which was an important map of northern Europe showing Greenland. Another important edition was issued at Rome in 1508; it contained an account by Marcus Beneventanus in which the New World is described and has a new map of the world by Johann Ruysch which shows the New World. The most important edition was produced at

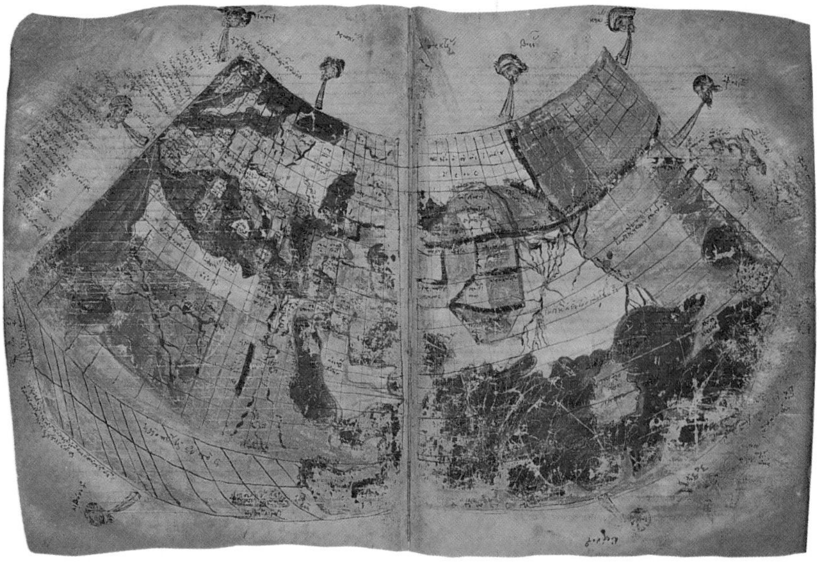

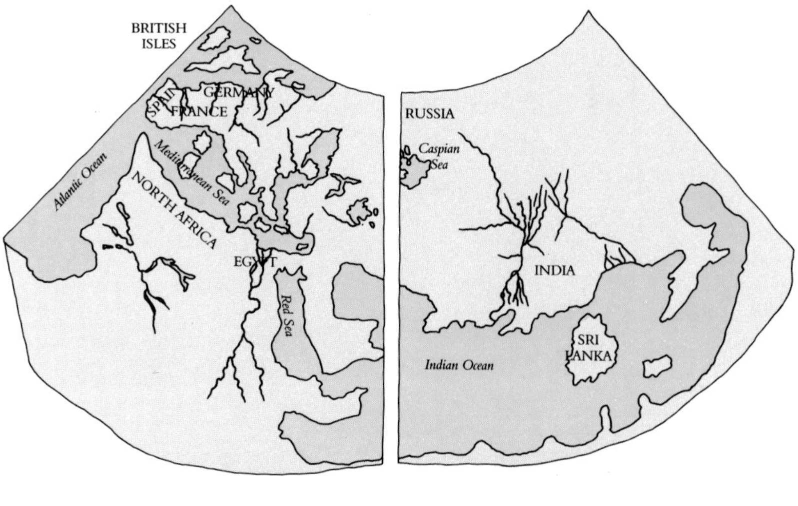

Ptolemy's description of the world was, of course, inaccurate: Africa was too broad and not long enough; India was too small and Sri Lanka too large; the Indian Ocean was landlocked; the size of the Earth was greatly underestimated, but his book is still recognized today as the greatest classical geography.

PREVIOUS PAGE: A zodiac ceiling by Lorenzo Costa adorns the Ducal Palace in Mantua, Italy.

Strasbourg in 1513, under the supervision of Martin Waldseemüller. It contained among others 20 maps showing geographical knowledge of this period, including one devoted specifically to the New World.

> ***The Earth is not a true sphere, but flattened at the poles and hence an oblate spheroid. The polar diameter of the Earth, which is 7899.806 miles*** **12 713.505 km**, ***is 26.575 miles*** **42.769 km** ***less than the equatorial diameter (7926.381 miles*** **12 756.274 km*****). The Earth has a pear-shaped asymmetry with the north polar radius being 148 ft*** **45 m** ***longer than the south polar radius. There is also a slight ellipticity of the equator since its long axis (about longitude 37° W) is 522 ft*** **159 m** ***greater than the short axis.***
>
> ***The greatest circumference of the Earth, at the equator, is 24 901.46 miles*** **40 075.02 km**, ***compared with 24 859.73 miles*** **40 007.86 km** ***at the meridian. The area of the surface is estimated to be 196 937 400 miles²*** **510 065 600 km².**

Most scientific geography ■ The ancient Greeks laid the foundations of scientific geography by their discovery of the roundness of the Earth and their calculations of its circumference and of the extent of the known world. Their work was continued by scholars of the Roman Empire writing mainly in Latin.

First Greek map of the known world ■ This was made by Anaximander of Miletus (*c.* 610–545 BC). At a later period the Greeks devised lines of latitude and longitude which were added to their maps. Greek knowledge of the world was greatly increased following the campaigns of Alexander the Great in 334–323 BC in the Middle East, Central Asia and north-west India.

Major source-book on Greek geography ■ The *Geography* of Strabo of Amasia in Asia Minor (*c.* 62 BC–25 AD) is a large-scale work in 17 books which contains detailed information on earlier Greek geographers whose writings have not survived. Among the most important of these is Eratosthenes, librarian at Alexandria, Egypt (*c.* 275–195 BC). A Latin translation of Strabo was published in Rome in 1472 and became well known in later revisions and editions.

In Western Europe during the medieval period the scientific geography of the Greeks was largely overshadowed by concepts derived from Biblical texts. The theory of a flat Earth was advocated by authors such as Lactantius Firmianus (*c.* 260–340 AD). During the same period Greek geographical writings were translated into Arabic and were the main foreign influence on Muslim geographers. In Renaissance Europe there was a great revival in the study of Greek geography. It was upon these foundations of scientific geography that European scholars built during the age of great geographical discoveries.

Earliest Latin work on geography ■ The earliest surviving work in Latin on geography is the *De chorographia* (On the description of regions) by the Roman writer Pomponius Mela (first century AD). Barthel Stein (1476/7–1521/2) devoted his inaugural lecture to this work in 1509 when he took up his appointment at the University of Wittenberg, Germany. This was the first official appointment of a geographer to a university.

Zones

Coldest and hottest regions ■ According to a well-known theory of Greek origin, the Earth is divided into five zones. The torrid equatorial zone is said to be uninhabitable because of the extreme heat. It is bordered on the north by the northern temperate zone and on the south by the southern temperate zone, both of which are habitable. The northern temperate zone covers the regions inhabited by man in the known world. The other two zones lie around the northern and southern polar regions and are uninhabitable owing to the extreme cold. This theory was very well known and influential during the medieval and later periods. It was restated by the Venerable Bede (*c.* 672–735) in his influential work *De Natura Rerum* (On the Nature of Things), Chapter 46.

Torrid and southern temperate zones ■ Macrobius (*c.* 395–423 AD) was the author of a well-known work in Latin entitled *Commentary on the Dream of Scipio* in which theories of these zones were discussed. It was thought that it would be impossible to travel through the torrid zone because of its extreme heat and that it would therefore be impossible to communicate with men living in the southern temperate zone. Some thinkers also found it difficult to conceive of men living in the southern temperate zone who, as it were, walked upside down. In the early 15th century Cardinal Pierre d'Ailly in his *Tractatus de Imagine Mundi* (Treatise on the Image of the World), Chapter 7, also pointed out a theological difficulty in so far as such inhabitants of the Antipodes would have no knowledge of Christianity. To get over such difficulties some thinkers suggested that the southern temperate zone was mainly covered by water or contained lands which were habitable but which were in fact uninhabited.

Arid and rainy regions ■ The famous Greek historian Herodotus of Halicarnassus in Asia Minor (*c.* 484–425 BC) in his *Histories* 2.26 and 3.10 refers to the extreme aridity of the Nile Valley in Egypt. The low level of atmospheric moisture in this region is a well-known phenomenon. In his *Histories* 2.19–27 Herodotus discusses the various theories put forward by Greek thinkers concerning the causes of the inundations of the Nile. This problem was much discussed by early geographers. Strabo in his *Geography* 17.1.5 gives the explanation as known to scholars of his day, that the inundations of the Nile were caused by heavy rainfall on the uplands of Ethiopia. It has been well known in modern times that torrential downpours on the Ethiopian Plateau have resulted in an annual rainfall of 30–40 inches *75–100 cm.*

Coldest zone ■ The Arctic zone was normally thought to be uninhabitable because of extreme cold, but some thinkers such as the English scholar Roger Bacon (*c.* 1219–1292) in his *Opus Majus* (Major Work) Book 4 discussed the possibility that the Arctic zone might contain temperate or warm zones. In the 16th century the Englishmen Robert Thorne and Roger Barlow thought that the Arctic contained an ice-free sea which could be sailed across, and this theory of an 'Open Polar Sea' was to influence projects for Arctic exploration.

Continents

The division of the Old World into three continents and the names of Europe, Asia and Africa are of Greek origin. This division into three continents did not find general acceptance among Muslim geographers who often preferred other ways of making divisions of the Earth. Al-Dimashqi of Damascus, Syria (1256–1327) described a number of ways in which divisions of the Earth could be made.

Largest and smallest ■ Chapter 5, Book 7, of Ptolemy's *Geography* describes Asia as the largest continent, Africa as the next largest and Europe as the smallest continent. Martin Waldseemüller published an edition of Ptolemy's work with updated material and also in 1507 a work entitled *Cosmographiae Introductio* (Introduction to Cosmography) in which for the first time he suggested that the name 'America' should be given to the new continent in view of the explorations of Amerigo Vespucci.

Largest ■ Of the Earth's surface 41.25 per cent, or 81 200 000 miles² *210 400 000 km²*, is covered by continental land masses of which only about two-thirds or 29.02 per cent of the Earth's surface (57 151 000 miles² *148 021 000 km²*) is land above water, with a mean height of 2480 ft *756 m* above sea level. The Eurasian land mass is the largest, with an area (including islands) of 20 733 000 miles² *53 698 000 km²*. The Afro-Eurasian land mass covers an area of 32 704 000 miles² *84 702 000 km²* or 57.2 per cent of the Earth's land mass.

Smallest ■ The smallest is the Australian mainland, with an area of 2 941 526 miles² *7 618 493 km²*, which, together with Tasmania, New Zealand, New Guinea and the Pacific Islands, is described sometimes as Oceania. Australia and New Zealand were unknown to Europeans in the 15–16th centuries.

Undiscovered southern continent ■ In order to counterbalance the land mass in the northern hemisphere it was thought that an unknown land must exist in the southern hemisphere, and this conception was sometimes connected with Ptolemy's concept of a land bridge connecting southern Africa and Asia. Important maps show a huge landmass in the southern hemisphere, and this concept continued until the 18th century when Australia was discovered by Europeans.

Oceans

The area of the Earth covered by sea is estimated to be 139 781 000 miles *362 033 000 km* or about 71 per cent of the total surface. The volume of the oceans is estimated to be 323 900 000 miles^3 *1 349 000 km^3* compared to 8 400 000 miles^3 *35 000 000 km^3* of fresh water.

Largest ▪ The largest ocean in the world is the Pacific. Excluding adjacent seas, it represents 45.9 per cent of the world's oceans and covers 64 185 600 miles^2 *166 241 000 km^2* in area.

The names of the Atlantic and Indian Oceans are of Greek origin. Muslim geographers describe the known world as being surrounded by the Encircling Sea (Al-Bahr A-Muhit), which is also sometimes called the Green Sea (Al-Bahr Al-Akhdar). Together with six other seas, it is described as one of the seven seas which surround the Earth, but sometimes a smaller number of seas is given.

First naming of Pacific ▪ The Pacific Ocean was first seen by a European when it was sighted by Balboa in 1513. He named it the Southern Ocean, but it was first given the name Pacific in 1520 during Magellan's ships' circumnavigation.

Greatest depth ▪ Aristotle (384–322 BC) in his *Meteorologia* II, I, stated that the Sardinian and Tyrrhenian seas were the deepest in the Mediterranean.

Estimates of heights and depths ▪ In theoretical discussions about the roundness of the Earth, Eratosthenes asserted that the greatest height of mountains did not exceed 10 stades, but Poseidonius of Apamea (*c.* 135–51 BC) argued that this figure should be 15 stades. These figures were also believed to apply to the greatest depths of the sea. Papirius Fabianus, a scholar of the reign of Emperor Tiberius, is also said to have held that the greatest depth of the sea was 15 stades, according to a report in Pliny's *Natural History* 2.105.

Ptolemy's ranking of gulfs ▪ Book 7, Chapter 5 of Ptolemy's *Geography* lists 10 gulfs in order of size, beginning with the Gangetic Gulf (Bay of Bengal) as the largest, followed by the Persian Gulf; Great Gulf (Gulf of Siam); Arabian Gulf (Red Sea); Ethiopian Gulf (Gulf of Guinea); Pontic Gulf (Black Sea); Aegean Sea; Maeotis (Sea of Azov); Adriatic Sea; Propontis (Sea of Marmara). The largest gulf in the world is in fact the Gulf of Mexico, with an area of 580 000 miles^2 *1 500 000 km^2* and a shoreline of 3100 miles *4990 km* from Cape Sable, Florida, USA, to Cabo Catoche, Mexico.

Most celebrated sea mirage ▪ Over the sea at Dengzhou in Shandong province there is a mirage which appears like multistorey houses and towns. People called it the 'sea-market'. The late Ming explanations of it were various: for example, it was the exhalations of sea monsters or the essence of sea-water condensing and then dispersing to form light.

PTOLEMY'S LISTINGS
in order of size with actual measurements

CONTINENTS	
Asia	**c. *16 900 000 miles^2* 43 771 000 km^2**
Africa	**c. *11 500 000 miles^2* 29 785 000 km^2**
Europe	**c. *3 700 000 miles^2* 9 583 000 km^2**
OCEANS AND SEAS	
Indian Ocean	***28 350 000 miles^2* 73 426 000 km^2**
Mediterranean	***965 000 miles^2* 3 499 350 km^2**
Persian Gulf	***90 000 miles^2* 233 100 km^2**
Bay of Bengal	***839 000 miles^2* 2 172 000 km^2**
Gulf of Guinea	***592 000 miles^2* 1 533 000 km^2**
Gulf of Siam	***92 000 miles^2* 239 000 km^2**
Red Sea	***170 000 miles^2* 440 300 km^2**
Black Sea	***159 000 miles^2* 411 810 km^2**
Aegean Sea	***69 000 miles^2* 179 000 km^2**
Sea of Azov	***14 000 miles^2* 36 260 km^2**
Adriatic Sea	***51 000 miles^2* 132 000 km^2**
Sea of Marmara	***4300 miles^2* 11 137 km^2**
ISLANDS	
Sri Lanka	***25 332 miles^2* 65 609.88 km^2**
Great Britain	***88 745 miles^2* 229 849.55 km^2**
Malay Peninsula	***70 000 miles^2* 181 300 km^2**
Ireland	***32 375 miles^2* 83 851.25 km^2**
	***land area 31 839 miles^2* 82 463.01 km^2**
Peloponnese	***8400 miles^2* 21 756 km^2**
Sicily	***9831 miles^2* 25 462.29 km^2**
Sardinia	***9196 miles^2* 23 817.64 km^2**
Corsica	***3367 miles^2* 8720.53 km^2**
Crete	***3207 miles^2* 8306.13 km^2**
Cyprus	***3572 miles^2* 9251.48 km^2**

Tides

Extreme tides are due to lunar and solar gravitational forces affected by their perigee, perihelion and syzigies. Barometric and wind effects can superimpose an added 'surge' element. Coastal and seafloor configurations can accentuate these forces. The normal interval between tides is 12 hr 25 min.

Greatest ▪ The greatest tides occur in the Bay of Fundy, which divides the peninsula of Nova Scotia, Canada, from the United States' north-easternmost state of Maine and the Canadian province of New Brunswick.

Best-known tidal bore in China ▪ The tidal bore on the Qiantang River off the city of Hangzhou in Zhejiang province was described with great vigour by a late Ming writer, Xie Zhaozhi: 'When one first sees it, it is a strip of blue-black vapour. When it is slightly nearer it is a vast expanse of white colour, with a sound like thunder. Its force is like that of a mountain, roaring and tossing itself about, and rushing forward in delirium. In an instant it reaches the shore, like a mountain collapsing or a house falling in ruins. In a few moments it is quiet again, and across the immensity of the river the sky and the water are an identical colour. When the tide comes in the foam spits straight onto the houses of the people who live by the shore, dripping down from the eaves as if there had been a sudden shower of rain . . .'

Islands

Largest ▪ Discounting Australia, which is usually regarded as a continental land mass, the largest island in the world is Greenland (now officially known as Kalaallit Nunaat), with an area of about 840 000 miles^2 *2 175 000 km^2*. There is evidence that Greenland is in fact several islands overlaid by an ice cap without which it would have an area of 650 000 miles^2 *1 680 000 km^2*.

Known largest ▪ Book 7, Chapter 5 of Ptolemy's *Geography* lists 10 islands in order of size, beginning with Taprobana (Sri Lanka) as the largest. (Like many other Greek authors Ptolemy greatly overestimated the size of Sri Lanka.) It is followed

TIDES ■ *The normal interval between tides is 12 hr 25 min. Mont-Saint-Michel, off the coast of Normandy, France, is a famous example of how tides can change the appearance of a place. At low tide a 3000 ft* 914 m *long causeway links it to the mainland, but at high tide it is transformed into an island.*

in order of size by: Albion (Britain); the Golden Chersonese (Malay Peninsula); Hibernia (Ireland); the Peloponnesus; Sicily; Sardinia; Corsica; Crete; Cyprus.

Freshwater ■ The largest island surrounded by fresh water is the Ilha de Marajó (18 500 miles^2 *48 000 km*^{2}), in the mouth of the River Amazon, Brazil. The world's largest inland island (*i.e.* land surrounded by rivers) is Ilha do Bananal, Brazil (7000 miles^2 *18 130 km*^{2}). The largest island in a lake is Manitoulin Island (1068 miles^2 *2766 km*^{2}) in the Canadian section of Lake Huron.

Mountains

Highest ■ The eastern Himalayan peak of Everest, 29 028 ft *8848 m* above sea level on the Tibet–Nepal border was not discovered to be the world's highest mountain for another 400 years after this period.

First book on origin of mountains ■ The first treatise written in Europe dealing solely with the origin of mountains was that of the Italian Valerius Faventies, written during the late 1550s. It was finally published in 1561, in Venice, and was a small pamphlet containing only 16 pages. The reasons Faventies cites for the origins of mountains (typical of thinking at the time) are: earthquakes, swelling of portions of the Earth moistened with water, uplifting power of air enclosed inside the Earth, fire, the soul of mountains, the stars, erosion, wind, moisture within the Earth being drawn towards the Sun, and the work of Man. Fracastoro (1483–1553) appears to have been the first person to realize that the strata found in high mountain ranges once resided beneath the sea.

Measurement of heights ■ It is recorded that the Greeks measured the heights of a number of mountains in Greece, with the aid of an instrument called the dioptra, an early kind of theodolite. Dicaearchus of Messene (*c.* 320 BC) is said to have measured the height of Mount Pelion in Thessaly, according to a report in the *Natural History* 2.65 of Pliny (23–79 AD). Dicaearchus is also reported to have measured the heights of Mount Cyllene in the Peloponnese and Mount Atabyrius in Rhodes. In his *Life of Aemilius Paulus*, Plutarch of Chaironea (*c.* 46–120 AD) mentions an inscription set up by Xenagoras, son of Eumelus, who had measured the height of Mount Olympus.

Greatest mountains ■ In his *Histories* Herodotus describes the Caucasus as the longest and highest of all mountains. At a later date, after the campaigns of Alexander the Great, the Greeks knew of the Hindu Kush (Paropamisus) and the Himalaya (Imaos or Emodus), and there was a well-known theory that, together with the Taurus Mountains of Asia Minor, the Hindu Kush and the Himalaya formed a huge chain of mountains stretching across Asia.

THE ORIGIN OF MOUNTAINS

Leonardo da Vinci (1452–1519) had not considered that any internal force played a part in mountain building. Rather he believed water erosion carved out the primitive crust into gigantic erosional remnants.

Major mountains of Europe ■ In his *Geography* Book 4, Strabo relates that Polybius of Megalopolis (*c.* 205–125 BC) estimated that the Alps could not be climbed even in five days, as compared with the mountains of Greece and Thrace which could be climbed in about a day if you travelled light.

Maximum height of mountains ■ Eratosthenes (*c.* 276–194 BC) asserted that the greatest height of mountains did not exceed 10 stades, but Posidonius argued that this figure should be 15 stades. The English scholar Roger Bacon (*c.* 1219–92) in his *Opus Majus* (Great Work) discussed estimates of the heights of mountains and concluded that the maximum height was 8 miles *12.8 km*.

At a later period, G. Reisch in his *Margarita Philosophica* (Pearls of Philosophy), published in 1508, estimated in a discussion in Book 7, Chapter 44, that the maximum height of mountains was 15 stades and the greatest depth of the sea was 30 stades. In 1550 Sebastian Münster in his *Cosmographia Universalis* (Universal Cosmography) Book 1, Chapter 16, estimated that the maximum height of mountains was 2–3 German miles.

Highest in Africa ■ Kilimanjaro (19 340 ft *5895 m*) has a permanent covering of snow. Although it can be seen across the plain for 100 miles *160 km*, it is not visible from the coast and sailors' descriptions of it were derived from hearsay. The valleys on the southern side of the mountain were intensively cultivated by banana farmers while the northern side was grazed by Masai pastoralists with large herds of cattle. Visiting hunters killed elephants around the mountain and sold their tusks to India for bridal bangles and to China for ornamental carvings.

Highest in the Middle East ■ Mt Damavand, south of the Caspian Sea in the Elburz Mountains, which is 17 996 ft *5610 m*; Mt Ararat, in the Taurus range, which is 16 569 ft *5165 ft*; and, in the Zagros Mountains, in Persia (Iran) Zard Kuh which is 14 590 ft *4548 m*.

Mt Ararat, in southern Turkey, was considered to be the mountain on which Noah's ark came to rest at the end of the Flood, and was called the mountain of Noah. Local tradition said that the ark was still there, but that God had decreed no one was to climb the mountain and see it. Nevertheless, people did try to climb the mountain. In 1474 a Venetian traveller got to its base and said it was 'very high and covered with snow, from the summit to the base, throughout the year. It is said that many persons have attempted to reach the top. Some have never returned, and those who have returned, say that it does not appear to them that a way up will ever be found.'

Rivers

Greatest rivers ■ The Greek historian Herodotus (*c.* 482–425 BC) in his *Histories* 4.48–50 describes the Danube and its tributaries and says that the Danube is the greatest river in the known world. Later in this discussion, however, he says that if the tributaries of the Danube are discounted, the Nile is the greater of the two rivers. (Modern lengths of these rivers are: Danube *c.* 1750 miles *2800 km*; Nile over 4150 miles *6695 km*.

Great Rivers of India ■ Strabo in his *Geography* 15.702, in connection with a description of India which had become better known to the Greeks after the campaign of Alexander the Great, says that the Ganges is the greatest of known rivers, with the Indus coming second, the Danube third, and the Nile fourth. The same judgement is given by Eustathius, Metropolitan of Thessalonica (12th century AD) in his *Commentaries* on Dionysius Periegetes (1143).

Volga ■ In his *Opus Majus* (Major Work) Book 4, Roger Bacon describes the Ethilia (Volga) as one of the larger rivers of the world and as being four times larger than the Seine; his information was derived from William of Rubruck (*c.* 1220–93) and other travellers.

Yangtze ■ Marco Polo (1254–1324) describes the Kiang (Yangtze) as 'the greatest river in the world, which is 100 days' journey in length'. (The modern length is 3430 miles *5488 km*.)

Amazon ■ In 1540–2 Francisco de Orellana travelled down the Amazon River from the Rio Napo to the sea, a distance of some 3000 miles *4750 km*, and gave the river its present name.

One of the first to see through earlier myths ■ Leonardo da Vinci (1452–1519) perceived the true source of rivers. In particular, he recognized the importance of pervious strata in synclinal folds and their value as reservoirs for rainwater percolating downwards into the Earth's crust.

First to recognize true origin of rivers ■ Conrad von Megenberg (1309–74) appears to have been the first to realize the true origin of rivers. He gave a brief account in *Das Buch der Natur* (The Book of Nature).

Least explored large river in Africa ■ In the 15th century, the Congo or Zaïre river could claim this record. The upper reaches were intensively used by Luba fish-farmers who sold dried fish on a large scale to the miners of the Central African Copperbelt. The middle bend of the river through one of the greatest of the world's rainforests was the home of many diverse Bantu-speaking peoples whose cultures were adapted to the economic exploitation of their aquatic environment as long-distance canoe traders. Access to the river from the Atlantic was barred by great rapids which prevented foreign exploration above the estuary. Portuguese sailors left rock inscriptions below the rapids in the 1490s.

First description of the Grand Canyon ■ Some of the Spaniard Francisco Vasquez de Coronado's men reached the land above the Colorado River and looked down on it in 1540, but were unable to descend. Two men who attempted the descent estimated the height of the rocks to be greater than the Giralda, the celebrated bell-tower of Seville Cathedral in Spain which is 275 ft *82.5 m* high.

Highest waterfall ■ The highest waterfall (as opposed to vaporized 'bridal veil') in the world is the Salto Angel in Venezuela, on a branch of the River Carrao, an upper tributary of the Caroni, with a total drop of 3212 ft *979 m* – the longest single drop is 2648 ft *807 m*. The falls were known by the native American peoples as Cherun-Maru.

Greatest waterfall ■ On the basis of the average annual flow, the greatest waterfalls in the world are the Boyoma (formerly Stanley) Falls in Zaïre with 600 000 cusec *17 000 m³/sec*. The flow of the Guaíra (Salto das Sete Quedas) on the Alto Paraná river between Brazil and Paraguay has at times attained a peak flow rate of 1 750 000 cusec *50 000 m³/sec*.

Largest waterfall ■ Musi O Tunia (known also as Victoria Falls), Zambia and Zimbabwe, are where the Zambezi river falls into a mile-wide chasm causing the

Knowledgeable people of the 15th century had a clear idea about the length of various rivers, though of course they knew nothing of the great rivers of the Americas, or of those of southern Africa. In the first half of the 14th century the great Muslim traveller and scholar Ibn Battuta roamed all over Asia and North Africa. He wrote of the Nile that it 'surpasses all rivers of the earth in sweetness of taste, length of course, and utility. No other river in the world can show such a continuous series of towns and villages along its banks, or a basin so intensely cultivated. Its course is from south to north, contrary to all the other great rivers.' Ibn Battuta named the five great rivers of the world as the Nile, Euphrates, Tigris, Sur Darya and Amu Darya, and added five others as also important: the Indus, the Ganges, the Jumna, the Volga and the Hoang-Ho or Saru, that is the Yellow River. Today we recognize the longest rivers of the world as being the Nile 4158 miles **6695 km**, ***the Amazon 4007 miles*** **6448 km**, ***the Yangtze 3962 miles*** **6380 km**, ***the Ob'-Irtysh 3459 miles*** **5570 km**, ***the Yenisey-Angara 3447 miles*** **5550 km**, ***the Hwang He or Yellow River 3393 miles*** **5464 km**, ***the Zaïre or Congo 2898 miles*** **46667 km**, ***the Parana 2794 miles*** **4500 km**, ***the Mekong 2748 miles*** **4425 km** ***and the Amur 2742 miles*** **4416 km**. ***Of the others mentioned by Ibn Battuta, the Euphrates is only 1748 miles*** **2815 km**, ***the Sur Darya 1911 miles*** **3078 km**, ***the Amu Darya 1627 miles*** **2620 km**, ***the Indus 1975 miles*** **3180 km**, ***the Ganges 1559 miles*** **2510 km** ***and the Volga 2290 miles*** **3688 km**. ***The Tigris and the Jumna are much shorter again.***

THE ORIGIN OF RIVERS

Contemporary views about rivers and their origin were dominated by ideas expressed in holy writs issued by the Christian church. Certain passages in the Bible were seen as proving that all rivers had their source in the oceans, thus:

All rivers run into the sea, yet the sea is not full: unto the place from which the rivers come, thither they return again.

(Ecclesiastes, i, verse 7)

'smoke that thunders' that gives them their name. Peering into the chasm on a sunlit day one can see fully circular rainbows.

Lakes and inland seas

Largest ■ Book 7, chapter 5 of Ptolemy's *Geography* describes the Indian Ocean as the largest inland sea, followed in size by the Mediterranean and the Caspian. Owing to a major geographical misconception Ptolemy believed that there was a land bridge between southern Asia and Africa and that the Indian Ocean was therefore a vast inland sea.

Modern measurement gives the largest inland sea or lake in the world as the Kaspiskoye More (Caspian Sea) in Western Asia and Iran. Its total area was in the 15–16th centuries 169 300 miles^2 *438 487 km*^{2}. Its surface has varied between 105 ft *32 m* (11th century) and 72 ft *22 m* (early 19th century) below sea level.

Freshwater ■ The freshwater lake with the greatest surface area is Lake Superior, one of the Great Lakes of North America. The total area is 31 800 miles^2 *82 350 km*^{2}. The freshwater lake with the greatest volume is Lake Baykal in Siberia, Russia, with an estimated volume of 5520 miles^3 *23 000 km*^{3}.

Biggest lake ■ Travellers around 1500 were often wildly astray in their estimates of sizes. In the 1470s an Italian traveller came upon the Caspian Sea, and said it was very large, maybe even equal in circumference to 'Mar Maggiore' in his native Italy. In fact Lake Maggiore covers 82 miles^2 *212 km*^{2} while the Caspian Sea at that time was 169 300 miles^2 *438 487 km*^{2}.

Deserts

Largest desert ■ Though the Sahara is the largest desert in the world it is not the driest. In Roman times strings of wells enabled horse charioteers and even trains of oxen to cross from one oasis to another or from one mountain village to another all the way from North to West Africa. By the fourth century Arabian camels began to be introduced which made travel faster and required the maintenance of fewer date oases. The use of the wheel was virtually abandoned in favour of camel transport.

Driest and hottest areas ■ The Middle East in 1500 had some very extreme climatic conditions. (In the *Timaeus* of Plato an Egyptian priest is reported as saying that Egypt never receives rainfall but is dependent on water from the Nile.) Aswan, in upper Egypt, has an average rainfall of 0.04 in *1 mm* per annum, Cairo 0.9 in *22 mm*, Jidda 0.98 in *25 mm* and Baghdad, Iraq, 5.95 in *151 mm*. In contrast, Rize in north-east Turkey has 96.14 in *2440 mm* a year.

In April 1444, in a port near Muscat, a Muslim traveller found it rather hot. He wrote that 'we felt during one night such excessive heat, that at daybreak one would have said that the heavens had set the earth on fire. So intense was the heat which scorched up the atmosphere, that even the bird of rapid flight was burnt up in the heights of heaven, as well as the fish in the depths of the sea.' This is no doubt a little exaggerated, yet the area does have very extreme temperatures, as modern records show. In July the average daily maximum is 36°C, and the minimum, that is the coolest at night, is 30°C. The absolute maximum is a scorching 45°C, which may have been what this traveller experienced. To add to his misery humidity at this time of the year is over 90%.

Most famous desert 'port' ■ Timbuktu, on the fringes of the Sahara, had a short canal linking it to the Niger River whence its food supply came. The city provided hostelries and banking services for camel caravans carrying rock salt from the greatest of the desert mines at Taodeni in the middle of the Sahara Desert. Timbuktu also sent grain to feed the slave miners in the salt quarries. The city dominated the gold trade from western Africa to the Mediterranean whence it imported textiles and fashionable Muslim clothing. The medieval gold supply came from the upper reaches of the Niger River. By 1400 this was supplemented by gold from the Akan forests, 600 miles *960 km* south of the city.

Most waterless ■ The capital of the Hurmuz kingdom in the 15th century was the Persian Gulf island of Jarun, which had no source of fresh water. Water was hence brought in boats from the mainland, and the island had huge reservoirs built on it, which – so it was said – held enough water to meet the needs of 18 000 people for a whole year.

Driest human settlement in Africa ■ The Taghaza salt mines in the Sahara were being worked from at least the 9th century AD. The town of Taghaza, including its mosques, was entirely built with blocks of salt roofed over with camel skins. All fresh food and water had to be brought in by camels. (The town and the mines were abandoned in the 1580s after repeated attacks from Morocco.)

Highest navigable lake ■ *Situated at 12 506 ft* 3811 m *above sea level, Lake Titicaca in Peru in South America is the highest navigable lake in the world. In the 13th century the Inca culture made its appearance in the region of the lake, and would dominate the area until the Spanish came in 1522.*

Earthquakes

Most popular view of the origin of earthquakes ■ Conrad von Megenburg described this in his *Das Buch der Natur* (The Book of Nature) published in 1475. He writes: 'The common people do not understand why this happens and so a lot of old women who claim to be very wise say that the Earth rests on a great fish called Celebrant, who grasps its tail in its mouth. When the fish moves or turns the Earth trembles. This is a ridiculous fable and of course is not true . . .'

First account of what earthquakes are ■ This was given by Conrad von Megenburg in his *Buch der Natur* (Book of Nature) (1475). He describes how they were generally believed to be due to mysterious exhalations (often poisonous) which built up inside the Earth. Such exhalations built up tremendous pressures inside caverns, such that eventually the cavern walls could not contain them. The battering of the cavern walls eventually reached such proportions that a passage to the surface opened up, throwing the mountains against one another. (Such a view was widely held from the time of Aristotle to the end of the 17th century.)

Worst death toll ■ The greatest chronicled loss of life occurred in the earthquake which rocked every city of the Near East and eastern Mediterranean *c.* July 1201. Contemporary accounts estimate the loss of life at 1 100 000. Less uncertain is the figure of 830 000 fatalities in a prolonged 'quake (*ti chen*) in the Shensi, Shansi and Honan provinces of China, of 2 February (new style) (23 January old style) 1556.

Most terrible earthquake to strike Constantinople ■ It began on the night of 13 September 1509 and continued at intervals for 45 days. During this time the population of Constantinople slept out of doors for fear of their houses falling on top of them. In the city alone, 109 mosques, about 1300 houses and part of the city walls collapsed, and about 5000 people lost their lives. There was much damage in other Turkish cities. In Corum, two-thirds of the population fled to the countryside.

Notable earthquake ■ On 15 February 1549 in eastern Qayin, Iran, a major earthquake destroyed two villages and caused 3000 deaths. The event was predicted by a local astrologer, who was himself killed in the 'quake.

Most frequent earthquakes ■ In the Fujian and Guandong provinces of China, according to the writer Xie Zhaozhi, 'the earth often moves. When such 'quakes occur the ground splits several tens of feet apart, and those unfortunate enough to encounter one may fall inside with their entire household. When the ground closes again, no crack or fissure remains, and one may excavate deeply but not locate them . . .' Xie Zhaozhi thought the reason that the earth quaked was that 'the great earth is fundamentally a kind of living creature with its own movements. The strange principle that it should *not* move would be even more inexplicable.'

Floods

Greatest land loss in Europe ■ In 1421 disaster struck the Low Countries when the serious flooding known as the St Elizabeth flood, because it occurred on that saint's day, overtook reclaimed lands so that 42 000 acres *16 800 hectares* of land was permanently lost.

Greatest land gain ■ Forty per cent of the Netherlands lies below sea level and without constant draining and dyking the sea would flood in. After record reclamation of land from the sea around 1200 amounting to nearly 40 000 acres *16 000 hectares* in a quarter of a century, the next great period of land reclamation was in the mid-16th century when new lands reached over 40 000 acres *16 000 hectares* in 25 years and to this was added further land claimed from inland waters.

Weather

Most disastrous cold spell ■ In the second half of the 15th century, the climate deteriorated over most of Europe and North America. Long harsh winters and late springtimes, followed by poor wet summers, resulted in poor crop yields and famine. Very large numbers of rural settlements in northern Europe were deserted during this period when the weather was especially poor. In most of Europe both winter and summer average temperatures fell by over 1.8°F *1°C*, and in Britain the yearly average decreased by 0.9°F *0.5°C*. These figures disguise the extraordinarily low temperatures experienced during some winters which earned this epoch its very graphic name, the 'Little Ice Age'.

The greatest effect of the climatic change was felt in Iceland and Greenland. The Norse community in Iceland was decimated by colder winters, increased rainfall, shorter summers and the advance of glaciers. The growing season became dangerously short and in some places land fell out of cultivation. Sheep and cattle were unable to find winter forage and large numbers of livestock died. Iceland survived medieval climatic change but European settlement in Greenland did not. The deterioration of weather was greater in Greenland than in Iceland. Links with the outside world became ever more difficult as pack ice spread down the coast. By the middle of the 15th century all sea routes to Greenland were practically impassable and famine became common, and the Norse community in Greenland eventually perished.

Most welcome climatic respite ■ In the period from 1500 to 1540 temperatures increased, rainfall diminished and the climate was characterized by sunshine rather than by snow and storms. In these milder, calmer conditions explorers set off from Spain and Portugal to the New World, to Africa and to Asia. It was, however, only a brief respite as, by the middle of the 16th century, the climate deteriorated again and the harsh weather of the 'Little Ice Age' returned.

Most disastrous drought ■ A 50-year drought at the beginning of the 16th century resulted in the abandonment of the north Indian city of Fatehpur Sikri. The city, which had been constructed as a local capital, was both large and imposing, but a severe and prolonged drought deprived it of a reliable water supply.

Longest drought ■ The drought of 1525 (2 June–15 August) was the longest ever recorded in Russia. For four weeks there was a haze so heavy that people could see neither the Sun nor the Moon. There were many fires in woods and fields and in villages and towns. The consequence of the drought was a rise in the price of bread by 7–10 times.

Most severe winters ■ *The most severe winters of the period were probably experienced in the middle of the 16th century. These harsh snowy winters were captured on canvas by Flemish and Dutch painters, for example in Pieter Bruegel's depiction of* Hunters in the Snow.

Worst hail storm on record ■ While Coronado's party was in California in 1541 they suffered from a terrible hail storm – the worst recorded in America. 'In a very short space of time a great quantity of hailstones, as big as bowls, or bigger, fell as thick as raindrops so that in places they covered the ground 2–3 spans (*c.* 18–27 in *23–66 cm*) or more deep.' The hail did much damage to the men, their horses and their equipment, breaking all their crockery.

First hygroscope ■ The hygroscope, a primitive device for measuring humidity, was first described in the notes of Nicolas Cryfts in 1450. Cryfts suggested that such a device could be made by placing dried wool on a pair of scales. The change of weight that would be observed would indicate changes in the humidity of the air. Leonardo da Vinci developed a more accurate hygroscope, probably basing his invention on Cryfts' work.

First modern rain gauges ■ Although a primitive form of rain gauge was known in India (*c.* 400 BC) the first modern rain gauge probably dates from 15th-century Korea. The device remained unknown in the West until several centuries later. Meteorological measurement was not practised in 15th-century Europe, although the more unusual weather conditions were recorded in chronicles, letters and so on.

Geographers

'Scholastic' geographer ■ This term is used to describe geographers who worked from classical and biblical reading rather than from actual experience. Cardinal Pierre d'Ailly of France was the leading theoretical geographer of the late 14th and early 15th centuries. His *Imago Mundi* (Image of the World) was written in 1410. It was printed in Louvain in Belgium about 1483 and was a most influential work. Columbus owned a copy which survives today with his marginal jottings. d'Ailly was familiar with the work of the Arab geographers and with Ptolemy's *Almagest*, but largely ignored them in favour of such rival classical sources as Aristotle and Pliny.

African geographer ■ Leo Africanus (Al-Hassan ibn Muhammad al-Wazzan) (1494–1552) was one of the best informed of the 15th-century geographers of Africa. He fled from Granada, in southern Spain, as a young child in 1492 when Castilian invaders overthrew the Muslim monarchy of the Nasrids and expelled them from Spanish soil. He travelled widely in northern Africa before being captured by Christian pirates in the Mediterranean and taken to Rome where he published a description of Africa for Pope Leo X and taught Arabic at the University of Bologna. His sociological analyses of the Saharan hinterland published after his death remained the best researched work on the region for many centuries.

Maps

World mapping ■ The first Greek map of the known world was made by Anaximander of Miletus (*c.* 610–545 BC). At a later period the Greeks devised lines of latitude and longitude which were added to their maps.

Most distorted ■ The great *mappae mundae* or 'maps of the world', such as the Hereford map shown here, take Jerusalem as the very centre of the world with the continents laid out symmetrically around the central point. Such maps were widely known and, for all practical purposes, absolutely useless.

Largest of the circular maps ■ The Mappa Mundi, or map of the world, in England's Hereford Cathedral is the largest and probably the most splendid of the surviving circular world maps which show Jerusalem as the centre of the world. It is 4.3 × 5.3 ft *1.3 × 1.6 m* and was completed in about 1275 by a monk called Richard of Haldringham.

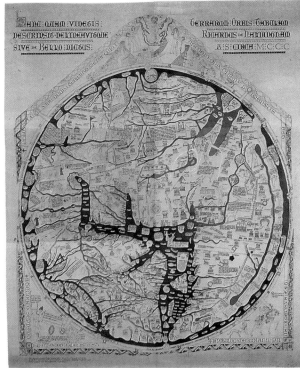

The Hereford Mappa Mundi is decorated with the figures of Christ and angels presiding at the Last Judgement. A Latin inscription around the border reads: 'The measurement of the world was begun by Julius Caesar.' Routes through Europe to the Holy Land are shown, including two crossing places through the Alps.

Cresques' maps included a drawing of Mansa Musa, a 14th-century Mandingo king of western Africa. These were the first reasonably accurate maps of Africa. They show Timbuktu in roughly the correct position, the Senegal River flowing westward from Timbuktu to the sea, and what would be the Niger River flowing eastward.

Africa ■ The earliest map showing the region of the Niger was that drawn by Angelino Dulcert of Majorca in 1339 from information provided by Jewish traders. The most famous early map of the Niger, which marks Timbuktu, was contained in the Catalan Atlas drawn by Abraham Cresques in 1375. He was one of the Majorcan Jews who had links with Europe through Sicily but also had strong commercial links with North Africa, who in this way were aware of both Arabic and European geographical knowledge.

Sea charts of West Africa ■ As the Portuguese extended their exploration southward along the coast of West Africa, they needed working charts which would enable merchant vessels to follow where the adventurers had led – for trade to follow the flag. The earliest sea charts were the work of Italians such as Andrea Bianco (1448),and Bartolomeo Benincasa (1468, showing the coast just southward of present-day Sierra Leone). Bartholomew Columbus, Christopher's brother, worked for a time as a chart maker in Portugal.

Scandinavia ■ The first map of Scandinavia is attributed to Claudius Clavus Svartbo, a native of the Danish island of Fyn. It is dated *c.* 1427 and became the source for northern Europe in the important world maps of Martin Waldseemüller (*c.* 1507) and the *Geography* of Ptolemy (1513).

First recording of lands in the west ■ Some historians think that Europeans may have discovered the Caribbean before Columbus. A large island of Antilia appears on sea charts of the Atlantic from 1424 onwards. Columbus wrote of it, saying: 'In the charts made in times past, there were depicted certain islands in that sea, especially the islands of Antilia more than 200 leagues (*c.* 600 miles *1320 km*) west of the Canaries and the Azores. The Portuguese do not forsake the opinion that it may be the island of the Seven Cities peopled by them when Spain was conquered (by the Moors) and they say that to escape that persecution seven bishops and many people embarked, and with their ships came to land at the said island, there each of them made his settlement, and lest the people should think of turning back they set fire to the ships.'

Oldest terrestrial globe ■ The first cartographer to produce a globe showing the whole round Earth was Martin Behaim of Nuremberg, Germany, in 1492. The east coast of Asia was shown in the position where the west coast of America is in reality located. It was not until Magellan's voyage in 1522 that the true extent of the Pacific Ocean began to be understood.

First map to name America ■ In 1507 Martin Waldseemüller of Nuremberg produced the first world map on which America appeared as a separate continent quite detached from Asia and separated from it by a wide ocean. The land mass which represented America had passages around it to the north-west. He also made use of the word 'America' for the first time on a map, derived from the name of the explorer Amerigo Vespucci.

Old and New Worlds ■ The earliest world chart to include both the Old and the New Worlds is that of 1500 by Juan de la Cosa who sailed with Columbus on his second voyage of 1493. The first printed map to show America (but not to name it) is the map made by Contarini in 1506.

The actual map drawn by Christopher Columbus has not survived, but the Turkish admiral and cartographer, Pirî Reis, acquired a copy from a member of Columbus' crew whom he had captured in the Mediterranean, and used it as a basis for his own world map which he made in 1513 and presented to the Ottoman Sultan Selim the Grim in 1517. Pirî Reis' copy is the only form in which Columbus' map, the first to show the Caribbean and parts of the coast of South America, survives.

Most important world chart ■ The Spanish *Padrón Real* was the official record of discoveries. It was drawn up in 1508 by royal order and was kept up to date from then on by cartographical experts in Seville. The most impressive of the surviving copies of the chart is kept in the Vatican in Rome and dates from 1529.

First modern atlas ■ In 1513 a book of maps was published at Strasbourg, France. It contained 47 maps: 36 of them were based on Ptolemy's maps and 11 of them were based on the results of sailors' growing knowledge. This book can be regarded as the first modern atlas.

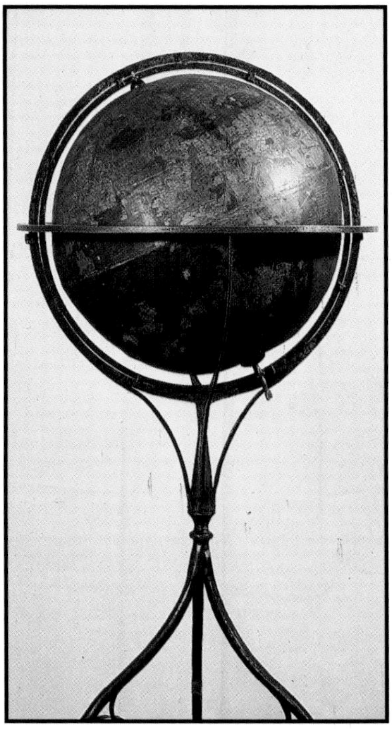

The spherical shell of Martin Behaim's globe of 1492 was 20 in 50 cm *in diameter. The map was drawn on strips of parchment which were then fitted and pasted onto the sphere. The globe was decorated with 111 little pictures of kings, saints, sailing ships and creatures of land and sea. Martin Behaim named it an* Erdapfel *(Earth apple).*

First globe showing the Antarctic and Magellan Strait ■ In 1515 Johann Schoner of Nuremberg, Germany, made a globe showing the then-hypothetical southern continent of Antarctica. It also showed a strait linking the Atlantic and Pacific, four years before Magellan set out on the round-the-world voyage that would prove the existence of such a channel, which now bears Magellan's name.

Europe ■ The first pictorial map of Europe is known as *Carta Marina of Olaus Magnus* (The Sea Map of Olaus Magnus) and was a woodcut published in Venice in 1539. It was produced by the Swede, Olaus Magnus.

Projection ■ The first use of the 'Mercator' projection which became the standard map projection for navigation was in fact by Erhard Etzlaub of Nuremberg, Germany, in 1511 in a map of Europe and North Africa. (Gerardus Mercator produced his world map in 1569.)

First maps by Mercator ■ Although the Flemish-born cartographer Gerardus Mercator (1512–94) would not draw his revolutionary world map with its new projection until 1569, he published his first world map in 1538. It was one of the earliest world maps to use the names of both North and South America, and he attempted on this map to represent the roundness of the Earth.

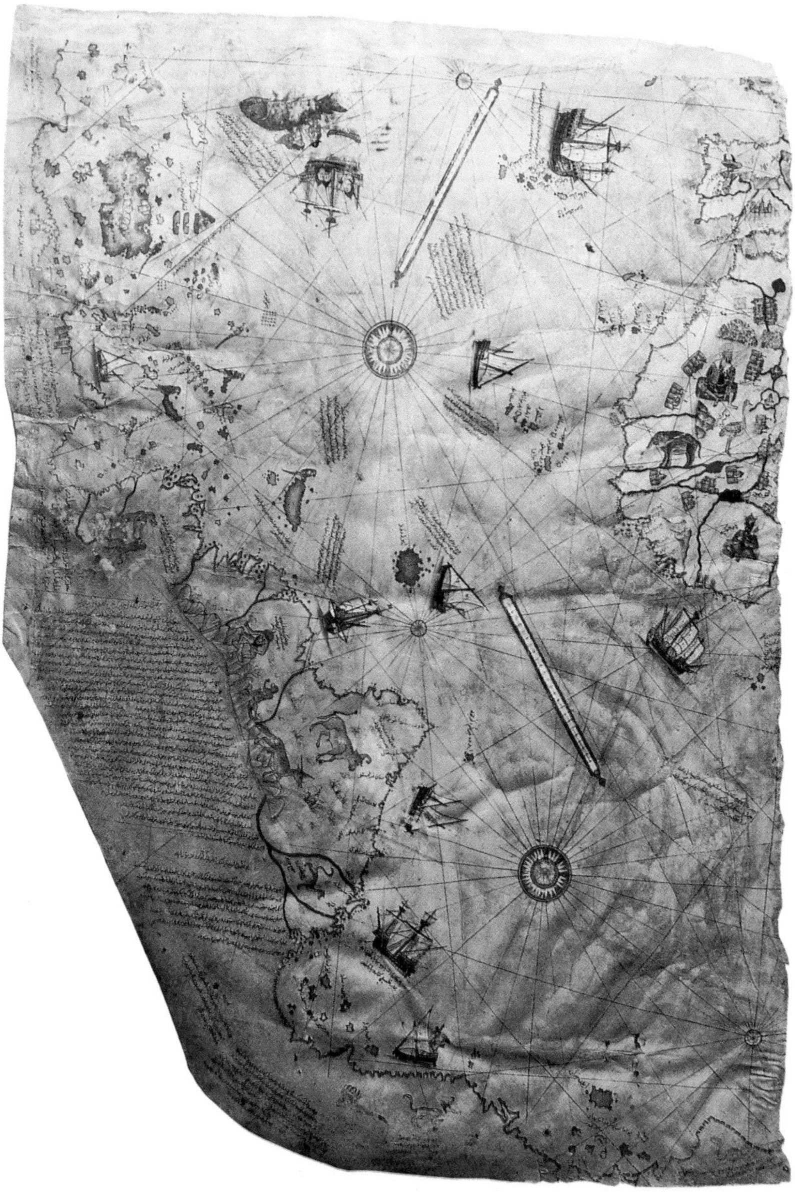

Map of Pirî Reis, the Turkish cartographer, showing Europe, the west coast of Africa and South America.

Geology

First observation of structure ■ The observation that many gems and other transparent minerals, when examined under transmitted light, exhibit small pores, streaks and fibres, was made by the German Hieronymous Cardanus in *De Subtilitate* (On detailed structure). He claimed that these were a simplified version of the organic structures seen in both animals and plants.

Most amazing contemporary belief ■ In the field of mineralogy this must be the supposed existence of male and female stones. Many ancient writers, including Pliny and Theophrastus, wrote concerning this point. Thus the brighter red and more pellucid form of carnelian was identified as the female form, while the deeper red or almost black variety was believed to be the male. Some writers even believed that stones could reproduce themselves!

Concretions were known by the ancients (e.g. Pliny) and by many philosophers of the 15th and 16th centuries as *aetites* or 'eagle stones'. They were colourfully imagined to possess the rare property of giving birth to young, a belief which presumably arose from their ability, once cracked open, to reveal small spherical layers inside. This was discussed by Leonardus Camillus, writing in 1505, and by Conrad Gesner (1516–65).

Greatest authority on mineralogy ■ Leonardus Camillus was physician to Cesare Borgia. He catalogued 279 separate mineral names in a work entitled *Speculum Lapidum* (A looking-glass of stones) which was first published in Venice in 1502. He held to the Aristotelian view that minerals in some way formed under the influence of heavenly bodies. The fact that more precious stones appeared to be found in tropical countries than in Europe was generally believed due to the higher altitude of the Sun and other heavenly bodies which therefore acted with greater power at the Earth's surface.

Most puzzling stone ■ Amber was considered to be a mineral from classical right through to medieval times. However, some writers (Aristotle and the author of *Hortus Sanitatis* (Garden of health)) said it was the product of a tree, while others (Georgius Agricola) saw it as a product of the Earth. The most remarkable book on this subject was *De Succino* (On Amber), written by the Swiss scientist Severin Gobels, in a part of which the complex structures so typical of the fossilized resin are seen as a complete allegorical exposition of the teachings of Christianity.

Saddest stone ■ The mineral onyx, according to the famous medieval herbal *Hortus Sanitatis* (Garden of health), was of vegetable origin and generated from the tears of the tree known as *onica*. When such tears hardened, they changed into onyx which, when placed in a fire, gave off a fragrant odour. The book also describes the familiar patterns seen in onyx which it explains as being due to them having been painted while the tears were still soft and plastic.

Most harmonious stone ■ The variety of gypsum known as selenite was widely held to change its lustre in harmony with the changing phases of the Moon, in some magical way reflecting the Moon's behaviour. Thus it attracted various names, such as *Lac Lunae* (lake of the Moon) and 'the Moon's Milk'. The German Georgius Agricola was among the first to realize its true nature.

Most highly prized metal ■ Undoubtedly this was gold. It was both a measure of value and a store of wealth. From the 13th century gold coinage was being revived in Europe; Florence and Venice were the leaders and their gold florins and ducats acquired the status of an international exchange medium.

Gold is a soft and malleable metal and so is easily worked. It may be found in veins of quartz, as in the example shown here.

Between 1493 and 1600 world production of gold was about 714 tons made up of 280 tons from the Americas, 255 tons from Africa and 148 tons from Europe.

Greediest ambition ■ Creating man-made gold was the most cherished dream of the greedy and the prime motivation of medieval alchemy. Chemical laboratories where alchemists competed to discover the secret were financed by the great kings and princes.

First to revive interest in minerals ■ After the 'Dark Ages', it was the 15th-century alchemists who began to study minerals. Their commonest belief was that rays from heavenly bodies – in particular the planets – penetrated the Earth and somehow produced metals within the crustal rocks. For instance, the English alchemist, Thomas Norton, writing in 1477 in his *Ordinall of Alchimy* says

> *For cause sufficient Mettals finde ye shall*
> *Only to be the vertue Minerall*
> *Which in everie Erth is not found,*
> *But in certain places of eligible ground:*
> *Into which places the Heavenly Spheare,*
> *Sendeth his beams directly everie yeare*
> *And as the matters there disposed be*
> *Such Mettalls thereof formed shall you see.*

First use of the name zinc ■ The first use of this term to describe the metal is attributed to Paracelsus (1493–1541) in 1530. He believed it to be a form of copper.

First to recognize origin of sedimentary rocks ■ The first person to realize that sedimentary rocks were produced by the wearing away of rock masses by running water was Georgius Agricola (1494–1555). He correctly determined that clastic rocks were formed in this way and also that some sedimentary rocks were precipitated out of percolating solutions.

First recognition of cause of strata ■ The first event to prompt philosophers to consider that the Earth's fossiliferous strata could have been laid down as layers was the eruption of Vesuvius in southern Italy in 1538, which built up a 270 ft *80 m* high cone in the Bay of Naples. They considered it likely that this took around 6000 years.

Gemstones

The hardest of stones ■ The name 'diamond' comes from the Greek for indomitable. This quality was transferred to the wearer who expected it to offer protection from wild and venomous beasts, and human enemies of all kinds. Likewise it drove off evil spirits in the night and was a prophylactic against insanity. Some lapidaries instruct the reader in conducting a test for adultery with the diamond. Diamonds were believed to be lethal if swallowed so they were not used medicinally. Saturn, the slowest-moving heaviest outermost planet with a reputation for causing hardship, was also given rulership over this most difficult to cut stone. Diamonds used in jewellery were most often 'pointed', cut into a four-sided double pyramid. Until the 14th century they were too hard to cut and only as the technology for cutting them developed was their full brilliance and corresponding market value recognized. India was the main source.

Favourite royal gem ■ Francis I of France was the monarch most fond of diamonds. The best diamond collar in his collection had 11 great stones which were alternately pointed and table-cut, with a diamond 'A' pendant which hung in the front.

First diamond engagement ring ■ The tradition of the diamond engagement ring began in 1477 when the Archduke Ferdinand of Austria gave one to Mary of Burgundy. The belief that a *vena amoris* (vein of love) runs directly from the brain to the top of the third finger of the left hand originated in ancient Egypt.

Largest known diamond ■ The *Koh-i-Noor* (Mountain of Light) was first recorded in 1304 when it was owned by an Indian prince; in the early 16th century it belonged to Babur (1483–1530) founder of the Moghul dynasty in India. When it was found it weighed 800 carats; after cutting it was reduced to 186 carats.

Most protective stone ■ The emerald was valued for its ability to foster understanding and improve memory. Royal children wore them from birth for protection from epilepsy. Emeralds were believed to give the power of seeing the future and to help find things that were lost. They were used to guard against evil spirits and venom.

Lapidaries, books about gems and minerals, were more directly derived from classical sources than any other type of medieval literature. The rediscovery of the classics in the 15th century made little difference to this area of knowledge. From Babylonian times metals were associated with planets and gems had probably also been connected with planets on the basis of colours. Egyptian tradition attributed stones to each day of the month, and also to each decan (ten degree segment) of the zodiac. The ancient Greeks mixed magic and science together in their writings on minerals. Like herbs, minerals had affinities with elements and were classified as hot or cold and moist and dry.

In the early Christian era writers passed on the information pertaining to medical uses of stones, both as amulets and as internal medicine, but deleted many of the more magical applications, substituting 12 sacred stones.

Most famous ■ In lapidary lore the most famous emeralds are the carved sunglasses which the Roman emperor Nero wore to watch gladiatorial contests.

Most sought after ■ Most emeralds were mined in Egypt. But the Colombian variety had better colour and soon became the most prized. When the New World emeralds were discovered by the Spanish in 1537 a substantial quantity was smashed by the men who mistakenly believed that extreme hardness was a quality the gems shared with diamonds.

Rarest profile ■ A mysterious religious image is the 'true likeness' of Christ that the Ottoman Sultan Bajazet II (1481–1512) gave to Pope Innocent VIII (1484–92). It was carved on an emerald and showed Christ's face in profile – an extremely rare feature in images of Jesus which are usually full-face. No trace of the emerald remains (it was probably lost in the sack of Rome in 1527) but numerous copies of the emerald portrait survive in paintings, engravings, and medals. In the popular imagination it was accepted as an authentic portrait from the life until the 19th century.

Most important quartz gem stones ■ The amethyst is the only purple gem stone, which may have caused it to be associated with wine. The name comes from a Greek word which means 'not drunken'. It had the useful prophylactic property of being believed the best protection against intoxification. It was one of the 12 sacred stones and signified the humble who died in Christ.

Most expensive medicine ■ Pearls, ground to a fine powder, were the most expensive medicine and a universal antidote to poison.

Finest jewels of the sea ■ Pearls were always highly prized as the jewels of the sea. Until the 15th century they were the dominant jewel. They were believed to be formed by dew drops: the superior white ones formed during the morning, the dark ones in the evening. They were good for the heart and effective against melancholy. Fisheries in the Persian Gulf were the main suppliers for Europe by way of Venice. They were looted from the Colombian coast by Spaniards 1517–19 and were eventually found off the coast of Venezuela and sent to Spain.

Most celebrated display ■ One of the most celebrated displays of pearls is that of the Cubaguan Pearls worn by Eleanor of Portugal in Titian's portrait of her.

Most frequently mentioned ■ Toadstone is the magical stone most frequently mentioned in inventories of jewellery. Usually it was set in a ring. The earth-toad, whose breath is poisonous, has a stone in the marrow of its head which must be removed when the moon is waning and kept in a linen cloth for 40 days in order to create a powerful amulet. The most effective stones were believed to be those taken while the toad was still alive.

A herbalist extracting the magical stone from the head of a toad. The toad-stone once extracted in this way might then be used in jewellery or in various magical recipes.

Best fake gems ■ These were manufactured by the Venetian glassworkers; the deep and intense colours required are characteristic not only of the finest glassware but also of the paintings of the Venetian master artists: Bellini, Giorgione and Titian.

Most dubious gems ■ Unicorn horn was worn in pendants as protection from poison by the great princes who could afford it. These are mentioned in inventories of the Dukes of Burgundy in 1456 and Henry VI of England, where it states that he put it in his drink. Others used them to touch the plates containing food. In addition to unicorn horn Anne of Burgundy's 1498 inventory includes serpent's tongue and toad stone which were kept in a crimson velvet purse.

Most misapprehended ■ For many centuries coral was the most misunderstood of precious substances. It was considered to be a plant which hardened upon exposure to the air.

Worst job ■ Diving for coral, which entailed dragging a net along the sea bed to entangle the sharp coral branches, was reputedly the worst of all possible jobs. In Naples, Italy, the main European centre, it was said that only a thief or a murderer deserved to be a coral fisher. Coral was nevertheless supplied in quantity for amulets, rosaries, and ecclesiastical objects.

Best love potions ■ Coral was regarded as one of the best love potions that money could buy. Its medical applications included arresting excessive bleeding, treatment of skin disorders, sore eyes, and dysentery.

Best storm protector ■ When bound to the mast with sealskin coral would calm storms at sea and, at home, when powdered and sprinkled on the roof it could avert lightning.

Most expensive pigment ■ Lapis lazuli is the semi-precious blue stone that is the source of the most expensive pigment used by painters to create the characteristic garment of the Virgin, her blue mantle. The price depended upon the intensity of the colour and was the most important factor in the calculation of the cost of a painting. It was also used for ornamental vases and furniture inlay (*pietra dura*).

Most expensive preparation ■ Of materials used in medicinal preparations bezoar (Persian for 'expelling poison')

Favourite royal gem ■ *Rubies were the favourite gem of Henry VIII; Hans Holbein painted him wearing his famous collar made of large balas rubies. Alternating flat-cut square and oval rubies are joined by pearl-studded gold links. He also wears large ruby rings and his hat jewels and buttons are diamonds.*

stones imported from the Orient were the most expensive of the 16th century. An animal stone of uncertain origin, it was ground into powder and ingested. The stone taken from the monkey was reputedly the most powerful, but various writers recommended different animals. Only in Portugal was the hog stone held to be superior.

Only clear vessels ■ Rock crystal, colourless quartz, was the only material suitable for clear vessels before the the discovery of the secret for making clear glass in the late 15th century. The Greek 'krystallos' means both rock-crystal and ice: the gem was formerly believed to be old glacial ice. It was an excellent material for magnifying-glasses and doctors used crystals held in sunlight for cautery (sealing tissue by burning). It was used for jewellery in Italy.

Most prominent craftsmen ■ Amber, the fossilized resin formed from the sap of trees, was used primarily for rosaries and crucifixes. The guilds of amber turners at Venice and Augsburg, Germany, were the most prominent craftsmen. The main source of supply was the Baltic coast of Prussia.

Richest mountain ■ The Chinese traveller Ma Huan who wrote about Sri Lanka in 1451 described a great mountain reaching to the skies near to the king's residence. 'This mountain,' he said, 'abounds with rubies and other precious stones.' These gems were being continually washed out of the ground by the rains and were discovered in the sands carried down the mountain by the torrents. Locally it was believed, he reported, that these precious stones had been made from the tears of the Buddha.

Most highly prized of all gems ■ Until it became technically possible to cut diamonds in the 14th century, rubies (red corundum) were the most highly prized gems. Burma was the main source. Their colour and relative softness made them more desirable than diamonds for jewellery. Like the emerald, the ruby is believed to bring joy and comfort. When worn around the neck, it would dispel sadness. Its virtues included aid to the heart, brain and liver.

LITERATURE

Earliest lapidaries ■ A lapidary is a treatise on precious stones. One of the earliest was that of Steinpreis, printed shortly after the year 1500. In it the author describes over a hundred different stones and establishes the fact that precious stones have peculiar virtues and properties. He also discusses how they should be treated.

Earliest lapidary to contain a chapter on rings ■ This was the lapidary of Erasmus Stella, entitled *Interpraetamenti Gemmarum Libellus* (Handbook on the interpretation of gems), written in 1517. He notes that the custom of wearing a ring on the third finger of the left hand was almost certainly derived from the Egyptians, who believed that a vein passed directly from this finger to the heart.

Most popular and influential ■ From the 11th century on this was one which reintroduced the magical properties of stones, *De Lapidibus* (About Stones) in Latin verse by Marbode Bishop of Rennes, France. Marbode describes the uses of 60 stones. The book was translated into six languages and inspired many more versions of the rhymed lapidary over the following three centuries. It was first printed in Vienna, Austria in 1511.

First renaissance lapidary ■ Included in his *De Vita Libri Tres* (Three Books about Life) Marsilio Ficino (1433–99) attributes the power of gems to the stars and gives instructions on engraving them to increase their power.

Most confusing name ■ The name carbuncle was used in medieval times to represent minerals as widely divergent as ruby, pleonaste and garnet.

First published description ■ The first description of the mineral bismuth to be published was given by Georgius Agricola in his book *Bermannus* (1530).

First printed mention of the word *geologia* ■ The word was invented by Richard de Bury, Bishop of Durham, and used in 1473. It had then a very different meaning from the current one. De Bury uses it as an opposite to *Theologia* (divine science), that is, 'earthly science', by which he meant Law (in the legal sense).

Earliest textbook on metallurgy ■ The *Pirotechnia* of Italian metallurgist and armament maker Vannoccio Biringuccio (1480–*c.* 1539) was published in 1540. It gave clear practical instructions on metallurgical and chemical processes, such as the smelting of gold, silver, copper, lead, tin and iron. Unlike earlier books, Biringuccio's work devoted little space to the fantasies of alchemy.

Fossils

Fossils were often known as 'Figured Stones'. Falloppio of Padua, writing in his *De Medicatis Aquis atque Fossilibus* (On curative waters and fossils) (Venice, 1564), considered that they were produced by vapours in a kind of strange fermentation process that took place in rocks where such fossils were found. This view was widespread during the 15th and 16th centuries.

First scientific view ■ The first person to realize that fossil shells could not have been left by the Biblical Flood appears to have been the Italian Fracastoro (1483–1553). He suggested that such fossils had lived and multiplied amongst the deposits in which they were found and, therefore, that the mountains must have been lifted above the sea.

Most heaven-sent ■ Belemnites were often referred to as thunderbolts. Their resemblance to arrowheads and their abundant presence in the soft strata of the Lias – a formation readily acted upon by the atmosphere, especially thunderstorms – led to the widely-held notion that they were formed in places often struck by lightning, thus emanating from the skies.

The universe

First suggestion that the Earth is in orbit round the Sun ■ Made by the Greek philosopher Aristarchus of Samos (*c.* 310–230 BC), whose writings have come down to us from his younger contemporary Archimedes of Syracuse.

Best known classical astronomer ■ Ptolemy's *Astronomy* is best known by its Arabic name meaning 'the Greatest', the *Almagest*. It was first translated into Latin in Spain in the 12th century and from then on was available to European readers. It was Ptolemy's work and the work of Aristotle which provided the framework for cosmological understanding up until Copernicus demolished it in the 16th century.

Most comprehensive book ■ The great Islamic astronomer Ibn Umar al-Marrakashi (died 1262) worked mainly in Morocco. His book *Jami al Mabadi Wal-Ghayat* (Of beginnings and ends) was possibly the most comprehensive work on both theoretical and practical astronomy of the time. It contained descriptions of instruments, trigonometrical tables, a catalogue of 240 stars for the years 1225–6, and latitudes and longitudes of 135 places, 34 of which he had recorded himself.

First modern book to support the heliocentric or Sun-centred theory ■ This was published in 1543 by the Polish canon Mikoaj Kopernik (Copernicus) (1473–1543). Fearing Church opposition, Copernicus hesitated to make his work known, and was finally persuaded to do so – by Georg Rhaeticus, professor of mathematics at the University of Wittenberg – in the last days of his life. It was entitled *De Revolutionibus Orbium Celestium* (On the Revolution of Heavenly Bodies) and teaches that the Earth moves round the Sun in a small circle or epicycle, the centre of which (the deferent) itself moves round the Sun in a perfect circle. The theory was strongly criticized as heretical by both the Catholic and Protestant churches.

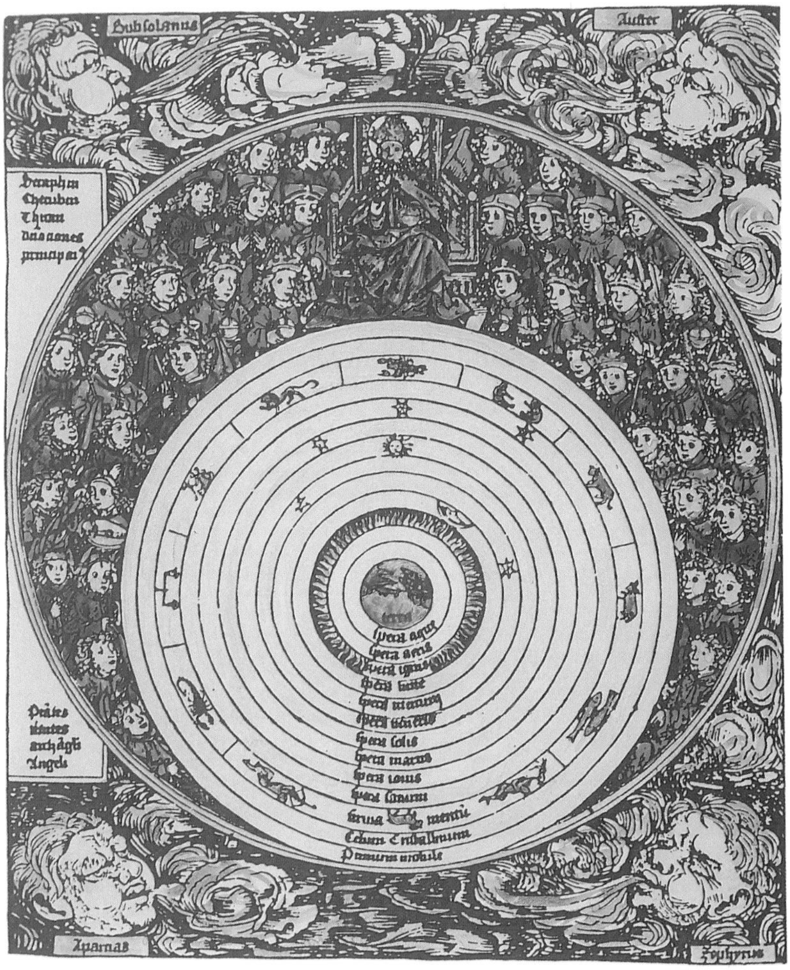

The medieval Cosmos is shown with Earth at its centre and the figure of God overseeing all creation.

Calendars

First reasonably good calendar ■ Drawn up before 420 BC by the Egyptians, this calendar was based upon the heliacal rising of the star Sirius (Sothis) – that is to say, the date when it could first be seen in the dawn sky. The 365-day Egyptian year was divided into 12 months of 30 days each, with five festival days.

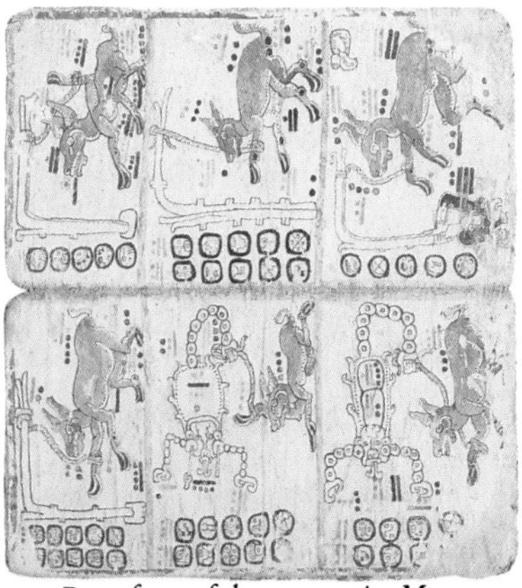

Part of one of the very precise Mayan calendars from the Yucatan in Mexico.

Greatest precision ■ The Maya astronomers of Central America determined in about the 6th century AD that the solar year was made up of 365.242 days. The real number as now recognized and used is 365.2422. They also calculated that a lunar month was 29.530 59 days. To adjust for inconsistencies they made corrections. In 687 all Maya cities had agreed to count the next new moon as the starting point of lunar cycles. In 756 they made a correction to allow for leap years. They also established a religious year of 260 days which ran alongside the solar year.

Moon

Distances of the Sun and Moon ■ The first scientific attempt to measure these distances was made by Aristarchus, *c.* 275 BC. His method was geometrical, and involved finding the time when the Moon is at exact half-phase. He also attempted to measure the real sizes of these two bodies in terms of that of the Earth. He concluded that the distance of the Sun was just under 3 million miles *4.8 million km* and its diameter 43 000 miles *69 000 km*, with the Moon's diameter 2300 miles *3700 km*. The Moon he was certain was the closest body in the heavens.

Moon's surface ■ The Roman writer Plutarch gave the first scientific description of the Moon's surface around 170 AD, in his essay *De Facie in Orbe Lunae* (Of the Face in the Orb of the Moon). He described 'deep places and ravines', and that 'just as our Earth has great depressions, so the Moon is opened up by great depths and clefts containing water or dark air, which the light of the Sun does not penetrate or touch'.

Earthshine ■ The Italian painter and scientist Leonardo da Vinci first noted that when the Moon is in its crescent phase, the 'unlit' side can often be seen shining faintly. Around 1480, Leonardo realized that this is due to light reflected on to the Moon from the Earth.

Eclipses

Last visible from London ■ There was such a total solar eclipse in 1140. The next (after 1492) would be in 1715.

Earliest recorded ■ For the Middle East, lunar eclipses have been extrapolated to 3450 BC and solar ones to 4200 BC. The oldest recorded total solar eclipse is on a clay tablet found among the ruins of the ancient city of Ugarit (now in Syria). A reassessment suggests that this records the eclipse of 5 March 1223 BC. Thus the first recorded eclipse of the Sun is probably that of 22 October 2136 BC, noted by the Chinese during the reign of the Emperor Chung K'ang.

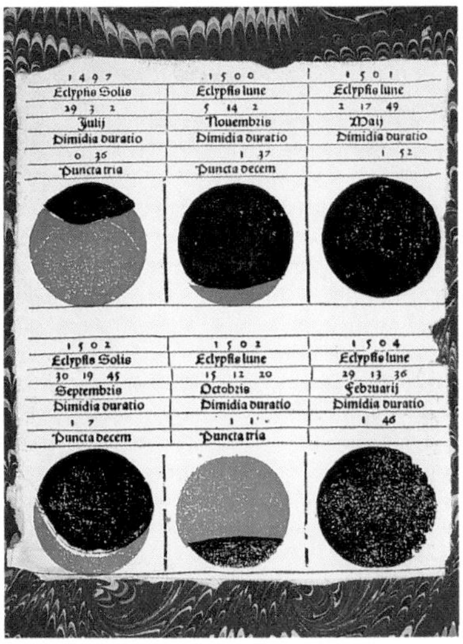

Calendar with eclipses, for the years 1497 to 1504, from an almanac said to have been used by Christopher Columbus.

First reliably predicted ■ On 25 May 585 BC the first of the Greek philosophers, Thales of Miletus (*c.* 624–547 BC), predicted correctly that an eclipse is likely to be followed by another eclipse 18 years 11 days later. Thales' prediction brought an abrupt end to a battle between the armies of the Lydians and the Medes; the soldiers were so alarmed by the sudden darkness that they concluded a hasty peace.

Only influence on a major war ■ This claim goes to the lunar eclipse of 413 BC. The Peloponnesian War was raging between the Greek city-states of Athens and Sparta, and the Athenian army which had invaded Sicily was in serious trouble. The Athenian commander, Nicias, decided upon evacuation, but delayed because the lunar eclispe was regarded as an unfavourable omen. By the time he tried to withdraw his troops it was too late. The Athenian fleet which was waiting was destroyed, and the soldiers were trapped. It was this defeat which led directly to the overthrow of Athens eight years later.

Planets

Brightest ■ By far the brightest of the five planets visible to the naked eye is Venus, which can often be seen before sunrise or after sunset. The only planets that are morning or evening objects but can never be seen throughout the night are Mercury and Venus.

Reddest ■ This is Mars. Its colour accounts for its name in honour of Mars (Greek, Ares) the God of War.

Slowest moving ■ Saturn takes 29½ years to travel once round the Zodiac.

Strongest influences ■ Planets were considered to have dominion over the different stages of human life from infancy to old age.

Comets

First recorded ■ The first records of comets are Chinese and date back well before 2000 BC.

Brightest ■ The brightest reliably reported comet was that of 1264, which developed a tail 100 degrees long; it was described by the English writer Francis Bacon as 'great and dreadful', causing 'vast disturbances and wars in England, Spain and in other lands in which many Christians were slaughtered'.

First records of Halley's Comet ■ The successive appearances of Halley's Comet have been traced back to 467 BC. It was first depicted in the Nuremberg Chronicle of 684 AD.

Only comet to be subject of Papal attention ■ In 1456, at the time the Turks were laying siege to the city of Belgrade, in what was later Yugoslavia, a comet appeared. Pope Calixtus III preached against it as an agent of the Devil; church bells were rung, and extra Ave Marias were ordered. Subsequently, the Hungarian general Hunniades was able to force Mehmed II and his Turkish army to raise the siege: so the Pope's intervention was seen as successful.

First recorded in tapestry ■ *The Bayeux Tapestry was woven on the instructions of the wife of William I. It shows the comet of 1066 shining down from above, while King Harold topples off his throne and the Saxon courtiers look on aghast.*

Greatest inspirer of predictions ■ The comet of 1472 which swept across 36 degrees, or one sixth of the sky, was called the 'great comet' and it inspired more predictions than any other comet of the century. Several astrologers correctly predicted the demise of Pope Paul II.

Greatest birth influence ■ Comets were believed to foreshadow the birth of famous persons whose sun or ascendant degrees would be the same as that of the comet. If a pregnant woman observed a comet it meant that her child would be quarrelsome or seditious.

Constellations

First list ■ The first list of currently accepted constellations was given by Ptolemy in the *Almagest* his astronomical text: 48 constellations were named. This list was still the accepted version in 1492.

Largest ■ *Argo Navis* (the Ship Argo).

Smallest ■ *Equuleus* (the Little Horse).

Only Zodiacal constellation named after an inanimate object ■ Libra (the Balance). It was formerly included in Scorpio, as *Chelae Scorpionis*, the Scorpion's Claws.

Direst personal prediction ■ If the star Arcturus in the constellation of Sagittarius is setting (opposite the ascendant) at birth it was thought to produce people who are driven by envy to commit grave crimes; their fate is to die in miserable torment fettered in chains in public dungeons.

Brightest ■ The brightest star in the sky is Sirius, in Canis Major (the Great dog).

First constellation of the Zodiac ■ This is Aries (the Ram). However, the shift known as precession had by 1500 transferred the vernal equinox (the point where the ecliptic cuts the celestial equator) into the adjacent constellation of Pisces (the Fishes).

Reddest bright star ■ Antares, in Scorpio (the Scorpion) holds this record. Other bright red stars are Betelgeux in Orion, Arcturus in Bootes (the Herdsman) and Aldebaran in Taurus (the Bull).

Star clusters

First list of star-clusters and nebulae ■ The first list was compiled by Ptolemy, and includes nine objects.

Brightest star-cluster ■ The Pleiades, in Taurus, are mentioned by Hesiod (*c.* 1000 BC) and in the Bible.

Fiery stars ■ The first suggestion that the stars are 'fiery' was due to the Ancient Egyptians, who believed that Sirius (which they called Sothis) was a sun.

Observatories

Most outstanding observatories ■ In 1420 the great Mongol ruler Ulugh Beg founded an observatory at Samarqand, Central Asia. This was inspired by earlier Muslim observatories, especially the one at Maragha in Azerbayjan. Important astronomical work was carried out at Samarqand, which is especially noteworthy for its huge astronomical instruments, including a meridian axis about 131 ft *40 m* long.

Ulagh Beg's great star catalogue was ready by 1439. Unfortunately, it was destroyed after his murder in 1449, by his son Abdallatif, whom he had banished upon astrological advice.

Most important Persian observatory ■ Nasireddin (1201–74) had his observatory at Maragha (now Iran). It was completed in 1259, and had a staff of 15, with a library of 400 000 books; the main measuring instrument was a quadrant. It was here that Nasireddin compiled his very accurate tables of planetary motion.

Greatest ancient observatory ■ This was Ptolemy's observatory at Alexandria in Egypt (*c.* 150 AD). Ptolemy brought classical science to its highest degree of perfection. After his death *c.* 180 AD, astronomy fell into decline, and was not truly revived until the time of the great Arab astronomers.

Earliest telescope ■ Although there is evidence that early Arabian scientists understood something of the magnifying power of lenses, their first use to form a telescope has been attributed to Roger Bacon (*c.* 1214–92) in England The suggestion of an optical device 'to see the Moon large' was made by Leonardo da Vinci, around 1490.

LITERATURE

Greatest astronomical book ■ In ancient times this was undoubtedly the *Syntaxis* (Order of parts) of Ptolemy of Alexandria (*c.* 120–80 AD) undoubtedly earns this title. It came down to 15th-century astronomers via its Arab translation as the *Almagest.* The book defines the geocentric or Earth-centred theory of the universe, and also gives a detailed star catalogue which was not surpassed for many hundreds of years.

Most widely-read textbooks on astronomy ■ In the 15th century these were *De Sphaera* (Of the Spheres) by Robert Grosseteste (1254) and *De Sphaera Mundi* (Of the Spheres of the World) by John Holywood of Yorkshire (usually known by his Latinized name of

Star map of constellations and zodiacal images drawn in about 1515 by the artist Albrecht Dürer, following the instructions of two German astrologers.

Sacrobosco). Sacrobosco died in 1256; his book was printed in Italy in 1472.

First printed astronomical ephemerides ■ These tables of the planet's positions were produced in Nuremberg, Germany by Bernard Walther (1436–1504) and his pupil and collaborator Johann Muller, better known as Regiomontanus (1436–76). They set up an observatory which included the first weight-driven astronomical clocks.

First star atlas ■ The first star atlas in which the stars are allotted letters in their respective constellations was that of Alessandro Piccolomini (1508–78), published in Italy in 1540.

First astronomical tables ■ The first astronomical tables published according to the heliocentric (sun-centred) theory were those of Erasmus Reinhold (1511–53) in 1551. Their accuracy is comparable with that of the older Alphonsine Tables, which were produced in 1252.

Oldest observatory ■ *The oldest building extant today is 'Tower of the Winds' used by Andronichus of Cyrrhus in Athens, Greece c. 100 BC, and equipped with sundials and clepsydra (water clocks).*

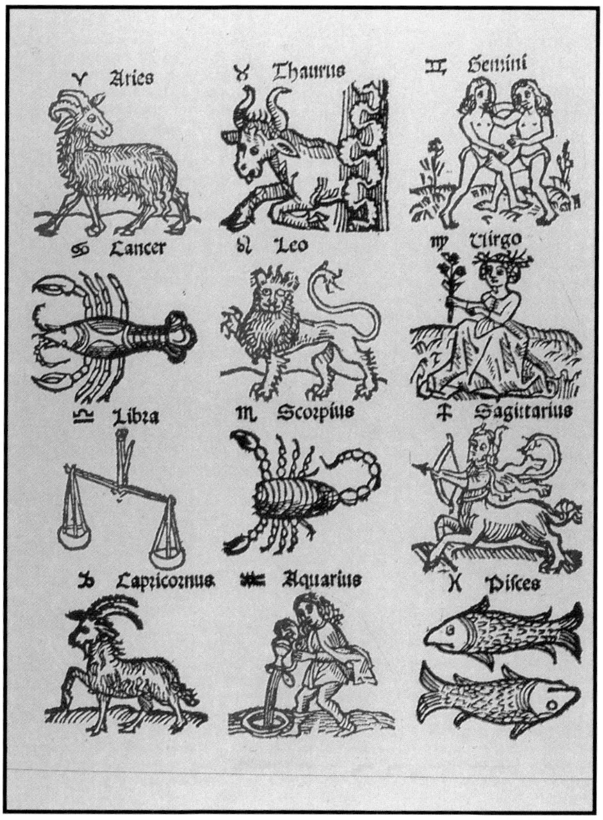

The twelve signs of the zodiac were divided into four groups which correspond to the cycle of changing seasons. Cardinal signs bring new beginnings; Aries for spring, Cancer for summer, Libra for Autumn, Capricorn for winter. Traditionally the Sun's entry into Aries was used for annual forecasts, but seasonal forecasts were made from the Sun's entry into any cardinal sign. The fixed signs follow the cardinal ones and are characterized by stability: Taurus, Leo, Scorpio and Aquarius. The flexibility of Gemini, Virgo, Sagittarius, and Pisces reflects the changeable weather between seasons.

Astrology

Most comprehensive explanation ■ Astrology explained the interrelatedness of things on Earth, as well as in the heavens. The belief in a natural law of correspondence and sympathy permitted speculation on all earthly things. There was as yet no contradiction between astrology and science; knowledge depended on proving God's existence as it was already understood. Scientific observation which was not bound by theological considerations, was tantamount to heresy. Because god was the Prime Mover of the planets, there was no real antagonism from the Church.

Outstanding predictions ■ Conjunctions of the slowest-moving outer planets Jupiter and Saturn, which occur every 20 years, portend great changes in the world; these could be used to locate events in history as well as the future. In 1456 Nicholas of Hungary was able to date the Great Flood of Noah's time 3223 years before Christ and he could also recognize that a great prophet, possibly the Anti-Christ, would arise as a result of a conjunction of 1562.

Greatest cause of predictions ■ The Great Conjunction of 1524 elicited more predictions than any other single phenomenon of the time; treatises by 56 astrologers which ran to 133 editions survive of the many that were published. Many expected that Earth would be destroyed by a flood such as the one that occurred in Noah's time. Others who were perhaps more astute – including the astrological sceptic and founding father of Protestantism, Martin Luther – interpreted the conjunction to refer to problems in the Church since Jupiter has dominion over both the Church and Pisces.

Most sensational prediction ■ The most sensational in the late 15th century was Johan Stöffler's 1494 treatise on the great conjunction of 1524. He was the first to alert the public of the potential hazards to men, estates and beasts of the sea. The Great Conjunction of February 1524 was truly exceptional; it involved all the planets and occurred in Pisces, a water sign. There were also 16 lesser conjunctions, also in water signs.

Most important influence ■ The most high-ranking clergymen consulted astrologers: Pope Julius II (1503–13) chose the time for his coronation according to the advice of astrologers. Likewise Pope Paul III (1549) (who issued the bull excommunicating Henry VIII in 1538) regularly selected the time for consistories (council meetings). Leo X (1513–21) established a professorship in astrology at the papal university at Rome.

England's most learned astrologer ■ Astronomers' star lists produced at Oxford, England, were also used by astrologers, for example Richard Fitzjames of Merton College. As warden, in 1497 he made astrological calculations to decide the best day to start the building of a new archway. The vaulting is carved with a magnificent series of zodiac signs.

Most astrologically-based decor ■ The Mughal ruler of India Humayun (1530–56) was well versed in scientific and mathematical matters and had a good knowledge of astronomy. He had built nine pavilions in which the different stars of each sky were represented. They were coloured to match the heavenly bodies: black for Saturn, red for Mars, golden for the Sun, white for the Moon and so on. The colour scheme of the public hall in the palace was changed each day according to the colour the astrologers fixed, and on the furnishings and even the dress of the servants was the symbol of the appropriate planet.

Most astrologically planned conception ■ A statuette of the planetary god Mercury made and consecrated in Venice is a unique survival which shows evidence of an astrologically planned conception. It was engraved with a horoscope for 15 June, 1527 at which time Mercury was in conjunction with the Sun and Jupiter. The moment had to be chosen some time in advance and the statuette deliberately completed at the time of the horoscope. Great wealth and minimum suffering were planned for the child since the benefic planets are prominent and the malefics are weak. A son was born to Maracantonio Michiel, the man who commissioned the work, seven months after the date of the horoscope. Either the young parents could not wait or the child was born prematurely. Mercury rules both merchants and scholars and in the horoscope Mercury is the source of wealth. Michiel was a well known humanist.

SIGNS FOR PREDICTION

Eclipses in Earth signs might signify rain or drought; the element of fire might bring terrible conflagration; air signs could indicate great wind. Earthquakes and crop failure were associated with eclipses. The degree of an eclipse could activate an individual's horoscope in an unpredictable manner, because of the disruption in heavenly routines symbolized by the cutting-off of light to the eclipsed body. Along with comets and conjunctions these were a mainstay of astrological prediction.

Most astrologers agreed with Aristotle's theories on comets: they were not celestial bodies but rather exhalations of vapours from the Earth which had congealed under the refining influence of the heavens. They were of the nature of Saturn, since they are cold and come from the Earth, but they were also of the nature of Mars which added the fire needed to propel them through the air. Depending on the signs in which the comet appeared and the position of the planets, it could bring good fortune or calamity.

Largest natal horoscope ■ *The natal or birth horoscope of Agostino Chigi, the banker, is one of the largest ever produced; it is a painted decorative scheme which fills the entire ceiling and vaults of a room in his palace in Farnesina in Rome. The painting of the sky, done by Raphael's associate Baldassare Peruzzi in 1511, shows the planets in their positions at the time of the patron's birth at 9.30pm on 29 November 1466.*

Most beneficent star ■ Spica was considered the most beneficent star, bringer of wealth and abundance. Its nature was Mars and Venus. Spica is a white binary star in the wheat held by the virgin of the constellation Virgo.

Most royal star ■ Regulus is the white triple star flushed with blue, that represents the heart of the lion in the constellation Leo. Known as a royal star from at least 3000 BC, its influence brings military or royal honours. The planetary nature is Mars and Jupiter.

Most dreaded of malevolent stars ■ Algol is a white binary variable star which represents the severed head of Medusa in the constellation Perseus. It was the most dreaded of the malevolent stars. With a planetary nature of Saturn and Jupiter it was believed to cause murder, sudden death or decapitation.

Horoscopes

Most common method of prediction ■ Most people did not know when they were born, so horoscopes of nativities were not always possible. Alternative methods of predicting the future were devised, the most common – and also most controversial – was Interrogation. If a question was asked at a suitable moment, the horoscope of that moment could furnish the astrologer with the answers. The most commonly asked questions concerned marriage, health and wealth. But astrologers were also able to find missing persons and stolen goods.

Best times of the day ■ The days of the week each had a planetary lord. Each astrological hour was also under the rulership of a different planet. The 24 hours of the day were not divided equally, but according to the length of the day from sunrise to sunset. If the lord of the hour was in a sympathetic position astrologers could forecast recovery from illness and answer questions of imprisonment, finding buried treasure or stolen goods, and hunting. The planetary lord of the hour was of vital importance for gathering herbs for medicinal purposes.

Greatest influence on temperament ■ Astrologers and their many followers believed that the dominant humour, or element, in a person's horoscope described his temperament. The airy, sanguine person was the most cheerful and even tempered. The fiery, choleric man was most easily angered. If predominantly phlegmatic, or watery, the person was apt to be overly obliging or weak-willed, while the earth element produced the gloomiest character, the melancholic. However, humanist theory emphasized the possibility that the melancholic temperament, if expressed with dignity, could also be the most creative.

Attacks on astrologers

Most significant ■ The condemnation of Simon de Phares, astrologer to Charles VIII of France, by the ecclesiastical court in 1491 and subsequent trial in 1494 by Parliament might claim this record.

Although his library contained nothing out of the ordinary, several of his books were burnt and he was censured for revealing thefts, hidden treasures, and men's secret thoughts. The import of this condemnation is that it is an indirect censure of the king for using astrology.

Charlatanism was a problem in Cologne, Germany. In 1488 all the books by Hartung Gernod were burnt and he was prevented from further practice because he could not convince the theological faculty of Cologne university that he was sufficiently knowledgable. In 1492 the same faculty recommended the arrest of a famous astrologer, Johann Lichtenberger, for predicting death by murder or hanging from a natal horoscope.

Most famous attack ■ The 12-volume work of the Italian humanist Pico della Mirandola questions the theoretical basis of astrology, but his real objection was that man was not accorded a sufficiently exalted position in the scheme of things. Pico convinced at least one astrologer to give up predicting, but even he was back in business by 1503. The fact that several astrologers had been able to predict the time of Pico's death to the day and hour appears to have been the most potent argument in astrology's favour.

LITERATURE

First to print *Ephemerides* ■ Johannes Muller (1436–1476) of Germany, usually known as Regiomontanus, was the first to print *Ephemerides* (tables of the planets' positions at different times). He also devised a system of determining the division of the heavens into houses which is still in use today. He was better at maths than he was at astrology. The king of Hungary asked him to find a time for the establishment of a university which would guarantee it long life and success; the university only survived for a few years.

Most incomprehensible almanac ■ *The Kalendar of Shepherdes*, translated from the French by a Scotsman, published in Paris in 1503, is only intelligible to a Frenchman with a fine eye for misprints and educated in Scotland.

Astrological best-seller ■ Giovanni Nannius of Viterbo, Italy, found the material for a best-seller in his astrological approach to the Turkish menace. His 1480 prediction was reprinted all over Europe until 1502. He linked the Anti-Christ with Mohammed, Islam with the Beast, and the Apocalypse with the fall of Constantinople in 1453. Christianity, he predicted, would dominate from 1480.

Animal kingdom

Largest and heaviest ■ The longest and heaviest mammal in the world, and the largest animal ever recorded, is the Blue or Sulphur-bottom whale (*Balaenoptera musculus*).

Largest on land ■ The largest living land animal is the African bush elephant (*Loxodonta africana*). The average adult bull stands 10 ft 6 in *3.2 m* at the shoulder.

Smallest ■ The smallest ungulate is the 'Royal Antelope', to be found in the west African rain forest. An adult is only 9¾ in *25 cm* high.

Smartest ■ The smartest animal in Africa is thought by people in the African savannah to be the hare (alias 'Brer Rabbit'), others give the title to the fennec fox ('Brer Fox') whose footprints on the sand are used to divine the future. The spider ('Anansi') is another contender for the title.

Fiercest ■ The Chinese writer Xie Zhaozhi reported that: 'the fiercest water-buffaloes are strong enough to fight with tigers, and the tigers are no match for them. In the Xuande reign period [1426–35] people tried pitting a water-buffalo against a tiger. The tiger attacked three times but could not strike home, after which the buffalo gored him to death.

Fiercest rats ■ European pests which accompanied the sailors to the New World flourished there. In Peru the rats became so fierce that 'no cat dare look them in the face'.

Noisiest ■ The noisiest land animals in the world are the Howling monkeys (*Alouatta*) of Central and South America. The males have an enlarged bony structure at the top of the windpipe which enables the sound to reverberate, and their fearsome screams have been described as a cross between the bark of a dog and the bray of an ass increased 1000-fold.

First Chinese description of a zebra ■ In 1226 the same Chinese writer who had described the giraffe also described 'a mule with red, black and white stripes wound as girdles around its body' which lived wild in the mountains of eastern Africa.

Strangest African animal ■ The lemur lives only on the island of Madagascar off the east coast of Africa. It is unknown elsewhere in the world.

Highest living ■ The Yak of Tibet and the Szechwanese Alps, China occasionally climbs to an altitude of 20 000 ft *6100 m* foraging.

Most mixed animal ■ Antonio Pigafetta who accompanied Magellan on his first circumnavigation in 1519 described the guanacos or southern llamas of South America as having the head and ears of a mule, the neck and body of a camel, the legs of a stag, and the tail of a horse. He gave the first European account of how local people caught these creatures, using captured young as decoys.

Noblest beast ■ When Friar Felix Fabri was travelling in the Holy Land in 1483 he saw the most noble of beasts, a unicorn, and described it thus: 'This beast is most singular in many respects. In the first place, they say that it is an exceeding fierce beast, and hath a horn set in the midst of its forehead, four feet (*1.2 m*) long, and so sharp and strong that, whatsoever it butts at, it either tosses into the air, or else runs him through, and pounds him against the rocks. His horn is wondrous brilliant, and the bone thereof is reckoned as costly as the most precious stones, and is set in gold and silver. He is so strong that he cannot be taken by any art or strength of those who hunt him; but it is said by writers on

The tapestry known as the Lady and the Unicorn *came from Boussac in France. It is one of the finest tapestries of the early 16th century. The six wall hangings have been interpreted in various ways, but probably represent the five senses, with the unicorn's actions indicating the sense illustrated.*

natural history that they place a young virgin in his way, who opens her bosom as he runs toward her, whereat he puts away from him all his fierceness, and lays down his head (in her lap), and is held thus entranced and, as it were, disarmed until he be taken and slain by the shafts of the huntsmen.'

First record of opossum ■ Cabeza de Vaca described an animal seen by him in 1528 in southern North America 'with a pocket on its belly, in which it carries its young until they know how to seek food; and if it happen that they should be out feeding and any one come near, the mother will not run until she has gathered them in together.' The word *opossum* is derived from the Algonqin language.

First printed reference to the American bison ■ Cabeza de Vaca in his narrative of his wanderings in America (1528–36) described how in 1534 he had seen 'cattle' and eaten their meat. 'I think,' he said, 'they are about the size of those in Spain. They have small horns like the cows of Morocco; their hair is very long and flocky like the merino's. Some are tawny, others black. To my judgement the flesh is finer and fatter than that of Spain. Of the skins that are not full grown the Indians make blankets, and of the larger they make shoes and bucklers. They come as far south as the sea-coast of Florida, from a northerly direction, ranging through a tract of more than 400 leagues (about 1200 miles *1900 km*)'.

Last wolves ■ The wolf had veen virtually eliminated in England during the 13th century, but the last few were thought to exist in the Yorkshire moors into the 15th century. There were still wolves in Wales and Scotland and in 1457 James II of Scotland passed a decree that required: 'Local magistrates sall gader the countrie folk three tymes in the year betwix St Mark Day and Lammas for that is the tyme of Quhelpis (whelping).'

First rhinoceros to reach Europe ■ A rhinoceros arrived at Lisbon 20 May 1515 after an eighteen-month journey around Africa from Goa. The first sculpture of the single-horned Indian rhinoceros in Europe was carved in the stone tower of Belem near Lisbon two years later.

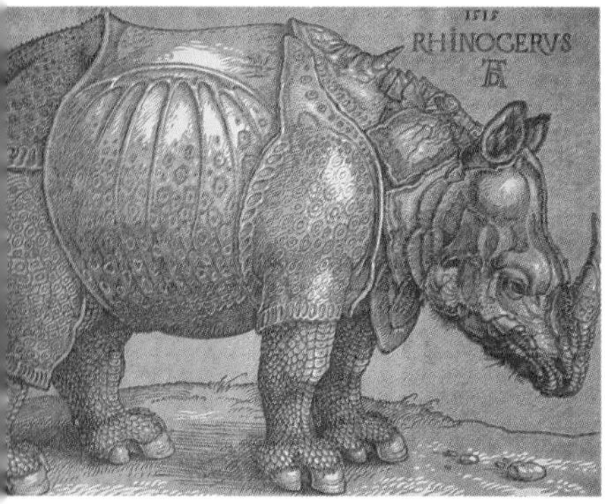

Albrecht Dürer was quick to produce a naturalistic wood-cut of the rhinoceros although he never saw it. The drawing which was a work of the imagination, especially in the armour plating which covers the body, rather than of observation, remained the authoritative text book image and model for the decorative arts for centuries. The inscription above the drawing refers to Pliny's first-century writings on the rhinoceros; he alleged that it was the natural mortal enemy of the elephant.

King Manuel I (1513–21) of Portugal who had come into possession of the rhino also had a plentiful supply of elephants and on 3 June 1515 attempted, without success, to verify Pliny's theory. He later decided to make a gift of the rhino to Pope Leo X (1513–21), to whom he had already given Hanno the celebrated elephant, and the rhino again set sail in December, stopping off in France to pay a state visit to Francis I and his queen. Unfortunately storms arose and both the ship and its valuable cargo were lost. An unverified report states that the beast was stuffed on the beach and continued the journey to Rome anyway.

Most popular elephant ■ Hanno, the elephant given by King Manuel of Portugal to Pope Leo X in 1514, became the most popular animal in Rome. Its arrival was celebrated in a ceremonial procession through the city, culminating in a reception at the Castle Santangelo. In an act of supreme irreverence, the elephant filled its trunk with perfumed water and sprayed Pope and Church dignatories three times just as the church bells began to ring and cannon were fired. When Hanno died in 1516 the Pope commissioned a monument to him from Raphael.

Giraffes

First Chinese description ■ A Chinese writer in 1226 described an animal called a *tsu-la* seen in East Africa. The animal was, he said, striped like a camel, the size of an ox, had a thick skin and was yellow in colour. It had front legs of 5 ft (*1.5 m*) high and hind legs of only 3 ft (*1 m*). Its head was high up and turned upwards.

Most deformed beast ■ The pilgrim Roberto da Sanseverino went from the Holy Land to Egypt in 1453 where he was shown a 'zaraffa'. He described it as immensely tall and 'lower at the rear end than at the front'. Its supple neck was, he reckoned, three arms' length and its head long 'with a pointed nose, eyes that are large and rather like those of an ox, large ears like a cow's, and on the top of its head two little horns like a goat's.'

Tallest land ■ The Giraffe (*Giraffa cameleopardalis*), which is now found only in the dry savannah and semi-desert areas of Africa south of the Sahara, is the tallest living animal. In the 15th century the giraffe grazed over most of the savannah regions of Africa. Chinese merchants of the 15th century were particularly astonished at their size and at least one was taken to China as a gift for the emperor. It appeared in contemporary drawings and writings about Africa before the first Europeans reached the Indian Ocean. Giraffes were further deemed to be curious because of their variable and often odd number of horns.

First account in a bestiary ■ The first account to enter bestiary lore was depicted in the *Dialogues of creatures moralised* printed in Holland in 1480. (It is illustrated and the giraffe bears no resemblance to a real one).

The Italian Simone Sigoli likened the giraffe to an ostrich 'save that its chest has no feathers but has very fine white wool.' According to Sigoli, a giraffe's head is like a horse's and so are its feet, but it has a bird's legs, two horns like a wether (castrated ram) and eats barley and bread – also like a horse. He summed it up: 'It is really a very deformed thing to see.'

Birds

Most common imaginary birds ■ Barnacle geese are creatures which seem only ever to have lived in the imagination; they are mentioned in most herbals though with increasing doubt before their final disappearance. The geese were believed to form in pods which grew on barnacle trees in the Orkneys, off the west coast of Scotland. When the pod ripened and fell off the tree into water, geese would emerge feet first. Those that fell to earth perished and came to nothing.

Most valuable ■ In 1396 a dozen white falcons from Greenland were accepted as an adequate ransom for a European prince by the Sultan of Turkey.

Largest ■ Chinese visitors to the east coast of Africa reported seeing camel-birds six or seven feet (*1.8–2 m*) tall. These it is assumed were ostriches.

Largest egg ■ The average Ostrich (*Struthio camelus*) egg measures 6–8 in *15–20 cm* in length, 4–6 in *10–15 cm* in diameter and weighs 3.63–3.88 lb *1.65–1.78 kg* (around two dozen hens' eggs in volume).

Sea swallows ■ Reaching the Pacific Ocean in 1519, Magellan's crew were the first Europeans to describe flying fish which they named *colindriny* (sea swallows). They said that they took off out of the water to escape predatory fish and could fly 'about the distance a man can fire a crossbolt'.

First sight of penguins ■ In 1519 Magellan's men saw strange animals on the offshore rocks along the coast of southern South America 'the like of which no Christian man had ever set eyes on'. They believed them to be a sort of black and white goose 'with the beak of a crow', which did not fly but lived on fish. They were the Patagonian penguins – seen by Europeans for the first time. Having no name for them, they called them *patos sin alos* (ducks without wings).

Toucan ■ Don Gonzalo Fernandez de Oviedo first recorded and described the toucan in his *Sumaria de la Natural Historia de las Indias* (Summary of the Natural History of the Indies) of 1525. Its closer association with humans may be accidental, the result of tame birds attracted to the areas of native groups.

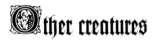

Other creatures

Largest ■ The largest reptile in the world is the Estuarine or Saltwater crocodile (*Crocodulus porosus*) of south-east Asia, the Malay Archipelago.

Strangest serpent ■ When the Italian pilgrim Roberto da Sanseverino was travelling through the desert to St Catherine's Monastery in the Sinai desert in 1453 he recorded seeing 'a serpent, large as a cat, long and sinuous, with four feet.' As Roberto approached it, the serpent scuttled off in a flurry of sand. (This creature was probably a monitor lizard, the largest of the lizard family.)

Most poisonous ■ The strongest animal poison comes from the puffer fish (*Diodon hystrix; Sphoeroides testudineus*) and when mixed with other poisons was used to turn people convicted of certain crimes into 'zombies'.

Most dangerous ■ Sailors and travellers by sea especially feared the fish Troys which according to Fra Felix Fabri in 1483, when it became aware of a ship, 'comes forth from the depths, and pierces the ship with his beak; for he has a beak fashioned like an auger, and unless he be driven away from the ship he bores through it. He cannot be forced away from the ship save by a fearless look, so that one should lean out of the ship over the water, and unflinchingly look into the eyes of the fish, while the fish meanwhile looks at him with a terrible gaze. If he who looks at the fish grows terrified, and begins to turn his eyes away, the beast straightway rises, snatches him down beneath the water, and devours him.'

First description of North American fish ■ When in 1541 Hernandes de Soto reached the area called the Rio Grande the Spaniards found that the Indians had linked the river to a lake by a canal so that fish would be entrapped in the lake ready for 'eating and pastime'. Among the fish described were *bagre*, 'the third part of which was head with gills from end to end and along the sides great spines very like sharp awls'; another was 'like a bream with the head of a hake'; the peel-fish had a 'snout a cubit in length (*c.* 20 in *50 cm*), the upper lip being shaped like a shovel'. The largest fish described was the *pereo*, 'the size of a hog, with rows of teeth above and below'.

First description of *belugas* ■ *Belugas* are the white porpoises of the salt-water St Lawrence and Saguenay fjord of Canada. In 1535 the French explorer Jacques Cartier described them: 'these fish are as large as porpoises, without any fins, and in body and head are formed like a greyhound, as white as snow, without a spot, and they are in that river in very great numbers.'

Greatest natural hazard ■ Drought and flooding were both important natural hazards in the Middle East, but worst of all may have been plagues of locusts. These are of course mentioned in the Bible, and were noted by travellers around 1500.

A swarm of locusts can cover many square kilometres, with each square kilometre containing up to 50 million locusts which consume up to 100 tons of vegetation a day. These devastating swarms can cover 60 miles 100 km *a day and consume all vegetation over a vast area in a few hours.*

Most dangerous ■ The world's most dangerous creatures (excluding Man) are the malarial mosquitoes of the genus *Plasmodium* which, if we exclude wars and accidents, have probably been responsible directly or indirectly for 50 per cent of all human deaths since the Stone Age.

Zoos

Oldest zoo ■ The earliest known collection of animals was that set up by Shulgi, a 3rd-dynasty ruler of Ur from 2097–2094 BC at Puzurish in south-east Iraq.

Most famous zoo ■ In the 15th century the most famous zoo was that of Ferrante, the Duke of Naples. Amongst his exotic creatures was a giraffe.

Most impressive zoological gifts ■ After each visit to foreign lands by the great Chinese fleets of the early 15th century, ambassadors returned to China with gifts for the emperor. Many of these were animals from their lands. The most impressive of such gifts was a collection of animals from Egypt. It included lions, tigers, oryxes, nilgais, zebras and ostriches. The emperor housed them all in the imperial zoological gardens in Beijing. In 1415 the ambassadors of Malinda in east Africa brought a giraffe to the emperor.

LITERATURE

Most widely read books ■ Bestiaries (treatises on animals) were the most widely read books about animals from the early middle ages. Fable, myth and ancient tradition were mixed together to present a moralised view of creatures. The medieval world view gave priority to God's preeminence and the individual's observations were subordinated to higher truths. As a consequence many of the animals in the Bestiary exist only in the popular imagination. The first account of a giraffe to enter bestiary lore was depicted in the *Dialogues of creatures Moralised* printed in Holland in 1480. It was illustrated but the picture bears no resemblance to the real animal.

First printed work ■ *The noble Life of Natures of Man, of Beasts, Serpents, Fowls and Fishes That Be Most Known* published by Laurence Andrew was the first printed book in English on animal life. It listed 144 known animals, 8 entirely unknown animals and 21 mythological animals.

Most comprehensive zoological treatise ■ The Swiss scholar (1516–65) Conrad Gesner's *Historia Animalium* (History of Animals), first printed in 1551, is the most comprehensive zoological treatise of the 16th century. Gesner followed Pliny in categorizing animals in sections on birds, beasts, and fishes and observed Aristotle's distinctions between viviparous (born live) and oviparous (egg-laying) species. All of the descriptions are accompanied with the visual evidence of his experience of animals. All of them are drawings made from life, except the genet for which he included the pelt of the dead animal. Gesner's work is a landmark in the study of natural history, important for the clearer picture of man's relationship to the other creatures in the world which was emerging in the Renaissance.

First natural history of the New World ■ It is to the credit of Gonzalo Fernandez de Oviedo y Valdes (known as Oviedo) (1478–1557) that we have an early European account of some animal species of the Americas. He noted the variation in native Indian dogs. He recorded that the tapir was mule size, dark skinned, hornless and good to eat. He claimed that the sloth took a day to travel fifty paces, sang by night, and lived on air. The anteater is not well described and Oviedo says it has the skin of a bear, no tail and feeds on ants (meaning termites). The manatee is demoted to being a fish, although Oviedo realized that it had a leathery skin and suckled its young. Of the birds of the West Indies and South America, he gives various comments, sometimes rather imaginative, as when the size of the humming-bird is described as no bigger than the top of the thumb. But however inaccurate such accounts, they must have been read back in Europe with amazement (and no doubt at times, amusement).

Plants introduced into Britain in the 15th and 16th Centuries

Artichoke	**Cynara scolymus**, *the globe artichoke; introduced from the Mediterranean.*
Blessed Thistle	**Carduus benedictus**, *medicinal herb and vegetable; introduced by monks from the Mediterranean.*
Cucumber, Cowcumber	*Cucumis sativus; not grown in Britain until 15th century.*
Cypress	**Cupressus sempervirens**; *introduced from the Mediterranean in early 16th century.*
Dittany	**Dictamnus albus**, *burning bush; introduced from southern Europe.*
Parsley	**Petroselinum crispum**, *culinary and medicinal; introduced from the Mediterranean in 15th or 16th century.*
Pomegranate	**Pumica granatum**; *introduced into Britain in the 1500s or earlier.*
Senae	**Coluea arborescens**, *bladder-senna, medicinal herb; introduced in early 16th century from the Mediterranean.*
Warden	*Variety of pear developed at Warden Abbey, Bedfordshire, in the Middle Ages.*

Plants introduced into Europe in the 15th and 16th Centuries

Amaranthus	*Ornamental and medicinal; introduced from New World.*
Beans	*A dozen different varieties were being cultivated. Kidney and runner beans from the New World were grown for food and as ornamental climbers.*
Carrot	**Daucus carota**; *orange-coloured strains introduced from the Middle East.*
Corn	*Term covered various forms of wheat; maize, known as turkey-corn, was brought from the New World in the early 16th century.*
Cress	**Lepidium sativum**, *garden cress; introduced from the New World.*
Endive	**Cichorium endivia**; *introduced from Asia.*
Melon	**Melo cucumis**; *came from Africa; water-melon was introduced from the New World in the mid-16th century.*
Nasturtiums	**Tropaeolum**; *introduced from the New World.*
Purselane	**Portulaca oleracea**, *salad vegetable; introduced from the Middle East around the 15th century.*
Rose	*Over 40 varieties grown; first musks and damask roses introduced in this period from Asia.*
Skerrot, Skirrit	**Sium sisarum**, *root vegetable; introduced from eastern Asia in the 15th century.*
Speradge	**Asparagus officinalis**, *asparagus; native but first cultivated forms appeared in the 16th century.*
Spinedge, Spinach	**Spinacea oleracea**; *introduced from Persia in mid-1500s.*
Sunflower	**Helianthus**; *introduced from the New World in the 1500s.*

Plant kingdom

Oldest ■ The oldest acknowledged tree was a Bristlecone pine (*Pinus longaeva*) which grew 10 750 ft *3275 m* above sea level on the north-east face of Mt Wheeler, eastern Nevada, USA. At this time it would have been 4600 years old.

British ■ Of all British trees that with the longest life is the Yew (*Taxus baccata*), for which a maximum age of 1000 years is usually conceded. The oldest known is the Fortingall Yew near Aberfeldy, Perthshire, part of which was still growing.

Earliest species ■ The earliest species of tree still surviving is the Maiden-hair tree (*Ginkgo biloba*), of Zhexiang, China, which first appeared about 160 000 000 years ago, during the Jurassic era. It has been grown in Japan since *c.* 1100 where it was known as *ginkyo* ('silver apricot') and is now known as *icho*.

An illustration from an Arabic translation of Dioscorides' Materia Medica. *Dioscorides was a fifth century Greek doctor who served with the Roman army.*

First classification ■ The Arab physician Ghafiqi of Cordoba in Spain (died 1165) was probably the first person to attempt the classification of plants, giving them names in Arabic, Latin and the Berber language of North Africa.

Best botanist ■ Abdullah Ibn al-Baytar of Malaga, Spain was regarded as the best botanist and pharmacist in the Islamic world. His two books *Materia Medica* and a collection of simples (materials composed of one substance, pure) and their properties were considered the best books of their kind.

HERBS

Most well-to-do households cultivated herbs in gardens near the house or kitchen; they were used for both culinary and medical purposes. Monastic communities grew them near the infirmaries. Brewers and vintners also kept special herbs for their flavours. Medicinal herbs were taken mixed with wine, infused as a tea, applied externally or they might be dried, powdered or even burnt depending on the nature of the affliction they were meant to treat. Essential oils were used for curative bathing. Herbs were classified according to temperament: heat, cold, dryness, and moistness were judged on a scale of 1 to 4. They were considered to be hot and dry, hot and moist, cold and dry or cold and moist in varying degrees. Since the cold and wet melancholic humour was the greatest threat to health, most healing herbs were hot and dry. The cold and dry herbs tend to be poisonous or narcotic (lethargy was considered to be a cold and dry distemper).

Great deforestation ■ The growing population of Europe put an enormous pressure on the forests. An average ironworks it is estimated consumed up to 5000 acres *2000 hectares* of forest in two years and caused such fuel shortages in its locality that some ironworks could only operate for one year in four. Other estimates suggest that 60–80 million tons of wood were used up in Europe every year – the equivalent of about a ton for every man, woman and child each year.

Most famous trees ■ People acknowledged the significance of certain great trees that were 'known' to be the place at which certain events happened or trees which were 'known' to be extremely old. In England, for example, at Clipston there was an oak where Edward I was said to have convened his Parliament in 1289; at Donnington Park, Newbury there was an oak which it was said the poet Geoffrey Chaucer had planted; in the New Forest one could see the 'actual' tree from which the arrow ricocheted to kill William Rufus. In Italy there were trees 'known' to have been planted by St Francis of Asissi.

Poisonous plants

Curare ■ Curare was the most lethal of all poisons to the pre-Columbian peoples and proliferated in the forest regions of South America. It was made from the sap of the toxic *strictinos toxifera* plant. The sap was mixed with other insect and animal venoms and was enormously efficient, arresting the action of the motor nerves and causing a heart attack on reaching the blood vessels of the victim. The South American Carib Indians used curare to poison the point of their hunting darts for use in blow pipes.

Calabar bean ■ In West Africa the most useful poison for ordeals or testing if a suspect was guilty was the 'Calabar bean' (*Physostigma venenosum*). Ground and mixed with water, the suspect who gulps it down will vomit it up immediately. Suspects so anxious they can only drink slowly eventually suffocate and die.

Most sadistic botanist ■ Pierandrea Mattioli (1501–77), a doctor living in Siena, Italy, used convicts as subjects for his experiments to determine whether the herb monkshood was poisonous. The results were positive.

Herbs

Hottest and driest ■ Of all the herbs, the hottest and driest were mustard, onion, chives and *rosa solis*.

Coldest ■ Most fruits, such as strawberries, pears and plums were cold and moist, but the coldest herbs of all were black hellebore, oak and poppy. Violets and roses were used as cold and moist medicines to treat ailments from hot and dry causes such as fever, inflammations, insomnia, restlessness and excesses of passion.

Coldest and driest ■ Hemlock and nightshade were considered the coldest and driest of herbs and also the most dangerous if abused or taken internally. Hemlock was applied externally to gout and other swellings to ease the inflamed tissue. An antidote to the accidental consumption of hemlock was offered by Pliny: 'Drink the strongest wine available before the hemlock reaches the heart.'

Holiest herb ■ Rosemary was believed to grow in height until it reached the same age that Christ attained on Earth, 33 years. Its reputation for compassion in healing and for purity was also seen as Christ-like. Tea made from its flowers was drunk to purify the body, and using the same to wash the face made the user whole and clean. Both the healing and aromatic properties of the herb led to its use in potpourri and incense in churches and sickrooms, as well as for strewing on the floor of courtrooms to protect innocent citizens from jail fever. Rosemary was classified as hot and dry, its medical application was therefore to diseases of a cold nature such as lethargy, falling sickness, yellow jaundice and obstructions of the digestive tract. Not only could it cure poor eyesight, but it was the most helpful stimulant of memory. The herb's classical association with remembrance was the underlying symbolism of the tradition of laying rosemary branches on the bodies of the dead. Rosemary also symbolized fidelity in marriage and was therefore woven into bridal wreaths. In the early 16th century Sir Thomas More associated it with friendship.

Most evil plant ■ Thorns, thistles and briars were believed to be evil, but the most evil was buckthorn from which the Crown of Thorns was fashioned at the Crucifixion.

Flowers

Earliest 'flower piece' ■ Hans Memling's vase of lilies, iris and columbine which was painted on the back of *A Man in an Attitude of Prayer* in 1490 claims this title. The white lilies symbolize purity, the blue irises heaven, while the dove-like shape of the columbine (*columba*, dove) represents the Holy Ghost. During the northern Reformation traditional devotional images of Christian martydom, such as the Crucifixion, were banned, and replaced by flower paintings. The outstanding characteristic of flowers, especially once they have been cut, is that they are dying.

Most important floral attributes of the Virgin ■ These were the white lily (chastity, purity), the violet (modesty), the rose (divine love), the carnation (divine love), and strawberries in blossom and bearing fruit represented the fruits of the spirit. Daisies were added in the late 15th century to emphasize innocence of the Child. The enclosed garden in which the Virgin was most often portrayed also symbolizes her virginity.

Edelweiss ■ The first recorded picture of the edelweiss was published in the *Codex Bellunensis* at Belluno in the Venetian Alps during the 15th century. Although Dioscorides described the plant and recommended it as a love potion, no one had illustrated it before.

Fuchsia ■ *The German Leonard Fuchs (1501–66) was one of the pioneers of modern botany. He identified and named the fuchsia, probably the first plant to be named after a living person.*

Most important flower ■ The tree peony was considered the 'king of flowers' in China. It symbolized high position, wealth and honour. The peony is the most commonly depicted of all flowers in Chinese art; found on vases, screens, and embroideries.

Strangest grass ■ Pedro de Castañeda, who accompanied Coronado across the plains of America in 1540–2, described with astonishment the grass of the prairies

Flowers were included in herbals for their medicinal uses; not until the 17th century do books exclusively devoted to flowers begin to appear. Apart from their practical uses, flowers had great importance as literary and religious symbols. Floral religious symbolism in painting was at its height in the 15th century; by the early 16th century natural observation began to dominate the artist's motivation. Every viewer would have recognized the meaning of the flowers depicted with the Virgin or Christ.

'which never failed to come erect after it had been trodden down'. He described how after '1000 horses and 500 of our cows and more than 5000 rams and ewes and more than 1500 friendly Indians and servants' tracked through the grass they would leave 'no more trace where they had passed than if nothing had been there – nothing – .' The Spaniards had to leave cairns of bones and cow dung to mark their trail.

LITERATURE

Most important books about plants ■ Herbals were essential to and written by physicians, and – until the 17th century – botanists.

Earliest plant drawings from nature ■ In herbals these are found in the *Livre des Simples Medicines* (The Book of Simple Medicines). The manuscript was made at Cluny *c.* 1480; it was a French version of a treatise compiled by the 13th-century writer Johannes Platearius who combined traditional Latin writings with newly discovered Arabic material to create the first dictionary of drug synonyms.

First known botanical woodcuts ■ These were published in 1475 by Hans Bamler of Augsburg, Germany, in *Das Buch der Natur* (The Book of Nature) by Conrad von Megenburg. This manuscript is also important because it is the first vernacular work of its kind.

Most important authority on herbs ■ From antiquity, Dioscorides, a first-century Greek doctor who served with the Roman army, was the most important authority. In *Materia Medica* he described the physical appearance and specific uses for over 600 plants and almost 1000 drugs. Manuscript copies of the work were illustrated, but until the 15th century most artists copied the plant pictures from other manuscripts instead of from nature with the result that the plants could not always be recognized.

Most popular herbal ■ The *Gart der Gesundheit* (The Garden of Health) printed by Peter Schoeffer at Mainz, Germany, in 1485 was the most popular herbal of its day and contained a large number of illustrations, mostly of plants. Its author, Joannes de Cuba, a Frankfurt doctor, claimed to have travelled with an artist in Italy, Greece, the Holy Land, Arabia, Babylonia and Egypt to research it. Herbals, descended from ancient Greek sources, were still important books of medicine. Other popular herbals were the *Herbarius latinus* (The Latin herbal) (1484), also printed by Schoeffer, and the *Ortus sanitatis* (The Garden of Health) (1491) printed by Johannes Meydenbach of Mainz.

Revival of natural botanical science ■ Otto Brunfel (1464–1534) published his *Herbarium Viva Eicones* (Images of Living Plants) in Strasbourg, now in France, in 1530. It was the first attempt to revive natural botanical science since antiquity. Although it is the first herbal illustrated with drawings which are true to nature, Brunfel still relies on Dioscorides and other earlier writers and the written descriptions lag behind the illustrations in accuracy. The illustrations were of such high quality that they were once thought to be the work of the artist Albrecht Dürer. Brunfel's contemporary, Jerome (Hieronymous) Bock (1498–1554) could not afford to illustrate the 1539 first edition of his work, the *Neue Kreutter Buch*, so he was forced to articulate. He thus surpassed Brunfel's work, at least in the text, and succeeded in coining a new word, 'pistil'. (There was, however, still not a word for petal.)

The 'King of Flowers' in China was the tree peony, which was used widely as a decorative symbol.

Earliest printed book in English with a definite botanical character ■ The translation of Bartholomew Anglicanus' encyclopedia *Liber de Proprietatibus Rerum* (Book of Botanical Properties) published by Wynkyn de Worde about 1495 claims this record.

First modern botanical treatise ■ The German humanist Conrad Gesner (1516–65) known as the 'Pliny of his age' because of his wide-ranging interest in natural science. He wrote a scientific treatise on botany which influenced Linnaeus in the 18th century in devising the system of classifying plants by genus and species. His *Historia plantarum* (History of Plants), along with 1500 original drawings and a large number of woodcuts, was never published in full. (The manuscript is now in a Swiss library.) The German Leonard Fuchs (1501–66) (after whom the fuchsia is named) also wrote a history of plants (*De Historia Stirpum* (History of Plants), published in 1542. These two books compete for the title of the first book of modern botany.

First printed illustrated herbal ■ The *Herbal of Apuleius Platonicus* 1481 edition was edited and printed by Johann Philippus de Lignamine, physician to Pope Sixtus IV. The work was a compilation of Greek medical recipes from around 400 AD. The pictures of the plants are accompanied by pictures suggestive of the conditions which they cure so that the user need not be able to read to consult the book. For example, the illustration of catmint includes a snake because the plant can be used as an antidote to the snake's venom.

A contender for the first printed herbal with illustrations is the *De Viribus Herbarum* (On the Potency of Herbs) of Macer Floridus, published at Milan in 1482. An unillustrated version from Naples in 1477 was certainly the earliest herbal to be printed.

Most mysterious manuscript ■ The Roger Bacon Cipher Manuscript has been called the most mysterious manuscript in the world. It was written in the 15th or 16th century in a code that has not been deciphered, except for some names of plants and stars. It includes over 400 illustrations, many of which are botanical or pharmaceutical. (Roger Bacon was a 13th-century English scientist with an interest in astrology and alchemy.)

Most important printed herbal ■ The German *Herbarius*, written in a Bavarian dialect and published at Mainz, Germany, about 1492, is the most splendid and also the most important early printed herbal of the period. Its 379 illustrations of plants were drawn from life. The entries are exceptionally well indexed in alphabetical order, by diseases, and other headings. Amongst the recommended remedies are the uses of marijuana (*cannabis sativa*): the leaves for stomach upsets, and the vapours for relief from headache. The German *Herbarius* was also the most plagiarized of all herbals; within five months of its appearance the drawings were being pirated by other publishers throughout Germany. Thirteen pirated editions survive.

First herbal printed in English ■ This was the illustrated Bancke's *Herbal* of 1525.

Most popular early printed English work on herbs ■ The anonymous *Grete Herball* of 1525 can claim this record. It is a translation from the French *Le Grand Herbier*, printed at Besançon in 1486, but includes an appendix on the use of wines. A recipe against melancholy at dinner parties instructs the reader to soak vervain leaves in wine and sprinkle the wine about the dining area. By contrast, the recommended use of willow (*salix*) leaves to put off the heat of fevers might be seen as good advice by modern doctors; salicylic acid is an important ingredient in aspirin.

the Human being

POPULATIONS • DIMENSIONS
DISASTERS • SICKNESS AND HEALTH

the guinness book of records 1492

Populations

The population of the world in 1500 was about 460 million, although without adequate statistics this estimate is little more than a guess. Europe had about 60 million people (some say 80 million), but we can be more confident that the population of England was a little over 2 million. The highest densities of population were found in China (65 persons per sq. mile, *25 ppsk*) and India (60 ppsm, *23 ppsk*). In Europe as a whole the average was 20 (*8*), and for England about 31 (*12*), although rural densities in parts of Kent and East Norfolk were over 52 (*20*).

Population

Least populated continent ■ It is estimated that in 1500 the total population of North America may have been no more than 10 million people. This compares with populations estimated at between 11 and 25 million in the Aztec empire in Mexico and 60 million in Europe. Asia, with of course a much greater land mass, had a far greater population. China alone had perhaps 200 million people in 1500, and India had 150 million a century later. Australia and Antarctica were unknown to the rest of the world.

WORLD POPULATION

DATE	MILLIONS
8000 BC	*c 6*
1 AD	*c 255*
1250	*c 254*
1500	*c 460*
1600	*c 579*
1990	*5 246*
2050 (projected)	*14 000*

Largest and smallest estimates of American Indian population ■ In 1492, north of the Rio Grande, that is, in continental North America, were at most 12 million, at least 1 million, people. Observers at the time under-estimated the true size of this population. Adding together their estimates over time is a problem, because the spread of record-keeping Europeans lagged behind the diffusion of new diseases which massively reduced the Indian population. Some ethnologists pin their faith to a depopulation ratio (arrived at by comparing the same area at different dates backward from its 'nadir').

PREVIOUS PAGE: Hieronymous Bosch's painting, The Garden of Earthly Delights. *The central panel shows 'The Sinful Descendants of Adam', creatures of combined human and animal forms.*

Europe ■ In 1500 the population of France was estimated at about 15 million people (rising to 16 million a century later). This was far greater than any other European country. In Spain there were only about 6 million (8 million by 1600). Germany was still a loose federation of states and not a single country and Italy was divided into states too.

Densest rain-forest populations ■ In the rain-forest environment, the densest populated settlements were along the central Amazon, in the realms of Machiparo, near the confluence with the Yapurá, and of Omagua, further downstream, where the members of Francisco de Orellana's expedition in 1542 reckoned that the populations could support armies of more than 50 000 men and where fortified riverside towns took several days to pass. Urban populations of up to about 50 000 had been sustained in Mesoamerican rain-forest cities during the 'Classic' period of Maya civilization, but those sites had been abandoned in about the 10th century.

Migration

Oldest homogeneous population ■ It is now believed that the settlement of Australia by Aboriginal peoples began some 60 000 years ago. Until the arrival of Europeans in the 16th or 17th centuries, these people lived and developed autonomously, isolated from the rest of the world. In 1500 they had had many, many centuries of this isolation and autonomy, in sharp contrast to the rest of the world.

Earliest settlers in America ■ Estimations about when humans first came to the Americas vary widely. A large group of scientists push the theory of a human presence as far back as 100 000 BC. However, this theory is not unanimously accepted. The South American population in 25 000 BC is fully proved by archaeological findings.

Oldest continuously inhabited South American settlement ■ The engineering and architecture of the Inca's imperialist period (1452–1532) was unsurpassed in the Americas and their town planning, based on a gridiron system, was far in advance of Europe. The frontier post at Ollantaybo, built *c.* 1500 in the Urabambo Valley, Peru, is the oldest continually occupied Inca town. It was designed in 18 rectangular blocks centred on an open plaza; each rectangle is subdivided into two square dwelling units, with individual central courtyards.

Oldest continually occupied settlement in America ■ The pueblo of Acoma in New Mexico was built on the summit of a rocky mesa 357 ft *107 m* high. It was reached by a broad stairway of 200 steps, a narrower stairway of 100 steps and then for the last 20 ft *3 m* by means of hand- and foot-holes in the rocks. Acoma had cisterns for collecting rainwater and snow, and land enough 'to sow and store a large amount of corn'. Coronado's men visited Acoma in 1540 and reported that there were then about 200 men (with their families) who were feared as robbers 'by the whole country round about'.

First naming of natives of America as Indians ■ Pope Alexander VI in his bull *Inter caetera* (Among other things) of 1493 granting Columbus' discoveries to the Spanish monarchs, named them thus.

Earliest European history of native Americans ■ The 'gentleman of Elvas', in Portugal, who in 1538 accompanied Hernandes de Soto, Governor of Cuba, on his journey through southern America, provided the earliest written history of the Indian nations of the area. They travelled through the lands of the Timuguas, Cherokee, the Muskogee federacy, the Choctaws, Chicksaws, Quapaws and Arkansas, and several branches of the Pani nation. The narrative of the expedition gives some of the first European descriptions of the habits, customs, buildings and artefacts of these peoples.

Last of the Mayans ■ The Mayan civilization, which had flourished in Central America in the first millenium, disappeared mysteriously in the 10th century without reason, overrun by the forest. There is speculation over the causes: overworked farmland, revolution, unknown epidemics, a drastic change in climate and even volcanic eruptions. The few survivors of the race emigrated northwards from Guatemala to the north and settled in Yucatan, where a new civilization grew up much influenced by the Mayan.

Greatest upheaval caused by food ■ In the mid-15th century, the Vakaranga of southern Africa abandoned their old tribal territories and trekked 300 miles (*480 km*) north to found a new kingdom of Karanga in what is now Zimbabwe. The reason was that salt supplies in their homeland had been exhausted.

North American people in Ireland ■ Christopher Columbus himself recorded in 1477 when he was in Ireland: 'Men of Cathay have come towards the east. Of this we have seen many signs. And especially in Galway in Ireland, a man and a woman of extraordinary appearance, have come to land on two tree trunks.' (Historians believe that these people could have been Eskimos blown across the Atlantic in their kayak during a hurricane.)

Last Jews in Spain ■ In 1492 the Jews were driven from Spain, the last recorded leaving on 2 August of that year. It is estimated that they had made up 5% of the population or about 300 000 people; some estimates are lower. In fact many Jews remained as nominal Christians, though following traditional rites. The Jews had been expelled from England in 1290 and from France in 1394. Often after their expulsion from a country the Jews were recalled for economic reasons when their financial expertise as bankers was needed. Between 1420 and 1471 the Jews of Mainz in Germany were expelled and recalled four times.

An Eskimo man drawn in about 1570 by the Englishman John White, whose drawings are judged the best made of the peoples of North America.

First Eskimos in England ■ In 1502 Sebastian Cabot took three Eskimos from northern Canada to England and paraded them proudly. They were described as 'flesh-eaters . . . who spake such speech that no man could understand them, and were in their demeanour like brute beasts'.

First Amerindians in Spain ■ In 1492 Columbus took several Indians back with him to Spain. His purpose was to train them as interpreters after showing them to his patrons King Ferdinand and Queen Isabella. Only seven of the Indians survived the voyage and five of them died within the year.

In 1495 Columbus sent 550 Amerindians as slaves to Spain. Only 350 survived the voyage and soon the others were dead in 'a land that did not suit them.'

First English ship to bring back Indians ■ The first ship was that of John Amayne in 1502 which also carried saltfish, hawks and an eagle. In 1509 a French ship brought back seven men who had been captured in their bark canoe. Six of them died very soon, but the survivor was taken to King Louis XII.

First American in Portugal ■ In 1501 Gaspar Corte-Real sent home to the King about 50 native American men and women from Newfoundland. They were at once seen as potential slaves and the Venetian ambassador to Lisbon noted that the men 'will be excellent for labour and the best slaves that have hitherto been obtained'.

Biggest re-settlement projects ■ The Incas arranged the internal colonization of their empire by re-settlement and the record project of the Cochabamba valley, where the Inca Huayna Capac (early 16th century) was said to have re-located 14 000 settlers from all over the southern Inca empire, from areas as far apart as Cuzco, Peru and Chile.

First white Americans ■ It was from the tough, desert-like areas of southern Spain, and particularly from Andalusia, that the greatest number of the earliest emigrants went to the Americas. They took with them their cattle and the skills and practices of ranching them which they had already developed. (See *Agriculture*.)

First European women to America ■ There is some evidence that the Vikings took women with them on their journeys to North America in the 11th century, but the first proposal that Spanish women should go to the colonies in the New World was not made until 1497, but in 1498 women accompanied Columbus, and from 1501 the Spanish Crown insisted that emigrants were married.

Towns and cities

Oldest ■ The oldest known walled town in the world is Ariha (Jericho). The radiocarbon dating on specimens from the lowest levels reached by archaeologists indicates habitation there by perhaps 2700 people as early as 7800 BC. The settlement of Dolní Věstonice, Czechoslovakia, has been dated to the Gravettian culture *c.* 27000 BC. The oldest capital city in the world is Dimashq (Damascus), Syria. It has been continuously inhabited longer than any other city in the world – for 25 centuries before the birth of Christ.

The oldest town in England is often cited as Colchester, the old British Camulodunum, headquarters of Belgic chiefs in the 1st century BC. However, the name of the tin trading post Salakee, St Mary's, Isles of Scilly is derived from pre-Celtic roots and hence *ante* 550 BC. The oldest borough in England is reputed to be Barnstaple, Devon whose charter was granted by King Athelstan (927–939) in AD 930.

Most urbanised populations ■ Over 50% of the population of Holland lived in cities and towns and in Flanders about 45% were town dwellers. Elsewhere the greatest part of the population of Europe lived in rural reas and, even if living in towns, often were still employed in agriculture.

Biggest cities ■ Population statistics for the world around 1500 are only rough estimates. In the early 16th century Constantinople (Istanbul) had a population of at least 100 000, some suggest as many as 400 000, while Damascus had 57 000, Aleppo up to 67 000, while by comparison Athens was about 12 500. Cairo, in Egypt, was very large – perhaps up to 400 000 or even 450 000 before the Ottoman conquest in 1517. The Italian traveller Varthema very early in the 16th century said it was as big in circumference as Rome, but with a much larger population. Rome in fact had about 100 000 inhabitants at this time.

In India, Vijayanagar (now Hampi) had upwards of 500 000 people. In Central America the largest city was Tenochtitlan (the Aztec capital in Mexico) with a population of possibly 150 000 or more, while South America's largest city, Cuzco in Peru, had 45 000 people. In Europe, Paris

A pictorial map of 1534 showing Constantinople, now Istanbul in Turkey, at the divide between Asia and Europe.

had a population of 225 000, and Naples about 125 000. But one of the largest cities was undoubtedly Beijing, in China, with some 672 000 people in about 1500. However Hangchow in China reputedly had a population of up to 1.5 million in 1279.

Largest Indian city ■ The largest city in India in 1492 was Vijanagar, the Deccan, south India. Vijayanagar (City of Victory) had a cultured and cosmopolitan population which welcomed Muslims and Europeans. The earliest European visitor to the city whose descriptions have survived was the Italian Nicolo dei Conti. He describes the city in 1420 as having a circumference of 60 miles *96 km*. He was very impressed by the strength of its fortifications. He considered the ruler Raya to be more powerful than any other monarch in India.

An Arab account of Vijayanagar in 1443 by Abdur Razzak describes the city as 'such that the eye has not seen nor heard of any place resembling it upon the whole earth. It is built that it has seven fortified walls, one within the other'.

Largest Japanese city ■ Kyoto, situated in central Honshu and residence of the emperor and shoguns (supreme military rulers) had a population of *c.* 200 000 in 1467.

The Bab Charni Gate into Damascus, Syria, the world's oldest capital city.

Last Inca city ■ *Machu Picchu, hidden in the Peruvian Andes, served as a refuge to Manco Inca, the last descendant of the Inca sovereigns, after the Spanish conquest. On the peak of a mountain range, 8250 ft* 2500 m *high, at whose foot runs the river Urubamba, it had many dwellings within a double fortress wall, and a fort on each of the two summits. Surrounding Machu Picchu were many terraces of cultivated land. In this city can be found the famous Intihuatana or sundial, made of stone, by which the winter solstice (21 June) was set, at which time the great worship to the sun god was held.*

Russia ■ In 1511 there were 41 500 houses in Moscow and a population of about 100 000. The city stretched for 5 miles *8 km* along the Moskva River. In comparison Novgorod (New City), one of its rivals, had only 5046 houses and a population of about 20 000.

Spain ■ An old Spanish saying picked out the most important cities of Spain; 'Toledo the rich, Salamanca the strong, Leon the fair, Oviedo the divine and Seville the great.' There were several other important cities in the 15th century, Valladolid was the capital. Madrid was still a small town and did not become the capital of Spain until 1560.

England ■ The population of London in 1500 was about 60 000 and the next largest town in England was Norwich with 12 700 people, followed by York, Bristol and Newcastle upon Tyne with around 10 000, and Exeter and Salisbury with 8000. Birmingham, Manchester and Liverpool were tiny villages.

Jewish ■ The city of Thessaloniki, then in the Ottoman Empire, now in Greece, had the largest Jewish population in the world. When the Jews were expelled from Spain towards the end of the 15th century, many migrated to the Ottoman Empire with the encouragement of the Sultan. Many of these settled in Thessaloniki. By 1550 over half of the city's population was Jewish.

Earliest record of Muslim settlements in India ■ The Arab geography the *Hudud al'Alam* written in 372 AH (983–2 AD)mentions the towns of Simur, Sindan, Subara and Kanbaya as having Muslim communities all with their own *jami masjids* (Friday mosques).

Greatest city in the Americas ■

WORLD'S MOST POPULOUS URBAN SETTLEMENTS

POPULATION	NAME	COUNTRY TODAY	DATE
>100	**Dolní Věstonice**	*Czechoslovakia*	*c. 27000 BC*
c. 150	**Chemi Shanidar**	*Iraq*	*8900 BC*
27 000	**Jericho (Aríha)**	*Occupied Jordan*	*7800 BC*
c. 5000	**Çatal Huyuk, Anatolia**	*Turkey*	*c. 6800 BC*
>5000	**Hierakonopolis (Nekhen)**	*Egypt*	*c. 3200 BC*
50 000	**Uruk (Erech) (now Warka) from 3800 BC**	*Iraq*	*3000 BC*
250 000	**Greater Ur (now Tell Muqayyar)**	*Iraq*	*2200 BC*
350 000	**Babylon (now al-Hillah)**	*Iraq*	*600 BC*
500 000	**Pataliputra (Patna) Bihār**	*India*	*400–185 BC*
600 000	**Seleukia (near Baghdad)**	*Iraq*	*300 BC–165 AD*
1 100 000	**Rome (founded *c.* 510 BC)**	*Italy*	*133 BC*
1 500 000	**Angkor**	*Cambodia*	*900 BC*
1.0–1.5 million	**Hangchow (now Hangzhou)**	*China*	*1279*

Tenochtitlan in Mexico was, in reality a conglomeration of two Aztec cities, Tenochtitlan and Tlatelolco, built within the lake of Texcoco and linked to dry land by three large causeways over the lake's waters: Iztapalapa, Tlacopan and Tepeyac. So the two cities were in fact separated by an arm of water and linked by a bridge. There were central monuments, large public buildings and numerous residential quarters. The exact size of the metropolis is unknown but it covered at least 4.6 sq miles *12 sq km* and had a population of more than 150 000, and perhaps as many as 500 000 divided among 80 distinct districts. The centre of the city, where the three causeways met, was impressive with many temples, playing fields, palaces and the 'altar of skulls'. (This area is now the site of Mexico City.)

First European–American towns ■ Santo Domingo in the Dominican Republic was founded in 1496 by Bartholomew Columbus, brother to Christopher. Negro slaves from Africa were introduced to the area in 1505 by the Spaniards and soon displaced the original Amerindian population. The first European city in Peru was Lima which was founded in 1534, the year after Pizarro had conquered the Inca empire for Spain. The Spaniards moved the capital of the area from the Inca capital of Cuzco in the highlands to Lima on the coast (the present capital of Peru). Their action lost Spanish control of the highlands for some decades.

Most corrupt city ■ The Portuguese Indian capital of Goa was a lavish and profligate town in the 16th century. Some men had dozens of Indian and African slaves, and used the female ones as concubines, or even employed them as prostitutes. Married Goan women were notorious for their extra-marital affairs. Most officials were dishonest. This scandalised the great missionary St Francis Xavier, who wrote in a famous letter of 1545 'here they are so accustomed to do what is not permitted that I see no remedy for it, since all go the way of *rapio, rapis* [Latin for I steal, you steal]. And I am astonished at seeing how those who come from there find so many moods, tenses, and participles for this poor word *rapio, rapis*.'

Dimensions

The true height of human giants is frequently obscured by exaggeration and commercial dishonesty.

The assertion that Goliath of Gath (*c.* 1060 BC) stood 6 cubits and a span 9 ft 6½ in *290 cm* suggests a confusion of units or some over-zealous exaggeration by the Hebrew chroniclers. The Jewish historian Flavius Josephus (born AD 37/38, died *c.* AD 100) and some of the manuscripts of the Septuagint (the earliest Greek translation of the Old Testament) attribute to Goliath the wholly credible height of 4 Greek cubits and a span 6 ft 10 in *208 cm*.

China ■ Cheng the Fourteenth from Taiyuan was eight Chinese feet tall, and of a build that was 'scarcely human'. If one Chinese foot = 14.1 English inches this indicates a height of about 9 feet *2.75 m*, but old measure conversions are notoriously unreliable, as there were many different Chinese 'feet'. Cheng is said to have killed two tigers by smashing one against the other.

Tallest in Africa ■ The Tutsi aristocracy of the East African highland kingdoms of Rwanda and Burundi grew tall on a diet fortified by the milk of their cattle herds while commoners who tilled their fields and fed on bananas were relatively short.

Most gigantic ■ To the people of Guanahani Island in the Caribbean the morning of 12 October 1492, brought a unique experience. Gigantic monsters came up out of the sea to their shores. When the sun was at its zenith (noon), there came out of these monsters canoes with men not like any they had ever seen before. The bodies of these men were covered all over and they had hair even on their faces. They spoke an unknown language, and they carried sticks so sharp that they cut into one if you ran a hand along them. The people of the island were relieved when the men re-entered the gigantic monsters and went away again.

Tallest in South America ■ After Magellan had been two months in Patagonia in present day Argentina during his journey around the world (1519) a huge giant 'ten spans high' (7 ft 6 in *2.25 m*) came to the shore. The giant, according to Antonio Pigafetta whose diary is the contemporary account of the voyage, 'was naked, and danced, leaped and sang, all the while throwing sand and dust over his head.' When the men approached him 'even the largest of us came only to midway between his waist and his shoulder.' The land took the name given by Magellan's men, from them: Patagonia, 'land of the big foot'.

Smallest people ■ There were and still are many causes of short stature in humans. These include genetic abnormalities, lack of appropriate hormones (e.g. growth hormone) and starvation. At this time, dwarfism, of whatever cause, would have been more pronounced than nowadays because of lower nutritional standards.

Shortest in Africa ■ The Pygmies of the equatorial rainforest lived in distant harmony with their farming neighbours and retained particular skills as Late Stone Age hunters. Early European traders on the west coast of Central Africa appreciated their ability to trap elephants and make charmed bracelets of elephant tail-hairs.

Monsters

Paedophogists ■ 'Under the Sui dynasty Ma Shumou and Zhu Can boiled up little children as a delicacy. During the Fire Dynasties Chang Congjian delighted in consuming human flesh. Wherever he went he would covertly grab hold of numerous children from among the common people to serve as his food. Both Yan Zhen and Dugu Zgnang shared this addic-

One cause of small stature was the administration of drugs. Dwarves were much in demand in the 15th century to appear in travelling fairs and at courts. Here, a court dwarf peers from a painting by the Italian Andrea Mantegna. Dealers would buy children and stunt their growth with drugs such as knotgrass. Thus they were kept undersized and looking older. The greatest number of such unfortunates was recorded in Italy and France although the practice was documented in most European countries during the 15th century.

tion. In Song times the mother of Yong Zhigao, one A-nong, had a cruel nature, and was fond of children's flesh. For every meal, she invariably killed a child.'

Europe's most enduring misperception of the native American people ■ This was that his body was hairy. Despite being told by Columbus and Vespucci that the Indians they encountered were smooth-skinned, most Europeans held to their belief in a 'wild man'. The probable explanation is that in certain areas it was an Indian custom to cover the body with down, which must have been noted by an early observer and passed on, spreading when it reached home. Ironically, the Indians themselves hated and feared a hairy man, even having a myth-figure to represent him.

MISCELLANEOUS

Longest living ■ The Chinese were obsessed with longevity. Almost universal use of the signs of the 60 year cycle meant that almost everyone knew their birth to the precise year. Late imperial records show no evidence of 'heaping' at multiples of 10 and 5. (These figures are not *completely* inconceivable, though some stretch credulity.) A man called Duo Gong was reputed to have reached 180 years in the Han dynasty and Zhao Yi in the Jin dynasty reached 200 years. A man from Shanghai reputedly reached 112. He ate twice as much as other people, and had a fleshy protruberance on his head. There was a man in Ziangching of 240 years of age, who no longer ate cereals, but only drank the milk of his great-grandson's wife. Huizhas, the monk who was the friend of the Loyal and Heroic Prince of Poyang under the Liang dynasty lived until the Yuanhe reign period in the Tang dynasty (806–820), at which time he was still alive aged 290.

Most persevering seducer ■ In the late 15th century a man from Shizhou in Taiynam prefecture, Sang Chong by name, had an outstanding method of seduction. He bound his feet from when he was young, became skilled in women's work, and dressed like a widow. He then travelled all over northeastern China, ingratiating himself with any family who had a fine daughter and, on the pretext of teaching her women's work, would have illicit sex with her. If she refused, he used a befuddling drug to overcome her resistance. Over a period of 10 years he debauched several hundred virgins in this way, until he was unmasked by a man with a passion for widows.

Most multiple births ■ 'Histories invariably record three boys being born at a single birth. This is keeping a register of uncanny (strange) events. There are also, however, cases of the parturition of four boys at the same time. I have personally witnessed this in Fuzhou [in Fujian], in the case of the wife of the military graduate Zhang Ma who was delivered of five sons at a single birth. In the year 1527, in Hejian, the wife – née Chan – of the commoner Li Gongwo gave birth to seven daughters at one time. This is something never recorded since records were first kept.'

WORST DISASTERS IN THE WORLD

DISASTER	NO. KILLED	LOCATION	DATE
Pandemic	*75 000 000*	**Eurasia: The Black Death (bubonic, pneumonic and septicaemic plague)**	*1347–51*
Genocide	**c.** *35 000 000*	**Mongol extermination of Chinese peasantry**	*1311–40*
Impact of Old on New World	**c.** *25 000 000*	**Spanish effect on Central America**	*1492–1592*
Earthquake	*1 100 000*	**Near East and eastern Mediterranean**	**c.** *July 1201*

In the *Collected Sayings of Chen Houshan* it says: 'There was the wife of a commoner in Tancheng who had 21 sons, including seven pairs of twins.'

Disasters

Biggest explosion ■ On 17 July 1490 lightning struck an old Greek church in Constantinople which the Turks were using to store gunpowder. The explosion killed 4000 to 5000 people, and destroyed many houses. The Turkish Sultan, Bayezid II, left the city when he saw the extent of the catastrophe.

Worst fire in Russia ■ Russian dwellings were mainly built of wood; stone houses only being erected for noble people. Thus Russian cities were constantly threatened by fire. The worst fire occurred in Novgorod lasting for 24 hours and killing 5000 people. On 21 June 1547 fire broke out in Moscow and much of the city was completely destroyed: 25 000 houses were burnt down, 1700 people lost their lives and more than 80 000 people were made homeless.

Medicine

Most prevalent theory ■ The 'four humours' theory of human biology had been evolving for 2000 years, based on thinking common to much of the ancient world. The Chinese in the 6th century BC had settled on six humours, later reduced to five, and Indians had elected for five. It was Empedocles in fifth century BC Greece who set the European standard of four. In simplified terms, the basic idea of the four humours was that human beings and their food contained within themselves the same four elements as made up the cosmos. These – air, fire, water and earth – manifested themselves in the human body in the form of 'humours' – blood, white bile, black bile and phlegm. Each of these four humours underlay a temperament: sanguine, bilious, melancholic and phlegmatic. Some people and some foods suffered from an excess of one or other of these elements, but good health could be achieved by maintaining an apparently simple balancing act. Clinical medicine reflected this; all diseases being under one of the four headings: hot, cold, moist and dry. The man of choleric (fire/bile) temperament was recommended to abstain from 'hot' foods and restrict himself to cool. Infants and the elderly (the over forties) were assumed to have a surplus of water/phlegm and instructed to avoid 'cool' foods.

It was not, however, as easy as it looked, because there was no straightforward dietary dividing line of the kind that would suggest itself to the modern mind, with fatty and starchy foods on the hot side and astringent ones on the cold. Although the Salerno school [see *Diet*] presumably had its own good reasons at the time, some of its classifications are now hard to fathom:

All pears and apples, peaches, milk and cheese,

The Four Temperaments: Bilious or Choleric (fire), Sanguine (air), Phlegmatic (water) and Melancholic (earth) from a 15th century German calendar.

Salt meat, red deer, hare, beef and goat, all these
Are meats that breed ill blood, and melancholy . . .

Greatest influence ■ The Church exerted the greatest influence on the practice of medicine of the time. There was a belief that disease was a punishment for sin. The general feeling was that everything worthwhile had been discovered, and scholars spent their time learning and considering the classical works such as those of Galen. No one thought to challenge the beliefs such as the idea that blood ebbed and flowed rather than circulated.

Best way to health ■ Medicines of an opposite nature to the disease were considered the best way to return the body to equilibrium. Fevers and afflictions which cause agitation originate from hot and dry causes and indicate excess choler; these were treated with cooling medicines such as coriander, white lead, allum or fresh roses. For diseases from cold causes, which are characterized by drowsiness and lethargy, warming medicines were prescribed like marjoram, myrrh, saltpetre, radish, garlic.

Most important astrological factor ■ This was the position of the Moon, the planet which stirs up the humours and determines the crisis points in any illness. The worst illnesses begin at the new Moon, when the hot Sun overpowers the liquid Moon and leaves the bodily functions at their weakest. The prognosis is usually better if the Moon is increasing in light (between new and full) and not as good if decreasing (past full and approaching the next new Moon). When the Moon was in the sign of Saturn it was considered the worst time to take medicine because its cold and dry nature would cause the humours of the body to congeal.

Most important for medical diagnosis ■ The sixth and eighth houses were the most important parts of the horoscope for medical diagnosis. Planets and signs in the sixth describe the health or illness of the patient and the condition of the eighth house determines survival.

Most dangerous time ■ Blood-letting to purge noxious humours was most dangerous when the Moon was in the sign that ruled the part of the body affected. Because the Moon is the fastest moving of the planets, completing a full orbit of the Earth in 29½ days, it changes its sign position every two days or so. Every physician would have needed an almanac in his possession to determine the Moon's precise position on any given day. The most competent would also have had an astrolabe to enable him to make a complete calculation of the horoscope.

Greatest medical debate ■ In the 15th century the greatest medical debate centred on methods of balancing fluids by purging. The three watery signs were best for purging; the Moon in Cancer or Scorpio was the best time for taking emetics, when the Moon was in Pisces it was the best time for taking laxatives.

Most influential medical book ■ The *Directory of Astrology made medical* by Jean Gavinet, a friar at Vienne, France, was written in 1431, and was printed in five editions between 1496 and 1614. Gavinet advised on the appropriate times for blood-letting and taking medicine or laxatives. Although he includes advice on maintaining good health based on balancing the patient's humours which could be known from study of the birth horoscope, most of the techniques employed were based on astrological calculations for the moment that the patient fell ill or when a urine sample was presented to the physician. The most obvious objection to these methods was that the doctor need never lay eyes or hands on the patient to predict recovery or death.

Bloodletting (from an Italian manuscript of about 1460) was a frequently used treatment.

Most important psychological factors ■ Psychology means knowledge of the soul. Since theology was the most important of the sciences and spiritual concerns were elevated over physical ones, the study of the soul was accorded a higher position in the intellectual world than the study of the body. Thus the most widely-held view in the early Renaissance of the make-up of Man's soul, which was a gift from God, was devised by philosophers. In the 11th century Avicenna determined that the soul consisted of ten wits. In the 13th century Thomas Aquinas reasoned that the body and soul depend upon each other and the body, by virtue of its perceptions, links the intellect to the material world. The five outward wits are also the five senses: sight, hearing, smell, touch and taste. The five inward wits were located in their own individual cells within the brain. These included the three centres of the brain recognized by the medical establishment: *fantasia* (common sense and perception), *imaginatio* (the storage facility for perceptions), *cogitatio* (decision and judgement-making from stored perceptions) plus *extimativa* (the ability to make instinctive or moral judgements) and *memorialis* (storage of accumulated moral and instinctive judgements).

For practical purposes, the character of an individual could be determined astrologically by the same criteria that defined his physical temperament. Complexion was a readily observable index to character, but alternative methods of observation could also give clues to those who knew how to read the 'divine imprints'.

Most far-fetched diagnostic technique ■ The location of moles on a person's body is one of the most far-fetched means of judging character and destiny, but it was widely practised in the Renaissance. Moles on the forehead were believed to produce a happy individual, moles on the nose were a sign of lust and extravagance: those found on the belly signified voracity. Moles on the face also had correspondence with other parts of the body. The famous astrologer and physician Giralamo Cardano (*b.* 1501) brought greater precision to the discipline by assigning astrological rulerships to moles in specific areas of the face and body.

Medical profession

Most controversial doctor ■ Paracelsus (1493–1541) – doctor, chemist, lecturer, astrologer, reformer and mystic – was known as the 'Luther of Medicine' and was the most controversial doctor of his time. Theophrastus Bombastus von Hohenheim adopted the pseudonym Paracelsus, which means 'beyond Celsus', after the Roman doctor who wrote the first systematic treatise on medicine. Paracelsus, son of a Swiss physician, became a legend in his day for burning the works of Galen and Avicenna (the ancient Greek and Arab physicians), a public act which cost him his position as professor of medicine in Basel

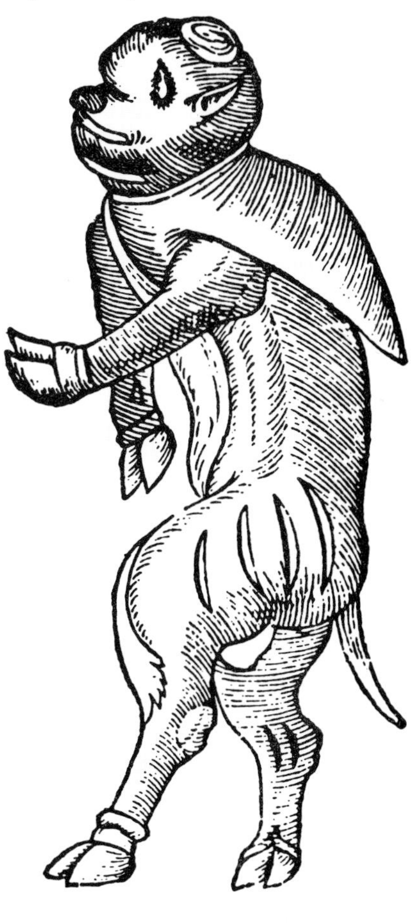

A hideous monster with the hands and feet of an ox and 'other very monstrous things' – an illustration from Ambroise Paré's book on Monsters and Marvels.

in 1528. He spent the rest of his life moving from place to place working as a doctor and writing on a wide range of medical subjects. He rejected the theory of the four humours, but accepted the four elements. He introduced the idea of three major principles which determine the form and faculty of all living things: sulphur (combustability, structure and substance), salt (solidity and colour), and mercury (vapour). As an alchemist he was concerned with chemical processes, but unlike most alchemists who were looking for gold, Paracelsus used chemistry to search for new medicines. He saw Creation as a divine chemical process and believed that Love was one of the foundations of medicine. His work marks the beginning of chemical medicine and the introduction of antimony, lead, mercury, arsenic, tin, copper, zinc sulphate, laudanum and alcoholic extracts into the pharmacopoeia. His emphasis on correct dosage and belief in the vital links between mind, spirit and matter in the creation of disease led him to treat the chemical process of curing diseases with substances of a nature similar to the disease. In this sense he can be seen as a forerunner of modern homeopathy.

He wrote eight books on the new disease of syphilis and offered a chemically altered and milder form of mercury (which is potentially poisonous) to cure it.

He was the first to understand the relationship between cretinism and endemic goitre, the first to write on miners' diseases and the first of the so-called 'modern' physicians to lecture in the vernacular (German rather than the traditional Latin).

Only very few people had access to medical care at the time. Physicians were scholars and so only found in the centres of learning. Surgeons – the craftsmen – were more widespread and there were more of them. They knew quite a lot about treatment of trauma, about fractures, reducing joint dislocations and applying red-hot cautery to wounds to stop bleeding. This last often caused infectious 'laudable pus' which was thought incorrectly to be a good sign of healing. These men were the casualty officers of the time. Medieval physicians did not often examine their patients. They listened to descriptions of the symptoms and after a cursory look at the patient would examine the various excreta such as vomit, urine and faeces.

Greatest surgeon ■ The French doctor Ambroise Paré (1510–90) was the greatest surgeon of the Renaissance. He resolved the fiercest controversy of 16th-century surgery by proving that the traditional methods of treating gunshot wounds actually harmed, rather than helped the patients. Instead of pouring boiling oil into the open wound he applied soothing applications of eggs, turpentine and rose-oil. However his greatest contribution to medicine was the abandonment of the practice of cautery to stop bleeding. Instead, for the first time since antiquity, he used ligatures to cut off the supply of blood. Paré was the inventor of artificial limbs and many new surgical instruments. He was the first to experiment with reimplanting teeth that had come out. His inventions include a device for treating women who suffered from hysteria, a condition which he saw as arising from natural causes, not demon possession. (See *Hysteria*.)

First English physician ■ Thomas Linacre (1460–1524) was the founder and first president of the Royal College of Physicians. His career marked the beginning of the medical profession in England. He travelled to Padua, in Italy, where he translated original Greek manuscripts of Hippocrates, Galen and Dioscorides and qualified as a physician. On his return he introduced the precise scientific methods of the ancient Greeks to medical students at Oxford and Cambridge. Thomas More was his pupil and Erasmus was his patient.

First professional medical bodies ■ From the 14th century all English craftsmen were required to join guilds, or trade unions. Most surgeons joined the Barber's Guild when it was incorporated in 1462. The Company of Barber–Surgeons was given corporate status in 1540, but the members wee not given the right to prescribe medicines.

The College of Physicians was founded by royal charter of Henry VIII in 1518. From 1540 physicians were entitled to practise surgery. In 1543 the Physicians' Act denied surgeons the right to practise internal medicine in any form. The professional organization of physicians in Padua was the direct inspiration for the English establishment.

Scotland was slower to organize than England, and had divergent interests. The royal incorporation of Barber–Surgeons in 1505 gave them the added bonus of sole manufacturing and retailing rights over whisky.

CHINA

First collection of medical case records ■ Medical case records are valuable sources of reference for doctors. A book entitled *Mingyi Leian* (Classified Medical Case Records of Noted Physicians) was compiled by Jiang Guang (1503–65), an outstanding physician, and revised and enriched by his son in 1552. It includes over 3000 case records collected from over 100 kinds of related literature covering 1600 years, and also including his own personal clinical experiences. It was the first and most comprehensive of its kind in the history of medicine.

Most comprehensive work on *materia medica* ■ The *Benco Gangmu* (Compendium on *Materia Medica*), consists of 52 volumes, lists 1892 kinds of drugs with detailed descriptions on their appearances, properties and uses. It also inclues 1100 illustrations and 11 000 recipes. It is composed of over 1 900 000 Chinese characters. The author, Li Shi-Zhen (1518–96), start¹ the writing of this work in 1522 and ˎ ompleted it in 1578, after his third revision. It was the result of his intensive study of over 800 related manuscripts and much on-the-spot investigation. It also deals with various branches of natural history, and has become the most widely studied and quoted book in the fields of medicine and natural history in the world.

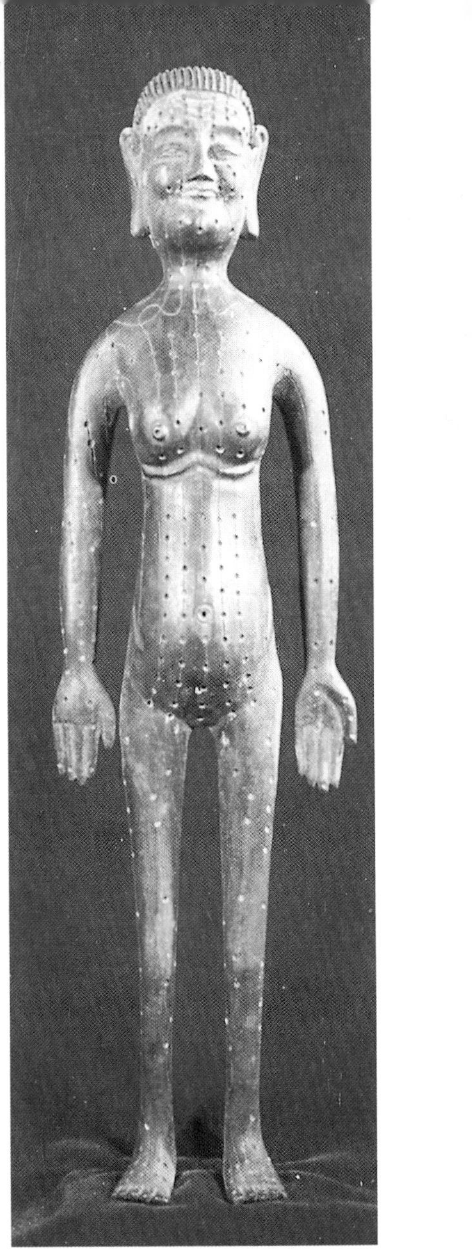

First medical models ■ *The first life-size bronze figure showing the location of channels and acupuncture points was cast officially in 1027 in China. In 1537, Gao Wu, an expert in acupuncture, designed and cast three figures, a man, a woman and a child, to show the respective location of channels and acupuncture points, particularly the differences in channels and acupuncture points in the body between men, women and children. These were not only the first bronze figures for acupuncture cast privately, but also unique medical models in the history of world medicine.*

First book on local *materia medica* ■ A book exclusively dealing with the *materia medica* of the Yuannan district, now a southern province of China, also known as the 'Kingdom of Plants', appeared in the 15th century. The author, Lan Mao (1394–1476), collected and summarized the medical experiences of the people of that district, including those of the minority nationalities. The book is therefore of considerable anthropological significance.

It was the earliest work of its kind in the world.

Most delayed publication ■ A voluminous work on *materia medica* entitled *Bencao Pinhui Jingyao* (Essential Collection of Herbs), an officially authorized book was compiled in 1505 by a group of 41 experts headed by the court physician Liu Wen-Tai under the order of the Emperor Qian-Lung. It consists of 42 volumes with 1815 medicinal substances and 1358 coloured illustrations and detailed descriptions. However, it was not published, owing to the death of the Emperor, for 432 years.

First woman medical writer ■ Although women physicians were a rarity. Tan Yuan-Xian (1461–1556) published a book entitled *Nuke Zayaõ* (Miscellaneous Talk of a Woman Physician) in 1510 when she was 50 years old. It contains 30 case records summarized from her many years of clinical work. It is not only the first book of its kind in the history of Chinese medicine, but also the earliest one written by a Chinese woman physician.

Most complete collection of prescriptions ■ A monumental work entitled *Puji Fang* (Prescriptions for Universal Relief) was compiled by a group of physicians headed by Teng Heng, a court physician, uner the patronage of Zhu Su, the fifth son of the Ming dynasty Emperor, Zhu Yuan-Zhang. It consists of 426 volumes with 61 739 prescriptions covering all branches of medicine of the time, and was issued in 1406. It was the most voluminous work of its kind in the history of Chinese and world medicine.

The Benedictine Priory of Christ Church

Canterbury, in England was set in the middle of the busy market town with about 4000–5000 inhabitants, and the meticulous medical records which have survived show a pattern of death not seen in later centuries. There was a hurdle in an individual's early 30s which had to be cleared. However, once this time of danger had been passed then there was every reason to be optimistic about reaching a European life expectancy of the mid 70s.

The reason seems to have been the fearful infectious illnesses which struck down many young people in their prime.

The priory had a large infirmary run by a senior monk, and it was staffed by laymen who worked as nurses and orderlies. There was also a resident physician and apothecary, as well as three laundrymen and a bathman. If necessary, specialist physicians and surgeons could be brought in from London.

This monastery might not have been exactly typical of medieval life. At first glance the community could have been thought to be above average in health matters. The monastic diet was a legendary one for the variety and quantity which set the refectory tables groaning. The monks' habits were made of good cloth, they had linen undershirts and drawers, and wool socks. In winter, leather and fur garments were made available. Drawers, shirts and socks were washed every two weeks (every three weeks in winter) and the monks washed frequently. Every year each monk got a new pair of shoes.

There was fresh water and the drains were adequate. It seems though that the general health of the monks was not especially good for the time. This was probably because of ignorance about many of the infectious diseases. Although the infectious nature of plague was known, and when someone died of it special precautions were taken to stem an outbreak, that of tuberculosis was not. TB would have flourished in the cloistered dormitory lives of such a close community and this is reflected in the record below.

Fatal diseases

Most meticulous health records ■ The religious houses of the period provide some of the best European medical statistics. However, they need to be interpreted with care, since it is not possible to place these causes of death alongside today's mortality rates. The monks were only able to describe patterns of illness and death rather than microscopically proven pathology. The monks though were skilled observers of what these diseases did to people.

Leading causes of death ■ The 15th century is infamous for its very high incidence of infectious diseases; together these would be the commonest cause of death in Europe. They included smallpox, cholera, plague, tuberculosis, sweating sickness and influenza.

These are reflected in the records from the Christ Church monks. They were spared from smallpox; cholera would probably be included in their diagnosis of 'dysentery'.

Diseases diagnosed in Christ Church monks dying between 1485 and 1507:

1. Tuberculosis (31%).

2. Sweating sickness (21%) (Possibly a collection of influenza-like conditions – see *Fastest fatal disease*.)

3. Plague (19%) (An infectious and severe febrile illness caused by a bacterium spread by rat fleas. Bubonic plague was the common form. The monks would be familiar with the clinical signs and symptoms of the disease, and they knew it was infectious.)

4. Dropsy (10%) (This is a description not a diagnosis. It means excess water in body tissue. The modern term is *oedema*. It is commonly seen in heart failure.)

5. Strangury (7%) (Strangulation or blockage of the intestines.) There would have been many abdominal catastrophes behind this single word of monastic diagnosis. These would have ranged from perforated appendix to cancer of the bowel. Tuberculosis can cause blockage of the bowel.)

Equal 6. (5%) Pleurisy (described with TB); Empyema (described with TB); Dysentery (In medieval times this was a description of diarrhoea with blood, mucus and pain. Without modern diagnostic means, as well as knowledge of bacteria – i.e. bacillary dysentery – all it is possible to say is that if these symptoms resulted in the death of a monk they could have been caused by very many diseases ranging from cancer to food poisoning.)

Equal 7. (2.3%) Paralysis. Fever. Hernia. Frenzy/delirium. Fistula-in-ano. The first four descriptions hardly need further explanation and would fit with many of the other illnesses described above. Fistula-in-ano decribes a condition around the anus in which there is an abnormal track or wound between the skin around the anus and internal tissues. It could have been present as a complication of many of the bowel conditions named above, as well as the ubiquitous tuberculosis.

Diseases

Worst epidemic ■ In the very year 1492 the plague attacked the population of Cairo. On one day 12 000 corpses were carried out of the city.

Worst pandemics ■ The highly contagious bubonic plague, commonly known as the Black Death, is thought to have been carried by the Mongols from Asia to Europe, where by the mid-14th century it had reached epidemic proportions. In the four years 1347–51 it cut Europe's population by as much as 40 per cent. The population, estimated at around 73 million in 1300, had dropped to around 45 million mid-century. Cold weather, poor harvests and periodic recurrences of the plague reduced the population still further, to perhaps 45 million by the beginning of the 15th century. Throughout the 15th century (and for another 300 years after that) the Black Death recurred sporadically all over Europe. Perugia in Italy was struck eight times, Hamburg, Cologne and Nuremberg in Germany each suffered ten epidemics. In some of these outbreaks as many as half the inhabitants died.

Most universal ■ According to Girolamo Fracastoro, a physician from

The doctor attending a plague victim covers his face; the patient's wife makes magic signs.

Verona in Italy, everyone had the disease of smallpox at least once in their lives. Those who survived were usually found to be immune to further contagion. The faces of most Europeans in 1492 would have shown the scars of smallpox.

First immunology ■ Variolation or inoculation was a method of inducing immunity to smallpox by directly infecting a person with matter from an active human smallpox scab. It was the very first of all immunological procedures. The first record of this method in the history of medicine of the world appeared in the Chinese medical book entitled *Duozhen Shiyi Xinfa* (Experiences of the Physicians of Generations for the Treatment of Smallpox and the Related Diseases) written by Wan Quan, a noted physician, in 1522. Later there appeared in China quite a few works dealing with this method in detail and several ways of practising it were described.

Commonest cause of death ■ Certainly in the Canterbury monastery, tuberculosis killed more people than any other disease. Tuberculosis was not understood at the time and so the monks must have been describing the pattern of symptoms. These would have been terrifying and unmistakable. Rampant tuberculosis of the lungs produces fever, night sweats, and above all an often massive, terrifying and fatal coughing-up of blood. (Now we know how tuberculosis behaves it is clear that some of the other 'leading causes of death' listed by the monks of Canterbury, might have had tuberculosis lurking behind the labels that the monks attached to a terminal illness. For example, tuberculosis can cause *empyema* (abscess) and pleurisy (inflammation of the membranes covering the lungs) as well as blockage of the intestine.

Fastest killer ■ The mysterious infectious disease known as English Sweating Sickness lays claim to being the fastest and most deadly disease of the time. On 22 August 1485, as King Richard III was defeated and killed at the Battle of Bosworth Field, rumours were afoot that a new and terrible disease was sweeping towards London from an outbreak in the Welsh borders. The rumours proved true; this first outbreak of English Sweats lasted five weeks.

The first person to describe the 'English Sweats' was an Italian diplomat called Polydore Vergil. He said it was a 'horrible pestilence, that struck as suddenly as a blow, and which no age could endure'. He said the disease killed in less than 24 hours and not one in a hundred evaded it. The English physician John Caius later wrote about the disease: 'It immediately kills some upon opening their windows, some while playing with children in their street doors, some in one hour and many in two.' The first symptoms were similar to those we would associate with influenza: high fever, headache, terrible aching joints and 'grief in the liver and stomach'. The sweating gave the disease its name, but this and the high temperature rapidly progressed to generalized body pains and a 'passion of the heart' (rapid heart-rate). Sufferers felt their bodies were on fire as they became delirious and confused, before lapsing into a final coma. Doctors were helpless and the disease spread faster than undertakers of the time could work; in some towns corpses were stacked up eight deep ready for burial. When the Sweats crossed to Germany it killed 5000 in five days.

We do not know what 'sweating sickness' was since it vanished around 1551. (There were five outbreaks in all.) It is probable that the disease brought about its own end. Whatever the agent was – possibly a virus – it killed its host so quickly that the invader simply had no time to establish itself, multiply, and then move on to another victim.

Best treatment ■ It was found that patients with the 'English Sweats' given water to drink and a rectal enema (known as a clyster) seemed to have the best chance of survival. Although it was not realized then, this was almost certainly because this treatment efficiently replaced lost body fluids.

Worst treatment ■ Some patients with the 'English Sweats' had fires built up around them, were covered in extra bedclothes and then had their well-meaning attendants lie on top of them. The only benefit from this would have been to produce a faster and more merciful end.

Greatest killer at sea ■ As ships began to make longer voyages, scurvy became rife amongst seamen. It is a deficiency disease and on long voyages, when fresh fruit containing vitamin C was not available, scurvy killed more men than did wars, storms and pirates put together, although in some ships poor sanitation was also a great killer. During his voyage around Africa in 1498, Vasco da Gama lost more than half his men fom scurvy.

Healthiest ships ■ Seagoing Chinese junks were far healthier than Western sailing vessels. Chinese sailors were protected by their diet against scurvy, the vitamin deficiency disease that killed thousands of European seafarers. Chinese ships carried salted and preserved vegetables and often had small gardens on deck to grow herbs and greens. Scurvy was described by the Chinese as far back as 1500 BC.

Most deadly ■ Malaria has probably been prevalent in Africa since before the first ocean-borne contacts with Europe and Asia. European sailors had little immunity to the bite of the malarial mos-

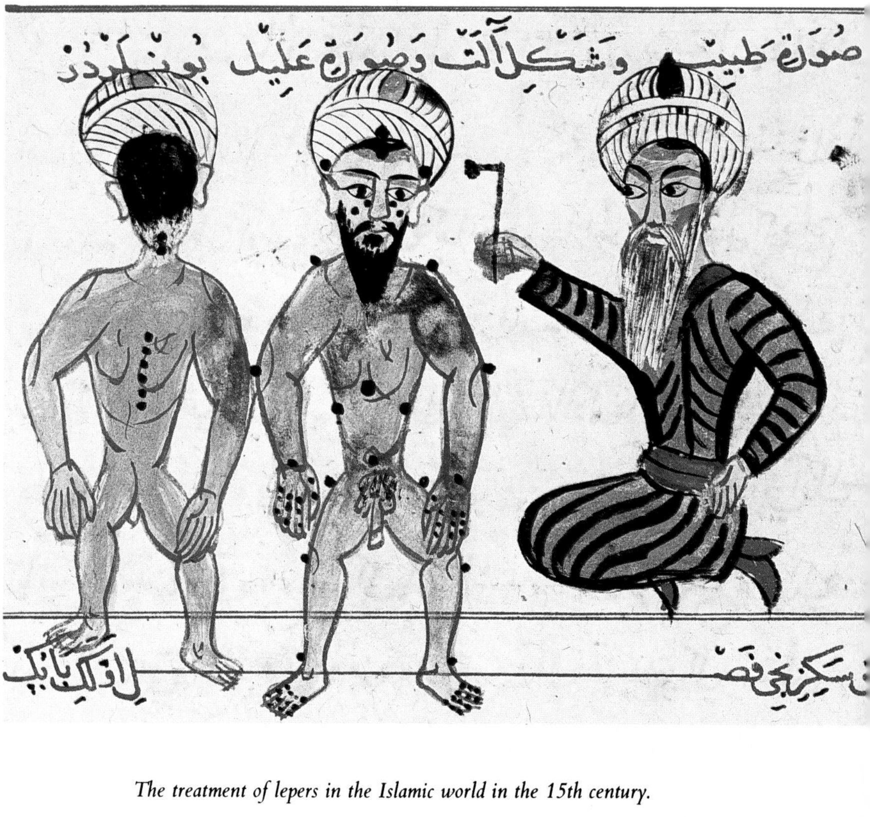

The treatment of lepers in the Islamic world in the 15th century.

quito and West Africa became known as the white man's grave, remembered in the saying, 'Beware and take care of the Bight of Benin: there's one as comes out for forty goes in.'

Most socially unacceptable disease ■ This undoubtedly was leprosy. Two common types are now known to have been diagnosed, but often less serious diseases such as scabies and inflammation of the skin were misdiagnosed as leprosy. Once the illness was confirmed the parish priest would administer the last rites and the unfortunate sufferer would be pronounced dead to the world, and instructed to live in God. This might mean confinement in a lazar house or simply banishment from the community. Lepers had to carry bells to warn others of their presence and to wear special clothes to make sure they were recognized. By the late 16th century most lazarets (houses for lepers) were closed or converted to other uses. The most remarkable property conversion of this kind was the hospital of St James the Less which Henry VIII turned in to a pleasure garden and retreat in 1547 in London. (It is now St James' Park and Palace.)

First work on leprosy ■ *Jiewei Yuansou* (Best Remedies for the Treatment of Leprosy), the earliest book exclusively devoted to leprosy in Chinese and Western medical literature, was written in 1550 by Shen Zhihwen, a doctor from a dynasty of physicians. It deals with the cause and symptoms of leprosy and contains 249 prescriptions. The exposition on the contagious nature of leprosy, including the droplets infection, the preventive methods for children, and the refutation of the superstitious belief that leprosy was incurable, are the most striking features in the history of leprosy.

First record of an effective treatment ■ The Chinese leprologist Shen Zhihwen was the first to record, in *Jiewei Yuansou*, the use of chaulmoogra seeds as a treatment for leprosy. Chinese physicians found the seeds a more effective remedy than any of the other drugs employed at the time. The use of chaulmoogra seeds for treating leprosy became widespread.

Most misunderstood disease ■ Hysteria was the most misunderstood of all diseases. From *c.* 2000 BC until the 20th century a set of miscellaneous symptoms ranging from paralysis, blindness, convulsion and various pains were grouped together and described as hysteria, an illness caused by the wandering of the womb through the body. The disease, it was thought, could only affect women because the *hystera*, the Greek word for uterus, and its malfunctions were obviously exclusively a feminine complaint.

Paracelsus (1493–1541) was the first to return to classical ideas of natural causes. In his 1525 *On the Diseases that Deprive Man of his Reason* he referred to Hippocrates, the Greek physician (*c.* 460–370 BC). In hysterics, he maintained, the womb suffered from excess cold caused by poison of the natural substance and upset of the chemical balance. The French writer François Rabelais (1483–1553) was also a physician; in his satire *Pantagruel* he describes the 'animal within the animal' whose movements deprive women of their sense. The great French surgeon Ambroise Paré (1510–90) disregarded the demon theories and also returned to classical science. He developed an instrument which permitted the fumigation (treatment with the smoke of curative herbs) of the uterus.

Greatest form of mass hysteria ■ Tarantism was a form of medieval dancing mania with its origins in the poor peasant communities of Taranto in southern Italy. A person – usually a woman – was supposedly bitten by the tarantula spider (one of the wolf spiders) and it was said that the symptoms of the poison could only be relieved by a ritual of fast dancing. This would continue at a furious pace until the victim collapsed exhausted. At this point the bite of the spider was considered 'cured'. It is almost certain that this was a form of mass hysteria rather than a reaction to a poison. It usually broke out around July or August, and victims would often start dancing again on the anniversary of their being bitten.

Nearest understanding of epilepsy ■ The most prevalent view of the cause of epilepsy was that it was caused by the Devil breathing upon the souls of those whose body chemistry was off-balance.

Paracelsus came the closest to defining a psychiatric concept of the disease. By 1530 the two books he wrote on the subject brought epilepsy into focus as a prime topic of discussion. He saw the element fire as a cause, and the thunderstorm of the rain which is its 'impression' is markedly like the convulsive seizures, therefore a natural link between man and the macrocosm. Terror before the attack (epileptics usually know in advance when they will suffer an attack) is comparable to apprehension before a thunderstorm. Lightning is like the flashing lights of the seizure experienced by the sufferer. The return of reason afterwards is much like the return of the Sun and calm after a storm. Paracelsus reasoned that the fire behind this was ruled by a certain star; we need only discover the constellation to know how to deal with its effects. He advocated treating epilepsy with gold and coral, rejecting the traditional therapy of mistletoe, blood from a decapitated man, or skull bones.

Commonest form of bone disease ■ Examination of medieval skeletons from archaeological sites indicates that joint disease was the commonest form of bone disease. By far and away most of this joint disease was caused by joint failure: osteoarthritis. In one examination of 250 medieval skeletons from the West of England nearly half had some form of bony change at their joints; and 50–60 per cent of those that did had osteoarthritis.

Rarest form ■ There are many bone diseases that are rarely found in archaeological material, including cancer of different types. However, only one possible case of rheumatoid arthritis has ever been found in many thousands of skeletons that have been examined, making it the rarest of all.

First book on stomatology ■ Stomatology is a branch of medicine concerning the mouth. The earliest extant book devoted to it is *Kouchi Leiyao* (Essentials of the Mouth and Teeth) written by Xue Ji, a noted Chinese physician, in the year 1529. It contains various kinds of diseases of the lip, tongue, teeth and throat, including lip cancer, with case reports.

Commonest disease ■ The commonest contagious disease in the world, then as now, would have been *coryza* (acute nasopharyngitis) or the common cold.

AMERICA

First recorded pandemic ■ For the 15th-century peoples of the Americas smallpox was the most deadly import of the Europeans. It reached Hispaniola in about 1518 and quickly killed perhaps half the indigenous Arawak population. It spread, even ahead of the Europen invaders: the Aztecs fell in huge numbers; the Incas, including the Inca himself and his successor, died of the disease. Smallpox spread everywhere, killing as it went. It is estimated that within two decades at most smallpox may have spread from the Great Lakes of North America to the pampas of Argentina.

Most deadly encounter ■ Within a few decades the indigenous populations of the Caribbean and the Americas had suffered terribly through the introduction of new diseases into their lands to which they had no immunity. These diseases included smallpox which raged through America by the early 1500s. Other killer diseases were influenza, diphtheria, bubonic plague and typhus brought by Europeans, and malaria, the greatest killer in history, and yellow fever which were carried across the Atlantic by African slaves. (Some claim that yellow fever was epidemic in Mexico during 1454.) The effect of these diseases was so great that the native population of the Greater Antilles had been wiped out by the 1540s. The Indian population of Mexico was probably about 25 million in 1500, and would be only one million a century later. The same pattern of disaster continued throughout the Americas.

Syphilis

First supposed appearance of syphilis in the Old World ■ Venereal syphilis has one of the most confused and complex histories of any major disease. Named first the 'Great Pox', and only later 'syphilis', it is believed to have appeared and spread widely in Europe and beyond during the few years after Columbus and his crews returned from the New World. It was claimed to be rampant in Paris by 1495, and one view is that it was spread into France and other countries by the multinational mercenaries in the army of Charles VIII of France, returning from the capture of Naples, and subsequent retreat. In any event, history claims its appearance in Germany and Switzerland by 1495, Holland and Greece in 1496, Britain by 1497, Hungary and Russia by 1499, China by 1502 and Japan by 1569. While various names were given to this condition by early medical writers in the 16th century, including the confusing title of French gonorrhea, it was Girolamo Fracastoro who gave the name *syphilis* to the condition in his poem *Syphilis sive Morbus Gallicus* (Syphilis or the French Disease), published in Venice in 1530. Fracastoro is also distinguished by providing the first good scientific description of typhus fever. (Was this epidemic disease described as syphilis truly its first appearance in Europe? Archaeological evidence is beginning to establish that it was not. There is now a syphilitic skull from York which predates the Columbus voyages, and other possible cases from East Anglia and London.)

Some authorities argue that syphilis existed from prehistory and was described in a Chinese medical treatise in 2637 BC and in a Japanese manuscript dating from AD 808, to name but two among many references from all parts of the then known world. It is possible that Columbus' men brought back a new strain which, in European bodies, evolved into a deadly venereal disease.

First explanations ■ Astrologers gave the first explanations of the origins of the disease in Europe. They attributed its appearance to the influence of the stars and the planets. Bartholomew Steber of Vienna wrote: 'It is a new disease caused by the conjunction of planets.' The first printed work on syphilis was by Grünpeck of Brückausen who in 1496 stated the disease was due to 'the unlucky work of Saturn and of Mars'. The Italian Coradin Gilini in 1497 elaborated on this: 'It is to the conjunction of Saturn and of Mars, which occurred 16 January 1496, at about noon, and which presaged a mortality among men; or else to the conjunction of Jupiter and of Mars, which had occurred 17 November 1494, in a warm and moist sign.'

Earliest illustration ■ The title page of Bartholomew Steber's treatise on syphilis (1497) is probably the earliest pictorial representation of the disease. This is a woodcut showing two doctors examining and applying treatment to two patients suffering from the disease.

First European syphilitic patient ■ Martin Alonzo Pinzón was the commander of the *Pinta*, one of the three ships sailing with Columbus to the Indies. He is reputed to have been the first known and recorded European syphilitic patient among those who returned from the voyage. He died from the disease on 20 March 1493, shortly after his return to Spain.

First person to name 'Syphilis' ■ Girolamo Fracastoro (1483–1553) was a physician of Verona and Padua. In 1530 he published a poem on the disease entitled *Syphilis sive Morbus Gallicus* (Syphilis or the French disease), in which he included the story of the shepherd boy, Syphilis, who cared for the sheep and cattle of King Alcithous: One summer the land suffered from terrible drought killing many of the animals; Syphilus cursed the Sun and the Gods for this and offered sacrifices to the King rather than to them. The Gods were furious and 'straight away an unknown pollution was born to flood the blasphemous earth. The first man to display the disfiguring sores over his body was Syphilus . . . he was the first to experience sleepless nights and tortured limbs, and from this first victim the disease derived its name and from him the farmers called the sickness Syphilis.'

First mention in print ■ Emperor Maximilian (1459–1509) issued an edict on 7 August 1495 which is thought to contain the first mention of syphilis in a printed document. The edict was first issued in German and then in Latin and states: 'Notably in our time there have been severe diseases and plagues of the people, to wit the *bosen blattern* [evil pocks] which have never occurred before nor been heard of within the memory of man.' The edict claimed that the disease and its spread were a result of blasphemy.

Albrecht Dürer's engraving of a syphilitic indicates the importance of zodiacal influences on health.

First descriptions of tuberculosis and congenital syphilis ■ Paracelsus (Theophrastus von Hohenheim, 1493–1541), Swiss physician and alchemist was the first physician to describe these afflictions. He was also first to treat diseases with doses of detoxified minerals such as sulphur, mercury and antimony.

Most complete description ■ John de Vigo (1460–1520) was the physician to Pope Julius II. In 1514 he devoted two chapters in his book on surgery to syphilis, the disease which he named *Le Mal Français* (the French sickness). He described in detail the symptoms he had seen and the treatments he had administered; this was unusual since most authors of his time had not actually seen or treated the disease. The first symptoms were ulcers on the genitalia; if these were not treated new ulcerations appeared and 'the skin became covered with crusted lumps. . . These eruptions affected especially the forehead, the head, the neck, the arms, the face, the legs and sometimes spread over the surface of the entire body . . . About a month and a half after the debut of the first symptoms, the patients were afflicted with pains, strong enough to tear from them cries of anguish.' Vigo considered mercury to be the best treatment for the disease.

Most common treatment ■ From the beginning, mercury was used to treat the disease. This was most usually administered in the form of an ointment, but it was also given by mouth, fumigation, and as mercurial plasters.

First to use Guaiacum as treatment ■ At the age of 15, Gonzalo Fernandez Oviedo y Valdes (1478–1557) was a page to Prince Juan, son of Ferdinand and Isabella, at Barcelona. In 1525, Oviedo wrote on the American origin of syphilis and he reasoned that there might be a cure for the disease, from which he was suffering, in the place where it had originated. Oviedo went to the Indies as Inspector of the gold mines, and is thought to have been the first person to use Guaiacum, an extract from Guaiac wood or Holy wood, in the treatment of his own disease.

THE DISEASE IN CHINA

First appearance ■ Syphilis was first brought into Canton, the sea-port in the south part of China, in 1502 as a result of the development of the sea route between the East and the West.

First description ■ This appeared in the medical book *Xu Yi Shuo* (Supplementary Discourse to Medicine) written by Yu Bian and published in 1522. In this book syphilis was named as the *Guang Chuang* (Red-berry Sore) because of the appearance of the disease.

First treatises ■ As a new disease syphilis caught the attention of quite a few physicians. *Yangmei Chuang LunZhi Fang* (Prescriptions for the Treatment of the Red-berry Sore) written by Han Mao in 1522 was the first work to be devoted exclusively to the disease. Among other works dealing with syphilis was the *Shisan Yian* (Shisan's Medical Cases) written by Wang Shisan in 1522, in which the author, apart from recording several cases of syphilis, also discusses the direct and indirect contagious infection of the disease and infection by unclean sexual intercourse.

Newest cure ■ The Chinese herbal medicine Smilax, a relative of Sarsaparilla, was used in treating syphilis in the early 16th century, a few years after syphilis was introduced into China from the West. In 1535, Smilax was exported to India, Turkey and Persia from China as a new drug. It was soon imported into Europe by Portuguese and other merchants and was called the 'China Root'. In order to promote its sale, the merchants claimed that Smilax could cure every sort of disease by a decoction of it. It leaped into sudden fame and became very popular, because it was said that it was used by the Emperor Charles V with benefit for his general health. It was then used in treating almost all kinds of disease, including syphilis. Andreas Vesalius, the physician and outstanding reformist in anatomy, concluded after having made investigations, in a letter to his friend Dominus Joachim Roelants in 1546, that Smilax was good for sufferers of syphilis and some other illnesses, but by no means a panacea. Vesalius was right in the way he applied his scientific spirit to the administration of drugs and also in his scepticism with regard to the pharmacology of his day and his distrust of authority. Actually, Smilax was used only as one of the ingredients by the Chinese physicians in treating syphilis, rheumatism and some other related diseases. Smilax fell into discredit later, being dethroned by Sarsaparilla, another popular drug imported from the New World.

Childbirth

Oddest cure for sterility ■ According to Johannes de Kethem in his *Fasciculus Medicinae*, sterility could be cured by both husband and wife drinking the saliva of a rabbit secreted whilst chewing greens. He also considered the use of a tampon, soaked in a solution of oil mixed with the powdered right testicle of a weasel, to be effective.

Earliest English text on obstetrics ■ A 15th century manuscript is thought to be the earliest text on obstetrics in English. Although the author is unknown, it is based on the writings of Roger of Parma, was printed in 1490, and deals with obstetrics and gynaecological subjects.

First book for midwives ■ Eucharius Rosslin was a German physician at Worms and later at Frankfurt. In 1513 his book *Die Rosengarten* (The Rose Garden) was published. Although this contained little original material, it was written especially for midwives and was the first work dealing with obstetrics apart from medicine and surgery. The illustrations included figures of the birth chair, the lying-in chamber and the positions of the foetus in the womb. The book was translated and published in English in 1540 under the title *The Woman's Book*. There were numerous editions of the book in Latin, English, Italian, German and French.

First cauterization of the umbilical cord ■ Tetanus (lock-jaw) in the infant was a common cause of death. It was usually caused by an infected umbilical cord. In 1540, Xue Ji, a well-known Chinese physician, recommended the use of a piece of heated iron to treat the umbilical cord as it is cut off. This method is described in his book *Nuke Cuoyao* (Essentials of Obstetrics and Gynaecology), and was considered by the author as the best way of preventing tetanus in the infant. It was the first such description in the history of Chinese and Western medicine.

Childcare

Best type of wet-nurse ■ One of the best early books on children's diseases is

that by Bartholomew Metlinger, *Regimen der Jungen Kinder* (The Regime for Young Children) which was printed in Augsburg, Germany, in 1473. After discussing the care of a newborn baby, he considers nursing and the choice of wet-nurse. According to Metlinger, the best type of wet-nurse should be at least 20 years old, at best 25, with her own child at least six weeks old: 'She should be well built; her face healthy in appearance, tanned; and she should have a thick neck, strong broad breasts, not too fat and not too thin but preferably well formed and fleshy . . . The wet-nurse should have good praiseworthy habits. She should not be easily frightened or worried and not small-minded or prone to anger.'

First use of artificial feeding ■ If the mother or wet-nurse were unable to provide milk, the infant was fed on cow's or goat's milk. Various methods were used which included sucking horns, cans with artificial nipples, and sugar lumps and bread rubbed in a piece of linen, shaped into an artificial teat. Use of the sucking horn was mentioned in a 14th century document but Bartholomew Metlinger's text of 1473 contains the first mention of the nippled nursing can and the artificial teat.

LITERATURE

First illustrated text on infant care ■ In 1429 the monk Heinrich von Louffenburg (*d.* 1458) wrote a poem, *Versehung des Liebs* (Care of the body), in which he included illustrations depicting the care of infants. He was the first to show a feeding bottle of the type still used today. The book was published in Augsburg in 1491.

First printed books ■ Paulus Bagellardus a Fleming (died 1492) was the author of the first printed book on children's diseases, published in Padua in 1472. The book is divided into two parts; the first concerns the management and care of babies in the first month, and the second is divided into 22 chapters and discusses the various diseases of children including wakefulness, eye diseases, ear diseases, diarrhoea, constipation and worms.

First English printed book ■ Thomas Phaer (*c.* 1510–60) has been given the title of 'The Father of English Paediatrics'. He recognized that paediatrics was a branch of medical learning which was almost totally neglected; his *Boke of Children*, published in 1544, was the first book on children's diseases to be printed in English.

Medicines and drugs

Drugs were widely used, and came from a multitude of sources. Most people did not have access to the few trained doctors around, and depended on folk healers and folk medicines. Folk medicines relied heavily on plants and herbs, and in fact many would have had a genuine beneficial effect.

Largest scientific study ■ Li Shizhen (1518–91) was one of China's most famous physicians. For most of his life, he worked to compile a huge catalogue of all substances of medicinal value, fully illustrated, and with detailed explanations of the origins and properties of each substance listed. His book contains 1 900 000 illustrations and 11 000 compound prescriptions for all known diseases. The title Li chose was *Bencao gangmu* (The Comprehensive Pharmacopoeia). (It was finally printed in 1596, three years after Li's death in 1593, and is still used today by traditional-style doctors in China.)

First modern pharmacopeia ■ Valerus Cordis (1515–44) published a new edition of Dioscorides' classical treatise on remedial medicine (*De Materia Medica*, On Medical Materials) which was so improved and expanded that it is thought to be the first modern pharmacopeia, or book of remedies.

Most used ■ Theriac (sometimes spelt theriaca) was one of the most used medicines, having been popular since ancient times. It was a mixture of substances, including viper's flesh, and many believed it possessed almost miraculous curative and antidotal powers.

Herbs in medicine

Most popular ■ *Angelica* was one of the most versatile herbs. Hot and dry by temperament, it was used as a prophylactic against pestilence and evil spells. It also worked as a digestive; chewing its leaves helped to prevent flatulence. When distilled, angelica can be made into perfume, and candied stalks were eaten as sweets. Angelica is linked to St Michael, and the archangel was believed to have appeared in a vision to explain the plant's extraordinary protective powers.

The seeds of the *plantain* were popular as a laxative. When swallowed they would absorb water and become bulky, like the modern-day high-bran foods which produce a well-formed stool.

Comfrey had many uses. It contains as astringent which helps wounds heal, and also contains mucilage, a hard and sticky substance which could be used as a support, not unlike the modern bone support of plaster of Paris.

Onions were popular for coughs and colds, since their powerful odour will make the mucous membranes of the ear, nose and threat run with mucous. These are then more easily coughed up.

Dandelion leaves were used as a diuretic – that is to cause more urine to be passed. This loss of body water is useful in conditions such as heart failure. (Dropsy was their word for the ankle swelling and other signs of cardiac failure.) Not only does dandelion contain a diuretic, but it also contains potassium – a substance which just happens to be lost from the body when some diuretics act.

Most bitter ■ *Artemisia* (wormwood) is the most bitter of herbs. The aromatic herb was named after the wife of King Mausolus; the tomb she built for him around 325 BC, at Halicarnassus, now Bodrum, Turkey – the Mausoleum – was one of the Seven Wonders of the Ancient World. Queen Artemisia was famous in the fourth century BC for her botanical and medical research. Dioscurides recommended eating the seeds of artemesia to expel worms. It was also used to treat melancholic distemper. It was recommended for those with weak livers. *Wormwood* was the best moth repellant in the herb garden. It was also employed as a charm against the dangers of travelling, a usage which survived into the 20th century in some parts of Europe.

Best antidote ■ *Rue* was known as the 'Herb of Grace' and was of primary importance as an antidote to poison and plague. It is the main ingredient in mithridate, named after its inventor, King Mithridates, a condemned enemy of ancient Rome who so successfully treated himself that he was immune to all poisons and had to ask his slave to stab him. Rue branches were used to sprinkle holy water before high mass and from the third century was mixed with holy oil for use at exorcisms. It was a favourite strewing herb for courtroom floors. Robbers of the corpses of plague victims sprinkled themselves with rue vinegar for protection. Its main culinary use was in pickling and salads. Both Leonardo da Vinci and Michelangelo used rue to heighten their creative vision. Rue is hot and dry and was also used in the treatment of epilepsy and hysteria (which was considered at the time to have its origins in the uterus). When mixed with myrtle leaves and wax, rue was applied to the face to treat pimples.

Consultations with a physician might take place in a pharmacy and the medicines prescribed would be mixed on the spot.

The Passau Herbal *published in 1485 contained 150 woodcuts of plants and explanations of their uses in medicine and the household.*

Most pungent ■ *Mint* was valued for its pungent oil which was used to stop milk from curdling and to aid digestion. Its hot and dry nature meant that it was a remedy for colds and coughs, giddiness, and headache. It was also a popular laxative. From Roman times it was associated with hospitality and its use as a fragrant strewing herb continued through the late middle ages.

Pennyroyal was by far the most favoured type of mint. Dioscorides prescribed it for counterbalancing excessive phlegm, the watery humour. When boiled in water and drunk it inhibited the desire to vomit. Applied directly to affected areas it eased the pain of gout and removed spots on the face. Pennyroyal was also used to treat leprosy. Its strong scent made an effective insect repellant; many people wore sprigs of mint to keep the fleas away.

Most popular with taverners ■ *Balm*, along with *ground ivy* and *costmary*, was used to flavour beer and wines and was therefore the most popular herb in monastic and taverners' gardens. Its hot and dry nature was considered an antidote to melancholy and could revive those who had fainted. Dioscorides claimed that balm leaves soaked in wine were an antidote to scorpion stings or mad dog bite; such leaves applied to a boil will cause it to ripen and break. Balm was also an important ingredient in Carmelite Water, a popular commercially prepared cosmetic. Its Latin name *melissa* alludes to its usefulness in attracting bees (*mel* = honey); the herb was also known as bee's leaf.

Tobacco – first European contact ■ Although Columbus became acquainted with a native plant of value, called *tabaco*, on landing in the New World, and he observed in Cuba (November 1492) both men and women smoking, it took European societies over half a century to understand its potential pleasure value. Indeed, it was first introduced as a medicinal herb, and it was noted that in Brazil it was used to 'loosen and carry off the superfluous humours of the brain'.

Most favoured scent ■ *Lavender* was valued as a tonic and heart cordial, as well as a guard against pestilence. It is also hot and dry. A 16th-century English herbal advises bathing the temples of migraine sufferers for relief from pain. Its oils were the most favoured for scenting the bath and making perfumes from Roman times; it was also used to make preserves, syrups and even varnish. The flowers were eaten in salads or candied. It was often used as a strewing plant and insect repellant.

Most important alchemy development ■ The Doctrine of Signatures was an idea devised by the alchemist and physician Theophrastus Bombast (1493–1541), better known as Paracelsus. It was the most important development in occult thought on the medical use of herbs. Every herb was believed to have been stamped by the Creator with a sign of its use; those shaped like a foot could cure gout, heart-shaped leaves were good for cardiac problems, maidenhair fern was an aid for the balding.

Diet

Most influential doctrine ■ 1526 saw the first (somewhat belated) English translation of the work that was the foundation of virtually all Western medicine from the beginning of the 12th century until well into the 18th. The *Regimen Sanitatis Salerni* (The Salerno Regimen of Health), published in 1480, was a unique synthesis of Greek, Arabic and Italian theories made in the late-11th century at the most famous and progressive medical school of the time at Salerno in south-west Italy. (It went in to 300 editions by the 19th century.) Except possibly in China, no other system of medicine in history has been so influential for so long. The Salerno Regimen was based on the simple proposition, no less appealing then than now, that it was possible to look younger and live longer on the right diet. Why, its theorists asked, were people dying younger these days when Adam had lived to be 930? And the answer, then as now, was that people were indulging in 'mis-diet' and 'much surfeiting'. Good and bad diets were formulated according to highly sophisticated principles, but Salerno was perfectly happy to have its teachings set out in popular terms.

Most popular diet-medicine ■ Great faith was placed on what a sick patient ate. Broths, milk and eggs were the most popular invalid diets, with milk being especially favoured for tuberculosis sufferers. (Milk is of course an excellent food, and would have nurtured those with TB and given them their best chance of survival.)

Health and diet books ■ Once printing from moveable type had been introduced into England in 1475, there was a demand for books on diet and medicine – not two subjects but one. In the first half of the 16th century, 32 major titles are recorded – not many by modern standards, but by no means inconsiderable when, at the beginning of the period, one of the most prolific of early printer-publishers, Wynkyn de Worde, was publishing no more than 10 books a year.

Anatomy

First standard textbook ■ The Italian anatomist, Mondinus, completed his *Anathomia* (Anatomy) in 1316. It was widely reproduced in manuscript and was first printed in 1478. It was the standard textbook on anatomy for two centuries, until Vesalius, *Fabrica De Humani Corporis* (The Structure of the Human Body) was published in 1543. Mondinus' book is regarded as a classic which had an enormous influence on medical thinking.

First human dissections ■ During the 14th and 15th centuries dissections of human bodies were few since the Church did not approve. Those that were performed were usually carried out on the bodies of executed criminals, often in front of spectators, as the ultimate punishment for the criminal.

Mondino de Luzzi (Mondinus) (1275–1326) carried out the first human dissections for anatomical purposes in 1315. This revolutionized the teaching of anatomy and Luzzi is considered by many to be the greatest of the medieval dissectors. He

The picture on the title page of Fabrica De Humani Corporis *(The Structure of the Human Body) printed in 1543, shows the young Vesalius demonstrating not only to his students and other physicians but also to councillors, nobles and representatives of the Church.*

would often lecture to students while assistants did the actual dissection.

Most public dissections ■ Flemish-born Andreas Vesalius (1514–64) and other surgeon–anatomists often worked in the open air with an audience. Special temporary wooden structures for seating spectators on such occasions were first used at Padua, in north-east Italy, by the anatomist Allesandro Benedetti and were dismantled at the end of a course of lectures.

Greatest of all medical books ■ The researches of Andreas Vesalius, combined with the outstanding drawings of the Flemish artist Jan Stefan Kalkar, are contained in the great treatise *Fabrica De humani corporis* (The structure of the human body), first published in 1543. This work, consisting of 659 pages with 277 plates, was produced from observations obtained through dissection, thus scientifically dealing with anatomy, and in many cases challenging Galen's ideas. Although the book was very popular, Vesalius received much criticism as he repudiated Galen whose works had been accepted for more than twelve centuries. Nevertheless, it has been acknowledged not only as one of the greatest of all medical books, but also as one of the most beautifully illustrated books of all time.

Like a modern textbook of anatomy, the *Fabrica* is divided into seven 'books'; the first on the skeleton, the second on muscles, the third on the vascular system, the fourth on the nervous system, the fifth on the abdominal viscera, the sixth on the thoracic contents and the seventh on the brain. This latter section on the brain is of a pioneering standard, as seen in the fine illustrations which accompany it.

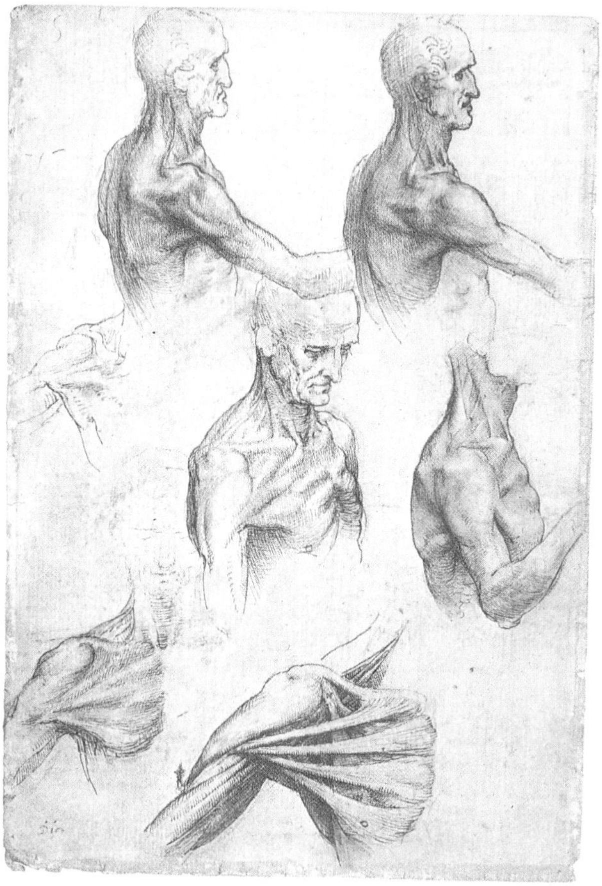

The great Italian artist Leonardo da Vinci, in one of his anatomical studies, showed how the muscles of the arm and chest function to create movement in the human body.

First papal approval of autopsies ■ Because of the Church's ban on the dissection of human bodies there had been little progress in the field of anatomy during the 14th and early-15th centuries. Pope Sixtus IV (1414–84), however, became the first Pope to approve autopsies, many of which were performed by the Florentine doctor, Antonio Benivieni. Notes from these were published in1507, after Benivieni's death, under the name of *De abidis morborum causis* (The hidden causes of disease). By the early 16th century dissection and autopsy could be performed without any obstacle.

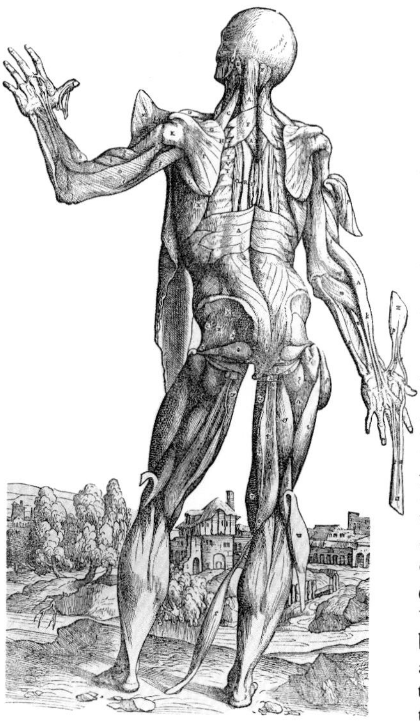

An illustration by the Flemish artist Jan Stefan Kalkar of Vesalius' book of anatomy.

ILLUSTRATION

Earliest printed picture of anatomical dissection ■ The first printed anatomical dissection scene is found in the French translation of Bartholomaeus Anglicus, *De proprietatibus rerum* (Of the properties of things), which was published in Lyons in 1482. The earliest known illustration of a dissection is in a 14th century manuscript of English origin.

Earliest illustrated anatomical book ■ Johannes de Kethem was a physician and professor of medicine at Vienna in the mid-15th century; his book, *Fasciculus Medicinae* (A garland of medicines), published in Venice in 1491, is the first anatomical book with illustrations. The book contains the best 15th-century depiction of the uterus.

Greatest medical artist ■ Leonardo da Vinci (1452–1519) illustrated all of the bones of the body to show how they work as levers to activate the muscles and was the first to accurately depict all of the vertebrae, as well as first to note the curvature of the spine. His interest in the flow of the blood led him to inject the vessels and internal organs to facilitate study; no one had done this before. The four-chamber structure of the heart was also first observed by him. His drawings include the moderator band on the right ventricle 300 years before physicians noticed it. When he studied a foetus in the uterus he made the novel observation that its source of nourishment was the placenta. From his work on the cadavers of men who had been hanged he was able to correct misconceptions about the erection of the penis by explaining that it was caused by the increased flow of arterial blood. Previous wisdom held that it was caused by 'pneuma', or vital spirit.

Most complete representations of the internal organs ■ A book by Magnus Hundt, printed in Leipzig, Germany, in 1501 is illustrated with several anatomical woodcuts; these include depictions of the head, face, neck, brain, palm of the hand, and skeleton. There is also an illustration of the internal organs which is thought to be the most complete representation of these organs as they were regarded in the 15th century.

Surgery

Least popular ■ Most surgery in the 15th and 16th centuries comprised wound dressing and the treatment of ulcers. Operations for hernias, bladderstones, facial disfigurements and cataracts, for example, were avoided since they involved considerable risks to the patient and thus to the surgeon's reputation. These operations, therefore, were often performed by itinerant 'cutters' who, after being paid for their work, fled leaving the patient to his fate. Some 'cutters', however, specialized in certain operations and became very proficient.

Most painful ■ Before proper anaesthetics the most painful operations must have been those done 'cold', and not the amputations and red-hot cauteries done in the heat of battles. The pain of these planned operations must be subjective; however, surgery for cataract, in which a needle was pushed into the eye to remove the opaque lens, must have been a dreadful price to pay for improved sight.

Fastest ■ 'Cutting for stones' was a service often provided by travelling fairs. The incision to remove kidney stones from the bladder was made in the perineum and the stone pulled out via this route between the top of the legs. The most highly regarded 'cutters' were the fastest operators for obvious reasons.

Foremost family of repairers ■ A family of laymen called Branca from Catania in Sicily were all involved in reconstructing noses which their patients had injured in feuds or through disease. They could also repair ears and lips by using flaps of skin from the forehead or cheek. Branca Senior used a flap from the arm to repair a nose, and his son Antonius perfected the method. Their work was first recorded in 1442. Elysius Calentius, a poet from Naples, reported that they could also restore a nose 'by infixing it upon the part of the nose of a slave'. In Calabria in Italy, four members of another family all did restoration to noses, ears and lips too. Vincenzo, his nephew Bernardino and his two sons, Paolo and Pietro were all involved.

Most influential surgeon–anatomist ■ The Flemish-born Andreas Vesalius (1514–64) did more than any other to bring surgery into the modern era. His work changed anatomy from an inexact description to a well-developed science. He was appointed Professor of Surgery at the University of Padua in Italy at the age of only 23. His appointment was given to him on the day after his graduation from the University. His duties included teaching anatomy and holding public dissections.

AMERICA

Best surgeons ■ The Inca doctors used many types of plants and herbs for treatment, some of which, for example quinine, have been passed to the Western world.

Most extraordinary surgery ■ The Inca surgeons of South America trepanned the skull of a patient to counteract disease. They pierced the bone and then took out the affected parts with their *tumis* or triangular knife. Many patients survived for years after surgery, X-rays showing that the bone healed in the posterior section of the skull where the incision had been made.

Painkillers

Most powerful painkiller ■ The only anaesthetics at this time were opium, mandragora (a narcotic obtained from the mandrake plant), and alcohol. Of these opium is the most powerful. It can be dissolved in alcohol; this mixture is known as laudanum. Opium was obtained from the opium poppy and it contained many drugs called opium alkaloids. Morphine is one of these – as is codeine.

Most powerful analgesic ■ The most powerful analgesic for use on the battlefield was a species of frog that the Chinese used. Its skin contains opioids that when rubbed on an injured person's skin relieve pain.

First transplant ■ *In keeping with the influence of the Church over medicine, there were many saints associated with healing. Two of the most famous were Saints Cosmas and Damian. They performed possibly the first 'transplant' – certainly the first one to be recorded in an illustration. The two saints – who had many surgical miracles attributed to them – are seen transplanting a black leg on to a white man who has had one of his amputated.*

LITERATURE

Earliest German surgical manual ■ Heinrich von Pfolspeundt's *Buch der Bundth-Ertznei* (Book of bandage treatment) was written in 1460 and is the earliest known German surgical manual. Pfolspeundt was a Brother of the Herman Order and gained his experience in a number of military campaigns between this order and the Polish kings. He discusses the management of wounds and other injuries, including the method of removing gunpowder from a wound, which is the earliest mention of war injuries from firearms in surgical literature. The book remained in manuscript form and was never printed.

First illustrated printed surgical manual ■ Hieronymus Brunschwig was born in Strasbourg, France, in 1450 and spent his life in the city as a wound surgeon. His book, published in 1497, is one of the first books on surgery to appear in print and the first to contain illustrations. These depict doctors and patients and show the costumes, furnishings and medical customs of the period.

First major book of surgery ■ Guy de Chauliac (1298–1368) was without doubt the best known, if not greatest surgeon of the Middle Ages. While he lived and worked in the 14th century, his reputation became more widely established with the printing of his manual of surgery in 1478. Entitled *La Pratique en Chirurgie du Maistre Guidon de Chauliac* (The practice of surgery of Master Guidon de Chauliac) was especially important for distinguishing various kinds of hernia and describing an operation for its cure. It also gives his views on fractures and on the management of contaminated wounds. Perhaps somewhat surprisingly, he also included instructions on dentistry.

Earliest reproduction of an amputation ■ The 16th-century German surgeon, Hans von Gersdorf, wrote a handbook of wound surgery which was published in 1517. The book contains a large number of illustrations including the earliest reproduction of an amputation, showing the use of an animal bladder as a pressure bandage enclosing the stump.

Most important book on Dreams ■ Giralamo Cardano (1501–76) was best

Oldest still used ■ *The Hôtel-Dieu in Paris is today one of the oldest hospitals in the world, having been founded by the Bishop of Paris in the 7th century. Even in 1492 it was eight centuries old. The conditions were typically crowded, with some patients two in a bed. With little in the way of effective treatment, death was an everyday event familiar to everyone and corpses were loaded into shrouds in full view of the rest of the ward.*

known in his day as a professor of medicine at Pavia, Italy, and for his works on mathematics, notably algebra. In the field of astrology he contributed both to medical lore and to the study of character. His *Liber de exemplis genituarum* (Book of birth signs) is a book of the natal horoscopes of 100 contemporaries including such eminences as Erasmus, Albrecht Dürer, and Henry VIII. He emphasized the effects of the fixed stars within the constellations upon personality. His treatise on the interpretation of dreams *De Somnis* (About Dreams) is the first methodical original departure in this area since the fifth century. Like many modern writers he recommended keeping a written record of dreams and studying it to gain understanding of the soul. The study of philosophy he considered was helpful in separating emotions from perceptions. He believed that if properly understood dreams could help a person to understand his present situation, although some dreams might refer to future events. His therapeutic approach is similar to modern psychological practice; he found his work on his own dreams helpful in coming to terms with the tragic death of his son. Dreams were tremors of the animal spirit which could have two possible causes, physical (such as food) or psychic (such as anxiety or memory). The book includes 50 chapters on the symbolism of dream imagery.

First naval surgical manual ■ A very rare text on wounds and their treatment was written in 1474 by Bartholomeo dal Sarasin, and was published in 1513. It was written in the Venetian dialect so it could be understood by sailors in the Venetian fleet. Bartholomeo relies on the healing power of nature; he states that for small, fresh and uncomplicated wounds caused by a sword or knife only a bandage should be used, and for deep wounds a pad and a bandage; medicines may be put around the wound but not in the wound itself. He also suggests that the wound should be bathed daily with warm wine.

Hospitals

Best ■ In the 12th and 13th centuries the running of hospitals was gradually transferred from the Church to local government. The greatest hospitals of the time developed from this period. They include St Bartholomew's and St Thomas's in London, Santo Spirito in Rome, and the Hôtel-Dieu in Paris.

Medieval hospitals were not like their modern counterparts. They cared for the sick, old and homeless, but also educated young children and took in travellers. This was often on a fee-paying basis.

There were very many of these institutions. In the later middle ages, London had about 34 hospitals and almshouses. Most of these were funded by wealthy businessmen who saw this as their Christian duty. Richard (Dick) Whittington (died 1423), a wealthy cloth merchant and mayor of London, is the best remembered of such men. However, the day-to-day administration was often inefficient and corrupt, and many hospitals had to close down. For this reason, many began to be run by the civil authorities – four of London's 10 leper hospitals were run by the mayor.

Other remedies

First whisky ■ How to distil spirits from wine had been discovered in the 12th century. The product, thought of as a medicine, was called *aqua vitae* (water, or elixir, of life). By the 15th century other spirits were being distilled from other materials, notably whisky from malt. The exchequer rolls of King James IV of Scotland show that whisky was being drunk at court around 1500, though not entirely for medical reasons. Most spirits, however, maintained the fiction in their names. 'Whisky' is from *uisge*, an abbreviated form of the Gaelic *uisge beatha*, meaning 'water of life', and *eau de vie*, and *vodka* have the same derivation. Brandy, a 14th-century product, takes its name from the German *gebrannnter Wein*, meaning 'burnt' or distilled wine.

Most welcome cure-all ■ Wine had since Greek and Roman times been used for medicinal purposes; it was one of the few things that could dissolve the variety of chemicals used in treating a wide range of illnesses. Since the publication of Arnald of Villanova's treatise, *Liber de Vinis* (Book of Wine) around the beginning of the 14th century, wine had become widely used as a restorative, an antiseptic and for the preparation of poultices. By the end of the 15th century, theriacs made by dissolving vegetable, mineral and animal ingredients in wines had achieved widespread acceptance as cure-alls. The main centre of their production was Cairo. Arnald of Villanova recommended that if ginger and cinnamon bark were put into wine, and then the mixture was distilled like rose-water, the resultant distillate could cure paralysis, was good for cold complexions and ailments, and beautified women, giving them white, subtle and pleasant complexions.

Most fraudulent ■ The powdered horn of a unicorn was undoubtedly the most fraudulent wonder drug of the era.

Other aids

First mention of dentures ■ The Roman poet Martial (died 104 AD) mentions false teeth in one of his epigrams, the earliest known reference.

Earliest dentures ■ From discoveries made in Etruscan tombs, partial dentures were being worn in what is now Tuscany, Italy as early as 700 BC. Some were permanently attached to existing teeth and others were removable.

First complete set of dentures ■ The earliest set of dentures in Europe were found in a grave in Switzerland, dated to the early 16th century. The unknown wearer was equipped with false teeth carved from the thigh bone of an ox, the upper and lower sets joined with wire.

First eyeglasses ■ Eyeglasses were invented in Tuscany in the 1280s. Their use spread rapidly but their social effects were masked at first by the Black Death in the 14th century. In the 15th century it became apparent, however, that the promotion of younger men was being slowed, since in any profession that demanded frequent reading ageing men could keep actively at work longer. (The skills in making lenses were to be of importance in the 16th century in the development of the telescope.)

Transport

ON LAND • AT SEA • NAVIGATION

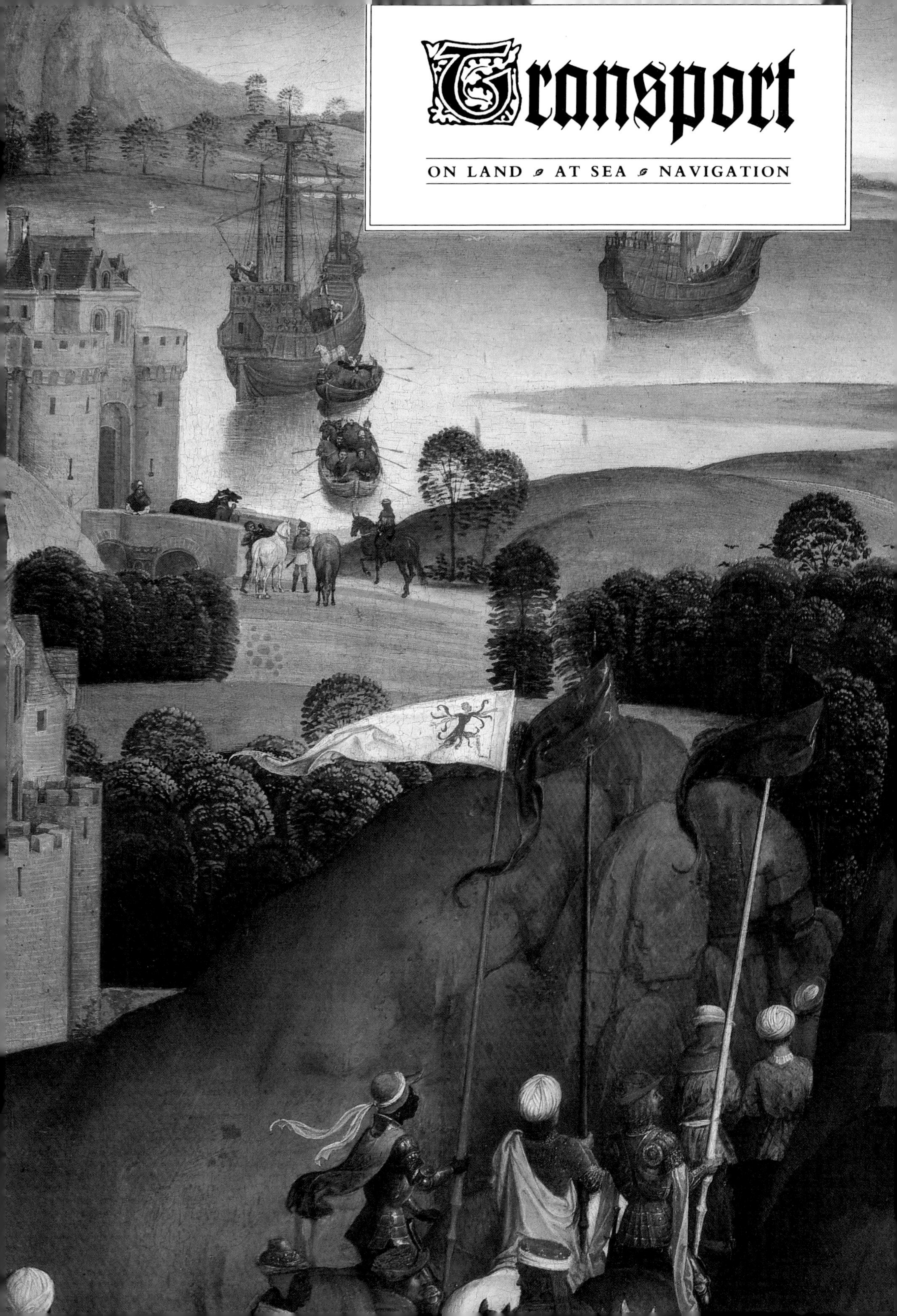

the guinness book of records 1492

Transport on land

Roads

Longest road network ■ The longest constructed road network in pre-Hispanic America was the *Inkario* of the Incas, comprising more than 12 420 miles *20 000 km* and stretching over more than 30 degrees of latitude from north to south, connecting what is now southern Colombia with Chile. In Mesoamerica, the longest known made-up road was that from Cobá to Yaxuná in Yucatan about 60 miles *100 km* long.

Inca roads followed the terrain for the wheel was unknown so they did not carry heavy traffic – transport was by foot and llama. In steep places the road might be cut out of the rock to form a sort of stairway. In flat places the road might become an avenue 23 ft *7 m* wide.

Highest paved road ■ The *Inkario* ran over passes 16 700 ft *5090 m* high between Huarochirí and Jauja, in present day Peru, as part of a lateral highway linking the coastal and highland road systems.

Highest tambo ■ A *tambos* is a way-station and warehouse along the Inca road system. The highest was Castillo Grande at Mallebamba, between Huamchuco and Conchucos, at over 13 000 ft *3960 m* above sea level.

Longest African caravan route ■ The Sahara was crossed by three main caravan roads which had been in operation since Carthaginian times. The longest of these ran from Tunis to Agades and was 1400 miles *2240 km* long. The other major caravan route from Marrakech, Morocco, to Timbuktu was about 1300 miles *2080 km* in length.

The most famous silk road ■ The silk route which linked China overland across the northern deserts to the Mediterranean, collapsed in the sixteenth century due to the new maritime trade routes. This extraordinary caravan route through the ages brought silks, spices, gold and wool, not least ideas, culture and civilization from one side of Eurasia to the other – the influences of many countries along the way may be seen from the designs picked up en route. Now the delicately woven silk stockings, finely embroidered satin bedspreads and sumptuous brocades, gold and silver ribbons and painted shawls were carefully packed and loaded not onto camels as in the past, but freighted aboard Chinese junks and transported to waiting European galleons, to sail west.

Greatest Indian road ■ The Sur Sultan Sher Shah, who deposed the second Mughal ruler Humayun from the throne of Delhi in 1530, had a major road, later called the Grand Trunk Road, constructed in north India. The road linked the Indus valley to the Bengal region in eastern India, and became a major linking route in the Mughal heartland.

Most mobile society ■ There was no road system in the Middle East and North Africa similar to that of the Romans. In these largely arid lands the camel was far more efficient than wheeled traffic for long-distance travel. The Islamic world in the Middle Ages was the most mobile society of any before modern times. The stimuli for this mobility were religious, commercial and political. Travellers were assisted by books that gave details of all the main routes throughout the Islamic world.

Earliest known pilgrim guide ■ *The Itinerary from Bordeaux to Jerusalem* was written in about AD 330. It gives distances between and locations of hostelries and places for changing horses or asses along the way. This book was copied, refined and reproduced in different forms over and over again during the next 1000 years or more.

First road maps ■ A 13th-century English monk, Matthew Paris, drew strip maps of routes for pilgrims to follow within England and south from Dover to Italy. These are regarded as the first usable road maps of Europe. Erhard Eyzlub, a compass maker from Nuremberg, Germany, compiled a road map in about 1500. Called *Der Rom Weg* (The Way to Rome), it showed the main travel routes to Rome by means of points from town to town from Denmark in the north to Naples in the south.

Busiest months ■ Although overland traffic could move through Europe at all times of the year, the roads were naturally better in the spring and summer months. The busiest months for trade were therefore from March to July. As the overland journey across Europe could take as long as three months, and merchant ships did not sail much in the Mediterranean in the stormy winter months, there were great fluctuations in trade patterns through the year. An Italian commentator, Guicciardini, writing in 1567, said that at that time there might be 500 ships in the river at Antwerp, with 200 passenger coaches and 2000 wagons a day loading from them. This may have been an exaggeration, and traffic may have been less 20 years earlier, but there were certainly about 40 road convoys a month from Antwerp in the busy seasons.

Highest passes ■ In the western Alps, for routes between Italy and France, this was that of the Great St Bernard (8111 ft *2472 m*). It was named after Bernard of Menthon, who had founded its celebrated hospice four centuries earlier. The monastery was at the height of its power, with 98 *curés* alone and many benefits, priories, farms and also lands abroad. In the central Alps, for Italy and the Rhine valley, the Septimer (7582 ft *2310 m*) was open, though difficult in snowy conditions. More frequently crossed was the Splügen (6945 ft *2116 m*). The San Gotthard (6936 ft *2114 m*) involved travellers and animals between Andermatt and Göschenen in crossing by a suspended gangway and 'the Devil's Bridge' in order to get round a steep cliff in the Schöllenen gorge. They made good use of the hospice. In the eastern Alps, for routes between Italy and the Danube, was the Brenner (4495 ft *1370 m*).

Postal system

Postal services ■ Postal services were organized whenever there was a strong central government in the Islamic world. There were many staging posts, usually 15 miles *24 km* apart. Couriers used mainly camels. Postmasters were responsible not only for the transmission of official letters, but also for providing central government with intelligence on the fiscal, economic and political situation in the provinces. In Mamluk times, 1250–1517, there was an efficient pigeon post – even using a special lightweight 'airmail' paper.

Newest postal system ■ In India, as elsewhere, messages were sent by an organized relay system of runners or on horseback with a changeover every few miles. Ibn Battuta (1304–68), the Arab traveller, reported that the foot messengers often reached their destinations faster than the mounted post. In 1528 the Mughal ruler Babur (1527–30) improved the service. He ordered that the road from Agra to Kabul be surveyed and every 36 miles *57 km* a station built where post-horses would always be ready to take the messages onward.

Fastest messengers ■ The pride of the Inca world was its postal system which was instituted by the 9th Inca, Pachacuti Inca Yupanqui (1438–71), in about 1450. There were two royal roads along which a regular postal service was maintained. The higher, or Andean, of 3250 miles *5200 km* length ran from the Ancasmayo river in Colombia to Tucuman in Argentina; it was completed in 1498. The Spaniard, Pedro de Cieza de Leon, travelled the entire length of it between 1547 and 1550. The shorter coastal road of 2520 miles *4032 km* led from Tumbes in northern Peru to Maule in Chile. The *Chasquis* ('he who receives, he who gives') postal runners of the Inca Empire ran an average of 1½ miles *2.4 km* per stage at altitudes of up to 17 160 ft *5232 m*. At each posting station was an *O'kla* (stone hut) in which two runners were stationed for periods of 15 days. At about every 10th *O'kla* was provided a *Tambos* (food station). The speed of communication from Quito to Cuzco, a distance of 1250 miles *2000 km*, was five days or an amazing 250 miles *400 km* per day or an average rate of 5¾ minutes per mile *3.6 min/km* over mountainous terrain!

Ice by post ■ A remarkable use of the postal service was the transport of ice for

PREVIOUS PAGE: A detail from Hans Memling's Embarkation of the Magi *provides a record of 15th century means of transport.*

cooling drinks. In Mamluk times five camel-loads were sent at regular intervals from Syria to Egypt, at the expense of the Egyptian treasury.

Carriers

Fastest European journey times ■ To Venice, by mail, the fastest recorded time from Rome is 1½ days for a journey of 360 miles *576 km*. From Paris it is seven days, from Barcelona in Spain, eight, from London nine, from Constantinople 15, and from Damascus in Syria, 28 days. A special courier could improve on these, if only because, at the end of the 15th century, it was customary to pay a decreasing fee according to the length of time taken. Ordinary mails depended more on their frequency and general standards than on the distance covered. They often took bizarre routes. The King of Portugal's ambassadors at Rome sent their letters to Lisbon via Antwerp, Belgium, hundreds of miles too far north.

Fastest journeys ■ On average a horse and rider can travel at about 15 mph *24 kph*. With regular changes of horse, a rider can achieve some surprising journeys. A relay of riders took only two days to cover the 400 miles *640 km* from London to Edinburgh in 1482.

The covered wagon or cart of 15th century European travel might be pulled by two horses or as many as six. Later, coaches had larger rear than front wheels which made travel considerably more comfortable.

Best adapted and fastest animals ■ In 1483 Friar Felix Fabri, a German monk and pilgrim, extolled the virtues of the camel as being 'especially well adapted and fitted for crossing the desert', reporting that it 'can go 100 Italian miles in one day'. The other great advantages he saw for the camel as a beast of burden in the desert are that 'it eats but little food, grazing on hay, bark and leaves . . . they are fond of foul water . . . and can endure thirst for many days, and, wondrous to tell, can go for 12 days without drink'.

First 'wagons' ■ The medieval cart was a heavy and cumbersome vehicle. Its suspension was primitive. In the 1400s the wagon body hung by straps from posts fastened to the axles. Court ladies travelled in *chars*, known in England as whirlicotes. The body rested directly on the wheels and two, four or six horses were harnessed. The covering was a leather or woollen canopy stretched over hoops. Until the 1400s front and rear wheels were the same size. The coach, which was more comfortable and had rear wheels much larger than the front wheels, could be pulled by a single horse. Hungarian coaches (named after Kocs, a town in Hungary where they were made in the 1400s) were admired throughout Europe for their lightness. (The first coach in England was made about 1555, by Walter Rippon for the Earl of Rutland. About this time the word 'wagon' (denoting a heavier working vehicle) appears in English.)

Longest-living transport contractors ■ A Scottish transport firm, Shore Porter Society of Aberdeen, was founded in 1498. In that year the town council decided to pay shore porters or *pynours*, as they were then called, to carry barrels from the quay to any part of the burgh. (The Society formed then continued for centuries as a partnership with a transport fleet, a furniture store, and a bonded warehouse.)

Most extraordinary way of transporting children ■ Europeans coming to America were astonished by the way Indian women carried their babies on their backs. This might be done in a baby-carrying basket, a kind of wooden bowl hung over the back. Carriers similar to this were used throughout the Americas by women who needed to carry their small children with them while they worked.

First description of *travois* ■ Pedro de Castaneda who accompanied Francisco Vasquez de Coronado across America in 1540–2, described the *travois* used by the Plains Indians: 'They travel with their tents and troops of dogs loaded with poles and having Moorish pack-saddles with girths. When the load gets disarranged, the dogs howl, calling some one to fix them right.' The dogs' loads were estimated at about 50 lb *20 kg*.

First pleasure sledges ■ Jaunting sledges pulled by donkeys or dogs were popular in Germany, particularly in the Nuremberg district. In 1452 there was an outcry against gambling and frivolity, and 52 of these jaunting sledges were burnt in Nuremberg market-place.

Waterways

Earliest port ■ The Phoenicians built harbours at Sidon and Tyre on the eastern coast of the Mediterranean as early as 1350 BC.

Largest port ■ The ports of Alexandria, Egypt, Genoa and Venice, in Italy, vied for the title of the Mediterranean's largest port in the 15th century.

Wealthiest northern port ■ The Venetians, who were very widely travelled, judged Antwerp, Belgium, to be the world's largest and wealthiest port in the 15th century. The Venetian ambassador described how 'everywhere there money flows with the sale of everything, and each man, no matter how low or lazy, becomes in his way rich'. By the start of the 16th century, Antwerp had a population of more than 100 000 and there were many hundreds of foreign businesses operating from the port.

Valuable cargoes ■ The most valuable cargoes regularly carried in European waters were those of the Venetian galleys. The pepper they carried sold at £200 a ton in northern Europe. This was at a time when a new ship could be built for £3–4 a ton. Precious metals were sent from the Red Sea port of Jidda to India in such amounts that objects of exceptional value were described as 'worth more than a Jidda ship'.

Major European merchant fleets ■ The fleet belonging to Venice was the largest at about 80 000 tons. That of the Hanseatic League came next at about 60 000 tons, about the same size as those of the towns of the future Dutch republic. The fleet of Genoa at about 30 000 was a poor fourth.

Size of fleets ■ Vessels commonly sailed in fleets. The reasons for this were various: cargoes were often only seasonally available; winds, notably the monsoons of Asia, rigorously determined the times at which ships could move; there was safety in numbers; if all the merchants departed and arrived together, no merchant could enjoy an unfair advantage over his fellows. In the West the biggest of these fleets were those entering and leaving the Baltic. They might comprise 100 or so vessels. Larger still were the fleets which fished for herring in the North Sea. These often numbered up to 500 craft.

Most taxed rivers ■ River transport was easy to tax, for a barge could not change direction as a cart could do. In 1500 there were as many as 70 tolls to be paid along the Rhine in Germany, and on the Seine in France it was said there was a toll to be paid by barges every 6–7 miles *10–12 km*.

Longest artificial waterway ■ The Chinese Grand Canal (Da Yunhe) was just over 1000 miles *1600 km* long: most sections were over 100 ft *30 m* wide. It ran from Hangzhou in the south to the capital at Beijing in the north, crossing five great rivers on its way. A clever system of lock gates and feeder streams allowed it to climb to 189 ft *57 m* above sea level near its mid-point. It was built between 600 and 1327 by a workforce rising above 5 000 000.

Highest-priority foods ■ In Ming China, the Directorate of Ceremonies had first call on Grand Canal transport and facilities. Next in line was the Directorate of Foodstuffs, who were entitled to priority over everyone else when transporting plums, loquats, bamboo shoots and the fruit of the strawberry tree – on ice – to the Imperial Court. (The Chinese had been using ice to chill and conserve food since about 600 BC, almost 2000 years before anyone else.)

China's capital city was in the north during this period, but its most important grain-producing areas were in the south. The artificial transport artery of the Chinese Grand Canal was therefore essential for the survival of the imperial state.

First Suez Canal ■ When Friar Felix Fabri on pilgrimage in the Holy Lands in 1483 came to the Red Sea he was relieved to find he did not need to cross it by ship as he had believed it to be joined to the Mediterranean. He greatly admired the ancient Egyptian attempt 'to bring the Red Sea into the Nile; wherefore they began to dig through the mountains of the isthmus at the head of the sea, to divide hills, cut through the midst of stones and rocks, and made a canal and waterway to the city of Arsinoe, which is also called Cleopatridis. This trench was first begun by Sesostris, King of Egypt, before the Trojan War, at a great cost, and afterwards Darius, King of Persia, attempted to make it, but left it unfinished. Afterwards it was completed with consummate art by Ptolemy II, yet in such a manner that the ditch was closed up and would open to himself alone. By this work the men of old meant to join together the East and the West . . .'

Panama Canal ■ The Spaniard, Gaspar de Espinosa, first proposed digging a canal with the help of 2000 native American workers from the Pacific to the Caribbean. It was 400 years before his vision became a reality.

Canoes

Largest in the Americas ■ Christopher Columbus first saw *canoa* (canoes) in the Caribbean during his first voyage of 1492–3: 'They have in all the islands very many canoes, after the manner of rowing galleys, some larger, some smaller; and a good many are larger than a galley of 18 benches. They are not so wide, because they are made of a single log of timber (carved and fire-burned from single great silk-wood trees) . . . a galley could not keep up with them in rowing, for their motion is a thing beyond belief . . . I have seen some of these canoes with 70, and 80, men in them, each one with his oar [actually paddle] as they face forward.' The largest he saw were capable of carrying up to 150 people.

Timbered canoes ■ A member of Columbus' second voyage (1493) reported that: 'The larger vessels have their sides constructed of timbers fastened together and are 80 ft *24.4 m* long . . . for oars they have broad boards, such as our bakers use for oven shovels.' In 1494 Columbus measured one dugout at 96 ft *29 m* and in 1502 young Ferdinand Columbus describes 25-paddle canoes 8ft *2.5 m* wide in the Bay of Honduras.

First to paddle across America ■ In 1513 Vasco Núñez de Balboa, commander of the coast of Panama, obtained some dugout canoes and paddled through the rainforest from the Caribbean to the Pacific, the first European to do so.

Speediest transport ■ When Mexico was conquered in 1521 it was estimated there were 50 000 canoes in the capital Tenochtitlan and other nearby lakes. Acailan (land of canoes) was a major trading place in the Chiapas province of south Mexico whose traders could, in a little more than a day, paddle the 100 miles *160 km* to the Gulf coast, although it would take nearly three days to paddle back.

First description of a *kayak* ■ Although kayaks would have been seen often, Master Dioise Settle, chronicler of Martin Frobisher's voyage of 1577, was the first to record this. He describes two types of leather boats of Baffin Island, Canada: 'The great sort are not unlike our wherries (actually an Umiak), wherein sixteene or twenty men may sit . . . the other boate (*kayak*) is but for one man to sit and row in with one oare.'

Greatest recorded native American armada ■ In March 1541 Hernandes de Soto met the Indian chief Aquixo who was souzerain of many towns and people along the Mississippi. Aquixo arrived with 200 canoes filled with armed men. They were painted with ochre, wore great bunches of white and coloured plumes, and carried feathered shields. The warriors – fine-looking men – stood erect from bow to stern in each canoe, sheltering the oarsmen. In the chief's barge Aquixo sat under an awning and issued orders to the rest. A contemporary Portuguese observer said 'it appeared like a famous armada of galleys.'

Earliest sea-going boats

Aborigines are thought to have been able to cross the Torres Straits from New Guinea to Australia, then at least 43½ miles *70 km* across, as long ago as 40 000 BC. They are believed to have used double canoes. The earliest 'vessel' surviving to this day is a pinewood dugout found in Pesse, Netherlands, and dated to *c.* 6315±275 BC, now in the Provincial Museum, Assen. The earliest representation of a boat is disputed between possible rock art outlines of Mesolithic skin boats in Høgnipen, Norway (*c.* 8000–7000 BC); Minateda, Spain (7000–3000 BC); and Kobystan (8000–6000 BC).

Most homogeneous boats ■ The people of the Maldive Islands, in the Indian Ocean, made their boats from a single species of tree, the coconut palm. The hulls, masts, sails and rigging all came from the timber or coir of the palm. It also provided the cargo.

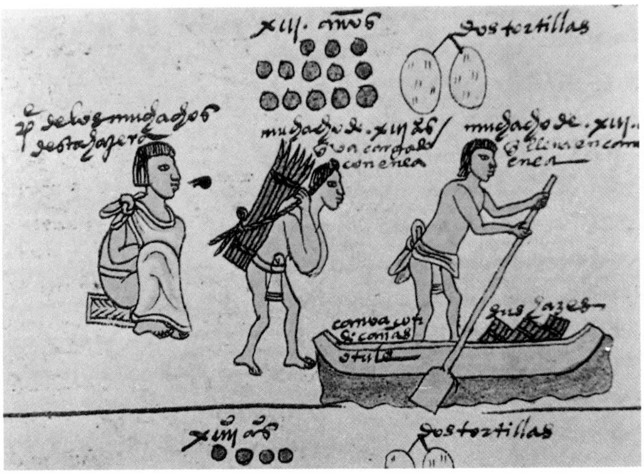

Possibly the earliest picture of an American dugout canoe was that in the Codex Mendoza *of about 1530.*

Oared ships

Most successful ▪ In the 15th and 16th centuries these were the 'great galleys' operated in the Mediterranean. They were armed merchant vessels, operating under sail as well as oars, and well able to defend themselves. They had a high reputation for safety and reliability, particularly those used by the Venetian Republic. Their maximum dimensions were length, stem to stern: about 135 ft *41 m*; breadth (hull only): 16–17 ft *5 m*.

Biggest in northern Europe ▪ Oared warships were very important in the Mediterranean, but less so in the rougher seas of the north. Nevertheless, the English and French monarchies used many oared fighting ships. Probably the biggest was Henry VIII's 800-ton *Great Galley* of 1515, perhaps also the last big clinker-built ship constructed in England.

Most power ▪ The traditional method for positioning oarsmen involved staggered rowing-benches, on which were seated several oarsmen, each man working his own oar. From about 1534 (at Venice), a new system was introduced. Now all the men on a bench worked the same oar. This simpler system allowed more men to be put to an oar, increasing speed and power.

Fastest ▪ Light war galleys could reach speeds of 7–10 knots, but only in short bursts of 20 minutes or so. Average speed under oars was about 2–3 knots in a day's voyage. The big canoe-like craft of southern Asia could probably match this speed. The great galleys of the Mediterranean also achieved remarkable speeds and could cover great distances very rapidly. These great galleys were three-masted and when at sea relied mostly on their sails, using their oars only over short distances and in emergencies. In 1509 there was a threat of war and galleys from Otranto, Italy, were ordered home from Southampton, England, urgently. They covered the 2500 miles *4000 km* in 31 days – a speed of over 80 miles *128 km* a day.

The oared ships of the Mediterranean did not depend on the oarsmen alone, but, as shown in this drawing of a Venetian galley by the Italian painter Raphael, they also used sails.

Last great galleys ▪ With the collapse of Venetian trade in the 15th century came the collapse of her superiority in shipping. The sailings of the last great galleys to North Africa ended in 1532 and to northern Europe three years later. In 1535, 26 great galleys totalling nearly 4000 tons had sailed from Venice; in 1557 only four galleys sailed.

Last surviving galley ▪ This is preserved in the Maritime Museum in Istanbul, Turkey. Called simply *Kadirga* (Turkish for galley), this 24-oar galley is

CHINESE SHIP CONSTRUCTION

Traditional Chinese ship and boat construction was (and remains) very different from that of Europe. Plank-fastenings were different, and the hulls had rigid watertight interior bulkheads that increased their strength and ability to survive. The largest ships were multi-masted, with tall, narrow lug-sails reinforced with horizontal battens. Some Chinese ships were flat-bottomed and bluff-bowed, but by no means all: keels and pointed bows were not uncommon, especially in sea-going vessels. The rudders of Chinese ships were large and could be raised or lowered to accommodate changes in water depth or to reduce leeway.

A view from the sea of the important and busy port of Genoa, in northern Italy (1481).

traditionally connected with Sultan Mehmet II, who conquered Constantinople in 1453.

First rudders ■ Rudders were first employed in Asian vessels, quite possibly Chinese junks. This invention allowed the efficient and simple control of the helm and was suited to directing the course of vessels of any size. The steering oar that had been employed previously and was to remain in use in the West until well into the 13th century limited the size of ships, as a steering oar could not be handled without the mechanical assistance of blocks, gears or quadrants. It is more than likely that the European age of exploration would never have begun without the introduction of the rudder from eastern seas.

First hydrodynamically efficient rudder ■ In addition to pioneering the use of rudders, the Chinese designed rudders that resembled latticework. The principle was that, by allowing water to flow through the rudder, control of the vessel could be maintained without the strain of pushing great quantities of water from side to side. The latticework or fenestrated rudder is believed to have been developed when it was seen that a rudder with holes was efficient and less demanding of the helmsman's strength; an invention was born. The design works admirably and is still in use, but the idea has not been widely adopted outside China.

First modern hull design ■ Chinese junks were built so that the greatest beam measurement was well aft rather than, as in European construction, about 40 per cent of the distance from the stem to the stern. Such a design reduces the drag of friction as the hull moves through the water and is today a favoured model for advanced racing yachts. Traditionally, Western sailing vessels' hulls were modelled after the shape of codfish or haddock, that is, widest towards the head, whereas the design of junk hulls was inspired by water birds. As birds, like ships, move on the surface of the water, the logic is clear.

First watertight compartments ■ As early as the 10th century (and possibly by the second century AD) Chinese junks were built with watertight compartments to allow the vessels to float even if holed below the waterline. Marco Polo was the first Westerner to marvel at this invention, which much later came to be adopted by shipbuilders around the world.

First stabilizers ■ The forwardmost watertight compartment on large Chinese vessels was often designed to permit water to flow in and out through holes drilled at the waterline. The purpose was to reduce pounding and pitching in heavy seas by allowing the compartment to flood when the bow plunged and to drain as the bow was subsequently lifted, thus lessening the violence of the motion.

This illustration in the 1497 charter of the German city of Hamburg shows a number of square-rigged ships.

Handiest sail plan ■ The fore and aft rigged lug sails of Chinese junks, unlike European square sails, could be handled by small crews working from the deck. Reefing the sails was uniquely simple and efficient; the full-length battens permitted quickly dropping a sail to reduce its area in heavy weather. The lowered battens and the unused parts of the sail would simply be lashed together along the boom. There was never any need for crew to go aloft. Junk sails could also be trimmed for maximum aerodynamic efficiency, as a sheet (controlling line) was attached to the end of each batten. On the largest vessels, masts were often staggered rather than placed along the centre line of the hull in order that no sail would blanket another when the vessels were running before the wind.

First skeleton-built ships in northern Europe ■ Although skeleton-built vessels from the Mediterranean had voyaged to northern Europe since the late 1200s, no ships of this type are known to have been built in the north before the 1400s.

SHIP CONSTRUCTION IN EUROPE

There were two great traditions of ship construction and rig in medieval Europe, which stayed largely separate until the 1400s. The typical seagoing vessel of northern Europe had a single square sail and a clinker-built hull. The square sail was well designed for sailing with the wind behind, but it was not very effective for sailing into the wind. Clinker construction involved building a hull from a shell of overlapping planks, fastened at the edges. The strength of the structure lay in the shell of planks, rather than in the frames inserted into it (see diagrams). The larger sailing ships of southern Europe and the Mediterranean had a single square sail on the mainmast (the square sail was a northern development, adopted in the Mediterranean in about 1300), but they also sometimes had a triangular lateen sail on a mizzenmast. The lateen had good windward sailing properties, and made the ship more manoeuvrable. The hulls of southern ships were skeleton-built (sometimes called carvel construction), made from pre-erected skeletons of frames on to which the planks were nailed, giving the hull a smooth appearance.

In the space of a few decades in the 1400s, these two traditions merged to produce a truly 'European' type of ship, using the same basic rig and construction technology. It was this type of ship that provided Columbus and the other early explorers with the means to cross the oceans – and gave them a better chance of coming back. The first step towards this was the adoption of the two-masted rig.

The Portuguese spread this construction technique to the north. The hull construction of their little skeleton-built

FROM 1-MASTER TO 4-MASTER C1400 TO C1480

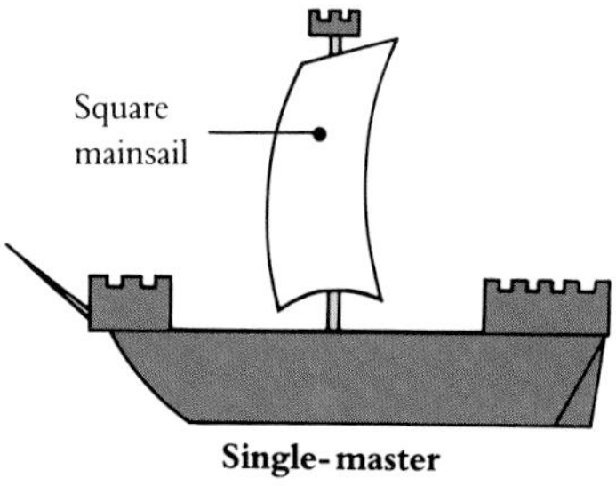

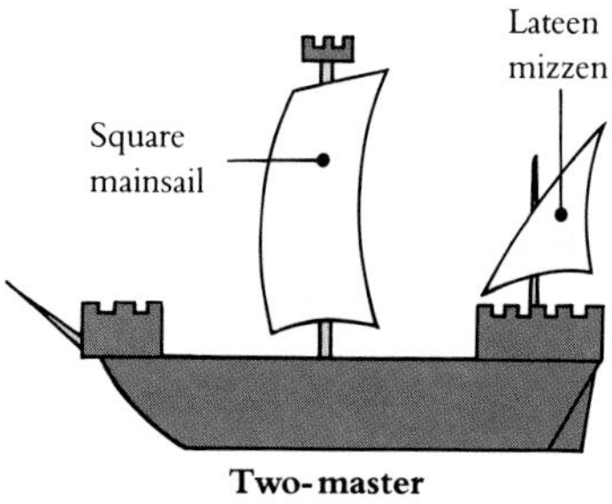

caravels was copied by northerners, probably because skeleton-building cost less in terms of skilled labour and materials than the clinker construction they had used hitherto. Skeleton-built hulls also seem to have been stronger and easier to repair. Northerners called the 'new' ship-types 'carvels', which is how the term carvel-built originated.

First carvel in northern Europe ■ The carvel constructed at Sluys in Flanders between 1438 and 1440 is the first known of its kind in the region. In 1439 Portuguese shipwrights built a *karveel* for the Duke of Burgundy near Brussels (now Belgium). The first English-owned carvel was probably the *Carvel* of Portsmouth, owned by the pirate Clais Stephens in 1450.

Greatest caravel before 1500 ■ Although most caravels were small vessels in the 1400s, some were very large. The greatest in northern Europe before 1500 was probably the 700-ton *Peter* of La Rochelle, in France. Seized at Danzig (now Gdansk, Poland), in 1462, this ship was studied by local shipwrights and became the means by which they learned skeleton construction. The *Peter* was a privately-owned vessel, but most of the very largest ships in Europe between 1400 and 1600 were those built by governments for use in war.

First two-masters in England ■ The 120-ton balinger *Anne* (a galley-type vessel) was the first two-master known to be built in England. She was built at Southampton in 1416. The idea for a two-masted rig may have come from the example of a number of large Genoese carracks that the English had captured.

First three-masters ■ The first clear evidence for a square-rigged three-master in northern Europe dates from 1436, when the royal balinger (sloop) *Petit Jesus* was rebuilt at Bursledon in Hampshire, England. This small 36-oar warship had a foresail, mainsail and mizzen. Two of Columbus' ships in 1492 were square-rigged three-masters: the *Santa Maria* and the carvel *Pinta*. The third, the carvel *Niña*, had only lateen sails to begin with. However, she was converted to square rig en route, in the Canary Islands. Square-riggers were much better than lateeners at sailing before the prevailing winds in the Atlantic and other oceans.

First 'European' ship ■ The combination of the three- or four-masted square rig with the skeleton-built hull produced a basic type of ship that was common to both northern and southern Europe. It was the first pan-European ship type. The first recorded ship of this kind was a carvel belonging to a Barcelona shipowner, Narcis Argullol. In 1453 he had a new set of sails made for his ship: square main and foresails, and a lateen mizzen. Sir John Howard's carvel (built at Dunwich in Suffolk between 1463 and 1466) is the earliest known example of the new type in England, although probably not the first actually to be built.

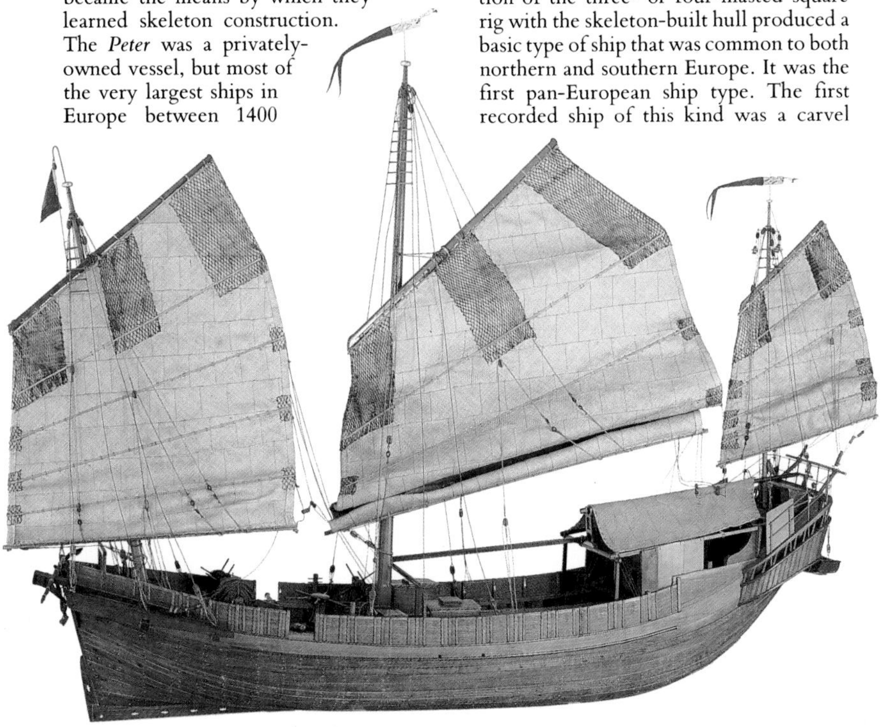

A model of a Chinese ocean-going junk shows how the sails could be worked by the crew from the deck.

THREE-MASTED SHIPS

The three-masted square rig was a 15th-century development. It combined the sailing qualities of the square main and foresails and the lateen mizzen. The new rig made ships much more manoeuvrable than the old one- or two-masters. Other masts and sails were added, such as topmasts on the lower masts, and a sail carried on a yard under the bowsprit. A fourth mast, the bonaventure ('good luck') mast, had appeared on large ships by the 1470s, perched on the stern and carrying another lateen sail. However, it was the three-masted square rig that was more common, and found even on very small ships. The development of the three-master did more than just facilitate the oceanic voyages: it set the pattern for European ship rig until the 19th century.

Largest ships

Largest ships in the world ■ Between 1405 and 1433, the Chinese emperor's Grand Eunuch, Cheng Ho, led a series of great fleets on voyages to Java, India and even East Africa. The biggest of his ships were probably the world's largest up until that time. These great ships each had five masts and were said to have been over 426 ft *130 m* in length. The biggest had 12 decks and could carry many hundreds of men. Their displacement has been measured at over 3000 tons. Domestic political pressure eventually killed off Cheng Ho's series of voyages, but had this not happened, it would not have been at all

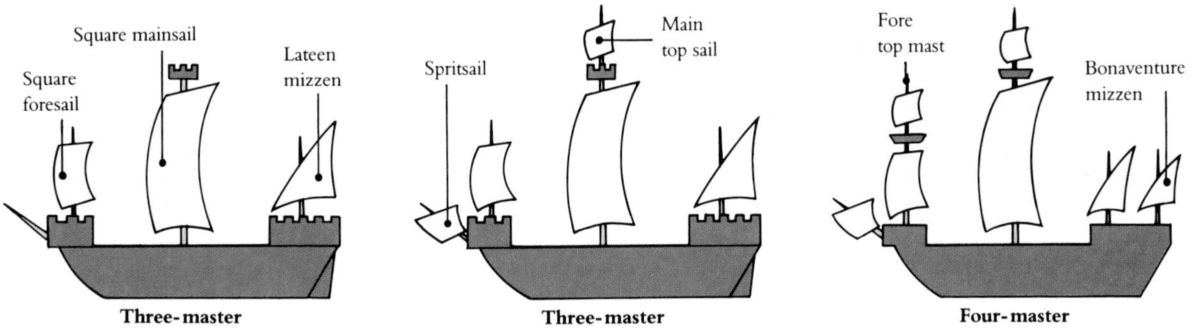

impossible for some of these powerful, seaworthy ships to have rounded the Cape of Good Hope and perhaps to have reached Europe. The first vessels on which Vasco da Gama made his voyage were tiny by Asian standards of ocean-going vessels. In 1510–11, the Portuguese fought and sank a great south-east Asian *jong* in the Straits of Malacca, which may have been over 1000 tons, that is over 10 times the size of some of da Gama's vessels.

Largest surviving Chinese ship ■ The *Quanzhou Ship* was discovered in the mud of Quanzhou Bay, Fujian Province, China. The hull of this great ship of the late 13th century survived only from the waterline down, but it is estimated that the overall length of the ship would have been 113 ft 6 in *34.6 m*, with a breadth of 32 ft 2½ in *9.82 m*, and a draught of 9ft 10 in *3 m*. Twelve great bulkheads divided the hull into 13 compartments. The hull bottom was V-shaped, with a keel and pointed bow. The ship had at least two, and probably three, masts.

Largest recorded Indian ships ■ The Italian traveller Nicolo Conti, who travelled in India and the East between 1414 and 1439, wrote that he had seen Indian ships with five masts, indicating that some Indian vessels of the 15th century were of great size.

Largest Japanese ships ■ The ships used to conduct the 'tally trade' between Japan and China 1404–1547 carried 150–200 people and had an estimated gross tonnage on 246 tons. The tally trade was established in 1404 when the Japanese were given a number of divided certificates (*kango*) which they had to produce on arrival in China and which had to match or tally with the half retained in Peking (Beijing) and Chekiang on the southern China coast. This enabled the Chinese to distinguish between official Japanese missions and ships belonging to Japanese pirates who had been active in the East China Sea since the 1350s.

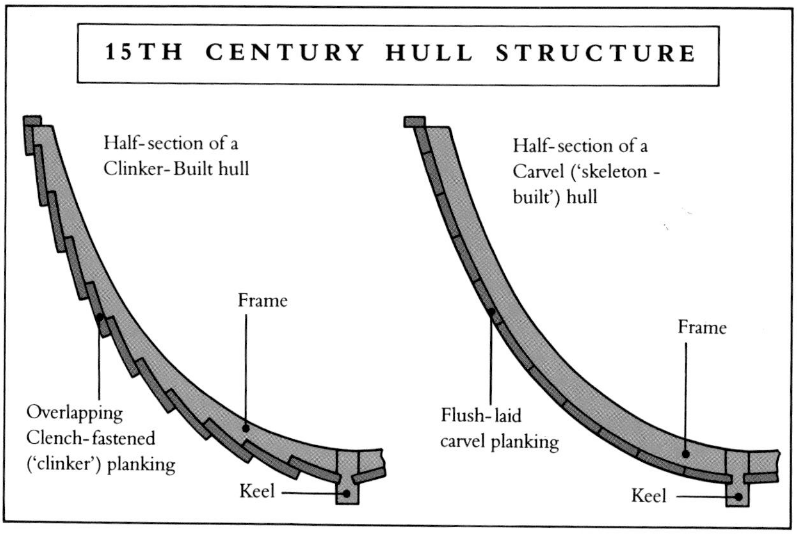

Largest English ships ■ The 1400-ton three-masted warship *Grâce Dieu*, constructed at Southampton between 1416 and 1420 for Henry V, holds this record. This huge warship never saw action, and was laid up in the River Hamble in Hampshire, to be destroyed by fire in 1439. (The bottom of her hull survives today in the Hamble mud: the keel is over 125 ft *38 m* in length.) The *Grâce Dieu* had an innovative three-masted rig, but her hull was built in the traditional clinker fashion. Each run of planks was three boards thick!

The *Henry Grâce à Dieu* (1000 tons) was constructed for Henry VIII at Woolwich near London between 1512 and 1514. Unlike the *Grâce Dieu* of 1418, this ship had a long and active career, before her accidental loss by fire in 1553.

Largest European sailing vessels ■ The 'hulks' of the Hanseatic cities of Germany could be up to 500 tons. They were used to carry freights like timber and grain from the Baltic. Bigger still were the high-built carracks of Genoa and Venice which could range up to 2000 tons.

Spanish caravels like these were often used on the early voyages of exploration.

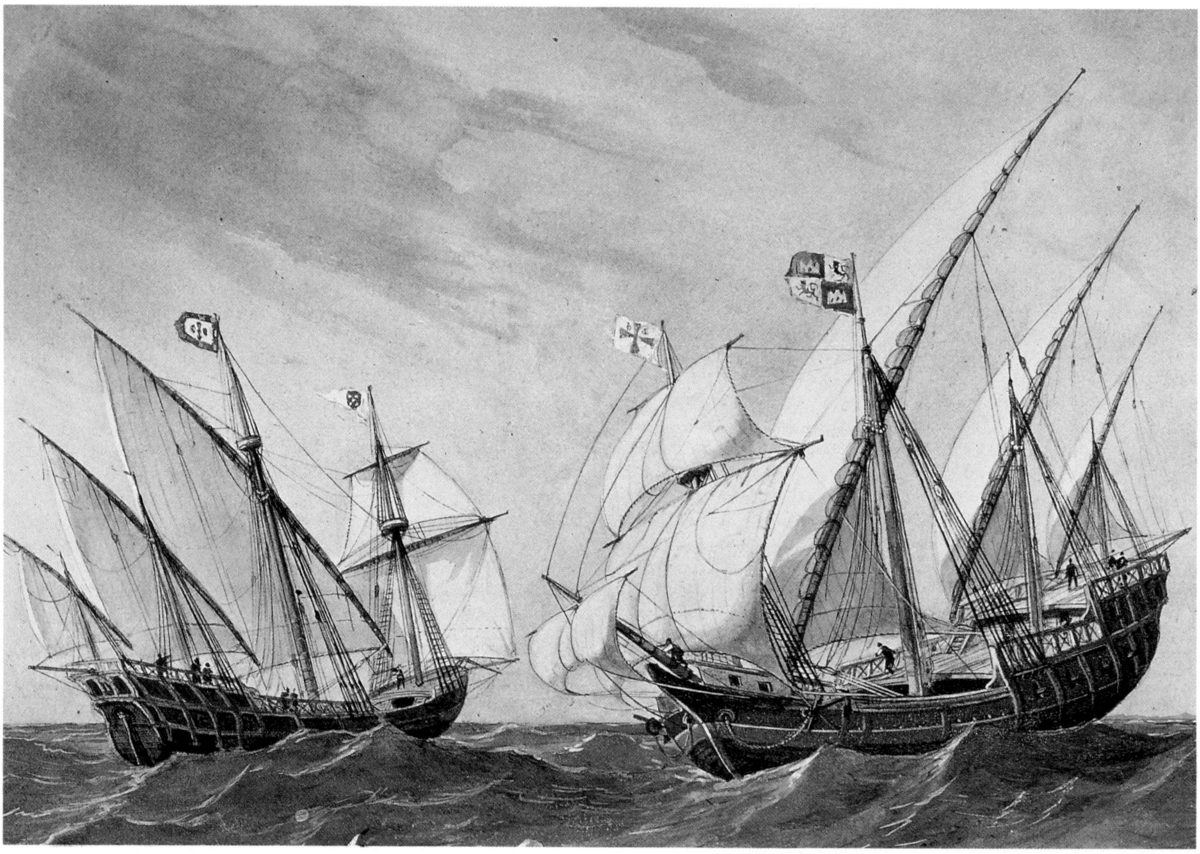

Fastest ships

European sailing craft ■ The caravels of Portugal and Spain were capable, like that of Columbus, of reaching 11 knots *13 mph*. This speed was not to be surpassed for centuries.

Fastest journey ■ Columbus set a time on the outward leg of his journey which was never beaten by his Spanish successors. He took only 72 days to reach the Bahamas.

Longest commercial voyage in European waters ■ The Genoese carracks carrying alum for use in dyestuffs from the eastern Mediterranean to the cloth manufacturing centres of the north and returning with textiles, made round trips of 7145 miles *11 500 km*. Venetian merchant galleys also took Mediterranean and oriental luxuries such as spices, silk and carpets to the ports of southern England and the Low Countries, in northern Europe. They could make the direct run home of 2485 miles *4000 km* non-stop.

Most expensive ship ■ All of the 'great ships' built to serve the pride and ambitions of royal masters were hugely expensive in contemporary terms, but perhaps none of them was more costly than the Scottish warship *Great Michael*, built for James IV in 1511. Her £3000 (Scottish) annual wages bill used up about 10 per cent of James IV's total income!

Most unsuccessful ship ■ As far as the Turkish sultans were concerned, this was the ship ordered by Mehmet the Conqueror (1451–81). He had been impressed by Genoese sailing ships, and ordered one to the same design to be built in his arsenal at Constantinople. On launching, it capsized immediately, and its Greek designer fled for his life.

First ships' hammocks ■ Until 1492 sailors slept on the decks of their ships or, in bad weather, down below on the cargo or ballast. They found in the West Indies that people used hammocks as beds and these were soon introduced as a comfortable, space-saving form of sailor's bed.

Largest anchor ■ The largest anchor may have been one of those belonging to Henry V of England's great ship *Grâce Dieu* of 1418 (see above). This iron anchor was 17 ft 2 in *5.23 m* long and its arms were 11 ft 5 in *3.5 m* wide.

Most remote sell-by date ■ When the new-style ships of the 15th century launched themselves onto the wide, unknown oceans of the world, their provisioning consisted mainly of preserved foods – brine-cured meats, dried peas and dried bread. 'Ship's biscuit', as the bread was called, was mass-produced from a flour and water dough baked to a state of such hardness that it was reckoned to remain edible, if not palatable, for as long as 50 years – provided the biscuit weavils did not get to it first. Sailors normally broke the bread down and soaked it in water to make a kind of cold porridge, and Columbus' son Ferdinand reported that, on his fourth voyage, 'the biscuit was so full of worms that, God help me, I saw many wait until nightfall to eat the porridge made of it so as not to see the worms.'

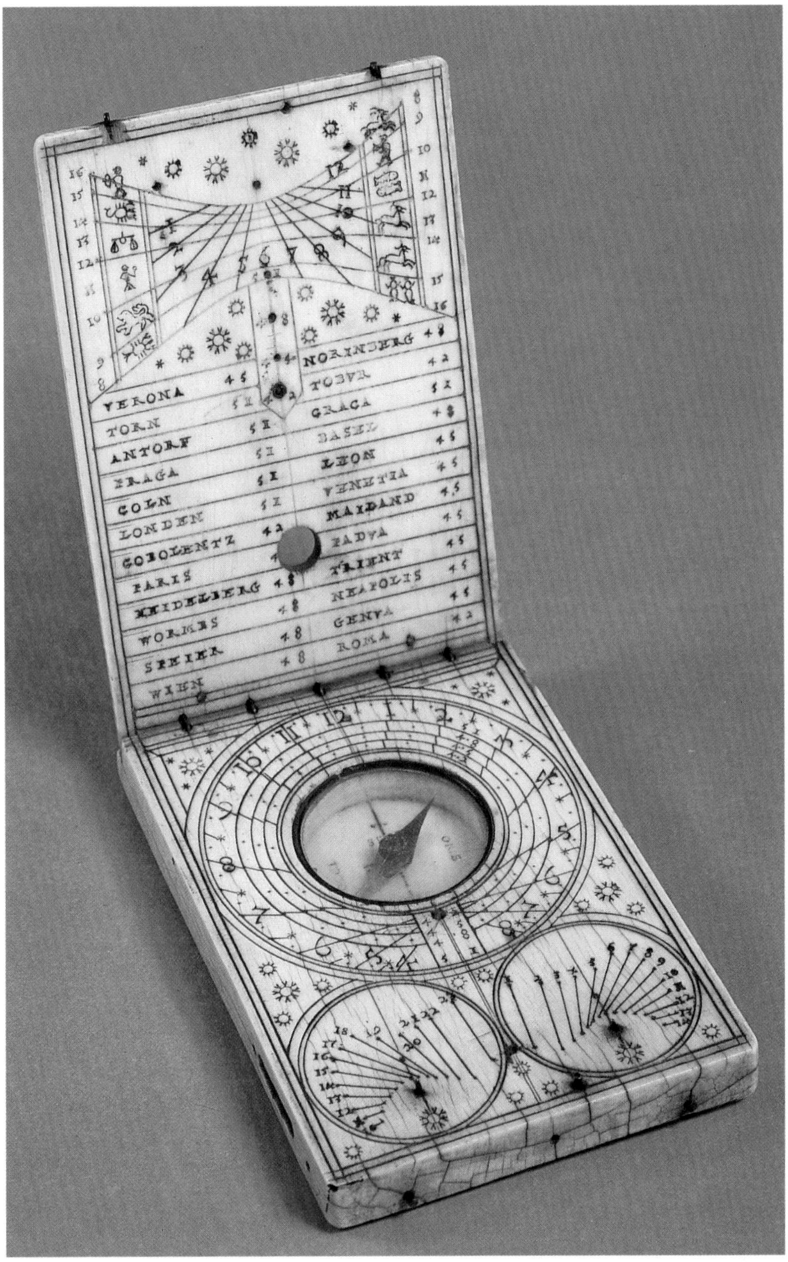

A German mariner's compass of the 16th century.

Navigation

Earliest compass knowledge ■ The Chinese Buddhist priest and astronomer Yi-hsing wrote of both the polarity of the magnetic needle as well as its declination in the eighth century AD. It was not until the 12th century that Europeans or even the Arabs recorded such knowledge. Although they could describe the properties of the magnetic needle, the writer Shen Kuo in about 1086 commented that it 'can be explained by nobody'.

Originally, the compass had been devised to guide Central Asian armies and travellers across trackless wastes of desert and steppe. It was a logical step to take it to sea. Unaware of the location of the magnetic pole, however, the Chinese assumed that the instrument indicated the direction of south. To this day, the Chinese name for compass translates as 'south-pointing needle'.

First European description of a compass ■ In 1269 a French crusader, one Petrus Peregrinus de Marocourt, described an instrument like a simple modern compass. It had a magnetized needle thrust through a pivoted axis in a box with a cover, and a cross index and a circle divided into the principal points of direction.

Earliest magnetic compasses ■ Although compasses in the form of floating needles were known in China, the Islamic lands and Europe by the 12th century, an important innovation was made in France in 1269 with the introduction of the dry needle; the familiar compass rose was added at the beginning of the 14th century. By the 15th century confidence in the compass was such that in Europe ships' masters used them widely.

NAVIGATIONAL INSTRUMENTS

Most European seafarers of the period 1450–1550 sailed only on coastal or short sea routes. Accordingly, the range of navigational instruments they used was limited to the magnetic compass, for finding direction; the sounding line and lead, for finding depth; the sandglass (hourglass) for measuring time, to help watch-keeping and in the estimation of speed; and the pilot-book, a written (later printed) record of coastal marks, currents and tides. Astrolabes, charts and other navigational aids were of great importance in oceanic voyaging, but it is uncertain how widespread their use was amongst the majority of seamen.

A tinted woodcut showing how the astrolabe is used to calculate latitude from the height of the sun.

Dead reckoning ■ European navigators commonly sailed by what was called 'dead reckoning'. This meant estimating from the strength of the wind and their understanding of their ship's performance, how far they had gone in the desired direction. Columbus was a master at this difficult and dangerous art. On his return from his second voyage in 1496, he found land within 35 miles *56 km* of where he wished after six weeks sailing a zigzag course at sea.

Finding longitude at sea ■ Johann Muller (Regiomontanus) described in 1474 a method of using lunar distances to determine longitude at sea.

First use of the sea quadrant ■ Mariners in the 15th century were the first to use a sea quadrant. It was a simple arc of wood or brass, with two sighting pinnules along one straight edge, which were directed towards a celestial body. A plumb bob attached to the apex swings across a scale graduated 0–90° to show an altitude reading.

First use of the astrolabe ■ Sailors could calculate their latitude by observing the height of the sun or stars with an astrolabe. This method was first used as early as 1429. In the Indian Ocean Arab navigators used the *kamal* for the same purpose.

Astrolabes like this may not have been widely available to sailors in the 15th century.

First tide tables ■ The monks of St Albans in England drew up the first known tide tables in the 13th century in order to give the height of the Thames at London Bridge. The first printed tide tables were published by Monsieur Brouscon of Brittany in France in the *Nautical Almanac* in 1546.

First European manual of navigation and nautical almanac ■ In 1484 King John II of Portugal convened a group of learned men to work out a method of finding latitude from observation of the sun. The work of this group was summarized in a manual entitled *Regimento do astrolabio e do quadrante* (The regimen of the astrolabe and quadrant). It was printed in 1509 but had been circulating in manuscript from before that date. It contained a list of latitudes from Lisbon to the Equator (most of them correct within one half degree), a calendar, and a table of the sun's declination for a leap year along with Pole Star observations.

Most famous manual of navigation ■ The Spaniard Martin Cortés' manual of navigation, *Breve compendio de la sphera y de la arte de navegar* (Brief compendium of the spheres and of the art of navigation), was published in 1551. It was not only the most famous 16th-century manual of navigation, it was also the most comprehensive.

First comprehensive pilot book ■ By the late 13th century the Mediterranean and Black Sea *portalans*, or directions from place to place for coastal traffic, had been gathered together into one book: *Il Compasso da Navigare* (The Navigational Compass). The directions go clockwise around the coasts from Cape St Vincent in Spain to Morocco. It also includes advice on open sea crossings of several hundred miles.

Earliest known rutter ■ In northern Europe the equivalent of the Mediterranean *portalans* were called *routiers* or rutters. The earliest surviving one describes the English coasts and the passages through the English Channel and the Straits of Gibraltar. The rutters also describe the tides, which in these regions are of far greater importance than in the Mediterranean.

GLOBES

Celestial globes, made of hollow brass and engraved with star positions and various celestial circles, were constructed in classical times and in the Middle Ages in Islamic lands, for the use of astronomers. Few were made in the medieval West but by the late 15th century their manufacture was greatly increased. Maps were glued to spheres made of lath and plaster (the first printed map was published in 1472). At the beginning of the 16th century terrestrial globes were produced as companion pieces.

Exploration and discovery

Exploration and discovery

Explorers and discoveries

Longest voyages ■ Before the circumnavigation of the world by a Spanish ship in 1519–22, the Chinese expeditions of a century earlier were the longest ever undertaken. Ming fleets sailed from China to the coasts of the Indian Ocean and adjacent seas, reaching East Africa, Arabia, India, Sri Lanka and the countries of Southeast Asia. Like Sindbad the Arab and Indian seamen crossed and recrossed the Indian Ocean, a journey of at least 4970 miles *8000 km*. Some even travelled as far as China.

Oceanic voyages took place pre-1500 from Indonesia to Madagascar. Polynesians at some uncertain date had spread all over the Pacific, from New Zealand to the Sandwich Islands and from Easter Island to the New Hebrides.

Largest fleet ■ Between 1405 and 1433, China sent enormous seagoing missions abroad for purposes of exploration and diplomacy. There were seven fleets in all during that period. The largest, that of 1413–15, consisted of 63 vessels of various sizes. 28 500 soldiers, sailors and officers were aboard. No fleet of exploration before or since has approached such a vast scale.

East Africa ■ A Chinese scholar who died in AD 863 reported on a land west of India, assumed to be the Somali coast. He called the land Po-po-la and described the customs of the people including how they siphoned blood out of their cattle and drank it raw. Po-po-la was described again by a writer in 1226, who said the people had many camels and sheep, and served heaven not the Buddha, meaning that they were Muslims. Imperial Chinese ships commanded by Cheng-Ho visited the northern ports of the East African coast in 1417–19 and 1421–2. Large quantities of Chinese porcelain had previously reached Africa as trade goods brought by Indian and Arabian merchants.

First European names ■ The Portuguese introduced their own names to the places they discovered. Some of them have endured: Madeira (*c.* 1420); Cape Verde (and islands) (*c.* 1456–60), and Sierra Leone (Mountains of the Lions from the roar of tropical thunder) (1460s).

AFRICA

First around Cape Bojador ■ The first Portugese ship to round the small bulge of land on the west African coast about 150 miles *240 km* south of the Canaries was captained by Gil Eannes in 1433. He returned after a calm and uneventful voyage, but most importantly he had conquered the fear that sailors had about what lay beyond the Cape in the waters then known by their Arabic name meaning 'the Sea of Darkness'.

African interior ■ Alvise da Cadamosto was a Venetian merchant who made two expeditions to Africa in 1455 and 1456. He visited the Senegal and Gambia rivers and travelled several days' journey inland. His account of his travels, *El libro de la prima navigazione per l'oceano a le terri de Nigri* (The book of the first ocean voyage to the land of the Blacks), written 10 years later and printed in 1507, was the first account of the African interior by a European.

PREVIOUS PAGE: The gold Inca death mask from Peru symbolises the end of a civilization in the Americas as the Old World discovered and explored the 'New'.

FIRST KNOWN VISITS BY EUROPEANS

Bahamas	*Christopher Columbus (Italian in Spanish service)*	*1492*
Bermudas	*Juan Bermudez (Spanish)*	*1515/1522*
Brazil	*Pedro Cabral (Portuguese)*	*1500*
California	*Spaniards*	*1530s–40s*
Canada	*John Cabot (Italian in English service)*	*1497*
Hudson's Bay	*Claimed by Sebastian Cabot (but disputed)*	*1508–9*
Labrador	*Norsemen*	*c. 986*
Newfoundland	*Norsemen*	*c. 1000*
Cape of Good Hope (South Africa)	*Bartholomew Dias (Portuguese)*	*1487*
Chile	*Ferdinand Magellan (Portuguese in service of Spain)*	*1520*
Cuba	*Christopher Columbus*	*1492*
Dominican Republic	*Christopher Columbus*	*1492*
Dominica	*Christopher Columbus*	*1493*
Fernando Po (off West Africa)	*Ferñao do Po (Portuguese)*	*1472*
Greenland	*Norsemen*	*982*
Grenada	*Christopher Columbus*	*1498*
Guadalupe	*Christopher Columbus*	*1493*
Haiti	*Christopher Columbus*	*1492*
Hawaii	*Shipwrecked Spaniards*	*1527*
Honduras	*Christopher Columbus*	*1502*
Jamaica	*Christopher Columbus*	*1494*
Japan	*Portuguese*	*1543*
Nicaragua	*Christopher Columbus*	*1502*
Paraguay	*Juan Diaz di Solis (Portuguese in Spanish service)*	*1515*
Philippines	*Ferdinand Magellan*	*1521*
San Salvador	*Christopher Columbus*	*1493*
St Helena (South Atlantic)	*Portuguese*	*21 May 1501 (St Helena's Day)*
Uruguay	*Juan Diaz di Solis*	*1512*
Venezuela	*Christopher Columbus*	*1498*
Virgin Islands	*Christopher Columbus*	*1494*
Zanzibar	*Portuguese (First sighted by Vasco da Gama 1499)*	*1503*

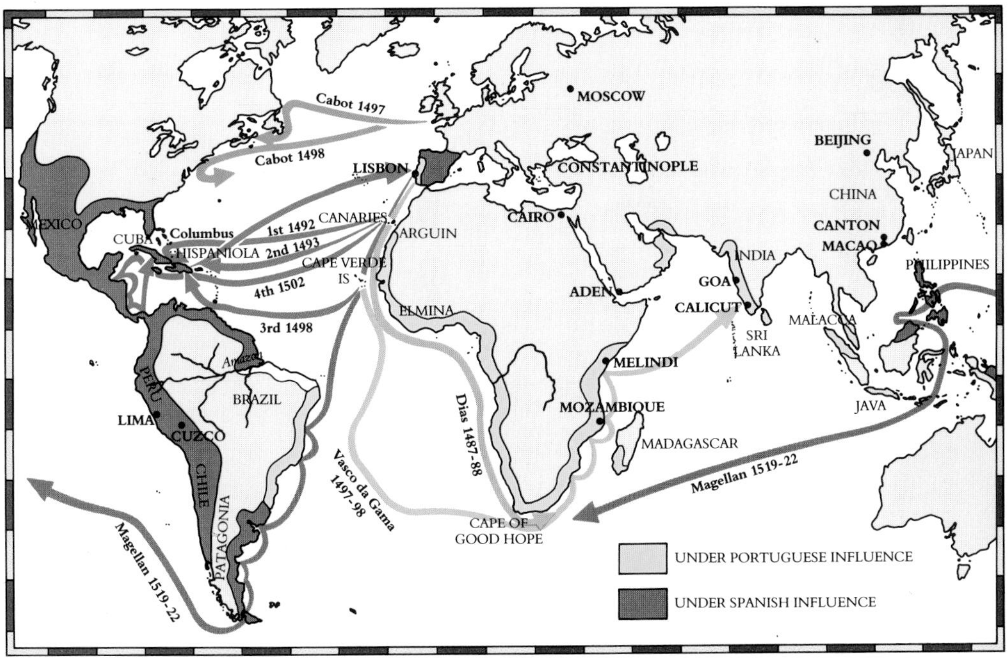

The claim to the deepest journey by a European into the interior of sub-Saharan Africa was implausibly made by Benedetto Dei of Florence, who said he had reached Timbuktu in 1470. In 1513 the Portuguese António Fernandes reached Chatacuy in the Zambezi valley and learned, perhaps from experience, of areas as far afield as Kwekwe in what is now central Zimbabwe.

First Europeans to Sierra Leone ■ In 1446 a Portuguese ship reached what is now Sierra Leone in West Africa. It was not until 1462 that a European ship reached what is now Liberia.

First royal contract for exploration ■ In 1469 King Alfonso of Portugal made a five year contract with a wealthy Lisbon merchant, giving him exclusive trading rights on the Guinea coast in exchange for exploration of 400 miles *640 km* of new coastline for each year of the contract at no expense to the king. Ferñao Gomes fulfilled his side of the contract and by 1474 had explored 2000 miles *3200 km* of coast, and grown rich as well.

Most effective explorer ■ The longest extent of African coast discovered by a single explorer stretched from St Cathérine in Gabon (1° 56′ S) to Walvis Bay in Namibia (22° 59′ S), explored by Diogo Cão da Vila Real of Portugal in two voyages, in 1482 and 1485–6. The claims made by Amerigo Vespucci of Florence, or advanced on his behalf, to have explored the coast of South America from roughly 8°N to up to 50°S in up to four voyages, probably between 1499 and 1504, are regarded as unreliable.

Across the Equator ■ Diogo Cão sailed from Lisbon in 1482 in a caravel small enough to be beached for cleaning and repairs and eventually reached the shores of the Kongo Kingdom in Central Africa. He failed to find gold or silver or islands suitable for colonization, but he opened the way for diplomatic and religious communications between Portugal and one of Africa's newest and most dynamic kingdoms. The route he had pioneered was, however, also followed by more piratical seamen interested in the catching of slaves.

First European inscription in Black Africa ■ In 1485 on his second voyage of discovery, Diogo Cão sailed up the River Congo to the limit of its navigation at Yellala Falls. On a rock above the rapids Cão and eight of his men carved an inscription with the arms of Portugal and their names.

Cape of Good Hope ■ It is believed that advance units of the great Ming dynasty fleets of the 15th century may have doubled the Cape many decades before the Portuguese, coming from the Atlantic, achieved that distinction. In addition to the Chinese possibility, some claim that ancient Phoenicians had gone around the African continent 2000 years earlier.

Earliest recorded deep-water voyage south of the Equator ■ This voyage was made by Bartholomew Dias of Portugal from an uncertain point on the African coast, probably about 23°S, into the zone of westerly winds, perhaps in about 38°S, which bore him to the discovery of the Cape of Good Hope and of some 300 miles *480 km* of coast beyond in 1487.

First European navigator in the Atlantic to reach South Africa ■ In 1488 Bartholomew Dias carried the coastal exploration of Atlantic Africa 2000 miles *3200 km* beyond the regions visited by Diogo Cão. Much of the land was barren and led only southward but he finally reached a cape which he called Cape of Good Hope. He landed there on 6 June and erected a stone pillar, or *padrao*, to celebrate the rounding of the southern tip of the African continent. Further exploration toward the east was delayed for a decade but eventually a route to India was opened in 1497 by Vasco da Gama. Later still, Dias' grandson, Paulo, obtained a royal charter which licensed him to conquer peoples whom his grandfather had visited while sailing along the coast of what is now Angola.

Madagascar first on sea charts ■ Although Arab navigators were probably visiting the island of Madagascar off the coast of eastern Africa from the eighth century, it did not appear on Arab charts until the 12th century. The first Europeans known to have sighted the island were Portuguese sailors in Diogo Dias' ship in 1500. The Cantino map of 1502 was the first European map to show Madagascar.

First printed description ■ Duarte Pacheco Pereira described southern Africa in 1506. His information came from Antonio de Saldhanha who landed at Table Bay in 1503.

INDIA

First Russian ■ Afanasy Nikitin, a Russian merchant from Tver, 100 miles *160 km* north of Moscow, set off for Persia with a team of merchants in 1466, down the Volga by ship. His ship was captured by the Caucasus prince's soldiers and he went by land round the Caspian Sea. Having crossed Persia he reached the Gulf and travelled on to India. There he travelled extensively before returning home. Taken ill on his way back to Russia, Nikitin died not far from Tver in 1474, unable to complete the last words of *Khozdeniye za tri morya* (Journey across Three Seas), the thrilling diary of his adventures.

First Portuguese ■ In 1487 two Portuguese, Covilha, a diplomat, and Paiva, a former spy, both of them Arabic speakers, set out to reach India 'through the land of the Moors'. Paiva disappeared but Covilha reached India and travelled back by way of East Africa and Egypt in 1490–1. From there he set off again for Ethiopia where he was later found by his countrymen living in great style.

300 days at sea ■ In 1497 Vasco da Gama, the Portuguese explorer, sailed to the Orient by the eastern route. He covered 3728 miles *5965 km* in 93 days out of sight of land just to clear the Cape of Good Hope.

Vasco da Gama's voyage from Lisbon to Calicut in India and back took a total of 300 days at sea and two years in all. Thereafter, heavy merchant vessels regularly followed the Cape route and brought silk and spices to Europe more cheaply than did the overland caravans of the Middle East.

His was the first crossing of the Indian Ocean in European ships. The ships were guided by a native pilot (probably a Gujerati Muslim) between Malindi and Calicut in May 1498. For long it was held that Vasco da Gama's pilot was the famed Arab navigator, Ahman Ibn-Majid. Recent research on Italian records concerning da Gama reveals however that the Asian pilot was taken back by da Gama to Portugal. Hence he could not have been Ibn-Majid, who remained in Asia to write his works on navigation.

First Europeans to enter the Red Sea ■ Diogo Dias and his Portuguese crew were the first Europeans to enter the Red Sea by ship from the east when, having rounded Africa, they sailed there in 1500.

AMERICAS

North America ■ In 986 AD a Norwegian, Bjarni Herjolfsson, by mistake on a journey from Iceland to Greenland, made landfall on a place well-forested and with low hills. It was not Greenland – it was probably southern Labrador. He is the first European known to have seen North America. In about 1000 Lief Erikson (son of Erik the Red) took Herjolfsson's boat and possibly some of his crew to follow their former route. He found a land that was 'full of great glaciers, and right up to the glaciers from the sea as it were a simple slab of rock.' They had probably reached modern Baffin Island. Erikson went south, probably to Newfoundland and Labrador. The expedition almost certainly over-wintered in North America before returning to Greenland in the spring.

English discovery? ■ The English ships *Trinity* and *George* may possibly have sighted North America in 1481. They were said to have been 'to search and find' the Isle of Brasil, which sometimes appeared on the charts far out into the Atlantic. In 1497, it was told to Columbus that John Cabot had seen this island 'found in the past by the men from Bristol, as your Lordship knows.'

Columbus' earliest Atlantic voyage? ■ Christopher Columbus said, when he was a sick man not long before his death in 1506, that he had been west and north of Iceland. He claimed to have been 600 miles north of it in February 1477. But he could not have been there in February as no ships went fishing then and no ship would sail so far north. Did he really mean that he went on a Bristol ship to southern Iceland and then transferred to a fishing vessel which took him round the northwest tip of Iceland? This is quite possible, but memory and imagination easily play tricks on a man with so much behind him.

First forecast of success ■ A horoscope cast for the Sun's entry into Libra in 1492 at Ferdinand and Isabella's court in Spain indicates the discovery of America. Jupiter, the planet of travel, rules the watery Pisces ascendant, 9th house, and midheaven showing adventure and discovery at sea. Jupiter is in the royal sign of Leo in the 5th house of ambassadors. Jupiter is with Mars which makes him more bold and daring and is also in opposition to Saturn in Aquarius showing danger and limitation. The part of the fortune is in the 9th house, indicating that substance or wealth comes from abroad. Columbus was actually looking for India; a modern astrologer would see that Neptune (not discovered until 1834) was at the midheaven and with the part of fortune. Not only does Neptune have dominion over the ocean, but it is also the planet of confusion and misunderstanding.

Longest deepwater voyage ■ In 1492 Columbus crossed the Atlantic, a distance of approximately 2640 miles *4250 km* and a duration of 224 days for the round trip. This was a journey unequalled since the Vikings had sailed to Greenland. From Norway, Greenland is a direct passage of 1491 miles *2400 km*.

First sight of the Americas ■ Sometime around 'two hours after midnight' on 12 October 1492 the lookout of the *Pinta*, one Rodriguez Bermejo, gave the cry of '*Tierra*!' ('Land ahoy!') and a cannon was fired as a signal to the other two ships. Bermejo was the first European to see the land of the Americas since the 11th century Vikings and should have received the prize promised by the royal sponsors of an annuity of 10 000 maravedi. However, Columbus claimed he had sighted land earlier in the evening and took the prize for himself. (It is unlikely that we will ever know exactly where it was that Columbus' ships made their landfall.) They waited until morning and then '. . . the Admiral went ashore in his armed longboat . . . and broke out the royal banner and the captains two flags with the green cross . . .'

Only surviving map made by Columbus ■ One of the maps made by Columbus during his four voyages to the New World survives. It is a rough sketch of the northwest coast of the island of Hispaniola. It was made during his second voyage and is dated December 1493.

Fastest ■ The fastest crossing of the Atlantic was made by Vicente Yánez Pinzón between the Cape Verde Islands and Brazil (probably Cape Santo Agostinho) from 6–26 January, 1500. This was the result of freak weather. Normally, the most reliable route was that from the

A woodcut of 1497 which illustrated the journals of Columbus shows his discovery of the New World.

In 1541 Spanish explorers first looked into the Grand Canyon.

Canary Islands to the Lesser Antilles, discovered by Columbus on his second Atlantic crossing (1493). Now dubbed Admiral of the Ocean Sea and Viceroy of the Indies, Columbus set out across the Atlantic with 17 ships carrying 1500 people. The crossing completed by Columbus between Gran Canaria and Martinique from 25 May–15 June, 1502 would long remain the record time for this journey.

North America ■ On 24 June 1497 John Cabot sighted land near Cape Breton (now Nova Scotia, Canada) from his ship, the *Matthew*. He moved up the Newfoundland coast and sailed back to Bristol in England early in August. He saw no people, but found a few signs of them, including a stick with holes at both ends, carved and painted with iron oxide. This was the first clear discovery of North America by a European.

Fastest journey ■ John Cabot crossed the Atlantic from Bristol to Cape Breton (now in Canada) in May–June 1497 in 35 days. He returned to England in August, after exploring some 500 miles *800 km* of North America's coast, from Cape Bauld in Newfoundland to Bristol in 15 days – a record he held for a long time.

First crossing of the Caribbean ■ Columbus sailed between a bay off the south coast of Cuba and Bonacca Island off the coast of Honduras from 27 to 30 July, 1502. Columbus claimed none of his pilots would be capable of repeating the feat.

First across America ■ Alvar Nuñez Cabeza de Vaca was the first European to walk across North America. Cast ashore in Texas in 1528 after the failure of a Spanish attempt to colonize the Gulf coast of Florida, he was made a slave by the people of the Galveston region. He learned local languages and, collecting a small group of other prisoners, set off westwards. He made a living as a medicine man and gradually built up a tribe of followers which won tributes from each Indian group they passed. They reached the borders of Spanish Mexico in 1536.

First geographical record of southern states of America ■ Following the return of Cabeza de Vaca from his travels in 1536, the Spaniards set out in 1538 under the leadership of Hernandes de Soto, first Governor of Cuba and Adelantado of Florida, to explore the interior of America – and seek the reported gold. The record of this journey by 'a gentleman of Elvas' in Portugal who accompanied de Soto and published the narrative of the journey in 1557, gave Europe the first geographical knowledge of what are now the states of Florida, Georgia, North and South Carolina, Tennessee, Alabama, Mississippi, Arkansas and Texas.

First black to explore America ■ When Cabeza de Vaca went on his great journey across America (1528–36) among his companions was one Estevan (or Estavanico), a negro slave. Estevan was one of the few men to survive and return to New Spain. He was later sold to Mendoza, the viceroy of Mexico. Estevan was the first black to have seen great areas of the American south. In 1539 he was sent north from Mexico with a Franciscan monk, Friar Marcos, to seek the 'Seven Cities' which the people had spoken of to Cabeza de Vaca. He was killed by Indians on this expedition.

Record journey ■ Hernandes de Soto, after making a fortune from Inca gold in the Conquest of Peru, aspired to conquer a similar empire in North America – if there was one. He landed in Florida in June 1539 and covered over 2000 miles *3200 km* in search of gold – more than any other North American explorer for a very long time. He went north to (what is now) North Carolina, over the Appalachian Mountains to the south and then zigzagging through the areas that are now Georgia, Alabama, Mississippi, Louisiana, Arkansas and Oklahama. He died in May 1542 on the return journey. His deputy's report conveyed something of the vastness of North America.

Grand Canyon ■ A party of Spaniards under Garcia Lopez de Cardenas, part of an expedition to the interior of America under the leadership of Vasquez de Coronado in 1540, were the first Europeans to look down into the Grand Canyon.

Most northerly Pacific exploration ■ From Central America Spaniards explored the west coast of North America in 1542. It is possible they reached as far north as what is now Oregon.

Early attempt to find the North-West Passage ■ Sebastian Cabot (son of John Cabot) made a famous voyage in 1508–09 in an attempt to get round the north of the newly-identified continent of North America. He probably got as far as Hudson Strait (60°N) before his crew made him turn back. There he found numerous masses of floating ice in the middle of July. He eventually reached England in May 1509, after wintering somewhere on the North American coast.

Nearest to Earthly paradise ■ According to a contemporary source, Friar Marcos who explored southern America in 1539, made the 'Seven Cities' of southwestern America sound as if they ought to have been 'the terrestial paradise'. Cibola, the largest, would 'contain within it two Sevilles and over' . . . 'the houses were very fine edifices, built with terraces and four storeys high'. There were also 'many wild cows (buffalo) in that country, and sheep and goats and rich treasures'. These stories created great hopes in the minds of adventurous young Spaniards in Mexico. It is said that the expedition of Coronado had greater hopes 'than any other expedition in all the colonial history of America'. They misunderstood the 'rich treasures' of the Indians and in 1542 returned to report the expedition as a 'total, dismal, ruinous failure'.

South America ■ The first recorded European voyage to the mainland of South America was Columbus's third Atlantic crossing; he set foot on the continent for the first time on the Paria peninsula of Venezuela, on 5 August, 1498. The tradition that he was beaten to this discovery by Amerigo Vespucci is the result of the misdating of Vespucci's voyage of 1499.

Yucatan ■ In 1517 a Spanish force based at Cuba were the first Europeans to reach Yucatan: 'a large town, and as we had never seen such a large town in the Island of Cuba, nor in Hispaniola, we named it Great Cairo.' The people were not welcoming and drove off the Spaniards. In February 1519 Hernán Cortés was sent with 11 ships and about 100 sailors to Yucatan and, though suffering losses, defeated their opponents – mainly because of the terror their horses caused the local people.

First official French exploration in Canada ■ in 1534 Jacques Cartier, a St Malo pilot who had already been to Brazil and 'the New Land' was commissioned by King Francis I to seek in 'the New Land certain islands and countries wherein there is said to be great quantities of gold and other things'. He reached Newfoundland (where he met French fishermen) and sailed into the Gulf of St Lawrence. He returned in 1535 and sailed 960 miles *1600 km* up the St Lawrence river to Hochelaga (where Montreal now stands). In 1542 Cartier on a third voyage tried to set up a settlement but the Huron peoples were now very hostile and the French retreated.

Brazil ■ The first recorded European voyage to Brazil was by Vicente Yánez Pinzón of Palos, Spain, arriving at 'Cabo de Consolación' (probably Cape St Agostinho) on 26 January, 1500. Pedro Álvares Cabral, making a long sweep into the Atlantic on his way to the Indian Ocean from Lisbon, arrived off Pta do Corumbaú on 22 April of the same year.

From there Cabral sent a ship back to Portugal to report, carrying some brightly coloured macaws. The land he had reached was later called Brazil from the brazilwood tree which produces a red dye and was already known from an Asiatic source.

Pacific ■ In 1513 the Spaniard Vasco Nuñez de Balboa crossed the Isthmus of Panama and was the first European to look out upon the Pacific Ocean. So excited was he by the discovery that he reputedly ran into the water in full armour. He named his discovery the South Sea and 'took possession' of it and the countries bordering on it for the King of Spain.

First official French voyage to North America ■ Giovanni da Verrazzano, leader of the first official French expedition to America, sailed south down the coast and landed in March, 1524 on the Outer Banks of what is now North Carolina.

First English voyage down the American coast ■ In 1527 an experienced sea captain, one John Rut, followed the coast of America southward from Labrador and Newfoundland as far as the Spanish West Indies. He was not well received there as he was regarded as an interloper in an area which the Spaniards saw as strictly their own.

First European down the Amazon ■ The Spaniard Francisco de Orellana, in 1541–2, using improvised boats, descended the 3000 miles *4800 km* of the Amazon from the Coca River to the Atlantic Ocean. He returned later to the Amazon and his death.

Frankest motives ■ Bernal Díaz de Castillo served in the Conquest of Mexico under Cortés, in which campaign he wrote an account from the point of view of an ordinary, though highly intelligent, foot soldier who had fought in no less than 199 battles. His *True History of the Conquest of New Spain* spelt out the motives of men like himself in the frankest terms: 'to serve God and His Majesty (Charles V), to give light to those who were in darkness, and to grow rich, as all men desire to do.' (These motives would be regarded by many as a summary of what guides all colonialists.)

LITERATURE

Earliest books ■ The Spaniard Oviedo y Valdes wrote *Historia general y natural de las Indias* (The General and Natural History of the Indies) and an Italian Spanish resident Peter Martyr (1459–1523) wrote *De Orbe Novo* (Of the New World, 1516). These were among the first European descriptions of the Americas.

ASIA

First white man known to have reached the Moluccas ■ This was Francisco Serrao, a captain in the unsuccessful Portuguese expedition of 1512–13, who completed the journey by native shipping after a shipwreck on the island of Lucipara. The previous record for the longest known journey in the same general direction was held by Girolamo di San Stefano and Girolamo Adorno of Genoa who reached Pegu in Burma in 1494.

China ■ Although Europeans had travelled to China in the days of the Mongol empire, it was not until Albuquerque, the Portuguese governor of the East, had captured Malacca in 1511 and established good relations with the Chinese traders that a Portuguese ship was sent to China to trade (at an island in the Pearl River) in 1514. They were not allowed to land, but traded profitably from their ships. Not long after, a Portuguese mission was sent to China, but their misguided behaviour (firing off salutes) and subsequent arrogance (building a fort and enslaving some Chinese), led to the Emperor sentencing 23 of the 'outer barbarians' to execution in 1523. The Portuguese then established themselves illicitly, but with Chinese connivance, at Macao.

First attempt to cross the Urals ■ At the beginning of the 16th century the Russian Prince Kurbskiy attempted to cross the Urals, the mountains separating Europe from Asia. After 17 days he gave up. (It was the legendary Yermak who crossed the Urals in 1581 and conquered Siberia in the name of the Tsars.)

Earliest references to a North Polar Passage ■ The earliest recorded hypothesis about the North Polar Passage was told to Pope Clement VII in Rome by a Russian envoy from the Novgorod republic in 1525. The envoy said, '. . . in northern Russia where the northern river Dvina flows into the sea, the sea coast extends eastwards so far that if, for example, a ship keeps to the coast on the right hand it may reach the Land of China by sea.' It was also reported in Moscow early in the 16th century that English and Dutch sailors had often heard of Russian seamen who reached the Ob River mouth by Arctic waters and even sailed further.

Magellan, sailing in the service of Spain, led the first expedition to circumnavigate the globe.

First Christian in Mecca ■ A 'gentleman of Rome', one Lodovico de Varthema, is credited with being, in 1503, the first Christian to visit the holy Muslim city of Mecca. He had been travelling in the Middle East and managed to attach himself to a caravan from Damascus bound for Mecca. There he described the Ka'aba as 'Similar to the Colosseum in Rome'. Varthema's adventures took him to India, Bengal and Malacca in Malaya. His reports on his journeyings are the first descriptions by a European of most of the places he visited.

JAPAN

First mention in European sources ■ Marco Polo (1254-1324), the Venetian traveller, records in his *Travels* the land of Chipangu, a corruption of the Chinese name for Japan, *Jih-pen-kue*. Tomé Pires in his *Suma Oriental* (Essence of the Orient), written 1512–15 (but not published until 1944) gives a Portuguese version of the Malay *Japun* or *Japang* from the Chinese *Jih-pen*.

First Europeans ■ In 1543 a typhoon blew Portuguese traders on their way to China to the shores of Japan. They were the first Europeans known to have visited Japan, and they found the Japanese most welcoming and avid for European goods. The Portuguese thought Japan 'one of the best and most suitable countries for gaining profit'.

Circumnavigation

First man ■ Few know the name Enrique, that of the Malay slave who was taken by Magellan from Malacca to Europe and subsequently accompanied that navigator on the first circumnavigation of the world (1519–22). When the Spanish ships reached the Philippines, Enrique knew he had returned to his home waters, for he could speak with the local people. When Magellan was killed in the islands, Enrique left the Spanish fleet and was not heard of again.

First ship ■ The Portuguese navigator Ferdinand Magellan (*c.* 1480–1521) began and Juan Sebastian del Cano (d. 1526) completed the circumnavigation of the world for the first time in 1519–22. They set off with 5 ships. Magellan and 250 men died on the way. In the summer of 1522 the *Victoria* with del Cano and 20 men aboard limped into the harbour of Sanlucar de Barremeda in southern Spain at the end of her voyage around the world.

Industry and commerce

FOOD AND AGRICULTURE • INDUSTRY
WEALTH • TRADE • MONEY
BANKING AND CREDIT

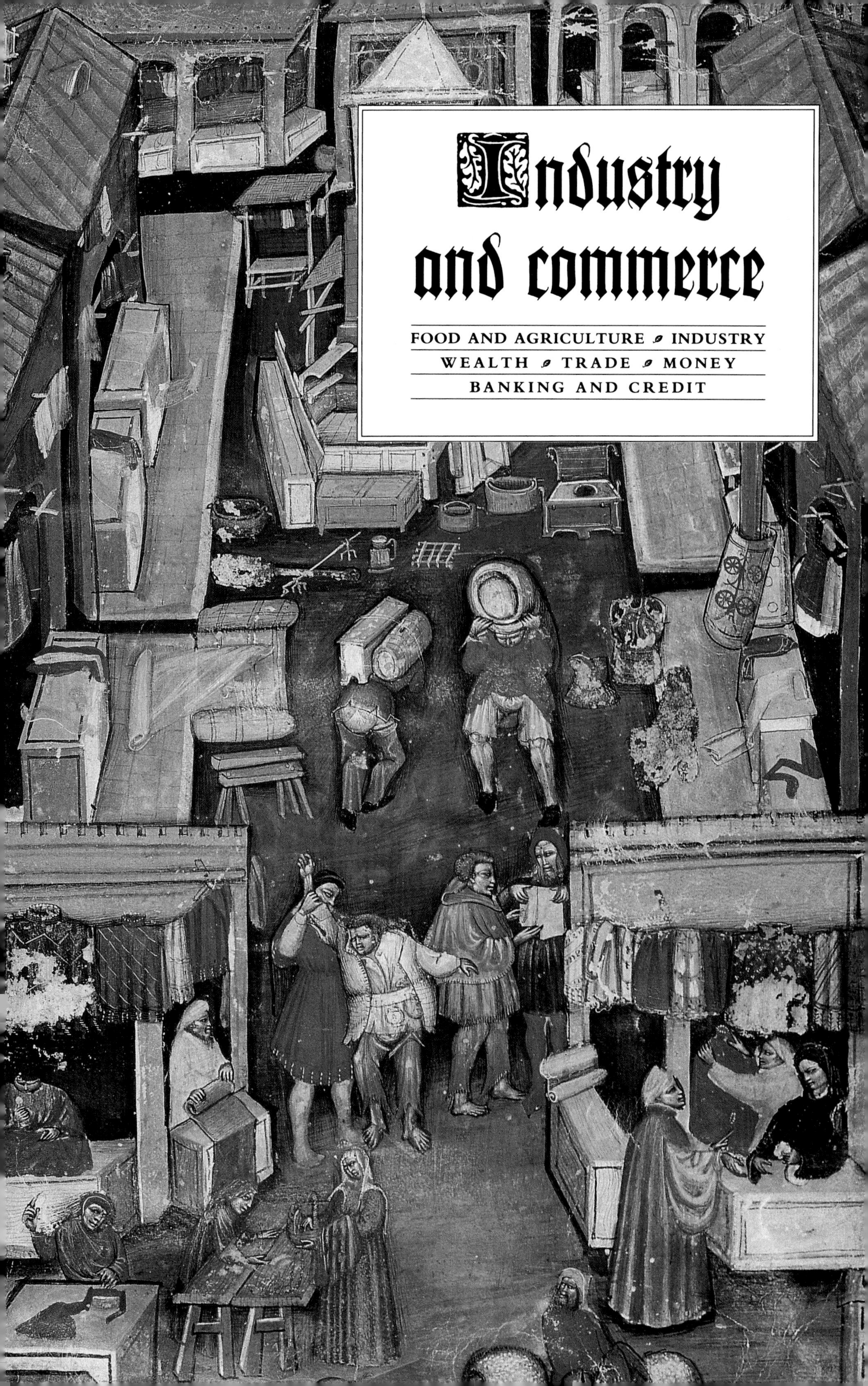

Agriculture

Origins ■ Evidence from Non Nok Tha and Spirit Cave, Thailand, tends to confirm that plant cultivation was part of the Haobinhian culture *c.* 11 000 BC but it is still likely that hominids (humans and their human-like ancestors) probably survived for 99.93 per cent of their known history without cultivating plants or domesticating animals. It has been suggested that reindeer (*Rangifer tarandus*) may have been domesticated as early as 18 000 BC, but definite proof remains lacking.

Domesticated livestock ■ The earliest known domesticated *food* animals were probably descendants of the wild goat (*Capra aegagrus = hircus*), which were herded at Asiah, Iran, *c.* 7700 BC. Sheep (*Ovis aries*) have been dated *c.* 7200 BC at Argissa Magula, Thessaly, Greece, and pigs (*Sus domestica*) and cattle (*Bos primigenius = taurus*) *c.* 7000 BC at the same site.

The earliest definite date for the horse (*Equus caballus*) is *c.* 4350 BC from Dereiska, Ukraine, USSR, but crib-biting evidence from southern France indicates that horses may have been tethered earlier than 30 000 BC.

Chickens were domesticated before 6000 BC in Indochina and by 5900–5400 BC had spread to north China, as shown by radiocarbon dating from a Neolithic site at Peiligan, near Zhengzhou, and also Cishan and Beixin. Chickens did not reach Britain until *c.* 150 BC.

Least domestication ■ The pre-Columbian South Americans had very few domesticated animals. Apart from the alpaca and the llama these included some small dogs, the turkey and the guinea pig. In the Andes the dogs were used for hunting, as sacrifices and as bed-warmers. The Aztecs of Central America ate them.

Livestock

Earliest domesticated ■ The earliest domesticated bird was the Greylag goose (*Anser*) of the Neolithic period (20 000 years ago) of south-eastern Europe and Asia Minor.

First Europeans to see a turkey ■ Columbus and his crews were probably the first Europeans to see the turkey. On his fourth voyage, in August 1502, they landed at Point Caxinas (Cabo de Honduras) and were brought food including *gallinas de la tierra* (chicken of the earth), a name which became commonly associated with the turkey. In 1519 Cortés had established that the coastal people from the island of Cozumel to Veracruz were raising many *gallinas*. Later, in 1525, when Cortés arrived at Trujillo, Point Caxinas, the natives also offered him fish and turkeys. As a tasty new attraction turkeys arrived in Europe in the as early 1500s. A pair were sent to Rome in 1520 and the turkey was known in France by 1528. The farming of turkeys in Europe began in Spain; they were intentionally transported there from 1511, and had become established by 1530.

Most misnamed bird ■ Soon after reaching Europe from the 'New Indies', turkeys were taken to England by the Mediterranean traders known as Levant or Turkey merchants, who had found them at one of their ports of call in Spain. Their correct name was *uexolotl* but the English (understandably, perhaps) preferred to say 'turkie cock'. Elsewhere, to people not quite *au fait* with the latest explorations, the Indies meant only one thing. Giving the credit to da Gama rather than Cortés, the French christened the new bird *coq d'Inde* ('cock of India'), later corrupted to *dinde* or *dindon*. In Italy it was *galle d'India* and in Germany *indianische Henn*. There were even some variants on the Indian theme – the German *calecutische Hahn*, Dutch *Kalkoen* and Scandinavian *Kalkon* – that quite specifically attributed the bird to Calicut, the place where da Gama first landed in India. It was ironic that even the Turks should call the turkey 'Indian' (*hindi*). In India itself, the new bird was called *Peru* – which was at least geographically closer to the mark than most, even if still a few hundred miles out.

Sheep ■ In 1467 Spain was home to 2 700 000 sheep – the equivalent of one sheep for every two people – which in autumn had to be herded from the Pyrenees and Cantabrian Mountains to winter pasture in the south, and then back again in spring. In the 1520s the number had risen to a record 3 450 000. As the sheep were taxed along the route, the figures for the flocks are recorded with some accuracy. Flowing along the 'roads' in their hundreds of thousands, they governed the entire life of the countryside. This inconvenient system (by no means unique to Spain) was known as transhumance and was necessary because, in many parts of Europe, it was the only way of keeping animals alive through the winter. It was not the cold that would otherwise have killed them, but the diet, because winter fodder in the cooler regions consisted of little more than dried beans, dried stems, chaff and straw. Although the sheep were reared primarily for their wool, they were also food providers – of milk while they lived and mutton when they died. Twenty ewes at this time could produce enough milk to make half a gallon *2.27 litres* of butter and 14 lb *6.35 kg* of cheese per week, and since at least 2 500 000 of Spain's 2 700 000 sheep are likely to have been ewes, the existence of butter and cheese 'mountains' cannot be ruled out. They would not, however, have been as large as in 14th-century England, where sheep (8 000 000 of them) outnumbered people by almost three to one.

Rabbits ■ In 1418 Henry the Navigator of Portugal sent colonists to Porto Santo, one of the Atlantic islands. They took with

Simon Bening, the artist of the Grimani Breviary, showed sheep shearers at work.

PREVIOUS PAGE: An Italian miniature of 1470 shows commercial activity in the streets of the clothing and furniture makers.

them a pregnant rabbit whose offspring multiplied so effectively that they made it impossible for the settlers to farm the island, and they had to move to the island of Madeira 12 leagues (*c.* 36 miles *80 km*) across the sea.

Greatest invasion of pigs ■ Being omnivores, pigs flourish if they are taken to a new area where the climate agrees with them. Columbus took eight pigs to the New World on his second journey in 1493. They bred quickly and their progeny spread to other islands and to the mainland by the end of the 1490s. Their numbers increased from Europe, the pigs multiplied rapidly and the quantity of pigs running wild was soon described as *infinitus*, a commentator reporting that 'all the mountains swarmed with them'. Pigs gone wild revert to their origins in a few generations and become the vicious, rangy creature known as the 'razorback'.

First sheep in America ■ Sheep were introduced to the New World during the second Columbus voyage (1493), having been put on board ship in the Canary Islands. Hispaniola (Haiti and the Dominican Republic) was the first land to receive livestock, followed by Cuba a few weeks later. Sheep arrived at the Panama Isthmus in 1521. Following the conquest of Mexico by Cortés in 1519–21, Spanish Churro sheep were introduced into New Spain, Mexico, in 1540. During the 1530s, the Spanish *conquistadores* expanded their empire into Peru, taking sheep as a basic meat supply. The explorer Coronado first pushed northwards along the Colorado River (New Mexico) in 1541–2, taking with him 5000 sheep and 500 cattle.

Newest method of stock-rearing ■ Cattle ranching developed in the semi-arid Andalusian plain of Spain in the late Middle Ages. In these dry plains new methods had to be used. Both the way in which stock were reared and the cattle themselves were very similar to the methods and stock of later Mexican and American ranching.

Unique cattle breed ■ The long-horned, long-legged, tough cattle which were bred for ranching in the semi-arid, rough grazing areas of southern Spain were unique in Europe. They were bred for their hides rather than for beef and dairy products. These cattle were half wild and were cared for on the free-range system very similar to the ranching methods later used in the New World.

First brands ■ The free-ranging cattle of southern Spain had been branded with their owners' insignia since the 10th century. These brand marks were registered and codified to prevent cattle-rustling.

Best baiting dogs ■ The Alaunts from Spain were highly regarded for hunting boars, driving cattle to the shambles (meat market) and as guard dogs.

First large dogs in America ■ Columbus and later the *conquistadores* took large European dogs with them to hunt down the native people as if they were animals. The dogs were clad in armour made from hides to protect them from the Amerindian arrows.

Largest fish farms ■ The Chinese had been farming carp since before 3000 BC, and in Europe every sizeable monastery had its *vivarium* or pond in which fish were kept alive until needed for the kitchen. But fish farming as a business began in France in the 13th century and reached its peak in the 15th, by which time the fishponds of Sologne, Brenne, Bresse and Dombes spread over almost 100 000 acres *40 000 hectares* of land. The fish farmed were mainly large ones such as carp and pike.

Horses

Horses for sale ■ In the summer of 1474 it is reported that 3200 Tartar merchants followed the Tartar Khan ambassador to Moscow and took with them more than 40 000 horses for sale.

Great increase ■ *The Spaniards took horses to the Americas in about 1500. Once acclimatized to the New World they multiplied so rapidly that by 1507 the import of horses into Hispaniola had to be banned. Elsewhere there were soon vast flocks of sheep, huge herds of cattle and ravaging armies of pigs. By the late 1500s it was said in Chile that: 'They do not count the number of their mules and asses, and whoever wants them goes into the country and catches them.'*

Least satisfactory horse-breeding ■ In 1495, Henry VII expressed concern regarding the shortage of good horses and mares in England and the fact that they were being sold abroad. As a consequence of this depletion, he prohibited their export. A further, positive, move to improve numbers and quality of English horses was made by Henry VIII, who had representatives who zealously searched other European countries for good horses. But in 1535 an 'Acte concernyng the breeds of Horses' still expressed anxiety at 'the greate decay of the generation and bredyng of good and swyfte and strong Horses which here to fore have been bredde in this Realme'. In an attempt to improve horse quality, an Act of 1540 named 30 shires and districts in which no person was allowed to put a stallion which was less than 15 hands high with mares or fillies.

Most impressive mule ■ The Chinese writer Xie Zhaozhi reported that 'in the Imperial parks there are also mules that fight with tigers. They are 8 ft *2.4 m* high and can despatch a tiger in three kicks. The eunuch Liu Ma obtained a black mule from the north-western barbarians that could cover 330 miles *528 km* in a day and kill a tiger with a single kick. Later on it was matched against a lion, and died after its spine was broken.'

LITERATURE

First veterinary manual ■ While veterinary knowledge was well established by medieval times, there was still much groundwork to be covered. Leonardo da Vinci had finished his studies on the *Anatomy of the Horse* by about 1499. Also, as a result of health problems in cavalry horses, King Alphonso V ordered the production of a reference work on veterinary medicine. This was produced by Manuel Diaz and printed at Castile in 1495.

Domestic plants

Edible plants ■ A book entitled *Jiuhuang Bencao* (Herbal for the Relief of Famine), composed by Zhu Su, the fifth son of the Ming dynasty Emperor Zhu Yuan-Zhang, in 1404, listed 414 plants which could be used against famine, among them 276 plants which were described for the first time. The book was the result of an on-the-spot survey of information obtained from the peasants and farmers. Each plant was not only described but also drawn in its natural environment. It was the first work of its kind in China and also the earliest in the world.

Leading domesticators of plants ■ Amerindians were among the world leaders in the domestication of plants. There are 120 species recorded as having been domesticated by them; between 30 and 70 edible plants were known in the Andean region alone. The domesticated plants of America included maize, kidney beans, the tomato, pumpkins, potatoes and sweet potatoes, the avocado pear, manioc and chilli peppers.

Highest productivity in the New World ■ The Taino people of the Caribbean islands where Columbus landed in 1492 had a most efficient method of farming. They built knee-high mounds or *cunocos* in which they planted manioc, sweet potato, pumpkins and beans. These crops grew together providing nutrients and shade for one another and resisting erosion. It has been estimated that this method may have been among the most productive in the world in terms of labour and output.

Earliest American fertilizer ■ The Iroquois of eastern America used fish heads and manure to fertilize their lands, and were later to advise the settlers on this. Others Indians used shells and fish as fertilizers.

New foods

From the New World to the Old travelled a great number of foods that had never been seen there before. Those of the new foods that could be raised in climatically favourable regions – and in the course of time this turned out to be true of most of them – eventually became so thoroughly naturalized in the Old World that many people today find it hard to believe that potatoes and tomatoes, for example, are in historical terms relative newcomers to Europe.

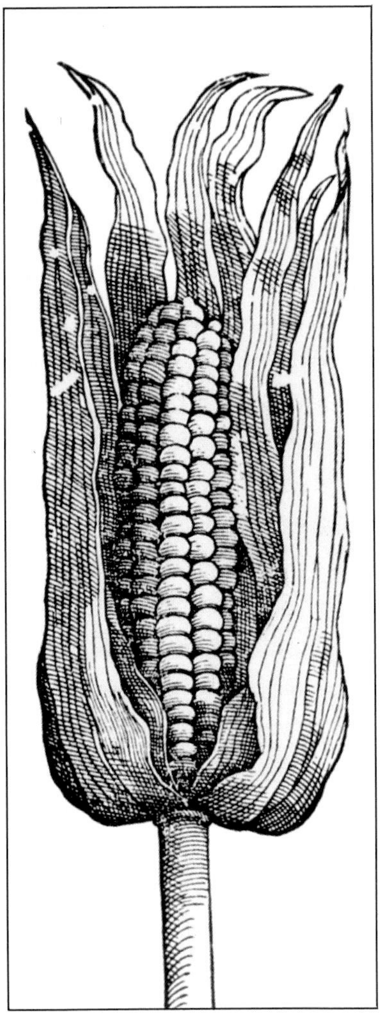

Maize was one of the most important crops to be brought from the New World to the Old.

Greatest west–east influx ■ From Central and South America to Europe and, via Europe, to Asia went: maize, tomatoes, avocados, potatoes, pineapples, papayas, kidney and butter beans, lima beans, scarlet runners, chocolate, peanuts, vanilla, sweet peppers, chillis, tapioca and the turkey. From the Americas to Africa went: maize, manioc, sweet potatoes and groundnuts (peanuts). From Canada to the Old World, somewhat later and through the agency of French explorers, went: the Jerusalem artichoke and 'French' beans.

Greatest east–west influx ■ Before America was discovered, 'east' and 'west' had different connotations. For centuries there had been a largely one-way traffic in foodstuffs from Asia to Europe via the Arabs. Some, such as rice, citrus fruits, peaches and apricots, had proved to be cultivable in Europe and along the Mediterranean shores of Africa, but others, like spices, remained items of trade. Despite the great diversity of the introductions, however, they had arrived one or two at a time, in fits and starts over a long period. By contrast, the foods native to or previously naturalized in Europe reached America in a flood. Among the crops and livestock that were now, for the first time, to be farmed in the New World were: sugar cane, bananas, rice and citrus fruits, wheat and cattle, chickpeas, coconuts and breadfruit. Also, to provide familiar food for the slaves who were being exported to the New World, a number of African crops were introduced, including yams, okra, cow peas and pigeon peas.

Widest range of food products ■ The introduction to China of maize, sweet potatoes and peanuts from the New World gave the Chinese the widest range of foodstuffs and ways of preparing them known to history.

Other early transfers of crops ■ Crops brought from America in the 16th century include the tomato (known as the love apple), which was brought from Mexico to Iberia between 1535 and 1554, and the avocado. The latter's Aztec name *ahuacati* was corrupted by the Spanish to *aguacate* which became *avocado* in English. The sunflower also came from South America, though the first European account of it was not given until 1568. Groundnuts (or peanuts) were carried to West Africa by the Portuguese, and to Asia by the Spanish, and had been introduced into China by the 1530s.

European crops were familiar enough in Asia, but the Portuguese introduced novel crops from America into India: tobacco, pineapples, red peppers and cashew nuts are examples. These were rapidly picked up by Indian growers and traders, so that tobacco was an important cash crop from late in the 16th century in Gujarat and later in many other areas.

First crops taken from the Old World to the New ■ Columbus took seeds of the main temperate cereal grains (wheat, rye, barley and oats) with him on his first voyage to Hispaniola but these crops had little initial success until they reached the drier uplands of Mexico and Peru. On his second voyage Columbus introduced sugar cane, which the Spanish had already taken from Asia to the Canary Islands. This was more successful and American sugar reached Spain in 1512. Bananas reached Hispaniola from the Canaries by 1516. The most successful Mediterranean crop to be exported across the Atlantic was citrus fruit, which was introduced into Hispaniola in 1493; it was being grown in Mexico by 1518 and had reached Brazil by 1540. Rice from Asia was being grown in Spain in the 14th century and was introduced to the West Indies in 1512.

Slowest new food to catch on ■ When Cortés and his Spaniards reached Mexico in 1519, they found that the Aztecs had already cultivated many heavy-yielding varieties of tomato. The name derives from the Aztec term *tomatl* or *xitomate*. The ones introduced into Europe in the following decades may have been orange-yellow in colour, hence the early Italian name *pomo d'oro* (golden apple). While the tomato probably arrived in Europe earlier, the earliest known mention of it by a botanist is in the herbal of Matthiolus in 1544. In Spain, the tomato was accepted almost immediately, but in Italy it took more than a century before it came to be used in soups and stews, and another century and a half before it was made into a pasta sauce. In France it was given the name *pomme* *d'amour* (love apple). Elsewhere, especially in northern Europe and North America, the tomato was believed to be lacking in nourishment and substance, and was blamed for causing gout. The enigma of the tomato is that while it was probably first cultivated in Mexico, the homeland of the wild forms is probably Peru and Ecuador. It is uncertain whether it travelled north as a weed or a cultivated plant.

Maize

Plant breeding ▪ By the time Columbus sighted America in 1492, its inhabitants had developed more than 200 different varieties of maize.

Introduction of maize as a major world food ▪ When Columbus visited Cuba in November 1492 he recorded that a type of grain like millet, but which was called maize, 'tasted very well when boiled, roasted, or made into porridge'. In fact this plant *Zea mays* had a long prehistory in the Americas, extending back to about 1000 BC. A number of major varieties of maize are known, and it has even been questioned whether the plant in the eastern United States could have been introduced into Europe by the Norsemen, prior to 1492. Nevertheless, maize became increasingly important in southern Europe, Africa and Asia after the 15th century. The first reference to maize in the botanical literature is in a herbal by Jerome Bock in 1532, and the first European illustration is by Leonard Fuchs in 1543.

Although it has been suggested that some New World plants may have been carried across the Pacific and thence got into Indian Ocean trade routes, it seems more likely that Magellan's expedition (*c.* 1480–1521) introduced maize into the East Indies and Philippines in 1519. The plant was then transported westwards into Asia. The history of maize in Africa is complex and has been much discussed. The Turkish conquest of Egypt in 1517 may have resulted in introduced maize cultivation, but it appears not to have reached Ethiopia until 1623. Following Portuguese landings in Brazil in 1500, it is likely that maize from there was subsequently taken and introduced to the Guinea coast of West Africa as a part of their trading expansion into that continent, and provide ship's stores for the slave trade.

Uses of maize ▪ As in its native land, maize was generally utilized as a cereal, not as a vegetable. In Italy and Romania, the flour was made into porridges or pastas like *polenta* and *mamaliga*.The first European settlers in North America preferred to use it for soft, pancake-like flatbreads (of which cornpone is probably the best known) and succotash, a stew of fresh or dried kernels cooked with beans. Africans ate their 'mealies' on the cob or ground into meal. In China, where it had become of considerable importance by 1550, a proportion of maize flour seems to have been mixed with wheat flour to make noodles when the wheat harvest was poor. In France and England, however, maize was considered food for hens, not humans.

First illustration of maize ▪ This appeared in the 1535 translation of Gonzalo Fernandez de Oviedo y Valdes' *Historia Natural y General de las Indias* (General and Natural History of the Americas). Oviedo was sent to America from Spain in 1513 to study plants.

Greatest impact on African agriculture ▪ One consequence of Columbus' voyage was to enhance farm production in Africa and speed up population growth. Maize brought the most far-reaching economic revolution to Africa in the decades after the first Atlantic crossing. West African millet and sorghum (a grain) farmers of the savanna first obtained Mexican-type maize seeds, known in England as 'turkey wheat'. Later, Brazilian-type maize was introduced to forest farmers, who adopted it for its heavy yields and because its cobs were naturally protected against birds.

First introduction of oilseed rape to England ▪ *The introduction of oilseed rape is not a new phenomenon. In response to the rising cost of imported olive oil English farmers began to grow rape from the 1530s, initially in eastern England under the encouragement of Dutch and French immigrants. The oil was used in preparing cloth and also for burning in lamps.*

Pecan ▪ Of those nut-bearing trees that are native to North America, the most important is the pecan (*Carya illinoiensis*), with a wide distribution from Illinois to Texas and south to Oaxaca in Mexico. The native name of *pecanes* or *paccan* was early adopted by Europeans. The Spanish explorer Alvar Nuñez Cabeza de Vaca was probably the first European, in 1528, to see the Indian exploitation of pecan-nut trees along the Guadelupe River in Texas. Lope de Oviedo, in 1533, similarly noted their use as food, and likened them to small walnuts.

Earliest peanuts ▪ Much of the world did not cultivate the groundnut until after 1492. The earliest cultivation seems to have been in Peru, but it had spread to Mexico as a cultivated plant by 700 AD. Early Spanish and Portuguese contacts with the New World resulted in its worldwide spread during the 16th century. It was introduced to the Malayan archipelago by Spanish explorers probably between 1521 and 1529. Portuguese contacts with Brazil by about 1500 resulted in the introduction of the crop to Africa, and thence eventually to India. It had been introduced into China by the 1530s. These early voyagers helped to establish different varieties of peanut in these different areas. Over the next two centuries the slave trade may well have assisted in its further distribution, including into temperate North America.

First example of colonial plantations ▪ The Cape Verde Islands were the West African archipelago on which the Portuguese pioneered the colonial planting of cotton and indigo (used to make a deep blue dye) tended by black slave labour. The associated spinning and weaving industry was modelled on African patterns of craft production and the skills were introduced from the African mainland. Slave cotton estates became the basis for subsequent 'Sea Island' colonization in the Caribbean and later for the plantation economy of the 'American South'. The first colonization of the Cape Verdes began one generation before Columbus attempted to colonize the island of Hispaniola in the Caribbean.

Tobacco first reached Europe ▪ When Christopher Columbus arrived in Cuba on 2 November 1492 he saw natives smoking rolled tobacco leaves. He brought seeds to Europe and it was being grown in Spain in the early 16th century. Although Ralph Lane, the first Governor of Virginia, and Sir Francis Drake are traditionally credited with its introduction to England, the plant was probably introduced some 20 years earlier. At first it was an object of curiosity in botanical gardens and used for medicinal purposes.

Yam ■ The largest food plant eaten in West Africa was undoubtedly the yam. The underground tubers of the African yam can attain several feet in length. Early farmers developed the crop from an indigenous wild vine by plant selection over several thousand years. The new yam harvest was celebrated with great ritual and ceremony and controlled by priests and kings.

First potato ■ The first potato to arrive in Europe from its American homeland was not the most widely known species, but the sweet potato, which took its name from the Haitian *batata*, and was brought to Europe by Columbus in 1493. It flourished in the warm soil of Spain and soon became known as the 'Spanish potato'. In the early days, recipes emphasized the sweetness, even to the extent of crystallizing it and serving it as comfits, rather like *marrons glacés*. It was also carried west to Guam and the Philippines by the Spaniards, and from there to China where it was well established in the 1560s. It was carried to Africa by the Portuguese.

First true potato ■ The true potato, *Solanum tuberosum*, was native to Peru, growing at heights above 11 000 ft *3300 m*. The Inca peoples preserved much of the crop by a freezing and drying process, the result being known to the Spaniards as *chunu*. The workers in the silver mines at Potosi subsisted almost entirely on *chunu* and their new rulers, recognizing its potential value in provisioning ships, introduced it to Spain. (Although Italy was relatively quick to adopt potatoes, elsewhere in Europe they were believed to cause either lust or leprosy, and did not become popular until the 1700s – in some areas considerably later.)

Most poisonous staple ■ Bitter yucca (*Manihot esculenta*, manioc), a bulbous root, was a staple food in large areas of South America, yet it contains a high content of prussic acid. For this reason it had to be treated by a very complex process before it was ready to eat. It was peeled, cut up, grated and pounded, and the pulp was then put into a squeezer to remove the liquid. The flour thus produced was then safe to eat, although fairly tasteless.

Vegetables

Most confusing new vegetable ■ The Central American capsicum 'pepper' bears no relationship to the *Piper nigrum* of India, But the Spanish had been looking for spices when they discovered the New World, and spices they were determined to have. In retrospect, it seems a pity that they should have applied the old name for real pepper, *pimienta*, to Central America's large, fleshy, sweet or bell 'peppers' – which, other than in the seeds, have little peppery taste – and gave the new name of *chile* (in English, chili or chilli) to the small, hot variety from Mexico (not Chile), whose pungency covers the scale from warmly glowing to outright inflammatory.

First hearted lettuce ■ Although lettuce has been known and eaten (often for its sedative effect) since the days of the Pharaohs and before, the variety common in early times resembled a loose-leaved cos. The modern type, bred to have a round, firm heart, was first mentioned and illustrated in the German *Krauterbuch* (Book of Herbs, meaning all kinds of leafy greens, including vegetables) by Leonard Fuchs, published in 1543.

Fruit

Most famous fruit-growing areas ■ In 15th-century England the county of Kent was already famous for its cherries, Hereford for its cider apples and Worcester for its pears.

First record of the papaya (pawpaw) ■ While the use of this plant in Central America must extend back into prehistory, it was not recorded until 1525 by the Spaniard Oviedo, who referred to it in his book *General and Natural History of the Americas*. After European contact it was taken to various parts of the tropics, and eventually even to remote parts of the South Pacific.

First bananas in the Caribbean ■ Bananas were first introduced from the Canary Islands to the Caribbean islands in 1516.

First European knowledge of pineapples ■ While the pineapple was first discovered by Columbus on Guadeloupe in 1493, it was found in Panama by 1502, and in fact subsequent European voyagers established its wide distribution in tropical America both north and south of the equator. The fruit was referred to by the Europeans as 'pines' because they looked like enormous pine cones, but the native names included *yayama* and *boniama*. Although the wild species of pineapple has a pebble-hard seed when mature, the Amerindians recognized and cultivated a seedless variety.

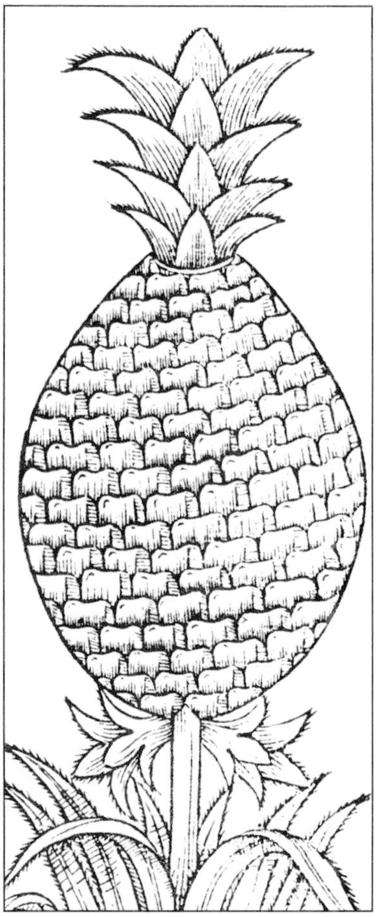

The pineapple was one of the new plants Europeans found in America.

First grapes (*Vinifera*) to America ■ The vine is perhaps the most important plant to have been transported to the New World. Although wine grapes were cultivated in the Near East by the fourth century BC, they did not reach the Americas until late in history. The Viking contacts with the New World do not appear to have introduced any species. Indeed, although the first wine and Vinifera grape were taken across at the end of the 15th century, the first recorded introduction to the eastern States had to wait more than a century.

Sugar

First cane sugar in America ■ While the sugar-making process was of Arab origin (the word comes from the Arabic *sukkar*), it was introduced to the New World by Europeans. On the second voyage of Columbus in 1493, cane cuttings were taken from the Canary Islands to Hispaniola. Early attempts to grow sugar cane were not successful, but profitable amounts were being produced by 1509. Cane was being grown in Mexico by 1520, with the first sugar mill being established there by Cortés in 1535. Cultivation spread fairly quickly to Venezuela, Colombia, Peru, Brazil and Puerto Rico. Contemporary with these developments, sugar technology and trading expanded from North Africa and Italy into northern Europe. The first sugar refineries to be built in England were established by Cornelius Bassine in 1544. Profits were low, owing to competition with the 'sugar bakers' of Antwerp, in Flanders.

When the Spaniards began cultivating sugar in the New World, there was a shortage of local labour which they resolved in the traditional way. Slaves were common in many parts of Europe, so they merely exported some – mainly from Africa – to the New Indies. It was, however, the Portuguese who in the next few decades embarked on large-scale slaving in Africa to supply the workforce for their own new sugar plantations in Brazil. By the end of the century, just under a million Africans had been landed in the Americas.

First island colony on the Equator producing slave-grown sugarcane ■ Slaves were brought to São Tomé from the nearby West African mainland kingdom of Benin. They served both as field hands cutting and pressing the sugar and as domestic servants in the houses of planters. The colonists were both Christian and Jewish Portuguese men who adopted African concubines and sired creole families which blended European and African languages and cultures. The island also became an important slave market from the 1470s and sold slaves to the gold miners of Elmina, Ghana, to the landed aristocracy of Portugal, to the merchant families of Lisbon and later to the new plantation colonies of the Americas.

Viticulture

Most important wine-producing countries ■ Wine was produced extensively throughout most of the countries of Europe south of about latitude 55°N. The main wine-exporting areas lay in coastal locations or along rivers, and the most famous were along the Rhine, the Loire, the region around Bordeaux, the northern and southern coasts of Spain, and the islands of the eastern Mediterranean.

Most northern limits of viticulture ■ Vines continued to be cultivated in Pomerania, Mecklenburg and Brandenburg as far north as the valleys of the Vistula near Bydgoszcz and the Oder just to the south of Stettin. Numerous vineyards were found in the region of Berlin, Germany. An anonymous Italian traveller in England in 1501 noted that vines were to be encountered frequently, and he suggested that wine could be made from them in the southern part of the country – but that the quality would probably be harsh!

Largest vineyards ■ Monasteries were amongst the largest and most important vineyard owners throughout the Middle Ages. Probably the most significant of all monastic achievements was the creation by the Cistercians of the 123-acre *50-hectare* vineyard of Clos de Vougeot, which for centuries was reputed to have produced the finest of all the wines in Burgundy. The Cistercians also owned what was one of the largest vineyards in Germany, the 62-acre *25-hectare* Steinberg belonging to Kloster Eberbach. In 1506 this abbey's warehouse at Cologne was reported to have held some 538 *stück* (approximately *7000 hectolitres*) of wine from its 1503 and 1504 vintages.

Earliest vintage dates ■ Vintage dates at the turn of the 16th century were somewhat earlier than those of half a century later, probably reflecting the warmer temperatures prevailing around 1500. However, they varied considerably. Thus, between 1485 and 1515 the earliest average annual date of the beginning of the grape harvest in north-east France, French Switzerland and south Rhineland was 12 September in 1495, whereas the latest was 20 October in 1491.

Best-known wine varieties ■ By the end of the 15th century, certain regions of Europe had become known for their production of wine from specific varieties of vine. Pinot Noir was already known as the great grape of Burgundy in the 14th century, but by around 1500 the Chenin Blanc, known locally as the Pineau de la Loire, came to be the preferred variety around Anjou; the Cabernet France, also known as the Breton, was the most popular variety from Tours and Orleans; and the Muscat began to be particularly popular in Alsace. In Italy, the 16th century saw vine growers concentrating on the grape varieties of trebbiano in Tuscany and the Marche, the vernaccia in Liguria, and the Schiava in the Po valley.

First New World vineyards ■ The explosion of energy reflected in the Iberian explorations and conquests of the 15th and 16th centuries led to the rapid spread of viticulture and wine-making outside their European heartland during the first few years of the 16th century. By the 1520s European vines were being cultivated by Spaniards in Mexico, and wine production then spread rapidly southwards so that it was to be found in Peru by the 1530s and Chile by the 1550s. (A little later, in the 1560s the Huguenots also attempted to cultivate vines and make wine in Florida.)

First detailed illustration of wine-making ■ The dawn of the 16th century sees the publication of many beautiful illustrations on viticulture and wine-making. Among the most detailed of these is a vintage scene from a Flemish Book of Hours of the Blessed Virgin *c.* 1500. In the background, grapes are being picked from vines trained up trees. There are then being carried in panniers on men's backs down to a courtyard where they are crushed in a screw press. The must is being poured carefully into wooden barrels for fermentation. Some of the new wine is then being sampled and offered by the owner to a friend or potential buyer.

Beverages

First coffee ■ This plant was introduced into Yemen from Ethiopia in the 14th century, and was domesticated around the Holy City of Mecca, Saudi Arabia, early in

In October the grape harvest kept everyone in the countryside around the vineyards exceedingly busy.

the 15th. Around 1500 it was introduced to Cairo, where it was used as a stimulant to enable mystics (*sufis*) to stay awake during their nightly devotions.

First wheeled plough ■ *Accounts of wheeled ploughs before the Middle Ages are unsubstantiated, but they appear to have been used in Europe from the 900s. Wheeled ploughs are recorded in England in 1523.*

Most protected crop ■ Cultivation of the wild coffee bush probably began in Ethiopia in the sixth century, but until the 13th beans were regarded mainly as something to chew. Then it was discovered how to roast and infuse them – and modern coffee had been invented. By the late 15th century, coffee was valued throughout most of the Islamic world as a stimulating substitute for the wine that was forbidden to Muslims.

For another 100 years the trade was a tightly controlled Arab monopoly; not a coffee bean was allowed out of Arabia without first being rendered incapable of germination. As a result, coffee remained rare in Europe until the monopoly was broken in the 1600s.

Most appreciated drink ■ The drink made of cacao was regarded by the Aztecs as the drink of the gods and its energy value was well recognized. Cacao was imported from warmer regions, often as a tribute. The beans were offered as sacrifices to the gods. The drink *chocolatl* (probably meaning bitter water) was made from ground cacao beans, a few grains of corn and water, and was beaten until it was frothy and drunk cold. Vanilla or honey was sometimes added as flavouring.

Most economically important Central American food plant ■ For nearly a century after the drink was introduced to the Spanish court, the Spaniards maintained a jealously guarded monopoly over production, preparation (which was exceedingly complicated) and consumption of cacao. It can be argued that cacao (*Theobroma cacao*) was the most important plant cultivated in ancient Central America and taken to post-Columbian Europe. The words cacao and chocolate are in fact derived from Mayan words. Indeed, the Amerindian communities who valued cacao believed the tree to be divine, and hence its name *theobroma* or 'food of the gods'. The beverage 'chocolatl' the Mexicans produced was very different to our own, being a mixture of cacao beans, maize and capsicum pepper. Chocolate arrived in Spain in 1520. With its growing economic importance to Europeans, its cultivation spread. First planted in Venezuela, Trinidad and the Windward Islands, it was transported eventually to Asia.

First hop-growing in Kent ■ Hop-growing was introduced to England by Flemish immigrants, though in other parts of northern Europe it went back to about 800 AD. Ordinary ale was slightly sweet and was often flavoured with honey or herbs. The effect of using hops was to clarify the wort, add a bitter flavour and a good head, and to improve keeping qualities. It was recommended that ale be kept only a fortnight, but beer could easily be kept for a month. For some decades, however, many people regarded hops as an adulterant. Henry VIII even tried to ban their use.

The principal grape ■ According to Dr William Bulleyn, writing just after this period, 'Barley is the principal vine grape of England, that our Malt is made upon and mother of our Beer and Ale . . .'

Last mead drinking ■ Mead was made from honey and in England the monasteries – where bees were kept for their wax, used for votive candles – were the great honey farms. Henry VIII's dissolution of the monasteries coincidentally put an end to large-scale honey production, and to the production of mead.

LITERATURE

Most important Islamic work on agriculture ■ The *Kirab-al-Filahah*, written by Ibu-al-Awwam Abu Zakariya Yahya Ibn Muhammed, was the most important work on botany and agriculture and its practical tips were highly influential. It advised that the best manure comes from bird droppings, but that these must not be water fowl's. Next in efficacy comes human excrement. Third: donkey dung; fourth: goat dung; fifth: sheep dung; sixth: cow dung; last: horse or mule dung. However, the use of ash from burnt vegetation is also recommended, especially when mixed with animal dung.

First printed agricultural textbook ■ This was the *Liber ruralium comodorum* (Book of rural activity) by Petrus Crescentius, printed by John Schussler of Augsburg in Germany in 1471. The first English agricultural text was Sir Anthony Fitzherbert's *Boke of husbondrye* published in 1523, which went through eight editions before the end of the century.

Feasts

Greediest Aztec consumers ■ In the

Seated for a wedding feast, a French noble family start their meal to the sound of trumpets from the minstrels' gallery.

palaces of the chiefs of the allied cities of Tenochtitlán, Texcoco and Tlacopan enormous quantities of food were consumed daily. The palace of Texcoco, for instance, is said to have absorbed daily tribute amounting to up to 2645 lb *1200 kg* of maize, 315 lb *143 kg* of beans, 32 000 cacao beans, 100 turkeys, 20 loaves of salt, 20 baskets of large chillies and another 20 of small chillies, 10 baskets of tomatoes and 10 baskets of squashes with, reputedly, 400 000 tortillas, in the reign of Nezahualcoyotl (1427–72). At Moctezuma's table in Tenochtitlán, more than 300 different dishes were reputedly served every day, after which his household ate from more than 1000 plates and received 'of jugs of foaming chocolate more than 2000 with infinite fruit'. The dishes served to Moctezuma included stewed fowl, stewed turkeys ('double-chin chickens', the *conquistador* Bernal Díaz said), pheasants, 'partridges of the country', quails, wild and domestic duck, venison, peccary, fried songbirds, pigeons, hares, rabbits, 'and many sorts of fowl and things that grow in this land'. 'I heard tell,' added Bernal Díaz, 'that they used to cook boys of tender age for him and, since he had so many different types of stews and other things, we were not able to see if it was human flesh or something else.'

The ruler would be seated before a low table, covered with a cloth. Four young, 'clean and beautiful' servants (as his chronicles state) would bring him water in a *xical* or ewer for him to wash his hands. Then two other servant girls would serve him his chosen dishes. Afterwards he would take various fruits, a cup of chocolate and a good pipe. The Spaniards agreed, however, that in spite of this vast feast offered to him the emperor probably ate frugally, picking a little from every dish.

Most lavish Turkish banquet ■ This was held in Constantinople in 1530 to celebrate the circumcision of three of Suleyman the Magnificent's sons. The festivities lasted 20 days from 17 July and featured public feasts, fireworks, circus acts, mock battles and debates.

Most cost-conscious banquet ■ On 6 January 1508, the Duke of Buckingham celebrated Epiphany by entertaining 459 guests and 100 members of his own household to midday dinner and evening supper. The total cost was just under £12. Those present consumed 6789 loaves of bread, 45 pitchers of wine and 259 flagons of ale; ling, cod, sturgeon, salmon, dogfish, tench, flounders, plaice and roach; substantial quantities of beef, veal, pork and mutton (including 12 whole sheep); three swans, geese, capons, peacocks and herons; various game birds including mallard, snipe and quail; chickens, rabbits, eggs, milk and butter; eels, lampreys and oysters. At this time, £12 was the equivalent of almost two years' wages for a labourer.

Largest kitchen staff ■ At the court of the Ming emperor of China there were 7874 kitchen servants to supply the imperial table and prepare state banquets.

Most useful basic food ■ Among the nomadic Bedouin of Arabia the date-palm tree was the central source of food. The fruit, along with camel's milk, provided the basic diet, and indeed dates were, along with camel flesh, the only solid food of the Bedouin. Its fermented beverage made a prized drink, and the crushed stones were used to feed camels. Over 100 varieties of dates were known to grow in the vicinity of the Holy City of Mecca, in what is now Saudi Arabia.

THE PERFECT PANTRY

c. 1460

. . . In the pantry, you must always keep three sharp knives, one to chop the loaves, another to pare them, and a third sharp and keen, to smooth and square the trenchers with.

Always cut your lord's bread, and see that it be new; and all other bread at the table one day old ere you cut it, all household bread three days old, and trencher bread four days old.

Look that your salt be fine, white, fair, and dry; and have your salt-plane of ivory, two inches wide and three long; and see to it that the lid of the salt-cellar touch not the salt.

Good son, look that your napery be sweet and clean, and that your table-cloth, towel, and napkin be folded neatly, your table-knives brightly polished and your spoon fair washed – ye wot well what I mean.

(*From* The Babees' Book)

Food preservation

First chilled foods ■ As early as 600 BC in the province of Shanxi, ordinary Chinese – not just the rich – spent some of their winter organizing a supply of ice for the summer. It was cut from rivers and ponds, and stored in icehouses kept cool by evaporation. In later centuries, great blocks of ice from mountains and frozen rivers were buried in underground pits that acted as giant refrigerators; the ice did not begin to melt until the summer sun penetrated the earth to a depth of several metres. So important was refrigeration to the Chinese that, by the second century BC, 94 'ice men' were listed among the 2271 kitchen staff in the royal palace of the Chou. Ice was used for keeping fish fresh, for chilling vegetables and fruit – especially melons – and cooling drinks. A third-century BC poem (The Summons of the Soul) mentions the pleasure of 'ice-cooled liquor, strained of impurities, clear wine, cool and refreshing'. And in Hangzhou by the 13th century (Marco Polo's day), among the many eating houses and restaurants – which included fish restaurants and Buddhist-style vegetarian restaurants – there were a number that specialized in iced foods.

Most advanced preservation technique ■ In South America the Incas used a complex technique for drying potatoes (*papas*). The potatoes were exposed to daytime sun and night frosts for 10 days. They were then covered with a layer of straw and trodden to press out any remaining water. They were further dried in the sun for another 10 days, although at this stage they were covered at night. This treatment reduced the original weight by a third and changed the potato into *chunu* which could be stored more easily.

Food preparation

Tastiest food ■ Two essential elements gave flavour to Aztec food: the tomato and the chilli. With these the Aztecs would make a sauce called *mole* that gave a strong and pleasant taste to any dish. Sometimes this *mole* was mixed with avocado to give a filling for corn tortillas (similar to today's *guacamole*). It was further flavoured with various aromatic plants and herbs and even flower petals.

First hot curry ■ When the chilli pepper reached India from South America, the palate-searing curry had its genesis. The 'hot' curries of earlier times, flavoured with white pepper and mustard seed, had been hot only by comparison with milder ones based on blends of cardamom, cumin, coriander and turmeric.

Newest Indian *haute cuisine* ■ When the empire of the Mughals was founded in 1526, a new cooking style was introduced to India, one that had its origins in the Islamic heartlands from which the invaders came. Notable new dishes from the 'Mughlai' repertoire included kebabs and the pellao (or pilau), while other introductions included the trick of mixing fruit into flesh dishes, the use of almonds, almond milk and rose-water, the garnishing of many kinds of food with wafers of beaten gold or silver and a passion – which soon developed into an addiction – for sweetmeats and desserts like *halwa*.

First barbecue ■ Shipwrecked sailors and other vagabonds of the Caribbean who took refuge on the island of Hispaniola in the century after its discovery learned from surviving Caribs the old island trick of smoke-drying meat on greenwood lattices over a small fire of animal bones and hides. The Caribs called the technique *boucan*, which later passed into French as *boucanier* and gave the outcasts their name of 'buccaneers'. In Spanish, the greenwood lattice became *barbacoa*, from which the word barbecue is derived.

Most generous gift of dogs ■ When Governor de Soto's party reached the town of Guaxulle, now in Tennessee, USA, the people, seeing that Spaniards went 'after dogs for their flesh, which Indians did not eat, gave them 300 of these animals'.

First chewing-gum ■ The Maya of Central America chewed chicle, the latex

MOST SURPRISING PIE

TO MAKE PIES THAT THE BIRDS MAY BE ALIVE IN THEM AND FLY OUT WHEN IT IS CUT UP

Make the coffin [piecrust] of a great pie or pasty. In the bottom thereof you make a hole as big as your fist, or bigger if you will. Let the sides of the coffin be somewhat higher than ordinary pies. Which done, put it full of flour and bake it, and being baked, open the hole in the bottom and take out the flour. Then, having a pie of the bigness of the hole in the bottom of the coffin aforesaid, you shall put it into the coffin [to stop up the hole], withal put into the said coffin round about the aforesaid pie as many small live birds as the empty coffin will hold, besides the [small] pie aforesaid. And this is to be done at such time as you send the pie to the table, and set before the guests: where, uncovering or cutting up the great lid of the pie, all the birds will fly out, which is to delight and pleasure show to the company. And that they be not altogether mocked, you shall cut open the small pie.

of the sapodilla tree. Gum-chewing was also known among ancient Mediterranean peoples, who chewed the gum of the mastic tree to clean their teeth and sweeten the breath.

Most popular stimulant ■ Coca was the most widely used stimulant in South America. Coca leaves and powdered lime were made into a ball which was moved about in the mouth. The use of hallucinatory drugs was also widespread.

LITERATURE

First printed cookery book (outside China) ■ This was the work not of a professional cook but of the librarian at the Vatican, in Rome, Bartolomeo de Sacchi, also known as Platine. *Platine de honesta voluptate et valetudine* (Platine on matters of honest pleasure and good health) dealt with the quality of various foods and how they nourished the body; how to prepare them; and the right sauces for them. It was, in effect, partly a cookery book and partly a guide to good health. Eat well, said Platine, but pay attention to what you eat and when you eat – and do not quarrel on a full stomach. The earliest Latin edition, not dated, has been attributed to 1474, the earliest dated edition being 1475. There were reprints in 1480, 1498, 1499 and after. The first translation into Italian was in 1494, into French in 1505 and into German in 1530.

First commercially printed English cookery book ■ Believed to have been *This is the Boke of Cokerye*, published in 1500, this was suitable, according to the anonymous author, for 'a prince's household'.

Most conscientious food writer ■ Lee Shizhen (1518–93), author of the great Ming dynasty herbal, the *Pencao Kangmu*, consulted 800 earlier works and took 27 years to complete his study of 1800 foods, plants and minerals. His book is still used by doctors today.

Wines and beer

First wine connoisseurs ■ There had been no tradition of fine wines since Roman times, and no attention paid to maturing. Most wine, indeed, was shipped and drunk within the year. But in the first half of the 16th century it began to be recognized that the sweet wines of Anjou lost nothing by being kept for two or three years, while Rhenish (Rhine wine) could be, and was, laid down for as much as six years.

First Madeira wine ■ The first consignment of 'Malvoisie [Malmsey] of the Isle of Madeer in Portyngale' arrived in London in 1537.

Largest pint ■ 'Jug' was the name for the various standard measures of the pint in Scotland, especially the 'Stirling jug'

This 15th century Italian butcher also baked his own raised pies on the premises.

TECHNICALITIES OF CARVING

THE ELABORATE RITUALS OF FEASTS OF THE NOBILITY, LIKE THOSE OF HUNTING, HAD A SPECIAL LANGUAGE

The termes of a Kerver be as here followeth:

Breke that dere – lesche that braune – rere that goose – lyste that swanne – sauce that capon – spoyle that hen – frusche that checkyn – unbrace that mallarde [duck] – unlace that conye [rabbit] – dismembre that heron – display that crayn – disfigure that pecocke – unjoynt that bytture [bittern] – untache that curlewe – alaye that fesande [pheasant] – wynge that partyche [partridge] – wyng that quayle – myne that plover – thye that pygion – border that pastry – thye that woodcock – thye all smale byrdes – tymbre that fyere – tyere that egge – chynne that samon – strynge that lamprye – splat that pyke – sauce that plaice – sauce that tenche – splaye that breme – syde that haddok – tuske that barbell – culpon that troute – syne that cheven [chub] – trassene that ele – trance that sturgion – under trance that porpose – tayme that crabbe – barbe that lopster. Here endeth the goodly termes of Kervinge.

(From Booke of Kerving, *published by Wynken de Worde in London in 1508.)*

which contained approximately 3 pts *1.7 litres* and became known as the 'Scots pint'.

MISCELLANEOUS

Most lurid adulteration scandal ■ In Venice in 1498 a number of small traders were charged with selling secondhand cooking oil which had previously been used as a 'curative' bath for syphilitic sufferers.

Earliest appearance of the table fork ■ In the 10th century the Byzantine nobility had used small gilt forks to pick up sticky sweetmeats, but it was not until 1518 that the first mention of them occurs in Italy, the country whose refined manners were the envy of Europe. Nor did the fashion spread until after 1700. In the meantime, the only eating implements for most Europeans continued to be fingers and knife, or spoon and bread.

Best-fed people in the world ■ From the 16th century, the Chinese population ate better, in terms of nutrition and quantity, than any of the other peoples of Asia, and almost certainly of the world. Grain production was sufficient to supply the population with approximately 600 lb *250 kg* per head per year, most of it used for food. Consumption of meat was low and of dairy products non-existent, but this was more than compensated for by a high intake of soy beans, which are richer in protein than equivalent weights of red meat and richer in digestible calcium than equivalent amounts of milk. Furthermore, the Chinese cultivated, and consumed daily, in winter as in summer, a far greater quantity and variety of fresh vegetables – and therefore of minerals and vitamins – than any other people in the world.

The Italian artist Domenico Ghirlandaio (1449–94) painted a man pouring wine from a vat into a pottery bottle for storage.

Industry

Oldest industry ■ The oldest known industry is flint knapping, involving the production of chopping tools and hand axes, dating from 2.5 million years ago in Ethiopia. The earliest evidence of trading in exotic stone and amber dates from *c.* 28 000 BC in Europe. Agriculture is often described as 'the oldest industry in the world', whereas in fact there is no firm evidence yet that it was practised before *c.* 11 000 BC. Recent excavations at La Tolita, Ecuador, have shown that platinum was already extensively extracted by the 2nd century BC. The earliest evidence for zinc mining is from Zawar in Rajasthan, India, and dates to about the time of Christ, as shown by dating of timbers from the mines.

Largest single industrial enterprise ■ The expansion of the Arsenal, the state dockyard of Venice, in 1473 when the Newest Arsenal was added to the New Arsenal, which in turn had been added to the Old Arsenal in 1303–25, made the whole complex the largest single industrial enterprise in Europe. The complex embraced docks, slipways, powder mills and a rope factory. The Arsenal built and repaired ships, and produced every sort of gear and weaponry. In 1436 an observer had described how a galley was prepared for service on an assembly line system, with weapons, munitions and gear being loaded aboard as it moved down a channel. In the 15th century covered slipways were constructed which could house 80 galleys. The labour force included every skill from shipwrights to female sailmakers, and in the 1500s rose to between 2000 and 3000 people.

Largest staff ■ The largest permanent civilian employer was probably the Chinese grain transport system. By 1432 there were about 160 000 permanent employees (mainly nion-combatant soldiers) transporting as much as 6.7 million piculs (about 800 million lb *360 million kg*) of rice over distances up to 1600 miles *2560 km*. By 1492 the average annual amount transported had fallen to 4 million piculs (about 480 million lb *220 million kg*).

First processing of alum ■ Alum salts were important in the making of glue, dyes and tanning agents. The technology for processing alum was brought to Europe from the Middle East by Bartolomew Perdix of Genoa in 1458. A second Italian alum factory (1465) was promptly monopolized by papal decree.

Unequalled output of cotton ■ In 16th-century India the production of cotton cloth was a major industry. The output was of a quality and on a scale unequalled elsewhere in the world.

First English paper mill ■ England was amongst the last countries in Europe to establish paper production. Paper mills were known in Spain and Italy from the 13th century, in France and Germany from the 14th. It was not until 1495 that John Tate set up his mill at Hertford.

First commercial production of coloured paper ■ Begun to be produced at Venice in the late 15th century, the *carta azurra* was tinted blue.

Paper in India ■ The first clear evidence of the manufacture of paper in India was when Sultan Zain ul Abidin of Kashmir (1416–67) returned from exile in Samarkand, Central Asia, with artisans who introduced paper-making skills. The manufacture of paper soon spread to other areas and before long Gujarat became the biggest producer of paper in India.

First large modern extractive industry ■ Salt was the first large modern extractive industry, involving gangs of skilled workmen and armies of labourers at all stages of production and distribution. In the mid-15th century, in terms of weight, salt was one of the three most important commodities of international trade, the other two being grain and wine.

obtained from the juice of sugar-cane by evaporation and draining off the molasses).

Ceramics

Most sophisticated product ■ In the 15th and 16th centuries China was the only country in the world able to produce porcelain. This sophisticated ceramic material is extremely hard, and can be made into vessels so thin that they are translucent. Chinese porcelain was finely

From the 16th century onwards a major export trade grew up between Europe and China, and a number of shipwrecks have given evidence of the amount of porcelain that was exported into the West. One ship was found to be carrying 25 000 unbroken porcelain objects – which eventually were sold in Amsterdam, their original destination.

decorated with painted patterns and figures, in colour, and its unique quality created a great demand outside China. Despite the efforts of the Ming government to restrict contacts with foreigners in the 15th century, large quantities of Chinese wares found their way as far afield as the east coast of Africa, and were in use at the Sultan's court at Constantinople. The secret of porcelain lies in its use of very

Most travelled dyestuffs ■ *The dyestuffs used in the Flemish cloth trade came mainly from distant places. Woad for the blue dye colour came only from France, but the red dye produced from the kermes insect came from Spain and the Middle East; true vermilion was brought from the Red Sea; and the red colour of the brazil tree came from as far away as Sri Lanka. The distances the dyes travelled and the demand for them made them as expensive as spices.*

Enormous quantities of salt were needed to preserve meat, fish, cheese and butter, one pound of salt to 10 pounds (*0.4 to 3.7 kg*) of produce being the average proportion.

First Russian salt mines ■ The first salt mines, up to 110 yd *100 m* deep were sunk in 1515 by the businessman Anika Stroganov in the Urals near the modern city of Solikamsk (the name means 'salts of the Kama river basin').

First production of refined sugar ■ The production of refined sugar was started in China by the people of the Fujian, now a southern province. It was recorded in 1522 in the book *Guangyang Zaiji* (Miscellaneous Notes of Guangyang) written by Liu Ji-Zhuang. Before that, people in China could only produce raw sugar or muscovada (unrefined sugar

THE IMPORTANCE OF SALT

Salts, in general, not only stimulate the taste buds but are a biological necessity. Human perspiration involves loss of natural body salts, and these have to be replaced from food. Raw meat is the best provider, but a diet largely based on cooked grain and vegetables (the diet of most of humanity throughout most of history) is seriously deficient and requires supplementing with mineral salt. Salt's fundamental importance is reflected in most of the world's languages. The word 'salary' is derived from the Roman 'salt rations'. In Russia, the word for hospitality (*khleb-sol*') literally means 'bread-salt'. To the Arabs, eating a man's salt creates a sacred bond. The salt of the earth, being true to one's salt, if the salt hath lost its savour . . .

pure china clay (kaolin) with additives such as quartz and feldspar. The vessels are then fired in kilns capable of reaching temperatures as high as 1400°C. Europeans tried repeatedly to find out how to make porcelain, but did not succeed for centuries.

A Chinese soft-paste porcelain bowl decorated with the lotus flower, made in the early 16th century. Such bowls were the envy of potters in Europe.

Newest art form ■ *Istoriato* (story) wares appear from *c.* 1515 in Urbino, eastern Italy. These plates with a characteristic bluish glaze, completely covered with scenes from history or mythology, are intended as art objects. These historiated plates are a new art form, the only contemporary art which had no antique precedent. The artists signed their names and the first, best and most famous of them was Nicola da Urbino (active 1520–37). The earliest attributed work is a set of 17 pieces (in the Correr Museum in Venice) made for Isabella d'Este in about 1524.

Finest northern European ceramics ■ German stoneware was the finest ceramic product of northern Europe. The grey salt-glazed pottery produced at Cologne reached its highest level of artistic distinction in the early 16th century. The relief decoration of foliage patterns was applied and the best specimens were mounted in silver.

Most celebrated French potter ■ Bernard Palissy (1510–90) was the most celebrated and admired French potter of his day. Also a naturalist with a predilection for reptiles, he was amongst the first to experiment with the casts of dead reptiles. By 1548 his 'rustic wares', plates shaped like ponds with casts of lizards, frogs and snakes glazed in a slimey green, were in regular production. He went on to provide special effects in the interior decoration of grottoes for châteaux. (Recently 5000 fragments of moulds and pottery were discovered during excavations at the site of his former workshop near the Louvre in Paris.)

Most ineffective industrial espionage ■ Porcelain, a hard ceramic substance much admired for its translucency and hardness, was only known in Europe from Chinese imports, but the quest for the secret of its manufacture was the greatest preoccupation of the pottery industry from the late 15th century. The first opaque white glass produced in the late 15th century, *lattimo*, was one of the best substitutes for most of the 16th century. Soft-paste porcelain seems to have been produced at Venice and Ferrara, in Italy, but the first European soft-paste porcelain which survives was made in the Medici factory only in the late 16th century.

Finest glazed earthenwares ■ Hispano-Moorish wares were the finest tin-glazed earthenwares in Europe for most of the 15th century. The tin glaze, first known in ninth century Baghdad, Iraq, and transmitted to Spain by the Moors, produces a white surface which is eminently suitable for decoration. In the 15th century the technique was refined. The finest examples, large lustred plates decorated with arabesques and Cufic script, were manufactured before the fall of Granada in 1492. After this date the patterns lose their liveliness. The technique was imported to Italy by way of Majorca, where it became known as *maiolica*.

First Italian *maiolica* ■ Italian maiolica production begins in 1454. Of the several centres where it was made, the Faenza potteries are the most famous, and from *c.* 1475 the best. The earliest extant example is a plaque in the Musée Cluny, Paris dated 1469. The characteristic colours, most of which were developed in the 15th century, are strong: dark blue, deep purple, turquoise, orange and bright yellow. From *c.* 1500 the colours soften and the motifs become more delicate. From 1520 maioloca decoration adopts the grotesques introduced by the artist Raphael.

First maker's marks ■ During the 16th century Italian maiolica makers became the first ceramicists in European history to use maker's marks.

Souvenirs

Mass production of pilgrim souvenirs ■ A pilgrimage to a miracle-working image of the Virgin Mary sprang up at Regensburg in Germany in 1519 and found the town unprepared for the influx of visitors. In that year 10 172 pewter badges and 2430 silver ones were made and sold at the church's shop, leaving many of the 50 000 pilgrims empty-handed and disappointed. The following year output was increased to 109 198 pewter and 9763 silver badges.

Record sales ■ At major pilgrim resorts like Cologne, Canterbury, Rocamadour or Mont-Saint-Michel, badges and other kinds of souvenirs were sold to pilgrims at the rate of hundreds of thousands per year. In 1466, 130 000 badges were sold to pilgrims in the space of two weeks at the Swiss monastery of Einsiedeln. In 1438 Johann Gutenberg, the inventor of movable type, then working at Strasbourg, undertook the mass production of metal badges in preparation for a great summer festival at Aachen in 1440.

Most valuable earth ■ To the Muslim population of Palestine the sale to pilgrims of souvenirs was a very lucrative business. However, even more profitable was the sale and export of 'the earth from which God fashioned Adam'. The soil of the Holy Land was dug up in huge amounts, loaded into crates and exported throughout Europe but also into Egypt, Ethiopia and anywhere else where Christians would buy it. The supply, it was said, renewed itself mysteriously so that in the course of a year the pits from which the earth was taken filled themselves up 'without any castings in or helpe of mannes hande'. The earth was sold not only as a relic (an object of reverence with possible miraculous powers) but also as a safeguard against epilepsy.

Glass

Premier producer ■ Venice was the unrivalled producer of fine glassware in the world. Removed to the island of Murano in the late 13th century because of the fire hazard, the skilled craftsmen made the first technological improvements in glassmaking since Roman times and raised glassmaking from a humble craft to a fine art. The elegant designs also increased in complexity and form throughout the 16th century. The glass of Venice was widely imitated, but never surpassed. The secrets of the glassmakers were most carefully guarded. The doge (ruler of Venice) forbade craftsmen to emigrate. Those who did were tracked down and assassinated.

Most sought after ■ *Cristallo*, clear glass, was the most desirable. Manganese, the secret ingredient which permitted the manufacture of colourless glass, was rediscovered in the 15th century, probably by Anzolo Barovier (*d.* 1460), a glassmaker who had connections with scientists at the universities of Padua and Venice. (Manganese was used in late antique clear glass.) He added the purple substance to the 'metal' in order to neutralize its naturally yellow hue. The first documentation of *cristallo* dates from 1460.

First millefiori glass ■ *Millefiori* glass, a revival of the patterned Roman glass technique, was made in the Barovier glasshouse in 1496. Short rods of coloured glass in a mould were arranged in patterns and embedded in molten glass of another colour. The patterns created are usually floral: *millefiori* is Italian for a thousand flowers.

Main supplier of lamps ■ The Venetians acquired the technique of enamelling glass from the Persians (who had learned it from the Chinese) in the 13th century. But by the late 15th century Venice had become the main supplier of mosque lamps. The earliest surviving Venetian mosque lamp was made for Sultan Quaytbay of Cairo, Egypt, (1468–98).

Best false jewels ■ The brilliant colours which the glassmen were able to produce made the finest false jewels; more complex multi-colour semi-precious stones such as agate and chalcedony were also simulated in the 16th century.

The processes of glassmaking were fully illustrated in a 15th century manuscript of the travels of Sir John Mandeville.

Textiles

Longest fibres ■ Silk was the only fabric in the Renaissance with fibres of a sufficient length not to require spinning to create usable threads. The fibres are obtained by unwinding the cocoon of the silk-worm which is spun into a continuous filament from glands in the front of the head; the average length varies from 100 to 550 yd *100–500 m*. The extreme fineness of the thread requires that several be twisted together in order to make suitable yarn for weaving. Unwinding the cocoon was the greatest problem facing the silk workers. The Italians devised water-driven mills to facilitate the process. For every 11 lb *5 kg* of silk produced 35 000 worms are required. 1800 miles *3000 km* of the filament weighs only 2.2 lb *1 kg*.

Fastest growing ■ Italy was the centre of silk production and the fastest growing textile industry of the 15th century. Throughout the country towns competed to establish production. In 1470 Galeazzo Maria Sforza issued legislation requiring that there should be at least five mulberry trees for every 15 acres *37.5 ha* of land in the countryside around Milan. The silkworm feeds only on the leaves of the white mulberry; a yield of 110 lb *50 kg* of silk from about half an acre or *hectare* of land is the maximum that could be expected.

Finest silks ■ Genoa was the leading producer of the finest Italian silks. In 1464 when the import of all silks to London was banned, the Genoese variety was excepted because its quality was unique.

Newest textiles ■ New varieties of textiles introduced into Italy in the 15th century include damask (woven patterns), shot silk (multi-colour weaving that appears to change colour in different light), and brocaded velvets (patterns created by shiny and dull surface contrasts). The manufacture of these very fine silk fabrics was made possible by the invention of the button loom.

Most elaborate textiles ■ In terms of the knots per inch *2.5 cm* and the variety of colours and material in the weaving, pre-Inca textiles were the most elaborate in the world.

First printed fabrics in Europe ■ Although fabrics had been printed in India since the fifth century, they did not reach Europe until the late 16th century. In the meantime fabrics patterned in black paint with wood blocks were made, but were not washable.

Greatest improvement in spinning ■ The only type of spinning wheel available until the 16th century was a large wheeled variety which came to Europe from India in the early middle ages. It remained in use for the softest fabrics, especially woollens until the 18th century. The saxony wheel was invented by Johan Jürgen *c.* 1530. It had a smaller wheel which permitted a harder twist in the thread. In addition it had a flyer which enabled drafting, twisting, and winding on simultaneously. The earliest illustration would appear to be the one in the German *Hausbuch* (Household Manual), but the exact date is not known. However Leonardo da Vinci had worked out the principle of the flyer for weaving plain textiles *c.* 1490; his drawings predate both the invention and the earliest illustration of the working model. Many of the other mechanical problems surrounding spinning and weaving which he addressed were not solved for another two centuries.

Minting

Greatest number from a single die ■ It has been calculated that, in the late 13th and 14th centuries, a mint worker could be expected to hammer out in excess of 70 000 coins from a single obverse die before it was finally discarded. The obverse die, which is usually the head side, was known as the 'pile' and was set into a wooden anvil. The reverse die, called the 'trussel', was held in the hand. A disc of metal was then placed between the two dies and the design was worked up by hammering. It was the trussel which received the hammer blow, therefore the ratio of dies used in the late 15th century was two reverse to one obverse.

First dies in steel ■ The Renaissance medallist and coin engraver Vittore Gambello Camelio (1460–1539) worked at the Venice Mint and at the Papal Mint in Rome. Famous for his contemporary medallic portraits, he is thought to have been the first coin engraver to cut dies in steel.

Earliest coining press ■ A certain Nicolo Grosso is reputed to have used a screw press at the Florence mint in 1500, but it was probably for cutting blanks. During the pontificate of Julius II (1503–17) the celebrated architect of the Italian Renaissance, Donato Bramante (1444–1514), is said to have invented the coining screw press. The press was first used to strike leaden papal bulls (seals attached to all the papal edicts). Cristofano Caradossa, an Italian goldsmith and

MINTING

With few exceptions 15th-century coins were still struck by hand and, although strictly controlled in weight and fineness of metal, were often misshapen and poorly made. (Many oriental coins, and certain European and Middle-Eastern coins, were cast in moulds.) The last quarter of the century saw the influence of the Italian Renaissance spread across Europe with coins, as always, mirroring in miniature the artistic, political and economic achievements of the age. The minting of a coin, whether ancient, medieval or modern, consists of three main processes: the production of the dies, the preparation of the coin blank and finally the actual striking.

medallist, is recorded as having used Bramante's press to strike medals. In 1506 Leonardo da Vinci also conducted experiments with a coining press and devised another which would cut out circular blanks of metal of all-over even thickness.

First European coin struck from African gold ■ The *cruzado* introduced in 1457 by Alphonso V of Portugal was the first modern European coin to be made from African gold, as the result of the Portuguese exploration around the west coast of Africa.

A model of a machine designed for coining money by the great artist-inventor Leonardo da Vinci. Such a screw press may have been used in Italy in 1500.

First coinage in America ■ The Spaniards, through their exploration and military occupation of the Central American regions, found incalculable wealth in gold and silver, particularly in Mexico and Peru. Mints were set up for the purpose of striking the metal into coin. This was a convenient form in which to transport vast amounts of bullion back to Spain. It could be said that coinage reached America as an export rather than an import.

Mining and mineralogy

Earliest description ■ Published in Germany around 1508, the small pamphlet entitled *Ein Nutzlich Bergbuchlein* (A useful mining booklet) was published anonymously. It gave the earliest description of the techniques of mining.

First description of assaying ■ A booklet entitled *Probierbuchlein* (Assaying booklet) was produced in 1510 by an unknown German writer. It described the process of assaying.

First systematic book ■ The first systematic book on mining and metallurgy was written by Vannucio Biringuccio, an Italian of Siena. The book was entitled *De la pirotechnia* (On pyrotechnics) and was published in 1540.

A miner pushing a wooden cart with solid wooden wheels out of the mine.

Greatest mining expert ■ This was undoubtedly Georg Bauer (1494–1555), known universally by his pseudonym, Georgius Agricola. He was the first person to cast aside earlier far-fetched speculations concerning minerals and set forth the theory of the lapidifying juice – the deposition of minerals by solution. This he did in a book entitled *De Ortu et Causis Subterraneorum* (On the origin and causes of minerals), first published in Basel, Switzerland, in 1546. Agricola states that the important processes involved in the formation of minerals are heat and cold, and *succus lapidescens* (a modern translation would be 'mineral-bearing solution'). (His greatest achievement, the massive treatise *De Re Metallica* (Of Metals) did not appear until 1560.) Georgius Agricola wrote the first systematic treatise dealing with mineralogy, entitled *De Natum Fossilium* (The Birth of Fossils).

Georg Bauer (1494–1555), better known as Georgius Agricola, was the greatest mineralogist of the age.

Earliest deep-shaft mining ■ Europe's earliest known deep-shaft coal mine is at Lounge near Coleorton, Leicestershire, England. Prop-lined underground galleries had long been used in siege warfare to undermine fortresses. Henry V recruited miners from the Forest of Dean, Gloucestershire, for his French wars.

In Central Europe Czech and Slovak deep silver mines, with ventilation shafts and horse-powered winch wheels, had been worked for generations. But the earlier English collieries used drift-mining, i.e. galleries driven into hillsides, while the underground galleries of Central European workings, illustrated in the 1490s *Kutna Hora Gradual* manuscript, were hewn from the living rock.

Oldest mining zones of tropical Africa ■ The Zaïre Copperbelt has been in continuous exploitation since the eighth century. The copper was cast into cross-shaped ingots for export and these were likened to windmills by the early European visitors who bought them on the Mozambique coast after 1500. One of the great copper-working centres of the 15th century was the town on the Zambezi River Igombe Ilede, which obtained at least some of its raw copper from Zimbabwe and turned it into personal jewels and ornaments.

West African gold ■ The Akan forest in the hinterland of the West African Gold Coast (now Ghana) contained the richest gold-bearing mineral belt in Africa and was first exploited in about 1400. The gold was bought from Akan gold washers and surface miners by long-distance Mande traders who travelled south from the Niger River with porters and donkeys to found a gold-trading market at Begho on the fringe of the forest. Myths about the 'silent' way in which trade was conducted by dumb barter probably do not reflect the thriving economic skills of the merchant 'caste' which governed the trade. By the 1470s the Akan trade was known in Europe and the long sea-route to the Gold

Coast was opened by the Portuguese. Over 10 000 oz *283 kg* of gold were shipped out each year, greatly adding to the European gold stock in the years preceding the conquest of Peru.

Greatest profit ■ By the early 16th century the Portuguese were reputedly exporting about 880 lb *400 kg* of gold from their trading posts at Mina and Axim (Ghana). They paid for the gold partly in cash and partly by barter, but in either case unfairly. It is reckoned that the profit they made was in the region of 500 per cent.

Earliest crude oil production ■ Crude oil was extracted and refined in the Sinai peninsula and at Kirkuk in Iraq. The most important source, however, was Baku on the Caspian Sea. The petroleum sources there were exploited from the ninth century onwards. In 1402, 200 mule-loads daily were drawn from the wells there.

Most important mercury mines ■ Near Cordoba in Spain, the mines employed 1000 men both in extracting the ore and in processing it on the surface. The mines were 410 ft *125 m* deep. These mines continued in production after the capture of Cordoba by the Christians in 1236.

Most important Indian silver mines ■ These were in the Indian Hindu Kush, at the towns of Panjir and Jariyana. Over 10 000 men were employed at Panjir.

First Spanish New World silver mines ■ The mines at Potosi in Peru were opened in 1545, and the mines of Zacatecas in Mexico were producing silver for export to Europe by 1548.

Biggest stone producer ■ France was richer in building stone than any other country in Europe and stone was one of the most significant of French exports. Paris is remarkable for having subterranean galleries due to the extraction of stone in the Middle Ages. There are 180 miles *300 km* of these galleries (as compared to 113 miles *189 km* tunnels on the Paris *Metro*).

Largest brickworks in Russia ■ The largest brickworks was the first built in Moscow under the supervision and according to the design of Italian architect Aristotle Fioravanti in 1475. For 20 years till 1495 it produced around 120 million red bricks for the Kremlin walls, its towers and buildings.

Most valuable cargoes ■ Although the scale of trade in precious metals from the New World to Europe cannot be known, it is safe to estimate that 80 per cent of the value of cargoes to Europe were made up of these materials throughout the 16th century.

Metalwork

Most famous of all time ■ In the years around 1500 the art of the European goldsmith rose to a level of excellence that has never been surpassed. Many of the most famous Italian artists began their careers apprenticed to goldsmiths: Ghiberti, Brunelleschi, Botticelli, Ghirlandaio, Verocchio. However, the most famous of all was the versatile sculptor Benvenuto Cellini (1500–71). In his autobiography (the most famous of the period) he describes many works made at Fontainebleau for Francis I of France and at Florence. His only surviving small-scale work is the exquisite gold and enamel salt cellar made in the mannerist style for Ippolito d'Este in 1540. The subject matter reflects the intended function of the piece: the sea god and the earth goddess symbolize the production of salt by their joint efforts. A temple with a triumphal arch is the pepper container, while salt is held in the ship. In eight niches on the base figures or busts represent the four seasons and the four times of day. A piece of ebony set in to the base was fitted with four ivory balls which allowed the salt to be wheeled about on the dining table.

Finest example of the goldsmith's art ■ Designed by the famous Portuguese poet and goldsmith Gil Vicente in 1503 a monstrance (a vessel which contained the consecrated host) modelled after the form of the south portal of the Convent of Belem near Lisbon was made of gold brought from East Africa by Vasco da Gama. The convent was established by the Portuguese King Manuel I in thanksgiving for the discovery of the trade route to India. Manuel's symbol, the armillary sphere (a celestial globe made of metal rings), appears six times on the hexagonal

Agricola's book about metals showed two types of mill for crushing gold-bearing ore.

stem which supports the figures of the 12 apostles. At the top of a triple *baldachin* (canopy) God the Father bestows his blessing.

Greatest German goldsmith ■ Wenzel Jamnitzer (1508–85) of Nuremberg was the greatest German goldsmith of the 16th century. His earliest surviving work is a table decoration of the type which replaced the *nef* (a miniature ship usually made of silver) as the favoured type of centrepiece. The Merkeltische of 1547–9 (now in the Rijksmuseum in Amsterdam) is named after the 19th-century merchant who saved it from the melting-pot. The work, over a yard *1 m* high, is a mixture of gothic and renaissance styles and represents a tour-de-force of the master's skills in moulding, engraving, embossing and enamelling. The insects, reptiles and plant forms that make up the decoration are cast from living fauna and flora.

Most elaborate table ornament ■ The *nef* (a miniature ship usually made of silver) was sometimes devised as a salt cellar; others held the master's cutlery and napkin. The Schüsselfelder *Nef* of *c.* 1503 is the best example of the type. The realistically conceived three-masted ship is peopled with sailors who are shown in the moment when the alarm has been sounded; tiny figures are at work unfurling the sails and hauling ammunition from the ship's hold. The ship itself is held aloft by a siren, the mythical sea-creature most feared by medieval and Renaissance navigators. (Columbus himself reported having seen three sirens en route to America.)

A goldsmith at work with his tools and the products of his trade on display around him in his workshop.

Earliest-known apostle spoons ■ Silver apostle spoons, with tiny figures of the apostles holding their emblems in one hand and a book in the other, were the most popular of several types of spoons bearing religious ornament on the terminals of the stems. They were manufactured in England and northern Europe from the late 15th century. English examples usually have haloes and the figures are gilded. The earliest single example dates from *c.* 1490. The first mention of apostle spoons is found in a will from York dated 1494 and describes a complete set of 13: one of each apostle and a large master spoon with a statuette of Christ. The Beaufort set was the earliest surviving example and was bequeathed to Christ's College, Cambridge, in 1509.

On the table of this wealthy Italian gentleman are glass goblets and a golden or gilded ornamental ship which may have held wine or his own cutlery and napkin.

Most famed coppersmith ■ The Emperor Maximilian granted Sebastien Lindenast (1460–1526) a monopoly on gilding and silvering copper, much to the consternation of coppersmiths. After the organization's strenuous protests it was decided that he should leave a patch of copper exposed on each piece he finished in order to prove that it was plated. Despite the imperial patent he was prosecuted and fined in 1527 for gilding copper. His masterpiece is the Männleinlaufen (Little men running) clock which was made for a church in Nuremberg. It includes figures of Charles IV, seven princes, a herald, a trumpeter, a trombonist and a drummer.

Most commonly used ■ Pewter, an alloy of tin and other metals, was the most commonly utilized metal for domestic wares of middle-class homes, dominating the market from the 15th century until cheap pottery of good quality became widely available three centuries later. The best pewter, made with copper, is lighter in colour and is the best alternative to silver. The worst, made with lead, is darker and potentially poisonous. In Europe the craft organized in the early 15th century and in England the Worshipful Company of Pewterers was established in 1473. From the 16th century taverners used pewter exclusively for pots and measures. An elaborate 'display pewter' intended for use on furniture and made with moulded relief work developed in Lyons, France, in the 16th century.

Most outstanding enamellers ■ The art of enamelling, fusing glass or vitreous substances to a metal surface at high temperatures, was the most effective way of adding colour to fine metal. A new technique of painting translucent colours over a white enamelled copper ground was developed at Limoges, France, sometime before 1479. Each colour required a separate firing in the kiln. Nardon Pénicaud (*c.* 1470–1543) was the most proficient early exponent of the technique. At least five other members of his family were also noted enamellers. Most of the enamel painters found the inspiration for their painted scenes in the prints of fine artists. The production of the small enamelled plaques marks the revival of Limoges's fame. From the 12th century Limoges enamels were the best in the world, but the craft had died out when the Black Prince ravaged the town in the massacre of 1371.

Foremost jewellery designer ■ The artist Hans Holbein (1497–1543) was the foremost designer of jewellery in Europe. His only real rival was another German artist, Albrecht Dürer, but Dürer gave up his work on jewellery under the influence of Martin Luther, who declared such things to be vanities unsuited to good Christian living. From 1537 Holbein was in the service of Henry VIII and he was the first to introduce Renaissance themes and style into England. He also supplied designs for practising jewellers. A sketchbook of nearly 200 designs for jewellery survives; many of the jewels in Holbein's court portraits can be found in it.

Most coveted and most famous jewel ■ The jewel known as the Three Brethren, three large, nearly identical balas rubies and a huge pointed diamond, was the most renowned jewel in Europe. It enters recorded history in the possession of John the Fearless (d. 1419). When his grandson, Charles the Bold (1433–77), Duke of Burgundy, lost the battle of Grandson, Switzerland, in 1476 it was seized by the Swiss. By 1506 it was in the possession of the Fuggers, a firm of German bankers from Augsburg. Both the Habsburg emperors Charles V and Ferdinand I decided they could not raise the necessary cash to purchase it. Henry VIII agreed to the price, but died before completing the purchase. Edward VI managed to pay for it but died in 1553 before acquisition.

Most sought-after antiques ■ Cameos are small stones, gems or shells of several layers of colour which were carved in relief so that one colour formed a background. They were sought after because they made excellent jewellery, but they were also mounted in precious metal on cups and vases. Classical cameos were sometimes recut and many complete fakes were also marketed. Glass imitations were made in Milan, Italy. Intaglios are similar but the stone is incised instead of modelled, making them the most suitable for seals. Intaglios were therefore most popular for use in signet rings.

First declaration of crown jewels ■ Crown jewels are inalienable heirlooms distinct from the personal collection of the monarch. The first declaration of such jewels dates from 1530 and was made by Francis I of France. (The distinction refers to the gems, not the settings because the pieces were refashioned in 1559 by his immediate successor, Francis II. No record of the appearance of the jewels survives.)

A 16th century lapidary illustrated this cutter of precious stones at work.

Greatest collections ■ Shrines of saints amassed the great collections of jewels – given by the faithful in gratitude for healing or payment for sins. The unparalleled wealth of display was calculated to impress. The great scholar Erasmus (1466–1536) visited the famous shrine of the miracle-working St Thomas Becket at Canterbury, England, in 1514 and described the treasure which was contained in a coffin of gold, concealed within a coffin of wood which could be lifted by ropes and pulley. The contents were displayed by the prior who pointed out each item, reciting the value of each object and its donor's name. Gold, the scholar wrote, was the meanest thing to be seen and some of the gems were as big as a goose's egg. In 1538, when Henry VIII dismantled the monasteries and confiscated their properties, he greatly enriched his treasury and brought to an end a long-standing traditional source of wealth for the Church in England. The booty from the shrine of St Thomas filled two huge chests with gold and jewels that were so heavy that eight men could hardly move them.

JEWELS AND THE JEWEL TRADE

Venice, because of her trade with the Orient, was the centre for gem trading until gems and precious metals from the New World began to flow into Europe. But the sumptuary laws (against conspicuous display) there assured that her citizens maintained a conservative appearance. Jewelled hairbands were outlawed in 1505, along with pearl-studded belts. Necklaces were limited to one row of pearls at a maximum value of 200 ducats. The laws were renewed in 1541 and 1548.

The status of the jeweller became so important that these craftsmen began to be known by name. Engravers and goldsmiths in full-time employment included Giovanni delle Corniuole for Lorenzo de Medici at Florence and Domenico dei Cammei at Milan. The family name of the famous artist Ghirlandaio came from the family's business: making high-fashion gold and silver wreaths for ladies.

From the 15th century, when gem cutting began to be exploited, jewellery design was radically changed as it depended far less on the metals than on the colourful gems. The first four decades of the 16th century is the age when jewellery design is most closely linked with the styles of the fine arts painting and sculpture. More jewellery was worn than ever before or after. The large-scale designs and emphasis on great pieces contrasts with the former preference for delicacy.

The workshop of a 16th century craftsman in precious metals.

Toughest of all rocks ■ Washed down from the Kunlun mountains of north west China, jade is known as nephrite. It is also known as the 'Stone of Heaven'.

There are two chemically distinct materials that the world officially recognizes as jade: nephrite and jadeite. Nephrite is harder than most steel; jadeite is slightly harder but not as tough as nephrite. Jadeite is not found in China, but was imported from Burma.

The long-favoured colour of jade in China is 'mutton-fat' white. The practice of staining jade brown or black dates from the early Ming period. Colour depends on trace elements in the stone – green, for example, is a favourite colour for jewellery. This prized material was given in order of merit to award Chinese athletes: first prize, jade; second prize, gold; third prize, ivory. Objects of superb jade craftsmanship adorned scholar's desks. Jade was worn in the form of hairpins, rings and necklaces by Chinese empresses and buried among the most precious possessions of the emperors.

Wealth

Largest jade treasure ■ Pacal the Great, lord of the Mayan city of Palanque, reigned between 603 and 684 AD and, like the Egyptian pharaohs, wanted to build himself a funeral crypt. Naturally he had it constructed in the Mayan style, with a funeral chamber covered by a pyramid commonly known as the Temple of Inscriptions. His will, which was fulfilled, was that he should be buried in the crypt surrounded by an immense treasure of jade pieces, sealed with a large triangular stone and covered in more slabs of stone. (This tomb was found to contain the largest trove of jade ever known in America: a life-size mask, ear pieces, necklaces, rings and even hands of jade.)

Largest gold object of the Inca world ■ The largest of recorded dimensions was the ritual 'chain' or 'cable' made of plaited maguey fibre interleaved with sheets of gold, reputedly 150 fathoms *274 m* long. It was kept coiled in the great square in Cuzco, Peru, except during an annual festival when it was dragged in the waters of Lake Urcos, 75 miles *120 km* to the south.

Greatest hauls ■ Gold was already being mined in America when the Spaniards arrived. When Hernán Cortés (1485–1547) conquered the Aztecs at Tenochtitlan, at Mexico, in 1519 he took approximately 2000 lb *900 kg* of gold from Moctezuma. The native goldsmiths melted it down and cast it into ingots and stamped it with the royal arms of Spain. The treasure of the Incas in Peru was the greatest single 'find'. When Francisco Pizarro (*c.* 1478–1541) defeated them in 1531 he took away 13 000 lb *5800 kg* of gold.

Largest item of tribute ■ In the Aztec empire this was cotton. From a total of 371 tributary communities, 123 400 cotton mantles were due annually to Tenochtitlán, the Aztec capital, together with 665 suits of quilted cotton armour, 12 200 tunics and skirts and 4400 bales of raw cotton. Other plentiful items included: maize (224 000 bushels, plus 256 bushels of a mixture of maize with cacao or sage); black beans, sage and purslane (168 000 bushels each); cacao (980 'loads'), salt (4000 loaves), chillis (1600 bales), incense (64 000 balls of unrefined and 3200 'baskets' of refined copal plus 16 000 rubber balls), feathers (33 680 handfuls of ornamental feathers plus 20 sacks of down), canes (90 000 including spear-shafts and smoking-tubes), lime (16 800 'loads'), skins (3200 deer, 80 ocelot), liquid amber (16 000 cakes and 100 pots), turquoise, gold, jade and copper. Of the rarest and most valuable item, jade, Tenochtitlán received only 21 necklaces and three large beads annually, whereas the total gold tribute comprised one shield, two diadems, two necklaces, 10 tablets, 60 discs and 60 bowls of dust.

Most expensive Turkish crown ■ The jewel-encrusted, three-tiered golden tiara which Suleyman the Magnificent (1494–1566, sultan from 1520) ordered from Venice, Italy, held this record. He could only pay for it after he had received the annual revenues of three provinces.

Most precious offering ■ Over four centuries pilgrims bestowed gifts of enormous value on the shrine of St Thomas of Canterbury, England. Most famous of all was an immense ruby given by a French king and described by a Bohemian pilgrim in 1465 as 'so precious that if a king of England were taken prisoner one could ransom him with it for it is said to be worth more than the whole of England'. By 1492 treasure at the shrine represented the largest accumulation of portable wealth in England.

Greatest gift ■ When Hernandes de Soto met Cofachiqui, the Indian queen of Carolina, USA, in 1538 she gave him a necklace of pearls. Seeing how the Spaniards admired them, she invited them to search in the sepulchres of her town and neighbouring abandoned towns for more pearls. The Spaniards found and carried away 350 lb *159 kg* weight of pearls 'and figures of birds and babies made of them'. Despite her generosity, when de Soto left Cutifachiqui, her town, he carried her and her female slaves with him. She travelled over 300 leagues (*c.* 900 miles, *2000 km*) with him and arranged for the Spaniards' loads to be carried between towns along the way. Eventually she slipped away from him and returned home. The pearls were later lost in the battle at Mauilla in Alabama.

Strangest art-related custom ■ The potlatch ceremony of North West Coast Indians was the strangest art-related custom. Social status depended on giving away wealth in the form of fine art and no

Three examples of the work of craftsmen of the Renaissance using amethyst, jasper and fine silversmithing.

Most outstanding treasure trove ■ *In a tomb in the city of Monte Alban, Mexico, the remains of nine bodies were uncovered: a high dignitary and his companions, possibly buried by a funerary offering of gold: 10 breastplates, a mask 2¾ in 7 cm long representing the god Xipe Lotec, 11 rings, a crown, five earflaps, armlets, tweezers and paper-thin sheets. There were also 24 pieces of silver: bells, rings, bracelets, false nails and a jug. A large discus with a gold facing and one of silver, symbols of day and night, dating from the Aztec times of the 14th and 15th centuries, were some of the best examples of their kind in pre-Columbian central America.*

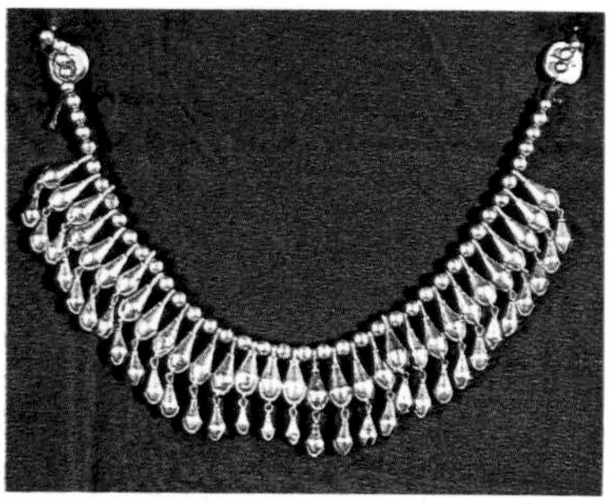

expense was spared as the most prominent members of the community attempted to outdo each other in generosity that led to poverty.

Most triumphant city ■ The wealth of Venice was based on dominance of traditional trading patterns in the Mediterranean and in particular of the luxury trade in spices, silks and carpets from the East. Together with Genoa, Venice controlled a great part of Europe's naval forces well into the 16th century. One of the greatest seaports of Europe, in 1500 Venice had a population of about 120 000, making it one of Europe's largest cities. It was described by a visitor at the end of the 15th century as 'the most triumphant city I have ever seen'.

Richest place in all the world ■ Malacca in southern Malaya was thus described in 1500. It was 'the mine of spices' to which all Asian traders were drawn as certainly 'as rivers flow to the sea'. To the entrepôt of Malacca went merchants from China and India, from Tunis and Japan. It gathered in goods from all these lands and dispersed them. Only Aden at the juncture of the Red Sea and the Arabian Sea competed as an entrepôt on the east-west routes with its 'unbelievable commerce', re-shipping spices westward, exporting gold from Africa, horses from Arabia and cloth from Europe.

Wealthiest monastery ■ In England the Benedictine abbey of Westminster, London, was the largest property owner, other than the Crown, in the land at the start of the 15th century.

Greatest shift of wealth ■ Between 1539 and 1546 Henry VIII sold off about two-thirds of the monastic property he had acquired through the abolition of the monasteries. He raised £800 000 in this way. This privatization created the biggest shift in English landowning since the Norman Conquest in 1066.

Wealthiest members of Great Zimbabwean society ■ Although it is not possible to measure the wealth of the king and 'barons' of Zimbabwean society, in southern Africa, it is known that they were clothed in foreign textiles from the Middle East and ate off celadon dishes imported from China. They paid for their luxuries with gold mined in the Shona gold-reefs and exported through the lowland emporium of Manikweni near the Mozambique port of Inhambane.

Wealthiest Englishmen ■ The richest men in England are revealed by a tax assessment of 1522. This did not cover the wealth of the King (whose income was estimated at about £40 000 a year in 1502–5) or the Church (with an income of something over £320 000 a year) or the aristocracy. Apart from the King and the royal family the richest men were London merchants. Sir Stephen Jenyons and Sir Thomas Seymour were rated at £3500, although their total wealth was much greater than this. Another London merchant, Robert Thorne the Younger (d. 1532) had a total estate worth around £20 000. Outside London, the richest man in 1522 was the cloth merchant Thomas Spring of Lavenham in Suffolk, whose goods alone were valued at £3200. Wealth was very unevenly distributed. In London those assessed at more than £100 constituted five per cent of the population yet owned 81 per cent of the wealth. The majority of the population owned virtually nothing. In Coventry, in the Midlands, for example, half the population were assessed as owning nothing, while the top 11 people in the town owned 44 per cent of the personal wealth.)

Wealthiest Frenchman ■ Early in the 15th century the name of the Frenchman Jacques Coeur was a byword for wealth. A proverb of the day said: 'Jacques Coeur does what he wants, the king what he can.' He was reputedly worth 500 000 florins and owned 30 castles, homes and estates in 50 villages, and copper, lead and silver mines. He amassed this wealth by trading directly with the Middle East and speculating in gold and silver. Not surprisingly, he was accused of embezzlement, false minting, treason and fraud and sentenced to death. Perhaps equally unsurprisingly, he managed to escape and fled to Rome. There he was appointed commander of a fleet being sent to the Greek islands to liberate them from the Turks. He died at Chios in 1459.

Extraordinary treatment of debtors ■ The Italian merchant Niccolo dei Conti who converted to Islam and travelled in the East between 1415 and 1439 reported this extraordinary treatment of debtors in Java: 'Debtors unable to pay their debts become slaves to those whom they owe, but others avoid this service by choosing death voluntarily in this way: they take a sword, go out into the streets, and kill everyone they meet until they encounter one who is better, who kills them; then the creditor of the dead man arrives and demands that the one who killed him must now pay his debts, and he is forced by the judges to comply.'

Greatest debt ■ A chronicler at the beginning of the 16th century recorded a debt of Prince Ury to his brother, the Russian tsar Ivan III, amounting to 315 000 roubles – a colossal sum.

Europe's wealthiest trading city ■ By 1550 Antwerp was handling up to 80 per cent of Flemish foreign trade. The volume of trade through the city was possibly three times as great as that through London. The trade items passing through Antwerp included cloth, spices, salt, jewels, minerals, wines, velvets, timber, furs, silks and saffron. The city's trading success spurred its growth, and Antwerp thrived as its rival Bruges declined because of the silting up of the River Zwyn. It had Europe's first real bourse, or exchange, in 1460, and a new building housing the bourse was built in 1531 (destroyed 1858). There were as many as 1000 foreign business houses in Antwerp at the beginning of the 1500s.

Outstanding wealth ■ An Italian description of England in about 1500 describes how '. . . in one single street [in London] named The Strand, leading to St Paul's, there are 52 goldsmiths' shops, so rich and so full of silver vessels, great and small, that in all the shops in Milan, Rome, Venice and Florence put together I do not think there would be found so many of this magnificence'. (In fact this street was not The Strand but Cheapside where, in 1491, a group of houses known as Goldsmiths' Row was erected.)

Most successful ■ The Medicis of Florence would certainly have been regarded as the most successful Italian, if not European, business families in 1450. They easily surpassed the rival families of the Strozzis and the Pazzis. Cosimo Medici (1389–1464) owned a banking enterprise and three companies manufacturing silk and wool in Florence. The Medicis also had outposts in Switzerland, Flanders, England and France as well as in other Italian cities. In the next decades they also acquired mining interests. Until 1474 they had what was a virtual monopoly on papal banking. The Medicis used their wealth to encourage art, literature and architecture, enriching Florence with splendid buildings.

Occupations

Greatest professional influence ■ An individual's character and profession could be most easily predicted from the planet which ruled the sign of the Sun at the time of birth; the theory of planetary children was the most popular astrological theme in the visual arts from the 14th century. Children of the Sun are kings, noblemen and stewards. Children of the Moon are common people, women, sailors, brewers, travellers, hunters. Children of Mercury are merchants, scholars, scribes, moneychangers and messengers; they can also be thieves or gossips. Children of Venus are tailors, embroiderers, musicians, perfumers, painters and sellers of women's clothing. Children of Mars are soldiers, butchers, physicians, hangmen, leather-workers and metal-workers; they can also be tyrants or thieves. The children of Jupiter are judges, men of law, churchmen and university scholars; they can also be clothiers, especially if they work with woollens. The children of Saturn are monks, miners, potters, undertakers, gardeners, herdsmen; they might also be beggars.

Most impressive job application ■ From *Leonardo da Vinci to the Duke of Milan, 1428*: Having, most illustrious lord, seen and considered the experiments of all those who pose as masters in the art of inventing instruments of war, and finding that their inventions differ in no way from those in common use, I am emboldened, without prejudice to anyone, to solicit an appointment of acquainting Your Excellency with certain of my secrets.

The name of the French merchant Jacques Coeur was a byword for wealth. But he fell from grace and ended his life in service at sea.

1. I can construct bridges which are very light and strong and very portable, with which to pursue and defeat the enemy; and others more solid, which can resist fire or assault, yet are easily removed and placed in position; and I can also burn and destroy those of the enemy.

2. In case of siege I can cut off water from the trenches and make pontoons and scaling ladders and other similar contrivances.

3. If by reason of the elevation or the strength of its position a place cannot be bombarded, I can demolish every fortress if its foundations have not been set on stone.

4. I can also make a kind of cannon which is light and easy of transport, with which to hurl small stones like hail, and of which the smoke causes great terror to the enemy, so that they suffer heavy loss and confusion.

5. I can noiselessly construct to any prescribed point subterranean passages either straight or winding, passing if necessary underneath trenches or a river.

6. I can make armoured wagons carrying artillery, which shall break through the most serried ranks of enemy, and so open a safe passage for his infantry.

7. If occasion should arise, I can construct cannon and mortars and light ordnance in shape both ornamental and useful and different from those in common use.

8. When it is impossible to use cannon I can supply in their stead catapults, mangonels, *trabocchi*, and other instruments of admirable efficiency not in general use – in short, as the occasion requires I can supply infinite means of attack and defence.

9. And if the fight should take place upon the sea I can construct many engines most suitable either for attack or defence and ships which can resist the fire of the heaviest cannon, and powders or weapons.

10. In time of peace, I believe that I can give you as complete satisfaction as anyone else in the construction of buildings both public and private, and in conducting water from one place to another.

I can further execute sculpture in marble, bronze or clay, also in painting I can do as much as anyone else, whoever he may be.

Moreover, I would undertake the commission of the bronze horse, which shall endue with immortal glory and eternal honour the auspicious memory of your father and of the illustrious house of Sforza.

And if any of the aforesaid things should seem to anyone impossible or impracticable, I offer myself as ready to make trial of them in your park or in whatever place shall please Your Excellency, to whom I commend myself with all possible humility.

Trade

Most sought-after trade ■ The commercial activity most likely to result in quick riches for European merchants was the buying and selling of high-value, low-bulk goods such as gold, precious stones, spices, silk, ivory, pearls and coral. Most of these came from Asian sources but, until the Cape of Good Hope was rounded, had to pass through the Mediterranean in order to reach the European markets. They increased greatly in add-on value as they travelled. The whole object of the Columbus voyage was to make contact with China and the great and rich world which was known to exist in Asia so that these goods could be brought directly by ship to Europe.

Most prized spices ■ The term 'spices' was used in the 15th century to include not only those used for preserving and seasoning foods but also a whole range of medicines, scents, dyes, waxes and gums. the most important spices in terms of value were various kinds of pepper, cinnamon, nutmeg and cloves.

Most desirable articles to the American Indians ■ In northern New England, when trading their furs with Europeans, the Indians appreciated fish-hooks, knives and other sharp metal articles above all else.

First Chinese merchants to visit Africa ■ Imperial Chinese ships commanded by Cheng-Ho visited the northern ports of the East African coast in 1417–19 and 1421–2. Large quantities of Chinese porcelain had previously reached Africa as trade goods brought by Indian and Arabian merchants.

First European settlement in Africa ■ The first permanent European settlement in sub-Saharan Africa was a trading fort and factory established on the orders of Prince Henry the Navigator of Portugal on Arguim Island off the coast of the modern Mauritania, probably about 1448. The factory was leased to private merchants who used it as a base to attract the Saharan gold trade.

Longest shopping trip ■ Vasco da Gama took over 10 months to cover the 7000 miles *12 200 km* around the Cape of Good Hope and reach the spice markets of south Asia. But he *did* reach them, and it was therefore the Portuguese, not the Spanish, who acquired a stranglehold over the spice trade.

Most lucrative expedition to India ■ Although only six of Cabral's royal fleet of 13 ships returned to Portugal from India in 1501, the sale of the cargoes of spices entirely covered the cost of the expedition. The effect of this new trade around the Cape of Good Hope on the old spice routes through the Levant was very speedy. When Venetian galleys went to Alexandria, Egypt, and Beirut, Lebanon, in 1504, the markets were almost empty. The Portuguese had bought up the supplies from the East. However, the trade recovered and 50 years later it was probably almost as great as before.

Greatest price increase ■ In the late 15th century pepper was in demand in Europe both as a preservative and as a flavouring. Pepper cost about 1 or 2 g of silver per kilogram in the producing areas of India and South-East Asia. By the time it reached Alexandria in Egypt it cost 10–14 g, in Venice it was 14–8 g, and the European consumer paid 20–30 g for each kilogram.

Rising food prices ■ In the 15th century the cost of living had been relatively stable throughout Europe, but there was a wave of inflation in the 16th century. In England, taking prices in 1501–10 as the base of 100, a basket of 12 food items (bread, ale, meat etc.) had risen to 180 by 1541.

Quickest valuation ■ A special commercial feature of the Malacca Sultanate of southern Malaya, which the Portuguese overthrew in 1511, was that ships requiring to leave the port urgently could sell their cargo *en masse* to a merchant consortium; to facilitate this, a committee of 'expert' merchants was used to make a rough and ready evaluation.

Most special gifts ■ The Arabian Peninsula was the only area in the world capable of exporting the gifts of the Three Wise Men: gold, frankincense and myrrh. Exports of all three took place from what is now the Sultanate of Oman. Other countries, such as India, produced and still produce two, but frankincense of quality occurs only in the northern valleys of Dhofar, Oman, where it was in earlier times exported by the Queen of Sheba.

Most important fisheries ■ Trade in dried and salted fish was very important to the economies of northern Europe. The fisheries of Skania, in southern Sweden, were the most important in Europe at the start of the 15th century but this importance declined and their place was taken by those of the North Sea during the century. This gave great benefits to the Netherlands and a contemporary Dutch saying went: 'The herring keeps Dutch trade going, and the Dutch trade sets the world afloat.'

First tourists to America ■ In 1536 a certain Captain Hore conducted a party of 30 young English gentlemen across the Atlantic to see the newly discovered lands for themselves. Originally planned as a fishing expedition, the journey was converted into a sightseeing tour of Newfoundland and the Gulf of St Lawrence. There were several misadventures: food ran short and one man was killed by another on shore and was then eaten for meat. The English party eventually met and overcame a French fishing vessel, took the ship and the stores and sailed safely home.

Strangest trading methods ■ Early Portuguese observers to the Indian subcontinent were astonished at some of the business techniques in use in centres like Goa. The practice of doing accounts 'by memory' rather than using an abacus seemed strange to them. Even stranger was a technique of bargaining wherein the two parties would make offers and counter-offers with the fingers of their clasped hands, which were concealed under a cloth, and thus hidden to curious passers-by.

Markets

Noblest emporium ■ In the mid-15th century Aeneas Piccolomini of Siena, in central Italy, praised Venice with its canals 'wide enough to admit a battleship with oars'. To this beautiful city came merchants and merchandise from all over the world so that there was not 'in Europe a nobler emporium'. The city, he commented, 'is all of brick . . . but if their power continues it will soon be all of marble'. Piccolomini reported enthusiastically on the wealth of the city where 'they say the pinnacle of the Campanile [bell tower] is gilded with 60 000 ducats' worth of gold . . . Daily,' he continued, 'that city grows, for there are no walls around it, only water.'

Largest African market ■ The city-state of Kano had one of the largest markets in Africa, serving the extensive textile and iron industries of post-medieval Hausaland (Nigeria). The caravan trade linked Kano to most parts of northern and western Africa. The ruling dynasty adopted Islam and invited philosophers, scholars, theologians and jurists to settle in the city. The most famous, Muhammad al-Maghili, was a royal adviser from 1463 to 1499. (Kano was still a centre of learning in the 19th century, when the first European visitor to Hausaland was asked if he could supply a work of classical Greek mathematics that had gone missing from the royal library.)

Biggest New World market ■ The market at Tlatelolco (near present-day Mexico City) was said to serve 20 000–25 000 people on a daily basis and up to 50 000 people every fifth day. According to a Spanish conqueror, the murmur could be heard four miles *6 km* off and the market square was bigger than any he or his comrades had seen in the Old World.

Largest shopping area ■ Many Islamic cities had vast market or bazaar areas, in which many shops and workshops were grouped together in one place or under one roof. The biggest of these was the Grand Bazaar or *Bedesten* in Constantinople. Construction was started soon after the conquest, in 1455, and was completed much later. It remained the centre of the town's commerce for 500 years. The original bazaar consisted of 140 shops under one roof, where the wealthiest merchants dealing in the finest and most expensive imported goods had their shops. It was strongly fortified to guard against robbery and fire. This market had 15 domes and was of great importance architecturally. Attached to it was a silk market with 200 shops. Four roads radiated out from the four gates of the bazaar, and this area also was roofed. This outer area had 12 large and 20 small gates, and over 1000 shops.

First commercial map-seller ■ Francisco Rosselli of Florence (1445–

1520) ran the first known map-shop in Europe. He sold not only sheet maps but also cartographic copper plates and wood-blocks. His stock included world maps, globes, sea charts and maps of individual countries, and his customers included some of the navigators on whose voyages the maps he sold were based.

First printed advertisement ■ The earliest printed piece of advertising to have survived was put up (probably in 1477) by William Caxton, England's first printer, who opened for business in the precincts of Westminster Abbey in 1476. It was for church service books which were 'to be had good chepe . . . empryntid after the forme of this present lettre'.

Slave trade

Seaborne slave trade ■ The first slaves to be brought from sub-Saharan Africa to Europe by sea were captured in the region of Cape Blanco and carried to Portugal by Antão Goncalves and Nuno Tristão in 1441 using ships equipped by Prince Henry the Navigator. In 1443 a fleet of six carvels brought about 200 men, women and children to be sold as slaves in Portugal at public auction. Thereafter slaves were brought to Europe at the rate of about 1000 a year until the end of the century.

First African slaves in the Caribbean ■ The Caribs and other native Americans were forced to labour for the Spaniards, but their numbers were quickly depleted by imported diseases and harsh treatment. European labour was seen as uncompetitive, so slaves began to be brought in from the Portuguese trading forts of West Africa. The first African slaves were shipped to the Caribbean in 1503, and from then on the trade grew rapidly. Until 1515 such slaves were purchased from the Portuguese in Lisbon, but from then on they were shipped directly from the Guinea Coast.

Most expensive slaves ■ African slaves were found admirably suited to the needs of the Spaniards in the Caribbean. They adapted well to the climate, and were able to endure physical hardship better than local people or Europeans. They had a fund of knowledge and skill about tropical agriculture from their homelands. They came from a continent where slavery was a familiar relationship. All these factors made them extremely valuable, and African slaves were three times the value of local slaves in the mid-15th century.

Comparative prices ■ At the auctions held in Portuguese Goa, in India, in the 16th century female slaves were paraded almost naked in the auction ring. They fetched the highest prices if they could sew, sing, dance and prove to a specialist that they were still virgin. Such women could fetch 30 *cruzados*. A fine horse from Arabia or Persia would sell for over 500 *cruzados*.

Wine trade

Most lucrative wines ■ The wines of northern Europe were generally light and dry, and unable to survive long in the barrel without turning sour. Generally they all had to be consumed within the year. In contrast the wines of southern Europe, particularly from the islands of the eastern Mediterranean and the Greek mainland, were much sweeter and higher in alcohol. This meant that they had a longer life, and could attract higher prices.

A tinted 15th century woodcut shows a wine grower checking the must (unfermented grape juice) of his harvest. Even at this time the wines of France had the reputation of being the best in the world.

Greatest consumption ■ The late 15th and early 16th centuries saw rapidly rising levels of wine consumption. In the late 15th century in parts of Germany consumption of wine per person is reported to have reached over 33 gallons *150 litres* per year, and by the middle of the 16th century average consumption in Vallodolid, Spain, was over 22 gallons *100 litres* per year. This rising tide of alcohol demand was fuelled primarily by an increase in the number of people living in towns. Increasingly in northern Europe wine began to be consumed by all levels of society, rather than just the élite, and there is some evidence that much wine quality consequently declined. In France the growth of Paris acted as a major influence on wine production, serving as the main market for most of the wines of northern France.

Most important trade routes ■ At an international level there were four main trade routes in the late 15th century: from the river valleys of western France to the north Eurpean ports of England, the Netherlands and the Baltic; from the Rhine and its tributaries northwards and eastwards to the Baltic and the North Sea; from the Mediterranean to northern Europe, either through the Straits of Gibraltar or via the Black Sea; and from Iberia westwards across the Atlantic to 'New Spain'. More locally, the rising urban demand was met by a constant flow of wine from the countryside surrounding most of the major urban centres.

Most significant wine importing countries ■ The countries of northern Europe, where it was difficult to produce large and reliable vintages of their own, were naturally the main wine importers. By 1492 the Netherlands and England were probably the two most important wine importers, but annual imports could vary dramatically from year to year. England's customs records, for example, indicate that only 4194 tuns were imported in 1509, in contrast to 17 518 tuns in 1521/2.

Most important wine port ■ Simon Bening's miniature of Bruges in Belgium dating from *c.* 1500 provides graphic illustration of the way in which wine was brought into one of the most important wine ports of northern Europe. Wine barrels were unloaded from lighters by a man-powered crane, with the ships which brought the wine from overseas probably being docked at the outer harbours of the city. One of the barrels is being filled up to compensate for wastage on the sea journey, and to minimize further oxidation and spoilage of the wine. Another barrel is being sampled, with a merchant offering the wine for tasting to a prospective customer. Nearby a carrier waits on his horse to transport the purchased wine.

Best-known Mediterranean wine ■ Numerous types of wine were encountered in international trade at the end of the 15th century. The main contrast was between the light wines of northern Europe, particularly from Bordeaux and the Rhine, and the sweet wines of the Mediterranean which were becoming increasingly important. Among the latter the best known were malmsey (or malvoisie) and romney (or rumney), both of which had traditionally been produced extensively in the eastern Mediterranean. These sweet wines also began to be made in large amounts in southern Spain during the 15th century.

'Best wine in the world' ■ By the end of the 15th century, the wines of Beaune in Burgundy were widely reputed to be the best in the world. This was certainly the view of Philip the Good, Duke of Burgundy, who claimed in 1459 that the wine of Beaune had a reputation as the leader of the best wines in all Christendom because of its good nature and excellence. It was certainly offered as a gift to the papal legate Georges d'Amboise when he made his official entry into Paris in 1501.

Dominant Spanish wine export ■ The final conquest of Granada in 1492 by Ferdinand II of Aragon and Isabella of Castille, the Catholic Monarchs, brought to an end the *Reconquista* of Iberia from the Moors and led to a resurgence of viticulture in southern Spain. The loss of Gascony to the French and the increasing preference for sweet wines led English merchants increasingly to venture to Spain for their supplies. In 1491, taxes on the export of wine from Sanlucar were abolished, and thereafter one wine in particular came to dominate southern Spanish exports: this was 'sack' from Jerez de la Frontera, the forerunner of sherry.

Last wine from eastern Mediterranean ■ The fall of Constantinople in 1453 led to the Muslim Ottoman Empire conquering the eastern Mediterranean, which had previously produced most of the high-value sweet wines in demand throughout Europe. Although some wine production and export continued from islands such as Rhodes, Cyprus and Crete during the 16th century, the eventual outcome was that northern Europe turned elsewhere for its imports of sweet, high-alcohol wines.

Earliest 'vintage' wines ■ In 1492 there was no such thing as a vintage wine. Most wine was consumed within the year in which it was produced, and even the sweeter, more alcoholic wines of the Mediterranean did not last for much more than a couple of years. However, during the 16th century numerous experiments were being undertaken in order to try to ensure that wines lasted longer. German tuns were one way in which this could be achieved, but Spanish wine producers were also experimenting with the addition of cooked wines to their normal products, and with the ageing of wines in barrels. It is also possible that the development of *flor* on the dry white wines of Jerez may first have been noticed during the 16th century. This served to protect such high-alcohol wines from the action of bacteria which would otherwise turn them to vinegar.

Most damaged wine trade ■ The year 1453 saw the final defeat of the English by the French at the Battle of Castillon near St Emilion in south-west France. Since the outbreak of the Hundred Years War, the Anglo-Gascon wine trade had been in dramatic decline. At the beginning of the 14th century between 90 000 and 100 000 tuns a year of wine were exported from Bordeaux, but by the 1430s this had dwindled to a mere 4000 or 5000 tuns a year. By the end of the 15th century, there had been some recovery in Bordeaux's exports to England to somewhere between 5000 and 10 000 tuns a year, but this was nevertheless only a fraction of what had once been the most flourishing of all European wine trade routes.

Largest tuns ■ During the late 15th century, German wine producers and merchants began to build huge barrels, known as tuns, for the storage of wine. These were regularly filled up, and because there was very little air in them compared with the vast quantities of wine they held, the wine lasted much longer than if kept in smaller barrels. In particularly fine vintages, when the grapes had a high sugar content, the wines couild last for a considerable time. Among the earliest recorded such barrels was the Strasburg Tun of 1472, and in 1500 monks at the Cistercian Abbey of Kloster Eberbach on the Rheingau inaugurated a barrel which could contain 15 500 gallons *70 000 litres*.

Currencies

Least knowledge of currency ■ When Europeans made the permanent discovery of North America they found a society which had no knowledge of money in any form. Trade had been conducted by means of barter: animal skins, cloth, coffee beans, tobacco and of course strings or woven belts of *wampum*. These served as a form of currency and consisted of threaded beads or discs made from shells. The word *wampum* was native North American in origin, meaning white and, if properly applied, referred to the white beads only, the black beads being known as *suckanhocks*. *Wampum* was usually shown with white and black beads either strung together or woven into patterns in the form of a belt. A string of *wampum* beads was known as *wampumpeag*. The beads were not merely used for trade but also as ornaments, a symbol of wealth, a talisman, or even regarded as semi-sacred.

First description of *wampum* ■ Jacques Cartier described in 1535 the most precious article the Indians of the island he named Montreal possessed: '. . . esognuy (wampum) which is as white as snow. They procure it from shells in the river in the following manner. When an Indian has incurred the death penalty or they have taken some prisoners of war, they kill one and make great incisions in his buttocks and thighs, and about his legs, arms and shoulders. Then at the spot where this esognuy is found, they sink it to the bottom and leave it there for ten or twelve hours. It is then brought to the surface and in the aforementioned cuts and incisions they find these shells, of which they make a sort of bead, which has the same use among them as gold and silver with us; for they consider it the most valuable article in the world.'

Most varied cash ■ Besides gold, silver and copper coins, other currency media also were used in Asia. Tin was commonly used for coinage in 15th-century Asia. In Bengal and Burma and elsewhere, cowrie shells, imported from the Maldive Islands, were used as small change. In Gujarat, almond seeds served the same purpose.

Cowries have been found in pre-dynastic Egyptian tombs and in Anglo-Saxon graves. Most emanated from the Maldive Islands and the Borneo-Philippines area where they were harvested in great numbers. Bronze replicas of cowries have also been found in Etruscan graves and gold replicas in Cyprus and Egypt. They were mentioned by both Marco Polo and Vasco da Gama, and in the more remote parts of the world continued as a currency for centuries.

Most widely used non-metallic currency ■ Of all the world's primitive non-metallic currencies the cowrie shell (*Cypraea moneta*) was the most prolific and widely spread. By the year 1492 it was accepted as a unit of exchange throughout parts of Asia, Africa, Europe and beyond.

The Moghul Empire valued a single cowrie at 0.000 39 (1/2560th) of a rupee. It is doubtful if cowries were ever used as money in the Americas, although they have been found in early burials which show no trace of European influence.

Coins

Longest circulating ■ Chinese bronze *ch'ien* or cash coins were first introduced in the T'ang dynasty. Early examples with the inscription K'ai Yuan, issued 618–26 AD, were still circulating in 1492 and continued to circulate until early in the 20th century. Cash coins were round with a square hole in the centre, enabling them to be strung together in lots of 100 or even 1000 (1000 cash were equal to one silver tael of 1.3 oz *37 g*). The type remained basically unchanged for over 1300 years. Other Chinese coins such a the Wu Ch'u money of the Han dynasty (first century

Right: Belts and strings of shell beads known as wampum were a currency in North America.

AD) probably had a sporadic circulation of nearly 2000 years.

Oldest coins ■ *The electrum staters of King Gyges of Lydia, Turkey, date from 670* BC.

Most widely used commercial coins ■ Ferdinand and Isabella of Spain introduced a new monetary system in 1497. The system included the eight-*reales* piece which was to become famous as the romantic 'piece of eight'. Few such pieces were actually struck before the return to Spain of Charles V in 1517. The type showing the Pillars of Hercules and the legend *plus ultra* (more beyond) was struck by Spanish-American mints from 1535. Later issues were struck in vast quantities. The coin provided an almost universal currency at the time. It was accepted in most parts of the world and was extensively countermarked and overstruck in many countries.

The later Latin-American denomination called a peso is really short for *peso de á ocho* (piece of eight).

Roman coins were still in use in some areas long after 1492.

Largest known true coin ■ In 1492 the largest known true coinage was the Roman republican *Aes Grave* (*c.* 269 BC), made in central Italy. The heaviest of these cast bronze coins was the multiple *Decussis as* (10 asses) which weighed 6 lb ¼ oz *2730 g*.

A shilling showing the boy king Edward VI who came to the English throne in 1547.

Smallest gold coin in circulation ■ King John of Aragon (1458–79) issued a gold quarter-florin which weighed 7/250 oz *0.80 g*. The *mas* was a tiny gold coin current in Sumatra between 1297 and 1760 under the sultans of Atjeh. Some examples contained less than 7/500 oz *0.4 g* of pure gold. In 1336 the Hindu dynasty of Vijayanagar rose to power in southern India and a gold *fanam* was produced weighing a mere 1/100 oz *0.3 g*.

Largest European silver coin ■ Archduke Sigismund's mint of Hall-in-Tyrol first struck a silver *guldengroschen* or *guldiner* in the year 1486. The coin had a diameter of 1 3/5 in *41 mm* with a thickness of 1/8 in *2.33 mm* and weighed 1 Troy ounce *31.3 g*. It was the precursor of the German *thaler* (a name which was later corrupted to 'dollar').

Smallest silver coin in circulation ■ In England, silver farthings of Edward IV's light coinage (*c.* 1464–7) and similar issues by Henry VII (minted *c.* 1490–4) would have been current in 1492. The standard weight of each is recorded at 3 grains – just 4/625 oz *0.194 g* with an average diameter of 3/10–3/8 in *7.5–9.5 mm*. The coins were produced in very small numbers and today few examples have survived. Small Indian punch-marked silver coins weighing as little as 53/10 000 oz *0.15 g* might still have been in circulation in the 15th century.

First successful pure copper in Europe ■ The Kushanas of India used copper for coinage (*c.* 100 AD) and the Abasid caliphs struck coins in copper throughout parts of North Africa from the seventh century. However, the first regular issue of copper coinage in the western world was in the form of the *cavallo* introduced by Ferdinand of Aragon in 1472 for the Kingdom of Naples and Sicily. The *cavallo* takes its name from the reverse type, a horse and the inscription *Equitas regni* (Justice reigns). Multiples of 2, 3, 4, 6 and 9 *cavalli* are known, which is not really surprising, for the unit was only equivalent to 1/200 *0.005* of a ducat. It was a token coinage without any intrinsic value, but couild be converted into good money.

Origin of the dollar symbol ■ North American coinage was inextricably linked to the Spanish eight-reales in more ways than one. The first emissions from the Mexico City mint in 1535 were eight-reales pieces struck on large thin blanks giving them the impression of a medieval coin, but later issues were struck on roughly shaped pieces of silver (cobs) hewn from cast sheets or cylinders. In addition to the eight-reales piece the mint also produced pieces of 4, 2, 1, 1/2 and even 1/4 reales. The two-reales and its fractions were simply bits of silver showing parts of a crudely stamped design. The term 'bits' has persisted through the centuries as a nickname for a quarter dollar. The main feature of the design on the 'cob' eight-reales was the figure 8 between two pillars. It is easy to see how, in written form, this soon took on the appearance of an 'S' between two lines – and so the dollar symbol was born!

A copper cavallo introduced by Ferdinand I as King of Naples.

The Cross of Jerusalem appeared on the observe of the Spanish gold escudo of Charles I and his mother Johanna. Charles was elected to the Holy Roman Empire as Charles V in 1519.

A gold double ducat of Ludovico Sforza minted in about 1495.

First African coins ■ The first coins minted in black Africa were produced by the Shirazi sultans of Kilwa, on the East African coast, towards the end of the 12th century. Silver and copper coins carrying the names of different sultans were minted at different times during the next 200 years. During the same period coins were also minted at Mogadishu, Somalia.

First numeric dates on coins ■ From early times coins were often marked with the year of the issuing monarch's reign or year of office. The Omayyad caliphs of Cordoba (North Africa and Spain) struck gold dinars 'dated' as 138 AH (756 AD) and in Damascus as early as 38 AH (659 AD). The Danish bishops of Roskilde issued silver pence dated 1234 AD (MCCXXXIIII) and there are isolated numerically-dated European coins up to the mid-15th century. The date 1474 on a Gelderland double-*vuurijzer* is the earliest known date in numerals on the Netherlands coinage. In Britain, the first numerically-dated coin was the Scottish 40-shilling piece of 1539, while the first English coin to bear a numeric date was the Edward VI gold half-sovereign of 1548 (MDXLVIII).

First portrait coin of the Renaissance ■ A gold ducat was struck for Francesco Sforza of Milan in Italy soon after 1450 but, not being thick or large enough for high relief, the coin was not a success artistically. Antonio Marescotti then engraved and struck a ducat of Borso d'Este in 1452. Little is known of this 15th-century medallist, Marescotti, except that he was working at the mint of Ferrara in Italy during the years 1444–62.

First thistle on Scottish coins ■ The national emblem of Scotland, the thistle head, first appeared on a base silver groat of James III of Scotland (1460–88) minted at Edinburgh between 1471 and 1475.

First use of the *tughra* on Islamic coins ■ The *tughra* or ornamental signature of the ruler which appears on many of the coins issued by Islamic countries was first used on an Ottoman coin by the emperor Suleyman bin Bayazid in 1404 AD.

First round silver farthings ■ These were issued in England on 4 August 1279 during the reign of Edward I (1272–1307). Before this farthings had been produced by simply chopping a silver penny into quarters – 'fourthlings'. Round silver halfpennies were not issued on a regular basis until a year later, although limited numbers of round halfpennies had been issued, on what seems to have been an experimental basis, from the reign of Alfred the Great (871–99).

First true Turkish gold coin ■ The gold *altun* was struck for the first time by Mehmet II in 1478 after the capture of Constantinople. The *altun* replaced the Venetian gold *zecchino* or sequin which had previously supplied all Turkey's currency needs in gold.

First gold sovereign ■ In England the pound sterling had been a denomination of account for centuries, yet a pound coin had never been minted. The year 1489 saw radical changes to the English coinage with the introduction of a magnificent gold pound coin. It was known as a sovereign after the design which featured the monarch enthroned in majesty. The reverse side of the coin displayed the royal arms set on a Tudor rose. The first issue of sovereigns weighed approximately 1/2 oz *15.5 g* of 23-carat gold and measured 1 3/5 in *41 mm* in diameter.

First silver shilling ■ Like the pound sterling, the shilling (12 old pence, equivalent to five new pence) had been money of account in England since Saxon times. A silver coin of that denomination was first struck in Henry VII's reign in 1503/4. It was initially known as a testoon from the Italian *testone* which seems to have inspired its design. Produced by the master engraver Alexander de Brugsal, it was the first English coin to bear a realistic portrait of the monarch.

Henry VIII's 'Crown of the Rose'.

First English crown piece ■ Henry VIII introduced a new denomination to the English coinage system in 1526. It was a gold coin called the 'crown of the rose' and was valued at four shillings and sixpence (about 22p). It was introduced as a competitor to the successful French *écu au soleil* but proved a failure and within a few months was replaced by the 'crown of the double rose' (valued at five shillings, 25p). This coin was a success despite being only 22-carat fineness, the first time an English gold coin had been minted below the standard 23¾ carat. (The more familiar silver crown did not appear in currency until 1551 during the reign of Henry's son, Edward VI.)

Paper money

Earliest ■ Paper money is an invention of the Chinese, first tried in 812 AD and prevalent by 970 AD.

Largest ■ The largest paper money ever issued was the 1-kwan note of the Chinese Ming dynasty issue of 1368–99, which measured 9 × 13 in *22.8 × 33 cm*.

Earliest surviving paper money ■ The concept of using paper in the form of a promissory note is attributed to T'sai Lun in 105 AD, during the Chinese Han dynasty. The earliest surviving paper note dates from the reign of Hung-Wu (1368–98 AD), who was founder of the Ming dynasty. Printed in black ink on mulberry bark paper, it measures 1 ft 2 in *360 mm* high by 9 in *230 mm* wide and displays two vermilion imperial seal stamps. The note proclaims that it is 'The Great Ming General Currency Precious Note' and continues to state that 'counterfeiters will be beheaded, informers will receive 250 liang in reward plus the entire property of the counterfeiter'.

Kublai Khan (1214–94), Mongol khan and emperor of China, supervises the distribution of paper money. Notes like these were current until the middle of the 15th century. Marco Polo, the Venetian merchant and traveller spent 17 years in the service of Kublai Khan and, on his return to Europe in 1295, told a great deal about his experiences of China and his route there in his very popular book of travels. His account of his travels was still circulating widely in Europe in the 15th century.

Banking and credit

Greatest inflation ■ Worst inflation of the period occurred in China where paper money had been in use since the ninth century simultaneously with copper and silver coins. Seventeen paper *caixas* (national currency) were valued at 13 copper *caixas* in 1378. But the central government – trying to 'balance the books' – started to print paper money so rapidly that 1000 paper *caixas* was valued at 13 copper *caixas* by 1448.

Most important French fair ■ From 1494 as trade picked up again between north-west Europe and the Mediterranean, and Tuscany was yielding financial power to Genoa, the quarterly fair at Lyons in France came to dominate all others. It served two purposes. First, agreement between merchant banks as to what was to be paid (accepted bills of exchange, and a fixed money of account – the *écu de mark* expressed as a fraction of the gold mark coin – set for each fair). Secondly, clearance of debts (either by set-offs – *virement des parties* – involving A and B directly or via a debtor C; or in cash borrowed from merchant bankers at a stipulated rate, the *dépôt de tent*). Credit would be given 'from fair to fair', sometimes 'across two fairs'. The system worked well. The fair lasted for upwards of three weeks for the financial part alone, starting at the Epiphany (early January), Low Sunday (the Sunday after Easter), early in August and at All Saints' (early November). Lyons was the occasion to settle bills on foreign countries (hostilities were suspended so that merchants of warring nations could attend). The Lyons fair was a pressure-group for Tuscan, Milanese and Genoese bankers: their financial arrangements had to be followed by France, south Germany, the Rhineland and the Netherlands.

Most entrenched corruption ■ Cosimo de'Medici (d. 1464) linked the struggle for political power in Florence's Council to conspicuous spending on public buildings for the city, also on taxes and works of charity. Cosimo got through 400 000 florins in this way. His son Lorenzo took this a stage further, seeing no difference between the state's finances and his own. If a war was to be funded, the necessary bonds were no longer low-interest paper secured on Florence's state debt, but instead high-interest loans made by current office-holders and their rich friends. Servicing these expensive loans could only be done by adding to the debt and weakening the value of the bonds that

A merchant and his wife check the cash and accounts.

Able, astute and embued with a love of art, Cosimo (1389–1464), 'the father of the Medici family', established the Medici domination of Florence, Italy.

carried it, or by raising taxes on the citizenry. This earned Lorenzo much dislike. The most flagrant single example of corruption, however, was enacted by his son Piero when Charles VIII led French troops into Tuscany *en route* for Rome. Piero secured the French safe conduct by means of bribes to local commanders so large that a sense of outrage was felt even by Medici supporters, who disowned him. Florence exiled the family for the next 18 years.

Most frequent form of long-term credit ■ In the countryside such credit was rare (farmers were lent corn in parts of Italy and Spain, or they could deposit savings with a notary and borrow against them). In the city a small businessman would often acquire credit by selling annuities. These were regular tax payments on land that got round the ban on usury by being limited to a maximum of 10 per cent of capital employed and by being redeemable; a Papal Bull of 1455 set out the conditions governing them. The businessman might buy land for development, sell it to home-builders and use the annuities he received (they ran for up to three lifetimes) to buy more land. A register of annuities in Antwerp dated 1545 shows the lower-middle class strong among the purchasers.

First Fugger loan to an Imperial borrower ■ Jakob Fugger, grandson of the founder of the Augsburg weavers and merchants, was not the first of his family to do business with royalty. (One of his brothers in 1473 supplied the Emperor Frederick III's entourage with 'good cloth and silks' for a visit abroad.) But the next royal transaction shows how they would conduct this business for the future. In 1487 Jakob, together with Antonio de Cavallis of Genoa, advanced 23 627 florins to Siegmund, Archduke of Tyrol, on the security of the best of the Schwatz silver mines and the whole province of Tyrol. The following year a further 150 000 florins was loaned, and until the entire debt was repaid the Fuggers received all the silver produced at Schwatz for what was a nominal price. They recovered their money in 1496 – deducting it from another loan made to Siegmund's successor as governor of Tyrol, the Emperor Maximilian I. Over the next century such lending gave Fuggers unmatched size and strength as a finance house.

Low-water mark for Medici bank ■ 1492, the year of Lorenzo de'Medici's death, saw the bank that had been founded by his great-grandfather about to join in a general collapse of banking confidence. Forty years earlier the Medicis had opened their 10th branch, a fine palace built by the family's adopted architect Michelozzo at Milan. Their assets then totalled some 100 000 florins, and an outstanding general manager, Giovanni Benci, ran a network that extended from Rome via Geneva, Lyons and Bruges to London. Medici trading dealt in staples such as wool and oil, and also luxuries for their richer clients. They were bankers to the Pope, with a branch that travelled with him to whichever of Florence, Avignon and the Vatican was his current seat. But Lorenzo earned Sixtus IV's anger by refusing him a loan in the 1470s – this led to the assassination attempt on Lorenzo in 1478. And by the following decade banks like the Medicis' were in difficulty because their north European branches found made-up goods and raw materials increasingly hard to obtain for Italy. Also the family name attracted loan-hungry kings such as Edward IV in England (Lorenzo had to close the bank's London branch), the very business it did not want.

First Imperial land-mortgage to Fuggers ■ Maximilian I, emperor from 1508, was soon involved in 10 years of war in Italy. He needed money to pay his Swiss mercenaries, but lacking credit and with only the deferred income from a tax voted him by the Imperial Diet to look to, had no means of raising cash. He was thus forced to mortgage his revenues as Count of Kirchberg and Lord of Weissenhorn to the Fuggers for 50 000 florins. It was a mortgage never redeemed. These lands mark the start of Jakob Fugger's massive acquisitions of property.

Least family-dominated finance house ■ The Welsers, one of the oldest trading firms in Augsburg, began very much as a family concern. Three brothers joined with one outsider (Hans Vöhlin). The brother named Lucas had three sons, Anton, Lucas and Jakob, each with a branch of the business called after him. Anton married Vöhlin's daughter in 1479. His firm of Welser and Vöhlin soon became established, dealing in silver. Even

Jakob Fugger II, head of the great German banking family was painted by Albrecht Dürer in 1518.

when they lent money to the emperor, the Welsers (unlike the Fuggers) never gave up trading. Another difference was in their partnership structure. Few of them were related more than distantly: the partnership articles of 1508 list 18 names, of which only four were immediate Welser/Vöhlin family. Control was spread across many individuals (the opposite case to Fuggers) who ran the factories themselves rather than delegate this. The Welsers therefore tended to have a well-informed if sometimes combative management style (several partners broke away in 1517).

First long-term French national debt ■ The fair at Lyons with its liquidity, reserves and various forms of credit was used by many French kings as a short-term loan source, usually on a fair-to-fair basis. By 1522 these loans became advances secured by the Crown and paid against income from the sale of rents on *l'hotel de ville de Paris* due to the royal account. Annuities on Paris were on sale eight years later.

Fastest international transfer of funds ■ In 1508 the League of Cambrai (the Habsburg emperor Maximilian I, Louis XII of France, Ferdinand of Spain, Pope Julius II and the rulers of Ferrara and Mantua) aimed to partition Venice's territories between themselves. It promised Maximilian subsidies of 170 000 ducats. In financial trouble as usual, Maximilian needed the money at once and all to be paid in Germany; however, the separate contributions were for payment in cities as far apart as Antwerp, Rome and Florence. Jakob Fugger used bills of exchange and succeeded in getting an interim sum to Augsburg inside two weeks. The balance followed within six weeks of the start – a record at a time when bills of exchange were not used internationally in northern Europe.

First lease of revenues – Spanish Crown to Fuggers ■ The three-year lease (1525–7) of dues from lands of the Knightly Orders of St Jago, Calatrava and Alcantara saw the start of a huge Spanish business for the Fuggers. This 'Maestrazgos' lease later included output of the quicksilver mines at Almadén (mercury was needed for a new process of treating silver). Genoa outbid Fuggers for a five-year renewal, but the German family took up the lease again subsequently and held it for 100 years. That part of Charles V's election debt that was assigned to Spain was paid off by the Maestrazgos lease.

Most powerful banker family ■ Death of a senior partner and the need to redistribute assets would be an (often unique) occasion for a company balance sheet. Jakob Fugger died in January 1526. The family was then at the height of fame and importance, owning mines and mining shares in the Tyrol (silver) and Hungary (copper), also land in southern Germany. Habsburg imperial debts formed its main assets (King Ferdinand of Austria alone owed 651 000 florins). The balance sheet drawn up in the year after Jakob's death showed 3 million florins standing to the Fuggers' account.

Largest capital held by one firm ■ Under Anton Fugger, the great Augsburg finance house enlarged its business capital. At end-year 1546 its claims on the Spanish Crown and on Antwerp alone totalled 2.75 million florins. In terms of profit-earning revenue Spain and Hungary contributed most (2.6 million, or almost 90 per cent of total net profit). The company's assets (7.1 million) left Anton and his nephews with a capital of some 5 million florins, the largest ever held by one firm.

Taxes

Highest figure for taxes paid in silver ■ The first Ming emperor tried to base China's money system entirely on paper notes and copper coins. All taxes reached the treasury in that form. Bullion mining was strictly controlled, and both silver and gold were banned from commercial transactions. Inflation soon weakened the value of paper notes; a shortage of copper currency held back what was then the world's largest economy. So despite the restrictions silver was much used. Western traders who came to China in the 16th century were left in no doubt that payment must be in silver. Because they bought large quantities of goods, their trade gave the economy a powerful stimulus. Figures for taxes paid in silver show this happening. In 1528 the treasury collected 1.3 million taels (107 473 lb *48 750 kg*). Some 11 years later the figure topped 2 million taels (165 344 lb *75 000 kg*) for the first time in China's history.

Science and technology

MATHEMATICS • CODES AND CIPHERS
ENGINEERING • CLOCKWORK • NEW
TECHNOLOGIES • THE WAR MACHINE

Mathematics

Oldest mathematical puzzle ■ dating from 1650 BC. This is the English version:

As I was going to St Ives
I met a man with seven wives.
Every wife had seven sacks,
and every sack had seven cats.
and every cat had seven kittens.
Kitten, cats, sacks and wives,
how many were going to St Ives?

Earliest measures ■ The earliest known measure of weight is the *beqa* of the Amratian period of Egyptian civilisation *c.* 3800 BC found at Naqada, Egypt. The weights are cylindrical with rounded ends from 6.65 to 7.45 oz *188.7– 211 g*.

The unit of length used by the megalithic tomb-builders in north-western Europe *c.* 3500 BC appears to have been 2.72 ± 0.003 ft *82.90 cm ± 0.09 cm*.

Most precise measures ■ To prevent fraud and to ensure fairness in trade attempts began in 1491 to establish uniformity in English weights and measures. In 1497 a new standard yard was defined by an octagonal brass rod one and a half inches thick, which was only 0.037 in *9.4 mm* short of the current imperial yard. Tudor standards for weights and measures were among the most precise and sophisticated in Europe.

The longest moment of all time ■ The medieval measures of time were concerned with the hypothetical fractional units of the canonical hour (any of those hours specifically appointed for prayers and devotions). In consequence, they are linked with Christian theology and the philosophical writers who were considered the authority. Thus, they have a history of great antiquity. In the measures of time, the smallest unit was the *atom* (from the Latin *atomus*, 'a twinkling of the eye'). According to one such authority, Papias (a bishop of Hieropolis, Phrygia in the second century), there were 22 560 atoms to the hour. His table of time read as follows:

PREVIOUS PAGE: The decorative technique of creating pictures from inlay of contrasting pieces of wood was used, in 1479, to decorate the study of the Ducal Palace at Urbino, Italy, with symbols of science and technology.

		MODERN EQUIVALENT
47 atoms . . . . . =	*1 ounce . . . .*	*(7½ seconds)*
8 ounces . . . . . =	*1 ostent . . .*	*(1 minute)*
1½ ostents . . . =	*1 moment . .*	*(1½ minutes)*
2⅔ moments . . =	*1 part . . . . .*	*(4 minutes)*
1½ parts . . . . . =	*1 minute . . .*	*(6 minutes)*
2 minutes . . . . =	*1 point . . . .*	*(12 minutes)*
5 points . . . . . =	*1 hour . . . .*	*(1 hour)*

The authority for the record-breaking moment may well be a 12th century figure, Honorious Augustodunensis of Autum, who divided the canonical hour into four points as opposed to the five points of Papius. He also had fewer atoms to the hour – 22 500 as opposed to the 22 560 of Papius. His particular table read as follows:

1 HOUR =	*4 points*
	or
	10 minutes
	or
	15 parts
	or
	40 movements
	or
	60 marks
	or
	22 500 atoms

However, the moment (which, today, has no specifically computable value) represented an even longer period of time according to another authority. The 1495 edition of *The Descrypcyon of Englonde* (a précis of a 14th century classic) stated, 'An hour containeth four points and a point ten moments.' A moment reckoned on this basis is the longest of all time.

Smallest weight ■ The smallest weight legally recognized in England was the *grain*. This equated to a dry barleycorn taken from the middle of an ear of barley. However, moneyers had even smaller divisions of weight and the smallest of these was the *blank*. There were 230 400 blanks to the grain! The full table was as follows:

24 blanks . . . . =	*1 perit*
20 perits . . . . =	*1 dwit*
24 dwits . . . . =	*1 mite*
20 mites . . . . =	*1 grain*
24 grains . . . . =	*1 pennyweight*
20 pennyweights . . . =	*1 ounce (troy)*
12 ounces (troy) . . . . =	*1 pound (troy)*

Most accurate census ■ The Europeans discovered an Incan society divided into nominal tributaries of 10, 50, 100, 500, 1000, 5000, 10000 and 40000. This decimal system was introduced by the Inca Pachacutec and it was said that the Inca knew exactly how many llamas and men were at his disposal. As there was no written system of recording, it was done using the *quipu*. This was an instrument of accounting consisting of a large central cord from which hung other cords like a comb. There were knots made at different heights along each of the 'teeth' and arranged in a decimal system – units at the lower end, then tens, hundreds, thousands etc. The cords were coloured differently to distinguish between the various utilities being accounted for, e.g. yellow for maize etc. Only the *quipucamayoc* who had created the individual quipu would be able to interpret his accounts. A single error in the counting could cost him his life, so they were rarely fallible.

The unique mathematicians ■ The Aztecs were the dominant peoples of Mexico from their arrival, *c.* 1200, until 1519 when, at the peak of their glory, they were overthrown by Cortés. Among their accomplishments was a unique and amazing system of mathematics.

A single number was considered neutral, but once subjected to the effect of a second number it became either good or evil. If it was good it was retained in the calculations, if it was evil it was rejected. If the secondary number was even, then the basic number was evil; if the secondary number was odd then the basic number was good. The Aztecs completely ignored fractions yet, despite this, were unfailingly accurate.

Take a trivial example: 35 × 10. 10 being even, therefore evil, means that 35 will have to be ignored in the subsequent calculations. By contrast, however, 10 × 35 has 10 accepted because 35 is good. In order to multiply either number by the other, the Aztecs would continue doubling the base number whilst simultaneously halving the secondary number (ignoring fractions) until that secondary number reached unity. Once unity has been reached all of the good numbers in the base column are added together and the correct result pertains:

(A) 35 × 10

~~35~~	:	10	(10 evil, reject 35)
70	:	5	(5 good, accept 70)
~~140~~	:	2	(ignore ½, 2 evil, reject 140)
280	:	1	(1 good, accept 280)
350			(Unity achieved, add together all good numbers)

(B) 10 × 35

10	:	35	(35 good, accept 10)
20	:	17	(ignore ½, 17 good, accept 20)
~~40~~	:	8	(ignore ½, 8 evil, reject 40)
~~80~~	:	4	(4 evil, reject 80)
~~160~~	:	2	(3 evil, reject 160)
320	:	1	(1 good, accept 320)
350			(Unity achieved, add together all good numbers)

Algebra ■ The origins of algebra are murky. Babylonians, Greeks and Indians can all claim to have been among the first to use an algebraic system. Influential work by the Islamic scholar Muhammad ben Musa al Khwarizmi (about 825) was widely read and translated into Latin by Robert of Chester about 1126. Leonardo of Pisa (Leonardo Fibonacci) was prominent in introducing algebra to Italy, where it was known as the 'rule of coss', or the 'great art'. Fibonacci's *Liber abaci* (Book of counting) (1202, 1228) played a key part in introducing Arabic numerals to Europe.

Luca Pacioli of Venice (1494) wrote the first printed book on algebra. François Vieta of France (1540–1603) gave algebra the name of the 'analytical art' and pioneered the use of letters for numbers. Vieta used vowels for unknown quantities and consonants for known quantities.

Plus and minus signs ■ The use of these signs in mathematics in Europe is attributed to Stephilius (Steifel), about 1536, but the multiplication sign was not introduced until the 17th century.

The most perfect shape ■ The circle was determined to be the most perfect shape; it has no beginning and no end and is therefore a most appropriate symbol for God. Leonardo da Vinci discovered that Man's proportions are also ideally suited to fit perfectly within the circle. The famous Vitruvian man in the Galleria della Accademia in Florence drawn by Leonardo *c.* 1492 is named for the classical architectural theorist Vitruvius whose work *De Architectura* was rediscoverd in the 15th century and first printed in 1486. The centralized plan was the most radical innovation in church design; a circular central space was created within a square building when it was covered by a circle in the shape of a domed ceiling.

Trigonometry ■ Trigonometry deals with the specific functions of angles. It was known to ancient mathematicians and astronomers in India, Arabia and possibly in Greece. The creation of trigonometry as a modern mathematical discipline was largely the work of the 13th-century Persian mathematician Nasir ad-din at-Tusi, and Johann Muller of Germany, known as Regiomontanus (1436–76), whose book on trigonometry *De triangulis* (Concerning triangles) was written in 1464, but was not published until 1533.

Earliest manual of double-entry bookkeeping ■ The *Summa de Arithmetica*, 1494, by the Franciscan Luca Pacioli of Venice, was the first instructional guide set out as such. Double-entry accounting had been in use in south Europe among merchants of importance for a century or more. It travelled north as 'quantities dealt in' became the point of interest for bookkeeping.

First study of probability ■ Before the eminent Italian physician, naturalist and mathematician Girolamo Cardano (1501–76) became famous and wealthy he supplemented his meagre income by gambling. For a two-year period in the early 1540s he was obsessed by games to the extent that his medical practice began to suffer. The skill and experience he acquired through chess, dice and card-playing led him to write the first study of the principles of probability. *Liber de Ludo Aleae* (Book of Games of Chance) includes advice for spotting loaded dice and marked or soaped cards. He recommended gambling as an antidote to melancholy, but warned that it was a possible cause of bankruptcy.

Codes and ciphers

Most useful secret inks ■ There are two types of invisible ink and both have been known since classical times. The first is organic fluids which reveal their message by gentle heating. Urine is one such fluid. The second is sympathetic chemicals. One chemical fluid which is colourless when dry is used to write the message and if a suitable reagent is painted over it the words appear in colour. In 1492, several invisible inks of both types were known and diplomatic correspondence made use of them.

Letter frequency ■ The Arabs were the first to discover the value of letter-frequency in codebreaking and by 1492 had been practising this art for nearly two centuries.

China's only known code ■ From the 11th century onwards the only known code was a list of 40 military statements ranging from a request for more arrows to the proclamation of a victory. Each statement was represented by a specific segment of poetry quoted in an otherwise normal despatch.

Greatest encylopaedia ■ The Egyptian Qalqashandi completed his massive 14 volume encyclopaedia in 1412. Written for the secretary class, it included sections on ciphers, codebreaking, invisible inks and symbolic attitudes and actions.

First European book ■ In 1518, 18 months after the death of its author, the world's first book devoted solely to the science of writing in code was published. Written by the Benedictine monk, Johan-

Portrait of the Italian mathematician Luca Pacioli of Venice who wrote the first book on geometry (and book-keeping) to be printed. He is surrounded by the tools of his vocation.

LEON BATTISTA ALBERTI'S CIPHER DISK

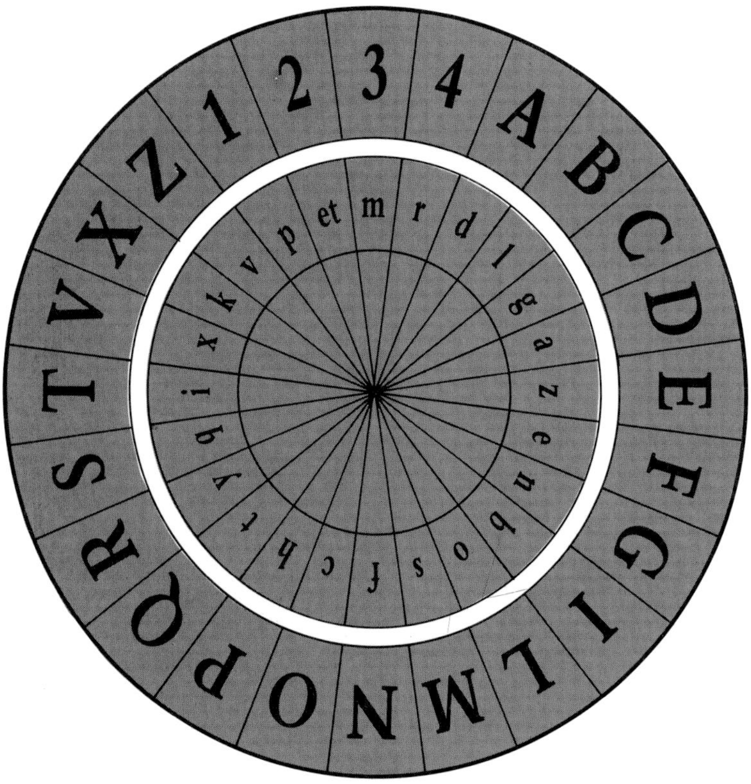

SECRET COMMUNICATION

By 1492, sophisticated secret communication was barely 25 years old. The vast majority of codes and ciphers employed a basic format which had been in existence for more than 3000 years directly traceable to an inscription carved, circa 1900 BC, *in the main chamber of a nobleman's tomb in Menet Khufu on the banks of the Nile.*

This format is the simple substitution of one character for another character, classically represented by the code of Julius Caesar. Caesar's code had the letter D representing the letter A, E for B, F for C and continued throught the alphabet to C representing Z. However, such codes are easily broken by a knowledge of the frequency with which individual letters occur in any language. For example, in modern English the letters B, G and V occur on average once in every hundred letters of standard text. That same average text will contain 13 Es and 9 Ts but the letter Q will, in all probability, be completely absent. This would not have been true for the English language of 1492. V would have occurred more than once as it was often used for the U. The letter I was not only used more frequently but it was also the ancestor of the modern letter J. The Q was in far greater evidence – witness white then spelt qwyt *and choir, believe it or not, spelt* queer!

Few users of codes were aware of the ease by which a knowledge of letter frequency could be utilized to break their systems such that when a code was broken this was generally ascribed to black magic.

One exception to the simple substitution rule of written communication is worthy of mention. This is the skytale *of the ancient Spartans. Identical batons were given to a general leading an army in a distant region and to his base commander. A strip of cloth wound round one baton was then written upon across the bandings so that, when unwound, it displayed meaningless strokes and dashes and only when rewound on its 'twin' did the message reveal itself.*

nes Trithemius, it contained tables of alphabets as models for encoding and gave instructions for complexity which went beyond that possible with Alberti's disk.

Greatest cryptologer ■ Born in Rome in 1404, the illegitimate son of a rich family of Florentine merchants, Leon Battista Alberti is rivalled only by Leonardo da Vinci as the Renaissance concept of the universal man. At the age of 63 he was asked, quite casually, by the Pope's secretary if he could produce an unbreakable code. The result was his famous cipher disk which immediatey rendered all simple substitution codes obsolete. This copper disk with its moveable inner circle enabled the sender to counter the threat posed by opponents possessing a knowledge of letter-frequency. Consider the disk as illustrated with the A = d. This meant that a letter A in the message should be interpreted as a D. However, if at an agreed point in the text the disk is revolved clockwise just one degree then the letter B now represents a D. The possibilities are endless and all that is needed is for the receiver and sender to possess identical disks and to agreee any sequence of changes they desire. Alberti's alphabet did not contain J, U and W whilst he ignored H, K and Y as being 'unnecessary'.

English code-breakers ■ In the 15th century the family of Thomas Phelippes, England's first great code-breaker who was to feature in the tragic saga of Mary Queen of Scots, were establishing themselves in London.

Code-breakers in Venice ■ The special conditions of Venetian society created a governing class very different from that of the other Italian communes or of the continental states. To counter any attempts at sole personal rule, the Council of Ten was established in 1310 to police the patrician order and to defend the existing regime. They maintained their control over the powerful and independent republic of Venice with the aid of a highly efficient secret police. Giovanni Soro, appointed cipher secretary in 1506, was the first great code-breaker of the Western world. So talented was he that, as early as 1500, the papal curia was sending him secret codes that no one in Rome could solve.

Engineering

Oldest machinery ■ The earliest mechanisms still in use are the *dâlu* – a water-raising instrument – known to have been in use in the Sumerian civilization which originated *c.* 3500 BC in lower Iraq and which are thus even earlier than the *Saqiyas* (water lifting devices) on the Nile.

Earliest crank mechanism ■ Piston engines work by operating a crank and connecting rod or crankshaft which transforms the reciprocating, that is back-and-forth motion, of the piston into the rotary, that is the circular motion of the wheels. Rotary motors transform their circular motion into reciprocating action by operating this crankshaft mechanism in reverse.

A similar crank handle was invented in

11th-century Europe. In 1206 the Islamic engineer al-Jazari, described a water-raising machine with a simple crank mechanism. The more sturdy and balanced form of the double-bearing crank was developed from a hand drill known as the 'bitstock'. The earliest known example of this was discovered in Jutland, Denmark, by archaeologists excavating a late-14th-century site. The earliest illustration of the bitstock is on a Paris guild seal dating from 1407. The combination of crank and connecting-rod, essential components in much modern machinery, first appeared in Italy about 1458.

Earliest flywheels ■ The flywheel is necessary to get over the 'dead-spot' which is the chief difficulty with crank motion. Its first mention in connection with large-scale machinery occurs in the treatise of an anonymous engineer in what is now Czechoslovakia, in about 1430.

Earliest conical valves ■ Automatically-operated conical valves were widely used by the Banu Musa, three brothers who worked in Baghdad, Iraq in the ninth century. They were used for switching, and controls of various kinds. They are first mentioned in Europe in the 15th century in the notebooks of Leonardo da Vinci. They are of course extensively used in modern machinery.

Most powerful windlasses ■ Large windlasses were the only devices capable of lifting weights to great heights and three still exist in England – at Peterborough Cathedral, Tewkesbury Abbey and Salisbury Cathedral. The one at Salisbury was used in the 13th century for construction of the tower. It has a treadwheel about 11 ft *3.3 m* in diameter, operated from the outside by rungs spaced around the rim. The barrel is 5 ft 9 in *1.75 m* long and 10¾ in *0.27 m* in diameter. The windlass was kept in use throughout the 15th–16th centuries for raising the bells and for maintenance.

Water power

There was a constant effort to increase the power and hence the output of water-mills. Power was increased by locating mills on the piers of bridges or mounting them on ships, in both cases to take advantage of the greater flow in midstream. Dams were built to raise the head of water above mills.

Most powerful mills ■ Ship mills made of teak and iron were moored on the Tigris and Euphrates in Upper Mesopotamia for producing flour for the cities of Iraq. Each mill contained two pairs of millstones and could produce 10 tons of flour every 24 hours, much more than any mills in 15th-century Europe.

Earliest recorded water-mills in Britain ■ These were built by the Romans near Hadrian's Wall to supply the garrisons with flour. In the Domesday Book, compiled in 1086, 5624 mills were recorded. Both water-mills and windmills were common in Europe in the Middle Ages and beyond.

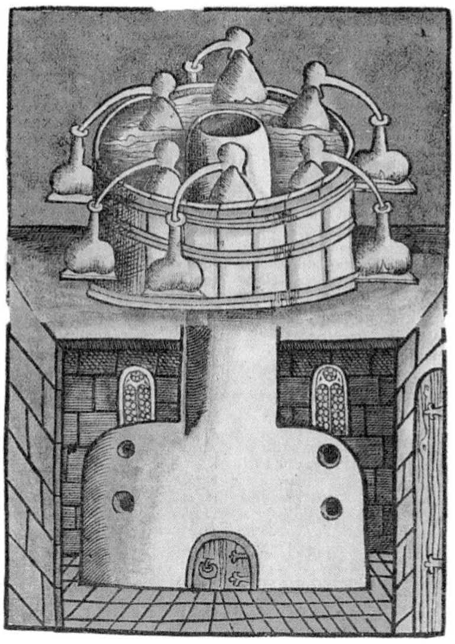

This woodcut of an alchemist's water bath illustrated a book in 1519.

First 'factory' milling ■ On the River Garonne in France three large dams were built across the river in the 12th century to provide power for mills. These were at Château-Narbonnais (16 mills), Bazacle (12 mills) and La Daurade (15 mills). (The first two continued to produce flour until the 19th century.) In medieval Paris there were 68 mills in the upstream section alone of the main branch of the Seine – a distance of 4757 ft *1450 m*.

Earliest water turbines ■ The late-15th-century drawings of horizontal water-wheels – notably those of Francesco di Giorgio Martini and Leonardo da Vinci – show the embryo pressureless turbine. Two essential components are present. First there is the jet, not as in earlier types open channels or chutes, but in the form of a nozzle. Secondly there is the shape of the buckets or vanes, with double curvature about a vertical axis, so that the change of momentum of the jet takes place largely in a horizontal plane.

Largest *noria* ■ The *noria* is a wheel for raising water. Its rim is divided into compartments, and paddles are fixed to the rim between the compartments. As the running stream turns the wheel the compartments fill with water and discharge their contents at the top into an aqueduct. The largest *noria* was at Toledo, Spain and was 135 ft *41 m* in diameter. *Norias* are still in

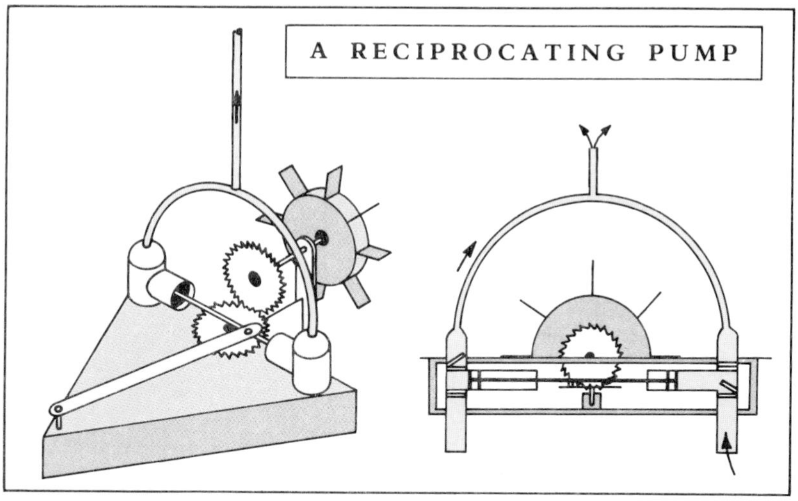

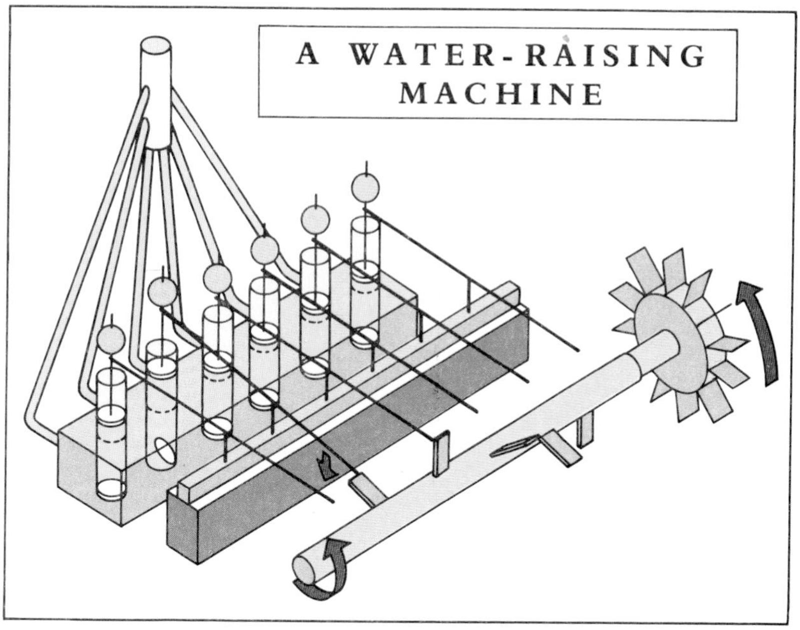

use in some parts of the world. Fine examples can be seen still at Cordoba and Murcia in Spain and at Hamah in Syria.

The great water wheel at Hamah in Syria.

Pumps

First piston pumps ■ These were invented in Alexandria, Egypt about 300 BC. The Greeks and Romans used small bronze pumps for firefighting. The cylinders stood upright in the water and the pistons were operated manually. The pumps probably had an output similar to that of a garden hose.

First true reciprocating pump ■ Described by the Arabic engineer al-Jazari in 1206, it was operated by a water-wheel. There were two horizontally opposed cylinder and suction pipes descending into the water. The delivery pipes were joined together above the machine to form a single outlet that discharged a strong jet of water to a height of 33 ft *10 m*.

Pump with the highest lift ■ The need for raising large quantities of water from mine sumps led to the development of the rag-and-chain pump early in the 15th century. A chain to which balls of rag or other materials were fixed at intervals was drawn continuously up a pipe that dipped into the sump. The machine was driven by horses or by water-wheels. A single stage was capable of lifting water from depths of 240 ft *73 m*; if three stages were used lifts of 600 ft *182 m* were attained.

First multi-cylinder machine ■ Taqi al-Din, in a book written in Syria in 1552, describes a six-cylinder 'monobloc' pump. Cams on the extended axle of a water wheel operated trip-levers that caused six vertical pistons to work in succession in cylinders cut into wooden block.

Windmills

Earliest ■ The earliest recorded windmills are those for grinding corn in Iran in the seven century AD.

Earliest in Europe ■ The windmill at Weedley, near Hull is dated 1185. It was also introduced for grinding corn.

The oldest Dutch windmill is the towermill at Zeddam, Gelderland, built in *c.* 1450.

Largest ■ The largest mills were introduced in the Netherlands in the 15th century for drainage. The movement of the sails was transmitted through two sets of gears to a large scoop wheel. Sometimes these *wipmolen* were used in a series of three or even four machines. Single machines could generate up to 50 hp.

Earliest gas turbines ■ Noticing the upward blast of hot air in chimneys, technicians of the late 15th century in Western Europe were setting in the flues small turbines geared to turn a spit. This was a particularly ingenious form of automation since the hotter the fire, the faster the roast would rotate.

Sundials

Earliest ■ Undoubtedly the earliest method of timekeeping was the sundial, the first being simple gnomons (vertical rods erected to catch the sun's rays). The use of this device goes back into remote antiquity.

The oldest gnomon known is a portable sundial from Egypt dating to about 1450 BC.

Earliest classic ■ In the 9th or 10th century the Arabs invented the sundial with its style directed towards the pole, i.e. parallel to the axis of the world. After the

Most famous Nilometer ■ *Used for measuring the annual rise of the Nile, the most famous Nilometer is that on Roda Island at Cairo, built 861 AD, it consists of a tall graduated column 19 in* 48 cm *in diameter and a height of about 33 ft* 10 m. *It is divided into divisions of one cubit each, the top ten of which are subdivided into 24 divisions. The column stands in a stone-lined pit about 20 ft* 6 m *square, with a staircase running down to the bottom. Connection is made to the Nile by three tunnels at different depths. The point on the column reached by the annual flood determined the tax levied on farmers in that year. Here, the Nilometer at Komombo temple, south of Cairo.*

MARKINGS OF SUNDIALS

Early timekeeping was done by noting the length rather than the direction of the shadow cast by the sun's rays. With a vertical gnomon on a horizontal table, or its reverse, a horizontal gnomon on a wall-plate, the length of the shadow at a given time varies from day to day; the tip of the sun's shadow describes a hyperbola. With 'simple' gnomons the marking out of dials to record the hours and other information is therefore a complex procedure demanding considerable mathematical skill. A wide range of different types of dials was constructed by the Greeks. The Greek knowledge was transmitted to the Arabs, who developed the skills of dialling.

Crusades this type of dial suddenly appeared all over Europe. These are the familiar sundials to be found in the gardens of old buildings and on the walls of churches and manor houses. The plates to which the styles are attached can be quite easily divided into hours by mathematical or constructional methods and the markings remain valid throughout the year.

The invention of the mechanical clock did not obviate the need for sundials. The variations to which even the best mechanical clocks are subject makes periodical checks essential, and such checks were only possible by using sundials.

Largest sundial ■ In sundials called noon-mark dials the light of the sun came through a hole pierced in the southern facade of a building as a thin shaft and precisely at noon crossed a meridian line on the floor. The hole can be considered as a hole at the end of a gnomon. The largest of such dials is in the cathedral at Florence, where it was installed in 1472. The hole in the cupola of the cathedral is 295 ft *90 m* above the floor.

Water clocks

Earliest ■ The sundial was of course useless at night or in cloudy weather, and the water-clock was introduced so that time could be recorded when the sun was obscured. The earliest type of water-clock was the simple outflow *clepsydra* (*clepysdra* means 'thief of water' in Greek), an earthenware vessel with a hole in its side near the base. This device was in use in Egypt and Babylonia before 1500 BC and the oldest surviving example, from Egypt, is dated about 1380 BC. This had a scale of hours graduated upon its inside, which must have been drawn by observation so that allowance was automatically made for the decrease in the rate of discharge as the water level fell.

Monumental ■ Water-clocks were gradually developed and made more elaborate and more accurate. An important innovation was probably due to the great scientist Archimedes (died 212 BC); this is an ingenious feed-back control system that enables the water-level in a cylindrical reservoir to descend at constant speed. A heavy float in the reservoir is connected to various time-recording devices. Large water-clocks incorporating this system were described in scrupulous detail by the Islamic engineer al-Jazari in a treatise completed in 1206. A Spanish Muslim called al-Muradi, living in Cordoba in the 11th century, described water-clocks that incorporated complex gear-trains.

Most complex ■ *A sundial made in Damascus, Syria, in the 14th century to adorn the main minaret of the Umayyad Mosque there displays time with respect to sunrise, midday and sunset, as well as with respect to the time of the afternoon prayer. It is the most sophisticated sundial known from the medieval period.*

Largest ■ The largest known water-clock, remains of which can still be seen, was built in the wall of a street in Fez, Morocco in 1357 AD. It is some 37 ft *11.27 m* long.

Mechanical clocks

Oldest ■ The earliest mechanical clock, that is, one with an escapement, was completed in China in 725 AD by I Hsing and Liang Lingtsan. Su Sung of the Emperor of China's court in 1088 described and illustrated his water-powered mechanical clock in his *Hsin I Hsiang Fa.*

The invention of the true mechanical clock, the most important machine invented in the Middle Ages, took place in western Europe towards the end of the 13th century. In order to allow room for the weights these clocks were mounted in towers or on walls; they were not portable. During the 14th century tower clocks became a feature of many towns and cities in Europe. Often mounted in the towers of churches, they incorporated dials, elaborate displays of automata, representations of celestial movements and bells that chimed the hours or shorter intervals.

The oldest working clock in the world, surviving today, is the faceless clock dating from 1386, or possibly earlier, at Salisbury Cathedral, Wiltshire, England. Earlier dates, ranging back to *c.* 1335, have been attributed to the weight-driven clock in Wells Cathedral, Somerset, England, but only the iron frame is original.

First weight-driven ■ Several clocks are described in the *Libros del Saber* (Books of Knowledge) compiled in 1277 under the sponsorship of Alfonso X of Castile with the express purpose of transmitting Arabic ideas into Castilian. One of the clocks consisted of a large sealed wooden drum, the interior divided into twelve compartments, with small holes between the compartments through which mercury flowed. Enough mercury was enclosed to fill just half the compartments. The drum was mounted on the same axle as a large wheel powered by a weight drive wound around it. Also on the axle was a pinion with six teeth that meshed with 36 oaken teeth on the rim of an astrolabe dial. The drum and the pinion made a complete revolution every four hours and the astrolabe dial made a complete revolution every 24 hours. This type of time-piece had been known in the Islamic world since the 11th century – at least 200 years before the first appearance of the weight-driven clock in the West. There is no doubt that the hydraulic escapement, i.e. the means to control the speed of descent of the weight, was effective. Similar clocks, probably inspired by the description in the *Libros del Saber*, came into use in Europe as cheap, reliable timekeepers.

Earliest Russian ■ The earliest mechanical weight-driven clock in Russia was completed in 1404 for the Court of the Great Prince in the Moscow Kremlin by a Serbian monk, Lazar. It had a round face with Slavonic letters instead of figures. The face rotated around a fixed hand. The clock struck the hours.

First alarm clock ■ The earliest known alarm clock was a German timepiece constructed in Wurzburg in about 1365.

First portable clocks ■ Spring-driven 'frame' clocks were first made in Burgundy about 1430. Because a spring weakens as it unwinds, the clock was not driven entirely from the spring. Instead a cord that was wound on to the barrel enclosing the spring went around a truncated cone called a *fusee*; the clock's drive was taken from the fusee. After the spring was wound the cord was at the narrow end of the fusee; as it unwound and the spring became weaker the leverage became greater.

First spring-driven 'plated' ■ Clocks in which the movements are enclosed between two plates, rather than inside an open framework as in 'frame' clocks, were invented in Belgium about 1450. The great significance of this alternative form of construction is that, when miniaturized, it could be used to create watches.

Watches

Watches appeared contemporaneously in a number of European centres in the last quarter of the 15th century. Very soon makers were vying with each other to produce small watches. Some were so tiny that they could be placed in a finger ring or in the hilt of a dagger – Francis I of France paid a small fortune for two of these in 1518.

Oldest ■ The oldest watch (portable clockwork time-keeper) is one made of iron by Peter Henlein in Nuremberg, Bavaria, Germany *c.* 1504.

A German mechanical clock of about 1520 which combined time-keeping with a complex automata arrangement for striking the hours.

First minute hands ■ These appeared on clocks in about 1480. By this time clocks were sufficiently accurate to necessitate this refinement.

Automata

Most astonishing ■ Reports of early automata are notoriously unreliable. An often-repeated story records that the noted German mathematician and astrologer Johann Muller, known as Regiomontanus (1436–76), built a wooden eagle which flew to greet the Emperor Maximilian on his arrival in Nuremberg in 1470 and perched on the town gate.

Chinese claims are even more astonishing:

'Emperor Hu of the Northern Qi dynasty [mid-sixth century AD] caused the monk Kingzhao to construct the Stage (Terrace) of Seven Precious Mirrors. It had 36 doors in each of which there was [the model of] a woman, each holding a lock. When one activated the mechanism downwards, all 36 doors closed automatically. If one pulled on the mechanism, all the doors opened and the women came out in front of them.

'In Tang times Ma Dengfeng made the Stage of the Empress's Toilette, in which the advancing and retiring, opening and closing, were all effected without human intervention. Towels and combs, perfume and powder came in succession. The onlookers considered it the handiwork of demons, and it was in truth of a skill unmatched at that time.

'Emperor Shun of the Yuan dynasty [c. 1333] himself constructed a Clepshydra Palace. He concelaed the water-reservoir in a casing, from which the water that provided the driving force fell after being lifted up to it. The Three Sages Palace was placed on top of the casing, and in the centre he set a Jade Girl who held up tallies according to the hour. Two gods in golden armour struck upon drums and bells without the minutest error. When the bells and drums sounded the hour, lions and phoenixes flew and danced at the sides, keeping time with the rhythm. On the sides of the casing were the Palaces of the Sun and Moon, in front of which flew six immortals. As midnight and midday made their transit, the immortals automatically advanced in pairs, crossed a bridge, and went into the Palace of the Three Sages, thereafter returning to take up their normal positions. The inspired craftsmanship and ingenious thought were unique to this one man since remotest antiquity.'

Flight

Tower-jumping ■ The earliest hang-glider flight in Europe may have been by an Italian mathematician of Perugia, Giovanni Battista Danti. He was reported to have 'flown' over Lake Trasimeno about 1490 after jumping from the top of a tower wearing artificial wings. One wing collapsed, and the would-be aviator crashed, with severe injuries.

First model helicopter ■ Leonardo da Vinci designed and flew a model helicopter about 1500. The machine had a helical screw turned by a spring; when wound up it proved capable of flying, and Leonardo demonstrated a cardboard model.

Aeronautical theory ■ The first real insight into the value of streamlining in a flying machine appears in Leonardo da Vinci's *Sul Volo degli Uccelli* (On the Flight of Birds) of 1505, a work containing many insights into gliding and soaring. Leonardo might have designed and flown a glider, had he not instead pursued the impossible goal of man-powered flapping flight. His designs for ornithopters reliant wholly on human muscle power were doomed to remain paper dreams.

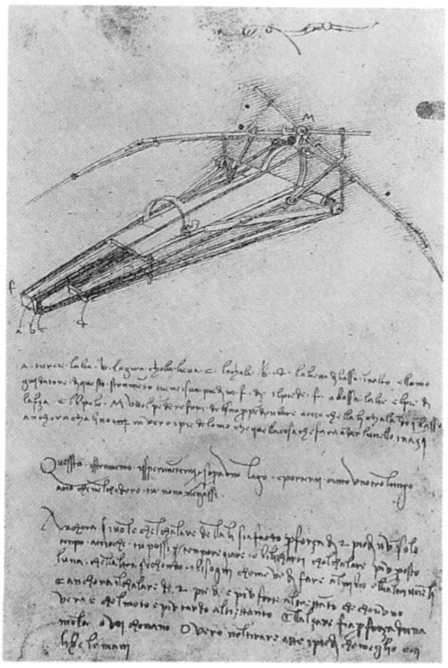

Leonardo da Vinci's notes and drawings of flying machines of about 1505.

First Scottish attempt at manned flight ■ In 1507 John Damian, the Italian Abbot of Tungland and physician at the court of King James IV of Scotland, was inadvertently left behind when a party of courtiers set off for France. Damian announced that he would fly after the travellers. Strapping on wings, he leaped from the walls of Stirling Castle. His flight ended predictably but, fortunately for Damian, without severe injury. Making light of his failure, he explained that it was due to his wearing wings made from chicken feathers, rather than those of an eagle.

Other inventions

Camera obscura ■ The earliest reports of this device, basically a darkened room with a pinhole to admit light which forms an image of external objects on a screen, date from the pre-Christian era. Aristotle (384–322 BC) seems to have been familiar with the principle. The camera obscura was familiar as an aid for artists by 1500. Roger Bacon and other medieval scientists described how the camera obscura worked, and Leonardo da Vinci drew one. The introduction of a lens instead of a pinhole was suggested by several scientists in the 1500s.

Newest glass-making method ■ The Romans had been excellent glass-makers, and although glass production collapsed in the wake of the fall of the Western Roman Empire, it seems as though some glass production survived throughout the medieval period in Europe. During the 15th century Venetian glass-makers developed a new method of making pure crystalline glass, one result of which was the production of glass containers which could be used for serving wine.

Printing

The invention of printing ■ Printing was the most far-reaching invention of the period, comparable in its revolutionary effects to that of photography or radio or television. Books were previously copied by hand and illustrated with illuminated miniatures, a costly and laborious process, and were mostly found in the libraries of monasteries, universities or wealthy private individuals. The cost of a bound manuscript in 1500 was equivalent to the monthly salary of an average court official. The essence of the invention was the use of movable metal type which could be re-used. Printing signalled the birth of the mass-media, enabling cheap reproductions of texts and images to reach a much wider public.

Several pre-existing factors contributed to its invention. Paper production, which came into medieval Europe through the Arabs in Spain, increased significantly in the 15th century. The screw press and wooden blocks, already used by papermakers, bookbinders and in the printing of textiles, were adapted to printing on paper, while the techniques of engraving and casting used by medieval goldsmiths and bookbinders facilitated the production of large quantities of accurately formed type.

Earliest dated type-set matter ■ The earliest printed document to bear an actual date is a papal bull of 1454 from Gutenberg's press.

First printing in Europe ■ Although printing had been known in China since the eighth century or before, it is now generally accepted that it was invented independently in Europe in the 15th century. Printing with wood blocks was invented in the first quarter of the century. The precise time and place for the invention of printing with movable metal type is still in doubt, but it probably occurred in Mainz, Germany about 1450.

First printer ■ Though Johann Gutenberg (?1397–1468) of Germany is usually credited as being the first printer to use movable type, this particular honour may belong to Laurens Janszoon Coster (?1370–1450) of Haarlem who printed from wood blocks in 1440.

The printer's mark or colophon of Fust and Schoeffer was a double shield hanging from a branch.

First book to carry a printer's name and mark ■ The Psalter of 1457 printed by Johann Fust and Peter Schoeffer, former associates of Gutenberg in Mainz, was the first book in which the name of the printers and the date of publication were recorded. It also introduced the printer's mark, a pictorial device inspired by the identifying marks used by merchants for their goods, an idea which was later widely adopted.

First printing presses outside Germany ■ These were initially set up by immigrant German printers. The press set up in Italy at the monastery of Subiaco, near Rome, in 1464, was the first outside Germany. In 1467 it moved to Rome. In 1469 Venice acquired its first press and rapidly became Europe's foremost city of printing. Paris, where a press was set up in 1470 in the cellars of the Sorbonne by the university librarian, Guillaume Fichet, became the third. By 1500 Venice had about 150 printing presses which had published about 3,750 volumes and Paris about 2,200 volumes.

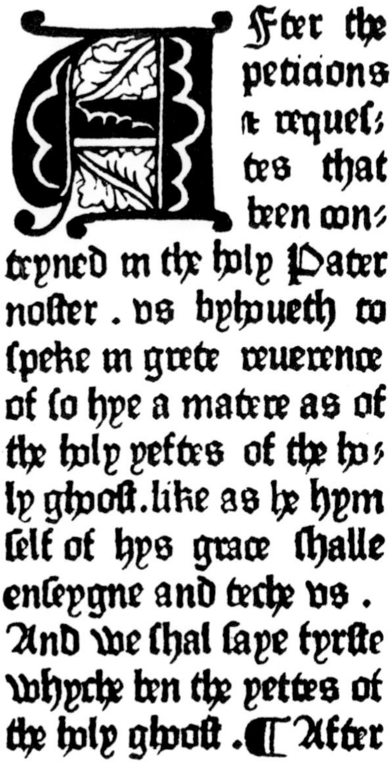

After the peticions & reques-
tes that
been con-
teyned in the holy Pater
noster. vs byhoueth to
speke in grete reuerence
of so hye a matere as of
the holy yeftes of the holy ghoost. like as he hym
self of hys grace shalle
enseygne and teche vs.
And we shal saye fyrste
whyche ben the yeftes of
the holy ghoost. ¶ After

First use of modern type ■ *The earliest printed books were set in gothic type, the lettering used in Germany. It was in Rome, in the late 1460s, that roman type was introduced, based on the rounded lettering favoured by Italian scholars, and the direct ancestor of the typefaces used today.*

First press in the New World ■ In 1539 Juan Cromberger, Seville agent of the German 'Great Trading Company' of Ravensburg sent a printing press to the capital of Spain's colony of Mexico. The press was established there by Juan Pablos (an Italian by birth), 100 years before the printing of the first book in North America.

First printing press in Asia ▪ The newly-established religious Order of the Society of Jesus (the Jesuits) set up a printing press in Goa in 1556.

Earliest English press ▪ William Caxton set up the first press in England in the precincts of Westminster Abbey, London, in 1476. Among the first books to come from it were a *History of Jason*, the *Dictes or Sayengis of the Philosophers* and the *Canterbury Tales.*

First printed book in English ▪ The *Recuyell of the Histories of Troy* – an account of the Trojan wars – was printed in Bruges, Flanders, for the English-born Duchess of Burgundy by William Caxton in 1474. Caxton, now famous as the first English printer, was originally a cloth-merchant, a career whcih took him to the cloth-producing centre of Bruges. Having learned something of the art of printing on a visit to Cologne, Germany, in 1471, he ran a press in Bruges from 1474–76 with Colard Mansion, a calligrapher and illuminator in the library of the Duke of Burgundy.

Most prolific printer ▪ Of the early English printers, Caxton's foreman Wynken de Worde was the most prolific. In 1500 he moved to 32 Fleet Street, London where he turned out nearly 800 books by the time of his death in 1534.

First book printed in Oxford ▪ Oxford's first printer was a German called Theodoric Rood who came to Oxford from Cologne. Scholars have identified 17 of his books, the earliest being *Exposito Sancti Hieronymi in symbolum apostolarum* (Exposition of St Jerome on symbols of the Apostles) by Rufinus of Aquileia, a work of the fourth century. Although the book itself is dated 1468, this is generally regarded as a misprint for 1478 because its two successors in the same type are dated 1479.

Symbols of death enter an early printing shop in 1499.

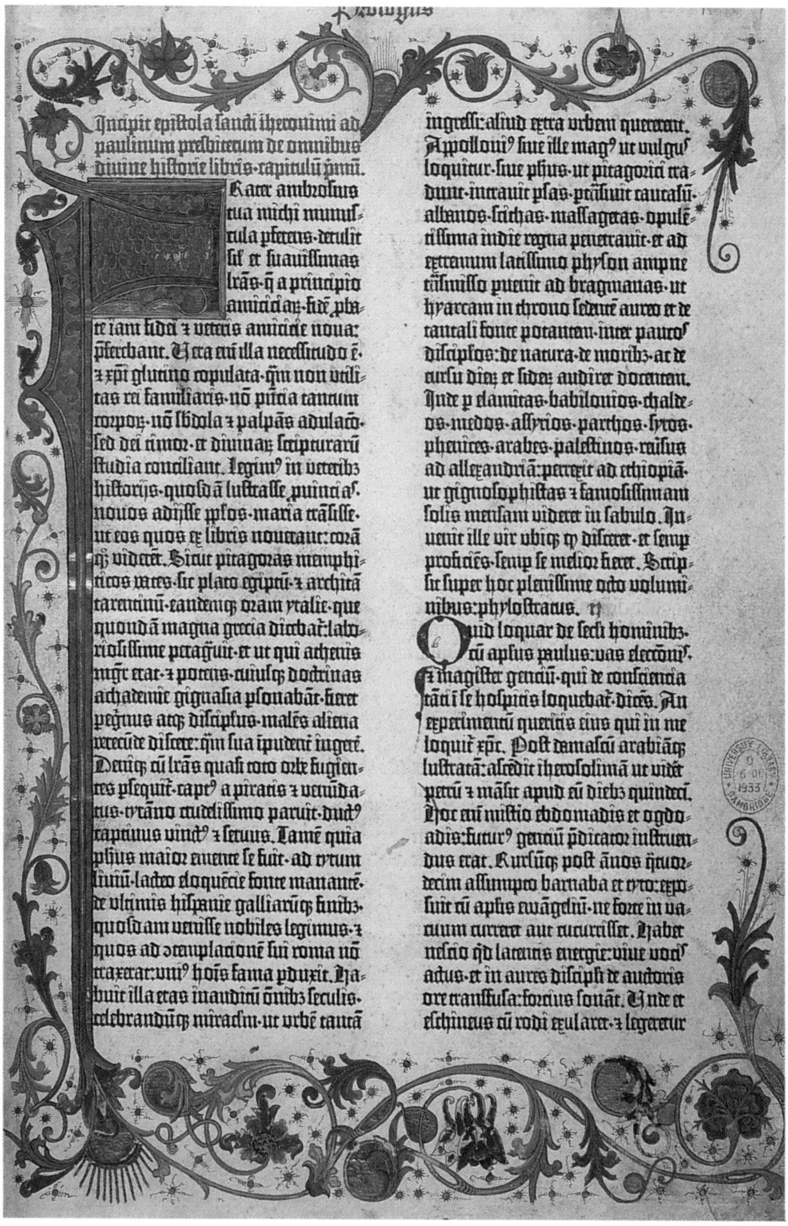

Prologus

Incipit epistola sancti hieronimi ad paulinum presbiterum de omnibus divine historie libris capitulum primum.

Frater ambrosius tua michi munuscula perferens detulit sil et suavissimas litteras que a principio amicitias fide probate iam fidei et veteris amicicie nova: preferebant. Vera enim illa necessitudo est et xpi glutino copulata que non utilitas rei familiaris non presentia tantum corporum non subdola et palpans adulacio. sed dei timor et divinarum scripturarum studia conciliant. Legimus in veteribus historiis quosdam lustrasse provincias. novos adisse populos maria transisse. ut eos quos ex libris noverant: coram quoque viderent. Sicut pitagoras memphiticos vates sic plato egiptum et architam tarentinum eandemque oram ytalie que quondam magna grecia dicebatur laboriosissime peragravit et ut qui athenis magister erat et potens cuiusque doctrinas achademie gignasia personabant fieret peregrinus atque discipulus malens aliena verecunde discere: quam sua inpudenter ingerere. Denique cum litteras quasi toto orbe fugientes persequitur captus a piratis et venundatus tyranno crudelissimo paruit ductus captivus vinctus et servus. Tamen quia philosophus maior emente se fuit. ad tytum livium lacteo eloquencie fonte manantem. de ultimis hispanie galliarumque finibus. quosdam venisse nobiles legimus et quos ad contemplacionem sui roma non traxerat: unius hominis fama perduxit. Habuit illa etas inauditum omnibus seculis. celebrandumque miraculum: ut urbem tantam ingressi aliud extra urbem quererent. Apollonius sive ille magus ut vulgus loquitur sive philosophus ut pitagorici tradunt intravit persas pertransivit caucasum. albanos scithas massagetas opulentissima indie regna penetravit et ad extremum latissimo phison amne transmisso pervenit ad bragmanas ut hyarcam in throno sedentem aureo et de tantali fonte potantem inter paucos discipulos de natura de moribus ac de cursu dierum et siderum audiret docentem. Inde per elamitas babilonios chaldeos medos assyrios parthos syros phenices arabes palestinos reversus ad alexandriam perrexit ad ethiopiam. ut gignosophistas et famosissimam solis mensam videret in sabulo. Invenit ille vir ubique quod disceret et semper proficiens semper se melior fieret. Scripsit super hoc plenissime octo voluminibus phylostratus.

Quid loquar de seculi hominibus. cum apostolus paulus vas eleccionis et magister gencium qui de consciencia tanti in se hospitis loquebatur dicens. An experimentum queritis eius qui in me loquitur xpistus. Post damascum arabiamque lustratam: ascendit ierosolimam ut videret petrum et mansit apud eum diebus quindecim. Hoc enim misterio ebdomadis et ogdoadis futurus gencium predicator instruendus erat. Rursumque post annos quatuordecim assumpto barnaba et tito: exposuit cum apostolis evangelium ne forte in vacuum curreret aut cucurrisset. Habet nescio quid latentis energie viue vocis actus et in aures discipuli de auctoris ore transfusa: fortius sonat. Unde et eschinus cum rodi exularet et legeretur

A page from the 42-line Bible printed in about 1455 by Johann Gutenberg.

First book in movable type ▪ The invention of movable type is usually credited to Johann Gutenberg of Mainz, Germany, who printed a large 2-volume Bible in or shortly before 1455, known as the Gutenberg Bible.

The edition is believed to have numbered some 200 copies, some on vellum and others on paper. It consists of 643 leaves printed in double columns of 42 lines of type, and is thus known as the '42-line Bible'.

Thus ende I this book whyche I have translated after my auctor as nyghe as God hath gyven me connyng to whom be gyven the laude and preysyng. And for as moche as in the wrytyng of the same my penne is worn, myn hande wery and not stedfast, myn eyen dimmed with overmoche lokyng on the whit paper, and my corage not so prone and redy to laboure as hit hath bet, and that age crepeth on me dayly and febleth all the bodye, and also because I have promysid to dyverce gentilmen and to my frendes to addresse to hem as hastely as I myght this sayd book. Therefore I have practysed and lerned at my grete charge and dispense to ordeyne this said booke in prynte after the maner and forme as ye may here see. And it is not wreton with penne and ynke as other bokes ben to thende that every man may have them attones. For all the bookes of this storye named the recule of the historyes of Troyes thus emprynted as ye here see were begonne in oon day, and also fynysshed in oon day.

From William Caxton in *The Recuyell of the Histories of Troye*, 1471

FIRST PRINTING PRESSES

c. 1450** . . **Mainz, Germany

1467** . . **Rome, Italy
1468** . . **Pilsen, Germany
1469** . . **Venice, Italy
1470** . . **Paris, France; Nuremburg, Germany; Utrecht, Netherlands
1471** . . **Milan, Naples, Florence, Italy
1472** . . **Cologne, Germany
1473** . . **Lyons, France; Valencia, Spain; Budapest, Hungary
1474** . . **Cracow, Poland; Bruges, Belgium
1475** . . **Lubeck, Germany; Breslau, Poland
1476** . . **Westminster, England; Rostock, Germany
1478** . . **Geneva, Switzerland; Palermo, Messina, Italy
1479** . . **Augsburg, Germany
1480** . . **London, England
1481** . . **Antwerp, Belgium; Leipzig, Germany
1482** . . **Odense, Denmark
1483** . . **Stockholm, Sweden

1525** . . **Iceland

Most famous printers ■ Anton Koberger of Nuremberg (godfather of the great graphic artist Dürer) was the most renowned printer at the end of the 15th century. He is said to have had 24 presses, employing 100 craftsmen, and carried on an immense international trade. His masterpiece is the *Nuremberg Chronicle* of 1493, illustrated by Dürer's teacher Michael Wolgemut. The most eminent early 16th-century printer was Aldus Manutius (*c.* 1450–1515) of Venice. His most famous publication was the *Hypnerotomachia Poliphili* (The dream battle of Poliphilus) 1499, a love-story written by a friar, although more significant for the history of books, was his revolutionary and influential 1501 edition of Virgil. This was a small octavo volume, a new format comprising a sheet folded into eight leaves, inexpensive and compact, in a new, close-set type, italic: effectively the first modern book. The Aldine press continued throughout the century, run by Aldus' descendants.

Wars

Longest ■ The Hundred Years War between England and France lasted from 1338 to 1453 (115 years). However, the nine Crusades from the First (1096–1104) to the Ninth (1270–91) extended over 195 years if seen as a single holy war.

Last crusade ■ After the fall of Constantinople in 1453 Pope Pius II strove to unite the bickering rulers of Western Europe in a crusade. By 1464 he seemed to be succeeding, summoned the Christian forces to meet in Italy at Ancona on the Adriatic, and took the cross himself to provide a gesture of leadership. But France was slipping into civil war, and the Italian states were so suspicious of one another that few provided contingents. When the Pope arrived, ill and exhausted, his servants drew the curtains of his litter so that he would not have to see the troops deserting his expedition. Pius died on 14 August 1464.

Armies

Oldest armed body in Britain ■ The Queen's Bodyguard of the Yeomen of the Guard was formed in 1485. The Honourable Artillery Company was formed from the Fraternity of St George, Southwark, London, and received its charter from Henry VIII in 1537.

Best troops of the Turkish sultans ■ The Turkish sultans' best troops were the Janissaries. They were mostly infantrymen, and also the personal slaves of the sultan. The word comes from Turkish *yeni ceri* or new army. To become a Janissary, you had to be either a foreign prisoner of war or a Christian lad forcibly recruited from the sultan's own lands (mainly from Greece and the Balkans). Military training followed conversion to Islam, work on a Turkish farm where you would learn the language, and training in carpentry, metalwork or other craft. Although the sultans' enemies feared the Janissaries, so too did the sultans themselves. They were forbidden to marry and have children – a prohibition intended to keep them loyal to their overlord. However, Janissary riots were quite common events. Originally archers, the Janissaries were one of the first bodies of infantry in Europe to adopt the new hand firearms. Mehmed II had 12 000 Janissaries in 1453 at the siege of Constantinople; in 1526 their disciplined fire destroyed the Hungarian cavalry at the Battle of Mohacs. The rest of the conscripts each year were selected to serve in the Ottoman administration and the palace service. Excellent careers were possible here, and many Muslim families bribed officials so that their children could be levied and so have a chance at these careers.

Most feared light cavalry ■ In Europe this record went to the Albanian *stradiots*, used by the Venetians from the late 1470s onwards, first during their wars with the Turks and then increasingly in European warfare. These hardy troops were lightly armed with short lances and swords, and they rode fast, small horses. It was not their custom to take prisoners and instead they cut off the heads of enemies who fell into their hands and carried them to the Venetian officials, demanding a ducat for each. The increasing use of such light cavalry in the late 15th century gave a new variety and a new ferocity to warfare. A similar, but less fearsome, category were the Hungarian hussars who were first used about the same time.

Oldest extant ■ *The oldest army in the world is the Pontifical Swiss Guard in the Vatican City, Rome, with a regular foundation dating to 21 January 1506, but with origins extending back beyond 1400.*

Most prized infantry ■ The Swiss pikemen who made up a third of the great French army which invaded Italy in 1494 could claim this title. For more than two centuries the independent herdsmen of the rural cantons of the Swiss Confederation had been developing a technique of fighting, with their 18 ft *5.5 m* pikes, in squares of 1000 men each. The tactic was developed not only as a defensive device to resist the cavalry charge, but was also used to attack the enemy. The Swiss squares could advance in a disciplined and rapid manner and overrun any other troops in the open. The heyday of the Swiss was the last three decades of the 15th century; in the great battles of the Italian Wars between 1500 and 1525 the Spanish found the answer in a combination of field fortifications to hold up the Swiss advance, arquebus and artillery fire from the flanks to break up the square, and finally cavalry charges to complete the work. The battles of Cerignola (1503), Marignano (1515) and Bicocca (1522) all showed that Swiss pike squares could be overcome by careful generalship. The nearest equivalent to the Swiss were the German *Landsknechte* raised by the Emperor Maximilian around 1500 and soon gaining a similar reputation to their more famous rivals.

Greatest Russian army ■ The Tartar-Mongol army at the end of the 15th century had about 300 000 fighting men. It occupied an area about 120 miles *190 km* in diameter and it took six days to go around the army.

Cruellest invaders ■ The Spaniard Bartholomé de las Casas (d. 1566) went to Hispaniola in 1502 as a colonist. In about 1508 he took his religious vows and, shocked by the brutal behaviour of his fellow Spaniards, reported their treatment of the local people as being 'cruelty never before seen, nor heard of, nor read of' Fernandez de Oviedo, chronicler of the New World, wrote in his *Historia general* that the 'conquistadores . . . could more accurately be called depopulators or squanderers of the new lands' who cause 'various and innumerable deaths . . . as uncountable as the stars'. Among Las Casas' accusations of brutality which he says 'all these I did with my own eyes witness' were occasions when the Spaniards 'made bets as to who would split a man in two, or cut off his head at one blow . . . They tore the babes from the mother's breast by their feet, and dashed their heads against the rocks . . . They spitted the bodies of other babes, together with their mothers and all who were before them on their swords.' As a formal punishment they would hang prisoners in groups of 13 'in honour and reverence of our Redeemer and the twelve Apostles' with their feet nearly touching the ground and then 'put wood underneath and, with fire, they burned the Indians alive'.

As the conquest continued the Spaniards forced people into near-slavery to search for gold; they hunted them down with dogs so vicious that 'in two bites they laid open their victims to the entrails'. They cut off the hands and noses of uncooperative Indians. Pedro Arias de Avila is reputed to have been responsible for the deaths or enslavement of two million Indians.

Greatest captain ■ Gonsalvo de Cordoba was nicknamed the 'Great Captain' because of his successes leading the armies of the Spanish kings against the Moors in Granada. After 10 years of campaigning the 'infidels' were finally driven out of Spain in 1492, and three years later Gonsalvo was sent to Italy with an army to oppose the French assault on Naples. He succeeded in driving the French out in 1496, but in 1500 at the Treaty of Granada France and Spain agreed to partition Naples. However, this compromise soon broke down and the Great Captain led the Spanish army to great victories over the French at Cerignola and the Garigliano in 1503. As a result Spanish rule in Naples was established for centuries to come, and Gonsalvo de Cordoba became the first viceroy until his retirement in 1507. His great skill lay in the organization and discipline that he imposed on his army, and his exploitation in battle of close cooperation between cavalry, infantry and guns. He was widely recognized in Europe as the greatest captain of his day.

Most warlike ruler ■ To the Aztec ruler Axayacatl is attributed the conquests of 37 communities during his reign of 13 years from 1469 to 1481. Ahuitzotzin (1486–1502) was credited with 45 such conquests in his 16 years. Moctezuma II (1502–20), who was the ruler at the time of the arrival of the Spanish conquerors, was credited with 44 in 18 years, but these were spread over a much wider area than those of his predecessors.

Most outstanding queen-warrior ■ When the Spaniard Hernandes de Soto trekked across America in 1539–42 in search of gold, he reported on a great ruler, the Senora of Cofachiqui (probably in what is now Georgia). For miles around 'she was greatly obeyed, whatsoever she ordered being performed with diligence and efficiency'. She was carried around her territory in a sort of palanquin by her nobles and was always accompanied by her slaves.

Last Roman soldier? ■ It is not inconceivable that, in 1492, the last Roman soldier was not only still alive but also was an Englishman. The Varangian Guard, a marine infantry corps of the army of the Eastern Roman (Byzantine) Empire, performed the same function as did the celebrated praetorian cohorts of the old Roman Empire. The Varangian Guard was raised in Sweden by Vladimir the Great, Grand Duke of Kiev, in the period 977–984, who transferred them to the service of the Eastern Roman Emperor Constantine VIII in 999. From 1066 onwards Englishmen were recruited and when the Eastern Roman Empire finally fell to the Turks in 1453 the Varangian Guard was exclusively English.

Fearless and without reproach ■ In an age of rapid transition in warfare when heavily armoured cavalry was giving way in the armies of Europe to mass infantry, many equipped with arquebuses, there were a number of chivalric figures who attracted attention as representatives of an earlier age. The most notable was Pierre Terrail de Bayard, *chevalier sans peur et sans reproche*, who was 18 years of age when he accompanied his king, Charles VIII, on the 1494 invasion of Italy, and fought with outstanding bravery in all the subsequent battles of the Italian Wars. Noted for his skills in individual combat and for his extraordinary ability in achieving great feats of arms with small numbers of followers, he became a byword for bravery and honour. When he was mortally wounded by an arquebus shot at the Battle of La Sesia in 1524, the opposing Spanish commander, the Marquis of Pescara, brought all his captains to the dying knight's side to pay their last respects to him.

Campaigns

First European foothold in Africa ■ In 1415 Henry 'the Navigator', a half-English prince of Portugal and the grandson of John of Gaunt, Regent of England, led a Christian army into battle against the Muslim king of Morocco at Ceuta. The followers of Henry were landed noblemen who wanted to win their spurs in battle and gain fertile lands beyond the barren shore of Portugal. Their territorial ambitions were frustrated, but the Christian appetite for overseas plunder had been whetted and the conquest was followed by expeditions into the Atlantic and down the African coast and colonial investment in the Atlantic islands which earned Henry the sobriquet 'the Navigator'. From the rocky promontory of Sagres, near the haven of Lagos in the Portuguese Algarve, Henry monitored the overseas expansion and by the time of his death in 1460 Portuguese seafarers had reached the green fringes of West Africa which they named Cape Verde. The raid on Ceuta is often seen as being the end of the closed European Middle Age and the beginning of the Modern Age of European expansion into the world.

Longest march ■ On 29 August 1494 Charles VIII of France left Grenoble at the head of an army of 22 000 fighting men to claim his rights to the Kingdom of Naples and overthrow the rival Aragonese dynasty. Having crossed the Alps, his march was held up for a month at Asti where he suffered a bout of smallpox. But on 6 October the army moved on across the Lombardy plain, over the northern Appenines into Tuscany, reaching Florence in mid-November. By Christmas he was in Rome and on 22 February 1495 his troops entered Naples largely unopposed. The sustained advance of this great army astonished contemporaries and permanently changed the political scene in Italy.

Most northerly march ■ The northernmost march of that period took place in autumn 1499–spring 1500 when a Russian army of 5000 soldiers sent by Great Prince Ivan III almost reached the Arctic Circle (the usual temperature in the area was probably −25°–−40°C). The soldiers moved on skis (they were called *Lyxhnoe voysko* – the skiing army and were armed with arquebuses and some light cannons). They were led by commanders Semen Kurbsky and Petr Ushatty. The army managed to cross the northern Ural mountain range and many frozen rivers, the Pechora among them. The Russians captured some native Siberian towns, reached the Ob River's mouth and came back having covered about 900 miles *1500 km*.

Furthest ranging ■ That recorded in the pre-Hispanic New World was undertaken by the Inca Tupac Yupanqui, who is said to have reached the River Bío-Bío in southern Chile from his 'capital' at Cuzco, in Peru, in 1486. In Mesoamerica, the corresponding record was held by the Aztec chief Moctezuma II (1466–1520) who, from Tenochtitlán, in Mexico, reached the River Panuco in the north and Xoconusco in the south. In a sense, this record was broken after the Spanish conquest by campaigns under Spanish leadership into Honduras under Hernán Cortés and into Guatemala under Pedro de Alvarado, both in 1524.

Unique overseas conquest ■ That reputedly undertaken by a native American Indian state of the Pacific islands known as Auachumbi and Ninachumbe, attributed to Tupac Inca Yupanqui, 10th supreme Inca, probably in the last quarter of the 15th century, was the only known overseas conquest. The episode has been dismissed as fabulous but the islands have been variously identified, for instance, as those of the Galapagos or Juan Fernandez.

Speediest ■ The great Ottoman Turkish conqueror Selim I (r. 1512–20) conquered all of modern Syria, Lebanon and Egypt in a dramatic campaign in 1516–17. These areas were ruled by the Mamluk dynasty from Cairo. Selim's formidable armies entered Syria on 28 July 1516, won a major battle near Aleppo on 24 August 1516, and had taken all Syria by September. The Ottoman armies then crossed the Sinai, with all their heavy equipment and cannon, in a remarkably short five days in January 1517, and took Cairo, the Mamluk capital, at the end of that month.

Most audacious ■ In a campaign of staggering audacity the Spaniard Hernán Cortés led a force of only 400 men and 16 horsemen to overthrow the great Aztec empire in Mexico.

Unsurpassed feat of arms ■ The Spaniards Francisco Pizarro and Diego Almagro led a force which overthrew the great Inca empire in 1531. The terrain in which the Spaniards fought was harsher than any they had encountered in Europe. The Andes dwarf the highest European mountains; the valleys are deeper and the deserts more arid than any the Spaniards had seen and the distances were far greater than for any European campaign.

First printed military map ■ A map printed about 1500 and made by someone signing themself simply 'P.W.' shows military operations in Switzerland during the Swabian War. Printed from copper plates, this is the earliest known printed map of a military campaign.

Battles

Bloodiest in ancient times ■ 250 000 men reputedly killed at Plataea (Greeks v. Persians) in 479 BC, and 200 000 men allegedly killed in a single day at Châlons, France (Huns v. Romans), in 451 AD.

Bloodiest in New World ■ In the pre-Hispanic New World this was probably the slaughter of 20 000 Caranqui Indians, whose bodies were flung into Lake Yahuar-cocha ('Lake of Blood'), near the Mira River, by order of Inca Huayna Capac (early 16th century). Inca warfare yielded higher casualties than that of Mesoamerica, where the object was to take prisoners.

Most decisive ■ Many battles of this period vie for the distinction of being the most decisive. One such was the battle of Chaldiron, near Tabriz, Iran, in 1514 in which the Ottoman Turks under Selim defeated Safavid Iran led by Shah Ismail and so stopped the westward march of this militant shia Muslim state. Another important victory was the successful siege of Constantinople by the Ottoman Turks in 1453, which ended the Eastern Roman or Byzantine empire. The Ottomans had an army of 80 000 regular soldiers, and huge artillery pieces. In Constantinople there were fewer than 7000 men to defend 14 miles *22.4 km* of walls. The siege lasted from 7 April to 29 May, which was a Tuesday. Even today Tuesday is still seen as

In a tapestry of the Battle of Pavia, troops of Charles V are shown attacking the French army.

inauspicious by many Greeks. Another decisive battle occurred at Panipat in north-west India in 1526, when Babur defeated the rulers of north India and so established the great Mughal empire. In Europe one of the most decisive battles was that of Nancy (5 January 1477) when Duke Charles the Bold of Burgundy, with his newly-created army of 10 000 men, was overwhelmed by a force of Lorrainers and Swiss infantry almost double the size. Charles and many of his men were killed, and this was both the end of his own expansionist plans and, because he died without a male heir, virtually the end of an independent Burgundian state.

Least predictable outcome ■ During the battle on the Shelon River in Russia in 1471 the 40 000 fighting men of the Novgorod area were defeated by 4000 men of the city of Moscow.

Greatest ■ In terms of numbers engaged, new ideas utilized and fierceness of the fighting, the greatest battle of the age in Europe has to be Pavia, in Italy (1525). The French army of about 35 000 men, led by Francis I himself, had advanced into the Duchy of Milan and laid siege to Pavia. The army had fortified itself in a strong camp, and the job of the Spanish commander, the Marquis of Pescara, with his slightly smaller force was to lure the French out of their encampment and break up the siege. He succeeded in doing this by an audacious march across the front of the French position in the face of the French guns. The French, scenting victory, came out in a disorganized attack and were defeated piecemeal by the more disciplined Spanish troops. Six thousand French dead were left on the field, including large numbers of French nobles. The famous Swiss infantry were shattered, Francis I captured, and French aspirations to rule Milan finally destroyed.

Largest armies to confront one another ■ When they met on the River Euphrates in eastern Turkey in 1473, the Iranian army, under the command of the ruler of Iran, Hasan the Long, numbered about 300 000, while the Turkish army, under the command of the Sultan Mehmed the Conqueror, numbered about 260 000. However, although Hasan the Long had more men, he had no guns, and he lost the battle when many of his men fled before the volleys of Turkish artillery.

One of the greatest massacres ■ In preparation for his attack on shia Iran in 1514, which culminated in the battle of Chaldiron, the Ottoman Sultan Selim decided to make sure there was no shia fifth column in his predominantly sunni Muslim empire. He killed 40 000 out of the 70 000 shia Muslims in the Ottoman Empire.

First major European–Indian battle in North America ■ In October 1540 Governor Hernandes de Soto reached the town of Mauilla in present day Alabama. A dispute arose between him and the Indians and battle took place. 'The Indians,' according to the contemporary record, 'fought with such great spirit that they many times drove our people back out of the town.' Eventually the Spaniards fired the town and then fought the Indians back into the palisade as they tried to escape; 'many, dashing headlong from the flaming houses, were smothered, and, heaped one upon another, burned to death.' About 2500 Indians and 18 Spaniards perished; 150 Spaniards received 700 arrow wounds; 12 horses were killed and another 70 injured.

Sieges

Longest ■ The longest ever recorded siege was that of Azotus (Ashod, Israel) which according to Herodotus was invested by Psamtik I of Egypt for 29 years in the period 664–610 BC.

Artillery initially served to shorten sieges, but by the early 16th century developments in fortifications were beginning to outstrip improvements in artillery, leading to a new emphasis on siege warfare. The great siege of Rhodes in 1522 when 650 Knights of St John and their followers held out for four months against 100 000 Turks was an example of this.

Europe's most magnificent siege ■ From 30 July 1474 to 27 June 1475 the siege of the German town of Neuss by Duke Charles the Rash of Burgundy with a force of some 22 000 men plus guns and siege engines was the wonder of Europe, 'the most magnificent siege for more than a hundred years . . . a school of honour . . . there are so many knightly combats'. Nine hundred tents housed the duke's household while he and leading courtiers had wooden mansions custom built. The camp was like a town with bakeries, brothels, tennis courts, inns, chapels and two large markets.

Greatest Ottoman siege ■ Suleyman the Magnificent succeeded his father Selim in 1520, and built the greatest fleet then seen. This was eventually used to establish what can be considered, because of the privation endured and, more importantly, the outcome, as the greatest siege. The siege of Malta resulted in eventual victory for the Knights of St John and Christendom itself was saved. Malta alone

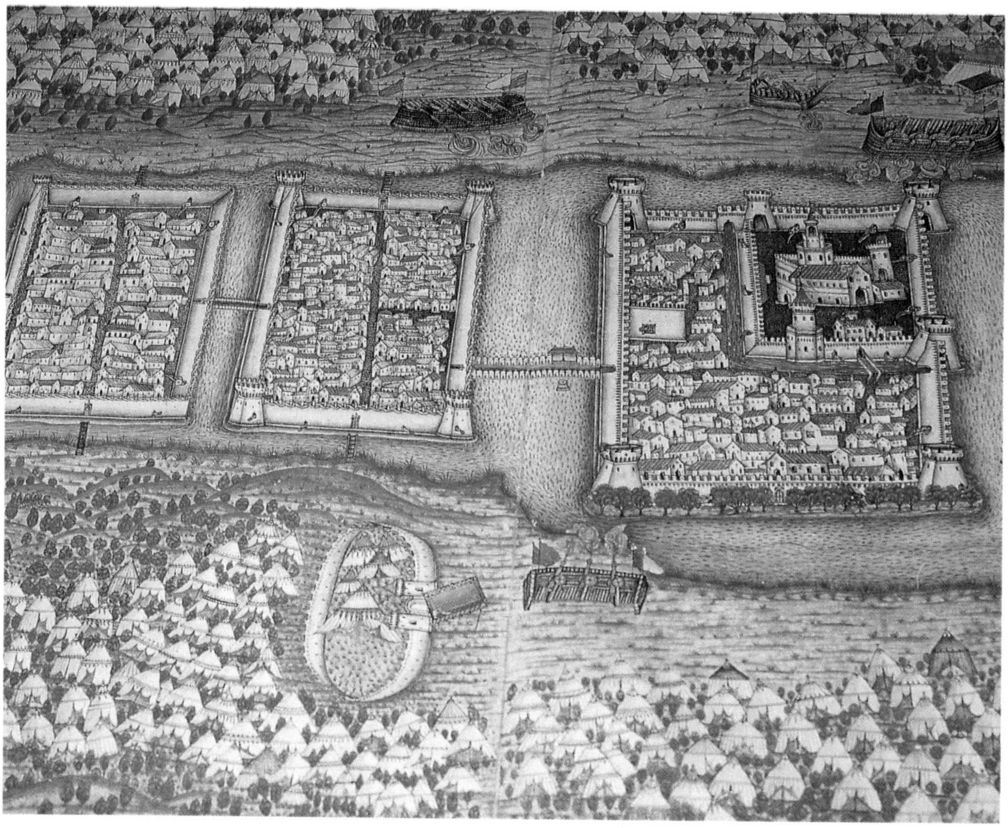

The battle plan for the siege of a fortress by the army of the Ottoman Sultan Suleyman the Magnificent in 1543.

stood between what was seen as the Christianity of the West and Islam of the East.

Worst siege ■ Since 1019 Novgorod, which had a charter of self-government, had struggled with Moscow for supremacy. In 1467 the army of Ivan III, the Russian Great Prince, besieged Novgorod for several months. When the siege was lifted it was reported that 48 000 people had died of hunger or been killed within the city, and as many as 250 000 were massacred or died of hunger in the areas around Novgorod devastated by the Moscow army.

A design for various siege weapons by the Italian master of the art of warfare, Francesco di Giorgio Martini (1439–1502).

Most complete destruction ■ The Aztec city of Tenochtitlán was systematically levelled to the ground at the command of Hernán Cortés in 1521. So complete was the destruction that any evidence of it is seldom found. He ordered a new city, now Mexico City, to be built on the ruins.

Most thorough sacking of a city ■ In 1527 the sacking of Rome by the forces of Charles V was perhaps the most brutal incident in the warfare of the age. It lasted for a month, during which time, day and night, the screams of men, women and children filled the streets, where their bodies were then left to rot. The soldiers gutted churches, palaces and hospitals and smashed and pillaged tombs. It is estimated that about half the population of the city died during those terrible days.

Arms and armour

Last of the archers ■ The longbow was best employed by large contingents of archers on the battlefield. Disciplined and rapid fire by well-trained archers could devastate both the knights and their horses, until armour became more sophisticated in the 15th century. As late as the 1470s Charles the Bold of Burgundy still maintained a much-prized corps of English archers, and the tradition of archery lasted in England for another century. But by 1500 the preferred weapons to provide mass infantry firepower were the new handguns and arquebuses.

Favourite weapon for princes' bodyguards ■ At the end of the 15th century the crossbow, which was essentially a sniper's weapon, very accurate and lethal at short range but difficult to use in a co-ordinated fashion, was enjoying a new lease of life as the favourite weapon for the mounted bodyguards of princes.

The 22 most secret arts ■ The *Ninja* of the mountain strongholds of Japan devised at least 22 arts: blow gun, mouth darts, miniature bows and arrows, gliding devices of bamboo and cloth, explosives, folding portable raft and paddle, climbing ladder, short chain for strangulation, blinding powders, water walking, swimming flippers, bamboo 'snorkel' tube, had claws for climbing and fighting, stars with spikes to throw or drop on the ground, firecrackers, a kite to penetrate castles or drop bombs, diving, sprint and long-distance running, jumping, disguise, horsemanship and way finding.

Horse artillery ■ The first large cannon were so heavy as to be practically immobile. Charles VIII of France (1483–98) introduced artillery mounted on wagons pulled by horses.

Artillery tactics ■ The first tactical theory for battlefield artillery fire may have been devised by Bartolomeo Colleoni (d. 1475). He devised a system by which field guns fired through gaps in the infantry ranks, the infantry re-forming while the guns reloaded.

Finest armour ■ The development of articulated plate armour which was invulnerable to arrows was one of the great achievements of the 15th-century arms

An army under attack uses both cannons and hand-held guns in an attempt to see off the advancing cavalry.

industry. It was this armour which maintained the importance of heavy cavalry in the armies of the period. The finest armour was made in Milan, in northern Italy, particularly by the workshop of the Missaglia family led by Antonio Missaglia, who died in 1495.

Best cavalry shields ■ The lightest, strongest African cavalry shields were made from oryx skin, and shone white in the bright sun. They were made by Berbers in the Sahara for use by camel-mounted warriors. The author of Kitab al-Istibsar wrote *c.* 1135: 'The best and most expensive shields are those made from the hides of the old females whose horns, through age, have grown so long that they prevent the male from mounting them.'

Most poisonous weapon ■ In North America this was undoubtedly the poisoned arrows of the Otapas tribe of California. The arrows had only to inflict a very small wound to make the body break out 'with an insupportable pestilential stench' before the victim died. 17 of Coronado's soldiers were killed in this way in 1541.

First and most famous description of scalping by a European observer ■ Jacques Cartier, on his second voyage up the St Lawrence River in Canada in 1535, was shown at Quebec by the Stadaconanas 'the skins of five men's heads, stretched on hoops, like parchment'. These came from Toudmamans (Micmacs) from the south, who waged war continually against his people. There is still debate as to whether scalping occurred in North America before the European arrival, or whether it was learnt by the native Indians from the Europeans. The fact that the word occurs in many Indian languages, but is not a common one in European languages, suggests that the practice was in use before the Europeans arrived.

War machines

Military engines ■ The largest military catapults, or onagers, could throw a missile weighing 60 lb *27 kg* a distance of 500 yd *450 m*.

Armoured vehicles ■ The first use of armoured wheeled vehicles, it appears, was during the wars of 1419–34 between the Bohemians and the Hussite religious dissidents. The Hussite leader John Zizka introduced armoured wagons to the battlefield. The wagons had raised wooden sides and carried small cannon, drawn up in circles with armoured boards slotted in to fill the gaps between wagons. Zizka's war wagons posed a challenging problem to attacking infantry or cavalry.

Wind-powered fighting vehicle ■ In 1472 the Italian Guido da Vigevano envisaged a tank-like vehicle driven by windmills, but such an unreliable machine was never tested.

Most imaginative war machine ■ The *ballista quadrirotis* or mobile arrow launcher which was drawn by two armoured horses was designed to fire arrows on the enemy from all sides, but it was never used in battle.

Hand-cranked tank ■ *Leonardo da Vinci's celebrated tank design of 1500 was massive, but relied on hand-cranked wheels. It is unlikely that human muscles could have propelled such a vehicle faster than a crawl.*

Guns

Earliest ■ Probably the earliest guns were constructed in both China and in North Africa in *c.* 1250. Cannon appeared in France in 1326, England in 1327. They were not at first very effective weapons because of the difficulties in casting the barrels and variations in the quality of gunpowder. In the 15th century, improvements in metal casting and, particularly, the 'corning' of gunpowder to make the particles all of equal size and composition, made the cannon a more formidable weapon. The 15th century also saw the introduction of 'case-shot' in which round, bullet-sized shots were fired from cannons, instead of single round balls.

Greatest guns ■ Europe around 1500 had many enormous guns. Most of them had been made in the first half of the 15th century when immature founding and powder-making techniques led to an emphasis on lobbing huge projectiles at castle walls. *Mons Meg*, one of the survivors of this generation of guns preserved at Edinburgh Castle, Scotland, was made for Duke Philip the Good of Burgundy in 1449. It weighs 15 366 lb *6961 kg* and fired a stone ball of 549 lb *249 kg*. It was said to throw a 19.5 in *0.63 m* bore.

Largest Russian cannon ■ The largest cannons which were ever put into action by Russian troops had barrels 24 ft *7.32 m* long. They were used during the three-month siege of the Swedish fortress of Vyborg on the shores of the Baltic Sea in 1496.

Biggest gun of all ■ Cast in 1453 in Edirne in southern Turkey for use in the siege of Constantinople, the largest cannon had, according to some contemporary estimates, a barrel 26 ft *7.36 m* long, 96 in *3.5 m* in circumference, weighing 49 tons and throwing cannon balls of 1331 lb *603 kg* and was described as 'a terrible and extraordinary monster'. It was the work of a Hungarian cannon-founder. It took a team of 60 oxen three months to pull it the 140 miles *234 km* from Edirne to Constantinople, and required 200 men on either side to hold it steady, as well as 50 carpenters with 200 assistants to prepare the bridges and roads for its journey. From it the Turks fired up to seven shots a day against the walls of Constantinople from 12 April to 29 May 1453.

Matchlock ■ The earliest firing mechanism for hand-guns was the matchlock, which appeared about 1425. The serpentine, an S-shaped pivoted arm which applied a glowing cord or match to a small charge of gunpowder in a pan at the side of the breech, was the first matchlock mechanism. It replaced the slow-burning match held in the gunner's hand. Using a matchlock gun, a soldier could keep his eye on the target while firing, instead of watching the pan to make sure he had touched the powder to set off the gun's main charge. The matchlock's disadvantage was that the match had to be alight constantly – a risk when powder was so close, and difficult in wet or windy weather. The wheel-lock that produced the spark to set off the gunpowder was invented by Johann Kiefuss in Nuremberg, Germany, about 1515. Its intricate mechanism brought a spinning wheel into contact with iron pyrites, held in the jaws of a spring-operated arm known as the dog. The contact sent sparks into the pan to ignite the powder. Wheel-locks were never widely used by infantry, being more appropriate for cavalry. Long heavy wheel-lock pistols, holstered and ready for use, had a considerable influence on tactics in northern Europe.

First firearms in Japan ■ Chinese copper-barrelled hand-guns were imported in 1510, but were not used in battle until 1543/1548. The Portuguese took

European muskets to Japan and these, called *Tanegashima*, were quickly copied and manufactured by Japanese gunsmiths. They were possibly first used in battle in 1549.

First matchlocks in Kabul ■ In 1519 Babur, who would become the first Mughal ruler of India, used guns against the fort at Kabul, Afghanistan. He wrote that the people 'had never before seen *tufang* (matchlocks), they at first took no care of them; indeed they made fun when they heard the report and answered it by unseemly gestures.'

The first use of the arquebus in war was by Spanish soldiers in Italy at Bicocca in 1522 and Pavia in 1525. The Spanish earned a reputation for formidable volley-fire. Filippo Strozzi improved the arquebus in the 1530s, giving it an effective range of up to 400 paces, and the French introduced weapons of standard calibre. It was these weapons, even more than the cannon, which gave the Europeans their great advantage in the Age of Discovery.

Most effective artillery ■ When Charles VIII of France invaded Italy in 1494 it was his artillery train which attracted most attention and was thought to be the cause of this unique success. These guns were not the great monsters of 50 years earlier, but rather medium-sized cannon and basilisks made of cast bronze and weighing 2–3 tons *2023–3048 kg* and firing 20 lb *9 kg* iron shot at high velocity on a level trajectory. Eight per cent of the total military expense of the French Crown was spent on this artillery train and its personnel and draught animals. But the creation of such a train was not unique to France in this period; the duchies of Milan and Burgundy had similar trains made up of mobile guns and they were also produced on a large scale in the Venetian arsenal for Venetian galleys as well as Venetian armies. In 1513 Henry VIII of England took 180 pieces of artillery to the siege of Tournai, in France, and these guns used up to 32 tons of powder a day.

The 'Tsar Cannon' or King of Cannon (now in the Moscow Kremlin) has a bore of 36 in 0.91 m *and weighs nearly 40 tons. By 1500, however, huge guns like this were no longer made.*

Earliest use of gunpowder in India ■ Gunpowder was used in South Asia before the Portuguese arrived. References to its use are found in the campaigns of the 15th-century ruler Sultan Mahmud Bigarh of Gujarat. The Portuguese, however, helped further spread of its use.

Mines and rockets

First explosive mine ■ Undoubtedly there were experiments with explosive mines, following on the medieval tradition of digging galleries under fortifications in order to bring the walls down, from an early stage in the history of gunpowder. But the first successful explosive mine is attributed to Francesco di Giorgio Martini, a noted Sienese architect and fortification designer, who brought down part of the wall of the Castel Nuovo in Naples in November 1495 with such a mine. This led to great loss of life amongst the French defenders and to the fall of the castle.

Earliest war rockets ■ In 1232 the Chinese fired war rockets at the Mongols during the siege of Kiai-fung-fu. This is the first known use of rockets in war. The first use of rockets in Europe, as recorded by the 17th-century historian Lodovico Muratori, was by the Paduan army in 1379 during a battle for the Italian island of Chiozza.

Conservation of the Mary Rose, *the earliest surviving broad-side firing warship, originally built in 1510.*

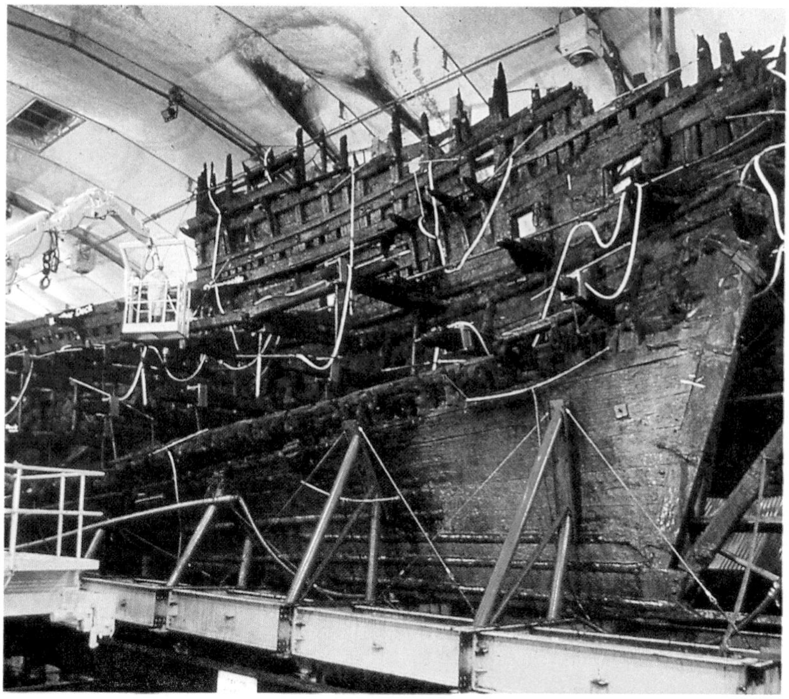

Newest weapon ■ Hand-held firearms had been an integral part of the development of gunpowder weapons since the 14th century, but in the early days they tended to be so heavy that they had to be supported on a tripod. By the end of the 15th century the arquebus with a flintlock mechanism was being produced on a very large scale. Named from the German *hakenbushe* (hook gun), it replaced the first hand-gun, a miniature cannon fired from the chest. The arquebus was a lighter, more mobile weapon, aimed from the shoulder. Around 1500, 18 000 arquebuses were kept in the imperial artillery stores in Innsbruck, Austria, and similar weapons were issued to the rural militia by the Venetian state. These guns were essentially for mass use; they were inaccurate but required little training to use. Their lead shot was able to pierce the best armour and soon the casualty rate of the knights began to rise as they confronted the murderous fire of the arquebusmen.

A compass from the Mary Rose: *with its bowl, box and lid.*

War at sea

Strongest Mediterranean naval power ■ The Ottoman Turks took over the sea as they took over the land. They drove the Venetians out of the Black Sea in 1484, they overran Syria in 1516 and Egypt a year later. They took Rhodes in 1522, moved into North Africa in 1529 and in 1538 defeated the combined Venetian, Genoese and Spanish fleets in the Ionian Sea.

A woodcut from Robertus Valturius's De re militari *(On military matters), printed in Verona, Italy in 1472. It was the first illustrated book to be printed there and only the second in Italy. The woodcut shows a contemporary warship and may have been made by Matteo de' Pasti.*

First European-Asian battle in eastern waters ■ In 1508 the Mamluk (Egyptian) and Gujarati (Indian) fleet defeated the Portuguese off Chaul on the northwestern coast of India. A year later the Portuguese under Francisco de Almeida were to defeat the Mamluk-Gujarati fleet off Diu.

First European–North American river battle ■ In June 1543 the new Governor of Cuba (successor to Hernandes de Soto who had died of fever) had seven brigantines (small vessels equipped for both sailing and rowing) constructed near the mouth of the Arkansas River. On 2 July 322 Spaniards and their companions boarded them and set off toward the sea, each brigantine towing a canoe. One boat was attacked by Indians and capsized with the loss of almost all aboard. Encouraged by success, the Indians attacked the other ships, one at a time. The battle went on day and night for three days until the Indians eventually turned back at the boundary of their own lands.

Guns at sea

The first gunports ■ About the beginning of the 16th century the lidded gunport was developed. Gunports were square or rectangular holes cut low down in the sides of a ship, equipped with hinged lids which allowed them to carry many more heavy guns, because they were set low down in the hull on gundecks, putting the weight of the ordnance closer to the waterline and so reducing its destabilizing effect. Warships now had the ability to fire broadsides of heavy guns. The invention of the gunport has been attributed to a French shipwright called Descharges, in 1501, but there is no definite evidence for this.

Earliest surviving broadside-firing warship ■ The *Mary Rose* was built for Henry VIII of England in 1510. She was a carrack of some 600–700 tons, and one of the largest ships in the English fleet. The *Mary Rose* was rebuilt in the 1530s, and lost on 19 July 1545, capsizing as she sailed out of Portsmouth to fight a French invasion force. Human error and mischance were probably the reasons for the disaster. The ship carried 14 large bronze and wrought-iron guns on each side, with perhaps four heavy bronze weapons firing forwards.

First known use of guns at sea in northern Europe ■ In the years 1337–8,the English royal ship *All Hallows Cog* was provided with a small cannon. However, guns had comparatively little effect on sea warfare until the 1500s. Ships were unable to carry many heavy guns because they could only be mounted on the open deck or up in the superstructures. Too much weight this high up would have made a vessel unstable.

India ■ The first recorded use of cannon at sea by Indian ships was in 1482 when Mahmud Shah II of Gujarat sent out a fleet against pirates 'on board of which he embarked gunners and musketeers'. In 1500 a Gujarat vessel fired several guns at the Portuguese. In 1503 the fleet of Zamorin reputedly carried 380 guns.

Medical services

First regulation of military medical service ■ Much more attention was paid to the military medical service by the Ming dynasty government than by previous dynasties in China. A series of decrees regarding it was promulgated. One of them issued in 1394 stipulated that soldiers on guard suffering from an acute or violent illness should immediately be sent back to the camp to be treated by a doctor. The punishments for delaying were 100 floggings for the lower officer directly responsible, 90 for the chief officer, and one month's suspension of salary for the head of the guard station.

Largest naval medical service ■ During the seven voyages abroad from China headed by Zhen He between 1405 and 1433, over 180 medical men, including court physicians, were attached to the junks to provide medical care to the sailors. Each junk had at least three medical men. Besides, there were also specialists in *materia medica* for drug identification in foreign trade.

Buildings and structures

TOWERS, SPIRES AND TOMBS
FORTIFICATIONS • RELIGIOUS BUILDINGS
BUILDINGS FOR LIVING • THE GARDEN
BRIDGES, CANALS AND DAMS
SPECIALIZED STRUCTURES

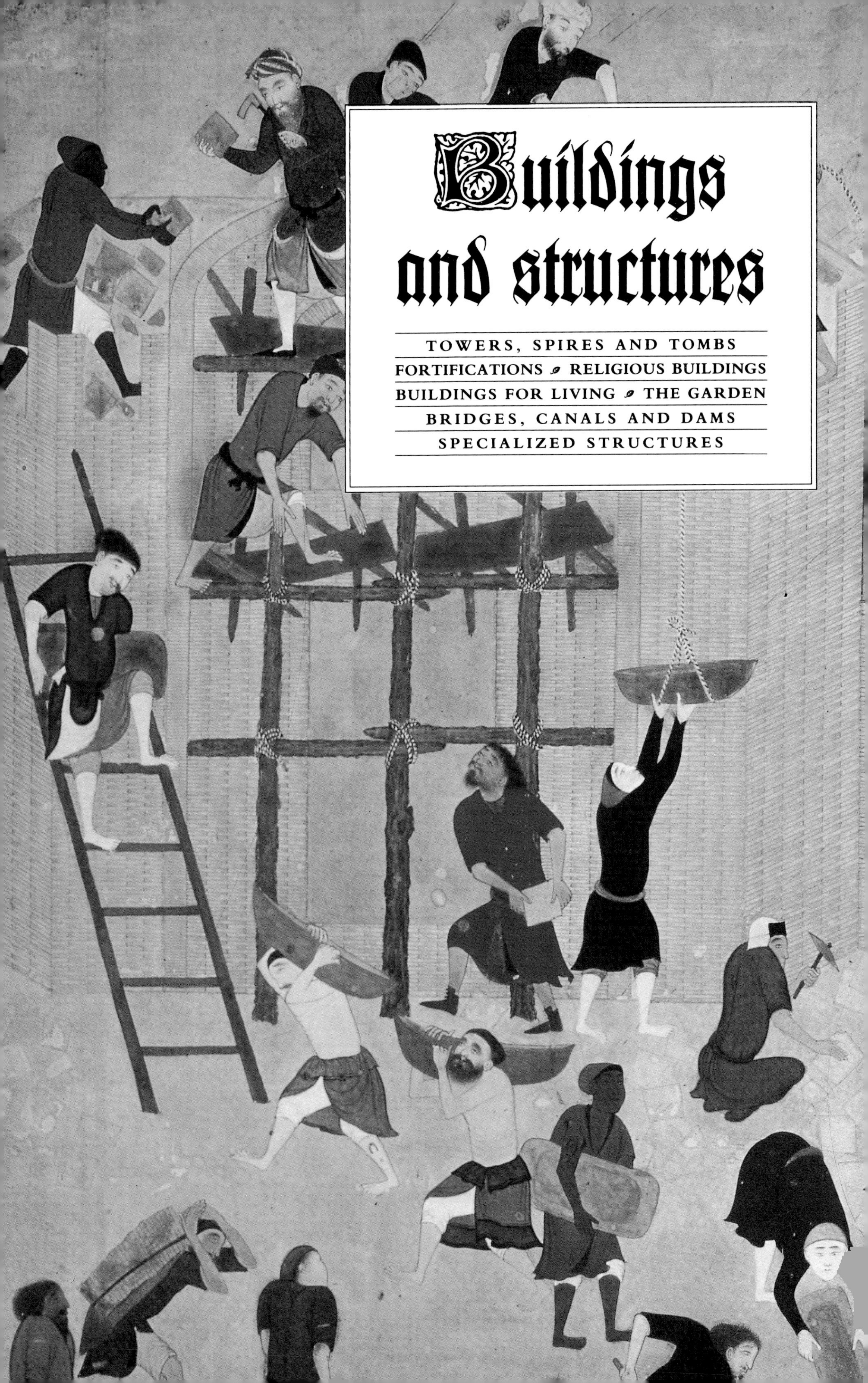

Towers, spires and tombs

Earliest structures

World ■ The earliest known human structure is a rough circle of loosely piled lava blocks found on the lowest cultural level at the Lower Palaeolithic site at Olduvai Gorge in Tanzania.

The earliest evidence of *buildings* yet discovered is that of 21 huts with hearths or pebble-lined pits and delimited by stake-holes at the Terra Amata site in Nice, France, thought to belong to the Acheulian culture of *c.* 400 000 years ago. The remains of a stone tower 20 ft *6.1 m* high originally built into the walls of Jericho have been excavated and are dated to 5000 BC. The foundations of the walls themselves have been dated to as early as 8350 BC.

The oldest free-standing structures in the world are now believed to be the megalithic temples at Mgarr and Skorba in Malta. With those at Ggantija in Gozo they date from *c.* 3250 BC.

Largest earthworks ■ Prior to the mechanical era these were the Linear Earth Boundaries of the Benin Empire in the Bendel state of Nigeria. It is estimated that the total length of the earthworks was probably between 4000 and 8000 miles *6400 and 12 800 km* with the amount of earth moved estimated at from 500 to 600 million yd² *380 to 460 million m³*.

The greatest prehistoric earthwork in Britain is Wansdyke, originally Wodensdic, which ran 86 miles *138 km* from Portishead, Avon to Inkpen Beacon and Ludgershall, south of Hungerford, Berks. It was built by the Belgae as their north boundary.

Tallest columns ■ The tallest load-bearing stone columns in the world are those measuring 69 ft *21 m* in the Hall of Columns of the Temple of Amun at Karnak, opposite Thebes on the Nile, the ancient capital of Upper Egypt. They were built in the 19th dynasty in the reign of Rameses II *c.* 1270 BC.

PREVIOUS PAGE: A Persian manuscript of 1494 shows slaves at work on the building site of a palace in Iran. Light-weight wooden scaffolding like this was widely used on all the great structures of the time.

Monuments

Earliest dated Islamic monument in India ■ The Shrine of Ibrahim (*Dargah La'l Shahbaz*)in Bhadresvar, Kachh, West India has an inscription dated 554 AH (1159–60 AD). The small stone structure is built using typical Gujarati stone construction techniques such as the corbled dome. Decorations to the columns and the mihrab are derived from the local traditional style but omit figurative motives.

Largest ■ The Mount Li tomb, belonging to Zheng, the first Emperor of China, dates to 221 BC and is situated 25 miles *40 km* east of Xianyang. The two walls surrounding the grave of Xianyang. The two walls surrounding the grave measure 7129 × 3195 ft *2173 × 974 m* and 2247 × 1896 *685 × 578 m*.

Largest North American ■ Before the coming of Europeans to the Americas many of the people of the continent built burial and temple mounds. Many of these were small, but a few were among the largest earth structures ever created. 'Monks Mound' is one of about 120 such mounds at Cahokia, Illinois. It has a volume of about 809 900 yd³ *623 000 m³* and covers an area of 16 acres *6.5 hectares*. All this earth was carried to the mound in about 1200 AD by people who had no work animals.

Most imaginative tomb ■ Of structures built in the mid-16th century, Sher Shah's tomb in Sasaram, India, may be considered the most imaginative. He died in 1545. The octagonal tomb 250 ft *75 m* wide, 5 storeys and 150 ft *45 m* high stands in the centre of an artificial lake some 1400 ft *420 m* square. It was designed by the architect Aliwal Khan.

Largest pyramid ■ The largest pyramid, and the largest monument ever constructed, is the Quetzacoatl at Cholula de Rivadabia, 63 miles *101 km* south-east of Mexico City. It is 177 ft *54 m* tall and its base covers an area of nearly 45 acres *18.2 ha*. Its total volume has been estimated at 4 300 000 yd³ *3 300 000 m³* compared with 3 360 000 yd³ *2.5 million m³* for the Pyramid of Cheops near Cairo, Egypt. The pyramid-building era here was between the 2nd and 6th centuries AD.

Oldest pyramid ■ The Djoser step pyramid at Saqqâra, Egypt was constructed by Imhotep to a height of 204 ft *62 m* originally with a Tura limestone casing *c.* 2650 BC. The largest known single block comes from the Third Pyramid (the pyramid of Mycerinus) and weighs *c.* 290 tons.

The oldest New World pyramid is that on the island of La Venta in south-eastern Mexico built by the Olmec people *c.* 800 BC. It stands 100 ft *30 m* tall with a base dimension of 420 ft *128 m*.

Largest henges ■ Great Britain's largest megalithic prehistoric monument and largest henge are the 28½ acre *11.5 ha* earthworks and stone circles of Avebury, Wilts. The earliest calibrated date in the area of this Neolithic site is *c.* 4200 BC.

The largest trilithons exist at Stonehenge, to the south of Salisbury Plain, Wilts, with single sarsen blocks weighing over 45 tons and requiring over 550 men to drag them up a 9° gradient. The earliest stage of the construction of the ditch has been dated to 2800 BC. Whether Stonehenge, which required some 30 million man-years, was a lunar calendar, a temple, an eclipse-predictor or a navigation school is still debated.

First square brick tomb in Bengal ■ The tomb of Sultan Jalal-ud-din Mohammed Shah whose reign lasted from 1414 to 1431 AD; known as the Eklakni Tomb, was built around 1425 in Pandua. It served as a prototype for the Islamic architectural style of Bengal, in India. The curved cornice used in this structure became a characteristic feature of the Bengali style. Other features such as the use of a string course to create a double storey facade, the engaged corner turrets, blind windows above the string course and the use of finely carved brickwork to decorate and give texture and form to the elevation are all characteristic of later Bengali tombs.

Tallest

Europe ■ In northern Europe church towers and spires reached record heights. Of those which were completed and survive, the tallest is that of Strasbourg Cathedral 465 ft *140 m*, completed in 1439 and designed by Ulrich von Ensingen. That of Ulm Cathedral, Germany, also by Ulrich, is actually taller – 530 ft *160 m* – but was eventually completed only in 1890. St Peter's, Louvain, Flanders, begun in 1425, had a tower of over 500 ft *150 m*, destroyed in a storm in 1606. St Waudru, Mons, begun in 1450, was to have had the tallest tower of all (600 ft *180 m*), but only the foundations were built.

Largest standing obelisk (monolithic) ■ The skewer or spit of Tuthmosis III brought from Aswan, Egypt to Rome by Emperor Constantius in the spring of AD 357. (It was repositioned in the Piazza San Giovanni in Laterano, Rome on 3 Aug 1588.) Once 118.1 ft *36 m* tall, it now stands 107.6 ft *32.81 m* and weighs 455 tons. The unfinished obelisk, probably commissioned by Queen Hatshepsut *c.* 1490 BC , at Aswan is 136.8 ft *41.75 m* in length and weighs 1168 tonnes.

Americas ■ The tallest recorded edifice in the New World was the Temple IV at Tikal, a Mayan city in the Peten region of Guatemala. Dedicated in AD 741 in the reign of Yaxkin Caan Chac, it still stands 212 ft *65 m* high from its base to the top of the roof-comb.

The tallest building in South America at the time of the Spanish conquest was probably the Pyramid of the Sun at the city of Moche (Trujillo, Peru), built by the Mochica people before *c.* AD 600. Its ruins stand 135 ft *40.5 m* high on a base measuring 440 × *250 ft 134* × *76 m*.

Tallest bell-tower ■ The 334 ft *97.2 m* high Torre del Mangia on the municipal building the Palazzo Pubblico in Siena is the tallest bell-tower in Italy. It dates from 1338–49.

Tallest tower in Russia ■ The Troitskaia Tower (Trinity Tower) in Moscow's Kremlin was 250.5 ft *76.35 m* high. Its construction was completed in 1495. In 1505–8 the Ivan the Great bell tower was constructed. It was 291 ft *81 m* high and its bell weighed 70 tons. The tower served as a watchtower, with observation of about 15 miles *25 km*.

Largest and most important *minar* (tower) ■ In India this was the tower built at the command of the King of Ghazni, Qutb-ud-din Aybak in 1199 to commemorate his victory over the Rajput ruler Prithvi Raj in 1191–2 AD. The top two levels were added later. It is similar in form and structure to minarets found in Transoxania erected as lighthouses in the desert to guide travellers, like the Kalyan minaret at Bukhara, Central Asia 1127.

The citadel at Aleppo in Syria is regarded as one of the most perfect examples of military building in the medieval Islamic world.

Fortresses, fortifications and castles

Earliest ■ The castle at Gomdan, in the Yemen, originally had 20 storeys and dates from before AD 100.

The oldest stone castle extant in Great Britain is Richmond Castle, North Yorks, built *c.* 1075. The oldest Irish castle is Ferrycarrying near Wexford, dating from *c.* 1180.

Largest ancient fort ■ The largest ancient castle in the world is Hradčany Castle, Prague, Czechoslovakia, originating in the 9th century. It is an irregular polygon with an axis of 1870 ft *570 m* and an average traverse diameter of 420 ft *128 m* with a surface area of 18 acres *7.28 hectares*.

Largest Old World fortress ■ The Moscow Kremlin was founded in *c.* 1147 on Borovitski Hill, which was protected on two sides by the Moscow and Neglinnaia rivers. Inside the Kremlin at the end of the 15th century there were cathedrals, the Russian Prince's chambers and two monasteries. Between 1485 and 1495 new walls and 18 towers of red brick were built under the direction of Italian architects. The Kremlin had an irregular triangle shape with a total surface area of about 70 acres *28 hectares*. The walls were 2436 yd *2235 m* long, 3.8–7 yd *3.5–6.5 m* thick and 5.5–21 yd *5–19 m* high, depending on the elevation of the land. They were pierced by 1045 loopholes. Six of the 18 towers of the Kremlin served as entryways with iron and oak gates; three had turrets with loopholes. On the Red Square side the Kremlin was protected by a water-filled moat. This moat was stone-lined and was fortified by additional low walls. All work on the Kremlin was completed by 1516. In 1538 a wall was erected around the Great Posad (the residential area of the city of Moscow) enclosing an area of 160 acres *64 hectares*.

Largest in British Isles ■ The total area of Dover Castle in Kent, covers 34 acres *13.75 hectares* with a width of 1100 ft *335.2 m* and a curtain wall of 1800 ft *550 m*, or if underground works are taken in, 2300 ft *700 m*. The overall dimensions of Carisbrooke Castle 450 ft × 360 ft *137 × 110 m*, Isle of Wight, if its earthworks are included, are 1350 ft × 825 ft *411 m × 251 m*. The largest English castle is the royal residence of Windsor Castle. It is primarily of 12th century construction and is in the form of a waisted parallelogram 1890 × 540 ft *576 × 164 m*. The largest castle in Scotland is Edinburgh Castle with a major axis of 1320 ft *402 m* and measuring 3360 ft *1025 m* along its perimeter wall including the Esplanade. The most capacious of all Irish castles is Carrickfergus, Co. Antrim, but that with the most extensive fortifications is Trim Castle, Co. Meath, built *c.* 1205 with a curtain wall 1455 ft *443 m* long.

Most perfect examples ■ The citadels in Syria, particularly those of Damascus and Aleppo, both of which have survived, can claim the title of the most perfect examples of medieval military building in the Islamic world. The Damascus citadel, for example, was built mainly of fine hewn masonry blocks. Although it was enlarged and strengthened from the 10th to the 15th centuries, it was mostly the work of Al-Adil, brother of Saladin, in the 13th century. A feature of his work is the huge towers spaced around the walls. A typical

THE WORLD'S TALLEST STRUCTURES
PROGRESSIVE RECORDS

HEIGHT ft	m	STRUCTURE	LOCATION	MATERIAL	BUILDING OR COMPLETION DATES
204	*62*	Djoser step pyramid (earliest Pyramid)	*Saqqâra, Egypt*	*Tura limestone casing*	*c. 2650* BC
300.8	*91.7*	Pyramid of Meidum	*Meidum, Egypt*	*Tura limestone casing*	*c. 2600* BC
331.6	*101.1*	Snefru Bent pyramid	*Dahshûr, Egypt*	*Tura limestone casing*	*c. 2600* BC
342	*104*	Snefru North Stone pyramid	*Dahshûr, Egypt*	*Tura limestone casing*	*c. 2600* BC
480.9	*146.5*	Great Pyramid of Cheops (Khufu)	*El Gizeh, Egypt*	*Tura limestone casing*	*c. 2580* BC
525	*160*	Lincoln Cathedral, Central Tower	*Lincoln, England*	*lead sheathed wood*	*c. 1307–1548*
489	*149*	St Paul's Cathedral spire	*City of London, England*	*lead sheathed wood*	*1315–1561*
465	*141*	Minster of Notre Dame	*Strasbourg, France*	*Vosges sandstone*	*1420–1439*
502	*153*	St Pierre de Beauvais spire	*Beauvais, France*	*lead sheathed wood*	*–1568*

tower was over 82 ft *25 m* high, 88 ft *27 m* by 43 ft *13 m* in plan, with walls 11 ft *3.4 m* thick.

Largest Inca fortress ■ Perhaps also largest in the whole of the New World, the fortress of Sacsahuaman in the Valley of Cuzco, Peru, was reckoned by Spanish observers to be easily big enough for a garrison of 5000 men plus supplies for a long siege. The three walls were almost 60 ft *18.3 m* high and 400 yd *366 m* long. A single stone still standing in the ruins of the lowest terrace is 28 ft *18.4 m* high and is reckoned to weigh about 360 tons – one of the largest stones ever used in any structure.

Strongest fort ■ At Sanaa in southern Arabia early in the 16th century the Italian traveller Varthema claimed that the fort had walls which were 10 *braza* high and 20 *braza* wide at the top, so that eight horses could gallop abreast around it. (A *braza* is about 26 in *65 cm*.) This seems to mean that this fort had bigger walls than the more famous Great Wall of China, which however is much longer and older.

Most famous fortress in Persia ■ There were many notable castles in 15th century Persia (Iran); over 70, for example, in the province of Fars alone. Most of these depended as much upon their sites on almost inaccessible crags as upon their fortifications. Alamut in the Alburz mountains was the main stronghold of the notorious sect of the Assassins. Alamut was finally captured by the Mongols in 1256 but its ruins can still be seen today.

Most extensive new chain in England ■ Henry VIII, having declared himself the Supreme Head of the Church of England in 1534 faced the wrath of European Christendom. To defend his lands he constructed the most extensive chain of fortresses built in Britain since the last days of the Roman Empire. There were 14 artillery castles and at least 10 block houses.

Shortest-lived ■ In 1480, William, Lord Hastings, a rich English nobleman who supported the Yorkist king Edward IV, began to build a castle at Kirby Muxloe in Northamptonshire. His dream 'home' was unusually decorated with red-brick patterning and had the first keyhole-shaped openings for guns. Meticulous accounts of its building were kept and survive. However in 1483 Richard III executed Lord Hastings on suspicion of treason and his new castle was never completed.

Greatest fortified cities

Turkey ■ The longest and most massive fortifications were the Byzantine walls of Constantinople. When the Turkish Sultan Mehmed the Conqueror (1451–81) captured the city in 1453, he refortified them and even added another fortress, known as the Castle of the Seven Towers, which was also to serve as gaol and place of execution for important prisoners.

Largest bastions ■ The creation of effective siege artillery in the later stages of the Hundred Years War (1422–53) led to rapid changes in fortification techniques. Between the 1450's and 1530 the bastioned trace was introduced into Italian fortification with thick low walls carrying guns and solid polygonal bastions projecting from the walls and providing the possibility of enfilading fire to protect the walls from assault. The largest of such bastions in this period was the double bastion at the Porta Ardeatina in the walls of Rome created by Antonio da Sangallo the Younger (1535–45) and containing 24 heavy guns. This bastion had deep underground chambers to prevent mining.

Largest in Africa ■ *The lowland enclose of Great Zimbabwe had a wall 60 ft* 18 m *high (behind which the king presumably held court). On the hill above, a highly fortified fastness could be reached through narrow stone gateways and protected from cliff-tops. The wealth of the Zimbabwe empire was based on a network of stone-built provincial courts controlling a sophisticated cattle economy which paid tribute to the king and his barons. The empire also benefited from extensive gold mining and traded with China. In about 1450 the Zimbabwe empire declined in influence and was replaced by the new Shona empire of Mutapa which controlled the trade-path linking the gold mines to the navigable stretch of the Zambezi River.*

Thickest walls ■ Urnammu's city walls at Ur (now Muqayyar, Iraq), destroyed by the Elamites in 2006 BC, were 88½ ft *27 m* thick. The walls of the Great Tower or Donjon of Flint Castle, in Wales, built in 1277–80 are 23 ft *7.0 m* thick.

Mesoamerica ■ The largest fortification was probably Quetzaltepec, captured by the Aztecs in about 1506. It had six circuits of walls, five of which measured 27.5 ft *8 m* deep by 16½ ft *5 m* high. Normally, Mesoamerican cities were lightly fortified, relying on natural defences, or enclosed by a modest boundary such as can be seen at Tulum on the Yucatán coast.

Domes

Greatest Turkish ■ The great Ottoman Turkish architect Sinan was born in 1489 near the town of Kayseri in Turkey. After serving in the army he became the Master Architect of the empire when he was 50. He designed a huge total of 364 monuments, including several outstanding mosques. Perhaps the best known of these is the Suleymaniye Mosque in Istanbul, built between 1550 and 1557, which has a dome 57.7 yd *26.5 m* in diameter and 28.8 yd *53 m* high. This, however, was not as large as the huge brick dome of the Orthodox Church of St Sophia or Hagia Sophia, completed in 537 AD under the emperor Justinian, which has a diameter of 102–105 ft *30.9–31.82 m* (it is slightly ovoid) and a height 183.5 ft *55.92 m*. It was converted to a mosque in 1453.

Largest ■ Brunelleschi's dome of Florence cathedral (1420–36) measures 138½ ft *42 m* in diameter and is the largest dome to have been built in the western world since ancient Roman times. Inspired by the largest dome of classical antiquity, that of the Pantheon in Rome, it employs a number of new building techniques based on those of ancient Rome and the near East, such as the use of a lightweight double shell and herringbone brickwork. It nevertheless has a medieval appearance because of its pointed shape, dictated by structural considerations, most notably the octagonal shape of the pre-existing gothic base.

Perfect hemisphere ■ The first dome built as a perfect hemisphere, like the Pantheon, was that of Donato Bramante's small Tempietto (S. Pietro in Montorio, Rome) of 1502.

Religious buildings

World's largest religious structure ■ The great temple complex of Angkor Wat built in Cambodia from the 12th century is a vast, decorated sandstone structure, originally dedicated to a Hindu god, but later used as a Buddhist shrine. The enclosure forms a rectangle 1425 × 1640 yd *1282 × 1476 m* with a moat 625 ft *187.5 m* wide. The main entrance is about 220 yd *198 m* long and has three pavilions with towers.

Largest *ziggurat* ■ The largest *ziggurat* (from the Assyrian *ziggurati*, summit, height) ever built was by the Elamite King Untash *c. 1250* BC known as the Ziggurat of Choga Zanbil, 18.6 miles *30 km* from Hafte Tepe, Iran. The outer base was 340 ft *105 × 105 m* and the fifth 'box' 91.8 ft *28 × 28 m* nearly 164 ft *50 m* above. The largest surviving is the Ziggurat of Ur (now Muquyyar, Iraq) with a base 200 × *150 ft 61 × 45.7 m* built in the reign of Ur-namu (*c. 2113–2096* BC) to three storeys surmounted by a summit temple.

Right: Brunelleschi's dome of the cathedral in Florence was constructed between 1420 and 1436 and has, ever since, dominated the city.

Churches

Biggest churches ■ Florence Cathedral (1296–1461) is 488 ft *149 m* in length, and was on its completion the largest church in the world. It was superseded by St Peter's, Rome (1506–1614), 610 ft *186 m* long – including the portico, 693 ft *21.5 m* long – still the world's largest church, with an overall surface area of 236 117 sq ft *22 067 sq m*. Santa Mariá de la Sede Cathedral, Seville, Spain (1420–1519), built in the earlier Gothic style, has, at 117 914 sq ft *11 020 sq m*, the largest surface area of any medieval church.

Most renowned basilica ■ Old St Peter's in Rome was built *c.* 326 by Emperor Constantine near where Christ's apostle St Peter was said to have been martyred. It was a huge simple building – its nave 200 ft *60 m long*. The basilica was pulled down in 1505 to make way for the new St Peter's.

Largest circular church ■ Santo Stefano Rotondo in Rome was built *c.* 468 and is still the largest circular church in the world.

Widest vaulted area ■ The aisleless 72 ft *21.6 m* wide nave of Gerona Cathedral in Spain (built 1312–1598) is the widest vaulted area in any European building.

Most beautiful ■ Friar Felix Fabri the German pilgrim of 1483 considered the Church of the Holy Sepulchre in Jerusalem to be 'more beautiful than all the other churches in the world from the variety of the nations who praise God therein'. However, as many do today, he found that very variety also rendered the church 'hideous and shocking' . . . 'Howbeit, there are seven different kinds of Christians in this church, whereof each has its own sect, its own ritual, and its own choir, together with various deadly errors even in the essentials of the faith.'

Most perilous building feat ■ The chapter house of the monastery of Batalha in Portugal (1402–1557) was vaulted, after two unsuccessful attempts, with a square vault of some 60 ft *20 m*. The work involved was so dangerous that it was said to have been accomplished by convicts condemned to death.

Largest crash ■ The Uspensky Cathedral in the Moscow Kremlin collapsed on 20 May, 1474, while building workers were completing the vaults. The Cathedral measured 147 × 126 ft *45 × 38 m* and its walls were 77 ft *23.5 m* high.

Mosques

Largest ■ The Great Mosque at Samarra in Iran begun in 847 is the largest mosque ever built, with its courtyard taken into account. It is made of burnt brick and has an unusual conical minaret. The mosque is 784 × 512 ft *235 × 154 m* and is enclosed by an outer *ziyada* (courtyard) more than a fifth of a mile square (*51 800 m*^{2}).

Largest Turkish ■ After the conquest of Constantinople by the Muslims in 1453, the Mosque of Mehmed the Conqueror was built. It was 145 ft *44 m* high and the central dome was 86 ft *26 m* in diameter. (This dome later collapsed in an earthquake.)

In the following century Sinan, Chief Architect of Suleyman the Magnificent, broke this record several times. The Prince's Mosque, built between 1543 and 1548, is 163.4 ft *49.5 m* high, with a dome 87 ft *26 m* in diameter.

East Africa ■ The Friday Mosque in Kilwa (Tanzania) was enlarged in about 1430 and was seen as the finest place of worship in eastern Africa.

Largest mosque in India ■ The Adina mosque built by Sikander Shah in 1374–5 was the largest mosque in India. It covered an area 501 × 285 ft *150 × 85 m* with a courtyard 400 × 130 ft *120 × 89 m*. The barrel vault is 70 × 34 × 50 ft *21 × 35 × 15 m* high at its highest point. The base of the structure is constructed from reused finely wrought basalt masonry whilst the vaults and domes are made up of small fired bricks. It has the first examples in India of the 'drop' arch and the barrel vault over a prayer chamber.

Largest pillared mosque ■ In India this was reputed to be the Adina Masjid in Patan, Gujarat. Built by Ulugh Khan, Governor to Alaudin Khalji it covered an area of 400 × 330 ft *120 × 99 m* and had some 1050 columns.

Largest Buddhist temple ■ *The temple of Borobudur, near Jogjakarta, Indonesia, built in the 8th century is 103 ft* 31.5 m *tall and 403 ft* 123 m.

Largest covered underground tank ■ Underground reservoirs are common in many parts of Central Persia and can be found under many of the mosque courtyards. The largest of such tanks was the reservoir built under the courtyard of the Cambay Jami Masjid. The mosque was completed in January 1325.

First Indian use of the foliated arch ■ This can be seen in the *mihrab* (prayer niche) of the Arhai-din-ka-Jhompura Mosque built by Abu Bakr of Herat in 1200 under the patronage of Qutb-ud-din Aybak. The surface decoration of the great screen at the Qutb Minar in Delhi erected in 1225 is identical to the screen at the Arhai-din-ka-Jhompura.

Largest ■ *The Great Mosque of Cordoba, Spain was the largest mosque building in the world, though in the 15th century it had been adapted for use as a cathedral, and is still so used today. Completed at the end of the 10th century, it covers an area of 238 500 sq ft* 21 942 sq m.

Largest temple ■ The largest religious structure ever built is Angkor Wat (City Temple), enclosing 402 acres *162.5 ha* in Cambodia (formerly Kampuchea), south-east Asia. It was built to the Hindu god Vishnu by the Khmer King Suryavarman II in the period 1113–50. Its curtain wall measures 4199 × 4199 ft *1280 × 1280 m* and its population, before it was abandoned in 1432, was 80 000. The whole complex of 72 major monuments, begun *c.* AD 900, extends over 15 × 5 miles *24 × 8 km*.

Oldest wooden building ■ The oldest wooden buildings in the world are those comprising the Pagoda, Chumanar gate and the Temple of Horyu (Horyu-ji, at Nara, Japan, dating from *c.* 670 and completed in 715. The wood used were beams from 100-year-old Hinoki trees.

Oldest Japanese temple complex ■ The Asukadera (present day, Angoin) temple about 15 miles *24 km* from Nara in central Honshu, was built in the late sixth century and was a major centre for the diffusion of Buddhism in Japan.

Earliest surviving stupa ■ The Asokan Stupa No 1 at Sanchi, Central India was erected around 250 BC. The brick hemispherical mound is crowned with an umbrella finial. A century later in the Sungan period (*c.* 185–70 BC) the stupa was encased in fine stone masonry increasing the hemisphere's diameter to 120 ft *36 m*. A larger and more complex finial was added along with elaborately carved stone railings and stone pavements on the circumambulatory route around the stupa.

Biggest Aztec temple ■ The rank of the biggest temple in the Aztec empire at the time of the Spanish conquest is disputed between the double temples of Tenochtitlan and Tlatelolco (of uncertain dimensions) and the temple of Quetzalcoatl in Cholula, which attracted pilgrims from all over Mexico and was ascended by 120 steps. The pyramid of Huitzilopotchtli at Texcoco had 117 steps and was reckoned next in size.

Largest ceremonial centre in the New World ■ At the time of the conquest by Spaniards this was probably that at Teotihuacan, erected north-east of Mexico City by about AD 600. It covers an area nearly a mile *1.5 km* long by over half a mile *1 km* wide. The next biggest sites known, at Chichen Itza in Yucatan and Tikal in Guatemala, are less than half the size. The ceremonial centre of Tenochtitlán was probably about 382 × 328 ft *115 × 98 m*.

Richest Inca temple ■ By repute, the richest temple in the Inca world, and therefore presumably in the entire hemisphere, was that of Curicancha, the Temple of the Sun, in Cuzco, Peru. Its perimeter of 400 ft *122 m* was surrounded by a garden 'in which the earth was lumps of gold and it was cunningly planted with stalks of corn that were of gold' and among other gold objects of art which crammed the interior, according to Spanish reports, were 'many tubs of gold and silver and emeralds'.

Largest and most complete sacred complex ■ In India this is the Ranganatha Temple, Srirangaam, in south India. Founded in the Chola period and extended substantially in the 13th century by Pandya and Hoysala rulers and again in the 16th century. The site now covers 155 acres *63 hectares* and is composed of seven concentric high walled rectangular enclosures. Gateways, axially located at the centre of each wall lead into the innermost sanctum. The size of the gateways increase from the innermost sacred areas – the largest being on the outermost gateways. The majority of the town's population lived in houses built within the three outermost enclosures. Shops line the main axial routes into the sacred central heart of the site.

Greatest use of ceramics ■ *Visitors to 15th-century Nanjing in China would be impressed by the gleaming white 'porcelain pagoda' constructed by the Yongle Emperor in 1412 in honour of his deceased father. Nine storeys high, it was entirely faced with porcelain bricks mass-produced by the imperial kilns at Jungdezhen.*

Greatest North American ceremonial centre ■ In about 1200 the great 'Monks Mound' of Cahokia, Illinois was an outstanding ceremonial centre. The nearby town which served it is thought to have been inhabited by as many as 40 000 people. Evidence shows that people may have travelled here from as far away as Lake Superior, Oklahoma and North Carolina. Other such centres existed in Alabama and Georgia. Hernandes de Soto reported such mounds when he trekked across America in 1539–42, but within two centuries the people of these lands and many of their structures had disappeared.

Cities

'Most beautiful' ■ When the great traveller, Ibn Battuta, visited Kilwa (Tanzania) in 1331 he described it as one of the most beautiful cities and the most elegantly built he had seen. At that time the architecture was of wood and reed but later a mosque of cut coral and a royal palace with a fine octagonal pool were built. It was one of the most influential of the medieval city-states of East Africa. It was the main over-wintering entrepôt for gold traders using the monsoon winds to reach the Mozambique coast. In 1505 the town was bombarded by a Portuguese naval squadron anxious to capture the monsoon lanes and dominate the seaways to India. The effects of the first cannon to be used in south-eastern Africa were devastating. The city was replaced first by Mombasa and later by Zanzibar as the prime haven of the east coast.

Finest in New World ■ In 1519 when the first Spaniards reached the Aztec capital of Technotitlan, in Mexico, Hernán Cortés wrote of it thus: 'The city itself is as big as Seville or Cordoba . . . there is one square twice as big as that of Salamanca, with arcades all around, where more than 60 000 people come each day to buy and sell . . . '

Most cultured ■ During the Middle Ages Rome had fallen into decay, factionalism and mob rule causing the exile of the Popes and restricting artistic patronage. In the 15th century civic stability was regained, the Papacy returned to the Vatican and Rome's regeneration as an artistic centre began. By 1500 it had superseded Florence, hitherto the cultural capital of Italy. Michelangelo, Raphael and others settled in Rome. Besides the Papal court, artists were attracted by the ancient Roman buildings and statues which it was increasingly considered essential for them to study. Among the first to do so were the 15th-century Florentines Donatello and Brunelleschi.

The first non-Italian visitor ■ The first non-Italian artist to visit Rome to study classical art was the Netherlandish painter Jan Gossaert in 1508. Thereafter Rome

Most important Indian Buddhist site ■ *Sanchi, Central India, has a large variety and number of monuments dating from the third century* BC *to the 6–7th centuries* AD. *The first known stupas were erected to enshrine the cremated remains of the Buddha and his disciples. Later memorial stupas were erected as votive objects.*

became a centre of artistic pilgrimage for artists from the north who aspired to the classically-inspired Italian style fashionable throughout Europe after 1500.

First archaeological treatise ■ In his *Roma instaurata* (Rome reconstructed) the Italian scholar Biondo Flavio (1392–1463) made the first attempt to produce a topographical reconstruction of ancient Rome. His work was built on by other scholars and in 1519 the great painter Raphael suggested an ambitious scheme of excavation to Pope Leo X.

From the little walled city of Nuremberg, Germany (shown in 1516) came some of the most significant ideas and influential people of the Renaissance.

Most magnificent complex ■ The Alhambra, standing on a narrow plateau rising almost sheer above the Darro river at Granada, in Spain, was completed early in the 14th century, it was the seat of the Nasrid dynasty and was in effect both a fortress and a small town. Its maximum length is 2 430 ft *740 m* and its maximum width is 720 ft *220 m*. There is water everywhere in the town and palaces, brought in by an aqueduct from the mountain range of Sierra Nevada. Because Granada was surrendered to Ferdinand and Isabella in 1492, the Alhambra remains today as it was in the days of the Nasrids.

First example of Renaissance town planning ■ The Tuscan village of Pienza, remodelled between 1458 and 1464 for Pope Pius II by the Florentine architect Bernardo Rossellino, was the first 'new town' to follow the aesthetic and philosophical principles set out in his *Ten Books on architecture* by the theorist and architect Alberti. In this respect it differed from medieval town planning, particularly since Alberti's ideas were based on ancient Roman writings, notably those of Cicero and Vitruvius.

Most complete destruction ■ The Aztec city of Tenochtitlán, in Mexico, was systematically levelled to the ground at the command of Hernán Cortés in 1521. So complete was the destruction that evidence of it is seldom found. He ordered a new city, now Mexico City, to be built on the ruins.

Fastest construction ■ The fastest building of a whole town was recorded in Russia in December 1551 when Sviyazhsk was built in a month. Preparations started in the summer of 1551 in the forest area near Uglich town 125 miles *200 km* north-east of Moscow. Timber amounting to 23 000 m^3 was floated down the Volga River to the mouth of the Sviyaga River. By that time a building site of 370 acres *150 hectares* had been prepared. The town, designed by the architect Ivan Vyrodkov as a base for the army of Ivan the Terrible (who was eager to take the Tartar city of Kazan), was to have fortified walls (filled with 200 000 m^3 of soil), seven towers, churches, dwelling houses, warehouses and other buildings. The town was completed by carpenters building *skorodom* (prefabricated houses – the term means a speedily-built house).

Largest hunting-lodge ■ *The Château of Chambord in the Loire valley (1519–47) was built for King Francis I of France by an Italian, Domenico da Cortona. Although ostensibly a hunting-lodge, it is effectively a vast palace with an imposing facade over 400 ft* 120 m *long.*

Palaces

Largest moat ■ From plans drawn by French sources it appears that those which surround the Imperial Palace in Beijing (see above) measure 54 yd *49 m* wide and have a total length of 3600 yd *3240 m*. The city's moats total in all 23½ miles *38 km*.

Largest ever royal palace ■ Hampton Court, Middlesex, acquired by Henry VIII from Cardinal Wolsey in 1525 was greatly enlarged by him and later monarchs. It covers 4 acres *1.6 hectares* of a 669 acre *270.7 hectares* site.

Largest unsupported roof ■ The hammer-beam roof of Westminster Hall – the only part of the Palace of Westminster in London to survive – is one of the largest unsupported roofs in the world – 250 × 70 ft 72 × 21 m.

Last and first ■ The last great perpendicular gothic ceiling is in the Chapel of Henry VII, suspended over the tomb which is the first Renaissance work in England. Richmond Palace, Henry VII's palace near London built in 1498 was the first Italian Renaissance building in England.

Most beautiful palace of renaissance? ■ Many buildings lay claim to this title. The Ducal Palace in Urbino, Italy was transformed in the late 15th century by Federigo da Montefeltro Duke of Urbino into 'the perfect setting for the complete man of the Renaissance'.

Largest rooms ■ The Salone del Cinquecento in the Town Hall of Florence, designed by Cronaca (1457–1508) in 1495, was the largest room of its day, measuring 58 × 24 yd *53 × 22 m* and heightened in the 16th century to 60 ft *18 m*. The Wladislaw Hall, Prague Castle, by Benedikt Ried (1493–1502), at over 52 ft *16 m* wide, is the greatest span to be vaulted in a medieval secular building.

Other buildings

Most northerly home ■ John o' Groats

Largest ■ *The Imperial Palace (Gu gong) in the centre of Beijing, the northern capital of China, covers a rectangle 1050 yd × 820 yd* 960 × 750 m, *an area of 177.9 acres* 72 hectares. *The outline survives from the construction of the third Ming Emperor, Yung Lo of 1402–24, but due to constant rearrangements most of the intra-mural buildings are far later.*

House, is the most northerly home in mainland Britain. It is said to have been named after a Dutchman who settled at this Scottish extremity in 1489.

First American 'apartment' houses ■ The Hopi and Zûni peoples of south-west America had since *c.* 1200 lived in planned villages in large terraced buildings. The largest of them, at Puebla Bonita, had about 800 rooms. As many as 1000 people may have lived there. These buildings were seen in 1540 by the Spaniards under Francisco Vasquez Coronado – who were very impressed by what they saw.

Tallest American houses ■ In 1540 Coronado's men saw houses in the village of Matsaki in New Mexico which were seven storeys high. Some of these house were used as fortresses: 'they are higher than the others and set above them like towers, and there are embrasures and loopholes in them for defending the roofs of the different storeys.'

First tea house in Japan ■ The tea ceremony, 'the Way of Tea', was introduced to Japan by Chinese Zen Buddhists and established as a ritual and art form in 1472. It was practised in an environment structured to generate calm by asymmetry of the space, warmth and texture of the surface, and the presence of works of art for contemplation which induces 'spiritual one-pointedness'. The first tea house, approximately 8 yd *7.5 m* square, was in Ginka kuji (the Silver Pavilion), home of Shogun Yoshimasa (reigned 1449–1474). The room had a built-in firebox in the centre for the tea.

First museum ■ The Conservatoire, was formed by the collection of antique sculpture given by Pope Sixtus IV (1471–84) to Rome's town councillors in 1471. The collection includes the most famous of all antique sculpture; the Etruscan She-Wolf, and a Roman copy in bronze of the Spinario (thorn-puller).

First purpose-built museum ■ The Belvedere Court, on the hillside behind the Vatican palace in Rome, was begun in 1505 by the leading Italian architect Donato Bramante for Pope Julius II (also the patron of Michelangelo and Raphael). Here, in elaborately decorated niches, was displayed the papal collection of newly-discovered and highly-prized antique Roman statues, including the *Apollo Belvedere* and the *Locoön*, still to be seen in the Vatican Museums. Both the concept of displaying art in this way, and the ideal of art it exemplified, were completely new and profoundly influential.

First works of African art brought to Europe ■ These were the Afro-Portuguese ivory carvings. About 100 of these survive, most of them are salt-cellars or spoons. Most are in the style of Nomoli figures of Sierra Leone.

First European display of American art ■ Mexican gold, silver and feather work was exhibited at Brussels in 1520. The objects had been sent to Charles V by Hernán Cortés. (No visual record survives of the appearance of the articles.)

Architects

First renaissance architect ■ The Florentine Filippo Brunelleschi (1377–1446) was the first architect to consciously use forms inspired by ancient Roman buildings, together with a mathematical system of proportions and a restrained use of materials. In, for example, the church of San Lorenzo, Florence (completed 1460s), he introduced the novel concepts of classicism and harmony which served as a springboard for later architects, first in Italy and then in northern Europe, where the renaissance style began to spread about 1500. Possibly the first such building in northern Europe is the Pavilion of Anne of Beaujeu in Moulins, France, of *c.* 1490.

Most imitated ■ Andrea Palladio (1508–80) built numerous churches, palaces, villas and public buildings in his native Veneto (the area around Venice) and wrote an important treatise, the *Four Books on Architecture*. His clear and classically elegant style, which revived ancient Roman ideas on symmetrical planning and harmonic proportions, was easily copied, and his influence – both formal and theoretical – pervades the subsequent architecture of the western world, most notably in Britain and North America.

First renaissance building ■ The portico of the Foundling Hospital in Florence, designed by Brunelleschi in 1419, is considered the first building in the renaissance style on account of its classically-inspired forms and a mathematical system of proportions.

First modern architectural drawing ■ The development of linear perspective, discovered by the Florentine architect Brunelleschi about 1415, allowed architects to set out their designs with new accuracy, but it was the introduction of plans, sections and elevations drawn to scale that revolutionised architectural practice. The *Ten Books on Architecture* (1452) by the architect and theorist Alberti (1404–72) recommends them, but the first evidence of their use is not until *c.* 1519 in the designs produced by the workshop of the architect and painter Raphael (1483–1520) for St Peter's, Rome.

Gardens

Most beauteous ■ In the Holy Land the gardens of Jericho were renowned for their outstanding beauty as Friar Felix Fabri recorded in 1483: '. . . as we went along between the dry stone walls of the gardens of Jericho, we saw most beauteous orchards, which are watered by the streams which run from the Fountain of

Elisha . . . In these gardens we saw many sycamores – tall trees. Besides sycamores, other trees grow there – both fruit-trees, and scented grape vines, and many fig-trees bearing exceeding sweet fruit, and likewise we saw there sundry kinds of flowers and roses of many different sorts, and we smelt delicious and fragrant scents, for the bushes and thorny shrubs bear especially fine roses and sweet fruits. Green herbs and pot-herbs also seem to grow there better than anywhere else, and all plants, and whatever grows in the soil there, flourish exceedingly.'

First Persian gardens in India ▪ The use of fountains, waterfalls and other sophisticated elements of traditional Persian garden design in Gujarat, western India, was carried out by a garden designer from Khurassan, Iran, at Halol, a suburb of the capital city of Champaner founded by Sultan Mahmud Bigarah in 1484.

Grandest ▪ Italian gardens were the grandest and most modern of all European gardens in the 15th and 16th centuries. There were three essential parts of a well designed garden: a *bosco*, woodland with tall trees, an orchard with symmetrical rows of fruit trees, and an *orto* – a small garden where herbs and flowers grew in organized beds. Larger estates would also have a *prato* or lawn. Art was combined with nature to create ornamental features such as topiary (shaped hedges), pergolas (a structure of columns or posts supporting a trellis on which climbing plants grow), grottoes (caves), mounts, labyrinths or mazes, tree houses, surprise water jets and automata (automatic devices) added interest and excitement to the vast pleasure gardens of the very wealthy. The entire garden would be enclosed with a high trellised wall covered with planting, and the parts were subdivided with hedges of myrtle, juniper, or box, clipped to varying heights.

The most rich, magnificent and ornamental garden in Europe ▪ This was identified by the Italian art historian Vasari as the garden of the villa at Castello Villa created by Tibolo *c.* 1540 for Cosimo de' Medici, Grand Duke of Tuscany, in central Italy. The focal point was a fountain of Venus by Giambologna placed in the centre of the main square garden surrounded by a labyrinth. The paths were surrounded by a pleached alley of citrus trees with their branches completely interlaced. The lemon terrace rose above on a higher plane, accessible by two flights of stairs which shaped the terrain in a monumental fashion. The grotto was famous for surprise fountains, shell mosaics, and animal sculptures.

The 'supreme statement of reality/illusion' ▪ The Dry Landscape Garden of Ryoanji, Kyoto, Japan of the 1480s is described thus. This walled garden emulates a seascape, formed by 17 rocks arranged into five groups. White pebbles, cover the ground between them and are raked to form the waves. The psychological compression created by the design is so perfect that the disruption of any element would weaken the composition. Although many have tried, no one has surpassed the design of this garden.

Most linked to nature ▪ Interest in landscape and the enjoyment of the countryside grew during the 15th century, inspired by ancient Roman precedent. One result of this was the construction of buildings which took account of beautiful views such as Pope Pius II's palace at Pienza in Tuscany (1464), and increasingly after 1500, of country villas. The most influential of buildings linked to nature are those built by Palladio in the mid-16th century in the environs of Venice, such as the Villa Rotonda at Vicenza.

Babur, the first Mughul ruler of India (1483–1530) is depicted, in a later manuscript, supervising work in his garden at Jalalabad.

Most favoured design ▪ Enclosed gardens were the favoured design in England at the turn of the 16th century. The records of 1520 from Thornbury Castle in Gloucestershire describe the most common arrangement of grounds of the late medieval manor house. High embattled walls surround a garden for strolling through, the orchard contained by a wooden fence, and the boundaries of the property marked by a thick hedge and ditch. The enclosed garden evolved from the earlier castle and fortified manors when necessity of providing protection from enemies or thieves was the highest priority in the layout of the grounds. In England, herbs became particularly important features in the knot garden when the monasteries were closed in 1535 and essential herbs could no longer be acquired from the monks. Garden furniture was also included in the design, seating was provided by benches under arbours of roses and raised beds planted with aromatic camomile.

First knot garden ■ Descriptions and illustrations of a knot garden occur in a poem, the *Hypnerotomachia Poliphili* (The Dream-battle of Poliphilus), written by Francesco Colonna in Italy in 1467, but first published in 1499. The interlaced knot pattern was a popular design element in all branches of the decorative arts from textiles to plasterwork and also found expression in the elaborately patterned clipped hedges and walkways of pleasure gardens. The *Hypnerotomachia* was a story about a dream garden, created on the Isle of Cythera (Crete), the home of the planetary deity who held dominion over gardens.

The Italian architect Palladio built the villa known as the Rotonda at Vicenza, near Venice in the mid-16th century. Its links to the open spaces and garden around it are integral to the design.

Loveliest roses ■ In 1483 Friar Felix Fabri, the German monk from Ulm, wrote of the famed roses of Jericho: '. . . even the Divine wisdom likens itself to a rose, and not to any rose, but to the rose of Jericho, where they are most lovely. Indeed, these roses are most beauteous, and feed the sight with their loveliness, rejoice the smell with their scent, delight the touch by their delicacy, cure the sick by their virtue, gladden the mournful by their colour, cause even serious men to admire them by their wondrous appearance, and prefigure the glories of paradise by their beauty. One of these roses has more than a hundred petals.'

Most famous Chinese garden ■ In the mid-14th to mid-15th century Ming period the garden designed by the scholar-artist Wen Cheng-Ming was the most outstanding. Wen's vision of the ideal garden included a courtyard pavilion beside a little pond widening into a great lake, stretching into the foothills of some ethereal mountains.

The age-old aim of the Chinese gardener was to re-create the effect of the totality of Nature in a garden. By the Ming dynasty the Confucian ideal of the retired scholar without portfolio was well accepted. It was a repressive autocratic dynasty when many gentlemen rejected public office and devoted their lives to the Arts, to contemplate Nature in the elegant setting of a garden. Chinese landscape painting and gardening are so inter-twined it is hard to appreciate one without the other. The closest analogy for a Westerner might be a walk through Chartres Cathedral. The Chinese garden lies between architecture and landscape painting.

Most celebrated French garden ■ The Archbishop of Rouen, Cardinal Georges d'Amboise laid out his garden at Gaillon between 1502 and 1509 on a terrace overlooking the River Seine. It was divided into four square beds with flowers, fruit trees and box or rosemary cut into figures. One square had the arms of France and another was laid out as a labyrinth or maze.

First French orangery ■ Louis XII and his queen, Anne de Bretagne, made a large, two level garden at Blois, in the Loire valley, France, between 1499 and 1515. Contemporary writers commented on the variety of fruit and vegetables, and the orange and lemon trees in tubs – possibly for the first French orangery. The orange, a native of China, was much sought after in Europe.

Largest Moorish garden in Spain ■ The original 12th century Alcazar (castle) in Seville was destroyed and rebuilt in the 14th century by Moorish architects. Its garden is the largest surviving garden that preserves the Moorish design.

First artificial garden ■ Early Chinese records describe a garden constructed by a rich man from Maoling, possibly as early as the first century AD. It was a mile and a half *2.4 km* across, within which poured tumbling streams of water, and there was a mountain of rocks over 100 feet *30m* high. Such artificial gardens were popular in China and in the late Ming era one is reported that had an imitation mountain made of wood with grottoes and peaks made of piled-up timbers. In this mountain 'not a scrap of stone, nor a cupful of earth' was used.

Quintessence of a water garden ■ Zhuo Zheng Yuan in Jiangsu province, China, constructed 1502–21, for a Court Examiner on his retirement is regarded as 'the quintessence of a water garden'. Much of it contains inter-linking pools, islands, bridges and streams. The buildings are arranged on the principle of 'borrowing views' so, as one moves about the garden, the vistas are planned for one's delight.

Greatest period of Zen art in Japan ■ During the Muromachi period (1392–1573) the Zen *shoguns* (warrior class) relied on the advice of the monks on every subject from 'taxation to tea'. Zen's appeal to the warriors lay in qualities which were most compatible with a military outlook: fortification of the will, and the emphasis on character building and self-salvation. Zen was the most instinctive and intuitive religion, and therefore the least rational and intellectual. Zen's greatest monuments are the temples within gardens designed for meditation. Most famous of the period is the great temple complex of Daitokuji, Kyoto. There are no flowers in the gardens so they are always in season.

First botanical garden (to survive) ■ Botanical gardens were originally started as physic gardens – belonging to university medical schools. The plants were grown to provide medicine. The oldest surviving botanical garden is that in Padua, Italy, begun in 1542.

Bridges

Oldest ■ Arch construction was understood by the Sumerians as early as 3200 BC and a reference exists to a Nile bridge in 2650 BC.

The oldest surviving datable bridge in the world is the slab stone single arch bridge over the River Meles in Smyrna (now Izmir), Turkey, which dates from *c.* 850 BC .

The clapper bridges of Dartmoor and Exmoor (e.g. the Tarr Steps over the River Barle, Exmoor, Somerset, England) are thought to be of prehistoric types although none of the existing examples can be certainly dated. They are made of large slabs of stone placed over boulders.

Oldest stone arch ■ The oldest known segmental arch bridge in the world, the An-chi Bridge at Chao-hsien in Hopeh, China, was built 605–16 AD. Its flat crown (rising only 23 ft *7 m* in a span of 122 ft *37 m*) was unmatched in Europe before the 1500s.

Longest single-span arch ■ *The Ponte del Castelvecchio at Verona, Italy, built in 1352–6 has three spans, the greatest of which is 160 ft* 49 m *long with a rise of 45 ft* 13.7 m. *The most daring of the medieval segmental arch bridges was the bridge over the Adda at Trezzo in northern Italy, built 1370–7. It consisted of a single arch 236 ft* 72 m *long with a rise of 70 ft* 21 m. *The bridge was deliberately destroyed in the course of hostilities in 1417; the abutments have survived.*

Mightiest in China ■ In the late Ming era Xie Zhaozhi, the Chinese miscellanist, stated that 'of all the bridges in the Empire' the Luoyang Bridge over a tidal creek in his province of Fujian was the greatest. 'It strides across the sea in a fashion that would make it seem beyond human powers to build.' The bridge was reckoned to be 3657 ft *1097 m* long and 15 ft *3 m* wide. It was built over a tidal creek and when the tides were angry it was 'always difficult to keep one's footing on it.'

Longest ■ The masonry bridge which was built in about 400 AD over the Tab river, near the town of Arrajan in central Iran, was 4920 ft *1500 m* long. In Europe the famous bridge at Avignon, southern France, built in 1177, was made up of spans each over 100 ft *30 m* in length. The total length of the bridge was 3000 ft *914 m*. Old London Bridge had a total length of 926 ft *282 m*. It was carried on 20 arches of roughly semicircular form supported on 19 artificial islands, which so restricted the channel that during the rise and fall of the tides the river rushed through in the form of rapids. The bridge carried a large number of houses and shops.

Highest masonry arch ■ In the Iranian province of Khuzistan, immediately to the east of lower Iraq where the river Karun runs through a gorge, a great stone bridge 245 ft *75 m* above the water level was built in about 700 AD. It consisted of a single arch, its stones held together by iron clamps set in lead. Remains of this bridge can still be seen.

Longest Inca ■ To cross the terrain of South America, the great road system of the Incas needed many bridges. To this end the Incas developed various techniques of bridge building. The simplest was the rope bridge (no more than a hemp rope stretching across a gully). The hanging wood bridge added a piece of wood to this rope. A traveller tied himself to this and pulled himself across. The hanging bridge was made of fibre ropes attached to pillars or stones on either side of the chasm or river. A four-rope bridge even had a reed floor between the two lower ropes. Floating bridges were made of mats laid on rafts. The longest of these bridges was probably that across the River Vilcas or Pampas on the way to Uranmarca, near Cuzco, Peru. It was estimated by Spanish observers at up to 360 ft *110 m* long, and wide enough for two horsemen to ride abreast. The more famous Huaca-chaca (Holy Bridge) over the Apurímac River at Curahuasi (which provided the setting for the novel and film *The Bridge of San Luis Rey*) stretched 250 ft *76 m* on cables as thick as a man's torso at a height of 125 ft *38 m* above the gorge.

Astonishing bridge foundations ■ The remarkable durability of concrete foundation work was demonstrated by the Pont Notre-Dame in Paris. This stone bridge was built in 1507 to replace a medieval wooden bridge. Its foundations were of mortar laid on top of piles driven into the river bed, and they proved so effective that they were reused 350 years later when the bridge was reconstructed.

First iron bridge ■ With its mastery of iron technology, China was able to lead the world in its construction of iron-chain suspension bridges over its many turbulent rivers and mountain gorges. One of these was built over the river Mekong at Baoshan in Yunan province, with a span of nearly 200 ft *60 m*. It was originally made using bamboo cables, but in about 1470 an engineer named Wang Huai converted it to iron chains. A contemporary poem speaks of it as 'woven of iron, a lonely thread running straight through the sky'. (The Chinese had been making such bridges since the beginning of the first millenium BC; the first European traffic-carrying suspension bridge was not built for another three centuries.)

Aqueducts

Longest ancient ■ The greatest of ancient aqueducts was the Aqueduct of Carthage in Tunisia, which ran 87.6 miles *141 km* from the springs of Zagouan to Djebel Djougar. It was built by the Romans during the reign of Publius Aelius Hadrianus (AD 117–38). Its original capacity has been calculated at 7 000 000 gal *31.8 million litres* per day.

Largest step well ■ Step wells are an indigenous building type in Gujarat, west-

The triple-tiered aqueduct Pont du Gard, built in 19 AD near Nimes, France, is 160 ft 48 m *high.*

ern India. Flights of stairs are linked to the well shaft so that one can walk down to water level. The subterranean depths offer a cool and quiet retreat whilst enabling a large number of people to reach the water at the same time.

The Rudabai step well is the largest to have been constructed in the 15th century. Located about 20 miles *32 km* outside Ahmadabad, at Adalaj, it was built as an act of charity by a local chieftain's wife. An inscription in the well states that it was completed in 1499.

Canals

Earliest ■ Relics of the oldest canals in the world, dated by archaeologists *c.* 4000 BC, have been discovered near Mandali, Iraq.

The earliest canals in Britain were first cut by the Romans. In the Midlands the 11 mile *17 km* long Fossdyke Canal between Lincoln and the river Trent at Torksey was built in about 65 AD and was scoured in 1122. It is still in use.

Longest canal in Islamic world ■ The great Nahrawan canal in Iraq irrigated all the lands along the east bank of the Tigris from above Samarra to about 100 miles *160 km* south of Baghdad. Its total length was about 200 miles *320 km*.

Deepest *qanat* ■ Found in eastern Iran, it is 1000 ft *328 m* deep at its source. *Qanats* are almost horizontal conduits that conduct water from underground water-bearing strata in the debris of mountain slopes to the better soils in the valleys. Generally *qanats* are 25-150 ft *7.6–45.7 m* deep and 3–5 ft *0.9–1.5 m* wide. Vertical shafts are sunk into the *qanats* at intervals of about 260 ft *80 m* for ventilation and the removal of spoil during construction. Believed to have originated in Iran from where they spread throughout the Muslim world and beyond, they had been in use for over 2000 years, providing much of Iran's water supply. These extraordinary feats of engineering were sometimes more than 12 miles *20 km* long and were graded so that water flows caused minimum damage.

First chamber lock ■ Sluices and simple gates may go back to 14th-century Dutch engineers, but the idea of the chamber lock is attributed to Leonardo da Vinci in about 1480, solving the problem of geting vessels from one reach of water to another.

First swinging lock-gates ■ The first swinging lock gates, known as mitre gates, are attributed to Leonardo da Vinci, who in 1498 was appointed state engineer in Milan. His drawings of the San Marco lock show mitre gates. Earlier gates in the ordinary or pound-lock (a Chinese invention of the 900s) rose vertically. In his five years in charge of Milan's canals, Leonardo brought together several important constituents of the modern canal; twin gates, stone-lined chamber, mitre gates with paddle openings controlled from above, use of windlass and chain to open the gates. Though his work no doubt made use of the innovations of others, his contribution to canal technology is still considerable.

First lateral canal ■ The first canal in Europe to run parallel to a river was the Bereguardo Canal in Italy. It was constructed between 1452 and 1458 by Bertola da Novate, engineer to the Duke of Milan, and was 11½ miles *19 km* long.

Earliest known North American irrigation ■ The people in the area which became New Mexico and Arizona irrigated their fields long before the 15th century. For example, it is judged that the inhabitants of the Salido Valley in Arizona controlled the irrigation of at least 250 000 acres *100 000 ha.* (Remains of irrigation ditches and canals have also been found elsewhere in the region.)

The commonest type of dam has always been the gravity dam. The tendency of the pressure of the water to cause fracture, slippage or overturning is resisted by the weight of the dam resting on its foundations. Until the 13th century this was the only type of dam known. Given suitable foundation conditions, however, a saving in material can be admired if the dam is curved in the upstream direction.

In southern Spain the dam across the Guadalquivir River and the mill-houses worked together to grind corn for 15th century Cordoba.

Dams

Earliest ■ The earliest known dams were those uncovered at Jawa in Jordan. These stone-faced earth dams are dated to *c.* 3200 BC.

Earliest Islamic ■ This was built in 677 AD at Taif in the Arabian peninsula. The Muslims inherited their skills in dam construction from their predecessors in the regions that they conquered in the seventh and eighth centuries. These regions comprised Spain, North Africa, Egypt, Syria, Arabia, Iran, Mesopotamia and Central Asia. The example of Roman engineers was particularly important because of the scale on which they worked and because their influence was relatively recent. Later the Muslims introduced a number of improvements in dam construction.

Longest in Europe ■ The dam built in the 10th century over the River Guadalquivir at Cordoba was 1400 ft *420 m* long. Like many Islamic dams it was used for hydropower. Downstream from it were three mill-houses each containing four mills, which continued to grind corn for Cordoba throughout the Middle Ages. (The mill-houses, without machinery, still exist.)

Earliest arched ■ An arched dam was built by the Mongols in about 1300 AD near Qum in Iran. It is 85 ft *26 m* high, 180 ft *55 m* long with a crest thickness of about 16 ft *5 m*. Its radius of curvature is 125 ft *38 m*. Arched dams were built in Christian Spain and elsewhere in Europe from about 1420 onwards.

First for hydropower ■ The Muslims were pioneers in the use of dams for hydropower. One of the first was the Band-i-Amir built over the river Kur in Iran between Shiraz and Persepolis in 960 AD. It was constructed throughout of masonry blocks set in mortar and strengthened with iron anchors set in lead. It was some 30 ft *9 m* high, 250 ft *75.25 m* long and wide enough at the crest for two horsemen to ride abreast. There were 10 *norias* (water-raising devices) and 10 mills below the dam. The water that it impounded was led into canals and irrigated 300 villages.

Earliest desilting sluices ■ The intro-

The total length of the Great Wall of China may have been as much as 6200 miles 9980 km.

duction of desilting sluices was another Islamic invention. In many Islamic dams in Spain the dam abuts on to a masonry wall on one side of the river which extends downstream for about 66 ft *20 m*. Between this wall and the river bank, part of the river's flow is diverted into the mouth of the irrigation canal. Sluices, usually two, were built into the wall. They served two purposes. During normal operation they were used as escapes to allow surplus water to drain back into the river; and occasionally they would both be opened to their fullest extent in order to desilt the approaches to the canal mouth. Such scouring sluices, closed with planks carried in grooves, are absolutely essential. Silt is bound to collect above dams and must periodically be removed if the canal intakes and the canals themselves are not to become hopelessly choked and obstructed. Such sluices were utilized on a grand scale by later Spanish dams.

First storage dams ■ The first and most impressive dam designed to create reservoirs for the storage of water was built by Spanish Christian engineers about 1260 in the reign of King James the Conqueror. The dam forms the reservoir of Almonacid and it is on the river Aquasivas about 25 miles *40 km* south of Zaragoza. It is some 100 ft high *30 m*, about as thick, and 340 ft *104 m* long.

Longest working ■ Eight Islamic dams on the River Turia in Valencia province, Spain are still working today. Designed for irrigation these dams have a low profile and very solid foundations, so that they had withstood the dangerous flash flood to which the river is subject for over 500 years. A further reason for their survival is their incorporation of desilting sluices. The dams and the canals associated with them still supply water to the Valencian rice fields.

Specialized structures

Longest statue ■ Near Bamiyan, Afghanistan there are the remains of the recumbent Sakya Buddha, built of plastered rubble, which was 'about 1000 ft' *305 m* long and is believed to date from the 3rd or 4th century AD.

Longest wall ■ The Great Wall of China has a main-line length of 2150 miles *3460 km* – nearly three times the length of Britain. Completed during the reign of Ch'in Shih Huang-ti (221–210 BC), it has a further 1780 miles *2860 km* of branches and spurs. Its height varies from 15–39 ft *4.5 m–12 m* and it is up to 32 ft *9.8 m* thick. Its width at the top ranges from 12–35 ft *3.7–10.7 m*. It runs from Shanhaikuan, on the Gulf of Pohai, to Yumenkuan and Yangkuan and was kept in repair up to the 16th century.

The longest of the Roman walls in Britain was the 15–20 ft *4.5–6 m* tall Hadrian's Wall, built 122–6 AD. It crossed the Tyne–Solway isthmus for 73½ miles *118 km* from Bowness-on-Solway, Cumbria, to Wallsend-on-Tyne, Tyne and Wear, being abandoned in 383 AD.

Most skilfully cut ■ Incorporated into the Hatrun-rumiyoc palace in Cuzco, Peru, is a famed block with 12 right angles on its face. There is another stone with 35 angles in three dimensions incorporated into Machu Picchu.

the Arts and entertainment

PAINTING AND DRAWING

SCULPTURE ❧ DECORATIVE ARTS

LANGUAGE, LITERATURE AND LEARNING

MUSIC ❧ ENTERTAINMENT

Painting and drawing

Most valuable ■ Valuations for three paintings by Leonardo da Vinci (*d.* 1519) in a Milanese inventory of 1525 place them, as far as can be judged, among the most expensive paintings of their day. The *Mona Lisa*, arguably the most famous portrait ever painted, was worth 100 *scudi*, as was the *Virgin and Child with St Anne* (both now in the Louvre, Paris). Even more valuable was the *Leda*, a mythological painting now lost and known only from copies, appraised at 200 *scudi*, and worth as much as its owner's house.

Largest altarpiece ■ The great retable which fills the entire apse of the Old Cathedral of Salamanca, Spain, comprises 53 panels depicting the life of Christ in an elaborate gilt frame. The work of Nicolas Florentino, a Florentine, it was completed by 1445 when he contracted to paint the fresco of the *Last Judgement* above it.

Leonardo da Vinci's portrait: the Mona Lisa.

PREVIOUS PAGE: In the painting by Jacopo del Sellaio (1442–93) the dress, interior decoration and decorative objects of the time are all clearly shown as the master of the house sits down to dine.

Greatest increase in ecclesiastical art and iconoclasm ■ Most art in northern Europe was religious and from 1500 the production of ecclesiastical art increased dramatically. In Zurich, Switzerland, alone records show that in the first 18 years of the century there was a 100% increase in production. The crisis of the Protestant Reformation which split the Christian church was also a crisis in art. Luther criticised the Catholic church for the amount of money spent on the building of St Peter's in Rome. The Protestant movement's greatest criticism of the increasingly realistic devotional painting and sculptures was that simple people treated the objects as if they were the real things, not simply images. Images were condemned by the most outspoken critics for causing idolatry. By the second decade of the century the same people who had commissioned works of art for churches were beginning to smash and burn them, along with the so-called miracle working relics of the saints. Zürich was the first city of many communities to 'cleanse' its churches. In Basel the most violent outburst of iconoclasm (idol-breaking) brought the city to the brink of civil war. In February 1529 iconoclasts stripped the cathedral and most of the churches of all images and, on Ash Wednesday, burnt them in the city square.

Largest ■ *The largest work of art – or at least of artifice – from the pre-Hispanic New World was a vast network of lines, spirals and shapes known as the Nasca lines, formed in the ground, stretching over the table-lands above the Rivers Palpa and Ingenio in Peru, covering an area some 60 miles* 97 km *long and several miles wide. It includes some huge figural compositions, such as birds and monkeys. The date and purpose of these patternings are unknown.*

Greatest loss ■ The Reformation in England caused the loss of more works of art than any other single factor in the country's history. In 1538 Henry VIII ordered the monasteries to shut down and sold them off. The booty included gold and jewels from the most famous shrines. But no profit was realized for anyone from the stained glass windows, sculptures and other objects that were smashed or burnt. Many manuscripts were also destroyed, but many were simply altered. The most important change required in the prayerbook was the removal of St Thomas of Canterbury from the calendar of saints: the best way to tell if a prayerbook was in England at the time of the Reformation is to look for erasures in the December calendar.

Largest icon ■ The icon known as *The Deeds of the Archangel Michael* was probably painted by the Greek Theophanes and his pupils in *c.* 1399. It measured 91.85 × 71 in *235.5 × 182 cm*. It was the patronal icon of the Kremlin Cathedral of the Archangel Michael in Moscow. In Russia the Archangel was venerated as protector and patron of soldiers, captain of the angelic host and

THE PRINCIPLE OF QI

The most important principle of all Chinese art and architecture is the principle of Qi – spirit. It is the first of the six essential principles codified by Xie He in the sixth century. For example a painting must vibrate. The qi of the painted forms must also respond to the real forms as they exist outside the painting. The complete principle is therefore one of consistency, harmony and also one of mystical realism, in which the artist catches the living spirit of nature itself. This idea is based on Taoism, whose goal is to become one with the universe.

defender of Christianity against the pagan hordes.

Biggest art export ■ The Portinari triptych (a painting consisting of three hinged panels) by Hugo van der Goes was painted in the Netherlands for the Florentine Tommaso Portinari, manager of the Bruges branch of the Medici bank in Flanders, for the altar of his family chapel in Florence, and shipped to Italy in 1483. Measuring 99 × 229 in *253 × 586 cm* it is the largest early Netherlandish triptych now in existence and, on its arrival in Florence, 16 porters were required to haul it across the city to its destination in the church of S. Egidio.

First art historian ■ The Italian artist Giorgio Vasari (1511–74) wrote the first narrative and critical account of Renaissance art in his *Lives of the most excellent painters, sculptors and architects*, published in 1550 and revised in 1568. It is perhaps the most important work on the history of art ever written, on account of its usefulness as a source-book and its extremely influential approach to the subject. Its basic theme is that the arts, decayed after the collapse of the Roman Empire, flowered again in 15th-century Italy, most notably in Florence, progressing to reach perfection in the art of Michelangelo in the 16th.

Art theorists ■ The critical theory of art, ignored since ancient Roman times, was newly formulated in Renaissance Italy. The Florentine Leon Battista Alberti (1404–72) wrote influential books on painting (1435), sculpture (*c.* 1463) and architecture (1452). These were followed by numerous theoretical works, including the notebooks of Leonardo da Vinci (1452–1519), the *Lives* of Vasari (1511–74). The important architectural treatises of the Bolognese architect Serlio (1475–1554), written between 1537 and 1551, and the north Italian architect Palladio (1508–80), published in 1570, in due course diffused the Italian renaissance language of architecture across the world.

Most important artistic centre ■ Rome, during the middle ages, had fallen into decay, factionalism and mob rule causing the exile of the Popes and restricting artistic patronage. In the 15th century civic stability was regained, the Papacy returned to the Vatican and Rome's regeneration as an artistic centre began. It increasingly drew artists from outside the city, and by 1500 these included such eminent figures as Michelangelo, Raphael, and the architect Bramante, all of whom were employed by the Popes and settled in Rome. Besides the Papal court, artists were attracted by the ancient Roman buildings and statues which it was increasingly considered essential for them to study. Among the first to do so were the 15th-century Florentines Donatello and Brunelleschi. Rome later became a centre of artistic pilgrimage for artists from the north who aspired to the classically-inspired Italian style fashionable throughout Europe after 1500. The first non-Italian artist to visit Rome for this purpose was the Netherlandish painter Jan Gossaert in 1508.

GREATEST ARTISTS

COUNTRY	NAME	DATES	OUTPUT
China	**Wu Wei**	1458–1508	*Painter*
Netherlands	**Hieronymous Bosch**	*c.* 1450–1516	*Painter*
	Pieter Bruegel (Elder)	1525–1569	*Painter*
	Jan van Eyck	*c.* 1389–1441	*Painter*
	Hugo van der Goes	*c.* 1435–1482	*Painter*
	Quintin Metsys	1466–1530	*Painter*
	Hans Memling	1430–1494	*Painter*
	Rogier van der Weyden	1400–1469	*Painter*
'Germany'	**Albrecht Altdorfer**	*c.* 1480–1538	*Painter, Engraver*
	Lucas Cranach	1472–1553	*Painter*
	Albrecht Dürer	1471–1528	*Painter, Engraver*
	Hans Holbein (Elder)	*c.* 1460–1524	*Painter*
	Hans Holbein (Younger)	1497–1543	*Painter*
'Italy'	**Leon Battista Alberti**	1404–1472	*Architect, Writer*
	Giovanni Bellini	1428–1516	*Painter*
	Sandro Botticelli	1444–1510	*Painter*
	Bramante da Urbino	1444–1514	*Architect*
	Benvenuto Cellini	1500–1571	*Sculptor, Jeweller*
	Filippo Brunelleschi	1377–1446	*Architect*
	Antonio da Correggio	1494–1534	*Painter*
	Luca Della Robbia	1397–1482	*Sculptor*
	Donatello	1386–1466	*Sculptor*
	Piero della Francesca	1416–1492	*Painter*
	Domenico Ghirlandaio	1449–1494	*Painter*
	Giorgione da Castelfianco	1477–1510	*Painter*
	Andrea Mantegna	1431–1506	*Painter*
	Michelangelo Buonarotti	1475–1564	*Architect, Painter, Sculptor*
	Andrea Palladio	1518–1580	*Architect*
	Pietro Perugino	1446–1524	*Painter*
	Raphael of Urbino	1483–1520	*Painter and Architect*
	Titian	1477–1576	*Painter*
	Giorgio Vasari	1511–1474	*Art historian*
	Leonardo da Vinci	1452–1519	*Painter and Sculptor*

Techniques

Newest technique ■ Until about 1400 the medium commonly used for easel painting was egg tempera, made from egg yolk diluted with water. Oil painting is traditionally said to have been invented by the Netherlandish painter Jan van Eyck (*d.* 1441), author of the *Arnolfini Marriage* and the Ghent altarpiece (St Bavo, Ghent), although it may be more accurate to say that he developed new ways of painting with oil, which was already used for limited purposes. Oil's slow-drying and light-refractive properties permitted the subtle blending and layering of colours to produce tonal effects which made paintings appear more true to life. By 1450 this highly sophisticated technique, of which van Eyck was the unrivalled exponent, was standard in the Netherlands and parts of northern Europe. Under Netherlandish influence, the oil medium was gradually adopted in Italy during the late 15th century, with Leonardo da Vinci, Piero della Francesca and Raphael among its foremost exponents. By 1550 it had become the principal medium for easel painting in Europe.

Most disastrous experiments ■ Leonardo da Vinci's fresco of the *Last Supper* (*c.* 1495–7) in the convent of Santa Maria delle Grazie, Milan, was painted in an unorthodox medium containing oil and varnish, as opposed to the 'true fresco' technique employed in Italy since the middle ages, in which water-based paint is applied to wet plaster. Already by 1517 it was beginning to perish. Since then it has been restored at least six times, making it one of the most frequently restored paintings. Another fresco by Leonardo, the *Battle of Anghiari* (1505–6) in the Town Hall of Florence, was painted in a sort of encaustic inspired by ancient Roman usage. One part of it dried too dark and the other melted, and it was eventually overpainted by the painter and art historian Vasari in 1565. It is now known only from early copies.

Most common supports ■ Throughout Europe, easel paintings (as opposed to murals) were produced on both wooden panel and canvas. Before 1500 panel was usually favoured for important and costly works, but after 1500 canvas was increasingly adopted, and by the end of the century had become the most common support. This was probably a consequence of growing public demand for pictures, since canvas was cheaper and could be more quickly prepared for painting than panel, and more easily transported.

Newest way of representing objects ■ Linear, or artificial, perspective is a quasi-mathematical system for representing three-dimensional objects on a two-dimensional surface. It assumes that receding lines at right-angles to the picture-surface appear to meet in a single point on the horizon, known as a Vanishing Point. Probably invented by Brunelleschi in early 15th-century Florence, it was developed and described by the architect and theoretician Alberti and, with more sophistication, by the painter Piero della Francesca in his treatise *De Prospectiva Pingendi* (On the perspective of painting) in the second half of the 15th century.

First aerial perspective ■ Burgundy (now in France) is credited with the late 15th century invention of aerial perspective, the use of blue tones for objects seen in the distance. Simon Marmion's (d. 1489) views of the Flemish countryside are pure landscapes. The Master of James IV of Scotland (who may be Gerard Horneboulte, d. 1540) show great advances toward a solution for the problem of depicting the middle distance.

Newest drawing techniques ■ The laborious early 15th-century technique of drawing with a stylus, usually made of silver, on specially prepared vellum or paper, was gradually replaced by new materials such as the quill pen, the brush, and most importantly, chalk. These allowed the artist to make rapid sketches and, in the case of chalk, to work on a large scale. This and the increased availability of paper led to the use of full-scale drawings (known as cartoons) for large paintings, which provided an accurate blueprint of the artist's original design. Cartoons were scaled up by means of a square grid superimposed over the original drawing, and transferred to the surface to be painted by dusting ground charcoal through pinpricks made on the outlines.

First 'exploded' illustration ■ Nowhere is the principle of objective observation which lies at the heart of the scientific method better exemplified than in the medical illustrations of the artist and inventor Leonardo da Vinci (1452–1519). In the course of dissecting and recording more than 30 human corpses he made several discoveries and developed drawing techniques which are still used by modern illustrators, most notaby the 'exploded' view which he pioneered in his drawings of shoulders and feet to demonstrate the structure of bones beneath the muscles. He was also the first to draw in cross section and to render organs as if they were transparent so that their position in relation to those behind them could be observed.

Most vibrant Indian paintings ■ In the late 15th century Persian influences, most obvious in the 'arabesque' line, transformed the staid conservative native Indian painting style in miniatures to produce the most vibrant paintings ever known on the sub-continent. The most vividly dramatic and elegant examples are the manuscripts in the Caurapancasika style, characterized by shallow space portrayed in a single plane and the use of bright primary colours. They were produced from the late 15th to the mid-16th century at a still unidentified centre between Delhi and Jaunpur. The group is named after a famous love poem which is the subject of one of the manuscripts; it concerns the unrepentant lover of a kings daughter who is about to be executed for his transgressions. The highly charged energy of the painting style reflects the emotional eroticism of the poetry.

Newest subject-matter ■ Renewed interest in ancient Greek and Roman literature led to the adoption of subjects from classical mythology in painting and sculpture, in which figures – imitating antique sculpture – were often shown nude or wearing ancient Roman costume. The first such works were Florentine and include Botticelli's painting of the *Birth of Venus* of *c.* 1480 and Michelangelo's statue of *Bacchus* of 1497. Among the first northern works in this genre were the Netherlandish paintings of Jan Gossaert, such as the *Neptune and Amphitrite* of 1516.

Earliest night scene ■ Geertgen tot Sint Jans 'Little Gerrit of the Order of St John' (*c.* 1460–1490) spent most of his short life in Haarlem, Netherlands, where he painted the earliest true night-time scene in European painting, *The Nativity of Christ*. The picture is illuminated by a non-solar light source – the body of the Christ child – creating the first optically correct and systematic rendering of forms and space not dependent on the light from the sun.

In about 1480, the Italian painter Sandro Botticelli (1444–1510) chose to paint this wonderful picture based on a story from classical mythology, rather than from the traditional Bible stories. It was the legend of the birth of Venus, the Roman goddess of love.

Portraits

Most popular pose ■ This, for portraits, was the three-quarters view, showing the sitter's head turned at an angle to the picture-surface. It appears to have been developed by early Netherlandish painters such as Jan van Eyck (*d.* 1441) and, under Netherlandish influence, was adopted in Italy – where previously the profile view had been preferred – during the second half of the 15th century. By 1500 it had become the standard portrait format in Italy as well as northern Europe, exemplified by Leonardo da Vinci's *Mona Lisa* of about 1503.

Earliest known Italian full length portrait ■ Moretto da Brescia painted the earliest known Italian full length portrait in 1526. The subject of *Portrait of a Nobleman* is unknown.

Most flattering portrait ■ During marriage negotiations it was common for a prince to be sent a portrait of his prospective bride and for his choice to be influenced by the beauty of the lady portrayed. King Henry VIII of England chose his fourth wife, Anne of Cleves, a German princess whom he had never seen, partly on the strength of her portrait (now in the Louvre, Paris) by Hans Holbein (1497–1543). When Anne arrived in England in 1540, the reality of her appearance so appalled the king that he soon divorced her.

First portrait sequence ■ The German painter Hans Holbein 'the Younger' (1497–1543) worked in Basel, Zurich and Lucerne in Switzerland before his first visit to England in 1526. There he painted portraits of several eminent figures, including Nicholas Kratzen, the king's astronomer, and Sir Thomas More's family. In England again in 1532 he painted the portrait group *The Ambassadors*, Thomas Cromwell, later Lord Chancellor, and in 1527, at the time of Francis I's visit to England, painted the organisers of the pageantry for the festivities surrounding the signing of the 'eternal' peace between France and England at Greenwich. This was the first portrait sequence made in England. In 1536 he was appointed painter to Henry VIII.

First American portraits ■ In 1505 Brazilian natives were drawn by Portuguese artists, and in 1529 Christopher Weiditz drew portraits of Aztecs brought to Spain by Hernán Cortés. Weiditz also produced an excellent medal of Cortés himself.

First portrait of Mehmet II ■ In 1479 the Italian artist Gentile Bellini travelled from Venice at the request of the Sultan himself to paint the portrait of the formidable conqueror of Constantinople.

Painters

Most famous ■ In 1450 the Italian writer Bartolomeo Fazio judged the four greatest painters of his day to be the Netherlanders Jan van Eyck (*d.* 1441) and Rogier van der Weyden (*d.* 1464) and the Italians Gentile da Fabriano (*d.* 1427) and Antonio Pisanello (*d.* 1455). The first two are still the most famous early Netherlandish painters. Gentile da Fabriano and Pisanello were sought after by eminent patrons throughout Italy, including the Pope, the King of Naples and the Venetian senate, but comparatively little of their work survives. By 1550, in the first edition of Vasari's *Lives*, Michelangelo (*d.* 1564), along with Leonardo (*d.* 1519) and Raphael (*d.* 1520) were the most renowned; they remain among the best-known painters of all time. The greatest Northern artist in Vasari's day was considered to be the German painter and draughtsman Albrecht Dürer (1471–1528).

Most prolific self-portraitist ■ *In an age when self-portraits were unusual, the German painter and graphic artist Albrecht Dürer (1471–1528) showed an exceptional fascination with his own appearance. He produced eight drawn or painted self-portraits, beginning at the age of 13, as well as numerous disguised self-portraits in his religious works.*

Greatest Venetian painters ■ Giovanni Bellini (Active *c.* 1460 – d. 1516) was the grestest Venetian painter of the 15th century; the jewel-like colours, use of light and atmosphere which distinguishes Venetian painting first appears in his work. The greatest painter of 16th century Venice is Titian (1487–1576). His early work is in the style of Giorgione and his later work has a 'painterliness', or freedom of brushwork, that was totally unprecedented.

Japan's greatest painter of all time ■ The *gaso*, or priest-painter, Sesshu Toyo (1420–1506) is considered to hold this title. He worked in the *haboku*, or 'ink splash' style which was practised in monasteries as a spiritual exercise for breaking through the barriers of the physical world; a few powerful splashes released from the painter's brush at the enlightened moment of deep meditation create an inspired landscape. Sesshu's personal style, is best represented in *Winter Landscape*. 1495. Unlike most Japanese painting, it is based on rugged, solid masses set in rational space instead of the more traditional poetic voids.

Greatest family of painters ■ The Japanese Kano family of artists represented the highest standards of professional painting from the 15th to 19th century; the number of geniuses in direct blood line is thought to be unequalled anywhere in the world. Their patrons from the outset were the military rulers. Kano Masanobu (*c.* 1434–1530), the accepted first generation, was the son of a samurai amateur painter. During the first two generations the style of the Chinese Song school of landscape was absorbed and naturalized to create the bold, decorative and assymetrical designs for which Japan is most famous. Their best large-scale painting was made for the sliding door panels and folding screens which formed the interior walls of Japanese houses.

First autobiographies of artists ■ The first artistic autobiographies were written by two Florentine sculptors and goldsmiths. Lorenzo Ghiberti (1378–1455) included an account of his life in his book on art, the *Commentaries*, of *c.* 1447. The *Autobiography* of Benvenuto Cellini (1500–71), written between 1558 and 1562, was inspired by the first edition of Vasari's *Lives* (1550) and is a spirited and colourful account of life in mid sixteenth-century Italy as well as of the process of artistic creation.

Miniaturists ■ The Persian miniaturist Bihzad is considered to be one of the greatest exponents of miniature painting. He was born in the 1450s and died in 1536 and was buried at Tabriz, in modern Iran. His works are regarded as being supreme examples of this art form, and he was recognized as a master during his lifetime. This meant he was lavishly rewarded by the Muslim rulers of the area, and especially by the powerful Shah Tahmasp, ruler of Safavid Iran.

The finest paintings produced in the English Renaissance are portrait miniatures. A specialist atelier established in 1496 was an offshoot of the school of illuminators in the Royal Library. In 1525 the entire Horenbout family (Gerard and his son Lucas and daughter Susanna) was recruited from the Netherlands where they had been the court painters. In 1531 Lucas was appointed King's Painter at a salary triple that of his immediate predecessor. At £30 per annum he made more than even Holbein. (At that time the daily wage of a skilled craftsman was sixpence (2.5p).) His duties included panel painting, designing jewellery, stained glass, tapestries, costumes for theatre and special occasions as well as book and document illumination. It was Lucas who devised the new form of the portrait miniature painted on parchment. The tiny portraits 1¼–2 in *30–50 mm* in diameter are of unprecedented spontaneity and liveliness and were painted without underdrawings. Three sittings, the second taking up to six hours, were required. 23 portrait miniatures are now attributed to him. He revealed his technical secrets only to Holbein, but both men died within a year of each other leaving no obvious successor. So Henry VIII again looked to the Netherlands where he found Lavinia Teerlinck, the talented daughter of the greatest miniaturist of the Ghent-Bruges school, Simon Bening.

First landscape painters ■ Landscape painting as a genre developed in 16th-century northern Europe. The German artist Albrecht Dürer (*d.* 1528) painted numerous watercolours of landscapes in the 1490s,but apart from such sketches, made for an artist's personal use, and landscape backgrounds in paintings of other subjects, there are no landscape paintings known before 1500. Up to 1550 most landscape paintings still had ostensible subjects, usually religious, but in the work of the German Albrecht Altdorfer (*d.* 1538) and the Netherlander Joachim Patinir (*d.* 1528) the setting became increasingly dominant and the figures insignificant. Landscape painting came to be considered a Netherlandish speciality, its foremost exponent being Pieter Bruegel the Elder (*d.* 1569).

Most prolific fresco painter ■ The Sistine Chapel ceiling (Vatican, Rome) measures 132 by 45 ft *40.2 m by 13.6 m* and was painted with scenes from the Old Testament by Michelangelo between 1508 and 1512. According to his early biographers he painted it without the use of assistants.

God creates Adam in a detail of Michelangelo's ceiling for the Sistine Chapel.

Even assuming that Michelangelo must have had someone to grind his colours and to apply the fresh plaster requisite to the fresco technique, this is a remarkable feat and unprecedented in an age when the delegation of areas of a large painting to assistants was the norm.

Women artists ■ The first women artists to hold prestigious appointments were Caterina van Hemessen (1527/8–1566) and Lavinia Teerlinck (*c.* 1520–76), who, both from Netherlandish artist families, enjoyed great fame. Caterina worked for the regent of the Netherlands, Mary of Hungary, and Lavinia became court miniaturist to Henry VIII, Edward VI and Mary of England.

Most maligned artist ■ Andrea del Castagno (1423–57) was reported by Vasari to have murdered Domenico Veneziano (d. 1461), but the putative murderer actually died four years before the victim.

Most emotive painter ■ Jacopo Pontormo's (1494–1556) expressive distortion of the human figure comes from mastery of his art. The Deposition at S Felicita, Florence is his masterpiece.

First known mentally ill artist ■ The Netherlandish painter Hugo van der Goes (*c.* 1435–1482), at the height of a successful career, retired to a monastery near Brussels. He continued to work, but suffered an attack of severe depression shortly before his death, described by the monastery's infirmarian Gaspar Ofhuys: 'He cried out incessantly that he was doomed and condemned to eternal damnation. He would even have injured himself had he not been forcibly prevented by his companions.'

Money first paid to see a painting ■ By 1530 visitors to St Bavo's cathedral, Ghent, Belgium were giving money to the church for viewing the folding altarpiece of the *Adoration of the Lamb* by Jan and Hubert van Eyck, completed in 1432. Measuring 12 × 17 feet (*375 × 520 cm*) when open, comprising 12 panels, eight painted on both sides, and containing a total of 252 figures, it is still probably the most famous early Netherlandish painting.

Earliest art academies ■ Around 1500 artists began to associate in groups which can very loosely be called academies, in the Medici Gardens, Florence, where the sculptor Bertoldo ran an informal school attended by the young Michelangelo, and around Leonardo da Vinci in Milan. (The first organized art academy with a teaching purpose was founded at Florence in 1563.)

Sculpture

First rediscovery ■ The Roman statue known as the Apollo Belvedere was found at Frascati, near Rome in Italy, in 1455. Pope Julius II had it placed in the Vatican in Rome in 1511.

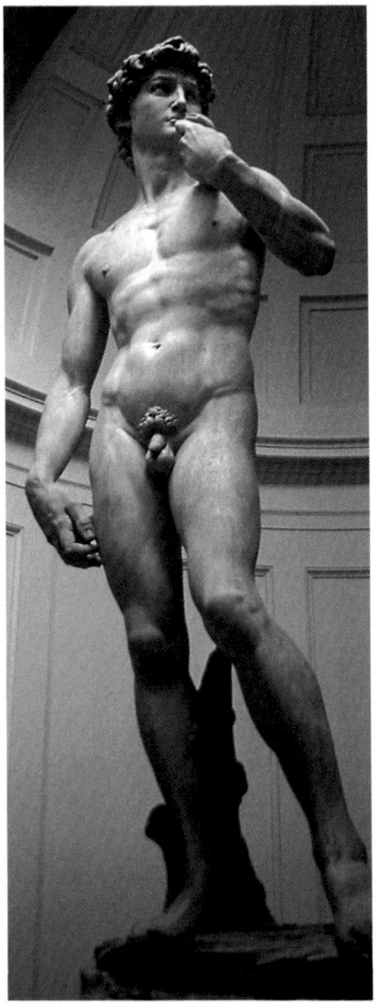

Largest male nude statue ■
Michelangelo's David, *completed in 1504 and set up outside the Town Hall of Florence (although now in the Accademia Gallery), was not only the largest statue of a nude produced since ancient Roman times, but also the first to be displayed in a public place. The marble giant, 13 ft 10 in* 4.10 m *high, also represents a technical feat in that it was carved from a block begun and apparently botched by an earlier sculptor.*

Hill figures ■ The largest human hill carving in Britain is the 'Long Man' of Wilmington, East Sussex, 226 ft *68 m* in length. The oldest of all White Horses in Britain is the Uffington White Horse in Oxfordshire, dating from the late Iron Age (*c.* 150 BC) and measuring 374 ft *114 m* from nose to tail and 120 ft *36 m* high.

Most refined, naturalistic sculpture in Africa ■ The lifelike bronze and terracotta heads, were produced at the religious centres of the Yoruba people of south-

western Nigeria 12th–16th centuries. Naturalism is a most uncommon feature in African representations of humans because realistic depictions were thought to be the most vulnerable to witchcraft. The quality of Ife work was so high that it was long presumed to be influenced by European Mediterranean art. The Ife were, however, the direct descendants of the Nok culture, the founders of the oldest tradition of sculpture known outside Egypt, and can justifiably be called 'classical' in their own right. Ife culture died out by the mid-16th century when the Europeans established a rival trade centre to the south and the Benin culture came to prominence to the east.

Most important archaeological find ▪ The rediscovery in 1506 of the large marble sculpture known as the *Laocoön*, a group of three figures being crushed to death by snakes was the most important archaeological find of the Renaissance. The anguished expressions of the figures was shocking to connoisseurs who believed that such emotionalism had no place in classical art. The debate over whether the subjects were suffering in noble silence lasted for several centuries. Michelangelo, who was most profoundly affected by the emotionalism of the piece, worked on its 16th century restoration. (Most of this work has now been removed.)

Most popular sculpture ▪ Luca della Robbia (*c.* 1400–1483) was the most popular sculptor of the 15th century. He invented a technique for enamelling terracotta sculpture which for 75 years remained the exclusive property of the workshop he established. The technique permitted large sculpture to be permanently coloured and was immediately exploited in interior decoration on walls, floors and ceilings; the most characteristic products were garlands of fruits and flowers. But Della Robbia's greatest artistic expression was in sculpture: the enamelled reliefs of madonnas mass-produced in moulds for the walls of well-to-do households. The Genoa Madonna of *c.* 1450 which survives in four copies is the finest. The communication between the mother and frightened child evokes compassion and tenderness and explains Della Robbia's reputation as the supreme sculptor of ordinary life.

Most ambitious project ▪ Michelangelo's tomb for Pope Julius II (S. Pietro in Vincoli, Rome) was begun in 1505. The original scheme was for an immense structure 34½ ft *10.5 m* long by 23 ft *7 m* wide, incorporating 40 figures, many of them over life-size. It was finally completed in 1545 by assistants on a much reduced scale. There are six statues on the finished tomb, of which only the *Moses* is entirely by Michelangelo.

First modern bronze-casting ▪ The elaborate technique of casting large statues in bronze, virtually forgotten since ancient Roman times, was revived by the Florentine sculptor Lorenzo Ghiberti (1378–1455), who first employed it in his over life-size statue of *St John the Baptist* (1414) for the Florentine church of Orsanmichele. It involved coating a clay model of the statue with wax, which was in turn coated with plaster, and then melted away through vent pipes (hence its name of 'lost wax' technique) to leave a narrow channel into which molten bronze was poured and left to solidify. The plaster coat was then removed to expose the bronze statue, and the finished surface produced by filing and polishing. Florentine expertise continued to be associated with bronze-casting throughout the 15th century, notably in the important commissions for equestrian statues in Padua and Venice from the Florentine sculptors Donatello and Verrocchio.

Newest art form ▪ Portrait medals, inspired by ancient Roman coins, showing the sitter's head in profile on one side and his or her personal emblem on the other, evolved during the 15th century in Italy and by 1500 had become fashionable across Europe. Their most famous exponent was Pisanello (1395–1455). Usually made of bronze, medals could be produced in quantity, and being small were easily portable, making them popular as diplomatic gifts.

Most advanced metal workers in Africa ▪ The bronze workers of Benin, Nigeria, operated under the protection of the *Oba*, or king, and lived in a separate quarter of the city. The most interesting and informative of their works are the plaques depicting historical and ritual events, which were made to hang in the Oba's house. A 16th century Benin plaque illustrates the *Oba* performing a sacrifice as he swings two leopards by their tails. Because of his divine kingship the Oba's feet are not meant to touch the ground, and are here formed by two serpent-like creatures which associate him with the sea god. The rectangular pictorial format is totally unlike any other native art in Africa. It has been suggested that contact with illustrated European printed books was the original inspiration. The Portuguese were the first Europeans to reach Benin, from 1485 they traded copper and brass for ivory carvings and slaves. From the early 16th century images of long haired, bearded Portuguese begin to appear in African art.

Luca della Robbia sculpted this panel for the hospital in Pistoia, Italy, appropriately showing the visit to the infirmary.

Two cast bronze heads of the queen mothers of Benin are equal to the finest bronzes made anywhere – at any time.

First modern equestrian statue ▪ The life-size monument in Padua commemorating the Venetian military commander Gattamelata was produced by the Florentine sculptor Donatello between 1443 and 1453, and was the first equestrian statue to have been cast in bronze since ancient Roman times. It also reintroduced the concept, inspired by ancient models such as the statue of the Roman emperor Marcus Aurelius, of the equestrian monument embodying a heroic ideal of power.

First renaissance sculptor in English works ■ Florentine sculptor Pietro Torrigiano (1472–1528) created the first renaissance works in England, where he was employed by King Henry VIII. His masterpiece is the bronze tomb of King Henry VII (1512–18) in Henry VII's Chapel, Westminster Abbey, London. He left England around 1522. Thereafter the Reformation cut England off from Italian influences circulating in continental Europe, and renaissance art had virtually no impact in England until after 1600.

First recorded fake ■ In 1496 Michelangelo went to Rome and was so overcome by what he found there that he began to make imitations of Graeco-Roman sculpture. One of his pieces (now lost) was sold as an antique and so is regarded as the first fake on record.

carvers was outstanding. Limewood, the most tractable of the hardwoods, was the most favoured medium. Tilman Riemenschneider (*c.* 1460–1513) was the most successful exponent of the school; he was at one time both the *Bürgermeister* of the town of Wurzburg and the master of a workshop employing 12 apprentices. The only one of his great altarpieces still *in situ* and intact is the *Altar of the Holy Blood* (1501–5) at the St Jakobskirche in Rothenburg. Housed within the altarpiece is the miracle-working drop of Christ's blood, the most prized possession of the church which attracted pilgrims from neighbouring towns. The central panel commemorates the Last Supper, the historic occasion when Christ instituted the Eucharist (holy communion) with the words 'This is my blood.' The artist has concentrated on telling the story rather than creating a devotional work. The figures of Christ and the 12 apostles are shown at the dramatic moment when Judas is revealed as a traitor. None of the figures is painted so that the possibility of simple people taking them for real persons is avoided. Although Judas, the most evil character in the scene, is focal when the work is seen in direct light, Riemenschneider knew that the movement of the sun during the course of the day would highlight other figures at different times and no one character would be given undue attention.

DECORATIVE STYLES

The renaissance style in the decorative arts, the single most important factor in design, was fully developed in the 15th century in Italy and spread in the 16th throughout Europe. The new style was based on Roman architecture and differed from the earlier gothic style in the preference for rectangular, solid forms over vertical, intricate and light elements. The architectonic quality of objects is emphasized by classical columns or pilasters. The dominant motifs are garlands, acanthus leaves, mythological creatures, **putti** ***(cherubs), and portrait heads, as found on classical cameos. Since the best architects, painters and sculptors were also designers of tapestries, makers of jewellery, furniture, and other decorative objects, the style was rapidly assimilated into the minor arts.***

The mannerist style evolved from the renaissance style c. 1520 in Rome and Florence and was absorbed by artists at court schools all over Europe: Paris, Fontainebleau, Prague, Mantua, London. It was the dominant style for most of the 16th century. The Sack of Rome in 1527 was the most important factor in causing the artists to disperse and transmit the new style to the other courts of Europe. The elements known from the Renaissance become elongated and often stylized in a precious manner. The figures maintain contorted postures and intricate decorative patterns of entwined lines became fashionable. The main difference between the earlier renaissance style and the mannerist style is the latter's appeal to the senses and emotions where the former is logical, calm and ordered.

Wood carving

Best North American sculptors ■ The Tlingit and Haida peoples were the best sculptors of large scale wooden objects in New World. They used stone tools, including jade, until the arrival of the Europeans when they began to use metal tools. Totem poles of spruce or cedar up to 69 ft *21 m* high served as clan memorials and indicators of the social position of the person who commissioned the work.

Unique design ■ The Tlingit 'x-ray' style most often found in woodcarvings and textiles is unique in the Americas; animal bodies are presented in an abstract flattened pattern which shows the internal organs as well as the limbs and normally visible parts.

Best sculpture in the north of Europe ■ The work of south German wood

Wall coverings

Most expensive wall covering ■ Tapestry was the most expensive mural decoration and also an excellent insulation for draughty stone buildings. In true tapestry the linen warp threads (the ones strung on the loom) do not show; the weft threads, which are woven in to carry the design, are beaten down to cover the warp. These were made from the highest quality materials – woollens, silk, gold, or silver.

Most sumptuous ■ The *Gideon Tapestries*, produced between 1449 and 1452 in Tournai (Belgium) (destroyed in the 18th century) were the most famous of 15th-century tapestries, and probably the most lavish ever woven. Commissioned by Philip the Good, Duke of Burgundy, for the prestigious chivalric Order of the Golden Fleece, they consisted of eight pieces, each measuring about 18.3 ft *5.6 m* high, with two about 50.5 ft *15.4 m* and the others about 36.7 ft *11.2 m* long, and cost the prodigious sum of 8,960 crowns. The highest quality materials were employed: thread of real gold for the yellows, and silk for the rest. To ensure their exclusiveness, the Duke paid an expensive copyright to the painter Baudouin de Ballieul for the cartoons from which they had been woven.

Undisputed tapestry centre ■ Until conquered by Louis XI of France in 1477, Arras was the undisputed centre of tapestry production. Between 1423 and 1467 the names of 59 high-loom weavers are recorded and the name of the town was synonymous throughout Europe with the finest woven hangings. Under French occupation the taxes and restrictions were so great that the best weavers emigrated. By the time Charles VIII restored full rights to the citizens in 1484 it was too late to save the craft. By 1491 only one master weaver was still working there. Tournai and Brussels then vied for eminence.

Most famous tapestries ■ The most mysterious and romantic tapestries of the period are six hangings of the Lady with the Unicorn; the series is now in the Musée Cluny in Paris. They were commissioned in the 1490s by Jean la Liste, a member of the high bourgeoisie, from a Brussels workshop noted for the *Mille Fleur* (thousand flower) backgrounds decorated with flowers and small animals. In each of the six hangings a fashionably dressed lady appears with a lion, representing nobility of blood, and a unicorn, representative of the new nobility. The most satisfactory explanation of the scenes is that the activities symbolize the five senses. (See *The Animal Kingdom*.)

Each piece of the 10 tapestries of the *Acts of the Apostles*, commissioned by Pope Leo X for the Sistine Chapel and woven in Brussels by Pieter van Aelst in 1515 from cartoons by the Italian painter Raphael cost between 1600 and 2000 ducats. (The original tapestries (of which several copies exist) are in the Vatican Museums, Rome, and the cartoons in the Victoria and Albert Museum, London.)

Earliest surviving printed wallpaper ■ Wallpaper was a cheap alternative to tapestry and from 1481 there is evidence of paper being pasted to walls for decorative purposes. By the 16th century it was widely used.

The 'Cambridge Fragments' discovered in 1911 in the Master's Lodge of Christ's College, Cambridge, are the earliest. A date of 1509 is confirmed by a text on the back which refers to the first year of the reign of Henry VIII. The black pattern is based on the pomegranate, the dominant motif found in Italian silks. The block from which the paper was printed measured 15.6 × 9.5 in *40 × 27 cm*.

First flocked paper ■ Paper printed with a textured raised pattern, designed to emulate velvet, was found in the archives of the Alte Kapelle in Regensburg, Germany, and dated *c.* 1450. The hunting scene in red raised upon a white background may have been used to decorate a wall.

Earliest surviving floral wallpaper ■ A piece of English wallpaper *c.* 1550 has a Tudor rose printed from a woodcut, in black upon a grey ground. (All wallpapers were made in small pieces; the commercially produced roll with repeat patterning was not invented until the 17th century.)

Finest tiles in the world ■ These were the glazed earthenware tiles made at kilns in Iznik, near Constantinople, Turkey. In the Islamic world tiles were used on walls, especially in mosques where they covered the inside and outside. In Europe tiles were used as flooring; important tile-making centres established in the 15th century in Naples and Faenza in Italy produced blue and white *maiolica*, as the technique was called when it appeared in Italy.

Most outstanding illusion ■ In Italy fresco painting was the kind of wall decoration most favoured by the wealthy. Mantegna's *Camera degli Sposi* (Chamber of the Bride and Groom) completed in 1471 is the most spectacular illusionistically designed room. A group portrait of the entire family, along with retainers and dwarf, was painted on a fireplace wall; the mantelpiece is artfully included in the composition as a platform for the group. The paintings, with views into the countryside in the background, are continuous on all four walls and the ceiling, giving the illusion that the walls have disappeared. The ceiling is the most dramatic feature; a cylindrical oculus seems to open to the sky and figures peer downwards at the viewer over the parapet while drastically foreshortened *putti* (cherubs) perch on the edge. A tub of flowers balanced precariously over the edge looks as if it were about to fall.

First intarsia ■ Intarsia, a decorative technique of creating pictures from inlay of pieces of different kinds of wood, was first developed in Siena, in Italy, on choir stalls. It soon became popular for walls and furniture. The *trompe l'oeil* (optical trick) decoration of 1479 in the study of the Duke's Palace at Urbino, Italy, is the finest. Nearly 30 kinds of wood have been identified in the illusionistic panels. (See *Science and Technology*.)

First complete grotesque' scheme ■ The *grotesque* is a kind of mannerist decoration which was often used for walls. It is based on ancient Roman wall painting and relief decoration. The word comes from *grotte*, the term used to describe the archaeological sites of recently excavated houses where such ancient decoration could be seen. In 1516 Raphael became the first to create a complete decorative scheme using grotesques both painted and in stucco relief; the room is Cardinal Bibbiena's in the Vatican. By the mid-16th century grotesques could be found everywhere in Europe and the motifs increased in popularity and fantasy as the range of objects to which they could be applied increased. Raphael's pupil Giovanni da Udine (1487–1564), who accompanied him on visits to archaeological sites of Roman houses, rediscovered the lost recipe for making stucco.

Furniture

Most important new craft ■ The development of joinery in Flanders in the late 15th century revolutionized furniture making and created a new specialist. The joiner's task was to fit panels of wood into the grooves of frames. The main advantage of this method of construction was that it prevented the boards from splitting and warping. The mortise and tenon joint was essential to the technique.

Largest bed ■ The Great Bed of Ware (now in London's Victoria and Albert Museum) is dated variously between 1463 and 1590. It measures 11 ft 1 in *332 cm* long, 10 ft 6 in *315 cm* wide and 8 ft *240 cm* high with its wooden canopy. Although the wealth of its carving suggests that it was made for a rich person, its earliest certain provenance is the Saracen's Head Inn at Ware. The practice of sharing a bed was commonplace, whether for family members or strangers staying in an inn. The carving exemplifies the decorative motifs of Tudor England: acanthus leaf, strapwork, lions' heads, and figured terms [pillars]. There are panels of intarsia (pictures created in inlaid wood) on the headboard.

Carpets

Finest ■ Oriental carpets were the finest in the Renaissance world: western interest in them first appeared in the 14th century and by the 16th century had become a passion. It was the one area of design and craftsmanship which was never surpassed by Europeans. The early oriental carpets which reached Europe were those woven by the Seljuk Turks in the northwest Anatolian peninsula or from Damascus, Syria. The finest of all were the knotted carpets made *c.* 1500 at the Safavid court in Persia (Iran).

Biggest, most beautiful and best preserved ■ The Holy Carpet of Ardebil holds all these records among Persian carpets. It measures 12.5 × 5.8 ft *11.5 × 5.34 m* and covers 72 yd^2 *61.5 m^2* of floor space. The knot count is 32 000 000. The intricacy and precision of the pattern indicates that a full-size cartoon was required to make it and identifies it as a member of the north Persian Medallion group of carpets. An inscription dates it precisely to year 946 of the Hijra (the Islamic era), or 1539–40 AD. Much speculation has arisen about the length of time it took to make: the most conservative estimate is three years.

Needlework

Earliest printed pattern books ■ Pattern books for lace, cut-work, and reticella (network) were written by Matio Pagano of Venice. They include *Giardinetto nuovo di punti tagliati* (New Garden of Cut-work Stitches) printed in 1542, and *Ornamento de le belle et virtudiose donne* (The Ornament of Beautiful and Virtuous Ladies), 1543.

Most carefully treated ■ *Carpets were so highly regarded in Europe in the 15th century that in paintings they appear on floors only in front of the Virgin's throne or in churches. In the 16th century they appear as altar coverings, but also begin to appear as secular table coverings or on balustrades, as in Vittorio Carpaccio's (c. 1450–1526) painting* The Legend of St Ursula.

These and other books were highly successful publications, and were printed in many editions within a very short time. (Very few pattern books for needlework survive because the owners pricked the patterns directly through the pages of the book onto the fabric.)

First true lace ■ Needle lace (needlepoint), the first true lace, was a Venetian discovery of the late 15th century. It developed from cut-and-drawn work which was used for the decoration of underwear, altar cloths and soft furnishings. It has an open structure which is created by the needle and a single thread worked in variations of the buttonhole stitch. It was known as *punto in aria* – a stitch in the air. Bobbin lace (pillow lace) was invented in Flanders in the late 15th century. It is created by looping and twisting several threads around pins arranged in a pattern on a padded roll. The finest was (and still is) produced in Brussels.

Earliest record of lace in England ■ The first indication of lace work in England is a complaint lodged in 1454 by the women of the Mystery (guild) of Threadworking about the importation of six Flemish women working in a new kind of thread and silk cut-work. The first specific mention of lace is found in the Act of 1463 of Edward IV which prohibits its importation, along with ribbons and fringes. However, among the finery surrounding Richard III at the time of his coronation in 1483 were 'fringes of Venice' and 'laces of white and venys gold'.

Crafts

Most impressive skills ■ The Incas had developed the highest levels of skill in ceramics, textiles and the working of precious metals in the whole of the Americas. However, Alonso de Carmona, who had lived in Mexico and Peru and was one of the Spaniards who accompanied Hernandes de Soto on his search for riches in North America in 1539–42 reported that in a burial house in what is now Georgia he saw carved and pearl-inlaid weapons which were among the finest pieces he had seen in the whole of the New World.

Oldest stained glass ■ The cathedral in Augsberg in Bavaria has a window in its clerestory which is believed to have been installed in the middle of the 11th century.

Most extravagant drinking vessels ■ The Schüsselfelder Ship is a most lavish example of a type of drinking vessel and table ornament found in wealthy households of the period. Made in Nuremberg in 1503, of partially-gilded silver, it is an intricate and accurate model of a galleon, complete with rigging, cannon, a moving rudder, a folding sundial and 74 figures engaged in various pursuits, such as eating and drinking, making music, playing cards, and climbing the rigging. It measures 31¼ in *79 cm* high and 17¼ in *43.5 cm* wide; the entire superstructure can be lifted off, permitting the hull to be filled with wine.

Shah Ismail, the founder of the Safavid dynasty in Iran in the early 16th century, killed an important opponent and then poured gold into his skull so that it could be used as a drinking vessel.

Most intricate basket-weaving ■ The high quality basket-weaving of the Pomo tribe of California was the most intricate in the world. They wove feathers and beads into grasses to produce the most delicate patterns; the tiniest baskets measure a mere ⅝ in *1.6 cm* in diameter and are known as 'jewel baskets'.

Manuscripts

Largest collection ■ In the 15th century the best books were still the ones that were made and decorated by hand. Such luxury objects were essential for the princely lifestyle. The first philosopher-prince, Federigo da Montefeltro (1422–82), Duke of Urbino, in Italy, owned a book collection that has been estimated to be larger than any European university's at the time. But it could have been even larger if he had purchased printed books. He declared that he would have been ashamed to own a printed book. A portrait by Justus of Ghent *c.* 1475 shows him in armour studying a manuscript.

A very splendid manuscript of the Koran made in 1545 and dedicated to the Sultan of Bokhara, now in Central Asia.

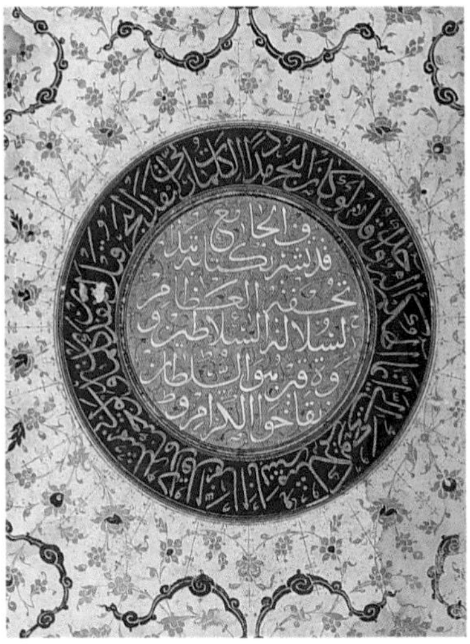

Largest manuscript ■ In 1492 this was the *Codex Gigas*, a Bible written in the 12th century in Bohemia, now in Czechoslovakia. With folios measuring 35 × 19.5 in *90 × 50 cm*, it is as big a book as can be made of animal skins.

Largest number ■ Books of Hours were produced in greater quantity than any other kind of manuscript. These were required by devout Christians for their daily devotions. The illustrative cycles for continental European books in the main daily sequence of prayers, the Hours of the Virgin, which were observed at intervals of several hours, follow a cycle of the events in Christ's infancy, beginning with the Annunciation; they end with the Coronation of the Virgin. For English users the preferred cycle of illustration is centred on Christ's final torments surrounding the Crucifixion. Many other prayers and devotions varied widely by geographical regions. The most extravagantly illustrated books might have up to 60 full page paintings.

Finest European manuscript ■ The Grimani Breviary made *c.* 1515 is the finest European manuscript of the period; it is a vast volume of 1664 pages with 110 miniatures. The manuscript is famous for its borders and the illusionistic treatment of space in the calendar scenes. It contains work by the greatest masters: Simon Bening, the Master of James IV of Scotland, and the Master of the David Scenes. By 1520 it belonged to Cardinal Grimani, but is was not made for him, and it is still not known who commissioned this most ambitious of Renaissance religious books.

Unique genealogy ■ The Genealogy of the Infante Dom Fernando of Portugal, 1530–4, is the only illuminated genealogy in Flemish art, and the largest manuscript produced in Flanders (21.8 × 15.4 in *559 × 394 mm*). It is also the best documented of all manuscripts ever produced, although it was never finished because of the death of the patron. The illustrations are the largest ever created by the greatest master, Simon Bening. The startlingly realistically painted family tree in the border of folio 2 shows the descent of the Portuguese kings from Magog, grandson of Noah.

Absolute embargo ■ Production of the Koran was totally unaffected by the new technology which transformed the production of other books. Since it was considered an act of heresy to print this most holy of all books of Islam, none were printed.

Longest Mayan manuscripts ■ The only illuminated 'manuscripts' in the New World were made by the peoples of Mexico. These were pleated screenfolds, made from the bark of the wild fig tree sized with lime and painted in earth colours for display in the houses of the rulers. Most were based on the ritual astronomical calendar which was sacred throughout Mesoamerica. There were 18 22-day months plus 5 dead days in the year. The Mayan manuscripts were the most ruthlessly destroyed and only four survive; the longest is the late 15th century Madrid Codex, which is made of bark paper and is 22 ft *6.6 m* in length. The illustrations are horoscopes which were used for divination. The first bishop of Yucatan, Diego de Landa, was the most zealous destroyer of the manuscripts which he claimed were works of the devil.;

Last illuminator ■ Simon Bening (1483–1561) was the greatest of the manuscript landscapists and the last of the great Flemish illuminators.

Book illustration

Finest printed pictures ■ With a long history of printing from carved wood blocks behind them, Chinese craftsmen in the 15th century were able to produce fine editions of books with illustrations on every page. One of the best examples is the edition of the play *Story of the Western Chamber* printed in 1499. Contemporary European printed books had much cruder pictures. By around 1550 Chinese printers were beginning to experiment with printing multi-coloured illustrations.

First European illustrated books ■ Before the invention of movable type around 1450, books were printed using a single wooden block for each page, which comprised both illustration and text. These so called block books continued in production throughout the 15th century. One of the most popular was the *Ars moriendi* (The Art of Dying), which appeared in at least 12 editions from 1450, in three languages: Latin, German and French. The earliest illustrated book with a text in movable type is thought to be *Der Ackerman aus Böhmen* (The Farmer from Bohemia) printed by Albrecht Pfister of Bamberg, Germany in 1460.

Albrecht Dürer's engraving for the Triumphal Arch and Procession, *1518.*

Biggest printed image ■ The Emperor Maximilian I commissioned in 1518 the *Triumphal Arch and Procession*, a series of prints by Dürer and others, intended when put together to form an immense design exalting the Habsburg dynasty, of which he was head. The *Triumphal Arch* alone consisted of 192 woodcuts, which combined covered an area of about 10 by 12 ft *3 by 3.6 m.*

Earliest European printed image ■ Printed pictures were not only used for book illustration but as inexpensive works of art in their own right. Many were religious images sold as souvenirs in pilgrimage-places, others were pasted onto boxes for decoration or used as shrines in households which could not afford paintings. Woodcuts, the earliest form of print, made from a wooden block, originated at the beginning of the 15th century in Germany or the Netherlands, and reached its height in the works of Albrecht Dürer, such as the *Apocalypse* of 1498.

Earliest engraving ■ Whilst engraving on wood was practised by the Chinese several centuries BC, the modern process dates from the 15th century with the earliest dated example of a woodcut coming from Memmingen, Germany, in 1423. The earliest known impressions from a metal plate date from 1452.

The earliest European known engraving is a *Flagellation of Christ* by the anonymous Master of 1446, bearing that date.

First book plates ■ Printed inserts to indicate the ownership of a book were first used in Germany in the late 15th century. The earliest surviving example was printed from a wood cut block 5.5 × 7 in *13.75 × 17.5 cm* for Johannes Knabbenburg, who was also known as 'Igler', which means hedgehog. The scroll above the picture of the tiny animal translates 'Hans Igler, May the hedge hog kiss you.' This unpleasant wish can be seen in the tradition of anathema, or curses, which throughout the Middle Ages were inscribed in books as a warning to prospective thieves.

Fashion

First international fashion ■ The rectangular silhouette of renaissance style in clothing began to take shape in the various courts of Italy in the last decades of the 15th century and by the turn of the 16th began to be emulated all over Europe: for the first time in history high fashion had become international. The great improvements in communication, most significantly the invention of printing, permitted new designs for needlework and jewellery in pattern books, and other illustrated materials, to reach across the continent more quickly than ever before. During the 16th century flamboyant German trends came to the fore; around 1550 Spanish influences predominated in dark sombre colours.

Most influential arbiters of fashion ■ The Church and the nobility exercised the greatest influence on styles of dress, imposing standards of decency on the general populace while ensuring that high fashion was the exclusive domain of the princely classes. Sumptuary laws (against

EUROPEAN DRESS

In all the countries of Europe three layers of clothing were standard, while the manner in which they were worn and details of style and convention varied enormously. Women wore underdresses, overdresses and an outer garment, usually a mantle. All men wore shirts and an overgarment, usually a doublet, on the upper body and hose on the lower body. The overgarment would have been a tunic which evolved into an overcoat. The difference between the sexes was strictly observed; transvestites were subject to burning at the stake. Headcoverings were the most telling of all items of clothing, subject to the most subtle of regional variations. Italian noblewomen differed from their northern European counterparts in their willingness to display their hair. In the north the women followed the teachings of St Paul more closely. In I Corinthians he writes:

'. . . let her wear a veil. For a man ought not to cover his head, since he is the image and glory of God; but woman is the glory of man . . . created for man. That is why a woman ought to wear a veil.' Most married women in most countries of Europe wore veils.

Corna, *horn-shaped headdresses, came into fashion c. 1450 from the north. By the mid-15th century the heavier style of headdress was on the wane and hair, whether real or false, was wrapped around the head with fine fabrics or gems braided into it.*

Jewels were knotted into **rete**, *hairnets made of silk and gold made for Italian ladies of the nobility. The* **rete** *came from the Spanish court in the last decades of the 15th century and increased in popularity in the 16th century.*

The **beretta**, *a brimless conical hat, was the preferred masculine headwear for most of the 15th century. About 1500 flat caps with jewelled brooches pinned on their turned-up brims became the most elegant headwear.*

Until c. 1500 the dominant style in French, Netherlandish, English and North German clothing is Gothic; the predominance of vertical and linear elements is seen in men's clothing and women's bodies are distorted into a long ogival gothic curve by their confining clothing. The difference between the silhouettes of men's and women's clothes is the most marked in France and Holland. The man's formed a top-heavy inverted triangle, while the woman's outline was a triangle resting on its base. Both contrast strongly with the Italian Renaissance rectangle which arrives in the north in the 1480s and is first to be seen in men's apparel. Not until the 1520s does women's fashion reflect the influence.

conspicuous expenditure and show) attempted to curb the most outlandish displays of middle-class wealth and offences to common decency, while the great dukes and duchesses continued to dress as they liked. Styles changed rapidly, but the clothing styles worn by the younger members of the wealthy ruling classes changed the most rapidly: often discrepancies of up to 20 years' difference in style can be seen in the same paintings when several generations are shown together.

Only fashion invention ■ The farthingale, or hoop-skirt, was the only new kind of clothing invented during the period. It first appeared in the 1460s and was greeted with cautious suspicion. Queen Juana of Portugal was the first to wear one; the wooden hoops – usually six – were then worn inside the skirt. By 1470 Queen Isabella (while still a princess) was wearing as many as 14 hoops on the outside of her skirts. The advantages were immediately apparent to the wearer, especially in the hot summers of Spain. By 1530 they were back on the inside of the skirts. The fashion spread quickly to the courts of Europe. In 1507 the hoop-skirt was prohibited in Venice.

Unprecedented immodesty in dress ■ The broad, rounded silhouette of the 1440–50s in European fashion gave way to a more sober look. In the 1450s bodices were closer-fitting and sleeves became tighter. Large patterns and bright colours characterize women's dress; lower necklines created a space to display jewels. By the 1480s the trend was towards revealing the human form in styles of unprecedented immodesty. Women's necklines plunged ever lower and the sleeves were split down their length. Young men abandoned their tunics and the tight-fitting hose extending to the waist displayed more of the masculine anatomy than ever before.

Most restrictive ■ Florence was the most conservative of all the important fashion centres in Italy and the laws restricting conspicuous display in clothing were the most severe. In 1464 Florentine women were forbidden to trade in any garment until it had been worn for at least three years. No more than two overgowns of silk could be owned at one time and only one overgarment could be dyed with *chermisi*, an expensive dyestuff imported from the East, and used to dye the robes of cardinals.

Most popular textile pattern ■ From 1420 to 1550 the most popular symbol on Italian textiles was based on the pomegranate. In the 1460s and 70s large scale patterns were used in the most fashionable dresses made for the ladies of the courts. But by the end of the century the patterns manufactured for clothing were greatly reduced in size and the larger patterns were used for making upholstery and other domestic requirements.

Most famous sleeve ■ Elaborate embroidery with gold or silver threads and even pearls and rubies was often used to enhance the appearance of the simply cut dresses; the most effective use of embroidery was on the sleeves of the garment, whether of men's or women's apparel. Most often the embroidery appears only on the left sleeve. Bona of Savoy had the most famous sleeve; she kept it with her jewels rather than in her wardrobe. The 1468 inventory describes a sleeve embroidered with a phoenix in rubies, pearls, and diamonds. It was valued at 18 000 ducats.

Most beaded article ■ A funeral blanket unearthed in the Mississippi Valley city of Cahokia, USA (population in 15th century about 35 000) was decorated with 12 000 shell beads.

First umbrella reported in North America ■ When Governor de Soto came to the town of Tastaluca (southern USA) the *cacique* or chief welcomed him in the piazza before his home. He sat on two cushions with his men around him, the Indians of the highest rank 'nearest to his person'. One of them 'shaded him from the sun with a circular umbrella, spread wide, the size of a target, with a small stem, and having deer-skin extended over cross-sticks, quartered with red and white, which at a distance made it look like taffeta, the colours were so very perfect. It formed the standard of the chief which he carried into battle.'

Headdresses

Most definitive feature ■ Headdresses were the most distinctive and expressive feature of the north European woman's wardrobe; they identified her age, social and marital status and regional origins. In Flanders the smallest details such as number of pleats and placement of the pins could identify the village of the wearer. The women of Brussels were unique in Flanders in maintaining the archaic custom of wearing veils over their necks. Elsewhere the chin veil was associated with the elderly or with professional men.

Tallest ■ The most impractical of all were the steeple headdresses of the 1460s. Reaching heights of up to 34 in (¾ of an ell *85 cm*), and trailing lengths of veils, they were an added hazard to mobility which was already complicated by the trains of dresses which were so long that wearers required a servant merely to move about. Agnes Sorel (d. 1450), first of the French royal mistresses to influence politics and fashion, wore trains that were longer by half than anyone else's and headdresses higher by half. Her household was more lavish than the queen's.

Fashion leaders

Most outrageous dresses ■ Bohemian (South German) men were the most outrageous dressers: their long, unkempt locks and loose, low-necked shirts set them apart from their more straight-laced European contemporaries. They are

These fashionable court ladies exhibit the use of the pomegranate symbol on textiles, elaborately embroidered sleeves and tall headdresses.

instantly recognizable in Italian paintings. The women correspondingly wore bright and ornate costumes and heavier jewellery styles than women of other countries.

German mercenaries serving with the Swiss army at the Battle of Grandson in 1476 adopted the style of the Swiss troops for patching their uniforms with cloth looted from the cities. The novelty of contrasting cloth appealed to the French court and a new fashion for slashing garments was born. The fad spread to all the courts of Europe.

A portrait of Maximilian I, Holy Roman Emperor, with his family in about 1515, shows various styles of head-wear.

Best dressed woman ■ Beatrice d'Este (1475–97), considered by many the most lovable of Renaissance princesses, had an international reputation for innovation in fashion. At her wedding in 1491 when she was 15, a tournament was held for which all the knights were dressed in green; as were the jousters and various others, including twelve 'wildmen'. In 1493 she amazed the citizens of Ferarra in central Italy when she appeared at a ceremony wearing a dress with the eight towers of the port of Genoa embroidered in small scale. She is known to have stayed up all night designing dresses on at least one occasion, when she produced a Turkish dress that was soon emulated by the other ladies at court. Her least successful experiment seems to have been an excursion into the realm of middle class headdress. When she and her sister Isabella appeared in Milan wearing Neapolitan linen *pannicelli* negative reaction from the local women was so strong that they went home and changed. Towering French headdresses made of silk and jewels were however totally acceptable. Within the first two years of her marriage the wardrobe at one of her residences included 84 gowns. She died in childbirth at the age of 22.

Most unaltering dress ■ Professional dress was the most conservative. Academic dress became distinct from lay dress in the 14th century and a European standard can be recognized in the 15th century. From *c.* 1450 hoods were a recognized, if archaic, feature. The round bonnet of the middle ages, the *pileus*, became fatter and rounder and by the turn of the 16th century the *pileus quadrata*, or square cap, which is still the standard today, had appeared at Paris. The robe that indicated a doctor (a scholar with a doctorate) however was an Italian development; the bell-sleeved gown with flap collar as worn by the theologian Marsilio Ficino (1433–99) in the late 15th century is the prototype of today's style. In the course of the 16th century black became the standard colour of academic dress for the universities of Paris, Oxford and Cambridge. Scarlet became associated with canon law, white with theology, blue with philosophy. Clothes indicated not only the faculty of the wearer, but also his status within it. Silk, gold and fur were reserved for the upper echelons.

Highest soles ■ High-heeled shoes are sometimes regarded as the least functional of footwear, worn for the sake of added height. In Venice *c.* 1480 the *pianelle* were constructed with soles which added a full 20 in *half a metre* to the height of the wearer.

Foremost devotee of the Moorish fad ■ René d'Anjou was the foremost devotee of the Moorish fad, one of several such foreign intrigues which occasionally swept through the courts. He had 21 pairs of Turkish shoes in his wardrobe and often dressed in a 'robe de Sarazin'. He also kept a Moor at court and had a zoo stocked with African animals.

Language

Earliest known today ■ The ability to speak is now believed to be dependent upon physiological changes in the height of the larynx between *Homo erectus* and *Homo sapiens sapiens* as developed *c.* 45 000 BC. The earliest written language discovered has been on Yangshao culture pottery from Paa-t'o, near Xi'an (Sian) in the Shaanxi (Shensi) province of China found in 1962 and dated to 5000–4000 BC. The earliest dated pictographs are on clay tablets from Nippur, southern Iraq, from one of the lowest excavation levels equivalent to Uruk V/VI and dated to *c.* 3400 BC. Tokens or tallies from Tepe Asiab and Ganji-I-Dareh Tepe in Iran have however been dated to 8500 BC. The earliest known piece of writing from the British Isles (*c.* AD 630) is a fragment of Irish uncial script in an ecclesiastical history.

Greatest linguistic diversity ■ Native Americans spoke about 2000 languages which can be grouped into 12 main stocks. Their linguistic diversity is greater than in any other part of the world. Cabeza de Vaca commented after his travels in 1528–36 that 'we passed through many and dissimilar tongues . . . although we knew six languages, we could not everywhere avail ourselves of them, there being a thousand differences.'

Unique absence of grammatical gender ■ Many native American languages recognize no gender based on sex distinction. Instead distinctions are based on other qualities: animate or inanimate; noble or ignoble; or relate to shape: round, flat or long.

Most complex ■ The following extremes of complexity have been noted: Chippewa, the native North American language of Minnesota, USA, has the most verb forms with up to 6000; Haida has the most prefixes with 70; Tabassaran, a language in Daghestan, on the Caspian Sea has 48 noun cases, while Eskimos use 63 forms of the present tense and simple nouns have as many as 252 inflections. In Chinese the 40-volume *Chung-wén Tà Tz'u-tien* dictionary lists 49 905 characters.

Most widely dispersed language family in Africa ■ The Bantu languages were spoken from Cameroun in West Africa to Natal in South Africa and Kenya in East Africa. Explorers were able to hire interpreters who could relatively easily learn the related languages of distant parts of the coast. In the southernmost parts of South Africa people who learnt the Bantu languages retained the unusual clicks of their own Khoi and San languages while adopting the grammar and vocabulary of the Bantu languages of wider communication.

Alphabets

Earliest ■ The earliest example of alphabetic writing has been found at Ugarit (now Ras Sharma), Syria, dated to *c.* 1450 BC. It comprised a tablet of 32 cuneiform letters.

Oldest letter ■ The letter 'O' is unchanged in shape since its adoption in the Phoenician alphabet *c.* 1300 BC.

Longest ■ The language with most letters is Cambodian with 72 (including useless ones).

Shortest ■ Rotokas in central Bougainville Island, Papua–New Guinea, has least letters with 11 (a, b, e, g, i, k, o, p, r, t and u).

Most and least consonants ■ The language with the most distinct consonantal sounds is that of the Ubykhs in the Caucusus, with 80–85, and that with the least is Rotokas, which has only six consonants. The English word 'latchstring' has six consecutive letters which are consonants, but the Georgian word *gvprtskvnis* (he is feeling us) has eight separately pronounced consonants.

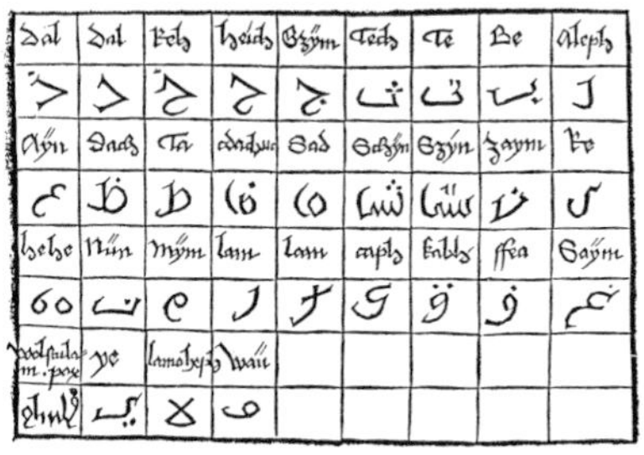

The Hebrew letters and their pronunciation were given by Erhard Reuwich in Bernard von Breydenbach's book of 1486.

Most and least vowels ■ The language with the most vowels is Sedang, a central Vietnamese language with 55 distinguishable vowel sounds, and that with the least is the Caucasian language Abkhazian with two. The record in written English for consecutive vowels is six in the musical term *euouae*. The Estonian word *jäääärne*, meaning the edge of the ice, has the same four consecutively. The name of a language in Pará State, Brazil consists solely of seven vowels – *uoiauai*.

Words

Longest ■ Length concatenations and some compound or agglutinative words or nonce words are or have been written in the closed-up style of a single word e.g. the 182-letter fricassee of 17 sweet and sour ingredients in Aristophanes' comedy *The Ecclesiazusae* in the 4th century BC.

The medieval Latin word *honorificabilitudinitas*, meaning 'honourableness', can be traced back to *c.* 1300. It was used by Shakespeare in *Love's Labours Lost* (1588) in the form *honorificabilitudinitatibus* and was often referred to as an example of a very long word.

Longest literary word ■ Non-existent books are sometimes mentioned in literary works. One of these is encountered in the class ribald work, *Gargantua and Pantagruel*, by the French writer, François Rabelais (*c.* 1490–1553). The 50 letters of the first word of its title, *Antipericatametaanaparcircumvolutiorectumgustpoops of the Coprofied*, make it contender for the distinction of being the longest word in contemporary Western European literature.

Languages that most influenced English ■ Throughout the ages, English has taken over words from other languages in order to supplement its own vocabulary. The 15th and 16th centuries were no exception. Most of the new words that appeared at this time came from Latin or French and include words such as *appropriate* (1525), *crisis* (1543), *dedicate* (1530), *education* (1531), *exhilarate* (1540), *habitual* (1526), *malignant* (1542), and *success* (1537) (from Latin), and *carob* (1548), *equip* (1523), *gallery* (1500), *gallop* (1523), *marmalade* (1524), *ruffian* (1531), *stratagem* (1489), *ticket* (1528), and *traffic* (1506) (from French).

Other western European languages were also important sources of new words in English. From Italian came *archipelago* (1502), *artichoke* (1531), *ballot* (1549), *bankrupt* (1539), *carnival* (1549), *cupola* (1549), *gondola* (1549), and *porcelain* (1530). From Spanish or Portuguese we have *armada* (1533), *cannibal* (1533), *canoe* (1555), *cocoa* (1555), *hammock* (1555), and *hurricane* (1555). Low German (the German of northern Germany) and Dutch contributed a significant number of nautical terms as well as general vocabulary, including *ballast* (1530), *deck* (1466), *dock* (1486), *lighter* (1487), *freight* (1463), *isinglass* (1545), *marline* (1485), *scrabble* (1537), *span* (1550), and *wagon* (1523).

In many cases, as with the words from Spanish or Portuguese, a single source of a borrowed word cannot be identified since parallel forms are found in more than one language. Many words could have entered English either from Latin or French, or from both languages, from Spanish or Italian, or from any of several languages, e.g. *scimitar* (1548) which could have come from French, Italian, Spanish *or* Portuguese.

THE END OF THE MIDDLE ENGLISH PERIOD AND THE START OF THE MODERN ENGLISH PERIOD

The development of English is traditionally divided into three periods, Old English or Anglo-Saxon (c. 450–1066), Middle English (c. 1066–1500) and Modern English (c. 1500 onwards). Columbus' voyage of 1492 came, therefore, at the boundary of the Middle English and Modern English periods. The first of these was characterized mainly by great changes in English grammar, and by the influence of French which became the language of official matters for nearly 300 years after the Norman Conquest. The later period was characterized mainly by the growth of the English vocabulary and its enrichment from many foreign sources, especially Latin, in the 16th century. The supreme influence of Latin was due to its long tradition as the language of learning, and to the renewed interest in Roman culture and civilization during the Renaissance.

Chief language of scholarship ■ At the beginning of the 16th century Latin, both in its spoken and written form, was the language used throughout Europe as the medium for communicating knowledge. Indeed, many people regarded the English language as crude and unsophisticated, incapable of expressing the abstract ideas that were found in the literature of the classical languages. This lack of confidence in English was shared by many translators of the period, one of whom, Sir Thomas Elyot, wrote in his *Doctrinal of Princes*: 'This little book . . . I have translated out of greke . . . to the intent only that I wolde assaie, if our English tongue mought receive the quicke and proper sentences pronounced by the grekes.

During the Renaissance, however, the demand increased for translations into English of the great works of the Latin and Greek civilizations so that they might become accessible to a wider population. This demand was met, and by the end of the 16th century English had at last become accepted as a language of learning.

In contrast with the few languages that had a great influence on English, there were many which had little or no influence during this period. For example, we have no evidence of words being taken from Finnish, Polish, Hungarian, Czech, Romanian, Bulgarian, Hindi, Chinese, or Japanese. Russian figures only from the 1550s when a few Russian words (e.g. *rouble* and *tsar*) are found in English texts about Russia.

First used in 1492 ■ The *Oxford English Dictionary* contains about 35 words in its 20 volumes for which 1492 is the date of the earliest printed or written example that has been found. Many of these words are no longer used (e.g. *disciple* 'to punish', *disheir* 'to disinherit', *hemplint* 'made of hemp', and *transitorious* 'transitory'). Others are dialect words (e.g. *milkness* 'milk yield', *tath(e)* 'dung', and *winnock* 'window'). A few are still used in the English language today, the most interesting of these being *maternal* (from French or Latin), *pomander* (from French), *resplend* (now a literary word meaning 'to shine brightly', from Latin), and *subscription* (in the sense 'act of signing one's name', also from Latin). Even these few examples of new words of the period illustrate the importance of French and Latin in the process of the enrichment of the English language in the 15th century. Although this trend continued into the 16th century, important contributions were also made by other languages as trade and communications developed.

First Indo-Portuguese linguistic borrowings ■ Several Asian languages contain substantial borrowings from Portuguese. These were frequently terms that referred to objects introduced into common use by the Portuguese, e.g. the table (*mesa*). Equally, the Portuguese borrowed terms from Indian languages, such as *chatim* (derived from *chetti*, or merchant). The word 'Canarim' was first used by the

Portuguese to denote the Konkani people of Goa. It then became the term used for those of Indo-Portuguese parentage and a common saying was 'every Canarim is descended from Vasco da Gama'.

Most detailed vocabulary ■ Hunters had most complex vocabularies for the beasts of the chase which categorised them by age, sex and behaviour. Each creatures' noise was defined as Sir Thomas Urquhart's translation of François Rabelais (*c.* 1494–1553) shows. Among these words were: barking of curs, bawling of mastiffs, bleating of sheep . . . tattling of jackdaws, grunting of swine, girning of boars, yelping of foxes, mewing of cats, cheeping of mice, squeaking of weasels, croaking of frogs, crowing of cocks, kekling of hens . . . changing of swans, chattering of jays, peeping of chickens, singing of larks, creaking of geese, chirping of swallows, bumbling of bees, rammage of hawks, chirming of linnets, croaking of ravens, screeching of owls . . .

IMPACT OF PRINTING ON THE ENGLISH LANGUAGE

The printing press was introduced by William Caxton in 1476. Caxton had studied printing in Cologne, Germany, (1470–72) and established a press in Bruges, in Flanders, where he printed the first book in the English language, before returning to England in 1476 to set up a press in Westminster.

The introduction of printing had two important effects on the English language. Firstly, it contributed to the standardization of the written language. Up until now, the spelling of English had been extremely diverse because it was recorded by hundreds of different scribes whose own spelling tended to be influenced by their knowledge of French and Latin. Printing led to the gradual establishment of orthographical norms, although some diversity continued for many years. Secondly, the production of printed books, together with a renewed interest in learning, led to an increase in knowledge and its communication which resulted in the enlargement of the vocabulary in the 16th centuries.

Writers who introduced most new English words ■ In the 16th century new words were introduced into the language mainly through the medium of writing. Although it is usually impossible to credit a particular person with the introduction of a particular word, two writers can be identified as having used very large numbers of new words. They were Sir Thomas Elyot (1490–1546) and Sir Thomas More (1477–1535). Sir Thomas Elyot promoted the use of English in scholarly works and translated the classics into English. He was also a philosopher and lexicographer. In his book on education, *The Boke Named the Governour* (1531), he consciously made use of new words in an attempt to enrich the English language. Words which first appear in his works are *accommodate*, *adumbration*, *encyclopædia*, *excrement*, *exhaust*, *experience*, and *exterminate*. Sir Thomas More, chancellor of England 1529–32), was also a student of Latin and a prolific writer. Some of the words which are first attested in his books are *absurdity*, *anticipate*, *combustible*, *contradictory*, *dissipate*, *exact*, and *explain*.

English pronunciation ■ The most significant changes in pronunciation during the second half of the 15th century related to long vowels as, for example, in the words m*ea*d, f*i*ve, d*ow*n, and r*oo*t. These were previously pronounced as the vowels in m*a*de, l*ea*ve, m*oo*n, and v*o*te. The first evidence we have of these changes, which formed the first stage of the so-called great vowel shift, is found in a poem, *The Hymn to the Virgin*, of which a phonetic transcription using Welsh orthography was made at the time. Scholars have dated this work as probably pre-1500.

Most influential variety of English ■ A characteristic feature of English until the end of the Middle Ages was its wide variety of dialects. They divided roughly into four areas, Northern (as far south as the Humber), West Midland and East Midland (as far as the Thames), and Southern (south of the Thames). Up until the middle of the 15th century it was not unusual for speakers in one part of the country to have difficulty in understanding speakers from other parts. One writer of the first half of the century expressed this problem as follows: 'The commen maner of spekyng in Englysshe of some contre [county] can skante be understonded in some other contre of the same londe.'

In the course of the 15th century it was the East Midland variety of English that gradually became the standard, especially the English of the London area, and this has remained the case up until the present day. The main reason for this was London's position as the focus of political and commercial life. The introduction of printing in London in 1476 also contributed to this process so that by the end of the 15th century it was difficult to tell from its language which part of the country a literary work had originated in.

New words from the New World ■ Many new words for previously unknown objects were introduced into European languages from the New World. These included the words for canoe, chilli, chocolate, hurricane, hammock, tomato, alpaca, llama, condor, pampa, puma, potato and tuna.

Place-names

Earliest ■ The world's earliest known place-names are pre-Sumerian e.g. Kish, Ur and Attara and therefore earlier than *c.* 3500 BC.

British ■ The earliest recorded British place-name is Belerion, the Penwith peninsula of Cornwall, referred to as such by Pytheas of Massilia *c.* 308 BC. The name Salakee on St Mary's, Isles of Scilly is however arguably of a pre-Indo-European substrate, meaning *tin island*. There are reasons to contend that Leicester (Roman, Ligora Castrum) contains an element reflecting its founding by the western Mediterranean navigators, the Ligurians, as early as *c.* 1200 BC. The earliest distinctive name for what is now Great Britain was Albion by Himilco *c.* 500 BC. The oldest name among England's 46 counties is Kent, first mentioned in its Roman form of Cantium (from the Celtic *canto*, meaning a rim, i.e. a coastal district), from the same circumnavigation by Pytheas. The earliest mention of England is the form *Angelcymn*, which appeared in the Anglo-Saxon Chronicle in AD 880.

Longest ■ The official name for Bangkok, the capital city of Thailand, is Krungthep Mahanakhon. The full name is however: Krungthep Mahanakhon Bovorn Ratanakosin Mahintharayutthaya Mahadilokpop Noparatratchathani Burirom Udomratchanivetmahasathen Amornpiman Avatarnsathit Sakkathattiyavisnukarmprasit (167 letters), which in its more scholarly transliteration emerges with 175 letters.

The longest place-name Taumatawhakatangihangakoauauotamateaturipukakapikimaungahoronukupokaiwhenuakitanatahu, the unofficial 85-letter version of the name of a hill (1002 ft *305 m* above sea level) in the Southern Hawke's Bay district of North Island, New Zealand. The Maori translation means 'The place where Tamatea, the man with the big knees who slid, climbed and swallowed mountains, known as landeater, played his flute to his loved one.'

Canada ■ There are two explanations of how Canada came to be so named, but both of them are attributed to Jacques Cartier, the Frenchman who sailed up the St Lawrence River in 1535. One version says that he heard the Indians frequently using the word *kanata*, meaning village and mistakenly took it as their word for the whole country. The other version says the name came from Cartier's misunderstanding of the Iroquois word for metals other than gold, *caignetdaze*.

Dictionaries and grammars

First lexicon for Eastern traders ■ In about 1300 a lexicon of words was produced, probably by the Genoese, to assist merchants trading with the East. It included Persian, Latin, Couman ('the language spoken and used throughout the empires of the Tartars, Persians, Chaldeans, Medes and Cathay').

First Greek grammar ■ Until the 15th century, no proper dictionaries or grammars of classical Greek existed. In 1478 Giovanni Crestone published a Greek–Latin dictionary and this made the study of classical Greek considerably easier for other scholars. In 1497 Urbano Bolzanio published the first Greek grammar written in Latin.

First Latin–Castilian dictionaries ■ Antonio de Nebrija, the foremost Spanish humanist, (1444–1522) produced a Latin–Castilian dictionary in about 1492. At almost the same time a similar dictionary was published by Alonso Hernandez de Palencia. Nebrija had also done much in Spain to improve the teaching of Latin after his return from ten years of studying in Italy.

First scholarly examination of manuscripts ■ In order to truly understand ancient manuscripts it is necessary to study them with great care: paying attention to the palaeographical evidence (handwriting), the orthography (spelling) and the 'usus scribendi'. It was the Italian scholar Angelo Ambrogini Poliziano (better known as Politian) (1454–94) who first conducted such work in a systematic way.

Recording

Most complex writing system ■ Japan's writing system is undoubtedly the most difficult for an outsider to master. At its core are several thousand characters borrowed from Chinese, but given Japanese pronunciations. Each one must be learned separately, and some are written with 10 or more strokes of the brush. Ordinary literacy requires the learning of something like 5000 characters. To make matters worse, whereas in Chinese each character usually has only one pronunciation, the Japanese give a character 2 or even 3 different pronunciations, and it is essential to learn when each one is appropriate. On top of that, there are two separate systems of *kana*, 50 signs used to give the sounds of grammatical endings and other particles found only in Japanese. Despite this, literacy in 15th century Japan seems to have been at least as widespread as in contemporary Europe.

Smallest ■ In the Tang dynasty people applied themselves to writing out edifying texts in minute characters. They inscribed the *Heart Sutra* (the shortest Buddhist sutra) on a copper coin, and also wrote 'Dynasty Great, People at Peace' on a hemp seed.

Unique system of recording ■ The most comprehensive system of recording information known in the pre-Hispanic New World was developed by the Maya, a people inhabiting what are now Yucatan and other parts of southern Mexico, Guatemala, Belize and Honduras, whose writing comprised pictographic, syllabic and phonetic devices from about the time of the birth of Christ. Nahua-speaking peoples of central Mexico used mnemonic pictographs and, to a limited extent, ideographs, while some South American peoples, including the Incas, used the knotted string known as the *quipu* for recording statistical information.

Earliest forms of shorthand ■ The commonest shorthand available in 1500 was an abbreviated Latin writing form, adapted from Roman models. Shorthand writing dates from the first century AD in Rome, and was used to record speeches in the Senate. Medieval scholars, including archbishop Thomas à Becket in England, used a shorthand system based on the Latin version devised by Marcus Tullius Tiro.

Bibles and other printed works

Earliest complete Bible printed in English ■ This was the Bible edited by Miles Coverdale, Bishop of Exeter (*c.* 1488–1569), while living in Antwerp, and printed in 1535. William Tyndale's New Testament in English had, however, been printed in Cologne and in Worms, Germany in 1525 while John Wycliffe's first manuscript translation dates from 1382.

Longest book ■ The longest book is the Book of Psalms, while the longest book including prose is the Book of the Prophet Isaiah, with 66 chapters.

Shortest book ■ The Third Epistle of John has only 294 words in 14 verses. The Second Epistle of John has only 13 verses but 298 words.

Longest and shortest psalm ■ Of the 150 psalms, the longest is the 119th, with 176 verses, and the shortest is the 117th, with two verses.

Longest name ■ The longest actual name in English language bibles is the 18-letter Maher-shalal-hashbaz, the symbolic name of the second son of Isaiah (Isaiah, Chapter VIII, verses 1 and 3). The caption of Psalm 22, however, contains a Hebrew title sometimes rendered Al-Ayyeleth Hash-Shahar (20 letters).

First Russian Bible ■ The first Russian edition of the Bible appeared in 1499.

Earliest almanac ■ The earliest surviving almanacs date from the 1100s. Almanacs by John Somers (1380) and Nicolas de Lynne (1386) were issued at Oxford. Georg Purback (1423–61), the

GREATEST AUTHORS AND BOOKS

COUNTRY	NAME	DATES	
Denmark	**Christiern Peterson**	**?1480–1554**	***Translator of the Bible***
Britain	**Alexander Barclay**	**?1475–1552**	***Poet***
	Miles Coverdale	**1488–1569**	***Translator of the Bible***
	William Dunbar	**?1460–1520**	***Poet***
	John Heywood	**?1497–?1580**	***Dramatist***
	Sir Thomas Malory	**fl. 1470**	***Author, translator of*** **Morte d'Arthur**
	John Skelton	**?1460–1529**	***Poet***
	Henry Howard, Earl of Surrey	**? 1517–1547**	***Poet***
	William Tyndale	**?1484–1536**	***Translator of the Bible***
	Sir Thomas Wyatt	**1503–1542**	***Poet***
France	**Nicholas Bartelemy**	**1478–*c.*1535**	***Dramatist***
	Jean Calvin	**1509–1563**	***Theologian***
	Guillaume Coquillart	**1450–1510**	***Satirist***
	Jean de Troyes	**fl. 1480**	***Chronicler***
	François Rabelais	**1495–?1553**	***Satirist***
	François Villon	**1431–?1480**	***Poet***
'Germany'	**Sebastian Brant**	**1458–1521**	***Satirist***
	Martin Luther	**1483–1546**	***Theologian***
	Hans Sachs	**1494–1576**	***Dramatist***
'Italy'	**Leon Battista Alberti**	**1404–1472**	***Humanist***
	Baldassare Castiglione	**1478–1529**	***Author of*** **The Book of the Courtier**
	Lorenzo de' Medici	**1449–1492**	***Poet, patron of the arts***
	Niccolo Machiavelli	**1469–1527**	***Historian and political writer***
	Michelangelo Buonarotti	**1475–1564**	***Poet***
	Poliziano (Angelo Ambrogini)	**1454–1494**	***Poet and dramatist***
	Georgio Vasari	**1511–1574**	***Biographer***
	Leonardo da Vinci	**1452–1519**	***Writer***
Netherlands	**Anna Bjinns**	***c.*1494–1575**	***Poet***
	Desiderius Erasmus	**1467–1536**	***Man of letters***

German scientist, published a printed almanac in 1457, and it appeared yearly for 30 years.

Europe's most elaborate printed book ■ In 1517 Arñao Guillén de Brocar, university printer of Alcala, Spain, completed the first printed polyglot Bible – one with different language versions of the text printed side by side. The first 'polyglot' Bible was written by Origen (*d.* 253). The Alcala Bible, known as the Complutensian Polyglot from Complutum, the town's ancient Latin name, contained Greek, Hebrew and Latin texts of the Old Testament, a Hebrew dictionary and other scholarly apparatus, the Latin text of the New Testament and the first printed Greek New Testament. Editorial work began in 1502, printing the six volumes took three years and cost the sponsor, Cardinal Fresco Jiménez (Ximenes), 50 000 gold ducats.

Best-seller ■ Described as a work whose 'circulation for a long time vied with and perhaps exceeded that of every contemporary production of the Press of lesser eminence than Holy Writ', *The Boke of St Albans* was first published in 1486. *The Boke* has enjoyed a continuous history of publication ever since. Essentially, it is an almanac with special reference to hawking, hunting and heraldry and was written by Dame Juliana Berners. Many of today's collective nouns were first recorded in *The Boke* and the book also contained the last real use of an Old English letter – the Y with a dot over it – in a major literary work.

Earliest encyclopaedias ■ The earliest known encyclopaedia was compiled by Speusippus (*post* 403–*c.* 338 BC), a nephew of Plato, in Athens *c.* 370 BC. The earliest encyclopaedia compiled by a Briton was *Liber exerptionum* (Book of excerpts) by the Scottish monk Richard (*d.* 1173) at St Victor's Abbey, Paris *c.* 1140.

Master François Rabelais, author of Gargantua and Rabelais, *has given his name to bawdy humour.*

Largest Russian encyclopaedia ■ Compiled under the direction of Metropolitan Macarius of Moscow in 1543–64, the 12 volume encyclopaedia had 27 000 folios. It was produced in the Kremlin workshops by dozens of clerks and covered all known world history. Six of its volumes were devoted to Russia. The clerks extensively copied and rewrote national chronicles, paying special attention to profiles of Russian princes, folklore and legends. It was illustrated by 10 000 pictures, many of them in colour, of buildings, costume, utensils, arms and armour of both the noble and the common people.

In the story of King Arthur and the Knights of the Round Table, Perceval dreams of two women who reprimand him.

Earliest newspapers in Europe ■ The first newspapers published regularly were the Roman *Acta Diurna* (Daily Events), news sheets posted in public places. The Chinese also issued handwritten news reports, but in medieval Europe news was spread almost wholly by mouth, via town criers and travellers, or occasionally by government decrees. The invention of printing in the 1400s gave fresh stimulus to news dissemination. The earliest surviving European news pamphlet was published in Cologne, Germany, in 1470.

In 1529 the Venetian authorities published broadsheets appealing to other Christian nations to come to their aid against the besieging Turks.

Books

Most popular book ■ The *Tai-Shang ganying pian* (The Responses of the Great Supreme) is usually recognized as holding the first place among all publications in the world. Written in China between the 3rd and 4th centuries, by the 16th century it had run through more editions than the Bible (and would go on to outclass both the Bible and Shakespeare). Many millions of devout Chinese believe that great merit can be gained from distributing it. The *Tai-Shang ganying pian* has as its purpose the elucidation of the doctrine of future retribution.

Most popular classical works ■ The invention of printing brought a flood of classical works onto the market. Before 1500 no less than 200 editions of Cicero's writings had been published. These books were edited by the best humanist scholars of the day.

First autobiography in English ■ Dame Margery Kempe (*c.* 1373–1440) was a pilgrim who visited all the holy places of England (Canterbury, Lambeth, Lincoln and York) and then in 1413 set off for the Holy Land, walking much of the way. There she visited all the holy places and then returned to England by way of Assisi and Rome. Her next pilgrimage abroad were to Santiago de Compostela in north west Spain and later to Danzig in Poland. Between 1436 and 1438 she dictated the story of her life to scribes. 'Here begyneth a schort tretys and a comfortabyl' are the opening words of the first autobiography in English. It was published in part by Wynken de Worde in London. (The full manuscript was lodged at Mount Grace Priory, a Carthusian priory in Yorkshire, and came to light only in this century.)

First printed book of riddles in English ■ *The Demaundes Joyous* was published in 1511 by Wynkyn de Worde. The selection of riddles was compiled and translated from a French source which includes more obscene and scatological material than the English version. The most familiar riddle to modern readers is probably 'Which was first, the chicken or the egg?' Most of the jokes are better than this one, however.

Early scientific books ■ The rise of interest in science led to the publication of numerous illustrated books on scientific topics. One of the earliest studies of anatomy, Vesalius' *Fabrica de humani corpori* (On the construction of the human body) was printed in Basel, Switzerland, in 1543. The first of the great flower books, Fuchs' *De historia stirpium* (On the history of plants) appeared in Basel in 1542.

Travel books

Most popular ■ Marco Polo's account of his journeys in Asia in 1271–3 and again in 1292 and his life in Peking are factual and on the whole accurate, but at the time they were regarded as no more truthful than the far more romantic and fantastic tales of Sir John Mandeville. His book, though mainly enjoyed as fiction, made far better reading and perhaps aroused more interest in travel and discovery, and did more to popularize the idea that the globe could be circumnavigated.

Earliest Chinese travel books ■ In 1434 Kung Chen published his *Record of the Barbarian Countries in the Western Ocean* and two years later Fei Tsin published *Triumphant Visions of the Starry Raft* – 'starry raft' being the term used for ships which carried ambassadors abroad from China. Fei Tsin also produced an illustrated book of foreign travel but sadly it has not survived. A Chinese Muslim interpreter from Yunnan, Ma Huan, published his *Triumphant Visions of the Boundless Ocean* in 1451. In 1520 *Record of the tribute-paying Western Countries* included compass directions and a mariner's chart.

African interior ■ Alvise de Cadamosto was a Venetian merchant who made two expeditions to Africa in 1455 and 1456. He visited the Senegal and Gambia rivers and travelled several days' journey inland. His account of his travels, *Il libro de la prima navigazione per l'oceano a le terri de Nigri* (The Book of the First Ocean Voyage to the Land of the Blacks) written 10 years later and printed in 1507, was the first account of the African interior to be written by a European.

First illustrated ■ The *Sanctae Peregrinationes* (Journey to the Holy Land) by Bernard Breydenbach, illustrated by Erhard Reuwich, was published at Mainz, Germany, in 1486. It is an account of the pilgrimage to Jerusalem made by Breydenbach, a wealthy German nobleman who took Reuwich with him to record the places visited. Reuwich made woodcuts of costumes and strange beasts, cities and sights, the most famous being a panorama of Venice which folds out to a leaf 57 in *145 cm* long plus its facing page. The *Peregrinationes* is also notable as the first printed book in which the illustrator's name is recorded.

Islamic pilgrims along the road to Jerusalem in 1486, as seen by the German artist – pilgrim Erhard Reuwich.

Most outstanding records ■ Many of the *conquistadores* but most notably Hernan Cortés and Bernal Díaz wrote of their experiences in the Americas in narratives of such excellence that they have hardly been surpassed in any language. Cortés wrote of the Aztecs: 'They lived almost as we do in Spain, and in as much harmony and order, and considering they are barbarous, and so far from the knowledge of God, and cut off from all civilized nations, it is truly remarkable to see what they have achieved.'

First study of America ■ The Spaniard Oviedo y Valdes' *Historia general y natural de las Indias* (The General and Natural History of the Indies) and the Italian who lived in Spain, Peter Martyr's *De Orbe Novo* (Of the New World) were among the first descriptions of the Americas.

Fiction

China's most famous war story ■ China's greatest warrior heroes lived during the Three Kingdoms period (AD 220–265). Tales about them were knit together and expanded in the huge 120-chapter novel *Three Kingdoms Saga*, which, as far as we know, first appeared in 1494. The earliest surviving edition is dated 1522. The novel mainly tells how the mighty warriors Guan Yu and Zhang Fei, and the wizard-like military strategist Zhuge Liang fought against the demonic wily warlord Cao Cao.

China's supreme bandit story ■ The most frequently banned novel in Chinese history is the long saga about bandits entitled *Watery Badlands*, also known as *Water Margin*. A brilliantly colourful, exciting, often violent and sometimes starkly brutal narrative, it has attracted a vast readership also for its championing of the notion that an individual can take up arms against gross injustice. A readily available inspiration for rebellion, it has rightly been feared by governments, both good and bad ones, but continues to be enjoyed for its thrilling tales such as Wu Song's bare-handed fight to the death with a man-eating tiger. The earliest known version was probably published during the late 15th or early 16th century.

Poetry

Last of the skaldic poets ■ The last Catholic bishop of Holar, Iceland, Jon Arason (1484–1551) was not only an historian but the last of the ancient Scandinavian poets known as the *skalds*. The skalds were court-poets among whose duties was the composition of verses suitable for recitation prior to taking the field of battle. They wrote in literary Norse, the West Norse language which was the common tongue of Norway, Iceland, Faroe, Orkney, Shetland, Greenland, a large part of the Hebrides and even parts of Scotland, Ireland and England from the time of the Vikings down to the 13th century. Literary Norse is deemed to have ended at the same time as Middle English (*c.* 1500).

Last great classical poet ■ The Persian poet Jami (1414–92) is considered to be the last of the great mystical classical Persian poets, whose predecessors included Sadi, and Omar Khayyam, best known in the west for his Rubaiyat. Jami was a great religious seeker, poet and prose writer, and was lavishly rewarded by Muslim rulers of the time. Persians often engage in poetic contests, where two or more rivals try to complete or cap a stanza by completing the verse in the correct style and metre. On one occasion a rival visited Jami and they engaged in this sort of contest. Jami surpassed himself and reached superhuman heights. After three days his rival recognized his inferiority to the master, his head fell on his chest, and he failed to reply – for he was dead.

Earliest Anglo-American literary work ■ In about 1510 the prolific English printer Wynken de Worde published a book called *Hyckescorner*. In this book the main character Hycke Scorner returns from an imaginary voyage to describe all the places he has seen, including the newly found lands of the Americas.

Syr I hau ben in many a countre
As in fraunce Irlonde and in spayne
Portyngale seuyll also in almayne
Freslonde flaunders and in burgoyne
Calabre poyle and erragoyne
Brytayne byske and also in gascoyne
Naples grece and in myddes of scotlonde
At cape saynt vyncent & in the new found Ilonde
I haue ben in gene and in cowe
Also in the londe of rumbelowe
Thre myle out of hell
At rodes constantyne and in babylonde
In cornewale and in northumberlonde
Where men sethe rushes in gruell
Ye syr in caldey tartare and Iude
And yͤ londe of woemen yͭ fewe men dothe fynde
In all these countres haue I be.

A new literary genre ■ At the turn of the 16th century a new literary genre appeared in Italy: poems in praise of gardens. In 1527 Erasmus (1466–1536) tried his hand at the new form and produced the *Convivium Religiosum* (The Sacred Banquet), a poem in which the forms of the natural world are given symbolic meanings.

Authors

Greatest compiler of bibliographies ■ Konrad Gesner (1516–65) of Switzerland was a prodigious bibliographer and encyclopaedist. In his *Bibliotheca Universalis* (Universal Library) (1545–55) he catalogued 'all known writings in Latin, Greek and Hebrew', mentioning more than 1800 titles and authors, and summarizing their content. He also compiled a natural history encyclopaedia, *Historia Animalum* (Natural History of Animals), from Greek and medieval sources, in which is included the first accurate description of medieval whaling. His unfinished *Opera Botanica* (Works concerning Plants) contained almost 1000 plant illustrations.

Most complex prose style ■ The Chinese literary prose style known as the Eight Legged Essay, was matured during the latter half of the 15th century. Used in the imperial civil service examinations of 1497, it came to dominate serious prose writing and influenced all kinds of literature and even theatre. Its unmatchedly intricate forms were a great help to setting out ideas with orderly logic and vivid impact.

Most famous West African writer-historian ■ Mahmud Kati of Timbuktu began his great chronicle of the Western Sudan, the *Taritch al-Fattash* in about 1519.

Libraries

Earliest ■ One of the earliest known collections of archival material was that of King Ashurbanipal at Nineveh (668–627 BC). He had clay tablets referring to events and personages as far back as the Dynasty of Agode *c.* 23rd century BC.

Largest Aztec library ■ The Aztecs kept their codices (their equivalent of books or manuscripts) in libraries called *amoxcalli*. The largest of these was in Texcoco and was destroyed during the Spanish conquest. Only four codices survive, and only one of those is pre-Columbian. The others are copies made in the Spanish period.

Oldest codex ■ The oldest surviving codex is Mayan and known as the Codex of Dresden. Made possibly in the early 1200s in the centre of the Yucatan, Mexico, it is a tract on divination and astronomy. Many codices were destroyed either by the people themselves or by the *conquistadores* or the Spanish priests, who considered them the work of the devil.

First great library founded once printing was established ■ This was probably the Royal Library now called the *Bibliothèque Nationale* founded by Francis I in Paris, *c.* 1520. Older great modern libraries include the University Library of St Andrews, Scotland, founded in 1456 and the Imperial Library at Vienna, Austria, founded by Frederick III *c.* 1440. Cambridge University Library was also founded in the 15th century.

First book fair ■ Probably the first book fair was that of Leipzig, Germany, which was instituted in 1545 though its fairs have been held since at least 1268.

FOUNDING OF LIBRARIES

1254 ... University Library, Salamanca, Spain
1337 ... University Library, Oxford, England
1436 ... Florence, Italy
1440 ... Imperial Library, Vienna, Austria
1446 ... Vatican Library, Rome
1456 ... University Library, St. Andrews, Scotland
1520 ... Bibliothèque Nationale, Paris, France

Schools

First compulsory education in Britain ■ In 1494, a Scottish act compelled all barons and freeholders to send their sons to school. (In England and Wales compulsory education had to wait 400 years.)

First foreign language school in China ■ After the intensive exploration of the world by the great Chinese fleets in the early years of the 15th century a school was founded in China to teach the languages of the 'Barbarians' whom the Chinese had visited. The school published bilingual texts such as a list of words in Malay and Chinese.

FOUNDING OF UNIVERSITIES

1221 .... Padua, Italy
1243 .... Salamanca, Spain
c. 1250 .... Oxford, England
1343 .... Pisa, Italy
1381 .... Cambridge, England
1385 .... Heidelberg, Germany
1409 .... Leipzig, Germany
1411 .... St Andrews, Scotland
1451 .... Glasgow, Scotland
1494 .... Aberdeen, Scotland

** The buildings of the University of Padua date from 1493–1552.*

Greatest number of universities ■ The countries with the most universities in Western Europe in 1500 were:

Italy	*20*
France	*18*
Germany	*16*
Spanish peninsula	*14*
Scotland	*3*
England	*2*
Others	*6*

Most famous university in tropical Africa ■ The great mosque of Timbuktu, on the edge of the Sahara, was the seat of a famed 'university' in the 15th century. Travelling scholars from as far afield as Spain and Egypt held seminars there.

Most sumptuous child's schoolbook ■ The schoolbook of Maximilian Sforza, son of Beatrice d'Este and Lodovico Sforza, is the most sumptuous child's schoolbook. Miniatures painted by Gian Pietro Birago depict the young scholar at work and play. The pictures must have been intended as moral training for the

Greatest centre of learning in the world ■ *In 1500 the academy attached to the great Mosque al-Azhar ('the bright or fair one') in Cairo has a strong claim to this distinction. The mosque was founded in 972. For centuries it was the greatest centre of learning in the Muslim world, and today ranks as the oldest university extant in the world.*

young prince who is shown in riding in triumph. Unfortunately his career did not turn out as gloriously as the picture would suggest.

Best selling school books ■ The most popular textbook used in 15th-century schools was a grammar, *De octo partibus orationes (Of the Eight Parts of Speech)*, by the 4th-century grammarian Donatus.

Most important occult science ■ In the late 15th century this was astrology. It was a university subject and had not yet been separated from astronomy, so it was still considered to be one of the seven liberal arts. Lecturers were attached to the most important medical faculties at Paris, Padua, and Bologna. The astrological system of thought also produced theories of history, as well as predictions of the future. Most astronomers were also astrologers; they were employed by kings and noblemen for their skills in prediction. Astronomical research was usually undertaken in their spare time.

Scholars

Greatest scholar of the northern Renaissance ■ Ordained a priest in 1492, Desiderius Erasmus (1466–1536) is acknowledged by this epithet. Born in Rotterdam, Netherlands, he lived in Paris,

It is said of Erasmus (1466–1536) that 'he did more than any other single man to advance the Revival of Learning'.

Oxford, Padua, Cambridge, Basel and Louvain (now in Belgium). His *Adagia* (Sayings) (*c.* 1507) contains more than 3000 proverbs collected from the works of classical authors. His *Colloquia* (Conversation) (1519) is usually regarded as his masterpiece. His commentary on the abuses of the Church in this and other work prepared people's minds for their ideas of the Reformation. His annotated *New Testament* (1516) is regarded as the first Greek text.

Italian musicians play brass and stringed instruments, while the children join in with bells and beating time.

Longest-lived 'blue stocking' ■ A speech made in Padua, in north-east Italy at her cousin's graduation in 1487 gives Cassandra Fedele of Venice some claim to be the first female academic, though she never had official status within the university. During the 1490s she enjoyed a prestige unmatched by any previous female intellectual, corresponding with European princes and numerous scholars. She died in 1558 at either 93 or 103, even the lower age being rarely approached at that time.

Instruments

Organs ■ By 1500 Europe had many large pipe organs with up to three manual keyboards plus a pedalboard. Among the most famous were the new cathedral organs of Rheims in France (1487) with 2000 pipes and Halberstadt in Germany (1495) with more than 1190 pipes and 20 bellows to supply the wind chest.

First trombone maker ■ The first known maker of trombones, and a famous player, was Hans Neuschel of Nuremberg, Germany, who died in 1503. He demonstrated instruments in Rome and made a set of silver trombones for Pope Leo X. He was succeeded by his sons Hans and Jörg.

First piano ■ Writing in Dijon about 1450, Henri Arnaut described musical instruments which had strings struck by hammers operated from a keyboard like the piano. But the plucking action of the instrument we call the harpsichord was much more popular and the piano had to be 'reinvented' in the early 1700s.

First harmonium ■ The church harmonium amazingly belongs to the same family of musical instruments as the mouth organ. The sound is produced by blowing air across flat metal reeds so as to make them vibrate. Mouth organists use their own breath, tongue and fingers but harmonium players have a bellows and keyboard to help them. The first keyboard instrument like this, the 'regal', was invented about 1450.

Oddest instrument ■ In the 1490s, we are told, Leonardo da Vinci performed before the court of Milan, Italy, upon a lyre made of silver and shaped like the skull of a horse. The great man apparently outshone all the other musicians present – his instrument must surely have outdone all the others as well.

First conductor's baton ■ The use of a light wand or baton by the director of music or conductor is usually thought to have been a 19th century innovation. In fact, a late 15th century painting by Melozzo da Forli (now in the Vatican) clearly shows an angel musician with a delicate baton, very similar to modern types.

Composers

Most famous ■ Writing in 1477 the theorist Tinctoris said that all experts were agreed that no music written before the 1430s was worth serious consideration. He attributed the 'new art' to the arrival of English composers, notably John Dunstable (*d.* 1453) on the continent. Throughout the period, serious music was dominated by composers from northern Europe. Dunstable the Englishman was followed by Guillaume Dufay (1400–1474), Johannes Ockeghem (*c.* 1420–1495) and, above all, Josquin des Pres (*c.* 1450–1521), all of them Franco-Flemings. A contemporary Italian called Josquin 'the Michelangelo of music'. In 1527 the Venetian authorities followed prevailing Italian fashion by appointing a Flemish composer to head the music of the city's most prestigious church, St Mark's. It already enjoyed a considerable reputation, but the installation of Adrian Willaert as *maestro da capella* brought Venice a long period of dominance in the musical life of northern Italy.

Most advanced musical theorist ■ In 1516 the Ming Prince Zhu Zaiyu was born in China. He used his wealth and leisure to carry out lengthy scientific investigations of the mathematical theory behind the tuning of musical instruments. He was the first to discover a way of tuning stringed instruments that made it possible to modulate easily from key to key without having to retune the whole instrument – this is what is now called 'equal temperament'.

Most popular tunes ■ Judging from the number of manuscript copies to have survived, the song *O rosa bella* (Oh, Lovely Rose) seems to have been among the most popular melodies of the first half of the 15th century. From the 1450s to the 1540s, probably the best known tune of all was *L'homme armé* (The Armed Man). Possibly composed by the Burgundian Antoine Busnois, it was used by no fewer than 24 composers as the theme for settings of the mass.

Earliest printed part music ■ In May 1501 the Venetian music printer Ottaviano Petrucci (1466–1539), published his *Harmonice musices odhecaton* (One hundred songs in harmonic music). Earlier printers had produced single line music; this is the first example of polyphonic music in print.

First music dictionary ■ When the Flemish music scholar Johannes Tinctoris wrote his *Terminorum Musicae Diffinitorium* (Definitions of Musical Terms) about 1473 it was the best book of the kind. In 1495 it was published at Treviso in Italy – the first music dictionary to appear in print.

Song

Oldest song ■ The *shaduf* chant has been sung since time immemorial by irrigation workers on the man-powered pivoted-rod bucket raisers of the Nile water mills (or *saqiyas*) in Egypt. The oldest known harmonised music performed today is the English song *Sumer is icumen in* which dates from *c.* 1240.

National anthems ■ The oldest national anthem is the *Kimigayo* of Japan, in which the words date from the 9th century, whilst the oldest music belongs to the Netherlands.

Most famous singers ■ In 1467 a 'talent scout' for the Church of St John Lateran, in Rome, Italy, held auditions in the cathedral school at Cambrai in northwestern France, centre for Europe's most famous boy sopranos. Agents for the popes' choirs often recruited here.

Most complex composition ■ A vocal part work by the Franco-Flemish composer Johannes Ockeghem (*c.* 1420–*c.* 1495) was considered a miracle by his contemporaries – it had parts for 36 different voices. Ockeghem's name is found in at least 44 variant spellings – Okeghem, Ockenheim, Okenghem, etc – a record of a different kind, perhaps.

Earliest ■ The music and parts of the text of a hymn in the *Oxyrhnchus Papyri* from the 2nd century are the earliest known hymnody. The earliest exactly datable hymn is the *Heyr Himno Smiður* (Hear the maker of heaven) from 1208 by the Icelandic bard and chieftain Kolbeinn Tumason (1173–1208).

Longest ■ The *Hora novissima tempora pessima sunt; vigilemus* by Bernard of Cluny (12th century), runs to 2966 lines.

Bells

Oldest ■ The tintinnabulum found in the Babylonian Palace of Nimrod dates from *c.* 1100 BC. The oldest known tower bell is one in Pisa, Italy dated MCVI (1106).

Great Britain ■ The fragile hand bell known as the Black or Iron Bell of St Patrick is dated *c.* AD 450. The oldest tower bell in Great Britain is one of 1 cwt *50 kg* at St Botolph, Hardham, Sussex, still in use but dated *ante* 1100. The oldest inscribed bell is the Gargate bell at Caversfield church, Oxfordshire and is dated *c.* 1200–1210. The oldest *dated* bell in England is one hanging in Lissett church, near Bridlington, Humberside, bearing the date MCCLIII (1254).

Ireland's oldest peal of bells ■ One of Ireland's oldest peal of bells was struck in 1492, and hangs in St Audoen's church in Dublin – this is the only medieval church in Dublin.

MISCELLANEOUS

Least musical monarch ■ Louis XII of France (1462–1509) may perhaps be saddled with this unenviable title. He was such a poor singer that his court composer Josquin des Prés wrote a special piece with a part, marked *vox regis* (literally 'the king's voice'), which held to a single note throughout the composition.

Most musical monarch ■ Henry VIII (1491–1547) was famous for his love of music. He composed anthems, masses and part songs and was a keen singer. His collection of musical instruments included 10 trombones or 'sackburrs', 14 trumpets, 5 bagpipes, no fewer than 76 recorders and 78 flutes.

First musical knight ■ Touring Italy in 1470, the 60-year old German organist Conrad Paumann, generally reckoned the foremost virtuoso of his day, was dubbed knight by Federico Gonzaga the Marquis of Mantua. Paumann is the first musician recorded as having received such an honour.

Drama

Earliest pantomime ■ The English stage pantomime has its origins in the Italian *commedia dell'arte*, a form of improvised theatre that began in the early 1500s. Its origins are obscure, but in 1530 it was described as a 'modern' dramatic invention. Mingling classical comedy, street theatre, farce and mime-shows, *commedia del'arte* troupes were active in Italy by 1545. The most famous were the Gelosi, led by Francisco and Isabella Andreini.

The Concert in an Egg, *one of the bizarre paintings of Hieronymous Bosch, shows a musical score.*

Most difficult animals to train ■ The late Ming writer Xie Zhaozhi reported that in the city of Chang'ar the beggars had performing dogs and monkeys, but also performing rats. 'Rats,' he commented, 'are extremely obstinate and unteachable, and I have no idea how they were trained.'

China's most famous play ■ The most celebrated drama of China is *West Wing*. It was created by Wang Shifu in the 13th or early 14th century, but the earliest surviving full edition was printed in 1498. So long that it would take a few days to perform, it is a love story proclaiming romance and free choice of Love. It has been both republished and banned far more times than any other play. Full of beautiful poetry, much sparkling humour and excitements a-plenty, it has been familiar to Chinese of all ages and social ranks and inspired a mass of later literature and entertainments.

First great Chinese revenge play ■ One of the most famous of all Chinese sagas was made into a huge drama called *Washing Silk-gauze*, written by Liang Chenyu around 1520. In no less than 45 acts, this tells how the King of Yue dedicated his life's energies to revenge against the rival kingdom of Wu. Also prominent in the plot is the love affair between Xishi, China's most legendary woman of beauty, and Fan Li, China's most celebrated merchant adventurer. Innovating a mixture of northern and southern song-music that became the rage throughout the empire, this drama inaugurated the Kunju genre of theatre, China's most refined and highbrow to this day.

First English secular play ■ Mystery and morality plays and masques formed the staple of theatrical productions until the advent of Nicholas Udall (1505–1556). His *Ralph Roister Doister*, probably written in 1531 when he was the headmaster of Eton, is not only the first English secular play but also the first English comedy.

Fastest-growing flower ■ The late Ming writer Xie Zhaozhi enjoyed watching conjuring tricks. One of the most amazing was known as 'instant flowers': 'A lotus seed is tossed into hot water. In the time that it takes to consume a meal, it sends forth sprouts and spreads its leaves. In the time that it takes to eat another meal, it brings forth a lotus flower, as big as a bowl of wine.'

In another trick, a small boy's stomach was cut open and a melon seed planted in it: 'In no time at all it produces small melons which, on being split open, prove to be edible.'

Fairs

Fair with the most destructive outcome ■ Carnivals could sometimes result in violence and rebellion, if the festive and the everyday got out of balance. After their June revels in 1513, 300 young peasants from country districts near Berne in Switzerland marched on the city and pillaged it to punish the *mangeurs de couronnes*. Berne was in the sway of a few very rich aristocratic families (the 'crown eaters' targeted by the peasants), at a time when religious strife disrupted all of Switzerland.

Most impudent target ■ Most city fairs were occasions for horseplay and satire. In charge of this was usually an 'abbey', a group of young people, mainly men, from a particular district, guild or profession. Lyons, France, (60 000 inhabitants) had about 20 such groups, each with its retinue of officers under an 'Abbot of Misrule', a 'Prince of Fools' or a similarly-titled leader. The men would install their officers on a float and join the civic procession issuing proclamations. (Rouen's abbey once announced a century of polygamy.) Satire and criticism could be very direct. The *charivaris* (masked gangs) named names of local wrongdoers, sometimes leading them along on an ass. Office-holders were frequent targets for these groups. Authority mostly let the misrule go unpunished, within a well-defined moratorium on law enforcement agreed by both sides. At Paris in 1516 the *Basoche*, an organization of justice clerks, staged a comic show depicting the King replaced at court by *Mere Sotte* (Mother Booze), who was taxing and fleecing the people.

Most frequent target of town charivaris ■ This was a domineering wife. She herself would not often be portrayed. Instead, her husband formed part of a float display in the city procession, seen having his beard pulled out or his private parts kicked. Well-known cases also would be taken through the streets on an ass, facing towards the tail. Panurge, in the story of Gargantua and Pantagruel by the French satirist François Rabelais (*c.* 1494–1553), is put off marriage by thoughts of an adulterous wife, but what troubles him as much is the prospect of being 'flayed' by her.

Occasions

Most extravagant party ■ In an age of conspicuous excesses, the Feast of the Pheasant held in Lille, in France, by Philip the Good, Duke of Burgundy, on 17 February 1454, was without a rival. Thirty-five artists, six joiners and a plumber were needed to design settings which included a wind orchestra playing from inside a pasty. The duke's table was served by two waiters blowing trumpets while sitting back to back on a double-headed horse, then by two men standing on one another's shoulders on an elephant, and by a choirboy riding a stag which sang the tenor part to his melody. The climax came when a live pheasant was led in by a gold and ruby collar, and the duke swore an oath to join a crusade against the Turks. He never did.

Most splendid fête ■ In June 1462 Pope Pius II arranged the celebration of the feast of Corpus Christi in Viterbo, an Italian town near Rome. In preparation he had the street leading from the citadel to the cathedral widened. Each cardinal was then given a section of the street to decorate in a great competition. There were floral arches, fountains of wine, luxuriant tapestries, orchestras, bands and choirs and even beautiful little boys dressed as angels swinging from ropes. Among the exhibits was a young man who, in impersonating Christ, sweated blood and filled a cup from a wound in his side. A tableau showed the Last Supper, while St Michael beheaded a huge dragon from which 'demons fell headlong baying like hounds'.

Indoor games

First English book ■ *The Game and Playe of Chesse* was the second book printed by Caxton and was published in 1474.

Oldest and most popular Chinese game ■ Of all the diversions ancient and modern known in China in the 15th and 16th centuries, 'the most enduring has been *go*' ('surrounding chess'). Its fascination is such that it was named 'the wooden bewitcher', and it 'can obsess men no less than alcohol or sex'. (*Go* is played on a board of 361 intersections. A slightly smaller version of the game on 289 intersections goes back to at least the early 10th century. The basic objective of the game is to surround one's opponent's pieces.)

Wari was played in West Africa in the 15th century.

Most popular game ■ Throughout Europe this was probably *primero*, an ancestor of modern poker. The bids were different and a hand consisted of four cards, with a deck of only 40 cards.

First known card game ■ About 1450 packs of cards comprising between 36 and 56 cards were common in western Europe. The first known game, *Piquet*, was said to have been invented by the famous French knight, Etienne Vignoles, before 1450 and employed 36 cards.

First playing cards in the New World ■ The sailors who went to America with Christopher Columbus are said to have thrown their playing cards overboard when terrified by a storm. Later they made new cards from the leaves of the copas tree, much to the interest of the Indians, and thereby introduced playing cards to the Americas.

Invention of trumps ■ The Arabs popularized fortune telling with the aid of Tarot cards in Europe around 1450 using 22 cards. These cards were added to the existing ones to form a pack of up to 78 cards and were used as trumps in play.

Sport

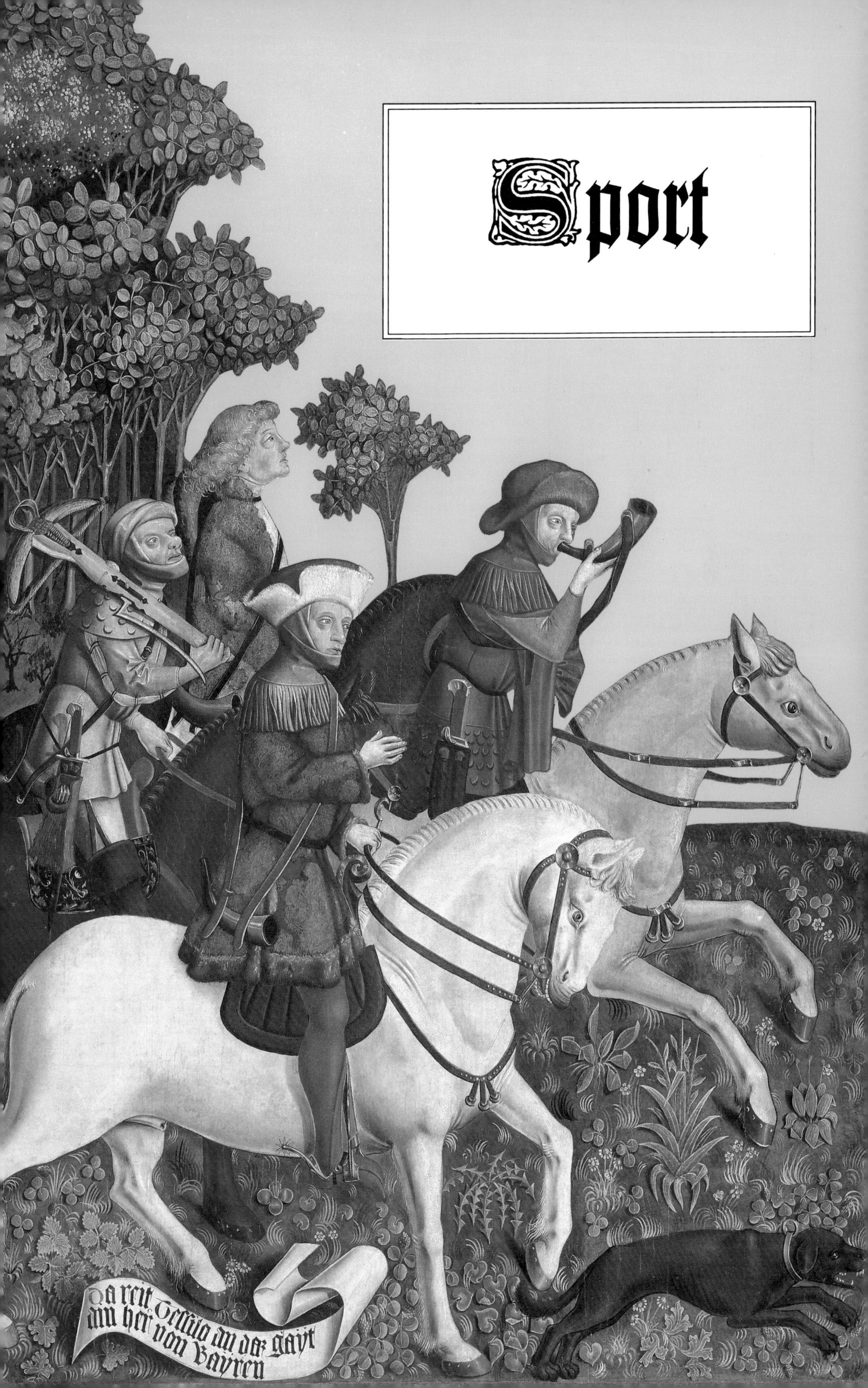
Da reit Tessilo an der gayt
ain her von Bayren

Sport

Sport stems from the time when self-preservation ceased to be the all-consuming human preoccupation. Archery, although a hunting skill in Mesolithic times (by *c.* 8000 BC), did not become an organized sport until later, possibly as early as *c.* 1150 BC, as an archery competition is described in Homer's *Iliad*, and certainly by *c.* 300 AD, among the Genoese. The earliest dated evidence is *c.* 2750–2600 BC for wrestling.

Target archery was common in every town and village in England during the 15th century. It was usually held each Sunday after morning service when all males between 16 and 60 years assembled at the butts. The butts were mounds of earth faced with a straw-filled canvas target about 18 in 45 cm in diameter. Two of these would be provided at a distance of 220 yd 201 m apart.

Government Acts of England and Scotland ensured that the archers kept up their practising in case of war, and were proclaimed several times between 1457 and 1483. The Scottish Act of 1457 said: 'Shooting at the butts is to be practised every Sunday from Easter to Allhallows (1 November), each man having to shoot six shots at least under fine of two pence to be paid as drink money to those present.'

Archery

Early competitions ■ By 1450 in Germany and Switzerland, the walled towns had long-established guilds of crossbowmen who were ready to defend the town against Turkish invaders. These crossbowmen practised each Sunday afternoon at the local target range and shot at about 130 paces. The winner received a prize of a hose or a pair of breeches and was appointed the buttmaster (who signalled hits) the following Sunday. Open competitions *Freischiessen* (free shooting) and *Schutzenfesten* (shooting festivals) were held several times a year.

Annual target shooting competitions were held in the Royal Animal Park in Prague (Czechoslovakia) with large marquees to accommodate up to 800 archers.

First inter-town annual contest ■ Competitions for target archery with the crossbow were held twice, and sometimes four times, a year in Lucca, Italy, in the latter half of the 15th century. There was also an annual contest between the two Italian towns of San Sepolcro and Gubbio.

First international competitions ■ In 1467 the crossbowmen of Zürich travelled by boat the 150 miles *240 km* to a competition in Strasbourg. 1504 saw Zürich send out hundreds of invitations to Schwabia, Bavaria, Tyrol, northern Italy and Flanders, and accommodation with food was provided free. The top seven bowmen received prizes. In 1540 about 1000 competitors took part in a contest in Liestal, Switzerland.

Popinjay shooting ■ *Papegai* (French for popinjay or parrot) shooting originated in Flanders and was the most popular form of competition in Holland, Belgium and northern France in the 15th and 16th centuries. The popinjay was made either of wood or leather and was placed upon a pole as high as 85 ft *26 m* and shot at by the crossbowmen. In 1512 when the future Charles V of Germany was 12 years old he was proclaimed king of the popinjay at the annual contest in Brussels.

Popinjay shooting was also popular in other parts of Europe such as Dresden, Germany, where the *Kronenbolzen* (Society of Crossbowmen) shot at a gaily coloured wooden eagle on top of a 13 ft *4 m* high pole. The bird was made up to 50 pieces and prizes were given according to the value of the piece dislodged by a blunt bolt.

Unequalled archer ■ Henry VIII of England used to have competitions with his 100 Yeomen of the Guard and often did well at shooting both informally and at their annual shoot at Totehill, London. In 1510 it was reported: 'His grace shotte as strong and as greate a lengthe as anie of his garde.' In 1513 he '. . . surprised his guard by clefting the mark in the middle'. In 1520, when he attended the Field of the Cloth of Gold outside Calais, Henry repeatedly shot into the centre of the mark at 240 yd *220 m*. Paul Jovius reported: 'No man in the Dominions drew the English bow more vigorously than Henry himselfe, no man shot further or with more unerring aim.'

Longest distances ■ Flight or distance shooting was the great interest of Persian and Turkish archers. They shot enormous distances with the stronger and larger Tartar crossbow. In Turkey the archers often exceeded 1000 *gez* (arrow lengths) 680 yd *622 m* and there exist today marble pillars at Ok Meydan (Place of the Arrows) in Constantinople to commemorate the distances achieved.

Most regulated ■ The followers of Confucius in 15th- and 16th-century China still followed the rules of archery practice as laid down in the Book of Sentences: 'An Emperor to shoot at 120 yards *110 m*, a King at 80 yards *73m*, a Mandarin at 70 yards *64 m* and a Man of Letters at 50 yards *46m*.' The tradition in China was that 'A Lord who could not hit the target was not an able and virtuous man.' Much of this philosophy spread into neighbouring countries such as Korea, Vietnam, Burma and Thailand. Archery was practised both on foot and on horseback in the Mongolian style.

Longest Japanese bow ■ The Japanese used two types of bow; the composite bow made of three strips of wood glued together and the *Yumi* (longbow) which could be up to 8 ft 6 in *2.6 m* long. *Kyūdō* (way of the archer) was performed on foot at targets of 90–200 ft *27–61 m* distance.

Most arrows ■ Archery was probably practised by all tribes in North America. The first explorer to mention archery skill was Le Moyne in 1539 on his expedition to east Florida. Speed shooting was the speciality of the Apaches of North America, who could have up to 10 arrows in the air at one time. The Pawnee of Nebraska, however, were fond of gambling with their arrows. The first shot across a certain marker qualified the shooter to collect all the arrows that had been previously shot.

Shooting at the Qabaq (a ball on the top of a pole) from horseback was a favourite sport of Sultan Mehmed II (1451–81); the most expert archer used the Parthian shot (shooting backwards).

Shooting

Earliest regulations ■ Regulations for competition shooting were formed at Magdeburg about 1450, at Leipzig in 1464

PREVIOUS PAGE: A nobleman goes out hunting escorted by three servants, one bearing a crossbow.

and at Basel in 1466. Competitors were allowed to use their own gun or one belonging to a near relative. They were allowed three practice shots and held their gun while in the standing position usually with the stock of the gun tucked under the arm. The igniter was required to light the fuse of the gun at a word of command from the competitor. Square or round boards were shot at and only hitting the target counted. Three misfires counted as a 'shot'.

First hand-gun societies ■ *Buchsenschutzen* (town hand-gun societies) became popular in the late 15th century and many town societies in Germany formed themselves into leagues.

The international Schutzenfest *or shooting festival held at Zürich in Switzerland in 1504 was probably the greatest shooting event of the time.*

First hand-gun society in England ■ The *hacquebut* was in use in England from about 1483 but received little encouragement until 1511 when Henry VIII (1509–1547) was monarch. In 1537 he issued a royal patent to the Guild of St George 'to shoot with longbow, crossbow and hand-gun at all manner of marks and butts and at the art of popinjay'.

Heaviest Scottish hand-gun ■ In Scotland in the early 16th century King James IV (1488–1513) shot at the butts with *Culverying* (a large hand-gun with a ¾ in *20 mm* bore weighing 30 lb *13.6 kg*), which required a rest and two men to handle it.

First hand-guns in Japan ■ The Portuguese introduced the hand-gun to Japan in 1543 and we learn that Lord Tokitaka's vassals were able to score 100 hits with 100 shots!

First rifling ■ Rifling is attributed to both Gaspard Kollner of Vienna and Augustas Kotter of Nuremberg in about 1498. They incorporated straight grooves in the gun-barrel to cause bullet spin and greater accuracy. By 1500, Emperor Maximilian I (1493–1519) possessed such a gun. Rifling did not become popular because it was commonly believed that the bullet was bewitched. *Der Hexenmamme* (Hammer of the Witches), published in 1487, describes the means by which the devil could influence marksmanship!

Most magic bullets ■ In 1522 it was stated that 'no devil could stay astride a spinning bullet of a sinful world'. As late as 1547, there was a supervised test at Mainz, in Germany, with lead and silver bullets. The latter had been suitably blessed and inscribed with a cross, yet not one hit the target at 200 yd *180 m*, while 19 of the 20 lead ones did! The makers of the lead bullets were accused of magic.

From 1420 there was a great interest in handguns for the defence of German towns. In 1420 the town of Eger held 'target shooting with hand-cannon', as also did Nuremberg in 1430 and 1433. In 1431 the council of Frankfurt-am-Main decreed that 'every burgher capable of bearing arms had to be equipped with a hand cannon'. Probably the earliest guild for **Buchsen** ***(hand-guns) was that founded at Lucerne, Switzerland, in 1446.***

About 1450 there were several major inventions related to the hand-gun. Gunpowder was manufactured in granular form, holding together the sulphur, charcoal and saltpetre for effective explosion. A metal bead was added to the gun barrel itself for a foresight, and a notch placed for a rear-sight, making for greater accuracy. Finally, springs were used in conjunction with a serpentine lever to ignite the charge. These advances took more than 30 years to be implemented, owing to superstition and prejudice against such innovations.

Longest range ■ Most of the early hand-guns were made in the Nuremberg area or in northern Italy. The typical 15th-century hand-gun was 36–51 in *90–130 cm* long and weighed 13–33 lb *6–15 kg*. The shooting range became longer as the hand-gun became more efficient. It had reached 230 paces in Zürich in 1472 and 245 paces at Eichstadt in 1477 while up to 280 paces was not unknown by 1550.

Closest targets ■ The Kofbibliothek Vienna code 2952 of about 1460 exposes the limitations of early hand-guns when it states: 'Shooting for hand-cannons at birds, animals and other objects to be at 16 paces' (virtually point-blank range!). Rapid improvement in range came within the next 20 years.

Most famous festivals ■ The *Schutzenfest* in Zürich in 1504 was probably the grandest and most famous event of its kind. It attracted no fewer than 405 *Buchsen* (hand-guns) from Switzerland, Austria and Germany with all visitors being freely housed and their travel expenses paid.

Boxing

Most unusual forms ■ The island of Flores in Indonesia had a unique style called *bajawah* boxing. It took the form of a ritual, where opponents were guided by a partner from behind who lightly held shoulders or arms as appropriate.

Tongan matches were arranged on a ritual challenge basis. Boxers would walk sideways in a stepped swagger. They bound their hands with cords for protection. Blows were handed out swiftly, sometimes delivering a blow and spinning on the heel and giving a backhander to their opponent with their other fist. When a boxer was knocked down, the song of victory was sung.

The *mokomo* (boxing) season in Hawaii lasted from mid-October to mid-January, when youths of different villages gathered to fight each other. A ring was formed by spears being placed in the ground and the fights were controlled by a referee with a stick. *Lua* was a combination of boxing, wrestling and bone dislocation. It was practised by the secret service warriors of Hawaiian chiefs.

Most notable Siamese duel ■ Boxing in Thailand claims an Indian origin. The combatants bound their hands, and perhaps their ankles, with hemp and glue. From 1411, in the kingdom of Siam, duels were fought with fists and feet with the winner drawing first blood. Fights often took place at village fairs. One Siamese duel is said to have lasted seven hours.

Mass fighting ■ Many cities and towns in northern Italy organized various types of mass fighting as a safety valve to civic stability. Townsfolk were given the opportunity to work out their grudges on one another by pitting one *contrada* (district) against another. Originally, mass stone fights were popular, but about 1280, the town of Gubbio substituted a *giuoco della pugna* (fisticuffs fight) while in 1291 Siena followed suit. In Pisa a great battle was fought in 1494; when Charles V, the Emperor of Germany, visited Siena in 1536 a contest was arranged in his honour.

Wrestling

First France v. England match ■ The most famous wrestlers in England were the Cornishmen who used hugging and heaving techniques from a standing position until one opponent was thrown. King Henry VIII went to Calais in France with his Cornish wrestlers, who stood behind their banner which depicted a wrestler in a hitch. The Cornishmen wrestled with the French, as did Henry VIII with Francis I of France on the same occasion. Henry challenged Francis with the words: 'Brother, we will wrestle.' Francis could not refuse. Henry had height and weight in his favour, but Francis tripped him in the French style and won the contest, although the English thought this an unfair trick.

Most styles ■ There were over 20 styles of folk wrestling in what later became the USSR. Belt wrestling was considered to be an Asian style and was known in Azerbaijan as the Turkish *kresh*, in Armenia as *kokh* and was also practised in northern parts of Russia and in Finland. Jacket gripping wrestling prevailed in Georgia and part of Armenia, and the modern Russian *sambo* wrestling gets its name from the two folk styles of *samozashchita* (self-defence) and *bez-orvschiya* (without weapons): Sam + b-o. The objective of jacket wrestling was to throw the opponent onto his back and then indulge in ground wrestling using severe locks.

Slipperiest wrestlers ■ The traditional Turkish wrestling of the Ottomans, called *yagli*, required the combatant to oil himself from head to foot and soak his leather breeches in water to make them supple. After 1453, the Sultans kept *gouressis* (free men from India and Tartary) of great strength as expert wrestlers, which gave rise to the expression, 'as strong as a Turk'.

Most terrible sport ■ In 15th-century Hindu southern India wrestling went under the name of *vajramushiti*. It was a wrestling-cum-boxing sport with the aid of spiked 'knuckle-dusters'. As the Hindu god of strength, Hanuman, held a club in his hand, the winner of a fight was often given a wooden club as a prize. A champion was known as a *Rustam-I-Hind* until beaten by another champion.

Greatest number of moves ■ When the Mughuls became established at Delhi in 1526, each prince had a 'stable' of wrestlers. The style employed was called *guile* and over 400 moves had to be learnt which led to the title of *pulwan* (expert).

Unique armoured wrestling ■ *Sumai* (struggle) was an early form of Japanese sumo wrestling and was popular in the 15th and 16th centuries with farmworkers as the feudal lords discouraged the Samurai from using it. The sport was more akin to the Mongolian belt style but allowed lethal blows and kicks. The Samurai had more interest in *yoroi kumi uchi* (wrestling in wooden armour). The first school for this style was founded in the 15th century. In Okinawa, *teguni* was the prevalent wrestling style in the 15th century. It was a grappling and rushing style fought in ordinary clothes.

First book ■ The first book wholly devoted to wrestling was anonymously published by Hans Wurm in Landshot, Germany, in 1507. German wrestling was a catch-as-catch-can style similar to that practised in most of France.

Sword art

Oldest swordsmanship school in Japan ■ The 15th century was a high point for *kenjutsu* (swordsmanship with steel blade) in Japan. Each *daimyo* (lord) would employ a master of the sport in his *dojo* (hall). By 1450 the Higuchi family were the principal teachers of the sword, and operated a *ryu* (school). Dozens of other schools were founded in the 15th century and great secrecy was attached to their methods. The oldest school was probably Tenshin Shoden Katori Shinu Ryu near Sawara city. Its master, Izasa Ienao, was instructor to Yoshimasa, the ninth Ashkaga *Shogun* (supreme military leader) (1435–1490).

Sharpest sword blade ■ The weapon used for *kenjutsu* was called a *katana* (regular sword) and techniques of *kiri* (cutting), *tsuki* (thrusting) were practised at clearly defined target areas. The *wakizashi* (short sword) and the *nodachi* (long sword) were also in vogue. *Iaijutsu* exponents were traditionally required to use a razor-sharp sword. Some samurai warriors who wished to test the sharpness of a sword lay in wait for an unsuspecting passer-by and tried to cut off his head with one sweep of the sword.

Most famous Japanese swordsman ■ Tsukahara Bokuden (1490–1571), who founded the Mutenkatsu school, was the most famous Japanese swordsman of the 16th century. He had previously studied at both the Katori Shinto and the Kage schools for 14 years. He was undefeated in 37 challenge matches using a steel sword, 17 challenges being fights to the death. Bokuden is said to have given his name to the *bokken* (wooden sword).

Most dangerous sport ■ *Yadomejusu* (art of arrow deflection with a sword) was only performed by the most proficient Japanese swordsmen. The height of admiration was won in ignoring those arrows that only just missed you. *Iaijutsu* (sword drawing) was another specialized art that was developed in the 15th century. A *bushi* (warrior) called Hayashizaki Jinsuke Shigenobu devised *iaido* (drawing of the sword in many different ways) and was the greatest exponent of this martial art in the 16th century.

Staff fighting

First Japanese wooden sword ■ Training with the steel sword was usually practised alone as it was too dangerous to fight an opponent. With the introduction of the *jojutsu* (fighting stick) and the *bokken* (wooden sword with the same weight and balance as a real sword) about 1530, the art of sword fighting advanced.

***Bojutsu** (art of the staff) was a Japanese sport in the 16th century, similar to the English quarter-staff fighting, with both hands gripping a **5 ft 1.5 m bo** (staff). In Okinawa the staff was **6 ft 1.8 m** long. Movements with the staff were extremely dynamic.*

Greatest exponents ■ The greatest exponent of the *yari* (spear) and *naginata* (halberd) in Japan was Choisal Ienad (died 1481). Kansuke Yorinori Yamamoto was another Japanese *yari* master (died 1561) who was commonly known as 'one-eyed' Yamamoto. His favourite practice technique was to cut water in a flowing stream.

Japanese Samurai swordsmen practising their art with swords that would have been razor-sharp.

Martial arts

First scientific approach ■ The background to Chinese unarmed combat or art of the *kung-fu* (empty hand) was the ancient Shaolin Temple boxing which existed in the 15th and 16th centuries. The Chinese were the first to develop their sport scientifically by studying the natural action of animals.

Most innovative styles ■ Various styles of unarmed combat prevailed, championed by various families. The *Ch'a Ch'uan* style was quite widespread, having a following in the north, but particularly in the south and west of China. The *Ch'en* style was created in the 15th century by Ch'en-chia-kou in Honan province. *Ta-sheng-men* was a *kung-fu* art based upon the movements of monkeys, incorporating crouching defensive positions and aggressive leaps, and was popular in the Hong Kong area in the 15th century. *Shauai-chiad* involved wrestling techniques of matwork, strikes, kicks and blocks and was found in north China.

Earliest disabling method ■ The taller Chinese of the north excelled in kicking techniques while the boating people of the rivers and coastal places leaned more heavily on wrestling styles. However, all secret society members were skilled in the identification of pressure points for disabling purposes.

First karate chops ■ In 1470 the second Shō dynasty of Okinawa, the west Pacific island, was established. King Shō Shir (*c.* 1477–1526) disarmed local lords and required them to live in the capital, Shuri. This state of affairs led to a great interest in *te* (hand fighting) by the Okinawans. The art of *tamashiwara* (trial by fist) was also developed, whereby the wooden armour of the occupying soldiers was broken by the force of a bare fist. These fighting techniques gave rise to the sport of *karate*.

Malayan dream ■ The legendary 15th-century Huan Tuah of Malaya has been credited with spreading a form of *jūjitsu* across the Malayan peninsula through his extensive travellings. *Bersilat* (self-defence) was akin to *jūjitsu*. Tradition has it that, in 1511, a woman by the name of Bersilat at the royal court dreamt of a fight without weapons. The omen was so potent that the royal army adopted a method of self-defence known as *Bersilat*. The art did not include kicking as this was considered very rude. It was not long before each village formed an army of Bersilat-trained warriors.

Greatest Japanese fighters ■ There were three forms of unarmed combat in 15th–16th-century Japan: wrestling, boxing and *yawara* (peacemaker), which was an early form of *jujitsu*. It was the duty of every *samurai* (warrior) to be proficient in these arts and he was feared because of his fighting ability.

Shadow fighting ■ *Kempo* (vigour of the fist) was a Chinese art imported into Japan. It combined boxing and unarmed combat styles mimicking the movements of animals. Its practice technique gave rise to shadow boxing and was popular with Japanese secret societies in the 15th and 16th centuries.

Wrestling was a popular spectator sport enjoyed by the nobility of Persia (now Iran).

Most deadly combat ■ *Kumi uchi* (grappling), which developed into sumo wrestling, was practised by the samurai. The objective was to force an opponent into unconditional surrender or, if not, kill him. Fights were organized to appease the gods at the annual harvest festival. At the Muso Jikidon School, wrestling in 80 lb *36 kg* wooden armour was practised. Choiisa Ienao was master at the school in the 15th century and devised 100 combat techniques called *yawara gi* (harmony). In the early part of the 16th century, the Takenouchi school was founded and it was here, in 1532, that Hisamori Takenouchi systemised *jūjitsu*.

Most severe training ■ In Japan of the 15th century the *samurai* went through a punishing seven or eight years of martial art training. They had to be expert in at least six arts: empty hand fighting, *bojujutsu* (staff fighting), *naginata* (halberd fighting), *hanbojutsu* (sword) and *kodachijutsu* (short sword skills).

Most efficient weapons ■ The Majaphit Sultans and their court officials of Indonesia found that a variety of weapon suitable to the individual was most efficient. The combined art of combat was called *penjjak silat*. At different courts in west or central Java, Sumatra, Bali, Celebes, Madura and Flores, several weapons were favoured: swords, axes, spears, sticks, sickles, chains, daggers. Unarmed combat was also employed.

Most unlikely weapon ■ When the Spanish arrived in the Philippines in the early 16th century they forbade the martial arts they found. These included a form of *jūjitsu*, wooden swords and daggers, the lance, the shoe art, the rope art, the fan art and the palm stick art, but the most surprising of all was the art of yo-yo. From behind a tree the warrior would direct his yo-yo and score a hit between the eyes of his antagonist. The yo-yo was also used for hunting.

Gymnastics

Highest performers ■ Touring round Europe was a small select band of rope walkers like the Spaniard who performed in front of Prince Edward in London in 1546, by sliding down a rope ('on his breast, head forward, arms spread out') that was attached to the spire of St Paul's Church. He probably used a grooved board. A little later a Dutchman performed a balancing routine on the weathercock of St Paul's, 'kneeling, standing on one foot and waving a streamer five yards long'.

Origins of the gymnastic horse ■ About 1450, the gymnastic wooden horse was introduced into Italy from the Arabs in Sicily. This apparatus was used for the winter pastime of *nel saltare cavalle* (to leap over a wooden horse).

Origins of jūjutsu ■ The Japanese nobles or warlords of the 15th and 16th centuries supported gymnastic and martial arts activities at their various courts. These were finger power exercises, pressure pushing head to head, hand against hand or foot against foot, and a system of isometric exercises. Also there was balancing on hands and fists and tug-of-war with a partner. Popular was *taijutsue* (body art), also known as *hakuda*, which was systemized by Hisamori Takenouchi in 1532 and developed into *jūjutsu*.

Running

Greatest endurance ■ The American Indian runners with greatest endurance were the Tarahumare of the north Mexican Sierra Madre at an elevation of 7000–8000 ft *2134–2240 m*. It was reported that when the Spanish conquered Mexico in 1519 they found the local *titlantic* (messengers) carrying hides covered in hieroglyphics. Hernán Cortés wrote that, within 24 hours of his landing at Chianiztlan in 1519, 'runners had described to Moctezuma, 260 miles *416 km* away, his ships, men and horses. The Tarahumare Indian could run from Guazapares to Chihuahua and back, a distance of nearly 600 miles *960 km* in five days.'

The Zuni of Arizona and New Mexico started training for running from the age of five. They had a reputation for never being beaten; their neighbours, Hopi, were also excellent long-distance runners. One of their number ran 120 miles *190 km* in 15 hours to deliver a message.

Fastest Americans ■ The Spaniard Cabeza de Vaca witnessed endurance races by trained runners, and described later: 'There is not a buffalo in the nations of Louisiana they cannot run down.'

Log runners ■ In Brazil near the mouth of the Amazon River live the Payacu Indians. From the 16th century there was a tradition of the sport of log-running for both men and women. The race by teams of runners took place along a prepared trackway up to 10 miles *16 km* long. Palm tree logs weighing 100–200 lb *220–440 kg* were shouldered. In the earlier stages stronger men were able to carry the logs 150 yd *135 m* before passing the log to a team member. As the runners tired the running stages became progressively shorter.

Weightlifting

Strongest weightlifters ■ The staggering weight of 1000 lb *454 kg* was reputedly lifted with one hand by an unknown athlete in China.

In southern Germany and Switzerland the most spectacular sport of the many *Schutzenfesten* (shooting festivals) was the stone lifting competition. Large stones with handles at either end were used for weightlifting, with lifting above the head the ultimate achievement. In 1470 at Augsburg Duke Wilhelm IV won the prizes in the running, jumping and weightlifting events. He lifted a stone of 400 lb *181 kg* with two hands.

Duke Christopher of Bavaria (1449–93) was a giant of a man, being 12 'shoes' tall – at least 8 ft 11 in *2.27 m* ! In the courtyard of the castle in Munich is a stone which weighs 400 lb *181 kg* and above it is an inscription: 'Duke Christopher of Bavaria lifted it in 1490 and threw it away from him.'

Lifting heavy weights among the Basques of France and Spain was popular in the 15th and 16th centuries. They lifted cylinders of stone weighing up to 440 lb *200* kg above their heads.

Hunting

Organized hunting is well over 5000 years old. In Mesopotamia the Sumerians hunted the lion, as various reliefs and the Uruk Stele show. In the 15th and 16th centuries the stag was the prize quarry in western Europe among the nobility, while the boar and bear were considered formidable prey owing to their ferocity. Other animals commonly hunted were the hare, fox, otter, badger and, in desert countries, the gazelle.

Most determined hunters ■ Prince Henry, the future Henry VIII (1509–47), hunted with his sister Margaret and Catherine of Aragon, and hunting soon became a passion with him. In 1519 the Venetian Ambassador reported that Henry tired out 8–10 horses while out hunting. His favourite method was to hunt *par force*, constantly tracking deer across country with *lymers* (scenting dogs), then using his buck hounds to wear down the quarry and finally releasing greyhounds to chase and pull down the victim. He would station relays of dogs and horses at strategic places to facilitate a hunt that could last until dusk and occupy up to nine hours. As king, Henry conducted a hunting progress from late June to mid-September each year and travelled from deer park to deer park across the country. With him went a retinue of his court followers: courtiers, huntsmen, a company of archers and many staff with dozens of carts laden with tents, dogs and *toils* (canvas or net fencing used to direct the deer along certain routes). These *toils* could be many miles long.

For his French contemporary Francis I (1515–1547) a typical grand hunt would involve 400–500 gentlemen riders, 200 mounted horsemen and grooms along with 100 pages. The king and gentlemen rode in smart red habits. The annual cost of his hunting amounted to the great sum of 150 000 crowns.

Most obsessive hunter ■ Maximilian I (1493–1519), the Holy Roman Emperor, was obsessed with killing hundreds of deer and other game and kept a detailed record of his achievements in a manuscript called *Geheime Jagdbuch* (Secret Book of Hunting) and another, *Weiskunis und Tierdank*, which describes his adventures in the hunting field. He kept over 1500 hounds. Maximilian organized great *Battues* (round-ups) using hundreds of local peasants, and shot at all kinds of game from elegant pavilions.

Most famed huntress ■ Diane de Poitiers (1499–1566), mistress of Henry II of France, was a renowned huntress. Almost daily she was out at daybreak for three hours of sport. She possibly hunted with Catherine de' Medici, wife of Henry II from 1533, who was also a notable huntress.

Most spectacular hunting ■ King Louis XII of France (1498–1515) was interested in hunting spectacles. He introduced the *venerie des toiles* (a semi-circular barrier at the edge of the forest), with the help of 100 of his archers who organized hunting matters for him. There he waited with his courtiers for the deer and other animals to be driven into the *toils* so they could shoot them at leisure.

Most unusual sport ■ King Ferdinand (1474–1516) and Queen Isabella (1474–1504) were both addicted to the hunt and Ferdinand actually died out hunting. The unusual sport of paddock coursing of deer was first introduced to Spain in the late 15th century. A screened avenue about 1600 yd *1500 m* was constructed and used for greyhounds to chase deer. The dogs were carefully trained for speed and large prizes rested upon the results of these races where the betting was unusually heavy.

Hunting dogs

Most uncommon ■ Francis I of France (1515–47) was an avid beagler and hunted hares on foot with a pack of *petits chiens de la Loire* (a kind of large beagle from the Loire.) Francis had lynxes at his court which were trained to catch hares and were transported on horseback pillion-style behind the huntsmen.

Most famous breed ■ In Germany, the Low Countries, Spain and Italy the mastiff dogs used in boar hunting wore spiked collars and padded dog coats of great thickness to protect them from the boars' tusks. The most famous breed of boar-fighting

Simon Bening's end of a stag hunt illustrated the months of November and December in the Grimani Breviary.

dogs was the extremely fierce mastiff Alaunts which originated in Spain.

Most unusual bed companions ■ In the 15th century, Prince John of Portugal had a passion for bear hunting and, being a somewhat eccentric character, slept nightly with his two favourite Alaunt mastiffs, Bravor and Rabez, on either side of him.

First pack of white hounds ■ Louis XI of France (1461–83) was a habitual hunter who spent the whole day from dawn to dusk in the hunting field. His daughter, Princess Anne (1460–1522), was just as enthusiastic as her father and during her regency (1483–9) set a lasting fashion of using pure white hunting hounds, instead of the usual grey and black ones.

A lady joins the occasion of hawking for herons and other water fowl in this Italian 15th century illustration of a treatise on hunting and falconry. Dogs were sent into the watery marshes to retrieve the fallen birds.

Largest number of cheetahs ■ In desert lands, the gazelle replaced the deer as the principal quarry. The Moors and Berbers of North Africa were fond of coursing gazelles with cheetahs. The cheetah was also extensively used to hunt in Persia, Kashmir and India for gazelle, tiger, wild pig and hare. The Mughul rulers of India from 1526 had kennels for over 1000 cheetahs.

Stickiest trapping ■ According to the Chinese writer Xie Zhaozhi the method used by mountain folk in China to defend themselves against tigers was to find a gap in a bank through which the tigers were accustomed to jump, and hang there a network of large ropes. 'When a tiger jumps into it, he will be caught in mid-air as he descends, entangled in the ropes, his four paws sticking into empty space, unable to make use of his power, or to escape.' Another method was to spread the ground with glue made from the pith of twigs and at right-angles to the tiger's paths. When the tiger's head encountered this substance, he would feel it sticking to him and claw at it without being able to get it off. At this point he would sit down and in an instant his entire body would be covered with the glue. He would then roar in anger and leap and thrash about until he died.'

Most effective way to shoot a tiger ■ According to the Chinese writer Xie Zhaozhi: 'When the northern barbarians shoot tigers, they need only two strong men to shoot them with their bows. When a tiger is shot *against* the nap of his fur, the arrow will penetrate, but if it strikes *with* the lie of the fur, it will not go in. Therefore the first bowman guides his horse to flee from the tiger while the second shoots from behind. If the tiger turns round, the bowmen reverse roles. Even numerous tigers can be immediately finished off in this way.'

Hawking

Best birds ■ There was a strict social order in Europe as to the suitability of a specific type of hawk for a particular person. An emperor should use an eagle, vulture or merlin, a king should use a gyr-falcon or tercel gyr-falcon, while a prince was allowed a falcon-gentle or tercel-gentle. For an earl, the falcon-peregrine was deemed suitable and for a baron a bustard. The knight was expected to use a sacre or sacret and his esquire a langere or laneret and so it went on: a marlyn for a lady, a hobby for a young man, a goshawk for a yeoman.

First books ■ *The Boke of Saint Albans*, of 1486, was the first book on hunting and hawking printed in English. The first French book, *Livre de l'Art de Fauconnerie* (Book of the Art of Falconry) by Guillaume Tardie, professor at the College of Navarre and tutor to Charles VII, was published in 1492.

Most selfish hawker ■ James IV of Scotland (1488–1513) was a keen hawker and even passed a law in 1493 to reserve heron hawking solely for himself.

Greatest royal hawker ■ Francis I (1515–1547) of France built a magnificent royal mews with over 300 hawks, a *grand fauconnier*, 50 noblemen falconers and 50 other falconers and many more in the lower positions. In the latter part of his reign it became popular to hawk with the ladies and, as one writer puts it: 'They eat a lot, drink a lot, laugh a lot and love the ladies.' Giovanni de' Medici, or Pope Leo X (1513–1521), was an inveterate falconer. He was said to have spent more time hawking than with affairs of the church.

Cruellest poaching law ■ The Duke of Burgundy, Philip the Good, who died in 1467, had a large hawking establishment with a Master of Falconry, 12 falconers, 24 valets (boys), 12 under-valets and six bird netters. To curb the theft of hawks a law peculiar to Burgundy was enforced. Anyone caught stealing a hawk had flesh ripped from his breast by the bird he stole.

Training school ■ There was a famous falconry training school at Marienburg, Germany, run by the Grand Master of the Order of Teutonic Knights. It supplied falcons to the aristocracy of all western Europe.

Most enthusiastic falconers ■ The Arabs and Turks of the Middle East and North Africa were the most enthusiastic of all hawkers. This enthusiasm spilt over into Spain which considered the art of hawking above that of hunting. The Arabs' prize hawk was the saker (similar to the large peregrine), which was used to hunt small gazelles in the desert. In combination with a greyhound, the hawk attacked the gazelle which enabled the greyhound to catch up with the faster gazelle and seize it.

Cockfighting

Most 'holy' cockpits ■ A favourite venue for cockfighting in England was the churchyard. As the cockfighting season went from September to May, many a battle took place inside the church. At York, the pit was adjacent to the cathedral, to satisfy the 'devotion' of the cathedral dean! At Canterbury, part of St Augustine's Monastery provided indoor facilities for fights. In 1535, Henry VIII had an indoor pit built at Whitehall, London, near the site of the present-day Prime Minister's residence, 10 Downing Street.

First recorded inter-county match ■ In England in 1546, such a match was held between Lancashire, Derbyshire and Hallamshire. Cocks were matched according to judgement of size.

Bullfighting

Most memorable Caccia ■ From Italy's earliest days *Caccia de Tori* (bullfights) had been held from time to time. The sport was particularly popular in Siena from about 1480 to 1590, when it was suppressed. The *Piazza* was boarded and each *contrada* (city district) led out its own bull into the arena. A huge decorated wooden machine was wheeled into a strategic position to serve as a refuge from the bulls when the tormenting of the bull began. In 1546 there was a memorable *Caccia* with the arena filled with bulls, wild beasts, stags, badgers, porcupines, foxes and hares.

America ■ There is a tradition that bullfighting took place in both Mexico and Peru before the middle of the 16th century.

Equestrian sports

Japan ■ The first known school of horsemanship in Japan, called *Otsubo*, was founded in the 15th century, to teach 50 different techniques. *Jo Bajutsu* (Japanese horsemanship), was a strict form of equestrian training, devoted to warfare, the aim being complete synchronization between horse and rider. Techniques of whirling on hindquarters, rearing, silent stalking and horse swimming were taught.

Dressage ■ The father of the new art of dressage was Battista Pignatelli of Naples, Italy, who, together with his protégé, Frederico Grisone, developed *c.* 1505 dressage movements for the heavier horse. They utilized the high step, elegant trot, vigorous canter and stretching jump.

Most brilliant royal display ■ When Henry VIII organized a great tournament in 1520, near Calais, 'the Field of the Cloth of Gold', he put on an outstanding display of horsemanship, to the 'delight and ecstasy of everyone'. He is said to have tired six horses while performing a thousand jumps! At another tournament, several thousand spectators watched Henry parade in blue velvet livery, followed by 24 pages similarly dressed. He then performed his equestrian routine on several white horses.

First French riding book ■ In Paris in 1533 Laurentius Lusius published his book *Hippiatrica Sive Marescalia* (Horseriding or Riding of Horses and Mares), which advised locking up a 'nappy' horse for 40 days to break its spirit. He also recommended the use of a clawed rod to move the horse forward and, in extreme cases, a heated bar under its tail.

Horse racing

Earliest racing stables ■ About 1450 there is a tradition that Queen Margaret of Anjou, wife of Henry VI of England, kept horses at Eltham Place and raced them. Before 1520, Henry had in his employ the Keeper of the King's running geldings named Davyson. Each Easter the king apparently held a horse race which gave rise to much betting at court. There were professional jockeys who were usually boys under 15 years of age. By 1530 there were four of 'the king's riding children' or 'running boys' at Greenwich and Windsor who rode Barbary horses. They wore 'ryding cappes of black veilvte and 22 buton of golde to garnish them'. There was even a bath for the Barbary horses and oil to rub their legs.

Most famous Irish racecourse ■ The most famous race track in Ireland is the Curragh which was certainly in use during the 15th and 16th centuries.

German races ■ In Augsburg, in 1470, there were no fewer than 466 entries for the horse races, most of whom were knights and burghers. The races were probably run around a large field and the knights' race was won by Duke Wolfgang von Bayern, who pocketed 45 gulden. The burghers had their own races according to status. At Ulm, in 1468, not only was a prize given to the winner but the last rider received a sow! In 1511 the Duke of Wurtemburg advertised his own race by printing and distributing handbills.

Oldest extant race ■ *By 1492 the* Palio *in Siena had been established over 250 years. The races were held over a three-lap semi-circular course around the city square which, in one place, had a steep descent and many nasty corners at which horses were invariably injured or even killed. In the late 15th century, race meetings were held on 20 March, 22 July, 15 August and 26 November. Preparation of the course began two months before the racing season. The jockeys even wore 'crash helmets', not so much to guard against falls, but to protect them against blows from other riders.*

Polo

Polo was a very popular game among the Persian nobility. The game originated in Persia, and was at first used as a form of training for the cavalry. In the 16th century the Englishman George Mainwaring described a polo game at the royal Persian court. Players assembled on 'some acres of ground . . . drums and trumpets sounded, there were twelve horsemen in all with the king; so they divided themselves six on one side and six on the other. Having in their hands long rods of wood about the bigness of a man's finger, and on the end of the rods a piece of wood is nailed on like onto a hammer. After these were divided and turned face to face, there came into the middle, and did throw a wooden ball betwen both companies and, having goals made at either end, they began their sport, striking the ball with their rod from one end to the other . . . and ever when the king had gotten the ball before him, the drums and trumpets would play one alarm.'

Largest permanent field ■ At Isfahan, the old Persian capital, there are remains of a polo ground 300 yd *274 m* long with stone goalposts 8 yd *7.3 m* apart. The game was called *chaugan gui* (stick-games), usually shortened to *chaugan* (stick with bent end).

Largest match ■ In the Citadel of Cairo, in Egypt, 600 mounted Mamluks would, on special occasions, play the game of *lanza*. An Irish monk who witnessed such a game in the mid-15th century said it was very like that 'played by shepherds in Christian countries with a ball and curved sticks except that the Sultan and his nobles never strike the ball unless they are on horseback . . . This resulted in many horses and knights being rendered unfit for active service in the future.' The audience, however, were extremely enthusiastic, especially when the Sultan played well: 'Whenever he would strike a ball the spectators would all cheer and praise him, sounding innumerable trumpets and striking countless harsh kettledrums.'

Most royal player ■ The first Mughul ruler of India was Babur (1494–1530), who was a keen polo player. The game was soon adopted by *nawabs* and *maharajahs* (nobles and princes). They appear to have played a 10-a-side game with much noise from kettledrums to create an air of excitement. Some furious betting also took place.

Strangest game ■ The Chinese game of polo, which was still played in the 15th and 16th centuries, was exported to Japan, where its nature was somewhat changed. *Dakyu* (polo) was practised to promote good horsemanship. It was played in a court 60 × 20 yd *54 × 18m*. There was only one goal which was a vertically placed board or sheet or cloth with an 18 in *45 cm* hole 7 ft *2 m* above the ground. The balls were 1½ in *4 cm* in diameter, coloured red for one team and white for

Polo was a favourite game amongst the Persian nobility, in what is now Iran. This picture illustrated a manuscript of about 1535.

the other. The bamboo polo sticks were 4 ft *1.2 m* long with the end split to take a silk net. There were 4–7 players a side with 7–12 balls allocated to each team. The balls were picked up in the net and thrown at the hole. If the game was a tie, a different-coloured ball was used for the play-off.

Swimming

First swimming schools ■ *Suiei jutsu* (swimming) was popular in Japan in the 15th and 16th centuries. The earliest school for advanced swimming was the Shinden Ryu, established by 1550, which taught a variety of techniques: *fumi ashi* (treading water), *inatob* (a quick exit from the water), *ashi garami* (wrestling in or under water) and *shusoku garami* (swimming with either hands or legs bound).

Earliest 'synchronized' swimming ■ The Egyptians swam in exhibitions for the Caliph. They performed a kind of synchronized upright swim carrying pots of fire above their heads.

Most unusual underwater sport ■ The Polynesians had a peculiar underwater walking competition and would walk as far as they could under water carrying a heavy stone. The place which they reached was marked with a peg and a distance of 70 yd *63 m* was common.

Most noted swimmers ■ The Cuma people of the San Blas Islands off Panama were accomplished swimmers by the age of five years. The coastal Inca tribes of Peru were as at home in the water as on land and were expert at underwater swimming.

First book on swimming ■ Nicholas Wynmann of Zürich, professor of languages at Ingolstadt University, Bavaria, wrote a book on swimming which was published in 1538. Wynmann recommends the breaststroke and running headers into the water. For learners he suggests swimming on rushes, cork or two inflated pigs' bladders.

Rowing and canoeing

First detailed course ■ In Venice there were often races for small ships and gondolas. The first details of a rowing course are those on the 15th-century Venetian canal: 'The race starts at Motta and goes along the Bacino of Santa Marco and then enters the grand canal. The course goes as far as Santa Lucia and here turns to reach Ca Foscari and then the bridge of Macchina where a floating stage is opposite the finish.'

First women's races ■ In 1493 a women's regatta was organized in Venice to celebrate the arrival of Beatrice d'Este, while in 1501 another was held for the visit of King Ladislav of Bohemia (1490–1516). Most of the competitors for the races came from the coastal village of Pellestrina, which had a tradition of female participation in sport.

First women coxes ■ The Sac and Fox Americans of the upper Mississippi region had a tradition of canoe racing with a woman holding the steering paddle.

First American 'regattas' ■ The Chipewyan tribe of Mackenzie Territory, Canada, even held canoe 'regattas'. Among the events was a tug-of-war between two canoes.

Most unusual sport ■ The 15th-century municipal records of Toulon in southern France state: 'It is the custom in the said town that on the second day of Easter seamen and country folk of the region arm boats for jousting at sea which are called *quintaines*.' Two boats each with at least four rowers approached each other head on. A man stood in the prow of each boat armed with a lance and shield. In the port of Cagliari, Italy, similar jousts were performed with swords and shields.

Football (SOCCER)

First professionals ■ The Prior of Bicester in Oxfordshire in the 15th century actually paid football money to the players who played on saints' days.

First regular teams ■ There appear to have been regular football teams or crafts guildsmen who hired the Brewers' Hall in London for annual functions before 1450.

> ***In Europe in the 15th and 16th centuries there were many regional styles of games. Some involved kicking (as in soccer) and others involved kicking, throwing and carrying of a ball (as in rugby football). In Italy, football became highly sophisticated at the end of the 15th century. Kicking games were usually played with a large ball often inflated, while carrying games mostly used a small ball.***

First aristocratic teams ■ The Medici family came to power in Florence in 1459 and became great supporters of the *Calcio*. *Calcio* became more sophisticated before 1490 when football costume came into use

In Italy Giuoco del Calcio *(game of kick or football) dates from the late 14th century in Florence. Before 1450 it was being played in the restricted area of the Piazza Santo Spirito and was described as a* battague *(battle). The game in Florence was most famous, but it was played in virtually all the towns of northern Italy from the 15th century.*

at games played in the Piazza Santo Spirito. From 1492 to 1494, Pietro de' Medici promoted *Calcio* among his nobility in his own palace courtyard. Public matches in the Piazza di Croce became popular and at least three games a year were played by aristocratic teams, two in June and one in August. In 1536 a grand game was played to celebrate the wedding of Alessandro de' Medici to Margaret von Pavia, daughter of Charles V, King of Spain and Emperor of Germany.

First description in England ■ A Scottish poet gave a description of street football in Lincoln around 1450, with the first instance of a prescribed number of players.

Four and twenty bony boys
Were playing at the ba'
And by it came sweet Sir Hugh
And he played o'er them a'
He kicked the ba' with his right foot
He catched it wi' his knee
And through-and-thro the jews' window
He gard the bony ba' flee.

The November slaughtering of pigs and other animals for winter sustenance gave rise to the use of inflated bladders for winter sport, as Alexander Barclay described in 1508:

They get the bladder and blowe it great and then
With many beans or peason put within
It ratleth, soundeth, and sineth cleare and fayre
With foot and with hande the bladder for to smite
If it falls to the grounde they lifte it up agayne
The sturdy plowmen, lustie, stronge and bolde.

Most popular match day ■ The most popular day of the year for football was Shrove Tuesday. In 1539 it was recorded that an annual game had been played 'time out of mind'. 'The shoumacres which tyme out of remembrance have geven and delyvered yerleye upon Teuesday commonly aculed shroft Teuesday, the citie at the cros upon the rood dee one ball of lether, cauled a foutboule.'

Earliest named ground ■ The school rules of Winchester School, England, at the middle of the 16th century include reference to pupils going for games to 'The Hill', which a little later is identified as the school playing field.

First designated football fields ■ In the east of England, in the counties of Norfolk, Essex and particularly in Suffolk, between the rivers Orwell and Alde, there were two types of 'Camping' in the 15th century. These were 'Savage Camp', a carrying-kicking game, and 'Kicking Camp', which was akin to soccer. The latter was played in a Camping Close or Camping Field with goals which were 20 yd *18 m* apart. Savage Camp was played for *snotches*, or points, for possession of the ball. Seven or nine *snotches* constituted a game.

First Italian rules ■ About 1500 the games of the Italian aristocrats were highly organized and played to huge crowds in the principal city squares. At the Santa Croce, Florence, the piazza was fenced around with a wooden palisade. It was 172 *braccici* (arm lengths) long by 86 wide and 2 high. The rules were flexible as to the number of players, but 19 and later 27 players aged 18 to 45 years took part and wore colourful costumes or kit. For a team of 27, there were five *sconciatori* (forwards), seven *datori* (half backs) and 15 *coridori* (scrum). The teams lined up in a pyramid formation, as in rugby football. *Alfiere* (standard-bearers) stood one at each end of the field and conducted a lottery to determine who should stand at the goal ends. Six referees sat aloft from where the ball was thrown in to start the game. Each time the ball passed beyond the palisade a goal was scored. A bugle sounded or drums rolled out and the players changed ends. The players were allowed to carry and run with the ball, but goals could only be scored by a kick or a punch from the hand. If the ball rose above head height, a *fallo* (fault) was called and two faults equalled a *caccia* (goal). A full game lasted about an hour.

On ice ■ Among the populace of Florence, *Calcio* was played throughout the winter, but particularly from January to March. Some celebrated games were played on the frozen river Arno in Florence, the first recorded on 10 January 1492, and others took place in 1514 and 1526. While under siege in 1530 by the forces of Charles V, a game of *Calcio* was played between the whites and greens to divert attention from their hunger. On 17 February, in subsequent years, a game was played to commemorate the event, with a heifer as a prize.

France ■ *La Soule au Pied* (football) was popular in Normandy and Brittany in France. The Easter games at Vieux-Pont, Normandy, commenced after the ball was kicked over the church roof.

China ■ *Tsu chu* (kick ball) was known in the third century BC and has been described as being played in four ways: around a field, in a field, with two goals and with one goal. The first and the last methods were played during the 15th and 16th centuries. In the 16th century a Tao priest from southern China developed the kicking game to include the use of shoulders, chest, bottom and stomach.

Most unusual games ■ The Japanese game of *Hakozaki-Gu-Notama-Seseri* was played annually, on 3 January, between two teams at the Hakozaki shrine in Fukuoka city. Two wooden balls were kept at the shrine, one representing the female and the other the male. To ensure a good harvest, the male ball was competed for and the team that entered the shrine with it handed it to the priest in charge with great honour to the winners.

The Chinese one-goal game was played by the military as a form of training and also by the nobility, particularly on the Emperor's birthday. Two bamboo poles, up to 10 yd *9 m* high, were erected and a silk cloth was draped between them. Centrally placed in the cloth, or net was a hole through which the 12 in *30 cm* diameter ball was to be kicked. Two teams took turns to score goals with the honour going to the winners and the indignity of a whipping for the captain of the losing side!

America ■ A simple football game was played by a number of native American tribes. It most likely began in Canada and then extended southwards along both the east and west coasts as far as present-day Carolina. The ball used for kicking was usually made of buckskin. It was 3–8 in *8–20 cm* in diameter, stuffed with hair and not perfectly round. Goals were usually two sticks set up in the ground or, in north Canada, a scratched line. The Micmac people of Nova Scotia had a small goal of two sticks forming a triangle.

Kick-ball-racing

Unique sport ■ Kick-ball-racing was peculiar to California, the south-western states of America and the northern parts of Mexico. A small ball 2–4 in *5–10 cm* of a soft material or wood was kicked or flicked along in races of 10 miles *16 km* or more.

Longest race ■ The Tarahumare Indians of Mexico were known as *ralamari* (foot-runners). Their favourite sport was kick-ball running. Districts or villages competed against each other with teams of four to 20 runners. At Carachic there was a 14 mile *22.4 km* course of which 12 circuits were often run with the leading runner kicking the wooden ball as far as 100 yd *90 m* ahead of him. The best runners could run a short race of 20 miles *32 km* in two hours or 40 miles *64 km* in five hours. Women sometimes competed in shorter races and were allowed to use sticks to propel the ball.

Bowls

Wooden bowls ■ Wooden bowls first appeared in western Europe in the early part of the 15th century, superseding those made of stone. Wood such a holly, oak, yew, ash, boxwood, ebony and bogoak were used; their irregular shape gave them a natural bias, and they were a little smaller than the modern English bowl.

Four types of bowling were played, with casting at pins or skittles being the most popular. The other forms were aiming at a peg, cone or jack, bowling through a ring and competitive distance bowling.

Bowling alleys ■ Bowling alleys were first recorded in 1455 and were associated with inns and ale houses. They took the form of narrow dirt strips in crowded towns, but were grass lawns in rural areas, and usually had pins or skittles to be knocked down. The upper classes began to build enclosed alleys with hedges by about 1475. Henry VIII took a portable covered bowling alley into France with him in 1513. He built a very fine indoor alley with windows on each side at Hampton Court, near London, in the early 1530s.

Scotland ■ In *c.* 1490 James IV is noted for playing *lang boulis*. He also played *kilis* (kayles) in Drummond Castle four years earlier, i.e. aiming bones at pins.

Polynesia ■ Early forms of bowling, called *ula maika* in Polynesia, using round flat stone discs 3½–4 in *7–8 cm* in diameter.

Canada ■ The indigenous peoples of Canada played an ancient bowling game called *chungka*. A stone disc, hollowed on both sides, was bowled some distance. Then the Indians would throw their spears, with the nearest being the winner.

Field handball

Largest playing area ■ The 16th-century historian Richard Carew wrote about the traditional Cornish game of hurling-to-goals. 'Hurling taketh his denomination from throwing of the ball. The game of hurling to goals is played with 15, 20 or 30 players who strip themselves into their slightest apparel and then join hands in rank one against another, match by pairs. They pitch two bushes in the ground 8–12 ft *2.4–3 m* apart, then the same at 100 to 120 paces off. Hurlers are bound to hurl man to man, not two set upon one. They must not butt nor hand-fast under the girdle. He who has the ball may only touch the other's breast.' Hurling matches were often held at weddings. 'Hurling to country' was a variation of the above game. The game was played between two villages or between town and village, some 3–4 miles *5–6 km* apart, across open country.

Knappen is named after the ball used in this game in Wales. It was commonly 3 in *7.6 cm* in diameter and was similar to that used in the Cornish hurling game. It was played across country between villages on Shrove Tuesday, with perhaps as many as 1000 participants.

Quoits

First quoits ■ In England, quoit was usually spelt *coyte*, *coit* or even *qucoit* and was played mostly by the common folk. At that time the quoits weighed 1–3 lb *0.45–1.36 kg* and old horseshoes were often used.

Most vile game ■ A game akin to quoits was *pennyprick*, in which a penny was placed upon a peg and competed for. The successful player who knocked it off claimed it. As this was a form of gambling, the 15th-century moralists condemned its practice. Roger Ascham says in his book, *Toxophilus* (On Archery), which was published in 1545: 'Quoiting be too ville for scholars.'

Volleyball

Earliest game ■ In many Italian cities at the end of the 15th century a throwing game was played with a large ball by two

Quoit-throwing at a pin or peg was popular in 14th-century England and probably in other European countries too. Horseshoe throwing was popular in Flanders in the 15th century, and went under the name of* coete. *In 16th-century Italy, they appear to have played the game with wooden discs of about 8 in* 20 cm *diameter and about an inch* 3–4 cm *thick with a hole in the middle. The ancient Swedish sport of* varpa *comprised throwing flat stones at a stick stuck in the ground. In India the* chakra *was a sharp-edged quoit used by foot soldiers, both in warfare and as a sport.

teams. The soldiers of the Medici of Florence were recorded as playing a game called *cacciata* in 1507 with a wooden arm protector which may be considered the earliest game of *pallone* (fist-ball). Antonio Scaino describes the game in some detail as played in the early 16th century. It was 'played with a wind ball very much lighter than *pallone* and with the fist armed with a slab of lead or iron . . . it was customary to bind the arm with a linen or wool cloth.'

The game of hand-ball played in Central America as illustrated by Christopher Weiditz.

First fist-ball ■ A volleyball game was played in Germany after 1517 under the name of *Faustball* or *Austball* (harvest-ball). There were usually five players a side striking a ball with their fists over a rope. The ball was allowed to bounce twice.

First Asian 'volleyball' ■ Games similar to volleyball were played in south-east Asia. In Thailand the game was called *takraw*, in the Philippines *sipak* and in Malaya *sepak*. It was played on a court of similar size to that used for badminton. The ball was large and light and made of wickerwork. It was played between two teams of three or more players and was first kicked into the air and then maintained aloft by the arms and hands.

Most popular sport ■ The Mexican Ball Game was well established and was the most popular sport in many parts of Mexico and Central America and in the present American state of Arizona. The game was normally played in a stone-built ball-court of which over 50 are known of in Mexico and over 100 in Guatemala.

Largest ball-court ■ In Mesoamerica the Great Court at Chichén Itzá (Yucatán) was probably erected *c.* 1200. The playing area is 480 × 120 ft *145 × 36 m* and the rings, thought to be targets for the bouncing rubber ball (which had to be struck by the players' elbows or heavy stone yokes worn around the waist) project from the walls 20 ft *6 m* high.

First description ■ Hernán Cortés, the Spanish conqueror of Mexico, saw a game played in 1520 which the Inca, Moctezuma II (1502–20), had arranged for his benefit. The report of this game was translated into English by Thomas Nicholas in 1578: 'Their ball is called *Villamaliztli*, and is made of the gumme which commeth from a tree called Villi . . . The gumme being kneded togither, and so made round, is as black as pitch, and somewhat heavie . . . but yet good and light to rebound, and better than our wind-balles . . . if the ball touch the wall it loseth. They may strike the ball with any part of their body, but there is always a penaltie if they only strike not with the buttoke or side, which is the finest play: wherefore they use a skynne upon each buttoke. They play so many to so many for a pack of mantels or according to the abilitie of the players . . . Court is called Tlachco (also the name of the game), and is a Hall long and narrow, but wyder upwards, than downewardes, and higher on the sides than the ends . . . they have certain stones like unto mylstones, with a little hole in the middest that passeth through the stone, the hole is so small, that scarcely the ball maye pass through . . . which seldome happeneth.'

Only game to require human sacrifices ■ It would appear that throwing a ball through the rings which usually supported the rope was a specialized game for only the most skilful. There are accounts of players being stunned by the ball and even killed. By 1550 the game was banned in Mexico owing to the human sacrifices, usually four at a time, associated with it.

Tennis

First purpose-built tennis court ■ This was at Poitiers, France, and existed in 1230.

First rules ■ In 1450 there were basically two types of tennis played: court and field. The nobility might have had walled courts varying in size to allow for singles, doubles or even trebles. Field tennis was played on any hard surface across an agreed line and could have three or more players on each side. Games were played with either the bare hand or a glove to protect the hand. Those who could afford it employed a server to put the ball into play. Scoring was usually by four points designated as 15, 30, 45 and game. When the ball bounced twice on the floor of the court a 'chase' was declared and marked. This had to be played off at the end of each game, the longest chase gaining the point. In field tennis the chase was marked where the ball was actually stopped.

Earliest record of rackets ■ The earliest mention of a racket appears in a Scottish poem by William Dunbar and dated to 1500: *'Sa mony rakkettis, sa mony ketche-pillaris, Sic ballis, sic nackettis and sic tutivillaris.'* (So many rackets, so many tennis players, such balls, such markers and such worthless persons.)

Unique Spanish ball ■ a unique feature of the Spanish tennis game was the use of a small air-filled ball of about 2 in *5 cm* diameter and suitably weighted.

Earliest tennis courts ■ The first French court was built in Paris in 1496. By about 1500, there were 100 courts in Paris, 40 in Orleans and 22 in Poitiers. Their walls were painted black to a height of 3 ft 6 in *1.05 m* to show up the ball, which was coloured white.

Tennis became very popular in Italy in the second half of the 15th century. The game was mostly played in the streets and town squares with only the nobility affording tennis courts. At the Duke of Milan's palace tennis was played from at least 1470. In 1472 we find mentioned the *Salla della Balla* (Hall of the Ball), the first recorded indoor tennis court.

James V of Scotland (1513–42) was playing tennis by 1526 and in 1539 built a tennis court at Falkland Palace which still exists.

Tennis was introduced late into Teutonic countries. About 1470 a tennis court

Henry VII was a keen player of tennis from as early as 1473. When he came to the throne in 1485 he seems to have built or rebuilt several tennis courts. The Greenwich Palace and Richmond Palace courts appear to have been indoor ones, while that at Windsor (shown here) had a viewing gallery and may have originally had a roof. Henry may have played in Westminster Hall, as old balls have been found lodged in the rafters. The Kenilworth Castle outdoor court was completed in 1493.

was opened at Gasthaus of the Krachbein in Frankfurt-am-Main and by 1500 there was a *Ballhaus* (court) in Badenhausen, Germany. King Ferdinand I of Bohemia (1536–63), a Spaniard, brought tennis to Vienna in the 1540s, but it was only played by the nobility. The first *Ballhaus* in Switzerland was built at Neuchâtel in 1537. A little later there was a court at Geneva. Both came into being through the influence of the French inhabitants.

First ship's court ■ The French king Francis I (1515–47) was noted as a strong player and was fanatical about the game. He built a number of courts, one at Fontainebleau, two at St Germain and a fine covered court at the Louvre in Paris in 1530. He even went to the length of incorporating a court on his new 2000-ton ship *La Grande Françoise* in 1532. It was located between the two castles in the waist of the ship and was overhung with awnings.

In the evolution of tennis, the origin was probably a ball-catching game between two or more players. This developed into a hand volleying game across a line until rackets came into use in the late 15th century. The game developed in France probably in the 12th century as a volleying game among monks and later the royalty. The game was widespread in the 13th century; it is said that Henry I of Castile, Spain (1214–17) died from playing a game of ball.

England's first internationals ■ In January 1505 England witnessed at Windsor its first international tennis match. Philip, the Archduke of Austria and the future King of Castile, played the Marquis of Dorset. The archduke played with a racket and had a handicap of 15; the marquis used his hand. Both Henry VII and Prince Henry were spectators. At Baynards Castle in Blackfriars, London, in 1523, Henry VIII teamed up with Charles V, the Holy Roman Emperor, in a match against the Prince of Orange and the Marquis of Brandenburg which appears to have resulted in a draw of 11 or 12 games each.

First tennis guilds ■ In 1457 there existed in Paris a guild of racket and brush makers but by 1547 they were replaced by the *Maîtres Paumiers d'Racquetiers* (Master Racket Makers). The guild successfully petitioned Louis XI (1461–83) in 1480; he raised an ordinance that first-class balls should be stuffed with dogs' hair or wool wadding and not sand and chalk which damaged the hands.

First book on tennis ■ *Cache* (chase or tennis) is a dialect word of Picardy in northern France. It was absorbed into German as *Katzball* and into Dutch as *Kaetspel* (game of chases). In 1476 a Flemish book was published called *Kaetspeel*, being a translation of an earlier French manuscript *Jeu de Paume Moralisé* (Moral View of Tennis).

Best exercise ■ Desiderius Erasmus of Rotterdam (1466–1536) discusses tennis in his *Familiarum Colloquarium Opus* (Work of Familiar Conversations),1524: 'No play is better to exercise all parts of the body than a game using the hand: but that is fitter for winter than summer . . . we shall sweat less as we play with the racket. Let us leave nets to fishermen; the game is prettier if played with the hands.'

Hurling

The Irish name for the game of hurling was *caman* and it was usually played in a field or *gortnahurla*, or over chosen ground or *greenanahurla* and perhaps in the churchyard or *killahurla* (church of the hurlers). In many parts of Ireland an inter-village game would be played on Sundays and would not reach a conclusion until the second or third Sunday of play.

First compensation ■ In Ireland the broad 3 in *8 cm* bladed stick was used, with a hard ball in winter and a softer one in the summer. In the 15th century, the game was extremely popular at Christmas and the New Year but was considered very dangerous. Many broken heads and shins were sustained, but happily Brenhon Law allowed for compensation of injury caused by stick or ball.

Golf

First prohibitions ■ Scotland is the home of golf and three early edicts prove its popularity in the Lowlands. The first edict was proclaimed at Edinburgh on 6 March 1457 and reads: 'Fute-ball and golfe be utterly cryed doune.' That of 1471 relates: 'Fute-ball and golfe be abusit in tyme cuming'; and in 1491 we hear: 'In na place of the real[m] be usit Fut-bawes, Goulf or uthir sik unprofitable sports.'

Earliest royal game ■ In each year from 1502 to 1506 there is a record of King James IV of Scotland (1488–1513) buying either golf clubs or golf balls, while in 1504 he played the earliest recorded game against the Earl of Bothwell.

In a letter from Queen Catherine of Aragon to Cardinal Wolsey, dated 1513, there is evidence of golf at the court of Henry VIII: '. . . and all his subjects be very glad, master almoner, I thank God, to be busy with the golf, for they take it for a pastime'. (Henry VIII's sister, Margaret, was married to James IV of Scotland.)

Most ancient and celebrated course ■ The Bishop of St Andrews in Scotland confirmed the right of the community to play 'gouf' over the links at St Andrews, about 1550. Another ancient course was Barry Links, near Carnoustie. In 1527, Sir Robert Maule (1497–1560) 'had gryt delight in haikine and huntine . . . lykenakes he exercisit the gowf and oftimes past to Barry Links quhan the wadsie (wager) was for a drink'.

Lacrosse

Huge playing fields ■ At least 48 native

The Flemish game of Kolven or Ground Billiards, shown here in a Book of Hours of about 1520, was related to golf.

American tribes played lacrosse. They played on a field as short as 165 yd *150 m* or as long as 1.5 miles *2.4 km*. There were goalposts at either end. The ball was about 3 in *8 cm* in diameter and was made either of wood or buckskin stuffed with hair. Playing rackets were 3.5–5 ft *1–1.5 m* long. Lacrosse was a fast running game, with the ball carried in the racket. The usual ploy to gain possession was to hit the opponent's racket and jolt the ball out.

Most widespread ■ The sport of double ball was played mostly by women of at least 31 tribes in southern Canada, America (except the south-east) and in north Mexico. It was most popular in the eastern states of America and on the Plains. It had some similarities to the lacrosse game.

Largest games ■ Two bases or goals were established from 300 yards to a mile *270–1640 m* apart. Each competitor had a stick 2–6 ft *60–240 cm* long. The Dakota tribe used two sticks. The Shoshoni and Painte had sticks with a forked end to catch the ball on. Two balls or billets were tied together about 4 in *10 cm* apart. The double ball was thrown from competitor to competitor and carried over the line for a goal. Up to 100 girls might play in a game, and sometimes married women were included.

Field hockey

First royal players ■ Hockey was played in the Lowlands of Scotland under the name of shinty. James IV of Scotland (1488–1513) is recorded as having enjoyed the game in 1507 and may have played it himself.

Longest games ■ In Persia hockey was considered to be the poor man's polo and was called *chauan gui* (stick ball). In Turkey, from about 1450, a variant of hockey was played called *holani* using a stick and a wooden wedge or cylinder of about 5 in *12* *cm* diameter. It was a village game without boundaries and play lasted from dawn to sunset. There appears to have been only one rule, that the players must not wear swords!

In the 15th and 16th centuries a form of hockey was played mainly by women throughout many parts of America and Canada. Over 60 tribes have been recorded as having played the game. Hockey sticks were 2.5–4 ft *750–120 cm* long while balls measured from a tiny 1.25–5 in *3–12.5 cm* in diameter. The game was played on a field 200–300 yd *180–270 m* long but sometimes as long as a mile *1640 m*.

Largest pitch ■ Around Addis Ababa in Ethiopia there was an ancient hockey-type game known as *ghenna* (birth). It was played with rough sticks and a hardwood ball or sometimes a woven leather one. Two pairs of trees, about a mile *1640 m* apart, were used as goals, and two referees were appointed.

Fencing

Earliest guilds ■ Ghent in Flanders (now part of Belgium) has the earliest tradition of fencing guilds in Europe. The Swordsmen's Society of Bruges was founded a little before 1450, but did not receive guild status until 1521. Until the early 16th century, many swordsmen's guilds of St Michael were formed by craftsmen and the lower middle classes in Flemish towns. Some of these guilds had connections with the Union of Acrobats, the wandering entertainers of the day.

Most towns in Germany had a fencing guild by the early 16th century. The oldest guild, incorporating swordsmen, was the *Bürgerschaft von St Marcus* at Löwenberg, which dates from the 14th century. The most famous German guild was the Fraternity of St Mark or *Marksbrüder*, which had its headquarters at Frankfurt and, by 1487, at Worms. It was here at the autumn fair that candidates sought qualification for membership. They fought on a scaffold stage which was set up in the market square. In 1480, the guild obtained a royal patent from Emperor Frederick III.

Earliest English fencing guilds ■ The first governing body for fencing in England was the Corporation of the Masters of Defence founded by Henry VIII before 1540. In that year, under the leadership of Richard Beste, late gunner at the Tower of London, and 19 masters and provosts, the London teachers of fence gained a warrant from Henry VIII 'to enquire and search in all parts of England, Wales and Ireland for persons of unsociable and covetous minds who keep schools of fence without due licence and without proper qualifications'. In 1544 the writer Roger Ascham wrote: 'There is sword play in everie towne, there is not only maisters to teach it, with provostes, ushers and scholars and other names of the arte and schole, . . . '

London's foremost arena ■ During the first half of the 16th century West Smithfield, outside the city walls, was the favourite resort for prize fights. The swordsmen's habit was to march from Blackfriars to Smithfield making terrible noises with their swords and bucklers (shields). The open area at Smithfield became known as Ruffians' Hall owing to the characters who assembled there.

First use of the word 'rapiere' ■ This French word describes a long sword. *Rapiere* was first recorded in France in 1474. About 1500 in Spain it was fashionable for courtiers to wear a light dress sword called an *espada rapera* (epée rapier). These two elements of French name and Spanish light sword gave rise to a long light sword, which was scorned when it reached England about 1530. Towards the middle of the 16th century, the shorter rapier came into fashion throughout Europe. In 1553, Camillo Agrippa of Milan, an enthusiastic swordsman but not a teacher of fence, wrote his book, *Trattatodi Asientia d'Arme* (On all the attempts at arms), which simplified and modernized the art of fencing. He recommended only four 'guards' and, more importantly, the use of the lunge as a thrust, for which the rapier was ideal.

Winter sports

Competitive skating is believed to have originated in Holland soon after the canals were built in the 12th century. Bone skate-blades were used in Holland until steel blades were inserted into bone or wood in the 14th century.

In northern Scandinavia stag hunting on skis was a popular winter sport in the early 16th century.

Best Dutch skaters ■ Friesland in north Holland had the reputation for the best skaters in the 15th and 16th centuries. A copper etching of 1533 by the Flemish engraver, Franz Nuijs, depicts San Joris gate at Antwerp with many pleasure skaters on the canal. It shows a line of skaters following a leader carrying a flag as if they were club members out on a skating trip.

Most blessed sport ■ Skiing in Scandinavia had the greatest number of gods and saintly patrons of any sport. Ull (also known as Skade) was the god of skiing and was depicted as a giant who excelled in ski-running, while Unduruddis was his goddess. St Hubert and St Eustace were also patron saints of skiing.

Earliest ski-troopers ■ From 1452 ski-troops existed in Sweden, Norway, Finland, Poland and Russia. These troops would sometimes indulge in competitive cross-country trials. These skiers would wear one long gliding ski and a short, fur-soled driving ski.

Most famous race ■ In 1520 Gustav Vasa, founder of the modern Swedish kingdom, left Sweden, which was under the yoke of the Danes, for exile in Norway. The inhabitants of Dalecarlia sent a skier after him in great haste to plead with him to return and fight the Danes, which he successfully accomplished.

Most popular winter sport in North America ■ The sport of Snow Snake consisted of sliding or tossing a snake (pole) a great distance along a frozen path. It was popular in the northern parts of America and in Canada and was played by over 30 tribes. The snake was called *Kow-w-sa* by the Seneca of New York state. It was a national winter game of the Iroquois who played with snakes 6–10 ft *1.8–3.05 m* long. The Menominee of Wisconsin reached distances of 300–440 yd *270–400 m* on a suitable course! A similar game was played by the peoples of north Texas and New Mexico, who slid polished bone or horn over flat hard ground.

Beastliest sport

An attempt to revive the Roman spectacle of brutal hunts, or *venationes*, failed miserably in Florence in 1459. A menagerie of horses, boars and a giraffe were assembled in a public square for the occasion. The Pope had even been invited. But the lions who were supposed to savage the other creatures lay down and fell asleep; the Roman technique of starving and torturing the beasts had been forgotten.

Religion and popular belief

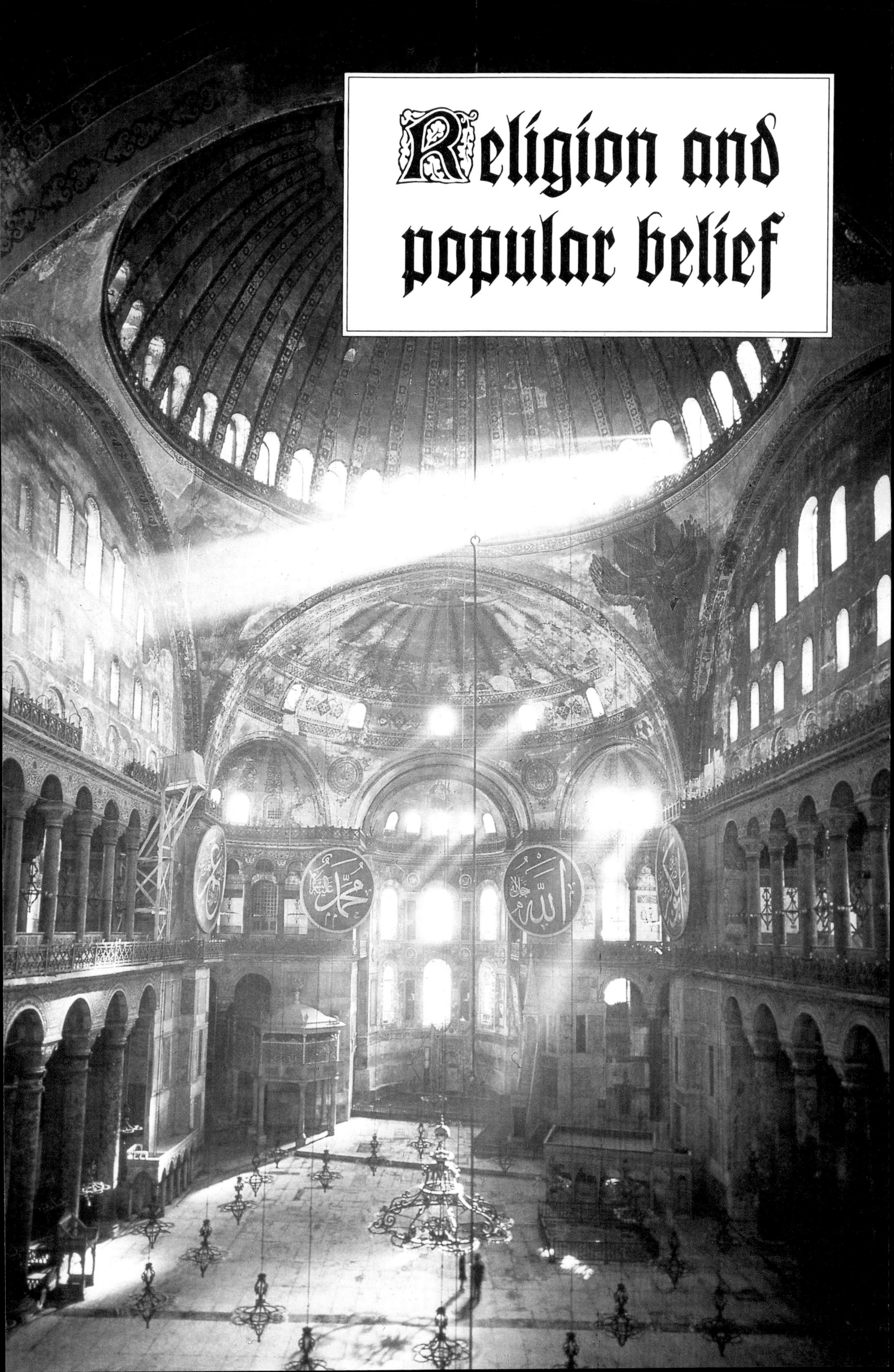

Religion

Site of an Ethiopian church dedicated to St George.

Christian missionaries

First Christian missionaries to China ■ In 1245 a Franciscan friar, John of Plano Carpini, was sent by the Pope to the Great Khan of China. John wrote an account of his experiences entitled *Description of the Mongols*, and one of his companions recorded the mission also.

The first French Christian mission was when William of Rubruck went to China at the behest of King Louis IX (later St Louis) in 1253. Over the next century several other churchmen visited China and wrote of their travels. This period of contact was broken in the 14th century by the break up of the Mongol empire and takeover by the native Chinese Ming dynasty in 1368. At the time of Columbus most knowledge about China would have been about a century old.

First African kingdom incorporated into western Christendom ■ In 1491 King Nzinga Nwuku of Kongo, central Africa, was christened with the foreign name of John. He failed however to unite the advantages of his European links with the internal political needs of his kingdom. After his death there was a struggle for the throne between traditionalists and modernizers. One of his 'sons', Alfonso, used the new religion in his bid for power and in 1506 gained a famous victory over his rival during which a celestial vision of Saint James and a host of angels was seen in the sky.

First black African bishop ■ One of the grandsons of King Nzinga Nwuku of Kongo was sent to Rome for his education and became the first black African to be appointed a bishop by the Pope. He took the title of the empty North African see of Utica which was then in the hands of Turkish Muslim rulers, and was sent back to the mission field in his native Kongo.

First missionaries to America ■ On Columbus' second voyage in 1493 he took with him on the 17 ships of his fleet some 1200–1500 colonists including five *religiosos* whose special responsibility it would be to convert the people of the New World to Christianity.

PREVIOUS PAGE: After the fall of Constantinople in 1453, the great Byzantine church of Holy Sophia was converted into a mosque.

Notable misconceptions ■ The first Europeans in Asia sometimes made amusing mistakes as they came to terms with new cultures and people. Early Portuguese in India kept trying to find aspects of Christianity in the Hindu religion. They hoped that the three major Hindu gods, Brahma, Visnu and Siva, were the same as the Christian notion of the Trinity, and that the way Hindus and Muslims engaged frequently in ritul bathing was something like baptism. This pattern had been set by da Gama himself in 1498, for he was taken to a Hindu temple which he thought was an eastern Christian church. The temple was full of images: 'this made da Gama and the rest take it for a Christian church'. On seeing a female deity, da Gama and the rest, taking it for an image of the Virgin, fell on their knees and prayed. Only one, João de Sala, who had some doubt of the matter, in making his genuflexions, said, 'If this be the devil, I worship God.' Only after the second Portuguese voyage were they disabused of this notion.

First in India ■ One of the tasks given by the Portuguese king to his captains was the discovery of the legendary tomb of the Apostle St Thomas, who was supposed to have died in India. This tomb was eventually located on the Coromandel coast of eastern India, near the modern city of Madras. It was extensively renovated by the Portuguese, as were other locations in the area associated with the Apostle.

Last Egyptian Christian empire ■ By the 16th century the lowland Christian kingdoms of the middle Nile were finally eroded by the advance of Islam, but the highland Christian empire of Ethiopia on the Blue Nile continued to flourish and to receive European visitors. Italian art influenced the evolution of the distinctive murals which decorated Ethiopian churches, and Christian Coptic monks illuminated manuscript editions of the gospels.

First of the great modern missionary orders ■ In 1534 the Jesuit Order was founded by Ignatius Loyola, whose conversion from a military and chivalrous life in Spain had occurred in 1521. Loyola's Order belonged to a group of clergy, technically known as 'clerks regular' (who were living according to a rule) as distinct from monks and friars. The Jesuits took vows of poverty, chastity and obedience but in addition they expressly put themselves at the disposal of the Pope. In an age when the centralized Church was disintegrating, they served as an aggressive arm of the Counter Reformation, and were especially active in the fields of education and conversion in newly-conquered countries, as in the West Indies and Central and South America. The character of the Jesuits is revealed in their organisation under a General (rather than the more usual Master or Master General) and unlike monks and friars they were spared internal divisions almost until our own day.

Ignatius Loyola (1491–1556), founder of the Jesuits.

Greatest saint ■ Born in Navarre in Northern Spain, Francis Xavier (1506–1552) was one of the founders of the new Jesuit Order in 1534. He is often known as the 'Apostle of the Indies'. He travelled to India in 1542, and later visited several areas of southeast Asia, and Japan (1549). He died on the island of Sanchon off the coast of China. During one month in 1544 in an area in southwest India he claimed to have converted over 10 000 people. In one of his letters in 1543 he noted that over 1000 children whom he had baptized 'God our Lord has taken to Himself in His holy glory before they lost their state of innocence.' In Goa, his body, still in a reasonable state of preservation, to this day attracts hordes of pilgrims.

Most communal god ■ The native peoples of North America had a very different view of God and society from Europeans. To them every part of the natural world was sacred: there was no division between humans and the world about them. This view affected their attitude to property and, therefore, each other. This attitude was described by a missionary who lived with the Delaware: 'The Creator made the Earth and all it contains for the common good of mankind . . . not for the benefit of a few, but for all: Everything was given in common to the sons of man.' American peoples did not own 'private property'; they had the use of what was available to all.

Pilgrimages

Largest ■ The largest routine gathering of people in the world around 1492 was at the time of the Muslim *hajj* or pilgrimage, to Mecca. This occurred on the same days of the Muslim calendar each year, and in the 16th century attracted about 200 000 Muslims each year from all over the Muslim world, that is from Morocco to Indonesia and even China. Those who died while on pilgrimage went straight to paradise.

Unmarried women were not allowed to perform the rites alone, so there was a profitable business in offering oneself in temporary marriage to aspiring female pilgrims. It was also meritorious to make it possible for someone else to go on pilgrimage. Sixteenth century Muslim Indian rulers financed huge ships which carried some thousands of pilgrims to Mecca each year, and vast camel caravans transported the believers from Damascus and Cairo. Muslims are required to make the pilgrimage to Mecca at least once in a lifetime if they can afford it.

Apart from the actual rites of the pilgrimage, Muslims around 1500 also visited a vast array of other places in Mecca sanctified by their association with the beginnings of Islam such as tombs and houses of the close companions of the prophet. Pilgrims usually combined a visit to Medina, to see the tomb of the prophet Muhammed, with the actual hajj to Mecca.

England's most popular shrine ■ In 1492 this was the brand-new St George's Chapel, Windsor Castle, in which had been installed two major attractions to pilgrims. One was the miracle-working tomb of King Henry VI (1421–71). The other was the body of a Buckinghamshire rector, John Schorn, long revered as an exorcist and as a protector against various ills and misfortunes. Both 'saints' were widely publicized by the distribution of countless pilgrim badges.

Most widely travelled pilgrim ■ Ghillebert de Lannoy, soldier and diplomat serving Philip the Good, Duke of Burgundy (1419–67), went on pilgrimage to Rome in 1450. On three occasions he completed the much more daunting journey to the Holy Land and twice travelled the long road to Santiago de Compostela in northwest Spain. He also visited what was looked upon in Europe as the last place on earth, St Patrick's Purgatory, a cave in remotest Donegal, Ireland, where those who dared to enter and spend a day and night amidst its unknown horrors would be purged of sin and, at death, go straight to heaven.

Most dangerous journeys ■ Around 1500 the hajj was a dangerous, long and expensive undertaking. Pilgrims from India could take a year to complete their journey and get back home, those from Southeast Asia or from North Africa much longer. Even those travelling on the great caravans from Cairo and Damascus could expect to be away from home for a minimum of 110 days, and up to 6 months was not uncommon. Travellers were often robbed by marauding Bedouin tribesmen, despite the efforts of the rulers of Arabia,

Greatest Christian pilgrimage ■ *All medieval maps give Jerusalem as the centre of the world. For pilgrims in every corner of Christendom the difficulties of the journey there and the appeal of the Holy Places made it the most highly-rated pilgrimage of all. Close behind were the pilgrimages to the burial places of the apostles St Peter and St Paul at Rome and St James the Great at Compostela in north-west Spain.*

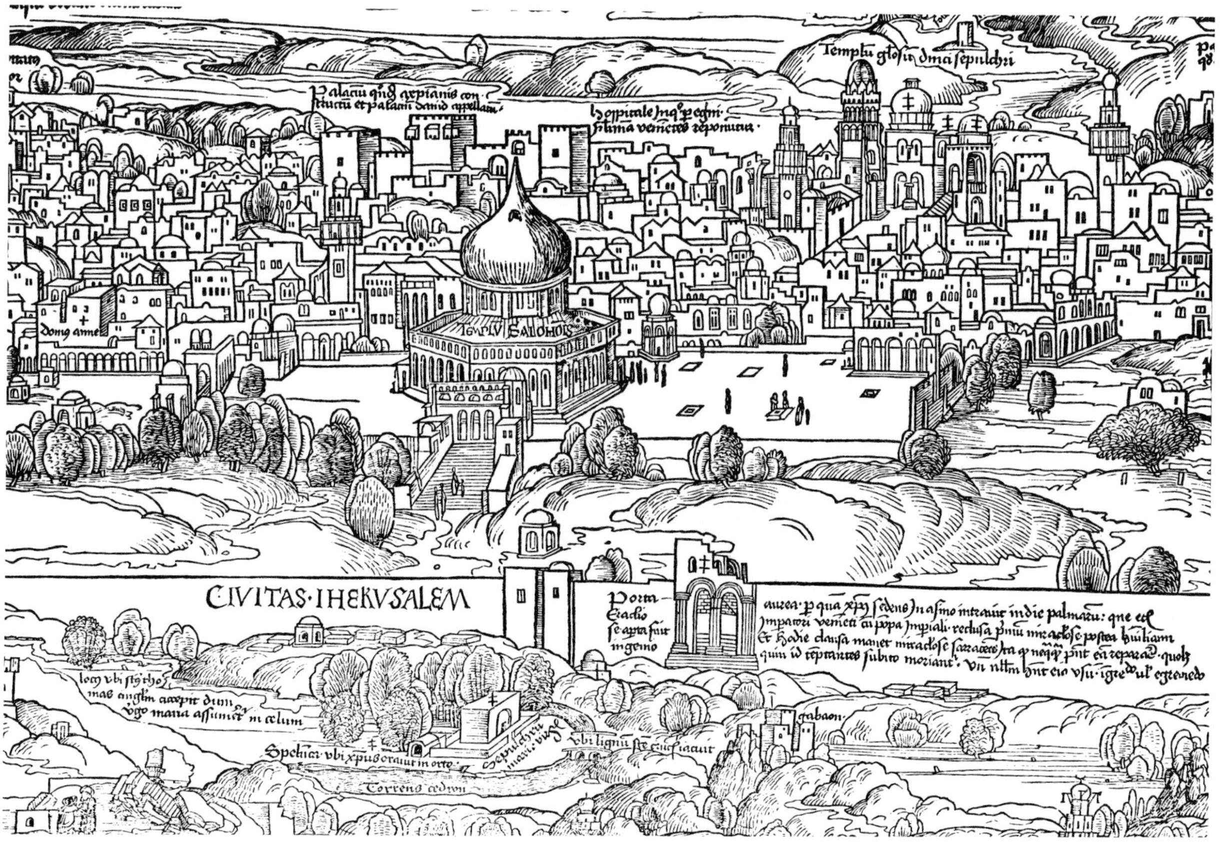

the sultans of Egypt until 1516, and then the Ottoman sultans, to provide escorts and security.

Most forbidden city ■ Only Muslims are allowed into the cities of Mecca and Medina; all others are turned away some distance from the towns. Nevertheless, there have been several adventurous Europeans who have disguised themselves as Muslims and so made the pilgrimage. In the first decade of the 16th century an Italian called Ludovico di Varthema made the hajj, and left an account of it.

Longest stay in Mecca ■ While many people visited Mecca at the time of the hajj, some Muslims stayed in Mecca for many years in order to study and pray at the most holy city in Islam. A stay of 24 years is recorded of one Indian saint in the mid-16th century who, on his return to India, became not surprisingly a very prestigious teacher of Islamic knowledge. Another famous saint of the same time did a total of 22 hajjs.

Most holy reflections ■ Christian pilgrims were motivated by a desire to see and above all to touch holy places and saintly relics. In the 15th century crowds grew so large at some shrines that personal contact became impossible. Images and relics were then exhibited from outdoor vantage-points to waiting pilgrims who held up little mirrors in the belief that, by catching the reflection of the saintly objects, the mirrors would encapsulate some of the virtues issuing from them.

Largest indulgences ■ Indulgences offered some relief from punishment due to sin, reducing the number of years of possible purgatory after death. Most places of pilgrimage had an indulgence attached to them which those who completed the journey automatically obtained. The largest accumulation of indulgences was to be had at Rome. Typically, an indulgence of 12 000 years was granted at St Peter's to pilgrims from abroad during any showing of the Vernicle (the kerchief of St Veronica bearing the impression of Christ's face).

Most pious souvenirs ■ Muslims who had made the pilgrimage were anxious to take back home some memento of their pious journey. Any item bought in the holy city of Mecca was automatically invested with extra prestige simply because it had been bought there. More specifically, the building called the Ka'ba, in the centre of the great mosque at Mecca, was newly covered each year with a very ornate cloth sent annually by the ruler of Egypt. After the pilgrimage season it was cut up into small pieces and sold to pilgrims, who paid high prices for such a valuable souvenir. The local rulers of Mecca, the sharifs, did well from similar items. They would send to Muslim rulers such items as a broom which purportedly had been used to sweep out the inside of the Ka'ba, or a little of the dust itself, and expect lavish monetary gifts in exchange. Equally valuable was a flask of water from the holy well called Zamzam. It was good to buy one's burial shroud in Mecca, and dip it in Zamzam water. Pious Muslims always kept the shroud with them so that it could be used to cover their bodies when they died.

Most precious treasure ■ Relics of Christ and his family and of other Biblical characters were scattered through Christendom and wherever they were placed they were regarded as treasures of the greatest importance. On the island of Rhodes, for instance, pilgrims would be shown – as 'the most precious treasure of all' – a 'spina' from Christ's Crown of Thorns. It was displayed in a tabernacle or casket made of crystal and silver and was 'most marvellously wrought'. The pilgrims were told that each year on Good Friday the Holy Thorn would flower and remain in bloom from the sixth to the ninth hour. The Knights of Rhodes and all the people of the island had, they said, witnessed this miracle themselves.

Finest 'prayer nuts' ■ A late Gothic fashion for 'prayer nuts' originated in the south Netherlands. These were large, hinged beads which could be opened to display scenes of the Passion (or Christ's final torments) surrounding the crucifixion. The finest to survive comes from Spain *c.* 1510 and is a rosary carved from boxwood with nine large beads, each showing a separate incident in the narrative cycle.

A diagram of Mecca painted on a Turkish ceramic tile with Arabic inscriptions giving explanations.

Most-carried processional item ■ This on Corpus Christi Day (the second Thursday after Easter) would be the host. Celebration of the Eucharist, that is, the doctrine that Christ's body and blood are present in consecrated bread and wine, was at its height in the late 15th century. The host would be processed under a *baldachin*, a canopy carried by civic dignitaries (six members of the council in Nuremberg, 1493; eight princes in Regensburg, 1532). Children strewing rose petals walked ahead. Frequent halts ('weather stops') were an opportunity to bless the harvest with sung antiphons, a note taken up by the greenery of the display with its branches, wreaths and lilies. The host was believed to heal sicknesses that were 'diabolical' in origin, such as epilepsy and hysteria. It also extinguished fires. Theologically this power was locked within the object itself; hence, to hold up the host in a monstrance was to frame it in the priest's hands and ensure that he controlled its emissions. Corpus Christi plays (at York and Chester in England, and elsewhere) embraced the whole history of mankind.

Human sacrifice

Record human ■ The biggest occasion of human sacrifice was reputedly the impressive dedication ceremony of the great dual Aztec temple of Tenochtitlán, Mexico, in 1487, when, according to various sources, between 20 000 and 84 400 captives were supposed to have been sacrificed. According to the Spanish one could see all of the city from the temple.

Highest tally ■ The 'more than 4000 souls, what with wives, pages and other servants' said to have been immolated at the burial of the Inca Huayna Capac in Cuzco, around the end of the first quarter of the 16th century is the highest tally of human sacrifice ascribed to the Incas on any one occasion.

Conversions

Last Muslims in Spain ■ In 1492 when Queen Isabella and King Ferdinand accepted the surrender of Granada, the last Moorish stronghold in Spain, it was agreed that the Moors might remain and practise their religion, convert to Christianity or emigrate to Africa. Ten years later this agreement was abrogated and all Muslims were ordered to convert to Christianity or be expelled.

Most necessary meat ■ The operations of the newly-established (1478) Spanish Inquisition made it necessary for even the most confirmed Christian households to ensure that Inquisitorial inspectors would always find pork in the *olla podrida* (a stew that, ironically, was derived from the Jewish *adafina*) or dried pork *chorizo* sausages hanging from the rafters. This was sure proof that neither Jews nor Muslims – to whom pork was religious anathema – lived in the house.

Record conversions ■ The biggest tally of converts in the evangelization of the New World was claimed by the first Franciscan mission, established in New Spain (Mexico) in 1524. The leader, Fray Martin de Valencia, claimed by June, 1531, that they had baptized more than 1 000 000 native Americans; a year later, Fray Toribio de Benavente, known as Fray Toribio de Motolinia, put the figure at over 100 000 for each of the 12 companions. In June, 1529, Father Peeter van der Moere, known as Fray Pedro de Gante, who had preceded the 12, claimed 14 000 baptisms a day.

Popes

Longest reigning ■ Pope Adrian I reigned for 23 years 11 months (772–795). His predecessor died in Rome on 24 Jan-

The Italian painter Pinturicchio (1454–1513) showed Pope Alexander VI piously at prayer in this scene of the Resurrection.

Lucretia Borgia daughter of Roderigo Borgia who became Pope in 1492, as Alexander VI.

Cesare Borgia was also openly acknowledged as the son of Pope Alexander VI.

uary 772 and Adrian I died on Christmas Day 795.

Shortest reigning ■ Pope Stephen II reigned for only 2 days in 752, and then died.

Longest living ■ The Sicilian Pope, St Agatho (*c.* 577 – January 681) reputedly lived for 104 years. He was Pope from June 678 until his death from the plague in Rome.

Youngest elected ■ Pope Benedict IX (*c.* 1020–1056) was elected Pope in 1032 when he was only 11 or 12 years old through simony (the practice of selling ecclesiastical preferments).

Last non-cardinal ■ Pope Urban VI (Bartolomeo Prignano, 1318–1389), the Archbishop of Bari, Italy, was elected Pope on 8 April 1377 and was the last Pope to be elected who was not a cardinal.

Most protracted election ■ The election of Pope Gregory X (Teobaldi Visconti) took 31 months from February 1269 to 1 September 1271.

Fastest ecclesiastical career ■ Giovanni de' Medici, second son of the Florentine banker and statesman Lorenzo, was declared capable of holding ecclesiastical benefices in 1483, at the age of seven and a half, and raised secretly to the cardinalcy at 13 after a deal that cost his father 95 000 florins. His family was driven from Florence in 1494 and he spent much of the next 10 years wandering in Italy and other parts of Europe in search of support. Emerging from adversity in 1513 he was elected pope as Leo X at the age of 37, and before he was technically a priest. A contemporary credits him with saying; 'Since God has given us the papacy, let us enjoy it'; but within five years he was facing Luther's challenge.

Most scandalous ■ Roderigo Borgia rose to the papacy on 11 August, 1492, as Alexander VI, after an election during which mules were seen carrying treasures from his palace to the residences of possible voters. By the time of his death in 1503 his policies and private life had scandalized Europe. His children – openly acknowledged rather than passed off as 'nephews' and 'nieces' – were used as pawns. Lucretia had been married three times before she was 20, one of her husbands having been strangled by an accomplice of her brother Cesare. A cardinal at 17, Cesare was released from his vows in 1498 to become the spearhead of his father's attempt to subdue central Italy by force, and earned the respect of Machiavelli for his ruthlessness. However, Cesare's political ambitions brought about his downfall. Like his father, he was very fond of his sister, Lucretia, and one of the delights that entertained the Pope, described by an accurate if indiscreet master of ceremonies, was an occasion when Alexander and Lucretia together enjoyed watching a concourse of vigorous stallions let loose on mares in one of the courtyards of the Vatican.

The family's reputation for using poison was probably not deserved: but since Cesare and Roderigo died within a few days of each and with similar symptoms, it was easy for scandal-mongers to believe that they had drunk a bottle of wine intended for another victim.

Monasteries

Greatest extent of English monastic life ■ In 1491 when Henry VIII was born, there were more than 800 religious houses in England. These included about 250 monasteries for monks, 280 houses of canons regular (where clergymen lived together), 170 friaries (convents of brothers of a religious order) and 130 nunneries. In them lived and worked about 4000 monks, 3000 canons regular,

3000 brothers or friars and 2000 nuns. So, out of a population at the time of about 2 million people in England, about 12 000 were in religious houses and a further 25 000 people worked for them as lay workers or farm workers. By the year of King Henry VIII's death in 1547 they had all been abolished.

Last religious house to be abolished ■ The last English religious house to be put down by Henry VIII was Waltham Abbey in Essex which was closed in 1540.

Northernmost monastery ■ The northernmost monastery in the world was Solovetskii monastery at 65° N founded on Solovetskii Island's Blagopoluchie Bay in the White Sea by Zosima and Savvatii, monks from the Kirill-Belozersk Monastery in the late 1420s. By the end of the 15th century around 100 monks lived in wooden cabins, surviving extremely cold and windy winters (usually minus 25/35° C) and short summers. The monks built several dozen saltworks in the area, produced and traded salt, hunted sea mammals and land animals, fished, mined mica and iron ore, and even grew vegetables.

First religious orders in the New World ■ The Dominican order was established by 1509, criticizing the settlers for 'the cruel and horrible servitude' imposed on the local population. In 1524 the Franciscans started to work in Mexico.

Religious persons

Most holy men of Central America ■ The Maya priests were famed for their wisdom and saintliness. They spent their lives making sacrifices and even practising self-mutilation, drawing blood from their own bodies. They were also concerned with seeing that other people did not sin against the gods, and with divining the future and with curing illnesses. The Maya priests had a monopoly on scientific knowledge; their training included the counting of the calendar (years, months and days), writing and tradition.

Most powerful ecclesiastic ■ Though the popes of the time generated more gossip, the most powerful ecclesiastic of the 1490s and 1500s was the Franciscan Ximenes de Cisneros, who became confessor to Queen Isabella in 1492, archbishop of Toledo and primate of Spain in 1495, cardinal and Grand Inquisitor in 1507. The latter position made him the only person whose writ ran in all the different kingdoms of Spain. Besides commanding an expedition to North Africa and conquering Oran in 1509, Ximenes founded a university at Alcala, played a vital part in reforming the Spanish clergy, and acted for a while as regent of Spain after the death of King Ferdinand in 1516.

Most extreme ascetic ■ In an age of religious extremes, Francesco de Paola presented the extreme of asceticism. From the age of 12 he lived in a cave in southern Italy, eating only fruit and vegetables, wearing a coarse hessian smock, and sleeping upright, slouched against the rock. But he also organized in 1474 a reform of the Franciscan order. Summoned to France by King Louis XI in 1483, he was welcomed with full honours at the court of Naples and at the Vatican, before proceeding to take up residence in a custom-built hermitage near the castle of Plessis, where Louis was dying. Francesco remained close to the French court, unaffected by the extravagance around him, frequently consulted by the courtiers about their personal problems and by royal ladies about their pregnancies. He was famed for his prophecies and miracles even in his lifetime. He died in 1507, aged 90, and was declared a saint 12 years later. (He became the patron saint of seafarers in 1943.)

Greatest memory for religious detail ■ Peter Rovenno, lawyer of the University of Padua, Italy, published in 1491 a treatise on memory training in which he claimed to be able to recite the whole of the canon law (four large folio volumes), 200 speeches, and 20 000 legal propositions by heart.

Most eccentric religious liberal ■ The Italian Giovanni Pico della Mirandola (1463–1494) dreamed of reconciling all world religions through a quest for the hidden mysteries underlying them. Beginning his studies at 14, he worked at five different universities and is supposed to have learned 22 languages before publishing his 900 propositions *De Omni Scibili* (On all there is to be Known) in Rome during 1486. His defence of occult magic offended the Pope as much as his sexual appetites outraged husbands, and he was imprisoned for a while: but on his release he died in Florence, robed as a Dominican friar.

Most scandalous unbeliever ■ Nicknamed 'the dregs of Italy' and formally consigned to Hell by the Pope in a public ceremony, Sigismundo Malatesta, ruler of Rimini until 1468, was said to have murdered two of his wives, attempted the rape of both his daughters and his son, and to believe that the soul died with the body. Though the more lurid details are creations of papal propaganda, Sigismundo's taste for the pagan stretched even the flexible toleration of the time to its limits: the church of San Francesco which he commissioned for Rimini looked like a Greek temple, was full of ancient relics, and contained a shrine to his mistress as 'the divine Isotta'.

New religions and sects

A new kind of Confucianism ■ From the year 1489 onwards the scholar, writer and mandarin Wang Shouren (1472–1529) developed a new variant of China's age-old principal philosophy, Confucianism. Stressing the importance of intuitive knowledge, he provided a radically new slant to the traditional body of more purely rationalist Confucian attitudes, and his Idealistic Confucianism swept through China, exercising a profound influence on later ages.

First stirrings of the Reformation controversy ■ In a sense the Reformation of the Church began not when Luther nailed his denunciation of the sale of indulgences on the door of Wittenberg parish church in 1517. Similar sorts of criticism of the established church had been made earlier. From the time when the Church was divided between rival popes, bitter critics of the ecclesiastical abuses were found in many parts of Christendom. Martin Luther, an Augustinian friar and teacher at the new university of Wittenberg, was obsessed by a conviction of his own unworthiness. This was resolved for him by the illumination that faith justifies not words and this interpretation of the New Testament became the basis of his theology and of the attraction his views held for many of his contemporaries. He translated the Vulgate into German, a task completed in 1534 which

Martin Luther as painted by Lucas Cranach.

became one of the most potent instruments of cultural unification in politically divided Germany. In many areas the tensions thus released led to the laity dismembering the property of the Church; in England. King Henry VIII dissolved the monasteries and shared the pickings with his friends.

New religion ■ Sikhism, a major religion especially strong in the Punjab, north India, was founded by Guru Nanak (1469–*c.* 1539). He became dissatisfied with the Hinduism in which he was brought up, and with Islam. His new religion and its holy book, the *Guru Granth Sahib*, rejected the Hindu caste system.

First Anabaptist: Thomas Munzer (*c.* 1489–1525) a German preacher, is regarded as the founder of the Anabaptists. His preaching of 'socialist' and mystical ideas and enthusiastic following brought him into conflict with the authorities from 1520 on, and he was eventually executed.

Religious books

Most valuable ■ Many Muslim rulers proclaimed their piety by sending valuable presents to Mecca. Some of these were for the rulers of the town, the sharifs, and some were meant to be distributed as charity to the inhabitants of the Holy City. Several 16th century Indian rulers copied out the Koran by hand, and sent the copy off to Mecca. Thus Sultan Mazaffar II of Gujarat (1511–26), in western India, made in his own hand two copies of the Koran, using gold water, and then sent them off to Mecca and Medina. He also made an annual grant to provide for the upkeep of the two books, and to pay those who used these copies for recitation.

Most successful ■ Thomas à Kempis' *Imitation of Christ* first circulated around 1418. This short guide to the Christian life achieved immediate acclaim, and was reprinted over 500 times between 1470 and 1500. Because of its small size, the *Imitation* was far more widely read during the 15th century than the Bible which was still too expensive for most readers to buy for themselves. It is generally agreed to have been the work of a German canon of the Augustinian order, Thomas à Kempis (1380–1471), but the author's undogmatic and very personal devotion has continued to appeal to Christians of every denomination. (The list of editions in the British Library Catalogue fills 151 columns.)

Most popular in England ■ John Mirk's *Liber festivalis* (Book of Festivals) was a collection of sermons and religious legends. Although composed before 1415, it continued to be so popular in England that it was reprinted no less than 19 times between 1483 and 1532.

Translations

First Latin Koran ■ Some parts of the teaching of Mohammed are believed to have been written down as early as 615 and revised by the Prophet himself in 622. The remainder was probably written down after his death in 632. The Koran was first translated into Latin in 1143 and thus became far more widely known in Europe.

First 'Peoples' Bibles' ■ Though printed Bibles remained large and expensive during the 15th century, a German translation had been printed in Strasbourg by 1466, an Italian version in Venice by 1471, and a French text in Paris around 1487. All sold well, and were soon reissued. By 1485 the archbishop of Mainz, Germany, Berthold von Hennenberg, was expressing concern that 'ignorant and greedy men had dared to translate the sacred texts into vulgar and incorrect German', and attempted to subject any future translation to the approval of the universities of Mainz and Erfurt.

First Finnish New Testament ■ Michael Agricola (1511–1557), generally regarded as the father of Finnish as a literary language, produced the first ABC book for Finns and completed the first translation of the New Testament into Finnish in 1548. A Swedish translation had appeared for the first time in 1541.

The universal belief in spirits was common to religion, astrology, magic and even such sciences as medicine and chemistry. If there were good spirits, there could also be evil ones. Belief in the Devil provided the most logical explanation of bad weather, bad luck, sudden death and other misfortunes in the intellectual climate of the late Middle Ages and early Renaissance. It was this outlook that permitted the greatest persecution that western civilization has ever seen of people who were believed to be the Devil's agents. During the 15th–16th centuries it is estimated that over a million witches, most of them women, were blamed for deliberate malaficium, or magically induced damage to others. Since confessions were most often extracted under torture it is impossible to know how many were really involved in witchcraft; most are not presumed to have been totally innocent. In this area of home medicines, it was part of every housewife's duty to know what herbs and remedies to use for the most common ailments. The use of ordinary charms, spells and talismans resulted in death for many innocent healers.

Popular belief

Most widespread belief ■ Almost everyone at this time believed in fairies. Treated well by humans, fairies responded kindly, but if they were treated badly they would respond in kind. They were reputed to torment livestock, steal babies and play tricks on an offender. Every country and language had its own name for the fairies: the English had the Brownies, the Germans the Kobold, the Russians the Domovoy and so on. To placate the fairies it was customary to put out a small bowl of milk or porridge each night – which was likely to have been consumed by the morning.

Most useful talismans ■ Talismans, images made under certain astrological influences, were commonly used for protection. A treatise was written in 1494 for King Ferdinand of Aragon by Jerome Torrella, later physician to Pope Julius II, that recommended the use of images of gold lions to prevent intestinal pains. Inscribed seals of fishes were similarly used to combat gout. Gold lions carved when the Sun was in conjunction with Jupiter could also cure the fear of thunderstorms.

Most frightening herb ■ The narcotic herb mandrake was the most frightening herb. From classical times it was believed that its humanoid-shaped roots were really a little old man who would cause harm to anyone who did not observe the proper rituals in digging it up. The author of *The Grete Herball* of 1526 clearly states that the little man is a myth, but both the man and a female mandrake are still illustrated in a gardening scene on the title page!

Most condemned popular beliefs ■ Amongst popular beliefs condemned by the learned and/or Church were:

✱ a belief that it was dangerous to plant crops at a full moon;

✱ it was unlucky to be born on Friday the 13th;

✱ it was unlucky to be born during the hour before midnight;

✱ that marriages contracted when the Moon was increasing in light worked best;

✱ the idolatrous practice by lay and clergy of fasting and genuflecting to the new moon;

✱ the practice of burning incense to Jupiter and Saturn on Thursday and Saturday, the days which they rule.

Most important factor in popularizing astrology ■ The invention of printing with movable type in the 15th century was the most important factor in making astrology popular; annual predictions became increasingly popular. Astrologers all over Europe competed with one another to forecast war, changes in government, religion, and weather. The main data they used was the horoscope for the Sun's return to the beginning of Aries, which marked the beginning of the astrological year. Ptolemy's writings on eclipses were held in the highest esteem, but newly discovered texts from Arab authors emphasized the greater importance of conjunctions.

Prophecy

Oldest means of divination ■ Chiromancy, the art of reading the length, depth and colour of lines of the hands and wrists, is one of the oldest means of divination and character judgement. In the early Renaissance, palmists read four principal lines – by the 17th century there were seven. The most famous chiromancer was the Italian Bartolomeo Cocle, who was also a metoscopist and physiognomist (teller of fortunes from the forehead and face). The accuracy of several of his predictions are verified by the historian Jovius. He died at the hand of Bentivoglio, the ruler of Bologna, for whom he had forecast exile and death in battle. The executioner was also his client; Cocle had once predicted that he would commit an ignominious murder.

Direst prediction ■ The great majority of the population of Russia feared that the end of the world would come in 1492. Theologians believed that the seven days of the world's creation corresponded to 7000 years of its existence, and calculated that the date of its end would be 1492. In 1524 a new Deluge (Flood) was predicted.

Most astonishing prophecy ■ Prophecies are recorded in many cultures. Few can be more amazing than that told by the Ojibwa people of Lake Superior, America of the Ojibwa prophet who dreamed in great detail of 'men who had come across the great water . . . their skins are white like snow, and on their faces long hair grows. These people have come . . . in wonderfully large canoes which have great white wings like those of a giant bird. The men have long and sharp knives, and they have long black tubes which they point at birds and animals. The tubes make a smoke that rises into the

The images of the Chinese zodiacal figures appear on this coin, used for divination in consultation with the Book of Changes.

air . . . from them come fire and . . . a terrific noise.' Following this prophecy a group of Ojibwa were sent down the St Lawrence waterway to investigate – and eventually saw their first white men – possibly Cabot's (1497) or Cartier's (1535) party.

Greatest soothsayer ever ■ In 1492, Jaune de Notredame had yet to be converted to Christianity and was still a reader of occult Jewish literature. It is this mixed Judaeo-Catholic background which played a vital part in the education of his amazing son Michel, who was born at noon on 14 December 1503 in St Remy de Provence, France. Michel – better known by the Latinized form of his surname, Nostradamus – is the most amazing of all astrologers. His famous work, *The Centuries*, contains detailed prophecies up to and beyond the year 2002.

Nostradamus wrote his predictions in a mixture of languages including French and Latin and set them down in four-line verses. He rarely used specific dates, preferring instead astrological terminology.

England's most famous prophetess ■ Ursula Southeil, a physically grotesque woman, was born in 1488 in a small cave in Knaresborough, Yorkshire. Known by her married name as Mother Shipton, she was genuinely clairvoyant, but most of the famous prophecies ascribed to her are, in fact, 19th-century forgeries.

Greatest prophetic forgeries ■ Dating from the 16th century, the so-called *Prophecies of St Malachy* contain a list of all future popes to a time which approximates to the dreadful 1999 associated with both Nostradamus and Mother Shipton.

Diagnosis

Most detailed study of lines ■ Metoscopy, the art of reading lines in the forehead, was also given astrological definition by Giralamo Cardano. His work, *Metoscopia*, is illustrated with over 800 woodcuts of case studies. The brow is divided into seven zones, each ruled by the planets, from Saturn at the top the Moon at the bottom. A large wrinkle in any given zone indicates personal qualities of the nature of the ruling planet. Health, wealth, imbecility, success in war or violent death could be recognized by reference to the manual.

Best illustrated physiognomy ■ Physiognomy is the art of judging character by the shape and expressions of the face. Amongst the early 16th-century treatises on the subject, the one published by John of Indagine in Strasbourg in 1531 has the finest woodcuts. Along with an author portrait by Hans Baldung Grien, are a long series of lively portraits that were copied by lesser artists over the following two centuries. The pictures demonstrate the large ears that betoken stupidity and ignorance and the small simian ears that betray instability and fallaciousness. Noses, eyes, chins and eyelashes provide similar clues to guile, vanity, intellect and adventurousness.

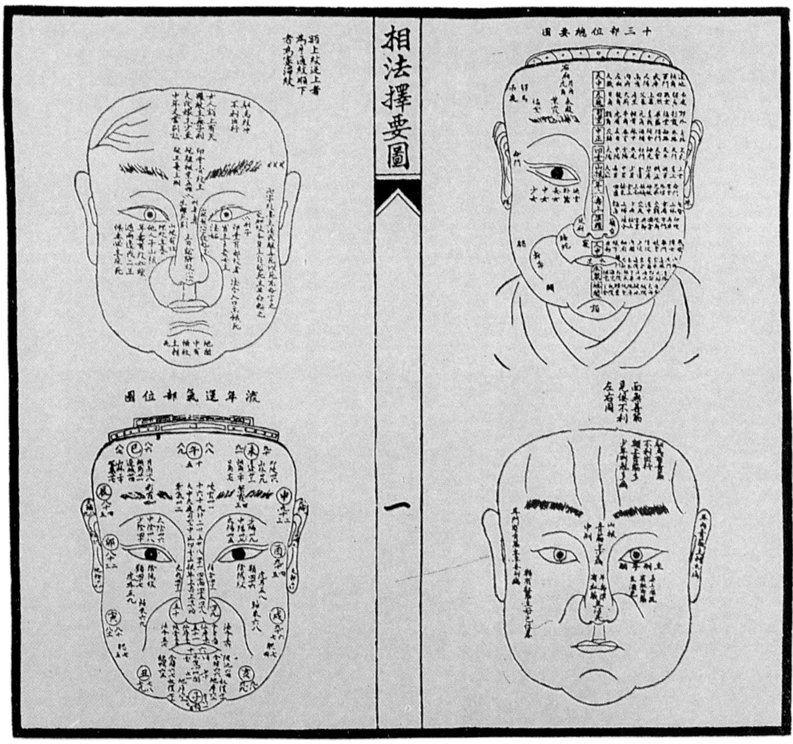

A double page from a Chinese almanac gives advice on the reading of parts of the human face – one of the means of diagnosis.

Newest learning ■ A flood of newly-discovered manuscripts from the East brought about a revival of magic in learned circles in Italy. The writings of Hermes Trismegistus, which were believed at the time to date from ancient Egypt, were translated by Marsilio Ficino in the 1460s at the request of Cosimo de' Medici and were of central importance to the growing movement. Modern scholarship has shown that Hermes was a mythical figure and that the writings were from a variety of Greek sources dating from the first to the fourth centuries; what they have in common is that they were aimed at keeping pagan religious practice alive at a time when Christianity was becoming the dominant religion. The secret mysteries accredited to Hermes gave instruction on drawing magical power into statues in the ancient Egyptian manner and also on realizing Man's innate divine powers by spiritually rising through the seven planetary spheres. The astrological cosmology was fundamental to these ideas; knowledge of the planets and their sympathetic substances was essential for the magician who had to know how and when to call upon the planet-god. Knowledge of the symbols was also required for writing the magical symbols which captured the power.

Witchcraft and sorcery

Between 1450 and 1700 at least 100 000 people in Europe and the British Isles were sentenced to death for crimes most people would now think could not possibly have been committed. The exact figures are disputed and some authorities estimate that the real numbers are in the millions. In the late 15th century, when witchcraft became associated with Devil worship, forcible suppression and extermination of witches was seen as the only reasonable response to the greatest crime against both God and

THE DEVIL

The personality of the Devil was generated in the popular visual imagination by practices endorsed by the Church. Mystery plays, the only experience of the theatre known to most people, frequently featured a huge hell-mouth. Every parish church would have had a Last Judgement, featuring demon and hellish torments, painted over the chancel arch. The Devil himself appears in plays such as Skelton's* The Necromancer *which was performed for Henry VII. His goat-like physical form derives from the classical satyr associated with Dionysiac rites which were much like the Witches' Sabbath. In the Great Catechism by the 16th-century Jesuit Peter Canisius the name of God appears 63 times, while the Devil's is mentioned 67 times.

In a fresco of about 1500 in the New Chapel of the Madonna of S. Brizio in Orvieto Cathedral in Italy Signorelli shows demons at work in Hell.

man. White magic was commonly employed for medical and other noble acceptable purposes and black magic was its sinister counterpart.

Cheapest witchcraft ■ Cursing, calling upon spirits to perform evil deeds, was the cheapest form of witchcraft and it was used by the poorest. In 1493 Elena Dalok appeared in court in London for bragging that everyone she had cursed subsequently died.

Most common spell ■ The most commonly practised method of causing physical damage to another was to stick pins in a wax image of the victim.

First identification of pacts with the Devil ■ Although belief in witchcraft and magic was ancient, the idea that the witch made a pact with the Devil was new. The Church supplied both the justification and the procedure for exposing and prosecuting them. The definitive proclamation was a Papal Bull of Pope Innocent VIII in 1484 and the *Malleus Maleficarum* (malleus = mallet or axe used for sacrificial slaughter; maleficium = crime) was published in 1486 by two Dominican inquisitors (judges in an ecclesiastical court). Their main concern was the rise of Devil worship in Germany and France. The importance of the idea of Devil worship was that anyone could perform evil deeds, not just those with natural psychic powers.

First official guide to witch-hunting ■ The *Malleus Maleficarum* (Hammer of Witches) was reprinted 14 times between 1486 and 1520 and its joint authors, the Dominican friars Heinrich Kramer and Jacobus Sprenger, were at the height of their prestige during the 1490s, being fêted by scholars in Italy and appointed to high ecclesiastical offices in Germany and central Europe by the papacy. Their order regarded them as two of its brightest lights. Beginning from the principle that witchcraft must involve a direct compact with the Devil, they worked systematically through the various forms it could take and suggested appropriate countermeasures, doing much to produce the 'witch-craze' of the next two centuries.

Malleus Maleficarum was intended as a handbook for inquisitors, but it served equally well as an 'encyclopedia' for anyone who wanted either to be informed or to learn the secrets for practical purposes.

Most likely to be a 'malefactor' ■ Those accused of witchcraft were most likely to be unattached, socially or economically dependent women and therefore the least powerful members of the community. The Church's explicit position was that women of all ages were much more driven by sexual passions, therefore more vulnerable to seduction by the Devil. Most of the accused were over 50 years of age, many of them senile, although many young attractive women were also convicted. On average, 75 per cent of those condemned to death for practising witchcraft were women; most of them were also unmarried. In Essex, England, Basel, Switzerland, and Namur (now in Belgium) over 90 per cent were female.

Largest prosecution of male malefactors ■ Men were more often accused of

A tinted woodcut made in Germany in about 1511 presents the seven deadly sins as demons. They represent, in order from top left to bottom right: the sins of anger, pride, envy, sloth, gluttony, lust and avarice.
These sins were believed to cause the spiritual death of the person who did not resist them.

witchcraft for political ends or at times of mass hysteria, when the community's anxiety might override stereotyped expectations. The largest prosecution of males at any court was at Aragon, Spain, where in the 16th century they account for 72 per cent of those prosecuted.

Most famous souls sold ■ The most famous of those who sold their souls to the Devil was Doctor Johann Faust. Several versions of *Hollenzwang* (Hell's Compulsion) printed in Rome between 1492 and 1503 were attributed to the black magician although he only began his occult practices in the 1520s. His legendary self-destruction served as a moral exemplar for opponents of Devil worship.

Mary of Nimmegen is the most famous woman to have sold her soul to the Devil. The Dutch miracle play named after her was printed in Antwerp by William Vorsterman (active 1512–43). It centres on the legend of a nun who runs away from her convent to spend 14 years frolicking with the Devil and then returns full of remorse to find that God's mercy is still available to her.

Unique belief ■ The idea of 'familiars', animals that performed evil acts at the witch's bidding, was unique to England. The first recorded mention of a familiar was in 1530 in Somerset; the animal was a toad.

Most dreaded weapon ■ Murder by untraceable means was the most dreaded weapon of witchcraft. Mabel Brigge of York was executed in 1538 for a Black Fast; the rite consisted of abstaining from foods containing milk or meat and concentrating upon the death of the victim. Although she claimed to have had previous successes, her fast against King Henry VIII and the Duke of Norfolk was not one of them. Nevertheless, her reputation was such that it took some time to quell the rumours of the king's demise.

Most amazing magical deaths ■ In China these events were 'facts' in the 16th century: 'sometimes people are killed but no blood appears. When a Great Monk [of the Buddhist faith] "demonstrates transmigration", this often happens. In the Tang dynasty, Zhou Gan was killed by the rebel Huang Chao, whereupon a white grease bubbled up several feet high. During the Yuan [Mongol] dynasty bandits stabbed Dong Boxiao, but all that was seen was a puff of white vapour striking upwards into the heavens, which one might describe as uncanny. When in Jin times Sima cut off the head of the Ministerial Secretary Shunyu Bo, his blood flowed in the reverse direction, rising into a column 23 feet 7 *in* high. When the state of Northern Qi put Hulu Guang to death his blood remained on the ground and could not be removed. This was due to the force of resentment [due to unjust accusation]. The same sort of thing happened when Chang Hong's blood turned into blue jade . . .'

Most royal witches ■ In 1483 Richard of Gloucester accused Queen Margaret, his brother's wife, and Jane Shore of witchcraft to cast doubt upon the legitimacy of the royal heir. He waved his withered and deformed arm as evidence of their evildoing, but all those present were aware that the defect was congenital. Henry VIII suspected Anne Boleyn of magical seduction because she did not produce a male heir for him.

Earliest reported case of mass possession ■ In an Augustinian convent near Cambrai, in northern France, in 1491 Sister Jeanne Potier was seized with a lustful passion for her confessor and the other nuns soon joined her. Although there were only three demons involved, it took the Bishop of Cambrai seven months to exorcise them.

Best prevention against witchcraft ■ The hanging of consecrated herbs over the threshold was the most popular preventative measure taken against witchcraft. Vervain, rowan and dill were the most commonly used, but amulets such as a horseshoe were also deemed effective.

Witch hunts

Greatest persecution ■ The persecution of witches on a great scale in England began almost a century later than on the Continent as printed accounts began to pour into the country. By 1542 the problem had become so widespread that Parliament imposed the death penalty for conjuration (effecting supernatural activity by spells), thereby creating legal grounds for prosecution. English Protestantism's emphasis on human sin and the concept of a personal Satan were the greatest contributing factors to the psychological climate that fostered mass persecution of witches. Protestant clergy were forbidden to perform the rite of exorcism, the Roman Catholic Church's best weapon against demon possession. All anyone could do was pray.

Largest witch hunt ■ In Trier in France, where 306 accused witches named over 1500 accomplices.

LITERATURE

Most useful magical handbook ■ The *Picatrix* was a popular magical handbook; it gives instructions for making astrological images for specific purposes such as escaping from prison, attracting a lover, destroying an enemy, or guaranteeing good health.

Rulers and law makers

ROYALTY AND HEADS OF STATE

NOBLES • GOVERNMENT • LAW

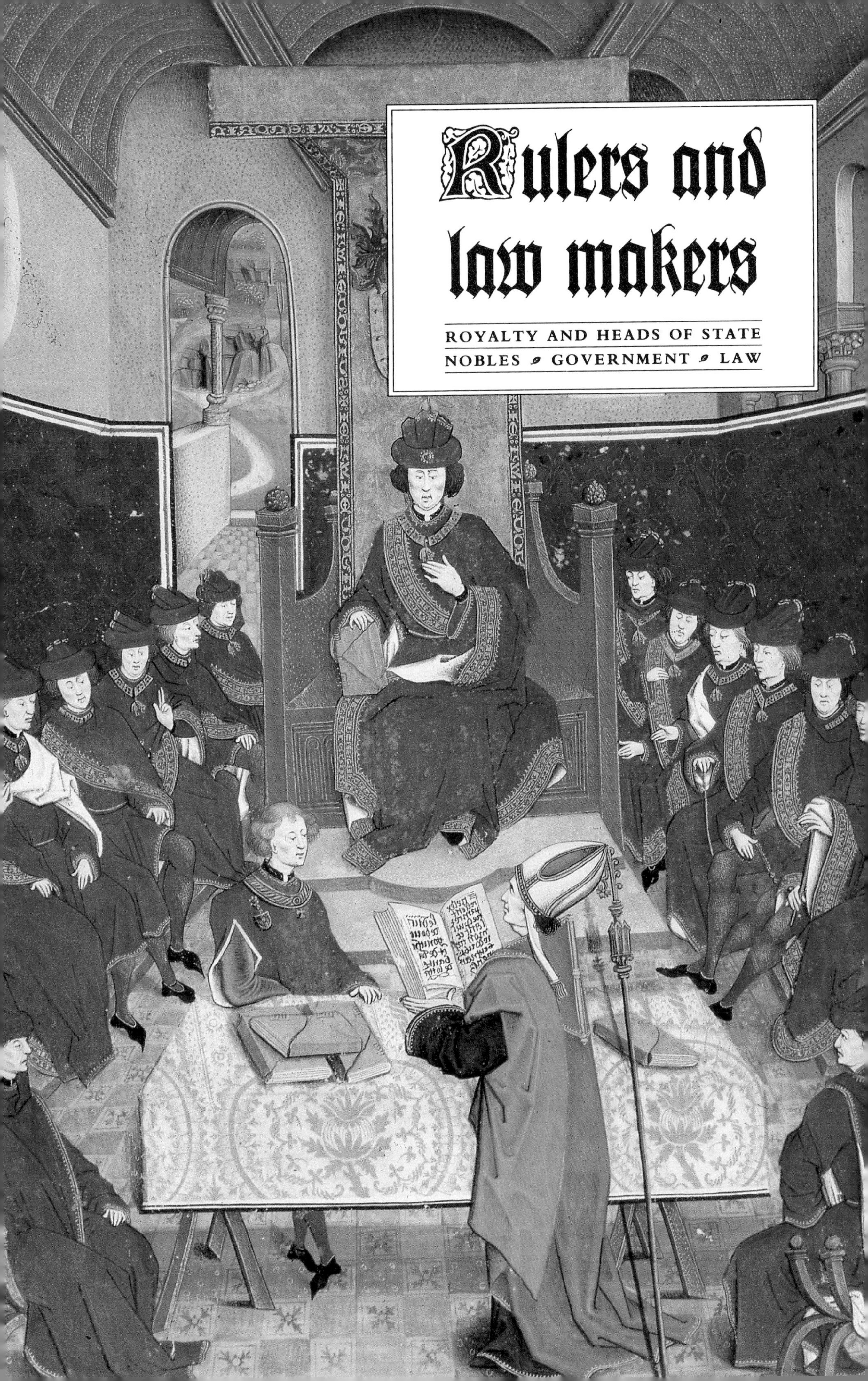

Royalty and heads of state

Royalty and heads of state

Oldest ruling dynasty ■ The present Japanese dynasty, despite various ups and downs and times when it held very little power, is conventionally and traditionally dated back to its foundation on 11 February 660 BC, though this could well be 600 years too early. The dynasty in 1500 had then been ruling for over 2000 years (on the traditional reckoning).

Oldest African dynasty ■ Since the decline of ancient Egypt, Ethiopia was governed by the longest-serving dynasty to rule in Africa. The political roots of the kingdom lay in the fourth-century Christianization of the highlands. By the 15th century the Coptic Christian king of Ethiopia was known as the 'Prester John of the Indies' and early European empire-builders sought to establish strategic and diplomatic links with him to counter the rising power of the Muslim Ottoman Turks. Western priests and mercenaries visited his court and helped the highland aristocracy survive the attacks of encircling Muslim enemies.

Longest all-time ■ The longest recorded reign of any monarch is that of Phiops II or Neferkare, a Sixth Dynasty Pharaoh of ancient Egypt. His reign began *c.* 2281 BC, when he was aged 6, and is believed to have lasted *c.* 94 years. Minhti, King of Arakan (Burma), is reputed to have reigned for 95 years between 1279 and 1374. The longest reign of any European monarch was that of Alfonso I Henrigues of Portugal who ascended the throne on 30 Apr 1112 and died on 6 Dec 1186 after a reign of 73 years 220 days, first as a Count and then as King.

Reigns

Longest reigns ■ Two Japanese emperors reigned for 36 years during this period: Go-Hanazono (1419–71) reigned, 1428–64 and Go-Tsuchimikada (1442–1500) reigned 1464–1500.

PREVIOUS PAGE: Charles the Bold, Duke of Burgundy, sitting with the assembly of the Order of the Golden Fleece.

Most unusual ■ The Mughul ruler Humayun, son of Babur the founder of the dynasty, had a most unusual reign. In the middle of it, around 1540, he was deposed by the Afghan chieftain Sher Khan, and had to flee to Iran. After the death of Sher Khan (now Sher Shah), Humayun managed to regain his throne after a gap of over a decade.

Most innovative ■ The Delhi Sultan Sikander Lodi (*d.* 1517) had a remarkable reign. He promoted Persian learning among the Hindu subjects of the Sultan, who were allowed to attend Islamic schools of learning (*madrasas*); an important musicological work, *Lahjat-i Sikandari* was the first recorded compilation of the *dhrupad* form; the first attempt was made to reconcile indigenous medical traditions to those of the Islamic *unani* school.

First in line of rulers

First emperors ■ With victory over the Moslem rulers of Delhi at the battle of Panipat in 1526, Zahir-ad-din Mohammed of Afghanistan (*c.* 1482–1530), popularly known as Babur (or Baber), became the most powerful man in northern India. He was founder of the Mughul empire. In 1547 Ivan IV 'the Terrible' (1530–84) was crowned, first Russian ruler entitled *Tsar* ('Caesar'), or emperor.

First 'All-Russian' ruler ■ *Tsar Ivan III called 'the Great' (1440–1505) ruled for 44 years (1462–1505). In 1485 he accepted the title All-Russia Prince and in 1492 proclaimed himself 'Sovereign of Russia'. The territory he ruled grew from about 155 500 sq miles* 430 000 sq km *to 1 081 000 sq miles* 2 800 000 sq km, *with a population of seven million people. During his rule the names* Rus *and* Moscovia *were replaced by* Russia.

First Prince of Wales ■ Born on 25 April 1284, the son of Edward I was named as the Prince of Wales in 1301 – the first English heir-apparent to bear the title. He succeeded his father to the throne as Edward II in 1307. Arthur Tudor, son of Henry VII was Prince of Wales in 1492, but he died in 1503 and his brother Henry succeeded him to the title. When Henry VII died in 1509, Henry became king as Henry VIII.

First Yorkist king ■ After six years of the English Wars of the Roses (1455–61) between the houses of York (the white rose) and Lancaster (the red rose), Edward IV was proclaimed king by the Yorkists, and defeated the Lancastrians at Towton. The Lancastrian king, Henry VI fled from England with Queen Margaret. Nine years later in 1470 the Lancastrians forced Edward IV to flee to Burgundy in France and Henry VI returned to the English throne for a year. In 1471 Edward IV returned to England. Queen Margaret was killed at Tewskesbury and Henry VI was imprisoned in the Tower of London where he soon died. The first Yorkists monarch was now secure.

First Tudor king ■ Victor at the Battle of Bosworth on 22 August 1485, Henry VII was the first of England's Tudor kings.

Crown of the tsars first used ■ The Hat of Monomakh, the crown of the Russian tsars, was, by tradition, sent with other insignia of imperial power by the Byzantine Emperor Constantine Monomakh to his grandson Prince Vladimir of Kiev. It is a golden crown adorned with delicate filigree work and emeralds, rubies and pearls, surmounted by a cross, and rimmed with sable. It was first used at the coronation of Tsar Dmitry, Ivan III's grandson, in 1498.

First Lord of the Isles ■ The title was created by King David I of Scotland and held, in turn, by two Scottish noble families. In 1493 it was forfeited to the Scottish crown, and since 1540 has belonged to the male heir of the Scottish crown.

First European rulers in America ■ Viceroys were appointed by the Spaniards in Mexico in 1535 and in Peru in 1543. These viceroys were head of the civil and military governments. They lived and governed in great style, with little interference or direction from Spain.

Greatest conqueror ■ Though he had been dead for 87 years, the Mongul emperor Timur the Lame or Tamberlane still fascinated western Europe in 1492. Striking north and east from Samarkand, he conquered the lands along the slopes of the Himalayas during the 1370s before turning southward to the Persian Gulf and westward to the Caspian in the 1380s. In 1391–6 it was the turn of South Russia, in 1398–9 that of North India; and from 1400 Timur struck westward again towards the Mediterranean in a series of campaigns which culminated in the greatest battle of the age, against the Ottoman sultan Bayezid at Angora in 1402. In a clash which may have embroiled 100 000 men on each side, Timur captured the sultan and ended as master of an empire reaching from the Dardanelles to Delhi, and from the Nile to the steppes of Central Asia. He was preparing to invade China at the time of his death.

Most improbable conqueror ■ 13 when he became king of France in 1483, short-legged and large headed, Charles VIII was described by contemporaries as

United Spain ■ *The marriage of King Ferdinand V of Aragon (1425–1516) and Queen Isabella I of Castile (1451–1504) in 1469 opened the way for the first united kingdom of Spain. The royal couple were known as the 'Catholic Kings'.*

'short, ugly, and with limbs so disproportioned that he looked more of a monster than a man'. Yet his reign saw the decisive defeat of a nobles' insurrection in 1486, the peaceful annexation of the independent Duchy of Brittany to France through his marriage to the heiress Anne in 1491, and the successful invasion of Italy in 1494. Marching south almost without opposition and conquering the kingdom of Naples without a battle, Charles was said to have 'won the war with the chalk of his billetting officers'. He died without a direct heir, aged only 28.

Most unsuccessful conqueror ■ Ruler of the powerful duchy of Burgundy, which reached from the North Sea to the Alps and encompassed modern Belgium, Holland and Luxembourg, as well as parts of France, Duke Charles the Bold became obsessed with dreams of wider conquest. In 1473 he attempted to persuade the Holy Roman Emperor to raise him to a new kingdom of Burgundy, and set about assembling one of the most formidable professional armies in contemporary Europe. Alarmed by these preparations, the Swiss cantons and the Rhineland cities formed a coalition against him: in spite of two crushing defeats in 1475 and 1476, Charles returned to the offensive in 1477, only to be defeated and killed at Nancy. Machiavelli used his defeat as proof that money did not always provide the sinews of war: but Charles' force was still uncoordinated, lacked a common language, and was unable to respond to surprise attacks.

Charles the Bold, Duke of Burgundy.

BRITISH MONARCHY RECORDS

LONGEST REIGN OR TENURE

KINGS

England: 56 years 19 days Henry III (1216–1272)
Scotland: 48 years 360 days William I (the Lion) (1165–1214)

SHORTEST REIGN OR TENURE

KINGS

40 days Sweyn Fork-beard, the Danish King of England (1013–14)
77 days Edward V 1483
6 months Duncan II of Scotland (May–November 1094)

QUEENS CONSORT

154 days Yoleta (1285–6) (Second Consort of Alexnder III of Scotland)

YOUNGEST TO START REIGN

KINGS

269 days Henry VI in 1422

QUEENS REGNANT

6 or 7 days Mary, Queen of Scots in 1542

LONGEST LIVED

KINGS

England: 68 years 19 days Edward I (1239–1307)

SHORTEST LIVED

KINGS

England: Under 13 years Edward V (Believed died in Tower of London on unknown date – July–September 1483)

QUEENS

Scotland: 7 years 5 months Margaret (c. 1283–c. 1290)

MOST MARRIED

KINGS

England: 6 times Henry VIII (1509–47)
Scotland: 6 Scottish kings had been married twice, but none thrice

QUEENS CONSORT

4 times Catherine Parr (c. 1512–1548) (Sixth consort of Henry VIII)

MOST CHILDREN

KINGS

England: 18 Edward I (1272–1307) 15 by Queen Eleanor and 3 by Queen Margaret
(Henry I (1068–1135) in addition to one or possibly two legitimate sons and a daughter had at least 20 bastard children (9 sons, 11 daughters) and possibly 22 by 6 mistresses)
Scotland: 12 Robert II (1316–1390) (the first 8 were legitimated by a subsequent marriage)

QUEENS CONSORT

15 Eleanor (c. 1244–90)

Most powerful rulers

Most powerful ■ In Iran, the Safavid dynasty, which came to power in 1501, was even more powerful, for they combined military and political success with a religious backing, which the Ottoman Turks did not do. The Safavids claimed that they were descended from the seventh Imam within the shia Muslim religion. Thus they could represent the Hidden Imam or Mahdi until he came back to earth.

Most powerful American rulers ■ The Inca empire stretched through the whole of present Peru, Chile, Bolivia, Ecuador and most of Argentina. It had a population of something between seven and nine million. The emperor of this great area was held by his subjects to be a god. His power was immense. Much of the land was state-owned; the state religion was imposed upon his peoples; provincial nobles were forced to spend part of each year in the Inca capital at Cuzco, thus linking them strongly to their ruler and weakening their own status. The Emperor Pachacutec was crowned in 1438 and dedicated himself to the service of his empire. During his reign he imposed Inca culture on people in the conquered towns, establishing schools for the noblemen. He imposed the decimal system on the tributary system and introduced a calendar based on the solar year. He died in 1471 and the Spanish found his mummy wrapped in sumptuous vestments, with eyes of gold in the sockets of his skull.

Most powerful women ■ Family membership of Iroquois society in the Eastern Woodlands of North America was determined through the female line. A male remained with his female family until marriage; then he joined the family of his wife. A woman could divorce simply by setting her husband's belongings outside the door of the long house. Political power in an Iroquois community came through a group of related families – *ochwachiras*. Through these the women named the representatives at tribal councils, but they also attended and influenced meetings of the ruling council. This relationship made Iroquois women among the most politically powerful in the world.

Most powerful imaginary monarch ■ From the 12th century onward news began to filter to Europe of a Christian monarch in the east of enormous power and wealth. Known as 'presbyter John' or 'presenter John', he was reported by a Syrian bishop in 1145 to be a direct descendant of the Three Wise Men, the Magi, who came to Jesus. A letter supposedly from Prester John circulated in Constantinople in which he described himself as exceeding 'in riches, virtue and power all creatures who do dwell under heaven.' His empire, where milk and honey flowed in abundance, was said to be vast. European explorers were sent eastward in the 13th century to link up with this amazing monarch but returned to report that 'not one-hundredth part is true of what is told of him'. Disappointed by the search for Prester John in Asia, his 'principal residence' began to be shown in Ethiopia, as it was on Fra Maura's map of 1459.

Most successful Incas ■ In military terms, the most successful were those of the 9th and 10th Incas, Pachacuti and Tupac Yupanqui, his son and successor, who was his general in the later years of his reign. Between them they were credited with the conquests of 42 distinct communities and established Inca hegemony from Quito, now in Ecuador, in the north to what is now southern Peru.

Last in line of rulers

Last Byzantine emperor to visit the West ■ Emperor John VIII Paleaologus came to Italy to negotiate a union between the orthodox church in Constantinople and the papacy. The painting of the procession of the Maji by Benozzo Gozzoli, done in Florence between 1459 and 1504, about 30 years after the visit, shows the Emperor arriving in Florence.

Last Byzantine emperor ■ Constantine XI Palaeologus came to the throne in 1449 and died during the successful Ottoman siege of Constantinople in 1453, and the line of Byzantine emperors, successors to the ancient emperors of Rome, came to an end. After the Ottoman conquest, some other members of the Imperial Byzantine family converted to Islam and held high office in the service of the Ottoman Sultans. Messih Pasha, who commanded the unsuccessful siege of Rhodes in 1480 was a Palaeologus.

Pisanello's portrait medal of John VIII Palaeologus, which was cast in 1438/9, ushered in a lasting style of modern realistic portraiture.

Last coronation ■ In 1452 Frederick of Habsburg (1415–93), crowned with the title Frederick III, became the last Holy Roman Emperor to hold his coronation in Rome. The first had been Charlemagne, crowned there on Christmas Day 800.

Last Czech king ■ In 1471 King George Podebrady of Bohemia (*b.* 1420, crowned

Charles V of Spain, who became Roman Emperor, rides with his rival Francis I of France.

1458) died. Today Bohemia is the Czech part of Czechoslovakia, then it was an independent kingdom. King George was the last native-born Czech to wear the crown; his successors were Hungarians or Germans.

Last Yorkist king ■ In 1485 Henry Tudor, the Lancastrian heir, defeated and killed Richard III (*b.* 1452; king 1483; *d.* 1485) at Bosworth Field and became himself King of England. He married Elizabeth of York, thus uniting the houses of York and Lancaster and ending the Wars of the Roses.

Last Aztec ruler ■ Cuauhtemoc succeeded Cuitlahuac, his cousin, who died of the smallpox epidemic introduced by the Spanish *conquistadores* in October 1520, after a reign of only four months. Captured on 13th August 1521, he was confirmed by the Spaniards as a puppet ruler but was deposed and put to death, allegedly for plotting against Spanish rule, during a campaign to Honduras, led by Hernán Cortés, probably on 28 February 1525.

Last duke ■ Charles the Bold, Duke of Burgundy (*b.* 1433 – duke 1467), also called *le Temeraire* ('the Rash') was killed at the Battle of Nancy. He was the last duke of a family whose lands included most of the modern Benelux countries as well as Burgundy in France. Their ambition, never achieved, had been to establish a new European kingdom.

Biggest electoral bribe ■ Who was to succeed Maximilian I as Habsburg emperor became a contest between Francis I of France and Charles I of Spain. The Imperial electors were openly bribed in merchants' acceptances handed over to them one by one in return for their vote. Francis could not find any backing in Italy, whereas Maximilian (already a client of the Fuggers in Germany) ensured that Charles would have financial support from the merchants most favoured by German electors. On Maximilian's death (January, 1519) what had previously seemed enough money (275 000 florins from the Welsers in Germany and three Italian parties) had to be increased as Francis grew desperate – he tried to bribe the Fuggers – and the florin weakened. Charles was advised to get a further 220 000. The eventual total sum raised came to over 850 000 florins and was written out in an itemized account headed 'Expenses incurred by the Emperor Charles for his election as King of the Romans'.

Cruellest successions ■ Many successions were bloody or cruel, but the succession of the Turkish Sultans were almost formally so. The Turkish Sultans began their reigns by fighting with their brothers. There was no orderly law of accession: the only rule was that the prince who seized the throne and eliminated the competition became Sultan. When Mehmed the Conqueror came to the throne in 1451 his first act was to strangle his infant brother. His son Bayezid II, who acceded in 1481, did not kill his brother Djem, because he had fled abroad, so he secretly poisoned Djem's son instead and personally executed Djem's chief supporter. Bayezid's son, Selim the Grim, became Sultan in 1512, after he had fought and killed his brothers, Korkud and Ahmed. Suleyman the Magnificent was luckier. He had no brothers and in 1520 became the Sultan unopposed.

Attributes of rulers

Youngest ■ Shah Ismael, the founder of the Safavid dynasty in Persia (Iran), was only 12 when he became Shah in 1501 and began over the next ten years, to expand his empire to include most of modern Iran. He claimed that he was God – and his followers believed him. He died in 1524. But his successor was even younger. Shah Tahmasp was only 10 years old at his accession. He ruled from 1533 to 1576.

Long-lived sultans ■ The Ottoman sultans were an immensely powerful and successful dynasty in the 15th and 16th centuries, helped by a remarkably long-lived series of rulers. Between 1481 and 1566 there were only three sultans:

The Ottoman ruler Suleyman I – known as the Magnificent or the Law Giver.

Bayezid II (1481–1512), Selim I (1512–20) and Suleyman I, known in the west as Suleyman the Magnificent, and to the Turks as Suleyman the Law-Giver, who ruled from 1520 to 1566. All of these rulers came to the throne when they were relatively mature men. Bayezid was 33 at his accession, Selim 42 and Suleyman 26.

Most handsome king ■ England's Edward IV (*b.* 1442, reigned 1461–70, 1471–83) attracted the comment of contemporaries for a number of physical and military accomplishments. Described as 'the most handsome among the elegant men of the world', he has been judged from his skeleton (his coffin was opened in

Portrait of the Ottoman ruler Mehmed II by the Italian artist Gentile Bellini.

1789) to have stood 6 feet 3½ in *192 cm* tall. An epic womanizer, he horrified his political advisers by marrying a widow for love, and later boasted of having enjoyed 'the merriest, the holiest, and the wiliest harlots in Christendom'. But he was also a man of action whose campaigns still interest strategists. A precocious exponent of accurate intelligence, rapid movement, and direct responsibility on the field, he commanded in nine victorious battles, the first of them – Mortimer's Cross – when he was only 18. Forced into exile by a coup in 1470, he returned to become the only king in English history to win a throne, lose it, regain it, and retain it to the end of his life.

Ugliest and cruellest ■ Edward IV's younger brother Richard had, by 1492, already gained his undeserved reputation as the ugliest and cruellest king in European history. The historian John Rouse had accused him of the murder of his nephews – the 'Princes in the Tower' – and described him as 'being born with teeth and black hair reaching to his shoulders, after being held for two years in his mother's womb'. Though these contemporary superlatives are now exploded myths, Richard (who came to the throne as Richard III in 1483) has at least retained the more honourable distinction of being the last English king to die on the battlefield, at Bosworth Field in 1485.

Most tragic queen ■ Margaret of Anjou (1429-82) married Henry VI of England in 1445 as part of the abortive quest for peace in the Hundred Years War. Margaret had by 1455 become the effective leader of the Lancastrian side in a struggle that was fast degenerating into war. In 1451 she seemed near to success after defeating the Yorkists at Wakefield and killing their leader Richard, but was herself defeated four months later at Towton and forced to flee to Scotland, then France. Returning 10 years later in another attempt to dislodge Edward IV, she was again defeated at Tewksbury (May 1471), her son Edward being killed on the battlefield and her husband Henry murdered in the Tower shortly afterwards. She had been 15 when she arrived in England and was only 41 when she left. Though lacking political finesse, Margaret was capable of inspiring great personal devotion, and was soon regarded in England and Europe as one whose trials had exceeded those of any heroine in a chivalric romance.

Most pious, successful, and bigoted ■ Isabella of Castile was fighting her half-brother Henry for her throne from 1468, when she was only 17. In 1478 she established the Spanish Inquisition. Victorious over her internal enemies by 1479, she turned in 1482 against Granada, the last surviving Muslim enclave in Spain, and completed its conquest in early January, 1492. In the same year she supported Columbus' plans for a westward voyage to the Indies, and ordered the Jewish community to accept conversion or leave Spain. Isabella had by her death in 1504 surpassed the achievements of any contemporary European ruler and remains one of the outstanding women of her own or any age.

Borgia papacy which Savonarola had repeatedly denounced had made his influence an embarrassment: he was discredited, tortured, and burned.

Craftiest king ■ Louis XI of France (1461–83) was described by a contemporary as 'the best person I ever knew at getting himself out of tight corner'. Defeated by a league of rebellious nobles in 1465, he divided and neutralized his enemies by making concessions to the leaders: captured by the Duke of Burgundy in 1468, he joined in the duke's campaign against Liège, which his own agents had been inciting to rebellion; faced in 1475 by the same coalition of England and Burgundy that had enabled Henry V to conquer France in 1420, he bought Edward IV off with a massive bribe and boasted that he had 'thrown the English out of France with free drinks and a good meal'. Outliving or outmanoeuvring most of the rebels who had faced him in 1465, he more than doubled the size of the French army and left a greatly strengthened monarchy to his son Charles VIII.

This picture of Louis XI, king of France 1461–83, with his counsellors was made in about 1470.

Most religious and reluctant ■ To contemporaries the strongest political career of the 1490s was that of the Dominican friar Gerolamo Savonarola, who was invited to Florence in 1489 to improve the quality of religious life. His fiery sermons offered moral leadership, while the death of the leading citizen Lorenzo de' Medici in 1492, and the incompetence of his successor Piero soon made Savonarola a centre of political attention as well. During the winter of 1494 Savonarola was called upon by the government as the only man who could advise on the reform of the constitution without provoking violence, and for the next four years was regarded by many observers as the ruler of Florence – a role which he constantly denied. By 1498 Florence's need to conciliate the

Cruellest ■ The semi-mythical Dracula was a fusion of two historical characters, Vladislav III and IV, both princes of Wallachia, in what is now Romania. The first, known to contemporaries as 'Dracul' or devil, played a real part in resisting the Turkish invasion of eastern Europe until his death in 1446. Vlad IV of Wallachia became known as 'the Impaler' from his love of impaling people on sharp spikes. In a six-year reign of terror (1456–62) he is said to have ordered more than 20 000 executions. According to one story, his palace at Tirgoviste was surrounded by a six-mile *10 km* hedge, with a row of his impaled victims in front of it all the way around. A thicket next to his palace was rumoured to have a corpse hanging from every branch, and anyone found trying to remove one would be hanged in its place. Enemies even claimed he fed on the flesh and blood of the victims and traditions about Vlad 'the Impaler' could have been the basis for the fictional Count Dracula. Vlad lost his throne in 1462. In the previous winter he had impaled the emissaries of the Turkish Sultan, Mehmed the Conqueror, who had come to collect the tribute money due from him, and then crossed the river Danube and either killed or cut off the ears and noses of the peasants on Sultan Mehmed's territory to the south of the river. The Sultan in reprisal led an army against him, forcing him to flee to Hungary.

Most isolated ■ The Ming emperors of China (1368–1644), 'the sons of Heaven', claimed universal sovereignty and lived in splendid isolation in the vast walled palace of the Imperial city of Beijing, surrounded only by the very influential court eunuchs.

Most astrologically influenced ■ The Mughul ruler Humayun (who came to the throne in 1530) was a great believer in astrology. According to the text *Qanun-i Humayuni*, he arranged his court ritual so that places were assigned to nobles on the basis of the zodiac; court dress also changed from day to day according to astrological almanacs.

Most tactless ■ Though only the fourth son of the Duke of Milan, Ludovico Sforza elbowed his nephew Giangaleazzo to one side in 1480 and assumed effective control of the duchy. His court, which welcomed both Leonardo da Vinci and Bramante, was one of the most brilliant in contemporary Europe. But by the early 1490s Ludovico's conduct had aroused the suspicion of other Italian rulers: in 1494 he invited the French to invade Italy in order to defend him, then grew alarmed by their success and turned against them. When the French attacked him in 1499, most of his subjects refused to fight: and when he attempted a comeback in 1500, his Swiss mercenaries also left him in the lurch. Ludovico ended his days in the French castle of Loches where his cell is covered from floor to ceiling with graffiti lamenting *J'ay tout perdu* (I have lost all).

Most decadent Turkish prince ■ This title must go to Alemshah, one of the sons of the Ottoman Sultan Bayezid II (1481–1512). His father sent him as governor to Manisa (western Turkey) where, despite his mother's attempts to reform him, he drank himself to death in 1503.

Most literary ■ All of the Ottoman Sultans of the 16th century, from Murad II (1421–51) to Murad III (1574–95) left volumes of poetry. A Turkish author in the century listed 'poetic talent' as one of the qualities which made the Sultans superior to all other monarchs.

The founder of the Mughal empire, Babur, was the author of an important autobiographical work in Turkish, the *Babur-nama*. The work reveals the ruler to have had a humanistic world-view, and provides an acute psychological portrait of the man. Babur's great-grandson, the Mughal ruler Jahangir, also authored an important autobiography, *Tuzuk-i Jahangiri*. These works are quite different from the official portrayals by court chroniclers.

Greatest beauty contest ■ In the early 1500s the Russian tsar Vassily III, the Great Prince of Moscow, chose a wife from a selection of 1500 maidens of noble families. He chose Solomonia, a daughter of the Saburov *boyars* (nobles).

Most married ■ Henry VIII of England (1491–1547) is famous for his many wives. The first was Catherine of Aragon (of Spain), whom he married in 1509 and divorced in 1533; then came Anne Boleyn, married in 1533, beheaded in 1536; Jane Seymour, whom he married in 1536 died only a year later; Anne of Cleves (in Germany) he married briefly in 1540; Katherine Howard he married also in 1540 and executed in 1542. Catherine Parr, his sixth wife whom he married in 1543, survived him.

Richest African king ■ In 1324 Mansa Musa, the emperor of Mali, arrived in Egypt on his pilgrimage to Mecca. He entered Cairo with 100 camels each carrying 300 lb *111 kg* of gold and was preceded by 500 slaves each carrying a gold staff weighing 60 oz *1.8 kg*. It is reported that he put so much gold into circulation in Egypt that he caused severe inflation. A Majorcan map of 1375 describes him as 'the richest and most noble king in all the land', and the legend of his wealth was still recorded on European maps of Africa as late as the 16th century.

The German painter Hans Holbein the younger (1497–1543) painted this portrait of Anne of Cleves to show to her future husband, Henry VIII of England. Henry agreed to the match but when he met her said the portrait was far too flattering and he did not wish to wed this 'Flanders Mare'. The marriage only lasted a few months and they parted by mutual consent.

Least married ■ After 1450, the Turkish Sultans almost never got married. The ladies who shared their beds and gave birth to their children were usually slaves. Thus most Ottoman princes and princesses have slave mothers, and even when they shared the same father – the Sultan – they usually had different mothers. Suleyman the Magnificent, however, married his favourite concubine, Hurrem Sultan, and she made sure that her favourite son, Selim – known as Selim the Sot – succeeded to the throne in 1566.

Largest ransom ■ In 1531 Francisco Pizarro, a member of the minor Spanish nobility, set out with about 100 foot soldiers and 62 horsemen to attack the great Inca empire. At Cajamarca Pizarro's tiny force faced 30 000 troops with the emperor Atahualpa at their head. Audaciously Pizarro seized the emperor. 'By having this man in our hands the entire realm is calm,' it was reported. Atahualpa ordered the secret removal of his rival and offered an enormous ransom for his own safety. When it was paid 24 200 lb *11 000 kg* of gold objects alone were melted down, one-fifth of what remained went to the King of Spain, and there was still enough for every cavalryman to receive 90 lb *41 kg* of gold and 180 lb *82 kg* of silver. Once the ransom was paid, Atahualpa was executed.

Narrowest escape ■ The closest a Turkish Sultan ever came to assassination was in 1492. When Sultan Bayezid II was returning from Albania with his army, a dervish with rings on his ears and round his neck ambushed him on the road. The dervish suddenly sprang forward shouting, 'I am the Mahdi.' He threw off his bearskin cloak and rushed at the Sultan with a drawn sword. The Sultan's bodyguards fled, but fortunately for Bayezid his vizier, Iskender Pasha, ran forward, smashed the dervish's skull and cut his body into pieces.

First use of famous phrase ■ *Le Roi est mort, vive le Roi* was first used in 1461 by the royal heralds to proclaim the death of the French king Charles VII and the accession to the throne of his successor, Louis XI.

Nobles

Most creations ■ The largest number of new hereditary peerages created in England in any year was the 54 in 1296.

Oldest order ■ The order which can trace its origins furthest back is the Military and Hospitaller Order of St Lazarus of Jerusalem founded by St Basil the Great in the 4th century AD. A date as early as 809 AD has been attributed to the Most Ancient Order of the Thistle, but is of doubtful provenance. The Order of St John in Scotland, founded in 1124, was suppressed in the 16th century. The prototype of the princely Orders of Chivalry is the Most Noble Order of the Garter founded by King Edward III *c.* 1348. The order of the Tower and Sword in Portugal dates from 1459, the Order of St George, Austria from 1470, the order of the Sword in Sweden and Norway from 1525. The Order of the Golden Fleece dates from 1429 in Spain and Austria.

First Heralds' College ■ In 1483 the English Heralds' College of Arms was founded as a royal corporation by King Richard III to make decisions in matters armorial, that is pertaining to the heraldic coat of arms that a family might bear. It consisted of the Earl Marshall of England, kings-of arms, heralds and pursuivants (junior heraldic officers). (The College of Arms still records proven pedigrees of those of noble birth and grants armorial bearings to new members of the House of Lords.)

Most urbane of noblemen ■ In about 1518 an Italian aristocrat completed work on his book which was only published a year after his death in 1528. Baldassare Castiglione's *Il Cortegiano* (The Book of the Courtier) depicts the ideal courtier and the perfect lady of the court. This ideal courtier should be of noble birth, be gracious in manners and be virtuous. He should have been a well-rounded educa-

Although Baldassare Castiglione (1478–1528) in his book, The Courtier, *showed great concern for outward appearances of dress and gesture, his real concern was with such moral values as sincerity and fidelity. 'The purpose of such a person is to serve a prince . . . and to convert him from any base ways into an instrument of his people's salvation.' To do this the courtier must 'seek to gain the good will and captivate the mind of his prince.'*

Most exclusive ■ *The governing families of Venice were the most exclusive ruling class in Europe. At this time they had admitted no newcomers to their ranks since 1381, and continued to exclude them for a further century after 1550.*

tion so that he would be as proficient in dancing, poetry and music as he was in the skills of war. He should be able to converse in Latin, Greek and the vernacular.

Most scandalous family liaison ■ Obsessed with his younger sister Isabelle and the father of three children by her, John V, Count of Armagnac in Southern France, attempted to persuade the Pope Nicholas V to allow a regular marriage. Excommunicated, driven from his estates by royal troops in 1455, and summoned to appear in Paris, John not only escaped but attempted to bribe two corrupt papal officials to forge the necessary dispensation for him. Though he was also suspected by King Louis XI of being in contact with English spies, he managed to secure the pardon of both the Pope and his king, and was killed in a pointless brawl on his own estates early in 1473.

Longest reigning shoguns ■ The title of shogun was originally given to generals sent to quell indigenous peoples in Japan's peripheral states, their name deriving from *seii tai shogun* (literally 'barbarian-subduing generalissimo'). The second, Ashikaga, shogunate lasted from 1338 to 1578. The longest shogun's reign during this period was that of Ashikaga Yoshihara (1511–50) who reigned between 1522 and 1547. At this time, powerless during the civil wars of the 16th century, the shoguns had little more than a ceremonial function.

Toughest political survivor ■ In an age when English statesmen often faced the option of turning their coats or losing their heads, the Earl of Oxford (John de Vere) managed to keep both his life and his integrity. Unreconciled to the Yorkist regime of Edward IV, who had killed his father and elder brother, he played a leading part in the attempt to reinstate Henry VI in 1470. Even after the defeat of the Lancastrians, he harried the south coast in a series of raids until he was captured in 1474 on St Michael's Mount and imprisoned in a castle near Calais. In 1483 Richard of Gloucester's coup and uncertainty over the fate of the 'Princes in the Tower' enabled de Vere to escape, along with his jailor, and join Henry Tudor. He survived to hold high commands in the Battles of Bosworth Field and Stoke, which concluded the Wars of the Roses.

Most celebrated assassin ■ Gianandrea Lampugnani, a young Milanese noble with two associates murdered the unloveable Duke Galeazzo Maria Sforza on 26 December 1476. Already steeped in classical ideals of civic liberty, the conspirators took mass to give their action Christian sanctity: Lampugnani's accomplices were killed by the ducal bodyguards, but he survived to give the torturers one of the best opportunities that even they had ever enjoyed. As they set about him with hot pincers, he was heard to murmur: 'Death is bitter, but fame everlasting.'

Most vile noblemen ■ Legends of powerful men who terrorized their neighbours are found in many traditions. In Europe, they took the forms of the aristocratic Bluebeard who murdered a succession of child brides and of the human vampire Count Dracula. The originals for both have been identified with 15th century noblemen. In 1440 Gilles de Laval, Seigneur de Retz (or de Rais) was executed at Nantes, France, for human sacrifice to devils and sexual perversion. He had confessed to the kidnapping and murder of more than 100 children and in Brittany, where his principal castle and estates lay, is thought to have been the original Bluebeard. (See *Cruellest rulers*.)

Most valuable exile ■ The exile of the 1490s whom other rulers were most eager to entertain was Prince Djem, son of Sultan Mehmed II. Defeated by his brother Bayezid in a contest for the Turkish throne, he fled in 1482 to Rhodes and was arrested by the Christian Knights of St John, who extorted 45 000 ducats annually from Bayezid for keeping him out of circulation. By 1492 Djem had become such an embarrassment that his brother agreed to pay Pope Alexander VI 150 000 ducats to keep his rival in custody. The Muslim prince became something of a favourite at the papal court, some of its younger members copying his dress. Removed from Rome by the French in 1494, Djem died early in the following year – probably from malaria but, contemporaries believed, from the slow poison of the Borgias.

Viziers

Unluckiest ■ In 1516, the Turkish Sultan, Selim the Grim, defeated the army of the Egyptian Sultan in Syria, occupied Syria and Palestine, and proposed to march in to Egypt. Huseyn Pasha, the vizier, objected, telling the Sultan that it would be impossible for the army to march across the waterless Sinai Desert. The Sultan reacted to this advice by cutting off the vizier's head. The vizier's advice also turned out to be wrong. The Turkish army crossed the desert without mishap and defeated the Egyptian army outside Cairo in January 1517.

Most scandalous ■ In 1541 Suleyman the Magnificent's Chief Minister or Grand Vizier, Lufti Pasha was dismissed. He had married one of the Sultan's sisters, and seems to have been sacked after quarrelling with her. According to one story, she lost her temper with him after he had refused to retract a command for a prostitute to be hung up by the legs and sliced in half. Different versions of the story were still being told a century later. Lufti Pasha himself claimed that he was not dismissed but retired voluntarily, in order to be free of the wiles of women. He commented: 'Bribes to officials are an incurable disease. Oh God, save us from bribes!'

LITERATURE

Most controversial political memoirs ■ Philippe de Commynes began his career as advisor to Charles, Duke of Burgundy, but deserted him in 1472 to join Louis XI of France in return for a bribe. During a long political career he knew personally or observed many of the European leaders of the later 15th century, including Edward IV, Richard III, and Henry VII of England, Louis XI and Charles VIII of France, Charles the Bold, Duke of Burgundy, Lorenzo de' Medici of Florence, and Emperor Maximilian I. Disgraced and imprisoned in 1487, he began the personal memoirs which are a major source for the history of the later 15th century: but they are so personal that historians still disagree about their value, many believing that they are a justification of his own defection to France.

Highest duty of a prince ■ Niccolo Machiavelli (1469–1527) wrote that the first duty of a prince is to master the art of war and wage it successfully. His great book *The Prince* was published in 1513, and was to become one of the most influential works in the history of Western thought.

When you enter your lord's place, say 'Good speed', and with humble cheer greet all who are there present. Do not rush in rudely, but enter with head up and at an easy pace, and kneel on one knee only to your lord or sovereign, whichever he be.

If any speak to you at your coming, look straight at them with a steady eye, and give good ear to their words while they be speaking; and see to it with all your might that ye jangle [chatter] not, nor let your eyes wnder about the house, but pay heed to what is said, with blithe visage and diligent spirit. When ye answer, ye shall be ready with what ye shall say, and speak 'things fructuous', and give your reasons smoothly in words that are gentle but compendious, for many words are right tedious to the wise man who listens; therefore eschew them with diligence.

Take no seat, but be ready to stand until you are bidden to sit down. Keep your hands and feet at rest; do not claw your flesh or lean against a post, in the presence of your lord, or handle anything belonging to the house.

Make obeisance to your lord alway when you answer; otherwise, stand as still as a stone, unless he speak.

The Babees' Book *c.* 1475

Most important book of manners ■ The Babees' Book was written in *c.* 1475 to instruct young princes and nobles in the courtesies of life. It was one of the most important of such tracts.

The words of Machiavelli (1469–1527) ring true across the centuries: 'Men are so simple and so ready to obey present necessities, that one who deceives will always find those who allow themselves to be deceived.'

Empires

Greatest ■ Between 1450 and 1550 the Ottoman empire not only expanded more rapidly than any other state at the time, but also became the greatest empire in the world in terms of territory controlled (see map). Mehmed the Conqueror (1451–81) not only conquered Constantinople in 1453, but also the Crimea, southern Greece, Albania, Bosnia, Hercegovina and much of Turkey. His grandson Selim the Grim (1512–20) conquered south-east Turkey and, in a single campaign in 1516–17, Syria, Palestine, Egypt and large parts of North Africa. By 1550, Selim's son, Suleyman the Magnificent (1520–66), had conquered Rhodes and most of the islands in the Aegean, Hungary, eastern Turkey and most of Iraq. Algiers too recognized the rule of the Turkish sultan. In 1529 Vienna was besieged and nearly taken.

The population under the control of the Ottoman empire was to increase from about 10 million in 1500 to nearly 30 million a century later.

Largest European world empire ■ By politically astute marriages rather than by conquest, the Habsburg dynasty had acquired, when Emperor Charles V (1519–58) came to the throne, an empire unequalled since that of Charlemagne of Rome. It embraced the Spanish kingdoms, Germany, the Low Countries and a large part of Italy. It rivalled for size the Ottoman empire which, though partly Asiatic, spread west into Europe in the 16th century.

Largest African ■ Askia Mohammed of Songhai gained power by a military coup in 1493 and became the greatest imperial ruler of late-15th-century tropical Africa. The Songhai empire inherited the state-building traditions of both the south Saharan Ghana empire of the 11th century and the upper Niger Mali empire of the 14th century. The Askia dynasty domi-

The Holy Roman Empire under Charles V and the Ottoman Empire circled the Mediterranean.

nated the Sudanic belt of West Africa almost from the Atlantic to the basin of Lake Chad and controlled much of the cloth, salt, rice and gold trade of the Sahara.

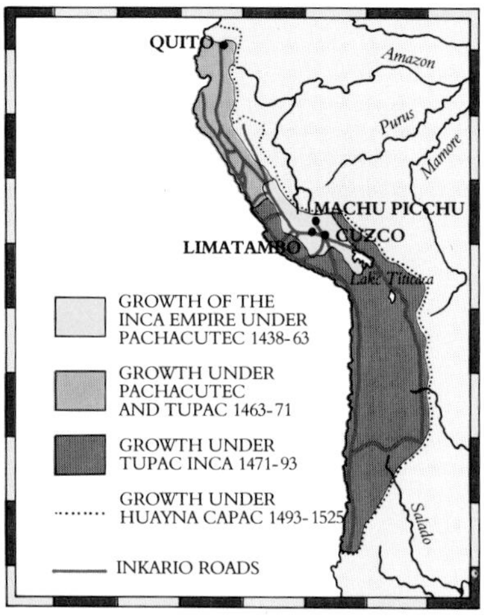

Shortest-lasting American empire ■ The Incas controlled what is today southern Colombia, Ecuador, Bolivia, Peru and the northern part of Chile when the Spaniards arrived. But this great empire of somewhere between 7 and 9 million people lasted little less than a century from 1438 when Pachacutec made conquests from Peru to present-day Ecuador. His son Tupac Yupanqui succeeded him in 1471 and extended the empire south to southern Colombia but had to defend the eastern frontiers from attack. He died, possibly from smallpox brought by the Spaniards, in 1527 and his son Huascar was proclaimed Inca in Peru, but his brother Atahualpa rose against him and violent civil war rocked the empire. In 1532 Atahualpa was finally victorious just as the Spaniards reached his territory and ended the 94 years of Inca rule.

Most populous ■ China, ruled by the Ming dynasty in 1500, was the most populous state in the world, having a population of up to 200 million. India, at this time not united, had about 100 million people. Ottoman Turkey was only about 10 million and Iran, on the point of being united by the Safavid dynasty, had only 4 million.

Most far-flung empire ■ For a period (1415–1580) the Portuguese possessed an empire which had possessions or rights in every known continent. It stretched from south China to the interior of Brazil and included outposts in Africa and North America. The Portuguese were the first nation in modern times to deliberately plan and undertake the sustained expansion of their dominions overseas.

Countries

Smallest country ■ Andorra, in the mountainous eastern Pyrenees, is only 190 square miles *300 sq km* in area. Under the *Paréage* of 1278 it was placed under the suzerainty of two co-principals – the Comte de Foix and the Bishop of Urgel.

Oldest country ■ Of the world's sovereign countries the oldest and most populous was China, where the Shang dynasty first ruled for six centuries from about 1750 BC.

England became sovereign in 927 AD when Æthelstan, King of the West Saxons and the Mercians, imposed direct rule upon Northumbria and maintained this until his death on 27 October 939.

Most recent ■ In the 15th century the country to achieve sovereignty and unity most recently was Spain, where the royal houses of Aragon and Castile had been united by the marriage of Ferdinand and Isabella in 1479.

Last English possession in France ■ English kings owned land in France from the Norman Conquest, and under Henry II (1154–89) English power extended across northern and western France. During the Hundred Years War, which ended in 1453, the English lost all their French territory except Calais, which remained English until 1558.

European settlements

Iceland ■ Although Iceland had been known to Irish Christian anchorites (hermits) who sought wilderness lands for their existence, it was Norsemen who in about 870 made the first settlement there. The Irish hermits were driven out and the habitable land was occupied over the next half-century. Some historians believe that as many as 25 000 people settled there. Most of them came from south-west Norway. Dependent on Scandinavia for their livelihood, they faced in the 15th century a deteriorating climate and fearful volcanic eruptions at home and lack of interest in their existence from Europe.

Greenland ■ From 982 AD Erik the Red, having been driven from Iceland, spent three years exploring the coast of Greenland. He returned in 986 with a small band of settlers. These first settlers lived a pastoral life as described in the 13th century: 'The farmers raise cattle and sheep in large numbers, and make butter and cheese in great quantities.' However, as with Iceland, changes in climate and in European politics led to the settlers abandoning Greenland from about 1410, although a few people may have remained.

First overseas colonies of Portugal ■ The indigenous Berbers of the Canary Islands were enslaved first by Portuguese planters and wine-growers and then by Spanish colonists who brought in both free immigrant and foreign slave labourers. The colonial model that evolved influenced the later Spanish colonization of America and many Canary Islanders became the followers of *conquistadores* who stopped at the Canaries en route to America. The most famous of these was Columbus himself, who sailed from the Canaries.

Africa ■ As the Portuguese navigators pressed further and further south along the west coast of Africa, they established trading forts and factories along their route. The first was at Arguim (off the coast of modern Mauretania) in about 1443. The factory was leased to private merchants who used it as a base to attract the Saharan gold trade. Then Elmina on the Gold Coast (Ghana) was established in 1503. Here the Portuguese traded with the local people for ivory, gold and slaves. (The Portuguese had had a foothold in North Africa since their conquest of Ceuta, and there were other European footholds there too by 1500.)

First Portuguese foothold in India ■ The first Portuguese fortress was erected on the island of Cochin (western India) in

A map of the Gulf of Guinea, West Africa, is decorated with Elmina Castle in what is now Ghana.

1503. It was known as Castel Manuel and was the headquarters of the Portuguese in India until their capture of Goa in 1510. The first Portuguese fortress built on the Indian mainland was at Cananor (City of Krishna) on the Malabar coast when in 1515 the local ruler allowed the construction of the fortress of Santo Angelo. Cananor was the major centre for the import of Persian and Arabian horses into India.

North America ■ In 1492 Columbus, with one of his ships wrecked, had to leave men ashore on Hispaniola (the modern island of Haiti and the Dominican Republic). Thus the first settlement was made by Europeans in the Americas for nearly 500 years, since the Vikings. When Columbus returned to Hispaniola in November 1493 he discovered that all the men had been killed by the local people.

In 1517 the lawyer, John Rastell, equipped two ships in London to install the first English colony in America. The masters of both ships incited the men to break off the voyage in Ireland. Rastell was left behind in Waterford and in 1519 published a short verse play including the lines:

O what a thing had been then
If that they that be English men
Might have been the first of all
That there should have taken possession
And made the first building a habitation
A memory perpetual.

In 1535 the Frenchman Jacques Cartier of St Malo got together the first colony of Frenchmen to attempt to settle in America. He had to report from his settlement near the site of Quebec that between November 1535 and April 1536 'we lay frozen up in the ice, which was more than two fathoms (6 ft *nearly 2 m*) in thickness, while on the shore there was more than 4 feet *1.2 m* of snow'. He returned to France as soon as it thawed in May. He tried again in 1541 but was again defeated by the winter climate and returned to France in 1542. It was more than half a century later before France succeeded in settling trading posts or colonies in North America.

First white Americans ■ Colonists of European descent soon began to feel themselves as separate from Europe, and by the mid-1500s royal officials were complaining of a generation of American-born Spaniards who 'neither knew their king nor wished to know him'.

Parliaments

Earliest and oldest ■ The earliest known legislative assembly or *ukkim* was a bicameral one in Erech, Iraq, *c.* 2800 BC. The oldest legislative body is the *Althing* of Iceland founded in 930 AD. The legislative assembly with the oldest continuous history is the Court of Tynwald in the Isle of Man, which was founded in 979.

Earliest in England ■ The earliest known use of the term 'parliament' is in an official royal document, in the meaning of a summons to the King's (Henry III's) Council, dating from 19 December 1241.

The French explorer Jacques Cartier in Canada in the winter of 1541–2. He and his party were driven away by the harsh North American climate.

Fewest meetings ■ The Cortes, the parliament of Portugal, was called by the king when he needed support and money. The vast profits of empire made it unnecessary to seek such support. The Cortes was called 25 times in 48 years by King John I (1385–1433), four times in Manuel I's 26-year reign (1495 –1521) and only three times in the 36-year reign (1521–57) of King John III.

First Russian parliament ■ In 1549 the first all-province council was summoned to hear the opinions of different social groups on the tsar's forthcoming decisions. This gathering is regarded as the prototype of the parliamentary system in Russia.

First use of the ballot box ■ The ballot box in which voting papers are placed during an election was first recorded as being used in England at the election of City of London aldermen (elected officers next in rank to the mayor) in 1526.

Civil service

Most highly governed ■ When the Spaniards reached the vast empire of the Incas in 1519, they found a nation more highly organized than most in Europe. The administration is calculated to have provided roughly 13 officials to each 100 people in a population of some 7–9 million.

Largest civil service ■ China had a salaried bureaucracy of some 100 000 men, among whom the most senior were recruited by competitive examinations.

First administrative use of printing ■ In 1454 indulgences (a document from the Church releasing a person from a punishment imposed for a sin) were printed with blanks left for the name of the recipient. This was one of the first ways in which administration (in this case of the Church) benefited from the technique of printing.

First African envoys to Europe ■ In 1427 two Ethiopian ambassadors were sent by the Negus Yishak to Aragon, Spain. In 1441 two Ethiopian delegates attended the Council of Florence and in 1452 an Ethiopian ambassador arrived in Lisbon, capital of Portugal.

First Russian embassy in Italy ■ In the year 1460 Vassily the Obscure sent an ambassador to Rome. The journey from Moscow to Rome at that time took 95–130 days.

First full-time ambassadors ■ From about 1450 the Italian cities of Florence and Milan appointed permanent representatives at each other's courts. Over the next century the employment of such full-time diplomats spread all over Europe. Latin was the language of diplomacy, but as early as 1508 French began to be used in some diplomatic documents.

English officials

Keepers of the Privy Seal ■ Of the 60 known Keepers of the Privy Seal since William Melton in 1307, that with the longest period of office was the Archdeacon of Oxford and Bishop of St David's, William Lyndwood, who held the seal for 11 years 5 months from 25 February 1432 to 18 July 1443.

Lord Chancellors ■ Of the 105 holders of the Chancellorship, the longest period of office was by the Bishop of Bath and Wells, Robert Burrell, for 12 years 3 months from 21 September 1274 to 17 December 1297.

Treasurers ■ The office of Treasurer was created by King Henry I in 1126. Of the 91 holders of the office the longest-serving was William of Ely for 19 years, under Kings Richard I and John from 1196 until August 1215.

Admirals of England ■ The longest tenure of this office has been 12 years 3 months by Richard, Duke of Gloucester (1452–85), from April 1471 when aged 19 to 25 July 1483, a month after he succeeded as King Richard III.

First English Attorney General ■ The office of Attorney General (the law officer appointed to act in all cases in which the state is a party) was created in 1378. William de Giselham was the first person to be appointed to the office.

Mayoralties ■ The mayoralty of the City of London dates from 1192 with the 20-year term of Henry Fitz Ailwyn until 1212. The most elections, since these became annual in 1215, has been eight by Gregory de Rokesley (1274/5 to 1280/1). The earliest recorded mayor of the City of

York, Nigel, dates from 1142. The first mayor to hold the title 'Right Honourable Lord Mayor' was in 1453, in which year the Lord Mayor's Show was first held. This is a procession which passes through the City of London.

First printed proclamations ■ From about 1505 government in England and in other countries came to depend on printed proclamations instead of the Town Crier, who survived where there were illiterate officials and population. Other public documents were likewise multiplied by the inventions of printing.

Symbols of government

Earliest national flag ■ The Danebrög, the national flag of Denmark, has been flown since 1219. Its design was chosen by King Valdemar II, who had seen a vision of a cross in a red sky. The red flag with its white cross has remained unchanged ever since.

The Danish flag, the Danebrög, is the oldest national flag in the world.

English royal standard ■ A uniform design for the English royal standard was achieved in 1405 and remained throughout the 1500s. Although earlier kings had personal banners, the English royal standard with its three lions (or 'leopards') appeared first in the 1100s. After 1340 French lilies were added, to mark the English claim to France. In 1405 King Henry IV reduced the number of lilies to three.

The English royal standard remained unchanged from 1405 until the accession of James I in 1603, when the Scottish lion and Irish harp were incorporated.

Most political plants ■ In England the rose came to be a political symbol. At the end of the War of the Roses (1455–85), when Elizabeth York married Henry Tudor (Henry VII), the Tudor rose of white and red was adopted as the emblem of the united houses of York and Lancaster, which had been symbolized by white and red roses. The lily was also recognized as a potent political sign. The flower's association with royalty led to its adoption as the *fleur-de-lys* of France which appeared on the English banner until the reign of Henry VIII.

Laws

Oldest statutes ■ The earliest surviving judicial code was that of King Ur-Hammu during the third dynasty of Ur, Iraq, *c.* 2110 BC. The oldest English statute in the Statute Book is a section of the Statute of Marlborough of 1267. Some statutes enacted by Henry II (d. 1189) and earlier kings are even more durable as they have been assimilated into the Common Law.

Earliest patent ■ The senate of Venice in 1474 created a protection for inventors whereby if they laid open (*patere*, to lay open) the secret of their invention their claim to priority would be recognized as a privilege and those who benefited would be required to reward them.

First Russian code of laws ■ The *Sudebrik*, the first code of law in Russia, was compiled in 1497. It secured the rights of feudal lords and was aimed against the feudal division of Russia.

First English game laws ■ In 1389 a law determined that those who did not possess land of a value of £2 or more could not keep dogs for hunting. A law of 1494 specifically forbade poaching.

German quality control ■ Although sulphur had for a long time been used to preserve wine and prevent its spoilage, the first legislation concerning the amounts of sulphur to be applied was apparently contained in a royal decree in Germany in 1487. This permitted approximately 3 oz *1 g* of sulphur per 30 pints *53 litres* of wine, and was achieved by burning sulphur together with wood shavings in barrels before they were filled.

English licensing laws ■ A statute of Henry VII in 1495 imposed nationwide restrictions on premises where alcoholic liquor was sold, less because of drunkenness than because customers were inclined to sit about playing games of chance when they should have been practising their archery. Fifteenth-century monarchs regularly tried to enforce such practice on their adult male subjects so as to ensure a supply of proficient archers in time of war.

Earliest street lighting ■ Paris was one of the first European cities to require citizens to show lights on the streets. An edict of 1524 directed Parisians to show a torch after 9 p.m., and lanterns were later fixed at street corners. Householders with homes fronting the street were responsible for hanging out lanterns.

First recording of births, marriages and deaths in England ■ Instituted by Thomas Cromwell in 1538, the ordinance required 'that every Sunday, in the presence of at least one of the churchwardens, the parson, vicar or curate should enter in the said book a written record of the dates and names of the weddings, christenings and burials of the preceding week'. The 'said book' became known as a parish register, and they are still kept by clergymen today.

First public standpipe ■ Sir Thomas More, humanist scholar and author of *Utopia*, was the leading champion of public health in England. During his term of office as Commissioner for Sewers he sponsored the Act of 1532 which established public standpipes in many towns and made polluting the water a punishable offence. In 1518 he established the practice of quarantining of houses where cases of the plague were detected. Houses were shut, sealed and marked, often to the annoyance of the occupants.

Sir Thomas More, Lord Chancellor of England, painted by Hans Holbein. He was one of the greatest scholars of the age.

Law breakers

Most lawless country ■ Although not based on statistics but on opinion, England was given this dubious title. The Venetian ambassador to Henry VII's court reported, 'There is no country in the world that contains so many thieves and robbers as England. Very few venture out alone in the country except in broad daylight, and still fewer dare go out at night, especially in London.'

Most notorious child murderer ■ Count Gilles de Rais (1404–40) is possibly the most notorious child murderer of all time. Records at the Archives of the Bastille show that he murdered 140 named victims and was suspected of killing a further 800 children. The bodies of children were purportedly essential for magic potions as well as simple healing of birthmarks, burns and carbuncles.

Most famous corsair ■ Hayreddin Barbarossa (Red Beard), a pirate from

western Turkey who settled in Algiers early in the 16th century, rose to become the city's ruler. In 1518 his brother Horuk was captured and beheaded. In 1519 Barbarossa sought protection from the Spaniards by offering the city to the Turkish sultan, Selim the Grim. In 1533, Suleyman the Magnificent appointed Barbarossa admiral of the Turkish fleet. Many other Algerian pirates also served as captains in the sultan's fleets. Barbarossa died in Constantinople in 1546.

Cruellest punishments for poaching ■ During the latter half of the 15th century, German game laws became more and more severe and finally reduced the peasants to hunting only 'vermin' like the fox, wolf and otter. For a first offence of killing deer the penalty was either a flogging or branding, but by 1517 the blinding of an eye or the chopping off of a hand was the punishment. Hanging was the punishment for a second offence.

The oppression by the German nobility after 1525 got even worse in some areas. Duke Ulrich of Württemberg had a poacher, who had to run while the hounds pursued him, sewn into the skin of a stag. The fanatical hunter Archbishop Michael of Salzburg had a poacher sewn into a fresh deer hide and thrown to the dogs in Salzburg's market square, where he was torn to pieces.

First guillotine ■ The guillotine is popularly supposed to have been invented by the Frenchman Dr Joseph Ignace Guillotin (1738–1814). But in fact he merely recommended the use of an implement variously known as the Halifax gibbet or the maiden. In 1492 the Yorkshire town of Halifax, England, had its own beheading machine and applied it as and when required by Halifax Law. That term is used to describe Halifax's application of summary trial and execution by the maiden for certain types of larceny.

Most horrid death ■ In 1542, some 10 maids in the Ming dynasty palace tried to kill the Emperor Zhu Hou-Cong by strangulation, in protest against his autocratic oppression. The emperor narrowly escaped with his life as the knot of the piece of silk used to strangle him was poorly tied, and the emperor was rescued by a court physician named Xu Shen. The maids involved in the event were arrested and sentenced to 'lingering death', which was carried out by dismembering their bodies and exposing them to the public. Xu Shen was promoted to be the Minister of Rites plus the Instructor to the Prince, the highest position that a Chinese physician could ever hold in the history of Chinese medicine. However, he soon fell ill and died. Before his death, he said that his illness was incurable, because it was caused by a great fear, and that when he was rescuing the emperor he had been greatly terrified that he would be put to death if he failed.

Gravest punishment for drunkenness ■ There can be few examples of a more fearsome punishment for the 'crime' of being drunk than that described by Father Sahugun in Aztec society: 'If a youth appeared intoxicated in public, or if he was found bearing wine, or lying in the street, or in the company of other drunkards, if he was a *macehualii* (common person) he was punished by being beaten to death with a stick or garotted before all the other youths assembled there; thus to serve as an example and to teach them to beware of drunkenness.' In Aztec society only the elderly were allowed to become intoxicated.

The Italian Dominican friar Girolamo Savonarola (1452–98) attacked corruption in religious and political life. In 1494 he led a revolt against the Medicis in Florence and established a democratic republic. However, in 1497 he was excommunicated for attacking the Pope and a year later was tortured, hanged and burned as a heretic in the main piazza of Florence.

Terrible punishment for adultery ■ The Aztec *Mendieta Codex* states: 'If a man and a woman were discovered committing adultery, or were strongly suspected, they were arrested and if they did not confess, were tortured, and after they had confessed to their crime put to death. Sometimes they were killed by their hands and feet being bound, and, once lying on the ground, were struck on the temples with a heavy, round stone in such a way that, with a few blows dealt, their heads were flattened like a pancake. Others were strangled with an oak garotte. Other times they burned the man and hanged the woman. Sometimes both were hanged, and if they were nobles, feathers would be put on their heads, and then they would be burnt. Or the judges could have them stoned to death.'

GENERAL

Basham, A L, *The Wonder that was India, Volume I*, Sidgwick & Jackson, 1987 and Taplinger Publishing Company Inc, 1968.

Burke, Peter, *The Renaissance Sense of the Past*, Edward Arnold, 1969.

Cambridge History of India, Volume IV, Mughal India, Delhi, 1968.

Clark, Sir George, *Early Modern Europe from about 1450 to about 1720*, Oxford University Press, 1975.

Fage, J D and Oliver, Roland (*eds*), *Cambridge History of Africa, Volume 3 1050–1600*, Cambridge University Press, 1977.

Hay, Denys and Elton, George, *Europe in the Fourteenth and Fifteenth Centuries*, Longman, 1989.

Koenigsberger, H G and Mosse, George L, *Europe in the Sixteenth Century*, 2nd Edition, Longman, 1989.

Lucena Salmoral, Manuel, *America 1492*, Facts on File, Oxford and New York 1990.

Rizvi, S A A, *The Wonder that was India, Volume II*, Sidgwick & Jackson, 1987.

Sansom, George, *A History of Japan*, Stanford University Press, 1988.

Spear, Percival, *A History of India, Volume II*, Penguin Books, 1978.

Thapar, Romila, *A History of India, Volume I*, Penguin Books, 1966.

Totman, Conrad, *Japan Before Perry*, Berkeley University Press, 1981.

UNESCO, *General History of Africa, Volume IV 12–16th centuries*, Heinemann, 1984.

Yamamura, Kozo (*ed*), *The Cambridge History of Japan, Volume III*, Cambridge University Press, 1990.

Chapter 1:
THIS WORLD AND BEYOND

Adams, F D, *The Birth and Development of the Geological Sciences*, Dover, 1990.

Beazley, C Raymond, *The Dawn of Modern Geography, Volume 5, I and II*, John Murray, 1897 and 1901. *Volume III*, Clarendon Press, 1906.

Broc, N, *La Geographie de la Renaissance 1420–1520*, Bibliotheque Nationale, 1980.

Crone, G R, *Maps and their Makers: Introduction to the History of Cartography*, William Dawson, 1978 and Shoe String Press Inc, 1978.

Geike, A, *The Founders of Modern Geology*, Macmillan, 1905.

Kimble, George H T, *Geography in the Middle Ages*, Methuen, 1938.

Mills, J V (*ed*), *The Overall Survey of the Ocean's Shores*, Cambridge University Press for the Hakluyt Society, 1970.

Wilford, John Noble, *The Mapmakers: The Story of the Great Pioneers in Cartography*, Alfred A Knopf Inc and Junction Books, 1981.

Chapter 2:
THE HUMAN BEING

Berdan, F, *The Aztecs of Central Mexico*, New York, 1982.

Blunden, Caroline, and Elvin, Mark, *A Cultural Atlas of China*, Phaidon Press, 1983 and Facts on File, 1983.

Cieza de Leon, P, *The Inca*, edited by V von Hagen, New York, 1982.

Crosby, Alfred W, *Columbian Exchange: Biological and Cultural Consequences of 1492*, Greenwood Press, 1972 and Greenwood Publishing Group Inc, 1973.

Dobyns, H F and Doughty, P L, *Peru: a cultural history*, 1976.

Driver, H, *The Indians of North America*, University of Chicago Press, 2nd Edition 1969.

Hammond, N, *Ancient Maya Civilization*, Cambridge University Press, 1982, (Rutgers University Press, 1982.)

Hourani, Albert, *A History of the Arab Peoples*, Faber and Faber, 1990 and Harvard University Press, 1991.

Katz, F, *The Ancient American Civilizations*, Weidenfeld and Nicolson, 1972.

Lewis, Bernard (*ed*), *The World of Islam*, Thames and Hudson, 1976.

Link, A S, *The American People*, 1981.

Lyons, Albert S & Petrucelli, R Joseph, *Medicine: An Illustrated History*, Harry N Abrams Inc, 1978.

McGrew, Roderick (*ed*), *Encyclopaedia of Medical History*, Macmillan, 1985.

Thomas, Keith, *Man and the Natural World: Changing Attitudes in England 1500–1800*, Penguin Books, London, 1983, *Man in the Natural World: A History of Modern Sensibility*, Pantheon Books, 1983.

Chapter 3:
TRANSPORT

Audemard, L, *Les Jongues Chinoises*, Volumes I–VI, Museum Voor Land-en Volkenkunde & Maritiem Museum, 1957–65.

Hurani, G F, *Arab Seafaring in the Indian Ocean*, Princeton, 1951.

Ta-san Din, Jose, *El Poder Naval Chino*, Ediciones Ariel, 1965.

Taylor, Eva, *The Haven-finding Art*, Hollis and Carter, 1956.

Tyler, J E, *The Alpine Passes*, Oxford University Press, 1930.

Worcester, G R G, *The Junks and Sampans of the Yangtze*, Inspectorate General of Customs, Shanghai, 1947–8.

Chapter 4:
EXPLORATION AND DISCOVERY

Andrews, Kenneth R, *Trade, Plunder and Settlement; Maritime Enterprise and the Genesis of the British Empire 1480–1630*, Cambridge University Press, 1985.

Boxer, C R, *The Portuguese Seaborne Empire*, Hutchinson, 1969.

Cameron, Ian, *Magellan and the First Circumnavigation of the World*, Weidenfeld and Nicolson, 1974.

Díaz, Bernal, *The Conquest of New Spain*, translated by J M Cohen, Penguin Classics.

Duyvendak, J J L, *China's Discovery of Africa*, Probsthain, 1949.

Fernández-Armesto, F, *Columbus*, Oxford University Press, 1991.

Hemming, John, *The Search for Eldorado*, Macmillan, 1978.

Mandeville, Sir John, *Travels*, (translated by Charles W R D Moseley), Penguin Classics.

Morison, S E, *The European Discovery of America*, 2 vols, Oxford University Press, 1971–4.

Parry, J H, *The Discovery of South America*, Paul Elek, 1979.

Parry, J H, *The Age of Reconnaissance: Discovery, Exploration and Settlement 1450–1650*, Weidenfeld and Nicolson, 1973 and University of California Press, 1982.

Peschel, O F, *Geschichte der Erdkunde bis auf Alexander von Humboldt und Carl Ritter, 2nd Edition*, R Oldenbourg, 1877.

Robinson, Francis, *Atlas of the Islamic World since 1500*, Phaidon Press, 1982 and Facts on File, 1982.

Quinn, David, *England and the Discovery of North America (1481–1620)*, George Allen & Unwin, 1974.

Sale, Kirkpatrick, *The Conquest of Paradise*, Alfred A Knopf Inc, 1990 and Hodder and Stoughton, 1991.

Scammell, G V, *The First Imperial Age: European Overseas Expansion c. 1400–1715*, Unwin Hyman, 1989.

Scammell, G V, *The World Encompassed: The First European Maritime Empires c. 800–1650*, Methuen, 1981 and University of California Press, 1981.

Spate, O H K, *The Spanish Lake: the Pacific Since Magellan, Volumes I and II*, Croom Helm, 1979 and University of Minnesota Press, 1979.

The Times Atlas of World Exploration, Times Books, 1991.

Zárate, Augustín de, *The Discovery and Conquest of Peru*, translated by J M Cohen, Penguin Classics, 1963.

Chapter 5:
INDUSTRY AND COMMERCE

Abel, Wilhelm, *Agricultural Fluctuations in Europe, 13–20th centuries*, Methuen, 1978.

Braudel, Fernand, *Civilization and Capitalism, Volume I*, Collins, 1973.

Carson, R A G, *Coins: Ancient, Medieval and Modern*, Hutchinson, 1982.

Carus Wilson, E M, *Medieval Merchant Venturers*, Methuen, 1967.

Challis, C E, *The Tudor Coinage*, Manchester University Press, 1978 and Barnes & Noble, 1978.

Chang, K C (*ed*), *Food in Chinese Culture: Anthropological and Historical Perspectives*, Yale University Press, 1981.

Chaudhuri, K, *Trade and Civilization in the Indian Ocean: Economic History from the Rise of Islam to 1750*, Cambridge University Press, 1985.

Coleman, Donald Cuthbert, *Economy of England 1450–1750*, Oxford University Press, 1977.

Davis, N Z and Zika, C, *Past and Present*, Oxford University Press, 1971.

Ehrenberg, R, *Capital and Finance in the Age of the Renaissance*, 1928.

Francis, A D, *The Wine Trade*, A & C Black, 1972 and Humanities Press International Inc, 1972.

Friedberg, R, *Gold Coins of the World*, The Coin & Currency Institute Inc, 1958.

Hale, J R, *Florence and the Medici*, 1977.

Hingston Quiggin, A, *A Survey of Primitive Money*, Methuen, 1949 and A M S Press Inc, 1949.

Hope, C E, *The Economy of Expanding Europe in the Sixteenth and Seventeenth Centuries (Volume 4)*, Cambridge University Press, 1967.

Johnson, H, *The Story of Wine*, Mitchell Beazley, 1989 and Simon & Schuster, 1989.

Junge, Ewald, *World Coin Encyclopedia*, Barrie & Jenkins, 1984 and William Morrow & Co, 1982.

Lachiver, M, *Vins, Vignes et Vignerons: Histoire des vignobles français*, Fayard, 1988.

Lloyd, T H, *Movement of Wool Prices in Medieval England*, Cambridge University Press, 1973.

Mayhew, N J (*ed*), *Edwardian Monetary Affairs*, British Archaeological Reports No 36, 1977.

Mitchell, S, and Reeds, B (*eds*), *The Standard Catalogue of British Coins: Coins of England*, Batsford, 1991 and Numismatic Fine Arts International Inc, 1991.

Monckton, H A, *A History of English Ale and Beer*, Bodley Head, 1966.

Nef, J U, *Rise of the British Coal Industry*, Frank Cass, 1966 and International Specialized Book Services, 1966.

Postan, M M (*ed*), *Cambridge Economic History of Europe: Trade and Industry in the Middle Ages Volume 2*, Cambridge University Press, 1987.

Price, M J (*ed*), *Coins: An Illustrated Survey from 650BC to the Present Day*, Hamlyn/Country Life, 1980 and Numismatic Fine Arts International Inc, 1980.

Raychaudhuri, T (*ed*), *Cambridge Economic History of India: (Volume I) c. 1200–c.1750*, Cambridge University Press, 1982.

Rich, E E, and Wilson, Charles Henry (*eds*), *Cambridge Economic History of Europe (Volume 5): The Economic Organization of Early Modern Europe*, Cambridge University Press, 1977.

Salaman, R N, *The History and Social Influence of the Potato*, Cambridge University Press, 1985.

Tannahill, Reay, *Food in History*, Penguin Books, 1988 and Crown Publishers Inc, 1989.

Unwin, T, *Wine and the Vine: An Historical Geography of Viticulture and the Wine Trade*, Routledge, 1991.

Wheaton, Barbara K, *Savouring the Past: The French Kitchen and Table from 1300 to 1789*, University of Pennsylvania Press, 1983.

Wilson, C Anne, *Food and Drink in Britain*, Constable, 1973.

Younger, William, *Gods, Men and Wine*, The Wine and Food Society, 1966.

Chapter 6:
SCIENCE AND TECHNOLOGY

Gimpel, Jean, *The Medieval Machine: The Industrial Revolution of the Middle Ages*, Gollancz, 1977.

Goody, Jack, *Technology, Tradition and the State in Africa*, Hutchinson, 1980 and Cambridge University Press, 1980.

Needham, Joseph, *Science and Civilization in China, Volume IV.3*, Cambridge University Press, 1971.

Steinberg, S H, *500 Years of Printing*, Penguin Books, 1955.

Chapter 7:
BUILDINGS AND STRUCTURES

Hill, Donald R, *A History of Engineering in Classical and Medieval Times*, Croom Helm, 1984 and Open Court Publishing Co, 1984.

Kubler, G, *The Art and Architecture of Ancient America*, Penguin Books, 1984.

Murray, Peter, *The Architecture of the Italian Renaissance*, Thames & Hudson, 1986 and Schocken Books Inc, 1986.

Rowland, Benjamin, *The Art and Architecture of India*, Penguin Books, 1953.

Sprague de Camp, L, *Ancient Engineers*, Tandem Books, 1977 and Ballantine Books Inc, 1988.

Chapter 8:
THE ARTS AND ENTERTAINMENT

Alberti, Leon Battista, *On Painting*, (*ed* M Kemp and translated by C Grayson), Penguin Classics.

Ariosto, Ludovico, *Orlando Furioso*, translated by B Reynolds, Penguin Classics.

Blunt, Anthony, *Artistic Theory in Italy 1450–1600*, Oxford University Press, 1940 and Oxford University Press Inc, 1956.

Cellini, Benvenuto, *Autobiography*, translated by G Bull, Penguin Classics.

Five Italian Renaissance Comedies, (*ed* Bruce Penman) Penguin Classics.

Grove Dictionary of Music and Musicians, *ed* Stanley Sadie, Macmillan, 1980.

The Jewish Poets of Spain Translated, Penguin Classics.

Rabelais, François, *The Histories of Gargantua and Pantagruel*, (translated by J M Cohen) Penguin Classics.

Vasari, Giorgio, *Lives of the Artists, Volumes 1 and 2*, (translated by George Bull), Penguin Classics, 1987.

Villon, François, *Selected Poems*, (translated by Peter Dale), Penguin Classics.

Chapter 9:
SPORT AND GAMES

Barber, R and Barker, J, *Tournaments*, Boydell Press, 1989.

Bradbury, J, *The Medieval Archer*, Boydell Press, 1989

Culin, S, *Games of the North American Indians*, Dover Publications, 1975.

Cummins, J, *The Hound and the Hawk*, Weidenfeld and Nicolson, 1988.

Eales, Richard, *Chess: History of the Game*, Batsford, 1984.

Finn, Michael, *Martial Arts: a Complete History*, Stanley Paul, 1988.

Strutt, J, *Sports and Pastimes of the People of England*, Methuen, 1903.

Trench, C C, *A History of Horsemanship*, Longman, 1970.

Trench, C C, *A History of Marksmanship*, Longman, 1972.

Chapter 10:
RELIGION AND POPULAR BELIEF

Ahmed, Akbar S, *Discovering Islam: Making Sense of Muslim History and Society*, 1988 and Routledge, Chapman & Hall Inc, 1989.

Basham, A L (*ed*), *A Cultural History of India*, Oxford University Press, 1983.

Burke, Peter, *Popular Culture in Early Modern Europe*, Temple Smith, 1978.

Burke, Peter, *The Italian Renaissance: Culture and Society in Renaissance Italy, 1420–1540*, Batsford, 1972.

Hay, Denys, *Cambridge Modern History (Renaissance and Reformation)*, Cambridge University Press.

Spencer, B, *Pilgrim Souvenirs and Secular Badges*, Salisbury Museum Medieval Catalogue Part 2, 1990.

Sumption J, *Pilgrimage: An Image of Medieval Religion*, Faber and Faber, 1975 and Rowman & Littlefield Publishers Inc, 1975.

Chapter 11:
RULERS AND LAW MAKERS

Castiglione, Baldassare, *The Book of the Courtier*, (translated by G Bull) Penguin Classics, 1976.

Machiavelli, Nicolo, *The Discourses*, (translated by L J Walker) Penguin Classics.

Machiavelli, Nicolo, *The Prince*, (translated by G Bull), Penguin Classics.

VICTORIS
CARPATIO
VENETI
OPVS